D1348247

THE LITERARY SPY

Spy

THE LITERARY

The Ultimate Source for

Quotations on Espionage

& Intelligence

Compiled and annotated by

CHARLES E. LATHROP

Yale University Press · New Haven and London

Published with assistance from the Mary Cady Tew Memorial Fund.

Designed by Sonia Shannon
Set in Monotype Bulmer with Scala Sans display by
Duke & Company, Devon, Pennsylvania

Printed in the United States of America by Edwards Brothers,
Ann Arbor, Michigan

Library of Congress Cataloging-in-Publication Data

The literary spy : the ultimate source for quotations on espionage and
intelligence / Compiled and annotated by Charles E. Lathrop
p.   cm.
Includes bibliographical references and index.
ISBN 0-300-10324-7 (cloth : alk. paper)
1. Espionage—Quotations, maxims, etc. 2. History, Modern—Quotations,
maxims, etc. I. Lathrop, Charles E.
PN6084.E82L58 2004
327.12—dc22   2003027624

A catalogue record for this book is available from the British Library.

The paper in this book meets the guidelines for permanence and durability
of the Committee on Production Guidelines for Book Longevity
of the Council on Library Resources.

10 9 8 7 6 5 4 3 2 1

То Мас

1913–1950

ВЕЧНАЯ + ПАМЯТЬ

Contents

Preface

Literary, *adjective.* Pertaining to letters of the alphabet *(obsolete)*. . . .
Of or concerning literature. . . . Bookish, pedantic.

Spy, *noun.* One who collects intelligence. . . . A person who discovers
information by close observation.

This work is based in part on my fourteen years' experience as a CIA analyst, speechwriter, spokesman, editor, manager, and amateur historian, as well as a few more years of study and research, reflection, writing, and teaching about intelligence. More important, it reflects the wisdom—and lack of wisdom—of users and practitioners of intelligence from ancient times to our own. The praise or condemnation of the various aspects of intelligence by qualified observers is included as valuable commentary on a much misunderstood profession. I have included remarks by singularly unqualified pundits when they are entertaining, when their remarks reflect the quality of discourse on the subject or, when they, like a broken clock, happen to be right. The rich literature of intelligence (or "spy fiction") also provides insightful and useful quotations for someone trying to make a point. And, solely for the amusement of the reader (you'll thank me for this), quotations from offbeat sources are sprinkled throughout.

How This Book Came to Be

After I became speechwriter for an unnamed director of Central Intelligence[1] several years ago, a warning and a revelation came my way. The warning was this: the DCI doesn't use quotations in his speeches, I was told; don't include them because he doesn't like them. Well, to a speechwriter, omitting such soundbites from a speech is rather like proposing the building of a house without windows. And because I suffered from the traditional curse of speechwriters—that is, not actually having much contact with the man whose message I was to craft into life—I didn't know whether the warning reflected the director's actual beliefs or was merely the bias of intervening satraps.

Moreover, even if a DCI thought he didn't like quotations, I reasoned that it was my duty to try to convince him of the impact of a pithy quotation. I knew that the business and history of intelligence, not to mention its literature, were a rich lode to mine. As it turned out, a quotation that I

---

1. Actually, that DCI had then and continues to have a name; I just choose not to reveal it here. We're funny about names in this business.

slipped as a test into the director's remarks to CIA senior officers[2] established that he would, in fact, use a good quotation. The trick, I thought, was finding the precisely appropriate quotation for the occasion, so I trundled off to the Agency's library to find the useful quotation book or books on intelligence that I expected to find there.

Then came the revelation: no such work existed. No one had done the gritty work of research for such a *Bartlett's* for Spooks. Its absence was a rude denial to students, researchers, historians, journalists, military personnel, all good people interested in the work and profession of intelligence. It hardly seemed fair; I found that most professions, and even many nationalities and ethnic groups, had their own quotation books—but not the "second oldest profession." Of course, my immediate concern was that my job as speechwriter, already frustrating, had just gotten harder, as I would have to come up with quotations on my own. And so, painfully and laboriously, I did. Even before I left the speechwriting job, I found myself addicted to collecting intelligence quotations as an adjunct of my voluminous reading in intelligence matters, and after several years' gestation *The Literary Spy* was born.

Who is the Literary Spy? And why is the Spy *Literary*? Here I use the tertiary American meaning of "literary" as "bookish" or "pedantic." The Literary Spy is me; it's you, the reader; it is anyone who wants to know more about intelligence and is willing to learn from diverse sources: historical, literary (relating to literature), polemical, serious, cheeky.

This book does not pretend to be comprehensive in the sense that the reader will find everything that is worth saying about intelligence. The typical Literary Spy who uses this book, whom I imagine to be a reasonable fellow (or lass), can be confident that most of what he or she expects will be here, as well as much that will surprise, astonish, titillate, vindicate, and perhaps even illuminate.

My own biases are evident throughout, but let me state them here: I believe that intelligence in all its aspects, including what is usually called covert action, is a vital resource and instrument of statecraft. I find no contradiction between the open, pluralistic, and democratic societies that are the hallmark of the Western world and the defense of such societies through the secret collection and evaluation of information and, when necessary, the use of covert means to effect a just foreign policy. Terrorism in our time, especially since September 11, 2001, has only confirmed the necessity of having an effective U.S. intelligence service—one that operates under responsible oversight, that obeys U.S. law, and that understands the moral underpinning of its existence.

Even so, those who consider intelligence something of an evil activity—you know who you are—will find the book useful. That lot will want especially to check "Critics & Defenders," where the critics are decidedly in the majority.

Another caveat: this is an American book, compiled with predominantly American sources and with the U.S. intelligence community as a frame of reference. Nevertheless, I have included, when appropriate, quotations from foreign perspectives, particularly the British, Soviet/Russian, and occasionally the Israeli.

How to Use This Book

The more than 3,000 quotations that compose this book appear within sixty-five categories arranged alphabetically. Within each category the

---

2. "Here is one of the most peculiar types of operation any government can have, and it probably takes a strange kind of genius to run it."—President Eisenhower (see Directors of Central Intelligence).

quotations are deployed generally in topically chronological order—quotations within a topic about the OSS, for example, are grouped together no matter when they were made. Occasionally I've juxtaposed particularly apt quotations out of time (Henry Stimson's 1929 comment that "Gentlemen do not read each other's mail" is followed quickly by Allen Dulles's 1963 retort that they do indeed).

At the beginning of each category I offer personal and provocative thoughts on the matter at hand. In addition, I have given in to the grievous temptation to comment on many quotations that have a high emotional content—stoking the fire, so to speak. This bad habit is most prevalent in the categories "Critics and Defenders" and "Traitors in Their Own Words."

Acknowledgments

First and foremost, my wife, Cathy, bore what often seemed a feckless task with love and encouragement; she and Marlene pushed me to aim high. Special thanks go to my four-year-old son, who didn't seem to mind that the Literary Spy's muse hit Daddy most often at his bath time.

I am indebted to many people who consistently provided much-needed support, encouragement, advice, and some particularly pithy quotations, especially Michael Warner of the CIA History Staff, CIA Museum curator Toni Hiley, CIA Historical Intelligence Collection curator Hayden Peake, Ed Mickolus, Ken Forstmeier, Scott Koch, and Lloyd Salvetti.

Several distinguished sources who appear herein gave me a morale boost when they expressed support for this project by e-mail: Christopher Andrew, Richard Betts, Phillip Knightley, Stephen Knott, Ernest Lefever, Arch Puddington, Tim Weiner, Nigel West, and Benjamin Wittes.

Many thanks to the good people at Yale University Press who took a chance on something we all agreed was a quirky project but that nevertheless might help people understand the mysterious world of intelligence. A special thanks to my talented editor, Heidi Downey, who endured much with grace and humor.

Finally, my deepest thanks to Professor Richard Shultz of the Fletcher School of Law and Diplomacy, who got me started (without knowing it) in intelligence. Dick, this makes up for my failure to call or write. I also wish to honor the memory of the late Colonel Robert Debs Heinl, Jr., USMC (ret.), whose *Dictionary of Military and Naval Quotations* (U.S. Naval Institute Press) was the inspiration for *The Literary Spy*.

It is customary at this point for an author to say that, despite all this wonderful help, any errors in the work remain his responsibility, and far be it from me to break with tradition. While a great deal of care was taken in assembling these quotations, inevitably there may be mistakes made in transcription, in attribution, or in epistemology (in most cases I was not present when the quotation was uttered). I shoulder the entire blame for such errors. Readers are encouraged to send complaints, compliments, and fully sourced suggestions for a second edition to LiterarySpy@hotmail.com.

A Final Duty

Like everyone who becomes a CIA officer, I signed upon my "entry on duty" an oath that I would submit for prepublication review anything I might ever write that had any relation to intelligence. This ensures that classified information is not disclosed. Unlike a few former CIA officers who have fought the obligations they have incurred, I have no problem with keeping such a promise. It is a reasonable condition of such employment, as no one signs the agreement under duress, and it is a reasonable measure for an intelligence agency serving a democracy to insist upon, even in those cases

when a CIA officer is long retired and no longer
has access to classified material. CIA's review of
this or any manuscript neither implies an endorsement of the author's views nor constitutes any au-
thentication of the information therein, and CIA's
clearance of the material certainly doesn't mean
that the Agency likes everything in it; it only means
that the Agency has reviewed the work and found
no classified information.

Glossary

Black Chamber	Informal term for the U.S. codebreaking unit shut down in 1929 by Secretary of State Henry "Gentlemen do not read each other's mail" Stimson.
CA	Covert action. Part of the shop talk of operations officers.
CAT	Civil Air Transport. Founded in 1946 by Claire Chennault with support from the Nationalist Chinese, this airline later became a CIA proprietary enterprise until its liquidation in 1973.
CENTCOM	U.S. Central Command.
Church Committee	U.S. Senate Select Committee to Study Governmental Operations with respect to Intelligence Activities. Chaired by Senator Frank Church (D-Idaho), the committee in 1975–76 investigated the activities and alleged abuses of U.S. intelligence services.
CI	Counterintelligence.
CIG	Central Intelligence Group, CIA's predecessor from January 1946 until CIA was created with the National Security Act of 1947.
cipher	A system for concealing a message by substituting symbols to represent individual letters.
cleartext	*See* plaintext.
code	A system for concealing a message by substituting symbols for words or phrases.
COI	Coordinator of Information, the small agency headed by William Donovan in 1941–42 that was the direct predecessor of the Office of Strategic Services (OSS).
covert action	Activities or operations conducted in such a way as to conceal the identity of the agency or nation sponsoring them. A term of the modern age; in most of human history, this was just part of normal statecraft.
cryptanalysis	Breaking a code or cipher to ascertain the original message (or plaintext).
cryptography	Devising a code or cipher to conceal messages.
cryptology	The science of devising, analyzing, and breaking codes and ciphers.
DCI	Director of Central Intelligence. Not just head of the CIA, the DCI also nominally heads the U.S. Intelligence Community and serves as the president's chief intelligence officer.
DDCI	Deputy Director of Central Intelligence. The DDCI often is a senior military officer. By law, the DCI and the DDCI cannot both be active duty military officers.
DDI	CIA's Deputy Director for Intelligence, who is responsible for the Agency's analytical

	product. In olden days (before the mid-1970s) the intelligence directorate (the DI) itself.
DDO	CIA's Deputy Director for Operations. As with DDI, DDO before the mid-1970s was used to refer to the directorate (the DO) itself.
DDP	Deputy Directorate for Plans, the name of CIA's operations directorate until renamed the DDO or DO (Directorate of Operations) under DCI James Schlesinger in 1973.
DI	CIA's analytical arm, the Directorate of Intelligence. Also known by old-timers as the DDI.
DIA	The Defense Intelligence Agency. Created in 1961 for reasons that are still debated.
DO	CIA's Directorate of Operations. Responsible for running spies and other forms of clandestine collection, and occasionally called upon to undertake covert action.
FOIA	Freedom of Information Act. The U.S. law that requires federal agencies to review and respond to requests for information and to justify withholding information. A boon to foreign intelligence services.
GPU	Gosudarstvennoye Politicheskoye Upravleniye. The blandly named State Political Administration was the successor of the Cheka, the first Soviet secret police and intelligence organization, and a predecessor of the KGB. See OGPU.
GRU	Glavnoye Razveditelnoye Upravleniye. The Main Intelligence Administration was the Soviet military intelligence organization.
G-2	Military designation for army intelligence. Can also refer to the chief of army intelligence.
HUMINT	Human intelligence. Information derived from espionage. Spies. Former DCI Richard Helms considered this term a "barbarism."
ICBM	Intercontinental ballistic missile.
IG	Inspector General.
INR	The State Department's Bureau of Intelligence and Research.
IRO	Information Review Officer. CIA and other U.S. intelligence agencies have IROs to review Freedom of Information Act requests and other petitions for the release of material currently or previously classified.
KGB	Komitet Gosudarstvenniy Bezopastnosti. The Committee for State Security was the premier Soviet intelligence service and CIA's chief rival during the Cold War.
Langley	Synonym for CIA Headquarters, located along the Potomac at the site of the now defunct village of Langley, Virginia—long since absorbed into the town of McLean. Not to be confused with Langley Air Force Base.
LXX	Designation for the Septuagint, the Greek Old Testament.
MAGIC	The U.S. codebreaking effort during World War II that decrypted Japanese diplomatic traffic.

MI5	The British counterintelligence service.
MI6	See SIS.
MO	Morale Operations. That branch of the Office of Strategic Services that engaged in deception and propaganda activities designed to undermine the morale of enemy soldiers. MO liked to hire journalists—who better to slant the news?
NIA	The National Intelligence Authority, a postwar body comprising the Secretaries of State, War, and the Navy, to oversee intelligence matters and to give direction to the Director of Central Intelligence, a position President Truman created in January 1946. The NIA was supplanted by the National Security Council when the NSC and CIA were both created by the National Security Act of 1947.
NID	The *National Intelligence Daily*. CIA's second current intelligence publication (after the PDB), created by DCI William Colby in 1973 to serve high-level officials under the level of the president and cabinet secretaries. Name changed to *Senior Executive's Intelligence Brief* in 1998.
NIE	National Intelligence Estimate. The National Security Act of 1947 required CIA to "correlate and evaluate" intelligence, and CIA's lead in developing NIEs evolved from that requirement. Once wholly CIA-drafted, today NIEs are the province of the National Intelligence Council, an independent body that reports to the DCI and that comprises talent from the entire intelligence community and occasionally experts from outside government service.
NKVD	Narodniy Komissariat Vnutryennikh Del. The People's Commissariat for Internal Affairs was Stalin's secret police and intelligence agency during the Soviet Great Terror of the 1930s, and it continued under a variety of names until the KGB was established after Stalin's death in 1953.
NRO	The National Reconnaissance Office, responsible for building and operating U.S. reconnaissance satellites. Its very existence was classified until 1992.
NSA	The National Security Agency. See SIGINT.
NSC	The National Security Council, established with CIA by the National Security Act of 1947.
OGPU	Obedinyonnoye Gosudarstvennoye Politicheskoye Upravleniye. The Unified State Political Administration was one of many incarnations of the Soviet secret police and intelligence service between its founding as the Cheka in 1917 and its swan-song as the KGB when the USSR collapsed in 1991.
ONI	Office of Naval Intelligence. Founded in 1882.
OSS	The Office of Strategic Services, created in 1942 by President Roosevelt under William Donovan, was America's first "full service" intelligence agency and the predecessor to CIA. Abolished by President Truman in September 1945.

PDB	*President's Daily Brief.* Created originally for President Kennedy as the *President's Intelligence Checklist,* the PDB is CIA's daily intelligence publication tailored for the president and distributed to him and to the top advisors he authorizes.
PICL	*President's Intelligence Checklist.* See PDB.
Pike Committee	U.S. House of Representatives committee, chaired by Otis Pike (D-New York), investigating U.S. intelligence activities in 1975. See also Church Committee.
plaintext	The text of a message before it is encoded or enciphered. Also called cleartext.
R&A	Research and Analysis, the analytic arm of the Office of Strategic Services (1942–45). Referred, often derisively, as the Chairborne Division, R&A was the forerunner of the Directorate of Intelligence (DI) in today's CIA.
R&D	Research and development.
S&T	Science and technology.
SAM	Surface-to-air missile.
SIGINT	Signals intelligence, known popularly as "electronic eavesdropping." The U.S. agency responsible for collecting SIGINT is the National Security Agency.
SIS	Secret Intelligence Service, also known by a previous name, MI6. The British foreign intelligence service.
SOE	Special Operations Executive, Britain's commando and covert action instrument during World War II. In Winston Churchill's words, SOE was to "set Europe ablaze."
SSU	Strategic Services Unit, the U.S. War Department's successor organization to the Office of Strategic Services. OSS was abolished in late 1945, and foreign intelligence and counterintelligence elements were preserved in SSU, which turned over these assets to the Central Intelligence Group in 1946–47. CIG became CIA in September 1947.
TASS	Telegrafnoye Agenstvo Sovietskovo Soyuza. The Telegraph Agency of the Soviet Union—the official propaganda arm of the USSR. KGB defectors have said that about half of TASS employees working outside the USSR were working for Soviet intelligence.
TRASHINT	Intelligence from trash. Not an officially recognized "INT" (means of intelligence collection), like HUMINT or SIGINT, the smelly art of TRASHINT offers huge potential payoffs: just think what your garbage reveals about *you.*
ULTRA	Code name for the British decryption operation that read intercepted German messages during World War II. Also refers to the decrypts themselves.
ZAPATA	CIA code name for the April 1961 Bay of Pigs operation.

THE LITERARY SPY

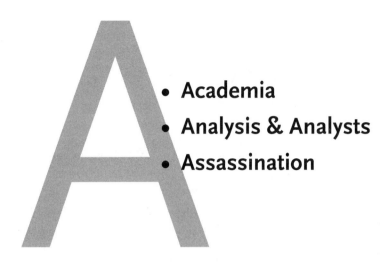

- **Academia**
- **Analysis & Analysts**
- **Assassination**

ACADEMIA

The Literary Spy knows that a country's intelligence services are never any better than that country's educational system. Not only are its spymasters and intelligence analysts recruited from the best schools, but the spooks often seek out academic experts to shed light on murky international developments. In a democracy, of course, academics have the right to shun contact with the same intelligence services that serve and protect that democracy, proving that advanced degrees are no guarantee of clear thinking.

See also: Analysis & Analysts; Collection; Intelligence & American Culture

"Some of the academics who were to accompany [Napoleon's] expedition [to Egypt in 1798] began to boast, a notorious failing of clever men leading unimportant lives. . . . Had Bonaparte known of their stream of leaks he certainly must have regretted the decision to encumber the expedition with so many professional talkers."

 JOHN KEEGAN on the "gossipy academic world" that helped inform London about the destination of Napoleonic forces in *Intelligence in War* (2003).

"Libraries have a much more important role to play than they have played in the past in buttressing spot intelligence with the scholarly element."

 ARCHIBALD MacLEISH, Librarian of Congress, letter to William Donovan, 29 June 1941; quoted in Troy, *Donovan and the CIA* (1981). Donovan, then Coordinator of Information—the predecessor of OSS—called on MacLeish to help find scholars to conduct intelligence research and analysis.

"Donovan . . . organized the government's first systemic utilization, in peace or war, of the knowledge, language capability, and area experience of the country's historians, economists, social scientists, anthropologists, geographers, and psychologists."

 THOMAS TROY, *Donovan and the CIA* (1981).

"At the same historical moment that General Groves and Professor Oppenheimer were recruiting the world's most eminent scientists to the Manhattan project, General William J. Donovan and Professor William L. Langer were conscripting the leading thinkers in a dozen scholarly disciplines into the Office of Strategic Services. . . . The erudite scholars of [OSS] did not paddle ashore in rubber dinghies or drop from the sky into enemy territory.

... In the last analysis, however, it was they more than their operational colleagues who laid the foundations of modern intelligence work.... One of the earliest achievements of this first generation of American intelligence analysts was to demonstrate that it was possible to secure the greater part of this vital intelligence not by dropping behind enemy lines but by walking over to the Library of Congress, where they did what scholars do best, namely, plodding through journals, monographs, foreign newspapers, and other published sources."

> **BARRY KATZ**, *Foreign Intelligence: Research and Analysis in OSS* (1989).

"General William Donovan used to say that intelligence is no more mysterious than McGuffey's *Second Reader* and just about as sinister. He meant that the world's libraries are filled with interesting information, and that scholarly research alone can produce much good intelligence. If scholars also have access to the data provided by espionage and reconnaissance, little of importance can be hid from them. Hence, thought Donovan, the primary tool of intelligence is the index card."

> **ANGELO CODEVILLA**, *Informing Statecraft* (1992).

"In such an environment [i.e., in a university] one might reasonably expect to find a number of people, students, faculty, alumni, and staff, who have a wide-ranging curiosity, a somewhat childlike desire to collect experiences and to see places, to know because knowing in itself is fun: that is, a number of people ideally suited for the rather unconventional life of an intelligence service, and in particular, of the Office of Strategic Services in World War II."

> **ROBIN W. WINKS** on the close association that universities like Yale have had with American intelligence, beginning with OSS, in *Cloak and Gown: Scholars in the Secret War, 1939–1961* (1987).

"It is a curious fact of academic history that the first great center of area studies in the United States was not located in any university, but in Washington, during the Second World War, in the Office of Strategic Services. In very large measure the area study programs developed in American universities in the years after the war were manned, directed, or stimulated by graduates of the OSS —a remarkable institution, half cops and robbers and half faculty meeting."

> **McGEORGE BUNDY** in 1964; quoted in Cline, *Secrets, Spies and Scholars* (1976).

"[OSS Research and Analysis] caused, in a sense, the reorganization of knowledge, promoted area studies, and was one of the reasons why American scholarship, which in the humanities and social sciences might have been thought to be behind that of Europe when the war began, emerged in the 1950s ... as predominant on the world scene."

> **ROBIN W. WINKS**, *Cloak and Gown: Scholars in the Secret War, 1939–1961* (1987).

"There is nothing at all discreditable or dishonorable in the projected activities [of] American academic personnel who collect intelligence in the course of their legitimate research in a foreign country.... Such intelligence work can be done by American academic persons with a completely clear conscience."

> Report of the Committee on Relations between Government Intelligence and Research Work and the American Universities, 1945; cited in Winks, *Cloak and Gown* (1987). This committee was formed by OSS analysis chief and Harvard history professor William Langer.

"The academic is all too apt to lack elasticity. He is generally an individualist, and when he thinks he is right he is all too prone to be impatient with the difficulties.... A real weakness of [OSS analysis] was undoubtedly the fact that it was of necessity so largely academic."

CIA National Estimates chief—and Harvard history professor—**WILLIAM LANGER** to Kermit Roosevelt, 5 March 1947; quoted in Katz, *Foreign Intelligence* (1989).

"The CIA research and analysis shops deserve a great deal of credit for realizing from the first that a symbiotic relationship exists between the scholars in government intelligence agencies and scholars elsewhere. This respect for scholarship is one of the main distinguishing features that has given CIA a marked superiority in intellectual quality over the Soviet KGB and other totalitarian intelligence services."

Former DDI **RAY CLINE**, *Secrets, Spies and Scholars* (1976).

"By 1948-49 CIA personnel came from seventy-seven different colleges and universities. There was, as yet, no public talk about 'invisible government,' no thought that a professor who acted as a contact point might be engaged in conflict of interest. The urgencies of the wartime campus simply extended, with hardly the hiatus of 1946, into the cold war and, at most universities, through the war in Korea, not to be questioned until the early 1960s."

ROBIN W. WINKS, *Cloak and Gown: Scholars in the Secret War, 1939–1961* (1987).

"Academic training leads you to look at the facts, to weigh the facts."

OSS and CIA veteran **HARRY ROSITZKE** in 1981; quoted in the *Washington Post*, 7 November 2002. Rositzke was a Harvard Ph.D. in philology who ran operations against the USSR.

"Academics who answered the CIA's call [in the 1950s] did so out of a patriotic desire to serve their country and out of a self-interested desire to obtain privileged, top-class information unavailable to them in the normal course of their university work."

JOHN RANELAGH, *The Agency* (1986).

"While CIA has experts in virtually all subjects of concern, there is a vast reservoir of expertise, experience, and insight in the community of university scholars that can help us, and through us, the American government, better understand problems and their implications for us and for international stability."

DDI **ROBERT GATES**, address at Harvard University, 13 February 1986; in *Studies in Intelligence* (summer 1986).

"One of the important differences between academe and the intelligence community [is that] in most universities one has the right to be wrong. Universities are built upon making mistakes; there could be no valid research were there not hundreds of feints, aborted projects, invalid conclusions. And one must not be punished, or intimidated, for mistakes honestly made. No government bureaucracy could hold to such a principle."

ROBIN W. WINKS, *Cloak and Gown: Scholars in the Secret War, 1939–1961* (1987).

"Another emergent heresy is that CIA analysts are influenced by academics and academic thinking to the detriment of realistic analysis. I am reminded of one venture we launched in the late 1960s to tap the knowledge and judgment of the best scholars of Chinese affairs. . . . The scholars were brilliantly knowledgeable of Chinese history, culture, and social structure, but they were as innocent as babes about current conditions, be they political, economic, or military. It invariably took the CIA Chinese experts at least a full day to bring the academic experts up to speed. . . . Most CIA analysts found academic people too inadequately informed about current developments to have much impact on their judgment."

Former DDI **R. JACK SMITH**, *The Unknown CIA* (1989).

"Intelligence analysts must provide answers in a timely fashion. Their work is useless unless it reaches policymakers before they have been forced by circumstances to act. Academic authors, by contrast, generally have the luxury of taking as much time as they feel is necessary to reach a conclusion. Similarly, academics typically work alone and on subjects of their own choice; intelligence analysts, meanwhile, are largely guided in their choice of topics by the requirements of others, and their work must be coordinated with others before it is completed."

ABRAM SHULSKY, *Silent Warfare: Understanding the World of Intelligence* (1993).

"If the United States is going to have markedly better intelligence in parts of the world where few Americans have lived, studied, or understood local mores and aspirations, it is going to have to overcome a cultural disease: thinking that American primacy makes it unnecessary for American education to foster broad and deep expertise on foreign, especially non-Western, societies. The United States is perhaps the only major country in the world where one can be considered well educated yet speak only the native tongue."

RICHARD K. BETTS, "Fixing Intelligence," *Foreign Affairs* (January–February 2002).

ANALYSIS & ANALYSTS

The primary job of intelligence is not, as one DCI put it, "to steal secrets" but rather to make sense of the secrets that intelligence does steal. Producing informed and timely analysis for the nation's leadership, the Literary Spy would argue, is the central reason intelligence agencies exist. It's the one major intelligence function that is an end in itself; all the others—collection, covert action, and counterintelligence—are means to this or other ends. Yet no one makes movies about intelligence analysis and analysts: it would be like watching paint dry.

See also: Academia; Collection; Espionage & Spies; Subcultures in CIA

"For in much wisdom is much grief: and he that increaseth knowledge increaseth sorrow."

Ecclesiastes, 1:18 (King James).

"When you know a thing, to hold that you know it, and when you do not know a thing, to allow that you do not know it: this is knowledge."

Attributed to Confucius (c. 551–479 B.C.).

"I am wiser to this small extent, that I do not think that I know what I do not know."

PLATO (427?–347? B.C.), *The Defense of Socrates.*

"If a man will begin with certainties, he shall end in doubts; but if he will be content to begin with doubts he shall end in certainties."

FRANCIS BACON, *The Advancement of Learning* (1605).

"The secret of being a bore is to tell everything."

VOLTAIRE, *Sept Discours en Vers sur l'Homme* (1738).

"Knowledge is of two kinds: we know a subject ourselves, or we know where we can find information upon it."

SAMUEL JOHNSON, 1775, in Boswell's *Life of Johnson* (1791).

"Given for one instant an intelligence which could comprehend all the forces by which nature is animated and the respective positions of the beings that compose it, if moreover this intelligence were vast enough to submit these data to analysis, it would embrace in the same formula both the movements of the largest bodies in the universe and those of the lightest atom; to it nothing would be uncertain, and the future as the past would be present to its eyes."

French mathematician and astronomer **PIERRE SIMON DE LAPLACE**, *Théorie Analytique des Probabilités* (1820).

"It is by comparing a variety of information, we are frequently enabled to investigate facts, which were so intricate or hidden, that no single clue could have led to the knowledge of them. . . . In this point of view, intelligence becomes interesting which but from its connection and collateral circumstances, would not be important."

GEORGE WASHINGTON, 1782; cited in Andrew, *For the President's Eyes Only* (1995).

"[Union General George] McClellan in mid-January [1862] found a couple of assistants who today would be called intelligence analysts . . . two young French aides-de-camp, Louis Philippe d'Orleans and his brother, Robert. Louis Philippe was the comte de Paris and pretender to the throne; Robert was the duc de Chartres. . . . This was doubtless the first time in the Civil War, and conceivably in any American war up to that time, that anyone was assigned analysis of intelligence as a full-time or principal duty; and the men McClellan found for that sensitive position, which today would require a security clearance not easily obtained, could not even take the oath of allegiance to the flag they were serving."

EDWIN FISHEL, *Secret War for the Union* (1996).

"It is a capital mistake to theorize before you have all the evidence. It biases the judgement."

Sherlock Holmes to Doctor Watson in Sir **ARTHUR CONAN DOYLE**, *A Study in Scarlet* (1887). Unfortunately, in intelligence work you never have all the evidence—but you're still expected to theorize without bias.

"We are suffering from a plethora of surmise, conjecture, and hypothesis. The difficulty is to detach the framework of fact—of absolute, undeniable fact—from the embellishments of theorists and reporters. Then, having established ourselves upon this sound basis, it is our duty to see what inferences may be drawn, and which are the special points upon which the whole mystery turns."

Sherlock Holmes in Sir **ARTHUR CONAN DOYLE**, "The Adventure of Silver Blaze" (1892). Here Holmes identifies the initial task of intelligence analysis: first determine what you *know*.

"An intelligence officer needs a well-balanced mind. As much of the news which he will get will be contradictory, questionable, and often entirely false, he must abstain from according too much faith to any reports which reach him. . . . The power of detecting true from false news is a great gift; it may be acquired by methodical reflection, by a careful comparison with analogous cases, by a just appreciation of the worthiness of the source from which it has been obtained, and by a knowledge of the characteristics and habits of the enemy. . . . When an officer is perplexed by conflicting statements and reports, so as to be unable to decide which contain the most truth, he must necessarily fall back on the law of probabilities. In his perplexity he will form several possible suppositions, and, when the most cogent reasons preponderate in favour of one over the other, there will be less danger of falling into error."

British Colonel **GEORGE FURSE**, *Information in War* (1895).

"Seek simplicity and distrust it."

ALFRED NORTH WHITEHEAD, British mathematician and philosopher, *The Concept of Nature* (1920).

"The function of the Intelligence Division is not merely to collect and pass on the Munchausen tales of spies and untrustworthy agents, but carefully to sift and scrutinise the intelligence they receive, and in putting it forward to indicate the degree of probability which attaches to it."

WINSTON CHURCHILL, First Lord of the Admiralty, November 1914; cited in Stafford, *Churchill and Secret Service* (1998).

"It is my business to know things. That is my trade."

Sherlock Holmes in Sir **ARTHUR CONAN DOYLE**, "The Adventure of the Blanched Soldier" (1926).

"Don't tell me what you think. Give me the facts and the source!"

JOSEPH STALIN to his intelligence officers; quoted in Andrew and Mitrokhin, *The Mitrokhin Archive* (1999). Stalin condemned intelligence analysis as "dangerous guesswork." Stalin was not the only national leader to consider himself his own best intelligence analyst.

"The historian must have a mulish obstinacy, a refusal to be gulled; he must be incredulous of his evidence or he will trip over the deliberately falsified."

SHERMAN KENT, *Writing History* (1941). Kent, a historian and wartime OSS analyst who later was in charge of producing CIA's estimates, could also have been describing the work of the intelligence analyst.

"In July 1941 [President] Roosevelt gave [William Donovan] the title of Coordinator of Information (COI). His first act was to set up the analytical branch. The OSS would have a brain (and a tongue) before it had eyes and ears."

ANGELO CODEVILLA, *Informing Statecraft* (1992).

"We have, scattered throughout the various departments of our government, documents and memoranda concerning military and naval and air and economic potentials of the Axis which, if gathered together and studied in detail by carefully selected trained minds, with a knowledge both of the related languages and technique, would yield valuable and often decisive results."

Coordinator of Information **WILLIAM DONOVAN** on the role of analysts in COI; quoted in Warner, *The Office of Strategic Services* (2000).

"We find that people with youth, good training, pliability of mind, and a lot of intellectual curiosity can learn the game from scratch in a rather short period of time, and they are the ones I am most interested in."

OSS official **SHERMAN KENT** to fellow historian Raymond Sontag, on recruiting for the Research and Analysis Branch of OSS, 4 August 1942; cited in Katz, *Foreign Intelligence: Research and Analysis in OSS* (1989). "R&A" was also known as the "Chairborne Division."

"During World War II, American academics and experts in the Office of Strategic Services . . . virtually invented the discipline of intelligence analysis—one of America's few unique contributions to the craft of intelligence."

CIA historian **MICHAEL WARNER** in Kuhns, *Assessing the Soviet Threat* (1997).

"Research and Analysis . . . proved in practice to be the heart of OSS intelligence. What was unexpected about OSS Research and Analysis was its remarkably effective use of publicly accessible information. From [open] sources . . . R&A provided exact details of the North African train systems ... predicted that the crunch for the Nazis would come in the area of manpower and not, as was widely assumed, in the area of food production ... demonstrated that the Axis powers would probably be able to maintain sufficient supplies of gasoline, oil, and lubricants for their needs despite Allied bombing.... The truth of these studies was shocking to the military: the idea that 'egghead' intellectuals could tell them something of practical use was a revelation."

JOHN RANELAGH, *The Agency* (1986). Today the military has its own "eggheads."

"There is little historical disagreement that R&A [Research and Analysis] was the most important unit in the OSS.... There was more respect for R&A outside OSS than there was inside the organization."

ROBIN W. WINKS, *Cloak and Gown: Scholars in the Secret War, 1939–1961* (1987).

"The Research and Analysis Branch [of OSS] prepared analytical reports on a bewildering range of problems: the condition of rail transport on the Russian front, the relation between aggression and business structure during the Weimar Republic, attitudes of the Roman Catholic Church in Hungary, the political ideas of Charles de Gaulle, the looting and damaging of artworks, the location of concentration camps in central Europe. Regional specialists studied the Communist Party of India and the puppet regime in Nanking, inflation in Burma and guerrillas in the Philippines, trade routes in the Congo basin and rival cliques in the Japanese Army."

BARRY KATZ, *Foreign Intelligence: Research and Analysis in OSS* (1989).

"[William Donovan's] unique contribution to American intelligence [was] that scholarship was its primary discipline, that the acquisition of information was to serve it, and that its paramilitary adventures were an adjunct to its authority and expertise in secret machinery."

Former DCI WILLIAM COLBY, *Honorable Men* (1978).

"Most of our intelligence came from good old-fashioned intellectual sweat."

General WILLIAM DONOVAN; quoted in Katz, *Foreign Intelligence: Research and Analysis in OSS* (1989).

"It is precisely when the resources are stretched and the tasks many, when the forces are evenly matched and the issue trembles in the balance, that good intelligence and sensitive interpretation matter most."

British historian DAVID DILKS describing analysis on the eve of World War II; quoted in Laqueur, *A World of Secrets* (1985).

"Imagination is sometimes baffled by the facts."

WINSTON CHURCHILL, 1941; quoted in Stafford, *Churchill and Secret Service* (1998). Sometimes it takes imagination even to see the facts.

"Discovery consists of seeing what everybody has seen and thinking what nobody has thought."

ALBERT SZENT-GYÖRGYI, Hungarian-born American scientist and 1937 Nobel Prize winner, *The Scientist Speculates* (1962).

"Since last November, I have pointed out the immediate necessity of setting up such [a centralized intelligence] agency to take over the valuable assets created by OSS. Among these assets was the establishment for the first time in our nation's history of a foreign secret intelligence service which reported information as seen through American eyes. As an integral and inseparable part of this service there is a group of specialists to analyze and evaluate the material for presentation to those who determine national policy."

> OSS director **WILLIAM DONOVAN**, memorandum to Harold Smith, director of the Bureau of the Budget, 25 August 1945; in *FRUS 1945–1950: Emergence of the Intelligence Establishment* (1996), document 3.

"There should be established a national centralized foreign intelligence agency. . . . Such a service should include in its staff specialists . . . professionally trained in analysis of information and possessing a high degree of linguistic, regional or functional competence, to analyze, coordinate and evaluate incoming information, to make special intelligence reports, and to provide guidance for the collecting branches of the agency."

> OSS director **WILLIAM DONOVAN**, paper on "A Centralized United States Foreign Intelligence System," attachment to Donovan's 25 August 1945 memorandum to President Truman; in *FRUS 1945–1950: Emergence of the Intelligence Establishment* (1996), document 3.

"The present American intelligence system [for analysis] represents a costly group of factories, each manufacturing component parts without a central assembly line for the finished product. This function of analysis and synthesis by a central intelligence agency represents the assembly line which has heretofore been lacking. . . . [Analytic] studies would be made in part at the request of individual departments of the Government. Within the central intelligence agency they would be drawn up by a staff of specialists with wide background and experience drawn from all phases of governmental and civil life. . . . A large proportion of the studies would deal with fields in which civilians are experts and military men are laymen, and

the staff should therefore contain a concentration of the best civilian talent available in the country."

> Strategic Services Unit Director General **JOHN MAGRUDER** in a report to the War Department on the proposed central intelligence agency, October 1945; in *FRUS 1945–1950: Emergence of the Intelligence Establishment* (1996), document 34.

"Synthesis."

> **WILLIAM DONOVAN**'s preferred term for what today is called "analysis"; see his memorandum of 13 September 1945 to President Truman, reproduced in Warner, *CIA Under Truman* (1994).

"Procedures are being developed to ensure that the items contained therein reflect the best judgment of qualified personnel in C.I.G. and the Departments."

> DCI **SIDNEY SOUERS**, Central Intelligence Group report, June 1946, describing the new *Weekly Summary*; reproduced in Warner, *CIA Under Truman* (1994).

"Any report of this nature is at best educated guesswork."

> Central Intelligence Group report "Soviet Capabilities for the Development and Production of Certain Types of Weapons and Equipment," 31 October 1946; reproduced in Kuhns, *Assessing the Soviet Threat* (1997).

"News does not become knowledge by the mere process of gathering."

> **ARTHUR DARLING**, *The Central Intelligence Agency* (1990). Collection is not analysis.

"You do not send a 200-page study to the White House when the request asked for a memorandum, nor do you send a memo to the operating officer who has requested an encyclopedia."

> **SHERMAN KENT**, *Strategic Intelligence* (1949). Know thy customer.

"An open mind and a willingness to accept new conclusions where the facts impose them are absolutely essential. Stubborn prejudice is fatal. Any intelligence officer who is unwilling to view new facts with an open mind despite firm convictions bred out of past experience is useless in our type of work."

> Former OSS officer **ALLEN DULLES**, speech in Boston, 16 November 1951; in CIA Historical Intelligence Collection.

"Don't start that paper on China by saying 'China is a great land mass'!"

> Attributed to DCI **WALTER BEDELL SMITH**; cited in Ranelagh, *The Agency* (1986). Junior analysts are very quickly disabused of the notion that our readers know only what we tell them.

"The obvious purpose of the SAMs was to blind us so we could not see what was going on there [in Cuba]. There they were with 16,000 men with all their ordnance equipment and then came the ships. There was nothing else to ship to Cuba but missiles. That was my argument. We didn't see the missiles. They were on the ships and we had no agents on the ships. We really didn't know what was on the ships, but some things you can deduce. That was one of them."

> Former DCI **JOHN McCONE** explaining in 1988 why he —alone at CIA and in the Kennedy administration—believed in 1962 that the USSR would try to put strategic missiles in Cuba; quoted in Schecter and Deriabin, *The Spy Who Saved the World* (1995).

"[In 1963] analysts were encouraged to learn to understand the concerns of policymakers, to package their finished intelligence in a relevant form, and to get it to the right people at the right time."

> CIA historian **ROBERTA KNAPP**, 1990; in CIA Historical Intelligence Collection. Knapp is describing DDI Ray

Cline's "new" doctrine—which every generation of DI managers replicates to varying degrees.

"Without [analysts] our scientifically produced information as well as that furnished by the tools of espionage would be of little use. For it is the patient analyst who arranges, ponders, tries out alternate hypotheses and draws conclusions. What he is bringing to the task is the substantive background, the imagination and originality of the sound and careful scholar."

> Former DCI **ALLEN DULLES**, *The Craft of Intelligence* (1963).

"You can't do a professional job on a subject if you're going to be passionate about it."

> CIA official **JOHN HUIZENGA** on analysis during the Vietnam conflict; quoted in Ranelagh, *The Agency* (1986).

"It is well documented and well known that for decades CIA analysts were skeptical of official pronouncements about the Vietnam war and consistently pessimistic about the outlook for light at the end of the tunnel."

> Former CIA official **HAROLD FORD** in *Studies in Intelligence* 40 (1996).

"President Johnson . . . wanted from us a list of U.S. gains and accomplishments in recent weeks in Vietnam. I accepted the task and passed it along to the Vietnam team. . . . Within fifteen minutes a deputation of six Vietnam specialists was outside my door. Their message was they refused to do the job. The Vietnam War was not going well for the United States, and they would not be a party to claiming it was."

> Former DDI **R. JACK SMITH**, *The Unknown CIA* (1989).

"Modern intelligence has to do with the painstaking collection and analysis of facts, the exercise of judgment, and clear and quick presentation. It is not simply what serious journalists would always produce if they had the time; it is something more rigorous, continuous, and above all operational—that is to say, something that somebody wants to do or may be forced to do."

> DCI **RICHARD HELMS** quoting the *Economist* in an address to the American Society of Newspaper Editors, Washington, D.C., 14 April 1971.

"A desk is a dangerous place from which to watch the world."

> **JOHN LE CARRÉ** [David Cornwell], *The Honorable Schoolboy* (1977).

"Keep giving me things that make me think."

> National Security Advisor **HENRY KISSINGER** to DCI William Colby; quoted in Colby, *Honorable Men* (1978).

"In my experience the CIA developed rationales for inaction much more frequently than for daring thrusts. Its analysts were only too aware that no one has ever been penalized for not having foreseen an opportunity, but that many careers have been blighted for not predicting a risk. Therefore the intelligence community has always been tempted to forecast dire consequences for any conceivable course of action, an attitude that encourages paralysis rather than adventurism."

> **HENRY KISSINGER**, *White House Years* (1979). Not sure what Henry's beef is—should not "daring thrusts" *always* be less frequent than inaction?

"The analytical side of the CIA . . . generally reflected the most liberal school of thought in the government."

> **HENRY KISSINGER**, *White House Years* (1979). And he doesn't mean that as a compliment.

"Nixon seemed more interested in the CIA for covert action than for intelligence analysis. Why not? Covert action was an extension of administration policy, while analysis often showed the policy to be unwise."

> Senior CIA official; quoted in Andrew, *For the President's Eyes Only* (1995).

"Intelligence is only useful if it is subjected to evaluation and analysis to put it into the context of ongoing U.S. national security and foreign policy concerns. It must be evaluated for accuracy and credibility in the light of its source or its collection method, for the validity and significance of the content, after being collated with other available data, and for its impact on U.S. interests, operations, or objectives."

> Former DDI **RAY CLINE**, *Secrets, Spies and Scholars* (1976).

"Before you become too entranced with gorgeous gadgets and mesmerizing video displays, let me remind you that information is not knowledge, knowledge is not wisdom, and wisdom is not foresight. Each grows out of the other and we need them all."

> Attributed to **ARTHUR C. CLARKE**.

"Analysts born rather than merely assigned to the job have a glutton's appetite for paper—newspapers and magazines, steel production statistics, lists of names at official ceremonies, maps, charts of radio traffic flow, the text of toasts at official banquets, railroad timetables, photographs of switching yards, shipping figures, the names of new towns, the reports of agents, telephone directories, anything at all which can be written down, stacked on a desk, and read."

    THOMAS POWERS, *The Man Who Kept the Secrets* (1979). Now we use computer databases, but the characterization still applies.

"The analysis came down firmly on both sides of the issue."

    Former DCI **ROBERT GATES** describing a 1980 CIA assessment of Soviet intentions; in Gates, *From the Shadows* (1996).

"It is not enough, of course, simply to collect information. Thoughtful analysis is vital to sound decisionmaking."

    President **RONALD REAGAN**, 4 December 1981; cited in CIA, *"Our First Line of Defense"* (1996).

"The analytic branch of the CIA is given to tweedy, pipe-smoking intellectuals who work much as if they were doing research back in the universities whence many of them came. It probably has more Ph.D.'s than any other area of government and more than many colleges. Their expertise ranges from anthropology to zoology. Yet, for all that, they can be wrong."

    Former DCI **STANSFIELD TURNER**, *Secrecy and Democracy* (1985). These days, smoking of all sorts is banned, and tweeds are out of favor.

"If there is a weakness in our intelligence analysis, it is in our ability to figure out what the leaders of a foreign power are going to do in any given situation. . . . As a country, we must develop a far deeper knowledge of other peoples' culture, religion, [and] politics than we possess today. Believe it or not, we are still essentially a provincial nation."

    Former DCI **RICHARD HELMS** in 1983; quoted in Ranelagh, *The Agency* (1986).

"Analysts cannot interpret information without hypotheses or a belief system. But this system may be wrong in the first place—for instance, it may err through wishful thinking (the Pollyanna syndrome) or, on the contrary, through excessive fear (the Cassandra syndrome). It may be affected by the stereotyped images one society has of another. There is frequently great reluctance to give up a hypothesis once it has been adopted, especially if much time and energy have already been invested in it. . . . One of the most frequent sources of error is mirror imaging, which also includes the assumption that what the enemy knows about its own side is more or less identical with what the observer knows."

    WALTER LAQUEUR, *A World of Secrets* (1985).

"Analysis, especially political analysis, is the Achilles' heel of intelligence."

    Former DCI **STANSFIELD TURNER**, *Secrecy and Democracy* (1985).

"A discipline such as intelligence involves competence not only in current affairs, in history and geography, in psychology and sociology, in economics, science and technology, but it should include firsthand experience [abroad]. Much thought has been given in recent decades to improving medical education, but very little to the acquisition of the skills and the knowledge needed in intelligence. Yet the quality of analysts will remain the decisive factor in intelligence in the future as it has been in the past."

    WALTER LAQUEUR, *A World of Secrets* (1985).

"A nation's intelligence community reflects the habits of thought of its educated elite from whose ranks it is recruited and on whom it depends for intellectual sustenance. The CIA is no exception. Its analytic staff, filled with American Ph.D.'s in the natural and social sciences along with engineers, inevitably shares the outlook of U.S. academe, with its penchant for philosophical positivism, cultural agnosticism, and political liberalism."

RICHARD PIPES in *Commentary* (October 1986).

"A [grave] danger lies in not having sufficient expertise about an area or a problem to detect and interpret important trends and developments. To make up for such deficiency, analysts tend to impose on the information the concepts, models, and beliefs that they have derived elsewhere. . . . The parochialism of those who know all the facts about a particular country that they consider to be unique, but lack the conceptual tools for making sense of what they see, is well known."

ROBERT JERVIS, "What's Wrong with the Intelligence Process?" *International Journal of Intelligence and Counterintelligence* (1986).

"These analysts are hardly James Bonds. They tell their friends and neighbors openly that they work for the CIA; by temperament they are more professorial than conspiratorial."

GREGORY TREVERTON, *Covert Action* (1987). Well, some of us read James Bond.

"The historian's 'use' [of evidence] does not involve any specific action . . . other than for himself: the act of writing a book or article, or perhaps delivering a lecture. The intelligence analyst's 'use' is predicated upon an assumption of some action, or denial of action, that reaches well beyond the self. This makes the analyst's task more difficult and it demands of him the greatest integrity. . . . The historian writes for himself, and if someone else likes what he writes, that is simply icing on

the cake. The intelligence analyst is a big boy, and he knows that his product is out of his hands, and open to abuse, as soon as he passes it along."

ROBIN W. WINKS on the difference between the historian's craft and that of the intelligence analyst, in *Cloak and Gown: Scholars in the Secret War, 1939–1961* (1987).

"CIA analysts—probably the best in the American government, perhaps even in our society—think clearly and write well. And while no human being can be truly objective, CIA analysts are trained to ask the hard questions and to resist pressures to come up with the estimates of reality that the policy makers want to see. . . . All Americans have a tremendous stake in the intelligence analysts' work."

ANTHONY LAKE, *Somoza Falling* (1989).

"*The Unknown CIA.*"

Title of 1989 book by former DDI **R. JACK SMITH**, referring to the Agency's intelligence analysts.

"*The Essential CIA.*"

Subtitle of 1976 book by former DDI **RAY CLINE**, *Secrets, Spies and Scholars*, referring to the Agency's intelligence analysts.

"The truth is that there is never enough good intelligence. We need all we can get of all kinds. Diplomatic reports, newspaper accounts, military reports, technical reports, espionage—they all form part of an intricate mosaic. Used with skill by an expert, they interact synergistically and establish approximate truth."

Former DDI **R. JACK SMITH**, *The Unknown CIA* (1989). What's hard is convincing policymakers, journalists, and the public that "approximate truth" is the best it's going to get.

"Probably the only political observer to predict, two years before his inauguration, that Carter would be the next president of the United States was a Soviet analyst who argued that Wall Street capitalists needed to install a puppet from the agrarian South in the White House to control the restless American peasantry. His foolish but accurate forecast is a reminder that the best predictions are not always produced by the best analysts."

> CHRISTOPHER ANDREW, *For the President's Eyes Only* (1995). Conversely, even the best analysts have their off days.

"The most difficult task that falls to us in intelligence is to see the world as it is, not as we—or others—would wish it to be."

> DCI **ROBERT GATES**, CIA Headquarters, 4 December 1991; in Gates, *Speeches 1991–1992* (1993). This is a profound philosophical—and political—distinction that goes beyond intelligence.

"It is quite normal for intelligence analysts both to see reality through their own intellectual constraints, and not to see the distinction between the constructs and the reality."

> **ANGELO CODEVILLA**, *Informing Statecraft* (1992).

"At the center of the intelligence machine lies the analyst, and he is the fellow to whom all the information goes so that he can review it and think about it and determine what it means."

> Former DCI **WILLIAM COLBY** in the *Foreign Service Journal* (January 1992).

"The DI's role in the post–Cold War world is likely to grow. The issues that are emerging—economics and trade, proliferation of weapons and related technologies, political instability and ethnoreligious strife—require the intellect of the analyst as much or more than the cloak and dagger of the spy."

> **MARVIN OTT** in the *Wall Street Journal*, 23 December 1992.

"There is in the post–Cold War world a greater proportion of mysteries—things such as Yeltsin's survival that even people in Russia don't know—than of secrets, which are things you can steal. And, the kinds of things policymakers need help on are often more mysteries than secrets."

> **JOSEPH NYE, JR.**, chairman of the National Intelligence Council; in CIA, *Symposium* (1994).

"Our committee questioned whether CIA needed to be writing studies on Evangelical Protestantism in Latin America, AIDS, or Norwegian whaling policy—matters better left to academic think tanks or to offices within the Department of State."

> U.S. Representative **DAN GLICKMAN**, then the immediate past chairman of the House intelligence committee, at a Georgetown University symposium; quoted in *Studies in Intelligence* (spring 1995).

"The national interest is not well served by an unimpeachably objective assessment that key officials judge to add little value to the policy-making process.... At the same time, the national interest is not well served by an assessment much admired by policy officials that does not meet the standards of sound analytic tradecraft."

> Former DDI **R. JACK SMITH**, *Studies in Intelligence* (fall 1995).

"The notion that the opinions of analysts should be the main product—when often they are not a useful product at all—is a recipe for having analysis ignored."

PAUL WOLFOWITZ, Undersecretary of Defense for Policy, 1989–93; quoted in *Studies in Intelligence* (spring 1995). This is why analysts are trained to argue on the merits of Evidence and Logic rather than on the basis of Rhetoric and Authority.

"[CIA] analysts did not have the foggiest notion of what I did; and I did not have a clue as to what they could or should do."

Ambassador **ROBERT BLACKWILL** explaining why early in his career he made it a policy never to read CIA analysis; quoted in *Studies in Intelligence* (1995 unclassified ed.).

"The ultimate purpose of U.S. intelligence is to enhance U.S. national security by informing policymakers and supporting military operations. Toward these ends, one of the most important functions of the intelligence community is to provide analysis gleaned from all sources (open and secret) and to package it in a timely and useful manner. Only the intelligence community performs this essential integrative function."

Council on Foreign Relations, *Making Intelligence Smarter* (1996).

"They [i.e., intelligence analysts] don't make connections. They don't see shapes forming in the sky. . . . A great intelligencer catches history in the act. We can't expect some little nine-to-five fellow on the third floor who's worried about his mortgage to catch history in the act. Can we?"

JOHN LE CARRÉ [David Cornwell], *The Tailor of Panama* (1996).

"Analysis is usually a messy affair, with incomplete information and often heated debates over what the available facts may really mean about the intentions of secretive adversaries in distant capitals. . . . Uncertainty, ambiguity, debate, and partial answers to tangled questions will remain an existential condition of the analytical process."

LOCH JOHNSON in *Intelligence and National Security* (October 1996). Messy, frustrating, and loads of fun.

"[In 1947,] the job of this fledgling CIA was 'to prevent another Pearl Harbor.' Fighting the Cold War came later. What became known as the Directorate of Intelligence was given the core mission. And it still has it! . . . Today's litany of newspaper and magazine articles advocating the end of CIA are almost all directed at covert action. The Directorate of Intelligence is rarely referred to. But, I repeat, that is where the core mission lies."

Former DCI **RICHARD HELMS**, rather surprising remarks at CIA's 50th anniversary ceremonies, 18 September 1997.

"The game is akin to putting a puzzle together without all the pieces, or a box top to guide you, and with several parts of other puzzles thrown in."

Senior CIA analyst **MARTIN PETERSEN** in *National Security Studies Quarterly* (spring 1999). And doing it in bad light as well.

"Getting knowledge out of intelligence information is like squeezing grapes into wine—there's a first pressing, a second pressing, and even the skins can be useful for something."

White House official with intelligence responsibilities, July 1999.

"Our analysts blend a scholar's mastery of detail with a reporter's sense of urgency and clarity."

> DCI **GEORGE TENET**, remarks at the opening of CIA's Sherman Kent School for Intelligence Analysis, May 2000.

"Electronic intercepts are great, but you don't know if you've got two idiots on the phone. And a picture may say 1,000 words, but it's still just a snapshot. There is no context."

> Senior CIA analyst **MARTIN PETERSEN**; quoted in the *Los Angeles Times*, 21 July 2000.

"Intelligence analysis—even the most rigorous— can never be error-free. Our analysts may have the best information available, but they seldom have the luxury of complete information before making a judgment. The glints and glimmerings of insight that they get from examining shards of information help them peer into the unknown. But getting some forecasts wrong is an unavoidable part of the intelligence business—a business built on uncertainty. . . . Our analysts are not in this business for headlines or kudos."

> DCI **GEORGE TENET**, remarks at Princeton University, March 2001. Good thing, too.

"On many subjects the [analytic] coverage is now only one analyst deep—and when that one goes on vacation, or quits, the account may be handled out of the back pocket of a specialist on something else. . . . Having half a dozen analysts on hand for some small country might be a good thing if that country turns out to be central to the campaign against terrorists, but those analysts need to be in place before we know we need them if they are to hit the ground running in a crisis. In most such cases, moreover, those analysts would serve their whole careers without producing anything that

the U.S. government really needs, and no good analyst wants to be buried in an inactive account with peripheral significance."

> **RICHARD K. BETTS**, "Fixing Intelligence," *Foreign Affairs* (January–February 2002).

"The most difficult challenge a CIA political analyst faces is establishing credibility with the audience. The first fact of life you must face is that your readers, regardless of their training, expertise, or track record, consider themselves excellent political analysts. Washington is a political town. What money is to New York and celebrity is to Los Angeles, politics and political analysis is to Washington. The mere fact your reader is employed here in a political position convinces him that he is both smart and politically savvy. Your readers may not argue physics with the boys in the missile shop or economics with the guys down the hall, but they most certainly will argue politics with you."

> Senior CIA official **MARTIN PETERSEN** to a class of analysts at CIA's Sherman Kent School for Intelligence Analysis, March 2002.

"Much is asked of you. We rely on your expertise as analysts to sort through enormous volumes of information and put together the pieces of some very important and complex puzzles. We also rely on you to point out where you have doubts, to admit what you don't know, and to question your own conclusions."

> Vice President **RICHARD CHENEY** addressing CIA analysts at their graduation from the Career Analyst Program, 8 November 2002.

"CIA is not the only agency doing this [intelligence] analysis; both the State and Defense Departments indulge in it. The critically important difference in the CIA analysis and that of other institutions is that the Agency product is independent of the occasional parochial interests of other government offices—including the various departments, notably State and Defense—and the executive agencies."

> Former DCI **RICHARD HELMS**, *A Look over My Shoulder* (2003).

"Your analysis will reach the top levels of government and is guaranteed to make a difference."

> CIA ad seeking intelligence analysts, in the *Economist* (September 2003). The first part of the statement is true more often than the second.

"Casting aside the perceived—and I must admit the occasionally real—excitement of secret operations, the absolute essence of the intelligence profession rests in the production of current intelligence reports, memoranda, and National Estimates on which sound policy decisions can be made."

> Former DCI **RICHARD HELMS**, *A Look over My Shoulder* (2003).

ASSASSINATION

The Literary Spy is a bit nonplussed by the wealth of quotations in this category, for it gives a distorted view of something that is rare among intelligence services, and indeed in the American experience it is a nonevent, despite the attention given it. We Americans, it turns out, are not very good assassins, and for this the Literary Spy is grateful.

See also: Covert Action; Plausible Denial

"If it were done when 'tis done, then 'twere well
It were done quickly: if the assassination
Could trammel up the consequence, and catch
With his surcease success; that but this blow

Might be the be-all and end-all here,
But here, upon this bank and shoal of time,
We'd jump the life to come. But in these cases
We still have judgment here; that we but teach
Bloody instructions, which, being taught, return
To plague the inventor: this even-handed justice
Commends the ingredients of our poison'd
    chalice
To our own lips . . ."

> Macbeth agonizing over the temptation to kill King Duncan, in **WILLIAM SHAKESPEARE**, *Macbeth* (1606), Act 1, scene 7. Macbeth, of course, talks himself into committing the murder and then regrets it.

"Assassination, poison, perjury . . . All of these were legitimate principles in the dark ages which intervened between ancient and modern civilizations, but exploded and held in just horror in the 18th century."

> **THOMAS JEFFERSON**, letter to James Monroe, 28 August 1789; cited in Knott, *Secret and Sanctioned* (1996).

"Mr. Consul Eliot and I arranged the neatest little parricide you can imagine, and I think I may promise a new and better-disposed Dey at present. . . . Perhaps you would be so kind as not to mention it specifically when speaking to the Admiral. 'A sudden regime change' is the term I have employed."

> Fictional British intelligence agent speaking of a "regime change" favored by His Majesty's Government in **PATRICK O'BRIAN**, *The Far Side of the World* (1984).

"If evil men were not now and then slain it would not be a good world for weaponless dreamers."

> **RUDYARD KIPLING**, *Kim* (1901).

"Mexico was the scene of the first known American-sponsored assassination attempt. During [President] Wilson's border war with Mexican bandits in 1916, the U.S. Army hired four Mexican citizens to poison revolutionary leader Francisco 'Pancho' Villa. The operatives were instructed by a member of General John Pershing's staff to drop poison tablets into Villa's coffee, but the attempt failed. Pershing apparently hid news of this mission, a cover-up that persisted until the 1980s. There is no known evidence showing that President Wilson was aware of the operation."

STEPHEN KNOTT, *Secret and Sanctioned* (1996).

"It's not the kind of thing we can have anything to do with. We don't wage war by those methods. We leave them to the Germans. Damn it all, we are gentlemen."

Fictional British spy chief R regarding the proposal to assassinate the king of a Balkan country in **W. SOMERSET MAUGHAM**, *Ashenden* (1927). Maugham was an SIS officer in World War I.

"We have not reached that state in our diplomacy where we have to use assassination as a substitute for diplomacy."

British Foreign Secretary **LORD HALIFAX** responding to a proposal in 1938 from the British military attaché in Berlin to kill Adolf Hitler with sporting rifles; quoted in Polmar and Allen, *Encyclopedia of Espionage* (1997).

"The important thing to know about an assassination or an attempted assassination is not who fired the shot, but who paid for the bullet."

ERIC AMBLER, *A Coffin for Dimitrios* (1939).

"I shall hear that cry all my life."

RAMÓN MERCADER, the Spanish communist who, on Stalin's orders and under the direction of Soviet intelligence, assassinated the exiled Leon Trotsky in Mexico on 20 August 1940 by driving an icepick into his skull; quoted in Andrew and Mitrokhin, *The Mitrokhin Archive* (1999).

"I think that the dropping of men dressed in civilian clothes for the purpose of attempting to kill members of the opposing forces is not an operation for which the Royal Air Force should be associated. I think you will agree that there is a vast difference, in ethics, between the time-honoured operation of the dropping of a spy from the air and this entirely new scheme for dropping what one can only call assassins."

British Chief of the Air Staff explaining why the RAF would not support SOE assassination operations, 1 February 1941; quoted in Lloyd, *Guinness Book of Espionage* (1994). The ethical distinction between dropping assassins to kill leaders responsible for an unjust war and the dropping of bombs on population centers is not explored.

"The elimination of Churchill must be an essential feature of any attack on British morale. It would no doubt have an infuriating and therefore temporarily invigorating effect on the population, but that would wear off. And there is no other statesman who could possibly take his place as the focus and fountain-head of British morale."

British assessment written from the perspective of the German Supreme Command, January 1942; cited in Peter Fleming, *Operation Sea Lion* (1957). Analysts today often prepare this kind of "red cell" memorandum to demonstrate the other side's thinking.

"Good morning: A very Happy Christmas to you all. Last night, in Algiers, Admiral Darlan was assassinated."

BBC broadcast on Christmas Day 1942 on the killing of the Vichy overseer of North Africa by a Free French assassin allegedly with British complicity; quoted in Stafford, *Churchill and Secret Service* (1998).

"Tally Ho. Let's get the bastard."

Cable to U.S. Army Air Force P-38 squadron assigned to intercept Japanese admiral Yamamoto's aircraft in April 1943; cited in Miller, *Spying for America* (1989). The P-38s got Yamamoto, who had been the mastermind behind the attack on Pearl Harbor.

"As a strategist, Hitler has been of the greatest possible assistance to the British war effort."

> **R. H. THORNLEY**, chief of the German section of the Special Operations Executive, arguing to the British leadership against Operation FOXLEY—SOE plans to assassinate Hitler in late 1944; quoted in the *Washington Post*, 24 July 1998.

"[British Foreign Minister] Eden and I flew home together by Gibraltar. As my presence in North Africa had been fully reported, the Germans were exceptionally vigilant, and this led to a tragedy which much distressed me. The daily commercial aircraft was about to start from the Lisbon airfield when a thickset man smoking a cigar walked up and was thought to be a passenger on it. The German agents therefore signalled that I was on board. Although these neutral passenger planes had plied unmolested for many months between Portugal and England and had carried only civilian traffic, a German war plane was instantly ordered out, and the defenseless aircraft was ruthlessly shot down. Fourteen civilian passengers perished, and among them the well-known British film actor Leslie Howard. . . . It is difficult to understand how anyone could imagine that with all the resources of Great Britain at my disposal I should have booked a passage in a neutral plane from Lisbon and flown home in broad daylight."

> **WINSTON CHURCHILL** on a German assassination attempt after his meeting with General Eisenhower in Algiers in June 1943; in *The Hinge of Fate* (1950).

"I shall shake my little finger, and there will be no more Tito."

> **JOSEPH STALIN** to Nikita Khrushchev, 1948; quoted in Andrew and Mitrokhin, *The Mitrokhin Archive* (1999). Yugoslav dictator Tito broke from Soviet control in 1948, and

Moscow plotted to assassinate him until Stalin's death in 1953.

"Georgi Sergeyevich, I've come to you from Moscow. The Central Committee of the Communist Party of the Soviet Union has ordered your assassination."

> Soviet assassin **NIKOLAI KHOKHLOV** to his intended target, the anti-Soviet émigré Georgi Okolovich, at the latter's flat in Frankfurt; quoted in Andrew and Mitrokhin, *The Mitrokhin Archive* (1999). Khokhlov decided not to use his weapon, a silent gun that fired cyanide bullets developed by Soviet intelligence, and instead defected.

"It's not difficult to get a Double 0 number if you're prepared to kill people. . . . It's nothing to be particularly proud of."

> James Bond in **IAN FLEMING**, *Casino Royale* (1953).

"In my job . . . I have another motto. It's 'live and let die.'"

> James Bond after being told that Americans prefer to "live and let live" in **IAN FLEMING**, *Live and Let Die* (1954).

"No assassination instructions should ever be written or recorded."

> CIA manual, part of declassified files on the 1954 overthrow of the Arbenz government in Guatemala; cited in the *New York Times*, 28 May 1997.

"The specific technique employed will depend on a large number of variables, but should be constant in one point: Death must be absolutely certain. . . . Absolute reliability is obtained by severing the spinal cord in the cervical region."

> CIA manual, part of declassified files on the 1954 overthrow of the Arbenz government in Guatemala; cited in the *Economist*, 9 August 1997.

"The attempted assassination of [Indonesian president] Sukarno had all the look of an 'operation' by the Central Intelligence Agency: everyone got killed except the appointed victim."

National Review editorial, 14 December 1957.

"It was part of his profession to kill people. He had never liked doing it and when he had to kill he did it as well as he knew how and forgot about it. As a secret agent who had the rare double-0 prefix—the license to kill in the Secret Service—it was his duty to be as cool about death as a surgeon. If it happened, it happened. Regret was unprofessional."

James Bond, "with two double bourbons inside him," thinking about life and death in **IAN FLEMING**, *Goldfinger* (1959).

"Bogdan Stashinsky was a nineteen-year-old student at Lwow University when the KGB recruited him.... On his first foreign assignment, Stashinsky intercepted Dr. Lev Rebet, a prominent Ukrainian émigré, on the steps of his Munich apartment. Thrusting a metal tube about the size of a cigar toward his victim, Stashinsky triggered a device that broke a glass ampoule and blew prussic acid into Rebet's face. The Ukrainian's blood vessels contracted exactly as if he had suffered a coronary spasm. Death was instant [and] as far as the coroner could tell, Rebet had died of coronary disease. Two years later, Stashinsky murdered Stefan Bandera, another Ukrainian émigré leader.... In 1961 Stashinsky defected and told West German officials about the KGB murder technique."

WILLIAM HOOD, *Mole* (1993).

"Difficult but honorable."

KGB chief **ALEKSANDR SHELEPIN** on the assignments given to KGB assassination specialists; quoted in Andrew and Gordievsky, *KGB* (1990).

"This was merely his job—as it was the job of a pest-control officer to kill rats. He was the public executioner, appointed by M to represent the community."

James Bond reflecting on an assassination assignment from M, the fictional chief of British intelligence in **IAN FLEMING**, "For Your Eyes Only" (1960).

"It was my honor to serve President Eisenhower as his Naval Aide during his second term.... [Once] he mentioned that the assassination of a certain dictator (Fidel Castro) had been hypothetically suggested to him. His reaction was that even if it would do any good, which he doubted, it was immoral in the first place and might bring on a wave of retaliatory assassinations which would be counter to world peace, his highest priority."

Vice Admiral **E. P. AURAND**; cited in U.S. Senate, *Final Report of the Senate Select Committee to Study Governmental Operations with respect to Intelligence Activities* [the Church Committee], Book IV (April 1976).

"It just makes every kind of sense to me that neither Eisenhower nor any other President ever said, 'I want that man assassinated.' What he would say is, 'I want that man got rid of.' Obviously, if he could have been kidnapped and kept some place for four or five years incommunicado, probably everyone concerned, probably any President, would have been much happier with that. But also any President, and notably, I think, Mr. Eisenhower, would have realized that if you go out to kidnap a guy in the middle of Africa and he's your enemy, the chances of his ending up getting killed are very good indeed.... So it never occurred to me that the President necessarily used the word 'assassination,' and it certainly never occurred to me that he preferred that means of solving the problem to others that would remove the character from the scene of action, but I have not the slightest doubt that he wanted Lumumba got rid of and he wanted it badly and promptly, as a matter of urgency and of very great importance."

> Former CIA operations chief **RICHARD BISSELL** in a 1976 interview; cited in Weber, *Spymasters* (1999). Patrice Lumumba was the prime minister of the Congo, and a problem.

"In high quarters here, it is the clear-cut conclusion that if [Lumumba] continues to hold high office, the inevitable result will at best be chaos, and at the worst would pave the way for a Communist takeover of the Congo, with disastrous consequences . . . for the interests of the free world generally. Consequently, we conclude that his removal must be an urgent and prime objective."

> DCI **ALLEN DULLES** in a cable to the Congo CIA station regarding Prime Minister Patrice Lumumba, August 1960; cited in U.S. Senate, *Alleged Assassination Plots* (1975).

"The phrase 'In high quarters' would have been understood by any senior Agency officer to be a reference to the President. The intent of the cable seemed as clear to me at the time as it does today. . . . The decision to plan moves against Lumumba was President Eisenhower's."

> Former DCI **RICHARD HELMS** on DCI Dulles's August 1960 cable directing the "removal" of Congo Prime Minister Patrice Lumumba, in *A Look over My Shoulder* (2003).

"The message [from DCI Dulles to the Congo CIA station on Lumumba's removal] was no doubt drafted in an intentionally ambiguous fashion to avoid attributing a decision to the president that

could become an embarrassment. . . . I believe, however, that if you had asked Eisenhower what he was thinking at that moment he probably would have said, 'I sure as hell would rather get rid of Lumumba without killing him, but if that's the only way, then that's got to be the way.' Eisenhower was a tough man behind that smile."

> Former senior CIA chief of operations **RICHARD BISSELL**, *Reflections of a Cold Warrior* (1996). He *did* liberate Europe.

"At some time during the discussion, President Eisenhower said something—I can no longer remember his words—that came across to me as an order for the assassination of Lumumba. . . . There was no discussion; the meeting simply moved on. I remember my sense of that moment quite clearly because the President's statement came as a great shock to me. . . . I was surprised . . . that I would ever hear a President say anything like this in my presence or in the presence of a group of people. I was startled."

> Former NSC staffer **ROBERT H. JOHNSON** in Senate testimony; cited in U.S. Senate, *Alleged Assassination Plots* (1975).

"Kennedy inherited from Eisenhower a system designed to ensure that major covert operations did not proceed without presidential approval. The plot to kill Castro was not a momentary aberration by a handful of agency deviants."

> **CHRISTOPHER ANDREW**, *For the President's Eyes Only* (1995).

"The plan to kill Castro had its genesis at a strange moment in American history, one in which the top officials of the U.S. government appear in retrospect to have been in the grip of what can only be called a murderous mood. Castro was the target of the most serious and sustained attempt, but he was not alone. In 1960 ... the CIA was also trying to assassinate Patrice Lumumba in the Congo, was at the very least considering the assassination of General Kassem of Iraq, and was deeply involved with a small group of dissidents in the Dominican Republic who were planning to kill Trujillo."

THOMAS POWERS, *The Man Who Kept the Secrets* (1979).

"The Committee finds that officials of the United States Government initiated and participated in plots to assassinate Patrice Lumumba and Fidel Castro.... Based on the record of our investigation, the Committee finds that the system of Executive command and control was so inherently ambiguous that it is difficult to be certain at what level assassination activity was known and authorized. This creates the disturbing prospect that assassination activity might have been undertaken by officials of the United States Government without its having been incontrovertibly clear that there was explicit authorization from the President of the United States. At the same time, this ambiguity and imprecision leaves open the possibility that there was a successful 'plausible denial' and that a Presidential authorization was issued but now obscured.... The chain of events revealed by the documents and testimony is strong enough to permit a reasonable inference that the plot to assassinate Lumumba was authorized by President Eisenhower.... There was insufficient evidence from which the Committee could conclude that Presidents Eisenhower, Kennedy, or Johnson, their close advisors, or the Special Group authorized the assassination of Castro."

U.S. Senate, *Alleged Assassination Plots: An Interim Report of the Select Committee to Study Governmental Operations with respect to Intelligence Activities* [the Church Committee] (November 1975). "Special Group" refers to the high-level committee that oversaw efforts to unseat Castro and that included Attorney General Robert Kennedy, Defense Secretary Robert McNamara, and DCI John McCone.

"I had a high degree of confidence that the gentlemen I was talking to in the White House [national security advisor McGeorge Bundy and assistant Walt Rostow] ... would not have given such encouragement unless they were confident that it would meet with the President's approval."

Former CIA operations chief **RICHARD BISSELL** in testimony to President Ford's commission on CIA activities (the Rockefeller Commission), on plans to assassinate Cuban dictator Fidel Castro during the Kennedy administration, 21 April 1975; quoted in Weber, *Spymasters* (1999).

"What would you think if I ordered Castro to be assassinated?"

President **JOHN F. KENNEDY** to *New York Times* reporter Tad Szulc, 9 November 1961; Szulc testimony cited in U.S. Senate, *Alleged Assassination Plots* (1975). Szulc replied that the United States should not engage in such activity, to which Kennedy said, "I agree with you completely." A Kennedy aide testified that the president also said, "Well, that's the kind of thing I'm never going to do."

"We cannot, as a free nation, compete with our adversaries in tactics of terror, assassination, false promises, counterfeit mobs and crises."

President **JOHN F. KENNEDY**, speech of 16 November 1961; cited in U.S. Senate, *Alleged Assassination Plots* (1975). He doesn't say we wouldn't try on specific occasions.

"I believe it was the policy at the time to get rid of Castro, and if killing him was one of the things that was to be done in this connection, that was within what was expected.... It was made abundantly clear to everybody involved in the operation that the desire was to get rid of the Castro regime and to get rid of Castro.... The point was that no limitations were put on this injunction."

Former DCI **RICHARD HELMS** in Senate testimony regarding pressure on CIA during the Kennedy administration to "do something" about Castro; cited in U.S. Senate, *Alleged Assassination Plots* (1975).

"The assassination of Castro by a Cuban might have been viewed [in Washington] as not very different in the benefits that would have accrued from the assassination of Hitler in 1944. . . . The truth is that CIA's experimentation with assassination was so out of the ordinary that none of the wild schemes developed by senior DDP officials and CIA technicians succeeded. No one was assassinated. The fact that assassination was planned and attempted shows more about the temper of the times than it does about CIA."

Former DDI **RAY CLINE**, *Secrets, Spies and Scholars* (1976). DDP was the CIA operations directorate.

"It is sometimes asked whether assassination should be ruled out absolutely. . . . Adolf Hitler is often cited as an example. Of course, the cases which the [Senate] committee investigated were not of that character at all. Tragically, they related to Latin leaders and black leaders of little countries that could not possibly have constituted a threat to the security of the United States. The only time when Fidel Castro permitted his island to become a base for Russian [*sic*] missiles, the only time during which it might have been said that he had become a threat to the security of the American people, was the one time when all assassination activity, plans, and plots against his life were stood down."

Senator **FRANK CHURCH**, introduction to U.S. Senate, *Alleged Assassination Plots* (1975).

"[The] CIA officials who managed the assassination attempts . . . were under enormous pressure to 'do something' about Castro. Nothing seemed excluded to them. And in those days covert operators did not march back to the White House to ask: 'Mr. President, when it says "remove" Castro, does that mean I can kill him? And can I have it in writing?' . . . Looking back at those assassination attempts now, and putting aside the nature of the act in question, what strikes one is their fecklessness. The agency that overturned governments never came close to killing Castro. . . . Yet part of the reason the attempts were so ineffective, I believe, is that CIA officers never quite had their hearts in them. They did not square with those officers' sense of their profession. If making revolutions, like making omelets, requires breaking some eggs, the same is true of making counter-revolutions. People will be killed, and some of those killings will be intentional. CIA officers accepted that as their profession. But targeting a single individual, a foreign leader, for killing was another matter."

GREGORY TREVERTON, *Covert Action* (1987).

"As Henry IV's cry 'Who will rid me of this meddlesome priest?' led to Thomas à Becket's death in Canterbury Cathedral, so the ambiguity with which covert policy vis-à-vis Castro was stated in this period led to vigorous efforts to achieve what the policymakers were thought to have meant, however they may have actually phrased their statements."

Former DCI **WILLIAM COLBY**, *Honorable Men* (1978).

"As these traitors, who have given important state secrets to the opponent and caused great political damage to the USSR, have been sentenced to death in their absence, this sentence will be carried out abroad."

KGB chairman **VLADIMIR SEMICHASTNY** approving a KGB plan to assassinate defectors, November 1962; cited in Andrew and Mitrokhin, *The Mitrokhin Archive* (1999).

"United States leaders should think that if they are aiding terrorist plans to eliminate Cuban leaders, they themselves will not be safe."

> **FIDEL CASTRO**, 7 September 1963; quoted in Powers, *The Man Who Kept the Secrets* (1979). Some have seized on this warning as evidence of Cuban involvement in the assassination of President Kennedy.

"There is no evidence that any of the three presidents [Eisenhower, Kennedy, Johnson] authorized or knew about . . . the CIA's assassination policy."

> **ARTHUR M. SCHLESINGER, JR.**, *The Cycles of American History* (1986). Note that Schlesinger calls it a policy of CIA's, not of the administrations it served.

"There has long been a rear-guard action by Kennedy loyalists to muddy the waters about the President's responsibility for the murder plots. . . . Somewhere among the winks and nods and grumbles of Presidential irritation must have been born an ember of conviction among high officials of the C.I.A. that perhaps what Kennedy actually meant, and actually wanted, when he said we have to get rid of Castro was . . . getting rid of Castro!"

> **THOMAS POWERS**, *New York Times Book Review*, 30 November 1997.

"I never lost sight of the irony that the same president who had canceled the air strikes and ruled out open intervention [during the Bay of Pigs operation] was now having his brother put tremendous pressure on the agency to accomplish even more."

> Former CIA operations chief **RICHARD BISSELL** on Robert Kennedy's impatience with CIA regarding Castro in *Reflections of a Cold Warrior* (1996).

"The best evidence [that the Kennedys were aware of assassination plots against Castro] is the lack of outrage exhibited by administration figures when the operations against Castro were finally made public; admittedly, this is of the 'dog that didn't bark' variety. Nevertheless, one would have expected major Kennedy administration figures, such as former Defense Secretary Robert McNamara, to express some outrage had they believed that the CIA had undertaken such an action without approval by higher authority; instead McNamara emphasized, in testifying before the Church Committee [of the U.S. Senate in 1975], his belief that 'the CIA was a highly disciplined organization, fully under the control of senior officials of the government.'"

> **ABRAM SHULSKY**, *Silent Warfare* (1993).

"I could understand in the case of Castro why a very few men might weigh the merits of disposing of one man at the same time two American Presidents had approved the Bay of Pigs—where many died and which could have resulted, in the event of civil war, in the death of thousands. But how those few men in CIA could have been so stupid as to make a connection with the Mafia for that purpose I cannot explain. A tenet of intelligence tradecraft is to avoid association with those who might later resort to blackmail."

> Former senior CIA operations officer **DAVID ATLEE PHILLIPS**, *The Night Watch* (1978).

"[On November 22, 1963, Robert] Kennedy called CIA director John McCone and asked him to come to Hickory Hill, a few minutes away from agency headquarters in Langley. Bluntly, Kennedy asked the nation's top intelligence officer if the CIA had killed President Kennedy. The deeply Catholic McCone swore the agency was innocent. . . . RFK later [said] that he had asked McCone 'in a way that he couldn't lie to me.'"

> **EVAN THOMAS**, *Robert Kennedy* (2000).

"Helms said . . . Robert Kennedy personally managed the operation on the assassination of Castro."

> Secretary of State **HENRY KISSINGER** to President Ford in White House memorandum of 4 January 1975, now declassified; cited in the *Washington Post*, 28 June 1998.

"Oh, I travel . . . a sort of licensed troubleshooter."

> James Bond, with the "00" license to kill, played by Sean Connery in the 1965 film *Thunderball*.

"One of the tasks of the intelligence service is to remove agents who are not needed any more by murdering them, poisoning them, or by some other means. A GRU agent may be shot or poisoned if it is feared that he is breaking down or is telling what he knows, or simply, if he knows too much. Or a warning may be received that a given agent is a foreign provocateur or that he may commit a provocation. Then orders are given to kill him and he is eliminated by any means."

> Soviet GRU Colonel **OLEG PENKOVSKIY**, *The Penkovskiy Papers* (1966).

"[We] did everything from plotting ways to poison the capital's water systems to drawing up assassination plans for US leaders."

> Former senior KGB officer **OLEG KALUGIN** on how he spent his time while posted to Washington, D.C., in the late 1960s and early 1970s; cited in Andrew and Mitrokhin, *The Mitrokhin Archive* (1999). Kalugin redeemed himself; he is now a U.S. citizen and intelligence consultant.

"[Congressional] investigations showed that while the assassination of foreign leaders had been considered several times, in only one case was it really attempted, and no foreign leader is known to have been killed or actually even injured as the result of a CIA plot—surely an almost unheard of record in the history of secret services."

> **WALTER LAQUEUR**, *A World of Secrets* (1985). Sometimes failure is a sort of success.

"There's nothing wrong with shooting, as long as all the right people get shot."

> Dirty Harry, movie cop played by Clint Eastwood, in *Magnum Force* (1973).

"In a different atmosphere . . . the congressional committees investigating the CIA might have been curious as to why the agency failed so miserably in its efforts to assassinate Lumumba and Castro. But in 1975 no one was interested in the inability of the agency to do what it was told to do, but only in the immorality of what it was told to do."

> **SAMUEL HUNTINGTON**, *The Promise of Disharmony* (1981).

"The [Church] committee's conclusion [in 1975] that the CIA had not actually participated in the successful assassination of any foreign leader was small consolation to the American public or to myself and the vast majority of CIA officers."

> Former senior CIA official **CORD MEYER**, *Facing Reality* (1980).

"In eight months of dramatic investigation, Senator Church had managed to determine that CIA had never assassinated anyone."

> Former DCI **RICHARD HELMS**, *A Look over My Shoulder* (2003).

"The involvement of the CIA in planning assassinations was not a momentary aberration of a handful of rogue agents who had jumped the reservation. The goals pursued by the agency—no matter how questionable—were those of the United States government. For at least a brief period, political assassination was regarded as a tool of American foreign policy."

NATHAN MILLER, *Spying for America* (1989).

"[The KGB's] Operational and Technical Directorate . . . had a laboratory that invented new ways of killing people, from poisons that could be slipped into drinks to jellies that could be rubbed on a person to induce a heart attack. A KGB agent rubbed just such a substance on Alexander Solzhenitsyn in a store in Russia in the early 1970s, making him violently ill but not killing him."

Former KGB general **OLEG KALUGIN**, *The First Directorate* (1994).

"No employee of the United States Government shall engage in, or conspire to engage in, assassination."

Executive Order 11905, signed by President **GERALD FORD** on 18 February 1976.

"[President Ford] outlawed assassination as an instrument of American policy—a most unusual step, even for a democracy."

RHODRI JEFFREYS-JONES, *The CIA and American Democracy* (1989).

"My own view of assassination is that I am against it for at least three good reasons: it's against the law of God, it's against the law of man, and it doesn't work—you just get another fanatic worse than the first one. . . . At the time and to put this in perspective—I'm not trying to excuse the things that were done, I am trying to put them in perspective—at the time this loose talk about assassination was going on [in the early 1960s], Castro specifically, Fidel Castro was shooting people every day

in front of the television cameras in the national stadium in Havana."

DDCI **VERNON WALTERS** in public remarks in Charlottesville, Virginia, 9 June 1976; in CIA's Historical Intelligence Collection.

"One was an assassin. The other was a Republican."

Retired CIA officer **CHARLES McCARRY** on the two kinds of men he never met in CIA; quoted in the *Washington Post*, 26 June 1977.

"No person employed by or acting on behalf of the United States Government shall engage in, or conspire to engage in, assassination."

Executive Order 12063 of 24 January 1978. President Carter's version of the prohibition on assassination is more expansive than Ford's—it proscribes using others who are not strictly employees—and was reaffirmed by President Reagan in E.O. 12333 of 4 December 1981.

"All right, all right. But there is to be no direct participation on our part. Give the Bulgarians whatever they need, show them how to use it, and send someone to Sofia to train their people. But that's all. No direct involvement."

KGB chief **YURI ANDROPOV** responding to Bulgarian entreaties for assistance in murdering Georgi Markov, an émigré opponent of the Zhivkov regime, in 1978; quoted in Kalugin, *The First Directorate* (1994).

"In September 1978, Georgi Markov, the dissident Bulgarian writer, was murdered on the streets of London. [He] was walking across Waterloo Bridge when he felt a sharp jab in his thigh. When he turned around he saw a man picking up an umbrella. . . . Markov soon developed a high temperature. Within three days he was dead. An autopsy discovered a tiny, poisoned pellet in his thigh."

MARK LLOYD, *Guinness Book of Espionage* (1994). KGB defector Oleg Gordievsky first revealed that the KGB provided the "umbrella gun" for assassinations to the Bulgarian intelligence service.

"Even the Soviets and the Bulgarians couldn't screw it up: We got our man."

> Former KGB general **OLEG KALUGIN** on the assassination of Bulgarian dissident Georgi Markov in 1978, in *The First Directorate* (1994).

"There was a moment during the Israeli invasion of Lebanon in 1982 when an Israeli sniper in Beirut had the Palestinian leader Yasir Arafat in his gun sight. The sniper, though, was under orders not to kill the Palestinian leader, because Israel felt that the world fallout would be too great—so he snapped a picture of Mr. Arafat instead."

> **THOMAS FRIEDMAN**, "The Summer of 1982," *New York Times*, 3 July 2001.

"There was an agreement in Lebanon not to liquidate Yasir Arafat. Actually, I am sorry that we did not liquidate him."

> Israeli Prime Minister **ARIEL SHARON**, who was defense minister in 1982; quoted in the *New York Times*, 1 February 2002.

"Killing people is wrong, but it happens, and if someone had polished off Idi Amin it would have saved a lot of people a lot of grief. But at the same time it must be a decision in the hands of people you can trust and who will not take such a decision lightly."

> Former CIA operations chief **RICHARD BISSELL** in 1983; quoted in Ranelagh, *The Agency* (1986).

"We received [in 1985] a draft secret executive order telling us to knock off terrorists in pre-emptive strikes. I told our folks to send it back and tell them: 'When the president revokes the executive order which precludes CIA from assassinations,

then we'll take this on.' That hit the guys on the NSC staff. They went ballistic."

> Former Deputy DCI **JOHN McMAHON**; quoted in Tim Weiner, "Rethinking the Ban on Political Assassination," *New York Times*, 30 August 1998.

"It is time for a reassessment of the current prohibition on political assassination. . . . Similar declarations are rare among other nations. Indeed, the absence of such declarations should alert us to the possibility that there are reasons to avoid taking this public stance."

> **DAVID NEWMAN** and **BRUCE BUENO DE MESQUITA** in the *New York Times*, 26 January 1989.

"Contrary to conventional wisdom, assassination is the most morally justifiable of all acts of war: If it is just to kill anyone in pursuit of a political goal, it is more just to kill an officer in the enemy army than a draftee, and *most* just to kill those who are orchestrating the contrary effort, namely the commanders-in-chief. The problems with assassination are practical: What will the killing of *this* individual in *these* circumstances accomplish?"

> **ANGELO CODEVILLA**, *Informing Statecraft* (1992).

"Scene: Uganda. Colonel Idi Amin has got possession of a nuclear bomb and plans at midnight to dispatch a low-flying plane to drop that bomb on Jerusalem. A CIA agent in the field communicates to Washington that Idi Amin will lie between the crosshairs of the agent's rifle at the airport before the bomb is dispatched. Should he squeeze the trigger? There are those, and Blackford Oakes [fictional CIA hero of ten of William F. Buckley's novels] was one of them, who would address that morally wrenching point by saying two things. (1) As to the particular question, yes, authorize the agent to shoot, in order to abort the destruction of Jerusalem and all that might then follow. But (2), do not then require as a condition of this decision that laws or rules be set down that embody that distinction. It isn't possible to write such judgments into law."

WILLIAM F. BUCKLEY, JR., introduction to *The Blackford Oakes Reader* (1995).

"This is a guy who has his ministers strip-searched before they come to see him. This is a guy who doesn't sleep two nights in a row in the same place. This is a guy who sends decoy motorcades around Baghdad every time he moves. It's a nonoption."

Former DCI **ROBERT GATES** when asked about the prospects for an assassination attempt on Saddam Hussein; quoted in the *Wall Street Journal*, 19 November 1997.

"If the president decides that he wants to change the government's policy barring assassinations there is no way of escaping the necessity of his first, openly, repealing President Ford's Executive Order —telling the world that we have decided to go back to the Kennedy era practice of, from time to time, attempting to commit political murder. Then, upon transmitting a secret finding to the Congress, he could order a specific assassination. Do we really want our country to do this? . . . It is hard to conceive of anything that would do more to undermine what America stands for in the world and do more to provoke anger and resentment . . . than to adopt the use of murder as a national policy."

Former DCI **R. JAMES WOOLSEY** in the *Washington Times*, 23 December 1997.

"With the single exception of the liquidation campaign against the terrorists who killed the Olympic athletes, the purpose of the Israeli policy of assassination has not been vengeance. Mossad operatives claimed in recent parliamentary subcommittee

hearings that revenge is an unworthy motive in battling terror. They explained that the only reason they used assassination was to frighten and deter terrorists and to disrupt their plans for future violence. But if that is the declared goal, it seems that the policy has not succeeded. Those who were assassinated were soon replaced and terrorism resumed, sometimes more ferociously than before."

Israeli journalist **YOSSI MELMAN**, "Israel's Darkest Secrets," *New York Times*, 25 March 1998.

"Perhaps you are wondering: 'Why not just quietly, without making a big public deal of it, send a couple of experienced guys named Victor over there to quietly arrange for Saddam to have an unfortunate shaving accident that results in the loss of the upper two-thirds of his head?' I am frankly shocked that you would even suggest such a thing. What you're talking about is assassination, which is a serious violation of international rules. On the other hand, it is perfectly okay to drop large quantities of bombs on a foreign country, as long as you are not specifically trying to drop one on the foreign leader, which of course under the rules would be assassination. These rules are made by lawyers."

DAVE BARRY, "Where Legal Eagles Dare," *Washington Post Magazine*, 19 April 1998.

"The service does not kill people or arrange their assassination."

Website of Britain's MI5, July 1998.

"I can tell you unequivocally what the policy is. If anyone has committed or is planning to carry out terrorist attacks, he has to be hit. . . . It is effective, precise, and just."

Israeli deputy defense minister **EPHRAIM SNEH** on assassinations; quoted in the *Washington Post*, 8 January 2001.

"The United States already takes actions clearly designed to remove foreign leaders. In the 1980s, we took actions clearly designed to remove Moammar Gadhafi. People may pretend that we don't do these things, but these are precisely the type of actions that we sometimes take. It is better policy to be more honest and recognize the president does and should have this authority.... [Existing] executive orders arbitrarily limit the options available to the president when dealing with terrorists."

U.S. Representative **BOB BARR** of Georgia introducing legislation that would authorize the president to order the assassination of a foreign leader; quoted in the *Washington Times*, 9 February 2001. But, Bob, if the president already can do it, why does he need this legislation?

"The president must, at long last, undo the idiotic Executive Order forbidding assassinations, that pious piece of paper from smug Jimmy Carter that has hamstrung our counterterrorist efforts lo these many years. If we identify the commanders of this operation, they should be killed."

MICHAEL LEDEEN, *National Review Online*, 11 September 2001. Actually, it was Gerald Ford who first prohibited assassination, and the ban has been reaffirmed by presidents—Democratic and Republican alike—since then.

"I want justice. And there is an old poster out West that I recall that said, 'Wanted, Dead or Alive.'"

President **GEORGE W. BUSH** speaking at the White House about Osama bin Ladin, 17 September 2001.

"The ban [on assassination] that was put into effect under President Ford only applies to heads of state. It doesn't apply to terrorists."

Former President **BILL CLINTON** on NBC, 18 September 2001.

"It's been in the paper now so I can talk about it. I authorized the arrest, and if necessary the killing, of Osama bin Ladin. And we actually made contact with a group in Afghanistan to do it. And they were unsuccessful."

Former President **BILL CLINTON** on CNN, 23 September 2001.

"Sixty-five percent [of those surveyed] think the law should be changed so the U.S. government can assassinate people in foreign countries who commit terrorist acts, and twenty-three percent disagree."

CBS–*New York Times* poll results released 24 September 2001. By contrast, 82 percent of respondents in a 1981 Gallup poll said assassinations were never justified.

"I think the executive order [banning assassination] was in response to the abuse of the power that a government should have ... to target execution at individuals who, if we don't stop them, will kill many more of us.... Our forces ought to have the power and the authority of the President of the United States to strike at bin Ladin and the small group around him directly. It's only the right thing to do. Frankly, in a tough situation, it's the moral thing to do, because it will save many more lives, both in Afghanistan and in the United States."

Senator **JOSEPH LIEBERMAN**, Democrat from Connecticut, on NBC's "Meet the Press," 21 October 2001.

"The gloves are off. The President has given the Agency the green light to do whatever is necessary. Lethal operations that were unthinkable pre–September 11 are now underway."

Senior George W. Bush administration official; quoted in the *Washington Post*, 21 October 2001.

"In my heart I'm often for assassination, but in my head [I'm] not. Until you can show me the firewall between those whose deaths you're positive would save a large number of lives, and those about whom you're not positive, then I think you're on a slippery slope to becoming the Borgias."

ANTHONY LAKE, former national security advisor to President Clinton; quoted in the *Washington Post*, 28 October 2001.

"*Every* U.S. effort to kill a high-ranking official since World War II has failed. This record is so poor that it would be hard to find an instrument of national policy that has been less successful in achieving its objectives than assassination (although price controls or election reform may come in a close second). . . . Indeed, there is reason to question whether [U.S.] intelligence organizations are even technically qualified for assassination. In every publicly known case in which the CIA has considered killing a foreign leader, the agency has outsourced the job. . . . It is hard to maintain control and quality when you subcontract assassination —as the record shows."

BRUCE BERKOWITZ, "Is Assassination an Option?" *Hoover Digest* (2002).

"The CIA fired a missile from an unmanned Predator aircraft over Afghanistan [on] Monday in an unsuccessful attempt to kill a factional leader who has vowed to attack U.S. service personnel and oust the interim government of Hamid Kharzai, according to administration sources."

"CIA Fails in Bid to Kill Afghan Rebel with a Missile," *Washington Post*, 10 May 2002.

"Bush administration officials described the missile strike on a car carrying six Al Qaeda operatives in Yemen on Sunday as a battlefield operation in the war on terrorism. . . . Other observers called it a targeted assassination, or even an extrajudicial killing—terms usually reserved for violations of human rights or international law. Such condemnation is not justified."

Washington Post editorial on what was reported as a missile strike from a CIA Predator unmanned aircraft, 6 November 2002. The *Post* condones assassination? It *is* a new world.

"We gotta assassinate Saddam Hussein. Why have we taken assassination off the table as a viable political tool? And yet they'll tell you the collateral damage of civilians is acceptable. But you're not allowed to assassinate the main pain in the ass."

Comedian DENNIS MILLER on "The Tonight Show with Jay Leno," 6 November 2002.

"We have more lawyers than Predator pilots."

Unidentified CIA official; quoted in the *Los Angeles Times*, 11 January 2003.

"There is no easy answer to the question of assassination. Clearly, boundless misery would have been avoided if Hitler had been struck down. . . . At least as much might be said had Stalin been eliminated before he established himself as the sole authority in the USSR. . . . This said, in peacetime the assassination of troublesome persons is morally and operationally indefensible. There are invariably other solutions, not the least of which is time—time for immediate and sometimes fierce tactical pressure to subside or for the problem to be reevaluated and another solution found. . . . In wartime, when air raids are coincidentally killing hundreds of noncombatants, I see no reason the assassination of enemy leaders such as Hitler and his immediate staff should be forbidden."

Former DCI RICHARD HELMS, *A Look over My Shoulder* (2003).

B
- **Bay of Pigs**
- **Budgets**

BAY OF PIGS

The lesson from the Bay of Pigs, sayeth the Literary Spy, is this: thou shalt not attempt covert actions that require everything to go right, because everything never goeth right. Indeed, so many things went awry in the planning and execution of this paramilitary operation—the attempt in April 1961 to mount an amphibious invasion of Cuba using CIA-trained and -equipped Cuban exiles—that one is tempted to conclude that covert action should never be attempted. That, considers the Literary Spy, would be the final mistake associated with a unique debacle.

See also: Covert Action; Failures; Plausible Denial

"I was never in on any of the consultations, either inside the Agency or otherwise. I think it was foolish, not because I would have decided it any differently, but at least on paper I knew more about amphibious warfare than anyone in the Agency. I had made twenty-six assault landings in the South Pacific, Southwest Pacific, and so on, of about the size, many of them, as the Bay of Pigs, whereas the Marine they had advising them had made one in his whole goddam life, and that was Iwo Jima, which

was three divisions abreast. . . . He just didn't know beans about what a small self-contained beachhead would be like."

> Former DDI **ROBERT AMORY** in a 1966 interview; cited in Weber, *Spymasters* (1999). A few days before the invasion, Amory told DCI Allen Dulles he knew something was up. Dulles told him, "You have nothing to do with that at all." To himself, Amory said "screw 'em," and he played tennis while President Kennedy was canceling the air strikes.

"In the planning of the Bay of Pigs, Operations deliberately failed to consult [the Directorate of] Intelligence."

> **CHRISTOPHER ANDREW**, *For the President's Eyes Only* (1995).

"Covert action, neither for the first time nor for the last, was a substitute for well-thought-out policy, that is, clearly defined objectives, and resources and techniques calculated to achieve those objectives. Instead, covert action was viewed as a magic bullet that in a single round could achieve a desirable objective without committing the United States militarily."

> **ROY GODSON** on the Bay of Pigs operation in *Dirty Tricks or Trump Cards* (1995).

"The plan receiving our recommendation was a landing that involved a combined amphibious/airborne assault during daytime, with concurrent tactical air support . . . near Trinidad, a city on the southern coast of Cuba near the Escambray Mountains. . . . [It] was deemed 'too noisy' by [President] Kennedy, and although he was willing to move ahead generally, he could not support a plan that he felt exposed the role of the United States so openly. Resorting to compromise, he gave the agency four days to rework the plans and come up with a 'less spectacular' alternative. It is hard to believe in retrospect that the president and his advisers felt the plans for a large-scale, complicated military operation that had been ongoing for more than a year could be reworked in four days and still offer a high likelihood of success. It is equally amazing that we in the agency agreed so readily."

Former CIA operations chief **RICHARD BISSELL**, *Reflections of a Cold Warrior* (1996).

"I stood right here at Ike's desk and told him I was certain our Guatemalan operation would succeed, and, Mr. President, the prospects for this plan are even better than they were for that one."

DCI **ALLEN DULLES** to President Kennedy before the Bay of Pigs operation, 1961; according to Theodore Sorenson, *Kennedy* (1965).

"I sincerely believed that, even with the plan's faults, as long as we were able to move ahead with the air strikes and destroy Castro's air force, the brigade would still win the day, at least to the extent of establishing a beachhead. It is also possible that we in the Agency were not as frank with the President about further deficiencies as we could have been. As an advocate for maintaining the President's authorization, I was very much afraid of what might happen if I said, 'Mr. President, this operation

might as well be made open because the role of the United States certainly cannot be hidden.'"

Former CIA operations chief **RICHARD BISSELL**, *Reflections of a Cold Warrior* (1996). But that's exactly what Bissell should have done.

"The only venue for a plan of this scope is a Hollywood motion picture studio. . . . I cannot understand [operations chief] Dick Bissell's and [DCI Allen] Dulles's failure to look more deeply into the facts bearing on this proposed plan. The best I can suggest is that Bissell's great success with the U-2 [spyplane] and CORONA [satellite] projects, and Dulles's determination to prove the Agency's capability, resulted in a collective suspension of judgment. . . . There was no way that a paramilitary force a thousand strong could be *secretly* recruited, trained and armed with an air force and the naval support necessary to ensure a successful landing. Aside from that, the island's geography did not lend itself to a broad scale of guerrilla activity. Equally to the point, the likely response of the Cuban people had not been thoroughly explored."

Former DCI **RICHARD HELMS**, *A Look over My Shoulder* (2003). Helms was Bissell's deputy at the time of the Bay of Pigs invasion but remained cut out of the planning or execution of it—something Helms apparently did not press.

"Timely and objective scrutiny of the operation in the months before the invasion, including study of all available intelligence, would have demonstrated to agency officials that the clandestine paramilitary operations had almost totally failed, that there was no controlled and responsive underground movement ready to rally to the invasion force, and that Castro's ability both to fight back and to roll up the internal opposition must be very considerably upgraded. It would also have raised the question of why the United States should contemplate pitting

1,500 soldiers, however well trained and armed, against an enemy vastly superior in number and armament on a terrain which offered nothing but vague hope of significant local support.... Cancellation would have been embarrassing.... However, cancellation would have averted failure, which brought even more embarrassment, carried death and misery to hundreds, destroyed millions of dollars' worth of U.S. property, and seriously damaged U.S. prestige."

CIA Inspector general **LYMAN KIRKPATRICK**'s report on the Bay of Pigs invasion, October 1961; quoted in the *New York Times*, 22 February 1998.

"The one report for which [CIA Inspector General Lyman] Kirkpatrick was never forgiven was his study of the Bay of Pigs.... [CIA operations chief Richard] Bissell and [DCI Allen] Dulles might talk of the canceled air strikes until the cows came home, but the failure which emerged with cool logic in Kirkpatrick's report was the CIA's own. The plan was either dishonest and cynical, depending on forcing Kennedy's hand, or plain dumb."

THOMAS POWERS, *The Man Who Kept the Secrets* (1979).

"The one point never to be forgotten about the Bay of Pigs was that the plans for that activity and its progress were meticulously reviewed for weeks before it came off by the President and the whole circle of his advisors, and in even more detail daily by a committee of the Joint Staff for the Pentagon and by a group in the Western Hemisphere Bureau of the State Department who were working actively on the political aspects of it.... If there's anything clear on the record of the Bay of Pigs, it is that lack of supervision and coordination was not the reason for failure."

Former CIA operations chief **RICHARD BISSELL** in a 1967 interview; cited in Weber, *Spymasters* (1999).

"It is incontrovertible that, without control of the air, the whole military operation was doomed. Even with control of the air it might have failed but without it there could not have been any chance of success. If, then, one wishes to learn what actually caused the military operation to fail, rather than what might have done so, the starting point must be an inquiry into why control of the air was lost and never regained.... The defeat in the air cannot be blamed on bad maintenance at Puerto Cabezas, or on a shortage of spare parts or fuel. It cannot be blamed on a shortage of B-26's, inasmuch as it proved possible rapidly to replace losses from the U.S. It cannot be blamed on the cowardice or lack of skill of the Cuban air crews, who by and large gave a good account of themselves. Nor can it be attributed to bad tactical decisions made either at Puerto Cabezas or in the Washington command post. The crucial defeat in the air was to no significant degree the result of bad execution. It was directly and unambiguously attributable to a long series of Washington policy decisions."

CIA operations directorate report, "An Analysis of the Cuban Operation," 18 January 1962. This was the rebuttal to CIA Inspector General Lyman Kirkpatrick's report.

"ZAPATA [the Bay of Pigs operation] was such a complex venture that by the time it had developed its own fatal momentum, the breakdown of almost any element in the plan might have doomed the entire effort."

Former DCI **RICHARD HELMS**, *A Look over My Shoulder* (2003). Helms, then a lower-level official uninvolved in the operation, marvels at how its planners failed to build in contingency planning for bad luck and missteps—Covert Action 101. Helms titled his chapter on the Bay of Pigs "Call It Hubris."

"A policy is bound to fail which deliberately violates our pledges and our principles, our treaties and our laws."

> **WALTER LIPPMANN** after the Bay of Pigs operation; quoted in the *New York Times Book Review*, 14 July 1996.

"Obviously you cannot tell of operations that go along well. Those that go badly speak for themselves."

> Former DCI **ALLEN DULLES**, *The Craft of Intelligence* (1963).

"Great actions require great determination. In these difficult types of operations, so many of which I have been associated over the years, one never succeeds unless there is a determination to succeed, a willingness to risk some unpleasant political repercussions, and a willingness to provide the basic military necessities. At the decisive moment of the Bay of Pigs operation, all three of these were lacking."

> Former DCI **ALLEN DULLES**, unpublished paper on the Bay of Pigs affair; cited in Bissell, *Reflections of a Cold Warrior* (1996).

"I think one simple failure of observation on the part of really all of us who were involved, including the President . . . and very definitely all of us in the CIA, was that despite reading the daily papers and listening to the radio, we didn't really grasp the extent to which it was believed by everyone else that . . . this was, in effect, an activity of the U.S. Government, which, to be sure, was using Cubans, but really only using them. Therefore, I believe that, just as a matter of fact, the concept of this as an operation, responsibility for which could be plausibly disclaimed by the U.S. Government,

had lost its validity many weeks before the invasion itself took place."

> Former CIA operations chief **RICHARD BISSELL** in a 1967 interview; cited in Weber, *Spymasters* (1999).

"If the United States was sure to be held responsible, then it made no sense to pay a price in terms of impaired operational capability for a result that could not be obtained. Yet that is exactly what we did. It was a major error. . . . Everyone in the Cuban operation moved forward without much debate, confident that the fig leaf of plausible deniability was still in place."

> Former CIA operations chief **RICHARD BISSELL**, *Reflections of a Cold Warrior* (1996).

"Until the Bay of Pigs—indeed, ever since the glory days of the OSS in World War II—the Agency had enjoyed a reputation with the public at large not a whit less than golden. . . . To a remarkable degree, this essentially naive and uninformed popular view of the CIA had been shared by the press and the Congress. . . . [The Bay of Pigs] was the start of the CIA's slide from being one of the most prestigious and admired agencies of the government toward one of its most denounced and condemned."

> Former DCI **WILLIAM COLBY**, *Honorable Men* (1978).

"You know, it was inevitable. . . . The fiasco, I mean. The disaster. If it hadn't been the Bay of Pigs it would have been something else, some time in the future. In 1953 [we] manipulated that crowd which toppled Mossadegh [in Iran] without any trouble at all. Then in 1954 we took care of Eisenhower's little problem in Guatemala. So easy, it seemed. All those successes just had to lead to a failure eventually, because the system kept calling on us for more and more even when it should have been obvious that secret shenanigans couldn't do what armies are supposed to do. . . . If it hadn't been this time at the Bay of Pigs, it would have been somewhere else, at some other time."

> Senior CIA operations officer after the Bay of Pigs operation; quoted in Phillips, *The Night Watch* (1978).

"The Bay of Pigs taught everyone, whether they were involved directly or indirectly, a lesson . . . that an organization like the CIA should not undertake such a mission, because they don't have the general staff system and the support mechanisms to underpin an activity of that kind and of that size involving that much support equipment, such as boats, airplanes, training camps, and all the rest of it."

> Former DCI **RICHARD HELMS** in a 1981 interview; cited in Weber, *Spymasters* (1999).

"Why did the CIA go along with a foredoomed plan? In part because the man running it, Richard Bissell, hoped that once it was underway the President would not dare let it fail. And why did [Kennedy aide] Arthur Schlesinger push upon the President conditions that guaranteed failure? Apparently in the hope that Kennedy would cancel the plan. Both sides seem to have looked upon the operation primarily as a lever on U.S. policy-making rather than as something with a life of its own. As for Kennedy, like other presidents he was willing enough to compromise between those who wanted to do something right and those who did not want to do it at all, by deciding to do it but not to do it right."

> **ANGELO CODEVILLA**, *Informing Statecraft* (1992).

"What are the lessons for the future to be drawn from this unhappy experience? Perhaps the main one is that the U.S. should not support an oper-

ation such as this involving the use of force without having also made the decision to use whatever force is needed to achieve success."

> CIA operations directorate report, "An Analysis of the Cuban Operation," 18 January 1962.

"We were self-deluded. It's pretty clear now that there was not a large body of people just waiting for a chance to turn against Castro. [We] went ahead on a set of assumptions which turned out to be faulty."

> Former CIA official **BOB REYNOLDS**, Miami station chief at the time of the Bay of Pigs operation; quoted in Reuters, 16 April 2001. That's what happens when CIA operators don't talk to CIA analysts.

BUDGETS

Just as "amateurs talk strategy, professionals talk logistics," the Literary Spy knows that in intelligence, the pros talk about funding. But only among themselves.

See also: Collection; Intelligence, the Missions of; Legislative Oversight

"Hostile armies may face each other for years, striving for victory which is decided in a single day. This being so, to remain in ignorance of the enemy's condition simply because one grudges the outlay of a hundred ounces of silver in honor and emoluments is the height of inhumanity. One who acts thus is no leader of men."

> **SUN TZU**, *The Art of War* (6th century B.C.).

"Knowledge is never too dear."

> Motto of Sir **FRANCIS WALSINGHAM** (1532–1590), Secretary of State and intelligence chief for Queen Elizabeth I; quoted in Polmar and Allen, *Encyclopedia of Espionage* (1997).

"No war can be conducted successfully without very early and good intelligence, [and] such advices cannot be had but at a very great expense. Nobody can be ignorant of this that knows anything of secret correspondence, or considers the numbers of persons that must be employed in it, the great hazard they undergo, the variety of places in which such correspondence must be kept, and the constant necessity of supporting and feeding this service, not to mention some extraordinary expenses of a higher nature, which ought only to be hinted at."

> JOHN CHURCHILL, the First Duke of Marlborough (1650–1722), responding to his critics about the costs of intelligence; cited in Sayle, "The Historical Underpinnings of the U.S. Intelligence Community," *International Journal of Intelligence and Counterintelligence* (spring 1986).

"No Money shall be drawn from the Treasury, but in Consequence of Appropriations made by Law; and a regular Statement and Account of the Receipts and Expenditures of all public Money shall be published from time to time."

> Constitution of the United States, Article I, section 9. This clause is cited by many who say that secret intelligence budgets are unconstitutional.

"The cost of maintaining the central intelligence agency will be considerably in excess of that which could be justified by a government department charged with more specific functions. No money value can be assigned to successful intelligence accomplishments. Budgetary standards of efficiency and economy are not generally applicable."

> Strategic Services Unit Director General JOHN MAGRUDER in a report to the War Department on the proposed central intelligence agency, October 1945; in *FRUS 1945–1950: Emergence of the Intelligence Establishment* (1996), document 34.

"It is of great importance that so far as it is possible under the law the amount of governmental expenditures for secret intelligence and the nature of the items of expenditures should be concealed. The War Department Budget is especially suited for this purpose."

> Recommendations of the interagency "Fortier Committee" to DCI Sidney Souers, 14 March 1946; in *FRUS 1945–1950: Emergence of the Intelligence Establishment* (1996), document 105.

"The funds appropriated for the activities of Central Intelligence are not large in terms of the total budget of the United States Government, nor in terms of the contribution which intelligence and operations can make to national security and the success of the United States foreign and military policy.... In general, CIA should be supplied with moderately increased funds over the next several years, limited primarily by the effectiveness with which they can spend their funds."

> "Joint Statement of Departments of Defense and State on CIA Budget for Fiscal 1951," memorandum to the National Security Council's Executive Secretary, 23 February 1950; in *FRUS 1945–1950: Emergence of the Intelligence Establishment* (1996), document 417.

"Mr. George Harvey, Chief Clerk, House Appropriations Committee ... opened the discussion by pointing out that since 1946 he was the only person on the House Appropriations Committee or its staff who has known each year the amount of the CIA budget or its location."

> CIA Legislative Counsel WALTER PFORZHEIMER, memorandum of 25 October 1951; reproduced in Warner, *CIA Under Truman* (1994).

"My official duties on the U-2 [spyplane] project commenced [in late 1954] with an initial organizational meeting ... at the Pentagon.... The question arose as to who was going to pay for the new airframe, which would probably cost in the tens of millions of dollars. I was sitting near the middle of the table, and as I turned to my right, everyone was looking in my direction. As I turned to the left, everyone on my left was looking in my direction as well. I got the point pretty quickly."

> Former senior CIA official **RICHARD BISSELL**, *Reflections of a Cold Warrior* (1996).

"'Ever seen one of these?' M abruptly fished something out of his waistcoat pocket. He tossed it halfway across the desk towards Bond. It fell with a faint clang on the red leather and lay, gleaming richly, an inch-wide hammered gold coin.... [M] tossed more magnificent gold coins on to the table in front of Bond [saying] 'we suspect that this Jamaican treasure is being used to finance the Soviet espionage system, or an important part of it, in America.'"

> **IAN FLEMING**, *Live and Let Die* (1954). M, James Bond's spy chief, later in the novel claims salvage rights to the rest of the treasure in order to finance British intelligence. A neat trick—did he have to inform the Parliament?

"Between 1953 and 1961, clandestine collection and covert action absorbed an average of 54 percent of the Agency's total annual budget."

> **ANNE KARALEKAS**, "The History of the Central Intelligence Agency," in Leary, *The Central Intelligence Agency* (1984).

"The total national intelligence budget works out at less than one-half of 1 percent of GNP.... The gross amount ought to be revealed because it is among the smallest of the many conjectural statements that have been published on intelligence expenditures. The general public would probably be reassured to know U.S. intelligence agencies give such good value for money if it were told the truth."

> Former DDI **RAY CLINE**, *Secrets, Spies and Scholars* (1976).

"In the mid- to late fifties, I think that about half of CIA's budget went into covert action, paramilitary and political and things like the Bay of Pigs and some other things. By the early seventies— and this was before the [congressional] investigations—that figure had sunk to something like 4 or 5 percent."

> Former DCI **WILLIAM COLBY** in a 1982 interview; cited in Weber, *Spymasters* (1999).

"I am seeking to obtain information on how much of the taxpayers' dollars you spend each year and the basic purposes for which it is spent.... I would assume that a reasonable place to look for [CIA's] statement of account would be in the Budget of the United States Government and while it may be in there, I can't find it.... The Index of the Budget for fiscal year 1976 under the C's moves from Center for Disease Control to Chamizal Settlement and to a little old country lawyer, it would seem to me that between those two might have been an appropriate place to find the CIA but it is not there. It's possibly in there somewhere but I submit that it is not there in the manner which the founding fathers intended and the Constitution requires."

> U.S. Representative **OTIS PIKE**, Democrat from New York and chairman of a House committee investigating U.S. intelligence activities, letter to DCI William Colby of 28 July 1975; quoted in Gerald Haines, "The Pike Committee Investigations and CIA," *Studies in Intelligence* (winter 1998–99).

"C.I.A. officials have trouble deciding what's sensitive and what's not. We are going to help them."

STEVEN AFTERGOOD of the Federation of American Scientists announcing that FAS was suing CIA to reveal the size of the U.S. intelligence budget; quoted in the *New York Times*, 20 May 1997.

"Abruptly abandoning 50 years of secrecy, the Central Intelligence Agency disclosed today how much money the United States spends annually for intelligence: $26.6 billion. . . . An agency spokesman said [the disclosure] was forced by a lawsuit under the Freedom of Information Act brought by the Federation of American Scientists."

New York Times, 16 October 1997.

"Let me be clear. I've not only been trying to cut your budget, I've been trying to out your budget. . . . But your budget by now is about as big a secret as my sexuality."

U.S. Representative **BARNEY FRANK**, Democrat from Massachusetts, speaking at CIA's "Gay Pride" event, 8 June 2000.

"Put it toward the cause."

A citizen who sent his $600 tax refund check to CIA in the wake of the 11 September terrorist attacks; quoted in the *New York Times*, 22 October 2001.

"We're talking about using leverage to force change in the right direction. A lot of that leverage is the color green."

U.S. Representative **JANE HARMAN**, Democrat from California, on using the budget to address perceived problems and shortfalls in the intelligence community; quoted in the *Philadelphia Inquirer*, 25 July 2002.

"The notion that secret intelligence budgets are bound only by the occasional need to break open another crate of money is pure Hollywood. Because some intelligence funds are unvouchered, there is stricter budgetary control in CIA than in any government agency I know, and throughout my tenure I remained tightfisted with the taxpayers' money."

Former DCI **RICHARD HELMS**, *A Look over My Shoulder* (2003). For Helms, "pure Hollywood" probably was the height of contempt.

- **Collection**
- **Compartmentation**
- **Counterintelligence**
- **Covert Action**
- **Critics & Defenders**
- **Current Intelligence**

COLLECTION

The gathering of information runs the gamut from reading newspapers at leisure to stealing secrets at great risk. It is the start of the cycle that ends with delivering intelligence to the nation's leaders, who often don't realize that many collection activities and systems are troublesome to establish and are the most expensive step in that cycle.

See also: Analysis & Analysts; Budgets; Counterintelligence; Espionage & Spies

"We have found the track of 32 men and 3 donkeys."

> Ancient Egyptian intelligence report regarding the border with Nubia, circa 2000 B.C.; cited in Keegan, *Intelligence in War* (2003).

"Bring me back reliable information."

> Inscription on a clay tablet, 1370 B.C., with instructions from the Hittite prince to his envoy bound for Egypt; cited in Haswell, *Spies and Spymasters* (1977).

"And the LORD spake unto Moses, saying
Send thou men, that they may search the land of Canaan . . .

And Moses sent them to spy out the land of Canaan, and said unto them,
Get you up this way southward, and go up into the mountain:
And see the land, what it is; and the people that dwelleth therein, whether they be strong or weak, few or many;
And what the land is that they dwell in, whether it be good or bad; and what cities they be that they dwell in, whether tents, or in strong holds;
And what the land is, whether it be fat or lean, whether there be wood therein, or not. And be ye of good courage, and bring the fruit of the land . . .
So they went up, and searched the land from the wilderness of Zin unto Rehob. . . . And they returned from searching of the land after forty days."

> Numbers 13:1–2, 17–21, 25 (King James).

"When [Moses's] 12 spies returned, it was clear that nine of them had gone with the wrong mindset. . . . Instead of useful details about the inhabitants they brought back nonsense about giants. They had no interest in fighting, and wanted to go back to Egypt. Their inadequately focused minds cost Israel 40 years in the wilderness."

> **ANGELO CODEVILLA**, *Informing Statecraft* (1992). Actually, it was faithlessness to higher principles, not inadequate intelligence, that kept that nation in the wilderness for so long.

"Knowledge must come about through action."

> Greek poet **SOPHOCLES** (495–406 B.C.), *Trachiniae*. This could serve as the motto of intelligence collectors.

"For years before [Hannibal] undertook his campaign against Rome, he had sent his spies into Italy and they were observing everyone and everything. He charged them with transmitting to him exact and positive information regarding the fertility of the trans-Alpine plains and the Valley of the Po, their populations, their military spirit and preparations and, above all, their disposition towards the government of Rome."

> **POLYBIUS** (208–126 B.C.) on the preparations of Hannibal (247–183 B.C.); cited in Sayle, "The Historical Underpinnings of the U.S. Intelligence Community," *International Journal of Intelligence and Counterintelligence* (spring 1986).

"He who is not lucky, let him not go a-fishing."

> **THOMAS FULLER**, 18th-century English doctor; quoted in Laqueur, *A World of Secrets* (1985). Successful collection involves roughly equal doses of careful planning and sheer luck.

"There is nothing more necessary than good Intelligence to frustrate a designing enemy, & nothing that requires greater pains to obtain."

> **GEORGE WASHINGTON**, writing from his experience as an officer in the French and Indian Wars, in 1766; cited in Andrew, *For the President's Eyes Only* (1995).

"Even minutia should have a place in our collection, for things of a seemingly trifling nature when enjoined with others of a more serious cast may lead to valuable conclusions."

> **GEORGE WASHINGTON**; cited in Miller, *Spying for America* (1989).

"The type of isolated observation, involving only a few spies, which has traditionally been employed to spy on other nations, has produced very limited results . . . [A] multiplicity of spies will enable us to penetrate to the best-protected secrets. . . . Moreover, the importance and accuracy of each piece of information collected by an army of agents can be more carefully analyzed in terms of the other pieces of information which verify or contradict it."

> **WILHELM STIEBER**, Imperial Germany's intelligence chief in the 1860s and 1870s; quoted in Richelson, *A Century of Spies* (1995).

"Data! Data! Data! I can't make bricks without clay."

> Sherlock Holmes in Sir **ARTHUR CONAN DOYLE**, "The Adventure of the Copper Beeches" (1892).

"I wish you simply to report facts in the fullest possible manner to me, and you can leave me to do the theorizing."

> Sherlock Holmes to Doctor Watson in Sir **ARTHUR CONAN DOYLE**, *The Hound of the Baskervilles* (1901). CIA analysts think this about NSA and especially DIA all the time.

"Let us get a firm grip of the very little which we do know, so that when fresh facts arise we may be ready to fit them into their places."

> Sherlock Holmes in Sir **ARTHUR CONAN DOYLE**, "The Adventure of the Devil's Foot" (1910).

"Success depends on sound deductions from a mass of intelligence, often specialised and highly technical, on every aspect of the enemy's national life, and much of this information has to be gathered in peace-time."

> **WINSTON CHURCHILL** on victory in war in *Triumph and Tragedy* (1953).

"The war taught us this lesson—that we had to collect intelligence in a manner that would make the information available where it was needed and when it was wanted, in an intelligent and understandable form."

> **HARRY TRUMAN**, *Memoirs*, vol. II (1956).

"The Council is generally acquainted with the Central Intelligence Agency's secret operations designed to produce raw intelligence. Although we are making every effort to develop these latter sources, our experience so far has been in general disappointing. . . . We must and shall devote our best effort to their improvement and to the exploitation of every reasonable chance for penetration. On a few rare occasions there have been really brilliant accomplishments."

> DCI **WALTER BEDELL SMITH**, memorandum to National Security Council, 23 April 1952; reproduced in Warner, *CIA Under Truman* (1994).

"No matter how important collection is, in the short and even the long run, it just doesn't cost very much. . . . It will probably always seem inconsequential to some of our less informed friends on the Hill—in both houses of Congress. They're accustomed to dealing in billions. What kind of impression can I make when I come along and ask for a few hundred thousand dollars and a bag of pennies? Believe me, I know the way they think up there. If there's no real money involved, it can't

be important, and they just won't pay much attention to us."

> DCI **ALLEN DULLES** to Richard Helms, then CIA chief of collection operations, in early 1954; quoted in Helms, *A Look over My Shoulder* (2003). Helms cited the case of a Russian spy the CIA was running at a cost of less than $4,000 a year but whose information had saved the Pentagon more than half a billion dollars in research funding. Soon, on Dulles's watch and perhaps to his relief, there would be plenty of costly collection systems, like the U-2 spyplane.

"We were flying from Moscow to Kiev, and it was during the day and I looked out the window and I saw some shapes. I had my sketch book, and I would put them down, and the flight attendant would walk by, and I would put a big nose and some eyes and make the whole thing into a funny face. So I had a whole book of funny-face cartoons at the end that I didn't know how to read."

> Cartoonist **HANK KETCHAM**, creator of "Dennis the Menace," on his 1959 trip to the USSR, for which CIA asked him to draw anything of interest he might see; quoted in Ketcham's obituary, *New York Times*, 2 June 2001. Years after his trip Ketcham met a CIA official who told him, "Hank, we haven't sent any more cartoonists on any more missions."

"Well, it's better than one of my first overseas assignments, which was to obtain a urine sample from a foreign minister."

> CIA officer at a station abroad after being kidded that going through the trash of a foreign embassy was not very glamorous work for an Ivy League graduate; quoted in Phillips, *The Night Watch* (1978).

"The Iron Curtain . . . had a triple impact on intelligence collection. It made intelligence difficult to get to, and difficult to get out once obtained; it made it difficult to keep contact with the agent who remained in hostile territory."

> Former DCI **ALLEN DULLES**, foreword to his edited volume *Great True Spy Stories* (1968).

"I was completely and hopelessly outgunned."

> Commander **LLOYD BUCHER** testifying to a naval court of inquiry regarding the attack and capture of the lightly armed intelligence collection ship he commanded, the USS *Pueblo*, by North Korean gunboats on 23 January 1968. Bucher and his crew spent eleven months in brutal captivity, suffering beatings and torture at the hands of the North Koreans. Quoted in Bucher's obituary, *Washington Post*, 30 January 2004.

"You can't always get what you want,
But if you try sometimes you just might find you
   get what you need."

> **MICK JAGGER** and **KEITH RICHARDS**, "You Can't Always Get What You Want," from the Rolling Stones' 1969 album *Let It Bleed*. The unofficial anthem of intelligence collectors.

"Collection is the hardest thing of all; it's much easier to plant an article in a local newspaper."

> Former senior CIA operations officer; quoted in Anne Karalekas, "The History of the Central Intelligence Agency," in Leary, *The Central Intelligence Agency* (1984).

"Once you accept the premise of no-holds-barred intelligence gathering, G. Gordon Liddy is what you end up with."

> **JEB MAGRUDER**, President Nixon's deputy attorney general; quoted in Andrew, *For the President's Eyes Only* (1995). To Magruder, that might have been high praise.

"There is no way to be on top of intelligence problems unless you collect much more extensively than any cost-accounting approach would justify. ... You might think you could do without most of what is collected; but in intelligence, in fact, as in ore-mining, there is no way to get at the nuggets without taking the whole ore-bearing compound."

> Former DDI **RAY CLINE**, *Secrets, Spies and Scholars* (1976).

"Intelligence work is not all fun and games but more often plodding perseverance in collecting what might appear to be trivia. ... Does it matter that a local Communist sometimes uses the alias 'Carlos'? Yes, it does if he someday goes to Europe and becomes a terrorist. Is it really important if a young Latin woman is having an affair with an intelligence officer from a [Soviet] Bloc country? It might be, if she later applied for a maid's job at the home of the CIA Station Chief, or gets involved with an American or Mexican official. Why bother to keep tabs on the international travel of a student radical; or will it be significant, years later, when his absence coincides with the period when a local guerrilla group has trained in Cuba? Is it notable if a political crackpot has a second apartment his wife doesn't know about? Probably not—unless an American ambassador has been kidnapped and the CIA is trying to assist local authorities in finding him. The list of trivia which might become vital in an unknown future goes on endlessly, and it must be recorded and made retrievable on demand, sometimes years later."

> Former senior CIA operations officer **DAVID ATLEE PHILLIPS** in *The Night Watch* (1978).

"Accurate and timely information about the capabilities, intentions and activities of foreign powers, organizations, or persons and their agents is essential to informed decisionmaking in the areas of national defense and foreign relations. Collection of such information is a priority objective and will be pursued in a vigorous, innovative and responsible manner that is consistent with the Constitution and applicable law and respectful of the principles upon which the United States was founded."

> President **RONALD REAGAN**, Executive Order 12333, 4 December 1981; reproduced in Warner, *Central Intelligence* (2001).

"In 1983, a delegation of Soviet scientists invited to tour a Grumman aircraft plant on Long Island were told they could carry no cameras and take no notes. Still, by putting adhesive tape on their shoes, the scientists were able to collect slivers of metal alloys being used for new U.S. fighter planes."

JOHN J. FIALKA, *War by Other Means: Economic Espionage in America* (1997).

"Clear policy objectives aid purposeful and discriminating intelligence gathering. Muddled thinking means muddled intelligence work."

Former SIS official GEORGE YOUNG, 1984; quoted in West, *Faber Book of Espionage* (1993). In the absence of guidance, the collectors often collect what they think is "neat stuff" but which often bears little resemblance to what analysts and ultimately policymakers need.

"In collection there is a far greater need for centralized control than in analysis."

Former DCI STANSFIELD TURNER, *Secrecy and Democracy* (1985).

"They wired up a cat [and] trained him to listen to conversations. . . . A lot of money was spent. They slit the cat open, put batteries in him, wired him up. The tail was used as an antenna. They made a monstrosity. They tested him and tested him. They found he would walk off the job when he got hungry, so they put another wire in to override that. Finally they're ready. They took it to a park and pointed it at a park bench and said, 'Listen to those two guys. Don't listen to anything else —not the birds, no cat or dog—just those two guys!' They put him out of the van, and a taxi comes and runs him over. There they were, sitting in the van with all those dials, and the cat was dead!"

Former CIA official VICTOR MARCHETTI; quoted in Ranelagh, *The Agency* (1986).

"Our final examination of trained cats [DELETED] for [DELETED] use in the [DELETED] convinced us that the program would not lend itself in a practical sense to our highly specialized needs. . . . We have satisfied ourselves that it is indeed possible [DELETED]. This in itself is a remarkable scientific achievement. Knowing that cats can indeed be trained to move short distances [DELETED] we see no reason to believe that a [DELETED] cat can not be similarly trained to approach [DELETED]. Again, however, the environmental and security factors in using this technique in a real foreign situation force us to conclude that, for our [DELETED] purposes, it would not be practical."

Released (and obviously redacted) CIA memorandum, "[DELETED] Views on Trained Cats [DELETED] for [DELETED] Use," March 1967.

"Most officials responsible for planning future collection systems have historically been the operators of the systems. Unfortunately, the operators are often the individuals in the intelligence cycle who have the least contact with the final users of intelligence."

BRUCE BERKOWITZ and ALLAN GOODMAN, *Strategic Intelligence* (1989). The authors are, as the British say, spot on. A job requirement for senior officials at intelligence collection agencies should be a rotation on a policy staff, preferably the NSC.

"Sometimes the solution to getting into position to collect intelligence can be as challenging as the collection itself. . . . For example, some of the more interesting earthbound approaches to collection have been telemetry-intercept stations in the Caucasus Mountains of Iran, large phased-array radar systems in the Aleutian Islands, and a tunnel bored under the Berlin Wall to tap Soviet bloc landlines."

> **BRUCE BERKOWITZ** and **ALLAN GOODMAN**, *Strategic Intelligence* (1989).

"In the pedestrian, but fast-growing and lucrative area of economic espionage, one of the most effective tools [is] 'TRASHINT,' the smelly but sometimes rewarding craft of sorting through a company's trash."

> **JOHN J. FIALKA**, *War by Other Means: Economic Espionage in America* (1997).

"Information saves lives, and . . . its collection is a risk worth taking."

> DCI **GEORGE TENET**, at the funeral of CIA officer Johnny Micheal Spann, who was killed in Afghanistan trying to glean intelligence from Taliban prisoners, 10 December 2001.

"So much has been revealed over the years about U.S. technical collection capabilities that the targets now understand better what they have to evade. State sponsors of terrorism may know satellite overflight schedules and can schedule accordingly activities that might otherwise be observable. They can use more fiber-optic communications, which are much harder to tap than transmissions over the airwaves. Competent terrorists know not to use cell phones for sensitive messages, and even small groups have access to impressive new encryption technologies."

> **RICHARD K. BETTS**, "Fixing Intelligence," *Foreign Affairs* (January–February 2002).

COMPARTMENTATION

A ship preserves its watertight integrity by means of a series of compartments that isolate any breach. Like-wise, the most sensitive secrets are compartmented—restricted to a relative few with a need to know—to minimize the possibility of damage from a leak and to make it easier to isolate and identify the source of the leak. The Literary Spy understands the paradox of compartmentation: it is just as important to identify whom a secret is to be kept from as to know whom it is for.

See also: Leaks; Secrecy

"It is essential for a general to be tranquil and obscure, upright and self-disciplined, and able to stupefy the eyes and ears of the officers and troops, keeping them ignorant."

> **SUN TZU**, on keeping one's own men in the dark, *The Art of War* (6th century B.C.).

"The Continental Congress protected intelligence sources and methods by authorizing deletion of the names of those employed by the committee or with whom it had corresponded."

> **EDWARD F. SAYLE**, "The Historical Underpinnings of the U.S. Intelligence Community," *International Journal of Intelligence and Counterintelligence* (spring 1986).

"His . . . name I have no desire to be informed of provided his intelligence is good & seasonably transmitted."

> **GEORGE WASHINGTON** to his intelligence chief Benjamin Tallmadge on the true identity of Tallmadge's spy "Culper," 27 June 1779; in the Sir Henry Clinton collection, Clements Library, University of Michigan. Washington didn't want to know and never found out.

"By the naming of names many good plans are brought to confusion."

> **RUDYARD KIPLING**, *Kim* (1901).

"It is well known that the free flow of information is the best stimulus of new knowledge and the elimination of error. But in the real world of government bureaucracy, sensitive intelligence information is compartmentalized; in other words, it is denied to as many persons as possible.... Compartmentalizing knowledge exacts a price."

WALTER LAQUEUR, *A World of Secrets* (1985).

"EDITH."

OGPU code name for, well, a woman named Edith. In the early 1930s, a female Soviet agent in Vienna was the first to identify Harold "Kim" Philby's potential as a spy for Moscow. Her name was Edith Suschitsky, codenamed EDITH. This was not an isolated case; during the war, the Soviet code name for Anthony Blunt, who with Philby was one of the infamous "Cambridge Five," was TONY. Andrew and Mitrokhin, *The Mitrokhin Archive* (1999). Andrew notes that the Soviets later improved their tradecraft.

"Compartmented intelligence became institutionalized during World War II, when the United States and Britain broke the Axis codes. Words such as MAGIC, ULTRA, PEARL, and THUMB were used to denote particularly sensitive intelligence, and access to it was tightly restricted by category. SCI [Sensitive Compartmented Information] functions on the theory that damaging security leaks can be kept to a minimum if those in the system know only what they need to know in order to perform their jobs. Security people are always talking about the 'need to know.' Compartmentalizing information is the way they restrict what is known."

WILLIAM E. BURROWS, *Deep Black* (1986).

"In an agreement dated January 23, 1941, the intelligence chiefs of the Army and Navy listed those eligible to see MAGIC [decrypted intercepts of Japan's diplomatic traffic].... [Army Chief of Staff George] Marshall interpreted the rules strictly and did not even entrust one of his closest assistants, Colonel Walter Bedell Smith, secretary to the general staff, with a key to the MAGIC briefcase."

DAVID KAHN, *The Codebreakers* (1996). Smith later was DCI under President Truman, responsible by law for the security of all intelligence "sources and methods."

"If you ever let drop one word of what you are going to learn today, I shall personally shoot you."

British intelligence officer to new personnel assigned to handle ULTRA [decrypted German messages], 1941; quoted in Winterbotham, *Ultra Spy* (1989).

"No action is to be taken on information herein reported, regardless of temporary advantage, if such action might have the effect of revealing the existence of the source to the enemy."

Warning on the cover of MAGIC summaries of Japanese diplomatic messages during World War II; cited in Kahn, *The Codebreakers* (1996).

"When we had [cryptologic] information that might enable a [U.S.] submarine to make contact with a Japanese aircraft carrier or task force, I went directly to the chief of ComSubPac and delivered it orally. I did not tell him how the information was obtained.... We kept no records. If I had a position in latitude and longitude, I wrote the figures in ink on the palm of my hand, and scrubbed my hands after I had delivered the message."

Former U.S. naval intelligence officer **W. J. HOLMES**, *Double-Edged Secrets* (1979).

"Information concerning the design and operation of collection systems is usually classified separately from the information actually produced by the system. For example, during World War II ULTRA intelligence was often disguised as being from some other source, such as human agents, so consumers often were unaware that they were even using SIGINT, let alone the nature of the technology that made it possible."

BRUCE BERKOWITZ and **ALLAN GOODMAN**, *Strategic Intelligence* (1989).

"In coded messages, countries had always to be referred to by symbols—Germany, for instance, was 'Twelve-land.' The practice was scrupulously observed throughout the war even though, on one festive occasion at an Istanbul hotel, when the orchestra played the German national anthem, the staff of the German embassy stood to attention and sang as one man: 'Zwölfte-land, Zwölfte-land, über alles!'"

Former SIS officer **MALCOLM MUGGERIDGE** in *Chronicles of Wasted Time: The Infernal Grove* (1973).

"Since any slight break would be disastrous, no constructive purpose would be served by cabling particulars."

ALLEN DULLES, OSS station chief in Bern, protecting his sources on the anti-Hitler opposition within Germany in a January 1944 cable to Washington; quoted in Grose, *Gentleman Spy* (1995).

"Conscious of security to the last, [Winston Churchill] gave General de Gaulle only forty-eight hours' notice of the liberation of France."

DAVID STAFFORD, *Churchill and Secret Service* (1998).

"We know too much. If we are going to get captured, I'll shoot you first. Then myself: After all, I'm the commanding officer."

OSS director Major General **WILLIAM DONOVAN** to his aide at Utah Beach, Normandy, 7 June 1944; quoted in Polmar and Allen, *Encyclopedia of Espionage* (1997). Donovan had broken the rules prohibiting ULTRA-cleared officers from putting themselves in danger of capture; at Utah Beach he and his aide briefly came under German machine-gun fire.

"Restricted, Confidential, Secret, More Than Secret, More Secret Than the More Than Secret, Most Extreme and Super-Secret."

OSS analysis chief **SHERMAN KENT**'s category of classifications by which one part of OSS (Secret Intelligence) denied information to another (Kent's Research and Analysis branch); cited in Winks, *Cloak and Gown* (1987).

"By virtue of just knowing about [cracked enemy ciphers], I automatically came into the category of those who must in no circumstances fall into enemy hands. . . . Thus, henceforth it became a positive duty, rather than just a negative inclination, to keep well away from the enemy."

Former SIS officer **MALCOLM MUGGERIDGE** in *Chronicles of Wasted Time: The Infernal Grove* (1973).

"Would it be possible for you to send us by Air Pouch one of those books you have giving people numbers and funny names, like 'fruitcake #385.' Frequently we find references to them here and no one knows who on earth is being referred to."

OSS employee **JULIA McWILLIAMS** (known later as the famous French chef Julia Child), dispatch from her post in Ceylon; quoted in *U.S. News and World Report* (3 February 2003). This is the only connection the Literary Spy has found between Julia Child and fruitcake.

"A . . . tragic outcome resulted from the decision not to disseminate [cryptologic] information concerning the positions of Japanese submarines late in the war. This information was given extremely limited distribution lest the Japanese should discover that their most sophisticated code had been broken. As a result, the USS *Indianapolis* never learned that there was a Japanese submarine in her path. The *Indianapolis* went down in fifteen minutes, and the total loss came to 883 men. . . . The source was so exceedingly valuable that it had to be protected at all costs, yet should such costs include, for example, the many lives aboard the *Indianapolis*?"

> Senator **DANIEL INOUYE**, foreword to W. J. Holmes, *Double-Edged Secrets* (1979).

"We had security that just would not quit. . . . The U-2, for example, was built and flying [in 1955] before the commander of the Air Force research and development command ever even heard of it. If you wanted to see one ticked-off Air Force major general, you should have seen this guy."

> **LEO GEARY**, a senior official on the joint CIA–Air Force project that produced the U-2 spyplane; quoted in Bissell, *Reflections of a Cold Warrior* (1996). Geary himself was an Air Force general. Now that's compartmentation.

"This case is of the highest possible importance and must therefore be handled on the lowest possible level."

> A "shrewd MI5 officer," according to **HAROLD "KIM" PHILBY**, *My Secret War* (1968).

"Burn Before Reading."

> U.S. military saying, highlighting the cynical extreme of compartmentation.

"The first major American-British intelligence success against the Soviet Union during the Cold War [was] the VENONA decrypts, which revealed the codenames and clues to the identities of several hundred Soviet agents. Remarkably, [President] Truman seems never to have been informed of VENONA at all. . . . Because of internal rivalries within the US intelligence community, even the CIA was not told until late in 1952. [Moscow], however, had learned of VENONA by early in 1947 from William Weisband, an agent in the US SIGINT agency, ASA. Thus, amazingly, Stalin discovered the greatest American intelligence secret of the early Cold War over five years before either the president or the CIA."

> **CHRISTOPHER ANDREW** and **VASILI MITROKHIN**, *The Sword and the Shield: The Mitrokhin Archive* (1999).

"The code names for most Agency operations are picked in sequence from a sterile list, with care taken not to use any word that might give a clue to the activity it covers. On some large projects, code names are occasionally specially chosen. . . . Occasionally the special code names come close to the nerve, as did MONGOOSE."

> Former DCI **RICHARD HELMS** on the operation that President John F. Kennedy and Attorney General Robert Kennedy intended to remove a particularly loathsome snake, Fidel Castro, in *A Look over My Shoulder* (2003).

"You aren't cleared for certain sources."

> CIA counterintelligence chief **JAMES ANGLETON** whenever he wished to end a debate on the reliability of a particular spy; quoted in Powers, *The Man Who Kept the Secrets* (1979).

"Because I might talk in my sleep."

> DCI **WILLIAM COLBY** explaining to an aide why he did not want to know the true names of CIA's Soviet agents; quoted in Schecter and Deriabin, *The Spy Who Saved the World* (1995).

"An intelligence document that is top secret, but not further restricted by a code word, is considered barely classified."

> Former DCI **STANSFIELD TURNER**, *Secrecy and Democracy* (1985).

"The special protection [accorded to ciphers] stems in part from the extraordinary damage that betrayal of cryptosystems can do. Knowledge of a cipher system can give an enemy insight into quantities of information, whereas knowledge of, say, a particular weapon is limited to that item."

DAVID KAHN, *The Codebreakers* (1996).

"If you're a spook and want to examine our satellite photographs of Saddam Hussein's favorite seraglio, you need a 'Talent Keyhole' clearance. But that's *compartmented;* if you've got no need to know, it matters not how much talent you have. They won't let you near the keyhole."

WILLIAM SAFIRE, "On Language," *New York Times Magazine*, 21 February 1999.

"Eye Only."

Handling instruction allegedly used for sensitive CIA cables to a particular station chief who was blind in one eye.

"In the secret operations canon it is axiomatic that the probability of leaks escalates exponentially each time a classified document is exposed to another person—be it an Agency employee, a member of Congress, a senior official, a typist, or a file clerk. Effective compartmentation is fundamental to all secret activity."

Former DCI **RICHARD HELMS**, *A Look over My Shoulder* (2003). Helms's dated and quaint references to typists and file clerks aside, the point is eternally valid: secret information is just secret, but secret compartmented information is *protected*. The downside of compartmentation, however, is that it makes the use and transmission of such material difficult; Helms goes on to say that "efficiency and secrecy are absolutely incompatible concepts."

COUNTERINTELLIGENCE

Having the best spies, the best collection systems, and the best analysts will not help an intelligence service if it leaks like a sieve. The Literary Spy submits that counterintelligence is the kidneys of national security:

necessary, but unheralded until something goes wrong.

See also: Espionage & Spies; FBI & Law Enforcement; Traitors in Their Own Words; Treason & Betrayal

"Conceal your dispositions, and you will be safe from the prying of the subtlest spies, from the machination of the wisest brains."

SUN TZU, *The Art of War* (6th century B.C.).

"The enemy's spies who have come to spy on us must be sought out, tempted with bribes, led away, and comfortably housed. Thus they will become converted spies and available for our service. . . . The converted spy not only brings information himself, but makes it possible to use the other kinds of spies to advantage. Hence it is essential that the converted spy be treated with the utmost liberality."

SUN TZU, *The Art of War* (6th century B.C.).

"As far as people who have been convicted of spying, if they are foreigners from a hostile country, Jews, Christians, or Persians who are Arab subjects, they must be decapitated. If they are bad Muslims, one has to inflict painful punishment on them and put them into prison for a long term."

Arab political treatise, 8th century; cited in Dvornik, *Origins of Intelligence Services* (1974).

"Smooth runs the water where the brook is
    deep;
And in his simple show he harbors treason.
The fox barks not when he would steal the
    lamb."

The Duke of Suffolk in **WILLIAM SHAKESPEARE**, *King Henry VI, Part II* (1590), Act III, scene 1.

"Inspire me, that I may this treason find! . . .
That we may know the traitors and the truth!"

> Marcus in **WILLIAM SHAKESPEARE**, *Titus Andronicus* (1590), Act IV, scene 1.

"Treason works ere traitors be espied."

> **WILLIAM SHAKESPEARE**, *The Rape of Lucrece* (1594).

"You must not dare, for shame, to talk of
    mercy . . .
Treason and murder ever kept together,
As two yoke-devils sworn to either's purpose,
Working so grossly in a natural cause . . .
. . . I will weep for thee;
For this revolt of thine, methinks, is like
Another fall of man. Their faults are open:
Arrest them to the answer of the law;
And God acquit them of their practises!"

> King Henry in **WILLIAM SHAKESPEARE**, *King Henry V* (1599), Act II, scene 2.

"His power went out in such distractions as
Beguiled all spies."

> Soldier in **WILLIAM SHAKESPEARE**, *Antony and Cleopatra* (1607), Act III, scene 7, on why Caesar's forces surprised Mark Antony's.

"As for his secret Spialls [i.e., spies], who hee did employ both at home and abroad, by them to discover what Practices and Conspiracies were against him, surely his Case required it: Hee had such Moles perpetually working and casting to undermine him. Neither can it be reprehended. For if Spialls bee lawful against lawful Enemies, much more against Conspirators, and Traitors."

> **FRANCIS BACON**, *The Historie of the Raigne of King Henry the Seventh* (1622); cited in Edward Sayle, "The Historical Underpinnings of the U.S. Intelligence Community," *International Journal of Intelligence and Counterintelligence* (spring 1986).

"It is a double pleasure to deceive the deceivers."

> **JEAN DE LA FONTAINE**, French writer, *Fables* (1668).

"There is one evil that I dread, & that is their Spies. . . . I think it a matter of some importance to prevent them from obtaining Intelligence of our Situation."

> **GEORGE WASHINGTON** in 1775; cited in Andrew, *For the President's Eyes Only* (1995).

"It is impossible to discover in every case the falsity of pretended friends, who would know our affairs; and more so to prevent being watch'd by spies, when interested people may think proper to place them for that purpose; I have long observ'd one rule which prevents any inconvenience from such practices. It is simply this, to be concern'd in no affairs that I should blush to have made publick, and to do nothing but what spies may see and welcome. When a man's actions are just and honourable, the more they are known, the more his reputation is increas'd and establish'd. If I was sure, therefore that my valet de Place was a spy, as probably he is, I think I should not discharge him for that, if in other respects I lik'd him."

> **BENJAMIN FRANKLIN**, while head of the American mission in Paris, responding to a warning from a friend about British spies, January 1777; quoted in *Studies in Intelligence* (1997). Thank heaven it was George Washington and not Franklin who was the American spymaster during the Revolutionary War, or we'd be singing "God Save the Queen."

"SIR,
    Nathan Palmer, a lieutenant in your King's service, was taken in my camp as a Spy—he was tried as a Spy—he was condemned as a Spy—and you may rest assured, Sir, he shall be hanged as a Spy.

I have the honor to be, etc.,
Israel Putnam
P.S. Afternoon. He is hanged."

Letter of 4 August 1777 from American General **ISRAEL PUTNAM** to the Tory governor of New York, who had warned that Palmer's execution for espionage would lead to British reprisals; cited in Bakeless, *Turncoats, Traitors and Heroes* (1998).

"I have no means of ascertaining the truth."

ROBERT E. LEE, in spring 1863, noting the effectiveness of Union counterintelligence; cited in Miller, *Spying for America* (1989).

"The very low estimate in which we hold spies should always make us distrustful of them. An individual who is ready to injure his own compatriots will not scruple to betray the enemy of his country, if the terms offered him are high enough."

British Colonel **GEORGE FURSE**, *Information in War* (1895).

"A spy in the pay of both sides is, generally speaking, hurtful to both. An individual suspected of double dealing may, nevertheless, be turned to account to convey false information to the adversary. To do this with some prospect of success demands a certain amount of finesse."

British Colonel **GEORGE FURSE**, *Information in War* (1895).

"Without her spies England is helpless."

Irish Republican Army leader **MICHAEL COLLINS**, 1920, during an Irish terror campaign against British intelligence operatives; cited in Stafford, *Churchill and Secret Service* (1998).

"We could not censor the mails. We could not censor the dispatches. We could not prevent the taking of photographs. We could not arrest Japanese suspects. There was nothing we could do to stop it, and all hands knew that espionage was go-

ing on all along, and reports were going back to Japan."

Captain **THEODORE WILKINSON**, director of U.S. naval intelligence, on the activities of the Japanese consulate in Honolulu in 1941; cited in Prange, *At Dawn We Slept* (1981).

"Make an example of someone at an early date for indiscretion, and continue to act ruthlessly where lack of security is concerned."

Commander **IAN FLEMING**, British naval intelligence officer and future creator of James Bond, to COI chief William Donovan, 27 June 1941; cited in Riebling, *Wedge: The Secret War Between the FBI and CIA* (1994).

"An insecure service is not merely useless; it is positively dangerous, because it allows a hostile agency to manipulate the penetrated organization, as the British, for example, manipulated German intelligence during World War II. MI 5 turned German agents in Britain, used them to feed false information to Germany, and thereby thoroughly confused the Germans as to the probable site and nature of the invasion of Europe. The Germans would have done better with no agents in Britain at all. . . . It is better to have no intelligence service at all than to have one which is insecure."

THOMAS POWERS, *The Man Who Kept the Secrets* (1979).

"Far the most interesting aspect, to me, of Intelligence operations was providing appropriate material (known as chicken feed) for transmission by enemy agents who had been turned around—that is, induced to go on functioning under control. This needed to be very carefully and subtly concocted; on the one hand, sufficiently high grade to impress their *Abwehr* masters, thereby building up their reputation; on the other, not so high grade that it gave away anything of major importance to us. . . . It was astonishing how, on both sides in the war, agents continued to be believed in even when they had been under control for years, and regularly sending grossly misleading information. The reason was, I think, that the officers controlling double-cross agents became in time very fond and proud of them. After all, they gave them their words, and built up their fictitious characters, so that they were as much the creation of their officer-controllers as the characters in a novel are the novelist's. If one of them was awarded an enemy decoration—as sometimes happened, again on both sides—it added lustre to the whole operation; and when the time came to blow a double-cross agent for some ulterior purpose, the controlling officers were as grieved as Dickens was when he felt bound to kill off Little Nell."

Former SIS officer **MALCOLM MUGGERIDGE**, *Chronicles of Wasted Time: The Infernal Grove* (1973).

"The weakness of security is not that it does not collect information but that the information it collects is not used. It is interesting to note that Alger Hiss was first accused of espionage in 1939, and that no effort was made to conduct an official investigation into the charges until 1948. This was equally unfortunate whether he was innocent or guilty."

REBECCA WEST, *The New Meaning of Treason* (1966).

"We must all bear in mind, if we cry out against the people who have abused their liberty in this country, that had we deprived them of that liberty without legal evidence against them we should have been taking steps which would, inevitably, have threatened the liberty of every one of us in Britain."

Sir **PERCY SILLITOE**, director of MI5 1946–53; cited in Robert Chadwell Williams, *Klaus Fuchs, Atom Spy* (1987).

"If you control counterintelligence, you control the intelligence service."

JAMES ANGLETON, longtime CIA counterintelligence chief, in 1949; quoted in Mangold, *Cold Warrior* (1991).

"Did you ever have or do you now have membership in, or support, any political party or organization which advocates the overthrow of our constitutional government in the United States?"

Question on employment forms for U.S. government service, 1940s–1970s. One supposes that at no time did anyone ever answer, "You betcha."

"We have to distrust each other. It's our only defense against betrayal."

TENNESSEE WILLIAMS, *Camino Real* (1953).

"A counterintelligence officer is someone who looks at himself in the mirror every morning and asks, 'I wonder who that man is working for?'"

Old joke in counterintelligence.

"Oh yes, I know of you. I read your reports."

NIKITA KHRUSHCHEV on meeting DCI Allen Dulles at a White House dinner, 15 September 1959; quoted in Jeffreys-Jones, *The CIA and American Democracy* (1989).

"I ask that in working with me you observe all rules of professional tradecraft and security and not permit any slipups. Protect me."

Soviet GRU Colonel **OLEG PENKOVSKIY**, letter making contact with CIA, August 1960; quoted in Schecter and Deriabin, *The Spy Who Saved the World* (1995).

"An anarchist and a crank who for some obscure reason is trying to get us into a war with Russia."

CIA counterintelligence chief **JAMES ANGLETON** on Soviet GRU Colonel Oleg Penkovskiy; quoted in Schecter and Deriabin, *The Spy Who Saved the World* (1995).

"I have already grown used to the fact that I note periodically some degree of surveillance and control over my movements. The 'neighbors' [the KGB] continue to study me. There is some reason for this KGB activity. I confuse and lose myself in guesses and suppositions. I am very far from exaggerating the dangers."

> Soviet GRU Colonel **OLEG PENKOVSKIY**, who was spying for CIA and SIS, in August 1962; in *The Penkovskiy Papers* (1966). Penkovskiy was arrested in October 1962 and tried and executed the following May.

"While much of the daily work of counterintelligence is laborious and humdrum, its complex and subtle operations are very much like a gigantic chess game that uses the whole world for its board."

> Former DCI **ALLEN DULLES**, *The Craft of Intelligence* (1963).

"The first of many writers to liken espionage to chess coined one of the least apt analogies in literature. . . . On the chessboard each piece is clearly visible and moves in a prescribed fashion. . . . There are no traitor pieces, no false knights, and even pawns never defect."

> **WILLIAM HOOD**, *Mole* (1993).

"I think if I were asked to single out one specific group of men, one type, one category as being the most suspicious, unbelieving, unreasonable, petty, inhuman, sadistic, double-crossing set of bastards in any language, I would say without hesitation: the people who run counter-espionage departments."

> **ERIC AMBLER**, *The Light of Day* (1963).

"In a free society the methods by which one combats subversion can vitally affect the health of the society as much as the subversion itself. Excesses cannot be dismissed, as some are wont to do, as

a small price to pay for security. For what is totalitarianism, against which we build dikes of security, except the systematization of excess?"

> **SIDNEY HOOK** in his introduction to Rebecca West, *The New Meaning of Treason* (1966).

"A double agent can learn not only what the enemy is thinking, but how he thinks, and therefore can know what his thoughts are going to be tomorrow and the day after that."

> **REBECCA WEST**, *The New Meaning of Treason* (1966).

"A wilderness of mirrors."

> Description of counterintelligence attributed to **JAMES ANGLETON**, legendary CIA counterintelligence chief. It comes from T. S. Eliot's poem "Gerontion" (1920). It also is the title of a 1980 book by David Martin on CIA counterintelligence.

"A dog returning to its own vomit."

> One definition of counterintelligence, from someone hostile to it and to James Angleton, quoted in Winks, *Cloak and Gown* (1987).

"Persons who work in a self-contained [counterespionage] unit are apt to develop theories which develop none the better for never being subject to open discussion."

> **REBECCA WEST**, *The New Meaning of Treason* (1966). What Dame West is saying is that CI officers tend to go batty.

"In a free society counterespionage is based on the practice most useful for hunting rabbits. Rather than look for the rabbit one posts oneself in a spot where the rabbit is likely to pass by."

> Former DCI **ALLEN DULLES** in his edited volume *Great True Spy Stories* (1968).

"She said the man in the gabardine suit was a spy. I said 'Be careful, his bowtie is really a camera.'"

> **PAUL SIMON**, "America," from Simon and Garfunkel's 1968 album *Bookends*.

"The function of the counterespionage officers is to question and verify every aspect of CIA operations; taking nothing at face value, they tend to see deceit everywhere. In an agency full of extremely mistrustful people, they are the professional paranoids."

> **VICTOR MARCHETTI** and **JOHN MARKS**, *CIA and the Cult of Intelligence* (1974).

"If some people were hurt in the process, I'm sorry! But this is not a game for the soft-hearted."

> Former DCI **RICHARD HELMS** recalling the internal hunt for CIA moles in the 1960s and 1970s; 1992 interview cited in Riebling, *Wedge: The Secret War Between the FBI and CIA* (1994).

"I sympathize with the victims, but that's part of the intelligence business. . . . You do not have rights in the intelligence field. The average officer accepts that."

> Former FBI official **SAM PAPICH** on the innocent victims of CIA molehunts; quoted in Mangold, *Cold Warrior* (1991). Sorry, Sam, the Bill of Rights still applies.

"We're often confronted with issues that you just don't find anywhere else. For instance, when you have Americans spying against the United States —what rights do they have? They still *do* have rights, but how do you determine what they are?"

> CIA lawyer, November 1998. Uh, check the Bill of Rights?

"The business of counterespionage is a Dantean hell with ninety-nine circles, and the men who dare its enigmas without exception have thick glasses, a midnight pallor, stomach ulcers, a love of fly fishing, and fretful wives."

> **THOMAS POWERS**, *The Man Who Kept the Secrets* (1979). Or at least three of the five.

"Counterintelligence is only as good as relations between the CIA and FBI."

> CIA counterintelligence chief **JAMES ANGLETON** in 1975; quoted in Riebling, *Wedge: The Secret War Between the FBI and CIA* (1994). This is not good news.

"Well, I went home with a waitress
The way I always do
How was I to know
She was with the Russians, too?"

> Rock balladeer **WARREN ZEVON**, "Lawyers, Guns, and Money," from Zevon's 1978 album *Excitable Boy*.

"After a while an intelligence-agent tended to see spies everywhere, rather as certain lunatics saw references to themselves in every newspaper."

> **PATRICK O'BRIAN**, *Treason's Harbour* (1983).

"There will always be penetrations. . . . It is a way of life. It should never be thought of as an aberration. Anyone who gets flustered by it is in the wrong business."

> CIA counterintelligence chief **JAMES ANGLETON** shortly before his death; quoted in the *New York Times*, 10 April 1987.

"Counterintelligence is to intelligence as epistemology is to philosophy. Both go back to the fundamental question of how we know things, both challenge what we are inclined to take most for granted, and both offer heavy advantage in debate to those who are skeptical of appearances."

> **THOMAS POWERS**, *The Man Who Kept the Secrets* (1979). One can never prove that any given intelligence service is *not* penetrated.

"[Counterintelligence is not for] those who believe that one ought to get everything out of a book on the first reading and move on, that one ought to interrogate a defector, deeply and thoroughly, and move on, that one ought to complete an operation, celebrate it quietly if successful or bury it deeply if not, and move on."

> **ROBIN W. WINKS**, *Cloak and Gown* (1987).

"In the world of CI there is seldom clear guilt or clear exoneration."

> **ANGELO CODEVILLA**, *Informing Statecraft* (1992).

"It is a commonplace of counter-espionage work that success comes and spies are caught not through the exercise of genius or even through the detective's flair for obscure clues, but by means of the patient and laborious study of records."

> Sir **JOHN MASTERMAN** of MI5 in 1975; cited in West, *Faber Book of Espionage* (1993). Or through the spy's own flubs, or by sheer luck.

"The first duty of a good inquisitor is to suspect especially those who seem sincere."

> Brother William in **UMBERTO ECO**, *The Name of the Rose* (1980). Can one fake insincerity?

"The CIA shall . . . conduct counterintelligence activities outside the United States and, without assuming or performing any internal security functions, conduct counterintelligence activities within the United States in coordination with the FBI."

> President **RONALD REAGAN**, Executive Order 12333, 4 December 1981; reproduced in Warner, *Central Intelligence* (2001).

"There are no friendly services. There are the services of friendly foreign powers."

> Anonymous CIA counterintelligence specialist during the era of counterintelligence chief James Angleton; quoted in Ranelagh, *The Agency* (1986).

"There is the danger of the counter-intelligence expert becoming so involved in the problems of hostile services, that he starts to see counter-intelligence cases through the eyes of the hostile intelligence service he has been studying so long. His judgement then goes. He sees ghosts where no ghosts exist. He invents ghosts to fit his theories. This has happened, and will happen again, and it can lead to disaster. Broadly speaking no highly intelligent, sensitive, counter-intelligence expert should be involved in this fascinating specialization for more than about twelve years. After that the 'Wilderness of Mirrors' starts to take over from common sense."

> SIS official **JOHN BRUCE LOCKHART**, "Intelligence: A British View" (1984); cited in West, *Faber Book of Espionage* (1993).

"You know, we really have no counterintelligence."

> Senator **SAM NUNN** to DCI Stansfield Turner; quoted in Turner, *Secrecy and Democracy* (1985).

"When you're catching spies, [it is said] you have a bad counterintelligence service; when you're not catching spies, you have a bad counterintelligence service. You can't have it both ways."

> FBI Director **WILLIAM WEBSTER**, 1985, after the John A. Walker, Jr., spy case; this quotation was displayed in the office of CIA's counterintelligence chief in 1996–97.

"K Mart has better security than the Navy."

> **JOHN A. WALKER, JR.**, the U.S. naval officer arrested in 1985 for espionage; quoted in Andrew and Mitrokhin, *The Mitrokhin File* (1999).

"I am appalled at the DO's handling of the Howard case [and] above all, an astonishing complacency about, seemingly an unwillingness to accept even as a possibility, a DO officer committing espionage for the Soviet Union."

> DCI **WILLIAM CASEY**, memorandum to CIA's Deputy Director for Operations, June 1986; cited in Gates, *From the Shadows* (1996). Edward Lee Howard was a CIA operations officer who spied for the USSR and escaped to Moscow in 1985.

"I have my own religion."

> Former CIA counterintelligence chief **JAMES ANGLETON** shortly before his death in 1987; quoted in Mangold, *Cold Warrior* (1991). So did Torquemada.

"The nightmare of every DCI is that his organization is penetrated. One lives with this every day."

> Former DCI **RICHARD HELMS**; quoted in Mangold, *Cold Warrior* (1991).

"With some chagrin, officials involved in the Pollard investigation recounted that Pollard had once collected so much [classified] data that he needed a handcart to move the papers to his car, in a nearby parking lot, and the [Pentagon] security guards held the doors for him."

> **SEYMOUR HERSH**, "The Traitor: The Case Against Jonathan Pollard," *New Yorker*, 18 January 1999.

"An agent is valuable because he tells you the truth about the enemy. A double agent is doubly valuable because he tells you about the enemy while letting you lie to the enemy. A triple agent is trebly valuable because in addition to the services of a double, he is the channel through which the enemy tells you lies that you already know to be lies, and which therefore disclose his deepest intentions."

> **ANGELO CODEVILLA**, *Informing Statecraft* (1992).

"[British turncoats Donald] Maclean and [Guy] Burgess slipped through a net that was, admittedly, full of holes; those who would like to live in a country where the nets catch all the 'moles' should go and live in the USSR. . . . Sometimes the price of liberty is eternal inefficiency."

> British diplomat **ROBERT CECIL**; cited in West, *Faber Book of Espionage* (1993).

"Some companies regard quality control as an opportunity to glory in the integrity of their product. Others think about quality control as little as possible, or even view it as a hindrance and a potential source of embarrassment. The U.S. intelligence system's approach to counterintelligence is of the latter kind. . . . The most important feature of CIA counterintelligence [is] a deeply ingrained resistance to independent quality control of espionage and covert action."

> **ANGELO CODEVILLA**, *Informing Statecraft* (1992).

"The problem with the world today is that nobody takes the time to do a really sinister interrogation anymore."

> James Bond, played by Pierce Brosnan, in the 1995 film *Goldeneye*.

"Of course, a polygraph is not foolproof; there are ways to 'beat the machine.' . . . Some cultures polygraph more effectively than others. Americans, because of our puritanical tradition of right and wrong, are good subjects. Arabs and Iranians, for example, are notoriously difficult, because lying under certain circumstances is culturally acceptable. . . . After all, the polygraph is a device devised by Westerners initially for use on other Westerners."

> Former senior CIA operations officer **DUANE CLARRIDGE**, *A Spy for All Seasons* (1997).

"For five years I was a colonel in the GRU, the Russian military intelligence agency, until 1992 [when] I defected to the United States. At that time, I was one of the top Russian intelligence officials in the United States.... During my career as a GRU spy stationed in the U.S., I grew to admire the FBI's and other US agencies' efforts to thwart foreign espionage. Despite the tireless work of the men and women of these agencies, I must honestly report to you that obtaining highly sensitive and classified information was not very difficult. For example, while [posing as] a reporter for TASS, I was invited to see the Stealth weapons. While I had the chance, I took pictures of the most sensitive parts of the bombers and fighters and sent them to Russia for analysis."

Former Soviet GRU Colonel **STANISLAV LUNEV**, testimony to the Military R&D Subcommittee of the House National Security Committee, 4 August 1998.

"It is truer of CI than of any other part of the craft of intelligence that no one has the resources, no one has the time, to really do it right."

ANGELO CODEVILLA, *Informing Statecraft* (1992). Well, that should help level the playing field.

"Any intelligence officer who assumes his service is penetration-proof is ignorant of intelligence history."

WILLIAM HOOD, *Mole* (1993).

"I was forever amazed at how much trouble people got into over sex. The CIA and Western intelligence services used sexual blackmail against our people, and we employed it even more frequently against our adversaries. Catching people with their pants down was a prime way of compromising them and recruiting them. As long as men would be men and women would be women, lust would play a role in the spy wars.... On the sexual espionage front, we usually got the better of the CIA and hostile Intelligence agencies for the simple reason that we were far more willing to use sex as a weapon, and generally had fewer scruples."

Former KGB general **OLEG KALUGIN**, *The First Directorate* (1994).

"This is going to be just as bad as the Rosenbergs."

CIA counterintelligence chief **PAUL REDMOND** upon being briefed in 1996 about possible Chinese espionage at Los Alamos National Laboratory; quoted in the *New York Times*, 15 March 1999.

"I've been thinking about your job and what you're trying to do. Anything I can do to help, just let me know."

CIA turncoat **ALDRICH AMES** to Jeanne Vertefeuille, head of the CIA counterintelligence team that eventually fingered Ames as a Russian spy; quoted in *Chicago Tribune*, 6 March 1997.

"One of the first rules of counter-intelligence is to protect an agent. Executing those double agents was a big mistake. From then onwards it was obvious that the Americans had a mole inside the CIA."

Former KGB officer **VIKTOR CHERKASHIN**, who was Aldrich Ames's first case officer; quoted in the *Sunday Times* (London), 8 February 1998.

"You don't catch spies by thinking like lawyers."

Assistant U.S. Attorney General **MARK HULKOWER**, Ames Prosecution Team, early 1995; this quotation was displayed in the office of CIA's counterintelligence chief in 1996–97.

"The extent of the damage [caused by Aldrich Ames] was due mostly to inexcusable laxity on the part of the professionals of the Directorate of

Operations and others at the CIA. It is an intelligence calamity of massive proportions."

DCI **JOHN DEUTCH**, "Moving Beyond Ames," *Washington Post*, 5 November 1995. With more to come!

"The only hostile foreign intelligence agency I thought I worked for was the CIA."

Frustrated veteran CIA operations officer forced to undergo several polygraph tests after Aldrich Ames's treason was revealed in 1994; quoted in *U.S. News and World Report* (11 June 2001).

"In any discussion of why spies are caught, one often overlooked [aspect] deserves mention . . . we are amazed at the poor level of tradecraft, even abject stupidity, displayed in many cases. . . . Since 1976, at least 16 of the [139] spies in our database telephoned or walked into the Soviet Embassy and asked if they would like to buy some secrets. In every case the FBI, who had intercepted the calls, met these would-be spies, bought what they had to offer, and then arrested them. In one case, the budding traitor threw a package of classified material with a note in it asking for money over the wall of the Soviet Embassy. The Soviets thought it was a bomb and called the Washington fire department. . . . Time and time again, these spies would engage in activities that any thinking person would avoid."

STAN TAYLOR and **DANIEL SNOW**, "Cold War Spies," *Intelligence and National Security* (April 1997).

"The biggest threat to each other's spies are agents coming over from the other side and snitching on them. . . . All the people whose names [I gave to the KGB] knew the risks they were taking when they began spying for the CIA and FBI. If one of them had learned about me, he would have told the CIA, and I would have been arrested and thrown in jail. Now that I was working for the

KGB, the people on my list could expect nothing less from me. It wasn't personal. It was simply how the game was played."

Former CIA operations officer **ALDRICH AMES**, who spied for Moscow and betrayed some two dozen U.S. agents; quoted in Earley, *Confessions of a Spy* (1997). Ames calls it a "game" to mask the essential difference, which was that the Soviets executed those who betrayed secrets that helped prop up the dictatorship. But why quibble?

"It may have been difficult for the CIA to find people like Ames when it was searching for people like Philby."

STAN TAYLOR and **DANIEL SNOW**, "Cold War Spies," *Intelligence and National Security* (April 1997). Treason knows no style.

"It is ideal for anyone interested in international intrigue, real-life spy stories, and worldly corruption."

CIA internal notice regarding a counterintelligence vacancy, June 1997.

"I'm a firm believer in giving them their full constitutional rights and then sending them to jail for a lifetime."

JOHN L. MARTIN, chief of the Justice Department's Internal Security Service, on what to do with Americans caught spying; quoted in the *Washington Post*, 31 July 1997.

"If someone with that kind of background can get a Pentagon secret clearance, what, it has to be wondered, might an undercover agent with a cleverly hidden past be able to do?"

Los Angeles Times editorial, 10 October 1997, on "pro-Communist, US-hating" Pentagon lawyer Therese Squillacote, arrested for spying for East Germany.

"By my view, in this country you have very powerful intelligence, counterintelligence community and law enforcement agencies. Unfortunately they do not have possibility to cover everything in this country, so they need support of American people, from everybody, to support them in their really very hard job."

> Former Soviet GRU Colonel **STANISLAV LUNEV**, testimony to the Military R&D Subcommittee of the House National Security Committee, 4 August 1998. Lunev was responding to a question about how the United States can protect itself from Russian intelligence.

"Security officers in the American government are not known for being particularly cosmopolitan. If one is well-schooled, curious, and well-traveled, it is not hard to appear a little unorthodox to security officials, who naturally prefer to see things uncomplicated, clean-cut, and all-American."

> Former CIA officer **REUEL GERECHT** in the *New Republic*, 1 February 1999.

"We should be adult enough to understand that major countries are going to be spying on us."

> **HENRY KISSINGER**; quoted in the *New York Times*, 14 March 1999.

"Do you know who the Rosenbergs are? . . . You know what happened to them? They electrocuted them."

> FBI agent during interrogation of Wen Ho Lee, accused of passing U.S. nuclear weapons secrets to China; March 1999 transcript cited in the *Washington Post*, 8 January 2000.

"We still have a problem with counterintelligence in this country. . . . There isn't very much being done."

> Former DCI **RICHARD HELMS**; quoted in Studies in Intelligence (unclassified ed., fall 2000).

"Recent changes in U.S. law now attach the death penalty to my help to you as you know, so I do take some risk."

> FBI affidavit of alleged communication in November 2000 between FBI counterintelligence expert Robert Hanssen and Russian intelligence officers; cited in the *New York Times*, 22 February 2001. Hanssen was convicted of spying for Moscow for fifteen years.

"Russian espionage is on the rise. The U.S. used to be Enemy Number 1. Now it is Priority Number 1."

> **OLEG KALUGIN**, former KGB major general and chief of KGB operations in the United States; quoted in the *Washington Post*, 24 January 2001. With priorities like these . . .

"We can no longer afford to focus our counterintelligence efforts only after an incident has sparked a full criminal case, because at that point it's too late. The damage has been done."

> DCI **GEORGE TENET**; quoted in *Government Executive* (February 2001).

"In any democratic society, counterintelligence is decidedly difficult and will never be perfect. It wasn't perfect in the totalitarian Soviet Union, and it certainly won't be in America."

> Former DCI **ROBERT GATES**, "The Moles Will Always Be with Us," the *New York Times*, 23 February 2001.

"You have to be a bit more paranoid in this business than you do when you're out in the normal world of business or commerce or law."

> Former DCI **R. JAMES WOOLSEY**; quoted by the Associated Press, 5 March 2001. Except that paranoids, of course, don't have real enemies.

"The federal government may as well put its faith in Wonder Woman's magic lasso than rely on the accuracy of the polygraph."

> Attorney **MARK ZAID**, whose clients have sued the FBI, the Secret Service, and the Drug Enforcement Administration over the use of the "lie detector"; quoted by the Associated Press, 25 April 2001. For those unfamiliar with Wonder Woman's superpowers: her magic lasso compelled the truth from anyone lassoed by it.

"I sincerely regret the adverse impact that this investigation had on you and the members of your family. It was not the intent of the FBI to either discredit you or to cause you or your family any embarrassment. If this has occurred, then I am sorry."

> FBI senior official **NEIL J. GALLAGHER** to a CIA officer wrongly accused of espionage; letter of 16 August 2001 quoted in the *Washington Post*, 11 September 2001. The CIA officer, who was suspended for twenty-one months, was targeted for activities later attributed to FBI counterintelligence agent Robert Hanssen.

"Joining the intelligence community is like trying out for a fraternity. The prospective employee must undergo a rugged pledge period during which his finances are examined, his neighbors questioned, his background searched and finally, after a heart-pounding, perspiration-inducing session with the polygraph operator, he is given thumbs up or thumbs down. Once he is admitted, except for a routine check every five years, his worries are over. Unfortunately, this method is nowhere near sufficient."

> **JAMES BAMFORD** in the *New York Times*, 28 August 2001.

"There is an actuarial certainty that there are other spies in U.S. national security agencies and there always will be."

> Former CIA counterintelligence chief **PAUL REDMOND**; quoted in *U.S. News and World Report* (10 September 2001).

"Simply put, security is not as valued within the [Federal] Bureau [of Investigation] as it is in other agencies.... Security policies are too often viewed as a nuisance to negotiate around, rather than [as] edicts with which to comply.... The FBI's failure to give human intelligence more protection than it does is somewhat at odds with its traditional desire to protect human sources."

> Report of a special panel, convened by the U.S. Justice Department and chaired by former FBI director and DCI William Webster, on the espionage of FBI officer Robert Hanssen, who betrayed some fifty sources to Moscow; cited in the *Washington Post*, 5 April 2002, and in the *New York Times*, 6 April 2002.

"Almost every spy that we have found, both in the CIA and the FBI, has been found with the aid of recruited sources of our own in other hostile intelligence agencies."

> Former FBI director and DCI **WILLIAM WEBSTER** in Senate testimony, 9 April 2002.

"No intelligence service can be more effective than its counterintelligence component for very long.... The bona fides of a spy can best be determined by a combined effort, with experienced field operatives and counterintelligence staff evaluating the operation itself, and the substantive analysts concentrating on the intelligence content. Neither element can function effectively without the support of the other."

> Former DCI **RICHARD HELMS**, *A Look over My Shoulder* (2003). This is one of the few instances in which a senior

CIA professional has acknowledged the crucial role of analysts in CI work.

"There are at least three, probably four, compromises and executions of assets of ours and one British in Moscow that aren't explained by anybody that we know about. . . . Jim Risen and I have reached the conclusion that Edward Lee Howard, Aldrich Ames, and [Robert] Hanssen were responsible for a certain number—and there was a lot of overlap between the three of them [but that] there had to be a fourth man."

Former CIA operations officer **MILTON BEARDEN**, who in a book with journalist James Risen (*The Main Enemy*, 2003) raised the possibility of a major traitor still at work at CIA or the FBI; interviewed on National Public Radio, 5 May 2003.

"THE OATH OF OFFICE. 'I, [name], do solemnly swear that I will support and defend the Constitution of the United States against all enemies, foreign and domestic; that I will bear true faith and allegiance to the same; that I take this obligation freely, without any mental reservation or purpose of evasion; and that I will well and faithfully discharge the duties of the office on which I am about to enter. SO HELP ME GOD.' *Said by all who enter on duty with the United States Government. Said by Jim Nicholson on 26 January 1982; Said by Earl Pitts on 18 September 1983; Said by Rick Ames on 17 June 1962; Said by Bob Hanssen on 12 January 1976.*"

CIA's Counterintelligence and Security Program, 2004.

COVERT ACTION

As with assassination, the Literary Spy was confronted with a disproportionate abundance of material on covert action: the conduct of activities designed to further a nation's foreign policy goals without showing that nation's hand. The popular notion that covert action is the central activity of an intelligence service is akin to the idea that a diplomatic service exists to shut down embassies. Sometimes it's necessary, but no one should be happy about the conditions that made it necessary.

See also: Assassination; Bay of Pigs; Collection; Espionage & Spies; Fact versus Fiction; Intelligence & American Culture; Legislative Oversight; Plausible Denial

"Generally speaking, there is no doubt that any idea or project that violates justice must be rejected by a man of integrity. But, Sire, State policy is not the same as private morality. . . . The sort of politics that upholds nations is different in almost every respect from the morality that governs private people. . . . And a king who alone wished to be absolutely just among the wicked and to remain good among the wolves would soon be devoured along with his flock."

PIERRE-AUGUSTIN CARON DE BEAUMARCHAIS (1732–1799), French writer and spymaster, pressing Louis XVI to approve a covert plan to aid the Americans in their rebellion against Britain, 1775; cited in *Studies in Intelligence* (1979).

"The philosophers have only *interpreted* the world in various ways; the point, however, is to *change* it."

KARL MARX, "Theses on Feuerbach" (1845). This quotation adorns Marx's headstone in Highgate Cemetery, London.

"The morality of the thing is not my concern. I present the state of fact, with the observation that action would greatly increase the chance of . . . success."

> Fictional British agent Stephen Maturin on whether London in 1803 should covertly aid Catalan succession to distract Spain from an alliance with France; in **PATRICK O'BRIAN**, *Post Captain* (1972).

"The English have burned our Capitol and President's House by means of their force. We can burn their St. James's and St. Paul's by means of our money, offered to their own incendiaries, of whom there are thousands in London who would do it rather than starve."

> Former President **THOMAS JEFFERSON** suggesting that the Madison administration retaliate for the burning of Washington, D.C., September 1814; quoted in Knott, *Secret and Sanctioned* (1996).

"Long before there was a Central Intelligence Agency, [President] Madison sent Joel R. Poinsett as a secret agent to Latin America and winked at his clandestine revolutionary adventures in Argentina and Chile; Madison's Secretary of State removed Poinsett's dispatches from State Department files lest Congress request them. The Madison and Monroe administrations used covert action to facilitate the annexation of Florida."

> **ARTHUR M. SCHLESINGER, JR.**, *The Cycles of American History* (1986).

"Covert action has been a tool of United States foreign policy for the past 28 years [that is, since 1947]."

> U.S. Senate, *Final Report of the Select Committee to Study Governmental Operations with respect to Intelligence Activities* [the Church Committee] (April 1976). Stephen Knott, whose *Secret and Sanctioned* (1996) chronicles the use of covert action by American leaders since Washington, calls the report historically distorted and myopic.

"We now have a pulpit to preach from which reaches a large audience and I consider it a very important gain."

> U.S. ambassador to Belgium **HENRY SANFORD** reporting to Secretary of State William Henry Seward that he had bribed the editor of a Belgian newspaper to tilt in favor of the Union during the American Civil War; quoted in Knott, *Secret and Sanctioned* (1996). Sanford directed U.S. secret service operations in Europe for President Lincoln.

"We can prevent a shooting war if we take the initiative to win the subversive war."

> **WILLIAM DONOVAN**, 1919, after visiting Soviet Russia; quoted in Pisani, *CIA and the Marshall Plan* (1991).

"They were all like that. They desired the end, but hesitated at the means. They were willing to take advantage of an accomplished fact, but wanted to shift on to someone else the responsibility for bringing it about."

> Fictional British intelligence agent, the autobiographical character in **W. SOMERSET MAUGHAM**, *Ashenden* (1927). The musings of Ashenden, a writer turned spy, could apply to, say, the Bay of Pigs. Maugham was an SIS officer in World War I.

"We're like people who have pushed a cart down a hill and jumped into it just as it gets going. We start it, but we can't stop it. We're caught up in something. We've got to go on. Our only hope is that the cart will one day arrive on the road at the bottom of the hill and stop of its own volition, so that we can get out."

> Fictional German spy in **PETER CHEYNEY**, *Dark Duet* (1942).

"Surprise, kill, and vanish."

> Motto of the Jedburgh teams, a joint commando enterprise between the OSS and Britain's SOE during World War II; cited in Miller, *Spying for America* (1989).

"We sleep safe in our beds because rough men stand ready in the night to visit violence on those who would do us harm."

GEORGE ORWELL [Eric Arthur Blair], BBC broadcast of 4 April 1942.

"[The] OSS mystique ... turned on the idea that even men of fine reputation, far from home, could find themselves doing bad things for a good cause."

MARK RIEBLING, *Wedge: The Secret War Between the FBI and CIA* (1994).

"This agency, as the sole agency for secret intelligence, should be authorized, in the foreign field only, to carry on services such as espionage, counter-espionage and those special operations (including morale and psychological) designed to anticipate and counter any attempted penetration and subversion of our national security by enemy action."

OSS director **WILLIAM DONOVAN**, paper attached to memorandum to President Truman, 25 August 1945; in *FRUS 1945–1950: Emergence of the Intelligence Establishment* (1996), document 3.

"The war had created the OSS and a strong covert capability. Truman never meant to obliterate the covert function, and his official disbanding of the OSS in 1945 was really a partitioning. ... What the President wanted was a peacetime covert organization."

SALLIE PISANI, *CIA and the Marshall Plan* (1991).

"Clandestine intelligence operations involve a constant breaking of all the rules of correct procedure according to which the regular government departments must operate. To put it baldly, such operations are necessarily extra-legal and sometimes illegal. No regular government department,

be it War, State or Navy, can afford to house such operations within itself or otherwise identify itself with them. Independence of association with them is therefore essential."

SSU director Brigadier General **JOHN MAGRUDER**, report on "Intelligence Matters" to Robert Lovett, Assistant Secretary of War for Air, October 1945; in *FRUS 1945–1950: Emergence of the Intelligence Establishment* (1996), document 34.

"For any U.S. agency to send unregistered clandestine operatives into a foreign country against which the United States is not at war ... not only runs directly counter to the principles upon which our country was founded but also those for which we recently fought a war."

OSS official (and later chief of CIA estimates) **SHERMAN KENT**, in a letter from 1945; quoted in Winks, *Cloak and Gown* (1987).

"Under the plan which you have approved, first priority is given to the development of a coordinated government-wide system and such secret intelligence operations as may be undertaken are operated on as adjunct. In this way secret operations are placed in their proper relationship to a general and much more comprehensive system of intelligence."

Budget director **HAROLD SMITH**, memorandum to President Truman, 28 November 1945; in *FRUS 1945–1950: Emergence of the Intelligence Establishment* (1996), document 51.

"If our measures short of war are going to be effective[,] we must select measures and use them not hit-or-miss as the moment may seem to demand, but in accordance with a pattern of grand strategy no less concrete and no less consistent than that which governs our actions in war. ... My personal conviction is that if we keep up our strength, if we are ready to use it, and if we select the measures short of war with the necessary wisdom and co-ordination, then these measures short of war will be all the ones that we will ever have to use to se-cure the prosperous and safe future of the people of this country."

GEORGE KENNAN, lecture at National War College, 16 September 1946; reprinted in Giles Harlow and George Maerz, *Measures Short of War* (1991).

"A review of the National Security Act reveals two provisions which might be construed as authority for CIA to engage in black propaganda or the type of activity known during the war as S.O. [special operations], which included ranger and commando raids, behind-the-lines sabotage, and support of guerrilla warfare. Section 102 (d) (4) provides that it shall be the duty of the Agency to perform for the benefit of existing intelligence agencies such additional services of common concern as the Na-tional Security Council determines can be more efficiently accomplished centrally. Section 102 (d) (5) provides that the Agency shall perform such other functions and duties related to intelligence affecting the national security as the NSC may di-rect. Taken out of context and without knowledge of its history, these Sections could bear almost un-limited interpretation, provided the service per-formed could be shown to be of benefit to an intelli-gence agency or related to national intelligence. . . . A review of debates indicates that Congress was primarily interested in an agency for coordinat-ing intelligence. . . . We do not believe that there was any thought in the minds of Congress that the Central Intelligence Agency under this authority would take positive action for subversion and sabo-tage. . . . Further confirmation is found in the brief and off-the-record hearings on appropriations for CIA."

CIA general counsel **LAWRENCE HOUSTON**, memoran-dum on "CIA Authority to Perform Propaganda and Com-mando Type Functions," to DCI Roscoe Hillenkoetter, 25 September 1947; in *FRUS 1945–1950: Emergence of the Intelligence Establishment* (1996), document 241. This document shows CIA's initial reluctance to take on re-sponsibility for covert action.

"[DCI] Admiral Hillenkoetter had thrust upon him at Christmas 1947 a responsibility and a duty to perform which he did not want in the Central Intelligence Agency. He took part in the prepara-tion. He did not object to the assignment of the task to him. He was reluctant nonetheless to in-volve the affairs of the Agency with the enterprise. The paper of the National Security Council on the subject, NSC 4-A, returned to its files. The di-rective to the Director of Central Intelligence, one of but three copies, remained closely guarded in the Director's office. . . . The reason for so great secrecy was altogether clear. Not only was the Union of Soviet Socialist Republics condemned in the directive for its 'vicious' psychological oper-ations against the United States. The Director of Central Intelligence was charged with planning and conducting under cover a similar attack upon the Soviet Union and its satellites."

ARTHUR DARLING, *The Central Intelligence Agency* (1990).

"The National Security Council . . . has deter-mined that, in the interests of world peace and U.S. national security, the foreign information ac-tivities of the U.S. Government must be supple-mented by covert psychological operations. The similarity of operational methods involved in covert psychological and intelligence activities and the need to ensure their secrecy and obviate costly duplication renders the Central Intelligence Agency the logical agency to conduct such oper-ations. . . . The National Security Council directs the Director of Central Intelligence to initiate and conduct . . . covert psychological operations designed to counteract Soviet and Soviet-inspired activities which constitute a threat to world peace and security or are designed to discredit the United States in its endeavors to promote world peace and security. The Director of Central Intelligence is charged with ensuring that such psychological operations are consistent with U.S. foreign policy . . . and that appropriate agencies of the U.S. Government, both at home and abroad (including diplomatic and military representatives in each area) are kept informed of such operations which will directly affect them."

National Security Council directive 4-A, 17 December 1947; reproduced in Warner, *CIA Under Truman* (1994).

"NSC 4/A was thus the first official charter for covert activity by any U.S. agency since the close of World War II. . . . The National Security Act of 1947 had said nothing about psychological warfare, covert action, or any secret operations; but a carefully controlled, limited program of anti-Communist activity was being discussed at the time of its passage by senior government officials. Like clandestine collection operations, covert action operations were not mentioned in the law. An elastic, catch-all phrase was included, referring to CIA's performance of 'such other functions and duties related to intelligence affecting national security as the National Security Council may from time to time direct,' and this clause was later cited as giving authority for covert actions."

Former DDI **RAY CLINE**, *Secrets, Spies and Scholars* (1976).

"Covert psychological operations may include all measures of information and persuasion short of physical. The originating role of the United States will always be concealed. . . . The primary objectives of such operations will be: (1) to undermine the strength of foreign instrumentalities,

whether governments, organizations or individuals, which are engaged in activities inimical to the United States; and (2) to support U.S. foreign policy by influencing foreign public opinion in a direction favorable to the attainment of U.S. objectives. No covert psychological operations will be undertaken unless they are fully consistent with the foreign policy and objectives of the United States Government."

DCI **ROSCOE HILLENKOETTER**, memorandum for the Assistant Director of Special Operations, 22 March 1948; reproduced in Warner, *CIA Under Truman* (1994).

"Political warfare is the logical application of Clausewitz's doctrine in time of peace. In broadest definition, political warfare is the employment of all the means at a nation's command, short of war, to achieve its national objectives. Such operations are both overt and covert. They range from such overt actions as political alliances, economic measures . . . and 'white' propaganda to such covert operations as clandestine support of 'friendly' foreign elements, 'black' psychological warfare and even encouragement of underground resistance in hostile states. . . . Lenin so synthesized the teachings of Marx and Clausewitz that the Kremlin's conduct of political warfare has become the most refined and effective of any in history. We have been handicapped however by a popular attachment to the concept of a basic difference between peace and war . . . and by a reluctance to recognize the realities of international relations—the perpetual rhythm of struggle, in and out of war. . . . Having assumed greater international responsibilities than ever before in our history and having been engaged by the full might of the Kremlin's political warfare, we cannot afford to leave unmobilized our resources for covert political warfare. . . . It would seem that the time is fully ripe for the creation of a covert political warfare operations directorate within the

Government. If we are to engage in such operations, they must be under unified direction. One man must be the boss. And he must, as those responsible for the overt phases of political warfare, be answerable to the Secretary of State, who directs the whole in coordination."

State Department Policy Planning Staff (headed by George Kennan), memorandum on "The inauguration of organized political warfare," 4 May 1948; in *FRUS 1945–1950: Emergence of the Intelligence Establishment* (1996), document 269.

"I should like to suggest that, since [the Department of] State will not go along with CIA operating this political warfare thing in any sane or sound manner, we go back to the original concept that State proposed. Let State run it and let it have no connection at all with us. It seems to me that this is the only thing that will satisfy State in any way and rather than try to keep a makeshift in running order, subject to countless restrictions which can only lead to continued bickering and argument, I think maybe the best idea is to go back and make the OSP [Office of Special Projects, later the Office of Policy Coordination] work for State alone."

DCI **ROSCOE HILLENKOETTER** to J. S. Lay, assistant executive secretary of the National Security Council, 9 June 1948; transcript reproduced in Warner, *CIA Under Truman* (1994). Hard as it is for some to believe, CIA really didn't want covert action in the beginning.

"This function [i.e., covert action] was fated to play a crucial role in coloring perceptions of CIA, but it was not one sought by the agency. CIA entered into covert action operations under pressure from leading U.S. officials of the day to support basic U.S. foreign policy."

Former DDI **RAY CLINE**, *Secrets, Spies and Scholars* (1976).

"1. The National Security Council, taking cognizance of the vicious covert activities of the USSR, its satellite countries and Communist groups to discredit and defeat the aims and activities of the United States and other Western powers, has determined that, in the interests of world peace and US national security, the overt foreign activities of the US Government must be supplemented by covert operations.

2. The Central Intelligence Agency is charged by the National Security Council with conducting espionage and counterespionage abroad. It therefore seems desirable, for operational reasons, not to create a new agency for covert operations, but in time of peace to place the responsibility for them within the structure of the Central Intelligence Agency. . . .

5. As used in this directive, 'covert operations' are understood to be all activities . . . which are conducted or sponsored by this Government against hostile foreign states or groups or in support of friendly foreign states or groups but which are so planned and executed that any US Government responsibility for them is not evident. . . . Specifically, such operations shall include any covert activities related to: propaganda; economic warfare; preventive direct action, including sabotage, anti-sabotage, demolition and evacuation measures; subversion against hostile states, including assistance to underground resistance movements, guerrillas and refugee liberation groups, and support of indigenous anti-communist elements in threatened countries of the free world. Such operations shall not include armed conflict by recognized military forces, espionage, counterespionage, and cover and deception for military operations."

National Security Council directive on Office of Special Projects, NSC 10/2, 18 June 1948; reproduced in Warner, *CIA Under Truman* (1994).

"[Frank] Wisner bears roughly the same relation to Cold War covert operations that Edward Teller does to the hydrogen bomb."

> NATHAN MILLER on the first chief of the joint State/CIA covert action enterprise, the Office of Special Projects —later the Office of Policy Coordination; in Miller, *Spying for America* (1989).

"My Dear Secretary: As you know, the Office of Policy Coordination of the Central Intelligence Agency, established under NSC 10, is preparing to discharge its mandate to conduct political warfare.... The Department of State considers that political warfare will be an important factor in the implementation of United States policies in the coming period. If effectively conducted, it may affect materially the possibilities for the achievement of United States objectives by means short of war. For this reason, considerations of foreign policy require, in the view of this department, that every effort be made to assist the Director of the Office of Policy Coordination in the implementation of his programs."

> Acting Secretary of State ROBERT LOVETT, letter to Secretary of Defense James Forrestal, 1 October 1948; in *FRUS 1945–1950: Emergence of the Intelligence Establishment* (1996), document 301. This letter was drafted by George Kennan of the Policy Planning Staff, as hinted by Kennan's favorite phrase for covert action, means or measures "short of war."

"No aspect of CIA operations has attracted as much public comment or as many screams of outrage as the operations now categorized as covert action.... The term 'covert action (CA)' slipped into the CIA intelligence lexicon sometime after the Agency was established in 1947. Although the various activities now encompassed by that coinage have been part of secret intelligence activity throughout history, the term was not used by OSS, nor do I recall seeing it in any of the wartime British

documents. The genesis probably came in December 1947 when the National Security Council [in NSC 4/A] made CIA responsible for 'Covert Psychological Operations.'... A subsequent National Security Council document [NSC 10/2 of 18 June 1948] dropped the 'Psychological' from the expression, and simply authorized CIA to carry out 'Covert Operations.' Because this term can be construed to embrace all manner of secret intelligence activity, it quickly evolved into the more accurate and restrictive expression 'Covert *Action* (CA).' The word 'action' is meant to distinguish CA from espionage.... Most of the results of successful CA operations are clearly to be seen—an election won or lost, a shift in the editorial position of a newspaper, the increased activity of an opposition party. In contrast, successful espionage goes unnoticed, with the victim unaware that a secret has been compromised."

> Former DCI RICHARD HELMS, *A Look over My Shoulder* (2003).

"We thought that we ought to have some facility for covert operations.... It ended up with the establishment within CIA of a branch, an office for activities of this nature, and one which employed a great many people. It did not work out at all the way I had conceived it.... We had thought that this would be a facility which could be used when and if an occasion arose when it might be needed. There might be years when we wouldn't have to do anything like this. But if the occasion arose we wanted somebody in the Government who would have the funds, the experience, the expertise to do these things and to do them in a proper way."

> GEORGE KENNAN on the development in 1948 of a U.S. covert action capability, in Senate testimony, 28 October 1975; cited in Leary, *The Central Intelligence Agency* (1984). That's the 1975 Kennan talking, not the 1948.

"As the international situation develops, every day makes more evident the importance of the role which will have to be played by covert operations if our national interests are to be adequately protected."

> GEORGE KENNAN, director of the State Department's Policy Planning Staff, memorandum to Frank Wisner, director of CIA's Office of Policy Coordination, 6 January 1949; in *FRUS 1945–1950: Emergence of the Intelligence Establishment* (1996), document 308.

"The principles governing the functions and general composition of CIA as reflected in the National Security Act of 1947 have been the subject of long debate. It was not casual that to one [agency] was given such widely different responsibilities as the production of national intelligence and the collection of foreign intelligence by clandestine methods. When the need for instituting covert operations in peacetime became apparent, again it was not casual that they should have been assigned to CIA and placed alongside their related activities, espionage and counter-espionage. To avoid the creation of a floating agency operationally inappropriate to any department and which was so directly dependent upon clandestine intelligence, it was natural to incorporate covert operations in CIA. . . . Clandestine intelligence and covert operations are characterized by both functional affinity and operational inter-dependence. They must be at least under the same general direction if ineffectiveness and even dangerous confusions are to be avoided. It is almost impossible to operate individuals, groups or chains of underground agents in the same area without their uncovering each other—unless they are very skillfully controlled by a central direction."

> Brigadier General JOHN MAGRUDER, former SSU director, memorandum to Secretary of Defense Louis Johnson, 22 December 1949; in *FRUS 1945–1950: Emergence of the Intelligence Establishment* (1996), document 408.

"Although the Agency was established primarily for the purpose of providing intelligence analysis to senior policymakers, within three years clandestine operations became and continued to be the Agency's preeminent activity."

> ANNE KARALEKAS, "The History of the Central Intelligence Agency," in Leary, *The Central Intelligence Agency* (1984).

"It is hardly an exaggeration to say that the policy of averting a third world war may depend on the strength and effectiveness of our efforts in the field of psychological warfare."

> President HARRY TRUMAN, letter to University of North Carolina president Gordon Gray, 31 May 1951; quoted in Pisani, *CIA and the Marshall Plan* (1991).

"The National Security Council approves . . . the immediate expansion of the covert organization established in NSC 10/2, and the intensification of covert operations designed [to place] maximum strain on the Soviet structure of power, including the relationships between the USSR, its satellites, and Communist China [and to] contribute to the retraction and reduction of Soviet power and influence to limits which no longer constitute a threat to U.S. security. . . . [The NSC] reaffirms the responsibility and authority of the Director of Central Intelligence for the conduct of covert operations."

> National Security Council directive 10/5, 23 October 1951; reproduced in Warner, *CIA Under Truman* (1994).

"NSC 10/5 redefines the Central Intelligence Agency's responsibilities in a field which was probably not envisaged at the time the National Security Act of 1947, under which the Agency was established, was framed. This is the field of cold war covert activities. . . . The presently projected scope of these activities has, during the past three years, produced a three-fold increase in the clandestine operations of this Agency and will require next year a budget three times larger than that required for our intelligence activities. . . . Given the necessary support, it will be possible for the Central Intelligence Agency to fulfill these requirements; but since they have resulted in such a large expansion in the Agency's budget and personnel strength, it should be noted that:

1. They are not functions essential to the performance by [the] Central Intelligence Agency of its intelligence responsibilities.

2. They were placed in this Agency because there was no other Department or Agency of the government which could undertake them at the time.

3. They will inevitably militate against the performance by [the] Central Intelligence Agency of its primary intelligence functions and are a continuing and increasing risk to its security."

DCI **WALTER BEDELL SMITH**, memorandum to the National Security Council, 23 April 1952; reproduced in Warner, *CIA Under Truman* (1994). In 1952, four and a half years after CIA was created, the DCI is still expressing misgivings about CIA's responsibility for covert action.

"The history of covert action might be loosely grouped into three categories. *Propaganda* can be no more than a little money distributed secretly to a few journalists in country *X* to get them to write articles favorable to the United States. . . . At the other extreme are covert *paramilitary operations,* secret military aid and training. . . . In between, *political action* attempts to change the balance of political forces in a particular country, most often by secretly providing money to particular groups."

GREGORY TREVERTON, *Covert Action* (1987).

"Careful studies had convinced us that first and foremost the army and secondly the people wanted the same things we did. Under those circumstances it's possible to achieve the results you want. . . . This operation had succeeded because the people, but most of all the army, wanted the same thing we did and therefore it was something that could be done by clandestine means. . . . If you don't want something that the people and the army want, don't give it to clandestine operations, give it to the marines."

CIA operations officer **KERMIT ROOSEVELT** on AJAX, the 1953 operation that restored the Shah of Iran to power; quoted in Ranelagh, *The Agency* (1986). Richard Helms reports that "at the time the covert action enthusiasts were celebrating their success [in Iran] and pondering further ventures, I never heard any discussion of Kim Roosevelt's advice, or even a reference to it." See Helms, *A Look over My Shoulder* (2003).

"Young man, if I had been but a few years younger, I would have loved nothing better than to have served under your command in this great venture!"

Prime Minister **WINSTON CHURCHILL** at seventy-eight after receiving a briefing in August 1953 from CIA operations officer Kermit Roosevelt on the just-concluded Iranian operation; quoted in Stafford, *Churchill and Secret Service* (1998).

"[The 1953 Iranian operation] did not prove that CIA could topple governments and place rulers in power; it was a unique case of supplying just the right bit of marginal assistance in the right way at the right time. Such is the nature of covert political action."

Former DDI **RAY CLINE**, *Secrets, Spies and Scholars* (1976).

"Most CIA covert wars did not begin as paramilitary operations. Rather, they began as secret political operations, then expanded as American purposes and foreign circumstance changed. The

1953 operation in Iran began as an attempt to use influence, tokens of American support, and small amounts of money to convince the wavering shah, in secret, that he was strong enough to dismiss his prime minister, Mohammed Mossadeq. Only when that political operation failed did CIA operatives turn seriously to organizing street mobs and armed force."

> **GREGORY TREVERTON**, *Covert Action* (1987).

"As a result [of] my interview with President Arbenz . . . I am convinced [the] Communists will continue to gain strength here as long as he remains in office. My staff fully agrees on this. Therefore, in view of [the] inadequacy of normal diplomatic procedures in dealing with [this] situation, there appears no alternative to our taking steps which would tend to make more difficult [the] continuation of his regime in Guatemala."

> **JOHN E. PEURIFOY**, U.S. ambassador to Guatemala, in a cable to Washington, 23 December 1953; cited in *Foreign Relations of the United States 1952–1954, Volume IV: The American Republics* (1983).

"Allen, the figure of 20 percent was persuasive. . . . If you had told me the chances would be 90 percent, I would have had a much more difficult decision."

> President **DWIGHT EISENHOWER** to DCI Dulles after being told the chances for success of the operation in Guatemala would rise from zero to twenty percent if Washington supplied aircraft to the rebels; quoted in Ranelagh, *The Agency* (1986). Ike approved CIA's request for the aircraft.

"Thanks, Allen, and thanks to all of you. You've averted a Soviet beachhead in our hemisphere."

> President **DWIGHT EISENHOWER** to DCI Dulles and CIA briefers after the Guatemala operation; quoted in Ranelagh, *The Agency* (1986).

"The [1953] Iranian operation was a squeaker. The situation was much in our favor, but even a bit of bad luck might have undone the intended result. At least as much can be said for the [1954] operation in Guatemala, where the prevailing conditions were less favorable. It, too, was a near thing. In planning secret operations, it cannot be assumed that any move will go unchallenged, that no misstep will occur, and that luck will always be on our side. In operations of a high level—and the ousting of Castro certainly qualified—contingency planning must take the possibility of failure, bad luck, or otherwise fully into account."

> Former DCI **RICHARD HELMS**, *A Look over My Shoulder* (2003).

"Iran and Guatemala . . . made the Agency's reputation and set the pattern for covert action in the years ahead. Small, cheap, fast, and tolerably secret, they encouraged Washingtonians to think other covert actions could be likewise."

> **GREGORY TREVERTON**, *Covert Action* (1987). A big mistake by April 1961.

"In retrospect, this approach to overthrowing governments *lowered* the United States' prestige. Potential targets—certainly Fidel Castro—learned that perhaps the U.S. was unwilling to send the Marines, and that if they just did not panic and defeat themselves, they could defeat the phantom 'rebels' and the U.S. would not actually intervene. In other words, the Guatemala operation is the sort of thing that works only once."

> **ANGELO CODEVILLA**, *Informing Statecraft* (1992).

"It's all down in black and white that the fundamental purpose of Central Intelligence is to prevent anything resembling another Pearl Harbor. And as of 1948 it's been equally clear that we have full responsibility—all of it specified in NSC 10/2, documented and legal—for most aspects of covert action operations. . . . I want you to be absolutely sure you understand how important covert action operations are right now. . . . I want you to be sure that everyone in operations has it firmly in mind that the White House and this administration have an *intense interest* in every aspect of *covert action.*"

> DCI **ALLEN DULLES** speaking to Richard Helms, then CIA chief of covert operations, in early 1954; quoted in Helms, *A Look over My Shoulder* (2003).

"Because the United States is relatively new at the game, and because we are opposed by a police state enemy . . . another important requirement is an aggressive covert psychological, political and paramilitary organization more effective, more unique and, if necessary, more ruthless than that employed by the enemy. . . . Hitherto acceptable norms of human conflict do not apply. If the United States is to survive, long-standing American concepts of 'fair play' must be reconsidered. We must develop effective espionage and counterespionage services and must learn to subvert, sabotage and destroy our enemies by more clever, more sophisticated and more effective methods than those used against us. It may become necessary that the American people be made acquainted with, understand and support this fundamentally repugnant philosophy."

> Lieutenant General **JAMES DOOLITTLE** in his *Report on the Covert Activities of the Central Intelligence Agency* to President Eisenhower, 1954; quoted in Ranelagh, *The Agency* (1986).

"In clandestine operations success or failure, life or death, may depend on meticulous attention to detail and timing. . . . Only perfection in performance is tolerable. If things can go wrong, they will, and every CIA officer should double-check and triple-check every detail of activity going on under his supervision."

> DCI **ALLEN DULLES**, 1956; quoted in Cline, *Secrets, Spies and Scholars* (1976). As Sherlock Holmes said to Doctor Watson, "Genius is an infinite capacity for taking pains" (Sir Arthur Conan Doyle, *A Study in Scarlet* [1887]).

"There is an aspect of covert political action that touches on the newly modish 'law of unintended consequences.' Some observers consider Operation AJAX [the 1953 Iranian operation] to have been an Agency mistake. . . . [The 1954 Guatemalan operation] is now thought by some to have fathered a Guatemalan regime which produced years of military brutality. However one may evaluate these speculations, it must be remembered that the Agency's role in Operation AJAX, as directed by the President, was to depose Mossadegh. The order to oust the Arbenz government also came from the White House. After any such successful operation, the continuing responsibility for establishing and nurturing a sound new government is not, and should never be, the ongoing task of an intelligence agency. This sort of nation building is the proper province of the State Department."

> Former DCI **RICHARD HELMS**, *A Look over My Shoulder* (2003).

"We have been unable to conclude that, on balance, all of the covert action programs undertaken by the CIA up to this time have been worth the risk or the great expenditure of manpower, money and other resources involved."

> President's Board of Consultants on Foreign Intelligence Activities, 1961 report to President Eisenhower; quoted in Allan Goodman, "Reforming U.S. Intelligence," *Foreign Policy* (summer 1987).

"What right do we have barging into other people's countries, buying newspapers and handing out money to opposition parties or supporting a candidate for this or that office?"

Former Secretary of Defense **ROBERT LOVETT** after the 1961 Bay of Pigs operation; quoted in Walter Isaacson and Evan Thomas, *The Wise Men* (1988). U.S. interests?

"Strictly speaking, paramilitary operations—such as supporting a secret army—should not be classified under covert action. They relate to covert action as war compares to diplomacy. . . . Unless the U.S. government was prepared to sponsor overt intervention in Cuba, the Bay of Pigs should have remained essentially a psychological warfare project rather than a military incursion."

Former senior CIA operations officer **DAVID ATLEE PHILLIPS**, *The Night Watch* (1978).

"You know, in intelligence work the operator falls in love with his operation—I don't care who it is or what his level is, whether it's Allen Dulles or a subordinate officer. And it's very difficult to be objective about your operation and say, 'We'd better drop it; it's not going to succeed.'"

Former CIA Inspector General **LYMAN KIRKPATRICK** in a 1967 interview; cited in Weber, *Spymasters* (1999). In his IG report of the Bay of Pigs operation, Kirkpatrick had lambasted CIA's operations directorate for, among many other things, not consulting with the analysis directorate.

"After the disastrous collapse of the Bay of Pigs invasion of Cuba, [President] Kennedy was determined to prevent Castro from succeeding in his attempt to ignite the fires of Marxist revolution throughout Latin America. . . . So it was that hope for genuine democratic reform and fear of successful Communist manipulation of the electoral process in Chile combined to persuade the Kennedy administration to decide upon a long-term program of covert assistance to the Chilean Christian Democratic Party. Such political funding had to

be kept secret to protect the recipients from propaganda attack, and much of the funding was handled through third parties so discreetly that the Christian Democratic leaders were not themselves aware of the true source. The only agency in the U.S. government authorized to distribute secret funds abroad for such political purposes was the CIA. Therefore at the highest policy level, the Kennedy administration directed the Agency to provide covert support to the Christian Democratic Party, and more than $200,000 was authorized and spent for that purpose in 1962."

Former senior CIA operations officer **CORD MEYER**, *Facing Reality* (1980).

"My idea is to stir things up on [the] island with espionage, sabotage, general disorder, run & operated by Cubans themselves with every group but Batistaites & Communists. Do not know if we will be successful in overthrowing Castro but we have nothing to lose in my estimate."

Attorney General **ROBERT KENNEDY** to President Kennedy, 4 November 1961; cited in Andrew, *For the President's Eyes Only* (1995).

"The weak point in covert paramilitary action is that a single misfortune that reveals CIA's connection makes it necessary for the United States either to abandon the cause completely or convert to a policy of overt military intervention."

Former DDI **RAY CLINE**, *Secrets, Spies and Scholars* (1976).

"[Defense Secretary Robert] McNamara expressed strong feelings that we should take every possible aggressive action in the fields of intelligence, sabotage and guerrilla warfare, utilizing Cubans and do such other things as might be indicated to divide the Castro regime. [DCI] McCone pointed out that all of these things could be done. . . . Attorney General [Robert Kennedy] queried the meeting as to what other aggressive steps could be taken, questioning the feasibility of provoking an action against Guantanamo which would permit us to retaliate. . . . It was [national security advisor McGeorge] Bundy's opinion that all overt actions would involve serious consequences throughout the world and therefore our operations must be covert at this time."

DCI **JOHN McCONE**, memorandum for the record of a 21 August 1962 meeting in Secretary of State Rusk's office; reproduced in McAuliffe, *Cuban Missile Crisis* (1992).

"We do disagreeable things so that ordinary people here and elsewhere can sleep safely in their beds at night. . . . Of course, we occasionally do very wicked things. . . . You can't be less ruthless than the opposition simply because your government's *policy* is benevolent, can you now? . . . That would *never* do."

"Control," in **JOHN LE CARRÉ** [David Cornwell], *The Spy Who Came in from the Cold* (1963).

"What are you? You are a common thug, a blunt instrument wielded by dolts in high places. Having done what you are told to do, out of some mistaken idea of duty or patriotism, you satisfy your brutish instincts with alcohol, nicotine, and sex while waiting to be dispatched on the next misbegotten foray."

Blofeld, the bad guy, to James Bond, in **IAN FLEMING**, *You Only Live Twice* (1964). This later became the view of many Americans regarding covert operators.

"I always felt, as did the President [i.e., Truman], that the CIG and later the CIA had no business to get involved in covert operations of a para-military type. After the very unfortunate experience in the Bay of Pigs campaign in Cuba, I was told, and I hope accurately, that the CIA would not conduct such campaigns in the future."

SIDNEY SOUERS, President Truman's first DCI, in a letter to CIA historian Ludwell Montague, 3 August 1964; quoted in Jeffreys-Jones, *North American Spies* (1991).

"The benefits of covert paramilitary action in peacetime tended to be favorably regarded on the basis of a romantic recollection of [the] wartime experiences of OSS. The totally different strategic situation in the 1960s and 1970s proved less congenial than wartime to large-scale guerrilla efforts by U.S. intelligence agencies. In this late period the OSS legacy turned out to be, at best, a mixed blessing, and in some cases a disaster."

Former DDI **RAY CLINE**, *Secrets, Spies and Scholars* (1976).

"The need for the United States to engage in clandestine activities will continue and so will the tension between this need and the need to preserve the asset in belief of our intentions and integrity. Similarly, the problem of secrecy and deception in a free society will continue. But it seems to me that all these problems are more the responsibility of the policymakers than of CIA and its particular mandate and powers. It was the policymakers who were fundamentally responsible for making covert action a fad."

ROGER HILSMAN, *To Move a Nation* (1967).

"Our 'active measures' [Soviet term for covert action] campaign [in the United States] did not discriminate on the basis of race, creed, or color: we went after everybody. Attempting to show that America was an inhospitable place for Jews, we wrote anti-Semitic letters to American Jewish leaders. My fellow officers paid American agents to paint swastikas on synagogues in New York and Washington. Our New York station even hired people to desecrate several Jewish cemeteries. . . . When the esteemed U.N. Secretary-General Dag Hammarskjöld died in a plane crash, I and my fellow officers did everything we could to fuel rumors that the CIA was behind it. . . . I had no qualms about stirring up as much trouble as possible for the U.S. government. It was all part of the job."

Former KGB general **OLEG KALUGIN** on his activities in the U.S. during the 1960s, in *The First Directorate* (1994). Today, Kalugin is a loyal U.S. citizen. What a country!

"Bear in mind that parameter of action is exceedingly narrow and available options quite limited. . . . Feel necessary to caution against any false optimism. It is essential that we not become victims of our own propaganda. . . . Urge you not to convey impression that Station has sure-fire method of halting, let alone triggering coup attempts."

CIA station chief, Santiago, Chile, to CIA Headquarters after receiving an order to "create a coup climate," 23 September 1970; in U.S. Senate, *Alleged Assassination Plots* (1975).

"[In September 1970] President Nixon had ordered me to instigate a military coup in Chile, a heretofore democratic country. Moreover, the knowledge of this presidential directive was to be kept from the U.S. officials most directly involved. Within CIA this directive was to be restricted to those with an absolute need to know. And I was to report to the President through Henry Kissinger. By what superior judgment was I to leave the White House and then decide that the President did not mean what he had just said? . . . I did not presume to have the authority to tamper with the President's obvious intent."

Former DCI **RICHARD HELMS**, *A Look over My Shoulder* (2003).

"Nobody expects the Spanish Inquisition! Our chief weapon is surprise—surprise and fear . . . fear and surprise . . . our two weapons are fear and surprise—and ruthless efficiency . . . our *three* weapons are fear and surprise and ruthless efficiency and an almost fanatical devotion to the Pope . . . our *four* . . . no . . . Amongst our weapons—amongst our weaponry—are such elements as fear, surprise . . . I'll come in again."

Monty Python's Flying Circus, BBC television, 1970; cited in *The Oxford Dictionary of Modern Quotations* (1992).

"What is clear is the signal conveyed to history by U.S. covert action. In retrospect, most reasonably objective observers conclude that Salvador Allende's experiment in Chile would have failed on its own terms. . . . Yet history's lesson is not that Allende would have fallen of his own accord. History's lesson is that the United States overthrew him in 1973. That is the lesson even if it is untrue in the narrow sense: Washington did not engineer his coup, nor did the CIA or the U.S. military participate in it. The fact of U.S. covert action muddied history's lesson."

GREGORY TREVERTON, *Covert Action* (1987). As Malcolm Muggeridge said of the Soviet show trials: everything about them is true but the facts.

"It sometimes seems that the best way to identify the most important lessons to be learned is to count the number of times a lesson must be relearned. There are three lessons to be relearned in respect to Chile. . . . If a major covert action is to be undertaken, ample time must be allotted for preparation; if any secret U.S. contact is made with an individual or group thought to be planning a coup or revolution, it will be all but impossible to convince the plotters that this contact does not indicate U.S. support; and, finally, unless the fate of the nation is at stake, an intelligence service should try to avoid being saddled with the command, 'do something, for Heaven's sake, do *anything.*'"

Former DCI **RICHARD HELMS**, *A Look over My Shoulder* (2003).

"This amendment will . . . abolish all clandestine or covert operations by the Central Intelligence Agency. . . . There is no justification in our legal, moral, or religious principles for operations of a U.S. agency which result in assassinations, sabotage, political disruptions, or other meddling in another country's internal affairs."

Senator **JAMES ABOUREZK** during the Senate floor debate on his proposed ban, 2 October 1974; quoted in Knott, *Secret and Sanctioned* (1996). The proposal received only seventeen votes.

"Should the CIA, even responding to a President's ukase, encourage a military coup in one of the few countries in Latin America with a solid, functioning democratic tradition?"

Former CIA operations officer **DAVID ATLEE PHILLIPS**, *The Night Watch* (1978). Depends.

"Covert action is the real reason for the CIA's existence."

PHILIP AGEE, *Inside the Company* (1975).

"In the mid- to late fifties, I think that about half of CIA's budget went into covert action, paramilitary and political and things like the Bay of Pigs and some other things. By the early seventies— and this was before the [congressional] investigations—that figure had sunk to something like 4 or 5 percent."

Former DCI **WILLIAM COLBY** in a 1982 interview; cited in Weber, *Spymasters* (1999).

"Covert action should not be confused with missionary work."

Attributed to **HENRY KISSINGER**, 1975; quoted in Miller, *Spying for America* (1989).

"One of the hardest things for outsiders to believe about CIA covert action programs is that only a few are big . . . and even fewer are big paramilitary projects. Most covert action projects are small scale—getting pro-U.S. books printed or anti-USSR articles published in newspapers, or providing funds and briefings to youth and labor representatives attending international meetings. . . . These projects have few risks attached and often involve only small sums of money. Most would be hard to construe as illegal, let alone immoral."

Former DDI **RAY CLINE**, *Secrets, Spies and Scholars* (1976).

"The charge has been leveled that the United States and, most certainly, the CIA have no business 'interfering' in the domestic political affairs of another sovereign nation, that their assistance to one side or another in an election there is not only illegal but immoral. Now, there can be no denying that 'interference' of this sort is illegal [but] espionage also is illegal under the laws of most countries, and yet most countries consider themselves justified by the inherent right of sovereign self-defense to engage in espionage. . . . Whether such illegal action also is immoral raises another question. The sovereign-state system of the modern world has long given to each state the moral right to use force in its own self-defense in such degree as may be necessary for that purpose. If such *military* 'interference' is accepted, then surely lesser forms of interference can be justified under the same conditions."

Former DCI **WILLIAM COLBY**, *Honorable Men* (1978).

"Clandestine operations have been condemned as immoral in principle and illegal in practice. This attitude naively sidesteps the problems of existing and, indeed, surviving in a world whose history continues to be determined by nations promoting their own interests at the expense of others. . . . If we decide that covert action is wrong because it constitutes meddling in other people's affairs, we should re-examine not only our intelligence programs but our entire foreign policy, our foreign aid program, and our tariff policies (to name only a few examples) because any aspect of each of these can have a profound effect on the internal affairs of any number of countries and very often is designed to have just such an effect."

Former senior CIA operations officer **DAVID ATLEE PHILLIPS**, *The Night Watch* (1978).

"I find it distasteful to discuss covert operations in print. . . . Of course, covert operations have their philosophical and practical difficulties and especially for America. Our national temperament and tradition are unsuited to them. Our system of government does not lend itself spontaneously to either the secrecy or subtlety that is required. We lack the elaborate conspiratorial apparatus of our adversaries. Those eager to dismantle our intelligence apparatus will have little difficulty finding examples of actions that were amateurish or transparent. But the men and women who have been prepared to carry out assignments in secret, with resources usually ridiculously inferior to those of our adversaries, under inhibiting restriction, deserve better of their country than the merciless assault to which they have been exposed—assaults that threaten to leave us naked in a vital area of our national security. . . . I cannot accept the proposition that the United States is debarred from acting in the gray area between diplomacy and military intervention."

HENRY KISSINGER, *White House Years* (1979).

"The most powerful government ever to fall as a result of American covert action was the administration of Richard Nixon."

CHRISTOPHER ANDREW, *For the President's Eyes Only* (1995). Andrew refers to the botched Watergate burglary.

"By 1976, the disclosures about official US participation in assassination attempts led President Ford to prohibit any further government involvement in political assassination. Since that time, however, neither the President nor Congress has forsworn the use of certain other types of operations, such as paramilitary activities, assistance in coup preparations, or the dissemination of deception and propaganda. As a result, when directed by the President, pursuant to US law, the Agency still . . . may engage in lawful activities that can result in the death of foreign nationals."

JONATHAN FREDMAN, CIA Office of General Counsel, "Covert Action, Loss of Life, and the Prohibition on Assassination, 1976–1996," *Studies in Intelligence* (1996).

"[CIA] learned a lesson in the investigations of the mid-1970s: when a President asks CIA to undertake a covert action because he cannot get public support for an overt policy, CIA will be left holding the proverbial presidential bag."

Former DCI **ROBERT GATES**, *From the Shadows* (1996).

"I can't imagine the United States saying we would not undertake any covert activities, and knowing at the same time that friends, as well as foes, are undertaking covert activity, not only in the United States but elsewhere. That would be like tying a

President's hands behind his back in the planning and execution of foreign policy."

President **GERALD FORD**, CBS interview of 21 April 1975, responding to a question about whether it was advisable to ban covert operations; cited in CIA, *"Our First Line of Defense"* (1996).

"The hostage crisis and the Soviet invasion of Afghanistan together converted [President] Carter to covert action as a major instrument of his foreign policy."

CHRISTOPHER ANDREW, *For the President's Eyes Only* (1995).

"Thus it was that the Carter administration, despite its dedication to human rights and its considerable reservations about the morality of covert actions, turned easily and quickly to covert devices."

Former DCI **STANSFIELD TURNER**, *Secrecy and Democracy* (1985).

"What America needed before Afghanistan, and needs now, is a significant upgrading of our military and intelligence assets. . . . A central element of that upgrading is a recognition that well-conceived covert operations abroad are politically necessary and morally right."

ERNEST LEFEVER, "Can Covert Action Be Just?" *Policy Review* (spring 1980).

"Six Phases of a U.S. Government Sponsored Covert Action: Enthusiasm—Disillusionment—Panic—Search for the Guilty—Punishment of the Innocent—Praise and Honor for the Nonparticipants."

Sign posted in CIA's Central American Task Force, 1982; cited in Clarridge, *A Spy for All Seasons* (1997).

"A nearsighted, illiterate Afghan could bring down a few million dollars' worth of Soviet aircraft."

CIA official discussing the advantages of providing Afghan fighters with portable surface-to-air missiles (Stingers), 1983; quoted in Richelson, *A Century of Spies* (1995). The United States began sending Stingers in 1986, and the Soviets quit Afghanistan in 1989.

"I strongly opposed a move by the Senate Committee on Intelligence to insert into the Intelligence Oversight Act of 1980 a requirement for 'prior' notification of all covert actions. . . . I felt it unreasonable to ask a person to risk his life and then tell him I was going to notify some thirty congressmen and their staffs about what he was going to do."

Former DCI **STANSFIELD TURNER**, *Secrecy and Democracy* (1985).

"[During the 1980s] what flowed out of CIA and through intermediaries to Solidarity [in Poland] was printing materials, communications equipment, and other supplies for waging underground political warfare."

Former DCI **ROBERT GATES**, *From the Shadows* (1996).

"The talent necessary for covert action is available in the CIA and must be preserved."

Former DCI **STANSFIELD TURNER**, *Secrecy and Democracy* (1985).

"Go out and kill me 10,000 Soviets until they give up."

DCI **WILLIAM CASEY** to CIA operations officer Milt Bearden, 1986, sending Bearden to Afghanistan to manage a covert program to provide arms to the mujaheddin; quoted by Bearden in the *Washington Post,* 12 December 1998.

"At an NSC meeting on August 14th [1986, DCI William] Casey reviewed what CIA had been doing to stir up trouble inside Libya and to keep Qaddafi off balance. . . . Our activities included launching balloons from ships of the Sixth Fleet . . . with messages to overthrow the government. When briefed on this [as Casey's deputy], I said to make sure that the leaflets were specific that it was *Qaddafi* that should be overthrown. CIA's experience with balloons was not unblemished, and I could just see strong winds carrying the balloons with a generic 'overthrow your oppressive government' [message] into Egypt where they would be picked up. I didn't think Egyptian President Hosni Mubarak would be pleased."

Former DCI **ROBERT GATES**, *From the Shadows* (1996).

"Covert interventions, by definition initiated in secret, nonetheless eventually become public, usually sooner rather than later. It is a manifestation of the paradox that secret decisions produce public results."

GREGORY TREVERTON, *Covert Action* (1987).

"A covert operation is, in its nature, a lie."

NSC staffer **OLIVER NORTH** in testimony to Congress, 1987; quoted in Miller, *Spying for America* (1989).

"It's hard for people in a free society to accept the fact that covert action is often necessary for a world power to survive. An American President faced with a potential threat to national security should have some alternative between doing nothing and waiting for a crisis to blow up in our face. The answer is covert action—but it has to be conducted along strictly legal guidelines."

Vice President **GEORGE H. W. BUSH**, *Looking Forward* (1987).

"Once covert interventions begin, no matter how hesitantly or provisionally, they can be hard to stop. Operational realities intrude, with deadlines attached. New stakes are created, changing the balance of risks and rewards as perceived by political leaders . . . the burden of proof switches from those who would propose covert action to those who oppose it."

GREGORY TREVERTON, *Covert Action* (1987).

"Covert action, when it has been successful, has not been an option chosen in lieu of diplomatic or military efforts. Rather, covert action makes sense only as a calculated addition to diplomatic and economic efforts—and only if it is backed up by the will to use overt military force if need be."

Senator **MALCOLM WALLOP**, "Covert Action: A Substitute for Clear U.S. Policy," in Walter Hahn, ed., *Central America and the Reagan Doctrine* (1987).

"The President may not authorize the conduct of a covert action by departments, agencies, or entities of the United States Government unless the President determines such an action is necessary to support identifiable foreign policy objectives of the United States and is important to the national security of the United States."

U.S. Code, Title 50, Chapter 15.

"In order to avoid congressional oversight of the Central Intelligence Agency and to evade the intent of the Boland Amendment, [Iran-Contra] secret operations were effectively placed in the White House, close to the President. A generation's admonitions to keep all covert operations as far from the President as possible were discarded."

Former DCI **JAMES SCHLESINGER** in *Foreign Affairs*, "America and the World" edition (1987).

"'Covert action' is a very imprecise, elastic term. It covers everything from having lunch with a foreign journalist in order to encourage him or her to write an editorial that may well have been written anyway to running elaborate, large-scale paramilitary operations over a time span measured in years. It is therefore hard to discuss this concept in a rational, meaningful way—especially in a public forum. In any such discussion, strong feelings about certain specific, limited types of covert action almost inevitably spread to, and becloud consideration of, other kinds of activity included under this far-too-encompassing label."

AMOS JORDAN, WILLIAM TAYLOR, and **LAWRENCE KORB,** *American National Security* (1989).

"While the Iran-Contra operation was ending in ignominy, the Reagan administration was simultaneously conducting in Afghanistan what became one of the most successful covert operations since the Second World War. There were two critical differences between Iran-Contra and Afghanistan. First, the secret help to the Afghan Mujahideen, unlike the arms supplied to Iran and the Contras, was in line with the publicly stated policy of the administration. Secondly, the Afghan operation, though far from flawless, was run by experienced CIA professionals rather than by the bungling amateurs of the NSC."

CHRISTOPHER ANDREW, *For the President's Eyes Only* (1995).

"In all attempts by one nation to influence the actions of another, the chain between intention and effect is imprecise. . . . The circumstances of covert action are particularly unpromising for neat calibration of effect. Revolutions and counterrevolutions are seldom tidy. . . . Yet I have been struck by the contrast between the free-wheeling image of covert action and the accountantlike auditing that is CIA practice. . . . Rather, it is the messy foreign policy in which covert action takes place that frustrates precise control."

GREGORY TREVERTON, *Covert Action* (1987).

"The very adjective 'covert' is a misnomer. Covert action is often easy to detect, always hard to control and in its nature illegal and immune to normal procedures of accountability. Covert action, moreover, is a weapon of marginal consequence in the scale of things. Its importance in the conduct of foreign affairs is greatly overrated."

ARTHUR SCHLESINGER, JR., "A Democrat Looks at Foreign Policy," *Foreign Affairs* (winter 1987–88).

"[Covert action] is an activity that has been assigned to us and accounts for less than three percent of our resources but which attracts the most heat, the most confusion, and generates the most ill ease and suspicion."

DCI **WILLIAM WEBSTER,** remarks of 15 January 1988; in *1988 Speeches.*

"At its height in the 1950s, covert action took up half of the CIA's budget. By 1990 it was taking only about 1 percent. Nevertheless, most books and journalism about the CIA deal chiefly with covert action (CA). In Congress, hearings on penny ante covert action pack hearing rooms, while few members or staff show up to deal with multibillion-dollar satellites. Why does CA draw so much attention? Because arguments about covert activity really are arguments about American foreign policy."

ANGELO CODEVILLA, *Informing Statecraft* (1992).

"Although covert action is not defined by law, the term has come to be understood to refer to activities conducted in support of national policy in such a way that the role of the United States Government is not apparent. Covert action, essential in our foreign policy, often supplies support for governments under siege whom we favor, and allows us to work in collaboration with governments who do not wish, for legitimate political reasons of their own, to have the U.S. role and involvement publicly known. From President Roosevelt forward, every president in my lifetime has endorsed and used covert action to support the foreign policy of this country."

DCI **WILLIAM WEBSTER**, remarks of 3 March 1988; in *1988 Speeches*.

"Covert action will probably never again be considered as a routine foreign policy tool."

ALLAN GOODMAN, "Does Covert Action Have a Future?" *Parameters* (June 1988).

"One of the dangerous attractions of covert actions abroad [is that] they appear to offer a means of containing communism without evident costs. Moreover, the public is also spared the knowledge that such actions may involve the United States in violations of human rights."

ANTHONY LAKE, *Somoza Falling* (1989).

"Covert policy usually is policy to which insufficient thought has been given."

ANGELO CODEVILLA, *Informing Statecraft* (1992).

"Once in a while, just often enough to give intelligence officers a false sense of confidence, a secret operation goes almost according to plan."

Former CIA operations officer **WILLIAM HOOD**, *Mole* (1993).

"Even if covert action were regarded as a normal tool of American statecraft, it would not necessarily mean that there should be more covert action in the post-cold-war era. Covert action should not become a substitute for political consensus or well-conceived policy. Unless the United States can develop such a policy and forge a national consensus, not much should be expected from covert action."

ROY GODSON, *Dirty Tricks or Trump Cards* (1995).

"I don't really know what to do with covert actions, quite frankly. It doesn't make sense to put them in a Central Intelligence Agency, but I'm not sure it makes any sense to put them anywhere else [and] it's not clear to me that there's a better alternative."

U.S. Representative **LEE HAMILTON** at a Georgetown University symposium on intelligence, 30 November 1994; quoted in *Studies in Intelligence* (spring 1995).

"I believe it is important that this country maintain a covert action capability that will provide policymakers with options between diplomacy and military action."

DCI **JOHN DEUTCH**, testimony before the House Committee on Intelligence, 19 December 1995.

"The professional competence of a clandestine service consists of, and is measured by, its ability to carry out operations secretly (or deniably), much as lawyers' competence consists in their ability to win cases, and doctors' in their ability to prevent or treat illness. The clandestine service may number among its members brilliant journalists, able warriors, and superior political analysts, but the professional skill for which . . . they are hired is the ability to organize and conduct operations covertly. . . . There is general agreement that decisions to undertake or continue specific operations are ultimately political, not technical or professional ones. Nevertheless, only professional covert operators can provide the assessments of capabilities, risks, and costs that define the choices open to policymakers."

> Former CIA operations chief **RICHARD BISSELL**, *Reflections of a Cold Warrior* (1996), from the chapter titled "A Philosophy of Covert Action."

"Covert action rarely has been 'career enhancing' in [CIA's] clandestine service."

> Former DCI **ROBERT GATES**, *From the Shadows* (1996).

"Many, probably most, [covert action] successes were successes only in the short run. Arbenz, for instance, was overthrown, but the long-term problems of Guatemala were not solved. Elections were won in several countries, but political parties and political systems were not permanently rejuvenated. Most covert action operations (like military operations) are directed at short-term objectives. Their success or failure must be judged by the degree to which these objectives are achieved. Their *effectiveness* must be measured by the degree to which achievement of the short-term objectives will contribute to the national interest. It can be argued that, although few uncompromised operations actually failed, the successful achievement of their short-term results made only a limited contribution to the national interest."

> Former CIA operations chief **RICHARD BISSELL**, *Reflections of a Cold Warrior* (1996), from the chapter titled "A Philosophy of Covert Action."

"The United States must retain the capability to do something in between sending in the Marines and sending in former President Carter."

> Former DCI **R. JAMES WOOLSEY** at the Council on Foreign Relations conference "The Future of the CIA," 18 February 1997, Washington, D.C.

"Covert action is a very small part of what the Central Intelligence Agency is supposed to do and it is not one of the basic and core issues of the Agency. . . . As a matter of fact, covert action is a function of the Central Intelligence Agency by fiat of the President. An executive order says the Agency should do that. But the President could take away that executive order tomorrow and that would be the end of that type of activity."

> Former DCI **RICHARD HELMS** interviewed on PBS, 20 October 1997.

"Two covert actions helped change the course of history and the Cold War. First, Radio Free Europe; [Lech] Walesa and [Vaclav] Havel both have said it was the most important thing the United States did during the Cold War. And [second,] the aid to the Mujahadeen that stopped the Soviets in Afghanistan. When people talk about covert action, they ought to talk about those two first and foremost."

> Former DCI **R. JAMES WOOLSEY** interviewed on PBS, 20 October 1997.

"Every American President of the post–World War II era [has] found America's covert capabilities indispensable—even when, like Carter and Clinton, they had originally been highly skeptical. The most frequent American covert operations were assistance to democratic parties or media in countries where radical or Communist groups, financed from abroad, threatened to become ascendant or sought to suppress free expression. On rarer occasions, covert operations financed paramilitary and even military resistance to takeovers by Communists or to forces considered to be a threat to our national security."

> **HENRY KISSINGER**, *Years of Renewal* (1999).

"Everybody thinks we sort of willy-nilly go out and undermine the government and do this and do that; that is simply not true. When a covert action is authorized, it is authorized by the President."

> CIA operations chief **JAMES PAVITT** in an interview with Reuters, 12 December 2000.

"If he were to be removed from the scene . . . I want you to understand I'm not recommending anything . . ."

> Western scholar briefing CIA analysts on a particular Asian leader, March 2001.

"I want the CIA to be first on the ground."

> President **GEORGE W. BUSH** on taking the war on terrorism to Afghanistan, 17 September 2001; quoted in the *Washington Post*, 1 February 2002.

"To: Ops guys. Stay strong. Head high. US public knows you're on the right track. Don't look back. Thanks for all you do."

> E-mail to CIA's public website (www.cia.gov) in response to the death of CIA operations officer Johnny Micheal Spann in Afghanistan, December 2001.

"Covert action has been referred to as the 'third choice'—an activity more aggressive than conventional diplomatic maneuvering and less drastic than military intervention. This is true, and the best possible reason for our government to retain a covert action capability. In seeking to maintain such a means, we must realize that today's world is far too sophisticated to permit covert action to be wielded about like an all-purpose political chain saw. At its best, covert action should be used like a well-honed scalpel, infrequently, and with discretion lest the blade lose its edge."

> Former DCI **RICHARD HELMS**, *A Look over My Shoulder* (2003).

CRITICS & DEFENDERS

The Literary Spy much prefers to live in a country where people are free to lambaste and even demonize the men and women who serve that country and who help protect it.

See also: Covert Action; Failures; Intelligence & American Culture; Legislative Oversight; Limits of Intelligence; "Rogue Elephant"; Successes; U.S. Intelligence "Community"; Warning, Prediction, & Surprise

"A shameful example of unbelievable incompetence. . . . We apparently had no idea of what was going on in a country just 2 hours flying time from the Panama Canal."

> **THOMAS E. DEWEY** criticizing CIA for failing to warn about impending anti-American riots in Bogotá in April 1948; quoted in Jeffreys-Jones, *The CIA and American Democracy* (1989). A congressional investigation found that there had been no intelligence failure.

"I have roughly a hundred pages of documentation covering incompetence, inefficiency, waste and Communist infiltration in the CIA, which I am holding in the hope that a committee will be established so that I can turn the information over to it."

> Senator **JOSEPH McCARTHY**; quoted in Knott, *Secret and Sanctioned* (1996).

"My briefing this morning was by the CIA and on various spooky activities, some of which I do not like. I shall stop them."

> **JOHN KENNETH GALBRAITH**, U.S. ambassador to India, journal entry of 29 March 1961 in *Ambassador's Journal* (1969).

"There are currently two schools of thought about our Intelligence Services. One school is convinced that they are staffed by murderous, powerful, double-crossing cynics, the other that the taxpayer is supporting a collection of bumbling, broken-down layabouts."

MI5 official **JOHN BINGHAM**, 1966; quoted in West, *Faber Book of Espionage* (1993). Many critics hold these mutually incompatible beliefs simultaneously.

"Life goes on."

DCI **RICHARD HELMS** to Agency personnel after *Ramparts* magazine's February 1967 exposé on CIA covert funding of anti-communist student groups; quotation in CIA's Historical Intelligence Collection.

"From my own personal experience, I know [that] most of the more extreme charges about the CIA were not valid. Although the people in CIA, in common with all other human beings, have made mistakes, the organization possesses a more able staff than most. . . . The United States, in fact, owes the men and women of the CIA an extraordinary debt."

ROGER HILSMAN, *To Move a Nation* (1967).

"Beginning in 1973, in the midst of Watergate and at the end of Vietnam, CIA confronted a new kind of investigative journalism, a newly aggressive Congress, and a President who both disliked the Agency and was himself dying a slow political death. CIA now had to face its past, a past of acting at the direction of Presidents, without them. Alone."

Former DCI **ROBERT GATES**, *From the Shadows* (1996).

"[In January 1975] I had to go before the redoubtable Bella Abzug . . . taking in the process a day-long tongue-lashing over why CIA had included her name among our reports from Paris about visitors to the Vietnamese Communist Delegation headquarters there, and telling her we would do it again if she visited an office abroad of an organization CIA was covering and which our troops were fighting."

Former DCI **WILLIAM COLBY**, *Honorable Men* (1978).

"A rogue elephant on the rampage."

Senator **FRANK CHURCH** speculating to journalists on CIA's past conduct, 19 July 1975; quoted in Treverton, *Covert Action* (1987). Though the Church Committee concluded in the end that CIA had never been a rogue elephant, the sobriquet stuck. Richard Helms in his autobiography *A Look over My Shoulder* (2003) remarked that "sensational charges linger longer than any after-the-fact proof that the allegations were false."

"[There is] nothing like an investigation of intelligence to bring loonies out of the woodwork."

GREGORY TREVERTON, *Covert Action* (1987).

"When I joined the CIA I believed in the need for its existence. After twelve years with the agency I finally understood how much suffering it was causing, that millions of people all over the world had been killed or had had their lives destroyed by the CIA and the institutions it supports. . . . I became the servant of the capitalism I rejected. I became one of its secret policemen. The CIA, after all, is nothing more than the secret police of American capitalism. . . . Not [even] the CIA . . . can forever postpone the revolutionary structural changes that mean the end of capitalist imperialism and the building of socialist society."

Former CIA "secret policeman" **PHILIP AGEE**, *Inside the Company* (1975). Meanwhile, capitalism lives.

"The most effective and important systematic efforts to combat the CIA that can be undertaken right now are, I think, the identification, exposure, and neutralization of its people working abroad. . . . Having this information, the peoples victimized by the CIA and the economic exploitation that CIA enforces can bring pressure on their so-often compromised governments to expel the CIA people. And, in the absence of such expulsion, which will not be uncommon, the people themselves will have to decide what they must do to rid themselves of CIA."

> **PHILIP AGEE** in the 1975 edition of *Counterspy;* cited in Phillips, *The Night Watch* (1978). The same issue of *Counterspy* identified the CIA station chief in Athens as Richard Welch. Welch was gunned down on his doorstep in Athens on 23 December 1975.

"Agency people are angry and disgusted with Victor Marchetti, Frank Snepp, and John Stockwell, but about [Philip] Agee they are cold and bitter, and if Agee turns out the hall light before opening his front door at night, and thinks twice about switching on his car's ignition, and doesn't accept candy from strangers, he is not being altogether melodramatic."

> **THOMAS POWERS**, *The Man Who Kept the Secrets* (1979).

"[During the 1970s] CIA was castigated for things it never did as well as for many things it had done under direct orders from several different Presidents of the United States."

> Former DDI **RAY CLINE**, *Secrets, Spies and Scholars* (1976).

"Sweeping attacks [and] overgeneralization against our intelligence activities jeopardize vital functions necessary to our national security. Today's sensations must not be the prelude to tomorrow's Pearl Harbor."

> President **GERALD FORD**, 19 August 1975; quoted in Andrew, *For the President's Eyes Only* (1995).

"They had charts on the wall, they had figures. And their conclusion was that in 10 years, the United States would be behind the Soviet Union in military capability, in economic growth. . . . It was a scary presentation. [But] they were 180 degrees wrong. These were the best people we had, the CIA's so-called experts."

> Former President **GERALD FORD**; quoted in the *New York Times,* 20 July 1997.

"What was omitted [during the congressional investigations of the 1970s] was any inquiry into the historical context. The Pike and Church committees simply rejected as not worth considering the notion that there had ever been a domestic or international emergency involving communism."

> **RICHARD GID POWERS**, *Not Without Honor* (1995).

"Those bastards down in Washington."

> Senator **WALTER MONDALE**'s description of CIA; quoted in *Time* (26 July 1976).

"CIA has in no way ever remotely approached becoming an American Gestapo or KGB. If we ever destroy it, as we have come close to doing in the past two years, the United States will be as naked and exposed in future international crises as it was when World War II came along. The price of such unreadiness in the last quarter of the 20th century would be a thousand times what it was at Pearl Harbor."

> Former DDI **RAY CLINE**, *Secrets, Spies and Scholars* (1976).

"There is no intelligence agency of any kind in the United States today."

> Senator **DANIEL PATRICK MOYNIHAN** in 1979; quoted in Laqueur, *A World of Secrets* (1985). Moynihan was speaking of the damage done to CIA by the congressional investigations of the 1970s.

"They have no compunction about fooling you."

> Secretary of State **GEORGE SHULTZ** suggesting to his staff that CIA had information on the Soviet shootdown of KAL 007 that it wasn't sharing, September 1983; quoted in Gates, *From the Shadows* (1996).

"I reserve a very special ring right in the heart of hell for those of my countrymen who, in the orgy of self-recrimination and self-doubt of the mid-70s in the United States, systematically and deliberately dismantled the intelligence capabilities of the United States."

> **CHARLES LICHTENSTEIN**, former U.S. deputy representative to the United Nations, January 1986; quoted in William Rusher, *The Coming Battle for the Media* (1988).

"The C.I.A. comes to this campus to recruit able-bodied men and women for invasions, subjugation and control of other countries beyond normal diplomatic means."

> Student protester at the University of Massachusetts at Amherst; quoted in the *New York Times*, 11 December 1986.

"The ambitions of publicity-thirsty senators have from time to time produced attacks more notable for their ferocity than for their logic. Professionally or ideologically frustrated CIA officers have occasionally resorted to damaging bouts of apostasy. The state of the political climate—whether 'Big Government' is in or out of fashion—and the temper of the press—whether it is out for blood or in a 'responsible' phase—have clearly affected the CIA's ability to avoid confidence-sapping scandals."

> **RHODRI JEFFREYS-JONES**, *The CIA and American Democracy* (1989).

"One significant part of the United States Government today is practically immune from the public scrutiny that prevents abuses. That is the Central Intelligence Agency. It spends billions of dollars and disposes of great power, with only occasional, inadequate accountability. . . . Logic and experience tell us that it is time to question the system of secret government. It is a system alien to American principles and defective in practice."

> **ANTHONY LEWIS**, "An Alien System," *New York Times*, 12 June 1990. Some people consider the *New York Times* fairly alien to American values.

"Recent international events have rendered the CIA an obsolete tool of national security policy. The CIA should be disbanded and its necessary functions spun off to the rest of the national security bureaucracy."

> Former CIA official and media talking head **VINCENT CANNISTRARO**, "The CIA Dinosaur," *Washington Post*, 5 September 1991.

"The U.S. has done as well as it has *despite* its intelligence."

> **ANGELO CODEVILLA**, *Informing Statecraft* (1992).

"Why does Congress put up with such ruinously expensive incompetence and, year after year, increase the CIA's secret budget?"

> **MARY McGRORY**, "Terminating the CIA," *Washington Post*, 3 December 1992.

"Some of the columnists who failed to foresee [George H. W.] Bush's demise [in 1992] castigated the CIA for failing to predict political change in the Soviet Union with greater accuracy than they themselves had shown in forecasting the outcome of a presidential election in the United States."

> **CHRISTOPHER ANDREW**, *For the President's Eyes Only* (1995).

"The question is why the CIA still exists. Perhaps it does not have any sophisticated equipment that would help its people discover that the Cold War is over."

MARY McGRORY, "Censurable Intelligence Agency," *Washington Post*, 28 October 1993.

"With a few exceptions, CNN provides real-time intelligence that rivals that offered by American intelligence agencies."

JOHN PIKE, *The National Reconnaissance Office* (1994). Does Ted Turner brief the President every morning?

"While you were an undergraduate screaming and yelling about our defense expenditures, some of us were doing what we could to avoid the need to *use* the American military . . . the kind of people who have offended you since you were at college are the people who won the Cold War and, at least for a while, gave the whole world immunity from a nuclear exchange. How this was done and how credit for it should be apportioned is something historians will decide."

Fictional career CIA operations officer Blackford Oakes to a liberal Senate staffer assisting an attempt to ban all covert action in **WILLIAM F. BUCKLEY, JR.**, *A Very Private Plot* (1994).

"It is the failure of Congress either to grasp or enforce the principle of congressional oversight that has given the CIA a license to commit excesses outside the law and human decency. Checks and balances do not apply in Langley. Did Congress ever make sure that anyone was disciplined for the staggering blunder of overestimating the Soviet economy, a bad guess we still pay for? . . . Like the Vietnam village, the agency has to be destroyed in order to save it. The CIA has to be reconstituted as an entity that reflects the Constitution and the democracy it's supposed to serve."

MARY McGRORY, "Treehouse Mentality on the CIA," *Washington Post*, 11 April 1995.

"CIA employees fit a certain mold. They all had really bad taste, they dressed badly, and they fit the stereotype of the ugly American."

ROSARIO AMES, wife of CIA turncoat Aldrich Ames, in 1995; quoted in Earley, *Confessions of a Spy* (1997). It's okay to betray your country as long as you look marvelous.

"Almost everyone, it seems, knows that the Central Intelligence Agency failed to anticipate the collapse of the Soviet Union. Indeed, the belief that the CIA somehow missed the single most important event of the twentieth century pervades virtually all discussions of U.S. intelligence these days, and may, in fact, be one of the few Cold War events about which both liberals and conservatives agree. . . . There is only one small problem: *The critics are wrong. The intelligence community did not fail to predict the Soviet collapse.*"

BRUCE BERKOWITZ and **JEFFREY RICHELSON**, "The CIA Vindicated," *The National Interest* (fall 1995).

"The buck never stops anywhere at the CIA . . . [It was] Harry Truman's worst idea."

MARY McGRORY, "Buck Up, CIA," *Washington Post*, 2 November 1995. Not the Air Force?

"The CIA remains a cancer on the American body politic. . . . The government [intends] to change nothing in the way the hidden monster of American intelligence goes about its business. . . . Covert action corrupts. Period. . . . President Clinton should begin the dismantling of this massive, outmoded and conscienceless machine."

JAMES CARROLL, "America's Covert Monster," *Boston Globe*, 9 April 1996.

"To say that the CIA and the KGB engage in similar practices is the equivalent of saying that the man who pushes an old lady into the path of a hurtling bus is not to be distinguished from the man who pushes an old lady out of the way of a hurtling bus, on the grounds that, after all, in both cases someone is pushing an old lady around."

WILLIAM F. BUCKLEY, JR., *The Right Word* (1996).

"The CIA exemplifies a great truth about life in Washington. If you goof up really spectacularly, you can expect to be rewarded."

MARY McGRORY, "CIA's Unlikely Exorcist," *Washington Post*, 7 May 1996.

"I was never worried about the CIA catching me. I knew how inept the organization was."

Former CIA officer and Soviet spy **ALDRICH AMES**; quoted in Earley, *Confessions of a Spy* (1997). Zero for two.

"Contrary to later allegations . . . CIA anticipated —and predicted—that by the mid-1980s a new Soviet leadership would be forced by economic decline to consider drastic changes in the system."

Former DCI **ROBERT GATES**, *From the Shadows* (1996).

"I guarantee you that forced to choose between the CIA and the *New York Times* as a source of reliable information, the country's elected leaders would take the *Times*. . . . Langley is an island in time. The CIA is a parody of what it once was. . . . If the CIA has effectively adapted to the times, that is one secret they've managed to keep."

RICHARD REEVES, "We Need Intelligence, Not a Joke CIA," *Los Angeles Times*, 24 November 1996.

"The Central Intelligence Agency . . . is close to incorrigible. Six years after the disintegration of the Soviet Union and end of the cold war, the C.I.A. is still struggling to get its bearings and still resisting reform. . . . Almost every aspect of the agency's activities requires further change. Nearly 50 years since the creation of the C.I.A., the agency's operations directorate retains an insular, arrogant culture that breeds a dangerous contempt for democratic principles and accountability."

New York Times editorial, "The Incorrigible C.I.A.," 8 December 1996.

"You would think that at a time when money is so tight that the president is considering cutting fuel assistance for the elderly poor by 25 per cent, there might be an interest in downsizing CIA's large budget and bloated work force, particularly in the light of its spotty history, record of resounding bloopers and the discovery of another spy in the ranks. . . . The CIA is one organization whose record seems to have little to do with its standing. . . . Why do we have such a vicious creature, with a mania for secrecy and so fleeting an acquaintance with common sense and democracy?"

MARY McGRORY, "Taming the CIA Beast," *Washington Post*, 15 December 1996.

"There has not been a foreign policy event since [the end of the Cold War] that the president could not have understood better by reading the daily press than by relying on the CIA."

Former U.S. ambassador **ROBERT E. WHITE**, "Too Many Spies, Too Little Intelligence," *Los Angeles Times*, 12 March 1997. Ambassadors don't get what CIA sends the President.

"When the dust settles and the arrow in his back hurts less, [Anthony] Lake may be glad he didn't get to be chief spook. The CIA needs a boss who can knock heads together, like Richard Holbrooke, our chief negotiator in Bosnia. Lake doesn't like secrets and secrets is what the CIA does. Its best kept secret is why it is still in existence."

MARY McGRORY, "Taking the 'Company' Line," *Washington Post*, 20 March 1997.

"The largest, most expensive and most thoroughly ridiculed intelligence service on Earth."

> **MARTIN WALKER** on CIA in *The Guardian* of London, 14 April 1997. Guilty on all three.

"The Senate is about to confirm another director for the CIA even though America found out about the collapse of the Soviet Union on CNN. America learned of the fall of the Berlin Wall on CNN. America found out about Saddam Hussein's invasion of Kuwait on CNN. Congress should fire the CIA and hire CNN."

> U.S. Representative **JAMES TRAFICANT**, Democrat from Ohio, on the House floor, 6 May 1997; quoted in the *Washington Times*, 7 May 1997.

"Without a clear and extraordinary mission, such as contending with the Soviet enemy, the CIA is a relic that the country does not need."

> **THEODORE DRAPER**, "Is the CIA Necessary?" *New York Review of Books*, 14 August 1997.

"I will not eat another bite of solid food until the President calls for a law to dissolve the CIA for its violations in disseminating drugs to African-American communities in the United States to raise money for political and covert intelligence operations."

> Comedian and activist **DICK GREGORY**, 27 November 1997. This is the "comedian" part.

"Why didn't the C.I.A. find this out? The question is why don't we learn to read. What's the State Department for? The political leadership in India as much as said they were going to begin [nuclear] testing. There's a tendency at the State Department to say, 'Gee, the C.I.A. never told us.'"

> Senator **DANIEL PATRICK MOYNIHAN** responding to criticism of CIA for failing to predict India's nuclear tests of May 1998; quoted in the *New York Times*, 13 May 1998.

"There is no political cost in attacking the CIA."

> Senior White House official; cited by Petersen in *National Security Studies Quarterly* (spring 1999).

"A principal policy goal of the Bush administration in the last days of the Cold War was to encourage liberalization in the Soviet Union, and especially in Eastern Europe, but at a rate that would not result in a crackdown by Soviet security forces. Our problem was, we did not know what rate of movement was sustainable. The CIA's analysis of the situation helped to keep our policy within sustainable bounds. Had there been an 'intelligence failure' in this case, we might still have a hostile Soviet Union facing us."

> **BRENT SCOWCROFT**, former national security advisor to President George H. W. Bush, letter to the *Washington Post*, 12 January 2000.

"The CIA . . . is a huge organization with simply too many people to get the job done. Departments overlap; in some smaller Latin American countries, US intelligence officers seem to be tripping over themselves. The importance of the private sector in the US means the best brains are recruited by big corporations for good money; the CIA must make do with second-rate material. Where the proportion of clever, charming officers in MI6 is nine out of 10, in the CIA it is closer to one out of 10."

> Former KGB officer **OLEG GORDIEVSKIY**, who defected to Britain's MI6, in the *Manchester Guardian*, 10 May 2000. Clever and charming can be a matter of taste; Kim Philby was both.

"The U.S. CIA is essentially a conspiracy organization that has made it its business to fabricate things. Nothing it says is worth listening to."

> North Korean radio broadcast, 8 May 2001. Was Mary McGrory working for P'yongyang?

"The 'intelligence failure' so horribly on display last week is the result of political and legal attacks on our spymakers going back to the 1970s witch-hunts of the Church committee. Americans need to understand that a key reason we don't have the intelligence we need to thwart terrorism is that we have spent many years actively discouraging good agents from getting it. . . . We only wish it hadn't taken . . . the blood of thousands of Americans for some of our elites to figure out that there are greater evils in this world than U.S. intelligence agencies."

> *Wall Street Journal* editorial, "Unspooking Spooks," 18 September 2001.

"It is a lamentably common practice in Washington and elsewhere to shoot people in the back and then complain when they fail to win the race. The loss of so many lives in New York and Washington is now called an 'intelligence failure,' mostly by those who crippled the CIA in the first place, and by those who celebrated the loss of its invaluable capabilities. What a pity that they cannot stand up like adults now and say: 'See, we gutted our intelligence agencies because we don't much like them, and now we can bury thousands of American citizens as an indirect result.' This, of course, will not happen, because those who inflict their aesthetic on the rest of us are never around to clean up the resulting mess. . . . The next time America is in a fight, it is well to remember that tying one's own arm is unlikely to assist in preserving, protecting and defending what is ours."

> **TOM CLANCY**, "First We Cripple the CIA, Then We Blame It," *Wall Street Journal*, 18 September 2001.

"The CIA's Directorate of Operations (DO) contains many dedicated men and women. But they work in a system locked in its Cold War past [that] rewards those who play the game at headquarters, not those who show innovation in the field. . . . I witnessed the DO in action [when] I accompanied what was described as two of the most savvy 'street-smart' operators in U.S. service with extensive Cold War experience to witness their surveillance tradecraft. After barely an hour of night-time driving through the dimly-lit streets of a large Third World capital, we pulled over on the side of the road, a CIA veteran using a penlight to examine a map—because we were lost."

> Former Senate staffer **RANDY SCHEUNEMANN** in the *Washington Times*, 27 September 2001.

"Much is expected of the Central Intelligence Agency these days, probably too much. As a pivotal front-line organization in the war against terrorism, the agency is supposed to detect and prevent new terror attacks, help locate and perhaps even kill Osama bin Laden and let President Bush know if the anthrax in the mail comes from Iraq—to mention only a few of Washington's expectations. These are lofty demands to make of an institution that before Sept. 11 was still struggling to reinvent itself a decade after the end of the cold war. As much as the nation may yearn for a crack intelligence service that can save the day, there is no such outfit in Washington at present."

> *New York Times* editorial, "The Spy Puzzle," 4 November 2001.

"Paradoxically, the news is worse than the angriest critics think, because the intelligence community has worked much better than they assume. Contrary to the image left by the destruction of September 11, U.S. intelligence and associated services have generally done very well at protecting the country."

> **RICHARD BETTS**, "Fixing Intelligence," *Foreign Affairs* (January–February 2002).

"Imagine a huge $30-billion conglomerate. It operates in one of the few businesses that might genuinely be described as cut-throat. Its competitors have changed dramatically, and so have its products and technologies. But its structure is the same as when it was founded, in 1947. Nobody leads this colossus (there is just an honorary chairman) and everyone exploits it. Demoralised and bureaucratic, it has just endured its biggest-ever loss. The response: the firm has been given even more money, and nobody has been sacked."

> "America's Intelligence Services: Time for a Rethink," the *Economist,* 20 April 2002.

"It is hard to go wrong criticizing the C.I.A. these days. When it comes to the agency, a Russian saying seems apt: 'If you see a Bulgarian on the street, beat him. He will know why.'"

> **JAMES RISEN**, "Kicking the C.I.A. While It's Down," *New York Times Book Review,* 24 August 2003.

"Unfortunately, you rarely hear a patient, careful, or thoughtful discussion of intelligence these days. . . . The question being asked about Iraq in the starkest of terms is: were we 'right' or were we 'wrong.' In the intelligence business, you are almost never completely wrong or completely right. That applies in full to the question of Saddam's weapons of mass destruction. And, like many of the toughest intelligence challenges, when the facts on Iraq are all in, we will be neither completely right nor completely wrong. . . . Based on an assessment of the data we collected over the past ten years, it would have been difficult for [CIA] analysts to come to any different conclusions than the ones reached in October of 2002. . . . Our analysts at the end of the day have a duty to inform and warn. They did so honestly and with integrity when

making judgments about the dangers posed by Saddam Hussein."

> DCI **GEORGE TENET**, remarks at Georgetown University, 5 February 2004.

CURRENT INTELLIGENCE

Current intelligence is the intelligence product that is delivered every day to the nation's top leadership. It is the extreme tip of the entire spear of intelligence as product, process, institution, and people. Current intelligence must be succinct yet leave out nothing essential, up to the minute yet thoughtful. The Literary Spy salutes those who work this minor miracle.

See also: Analysis & Analysts; Warning, Prediction, & Surprise

"Of making many books there is no end . . ."

> Ecclesiastes 12:12 (Revised Standard).

"Let thy words explicit be."

> **DANTE**, *Inferno* (1320), canto X. Other translations say our words should be "clear," "counted," or "choice"— all good attributes of current intelligence.

"It is now 3 days since I have received any intelligence. . . . It is of such importance to me to be regularly informed that I must request you will send expresses daily."

> **GEORGE WASHINGTON** to his generals, 4 October 1778; quoted in Miller, *Spying for America* (1989).

"An essential point is not to keep back any intelligence of great consequence, waiting until it has been corroborated from other sources, but to communicate it without delay to the chief of staff or other officer concerned. The earliest possible information is what is wanted; not only therefore has the news to be got, but the means for transmitting it must be well organized and swift."

British Colonel **GEORGE FURSE**, *Information in War* (1895).

"Why have you not kept me properly supplied with news? Volume should be increased at least five-fold and important messages sent textually."

WINSTON CHURCHILL during the 1943 Casablanca conference to his intelligence chief; quoted in Stafford, *Churchill and Secret Service* (1998).

"Intelligence reports find their literary merit in terseness and clarity rather than in expressive description. . . . Proust, Joyce, or Gertrude Stein would all be equally out of place. . . . Sobriety is imperative. All parading of erudition which might have been spared without inconvenience is odious."

OSS guide for writing intelligence reports; cited in Katz, *Foreign Intelligence: Research and Analysis in OSS* (1989).

"A President has to know what is going on all around the world in order to be ready to act when action is needed. The President must have all the facts that may affect the foreign policy or the military policy of the United States. . . . On January 20, 1946, I issued an Executive Order setting up the Central Intelligence Group. . . . Under the new intelligence arrangement I now began to receive a daily digest and summary of the information obtained abroad. . . . Here, at last . . . a practical way had been found for keeping the President informed as to what was known and what was going on."

HARRY TRUMAN, *Memoirs*, vol. II (1956). Truman established CIG on 22 January (not 20 January) 1946.

"The CIG [Central Intelligence Group] daily intelligence summary had a specific, receptive reader, President Harry Truman. When CIG was first be-

ing organized, Truman began asking almost daily, 'Where's my newspaper?' It seemed almost that the only CIG activity President Truman deemed important was the daily summary. . . . It became apparent there was no established criteria. No one in the White House had told the Central Intelligence Group what was important for the president to see. This startled me considerably, but I later came to recognize it as a persistent problem in the relationship between intelligence people and people who make policy. Rarely is there guidance. The process is usually carried out by feel, one of the reasons intelligence work is often termed an art."

Former DDI **R. JACK SMITH**, *The Unknown CIA* (1989).

"Secretary [of State James F.] Byrnes . . . pointed out that he is responsible for reporting to the President on matters of foreign policy. [DCI Sidney] Souers explained his understanding was that the President wanted him only to go through the dispatch traffic and make a digest of significant developments. Admiral Souers emphasized that there was no intention that he should interpret these dispatches or advise the President on any matters of foreign policy. His report was intended to be purely factual. . . . Secretary Byrnes stressed the fact that it was his function to furnish the President with information on which to base decisions. [The President's personal representative] Admiral [William] Leahy expressed his understanding that the President wanted the information from all three departments (State, War and Navy) summarized in order to keep him currently informed. Admiral Leahy pointed out that Secretary Byrnes presents the viewpoint of the Department of State while the President would like to receive significant information in all three departments in a single summary."

> Minutes of the first meeting of the National Intelligence Authority, 5 February 1946; in *FRUS 1945–1950: Emergence of the Intelligence Establishment* (1996), document 140. This early discussion focused on the most important aspect of current intelligence: what does the President want and find useful?

"The Director of Central Intelligence will give first priority to the following tasks: a. Production of daily summaries containing factual statements of the significant developments in the field of intelligence and operations related to national security and to foreign events for the use of the President . . ."

> National Intelligence Authority Directive No. 2, "Organization and Functions of the Central Intelligence Group," 8 February 1946; in *FRUS 1945–1950: Emergence of the Intelligence Establishment* (1996), document 142.

"In trying to meet the needs of several levels requiring [current] intelligence with one series of reports . . . we are not fully meeting the requirements of any. We appear to be overwriting for some and underwriting for others. I propose that we prepare a special daily for the President, so written that it should reach the President regularly, in its original form, and without the need for any preliminary annotations by aides. This will require very special selection and editing."

> Internal CIG memorandum by planning chief **DONALD EDGAR**, 13 January 1947; in *FRUS 1945–1950: Emergence of the Intelligence Establishment* (1996), document 182. Edgar was anticipating the *President's Daily Brief*—which was created for President Kennedy and has served since as the only document prepared for the president that isn't annotated by aides.

"Adm. [James] Foskett delivers the Daily Summary to the President during the afternoon. Usually the President takes it with him on leaving his office and reads it during the evening. It serves as the basis of discussion of foreign problems with Adm. [William] Leahy the following morning. The President considers that he personally originated the Daily, that it is prepared in accordance with his own specifications, that it is well done, and that in its present form it satisfies his requirements. . . . The President normally reads every item in the Daily with interest."

> Central Intelligence Group memorandum of 26 February 1947; reproduced in Warner, *CIA Under Truman* (1994).

"CIG is required to produce current intelligence for the use of the President, the members of this Authority, and a few others. These are the Daily and Weekly Summaries. Personally, I feel that these summaries are pretty poor, and we are now endeavoring to make changes in them to increase their value. Any suggestions or ideas to make them better would be warmly received."

> DCI **ROSCOE HILLENKOETTER**, report to the National Intelligence Authority, 26 June 1947; in *FRUS 1945–1950: Emergence of the Intelligence Establishment* (1996), document 319. Admiral William Leahy, President Truman's personal representative on the NIA, responded by saying that the "President was pleased with the contents of the daily summaries, and further he read these summaries every day." Current intelligence producers and readers often disagree on the quality of the product.

"[CIA's] Daily Summary is probably as good a document as can be brought to the attention of its most important half dozen readers. . . . Because of the importance of the Daily's top half-dozen readers, its snob appeal will be enormous. Many officers of the government will want to be on the distribution list for the sake of the company they will be keeping, or out of idle but pardonable curiosity. Those with the least reason to be on the list are likely to be the ones worst served by the document and most critical of its fancied shortcomings."

SHERMAN KENT, former senior OSS analyst, memorandum to DCI Hillenkoetter, 9 February 1948; in *FRUS 1945–1950: Emergence of the Intelligence Establishment* (1996), document 339. The DCI had asked Kent to critically review CIA analysis. In 1950, Kent was brought to CIA to help run the Board of National Estimates.

"Intelligence organizations must also have many of the qualities of those of our greatest metropolitan newspapers. After all, many of their duties have a close resemblance to those of an outstanding daily. They watch, report, summarize, and analyze. They have their foreign correspondents and home staff. Like the newspaper they have their privately developed hot sources; their speedy and sure communications. They have their responsibilities for completeness and accuracy—with commensurately greater penalties for omission and error. They have their deadlines. . . . They even have the problem of editorial control and the difficulties of reproduction and dissemination. In these terms it is fitting that intelligence organizations put more study upon newspaper organization and borrow those phases of it which they require."

SHERMAN KENT, *Strategic Intelligence* (1949).

"Intelligence organizations . . . must maintain small forces of decorous and highly intelligent salesmen who not only push the product and appraise consumer reaction to it but also discover new consumer problems with an eye to the development of new products."

SHERMAN KENT, *Strategic Intelligence* (1949). Kent anticipated the PDB briefer—the CIA officer who delivers and explains the *President's Daily Brief.*

"The imposition of a word count forces the intelligence producers to be clear in their thought and concise in their presentation, and it enables the hurried consumer to consume while he runs."

SHERMAN KENT, *Strategic Intelligence* (1949).

"As the intelligence facility of the National Security Council and the President, the Central Intelligence Agency must continually and systematically report all developments, political, economic, military, and otherwise, which materially affect or have a bearing upon United States national security and objectives abroad. . . . CIA's Daily and Weekly Summaries . . . are the only ones designed primarily for the President and the National Security Council."

DCI **ROSCOE HILLENKOETTER**, report to the Executive Secretary of the National Security Council, 27 December 1949; in *FRUS 1945–1950: Emergence of the Intelligence Establishment* (1996), document 407. CIA's practice of aiming high in its daily publications is an old one.

"Regardless of our views of the merits of the [CIA] Summary, every indication is that the President likes it and wants it."

Internal State Department memorandum on the CIA Daily Summary, 19 January 1950; in *FRUS 1945–1950: Emergence of the Intelligence Establishment* (1996), document 411. State had objected that CIA used information in State cables to comment on developments affecting U.S. foreign policy, which State said it alone should do.

"Dear Bedel:

I have been reading the Intelligence Bulletin and I am highly impressed with it. I believe you have hit the jackpot with this one.

Sincerely, Harry Truman"

President **TRUMAN** to DCI Walter Bedell Smith, 6 March 1951; reproduced in *Studies in Intelligence* (1995).

"First impressions [subject to] later revision."

> DCI **WALTER BEDELL SMITH**'s characterization of current intelligence; quotation in CIA's Historical Intelligence Collection.

"[DCI Allen] Dulles had a good feel for current intelligence—he wanted brief, colorful, snappy items with dramatic quality."

> Former DDI **RAY CLINE**, *Secrets, Spies and Scholars* (1976).

"[General Chester Clifton, President Kennedy's senior military aide] pulled out of a folder a series of intelligence publications that were daily coming in down there from all over, and he said, 'What I need is something that will have everything in it that is worth the President's attention, everything that is worth his knowing.' . . . What he was doing was laying out what I had been thinking all along, a single publication, no sources barred, covering the whole ground, and written in the President's language rather than in officialese. . . . We turned out a live issue [three days later], Clifton took it to the President, the President read it . . . and liked it. It has been in business from then on."

> **RICHARD LEHMAN**, CIA's former director of current intelligence, on creating the *President's Intelligence Check List*—later renamed the *President's Daily Brief*—for President Kennedy in June 1961; CIA oral history interview, February 1998.

"JFK asked for a single, concise summary of the most important 'all source' reports from the intelligence community. The result was a daily document that included summaries of *all* the most highly classified and sensitive intelligence of the preceding twenty-four hours. . . . At the outset, the JFK briefing was known as the 'President's Intelligence Check List,' otherwise, PICL—pronounced 'Pickle' by those involved in preparing the document. In time this evolved into the 'Presi-

dent's Daily Brief,' otherwise the 'PDB.' As I recall it, President Eisenhower had wanted his daily summary at reveille. JFK liked to read the Pickle on arrival at his desk. President Johnson wanted the PDB in late afternoon and often read it in bed. Neither [DDI] Jack Smith or I was ever sure how often Nixon even glanced at his PDB."

> Former DCI **RICHARD HELMS**, *A Look over My Shoulder* (2003). Note the respectful use of "President" with Eisenhower and Johnson, the chummy "JFK," but lastly there's just "Nixon."

"President Kennedy . . . entered enthusiastically into an exchange of comments with [the PDB's] producers, sometimes praising an account, sometimes criticizing a comment, once objecting to 'boondocks' as not an accepted word. For current intelligence people, this was heaven on earth! A president who read your material thoughtfully and told you what he liked and did not like!"

> Former DDI **R. JACK SMITH**, then editor of the *President's Daily Brief*, in *The Unknown CIA* (1989).

"The President desires that his daily intelligence report be made available on a daily basis to the Secretary of State and the Secretary of Defense. . . . Because the usefulness of the [President's Intelligence] Checklist might be diminished if this report were too widely circulated, the Director of Central Intelligence should arrange delivery so that the report is read by the two Secretaries only. The President's Checklist is a very closely held report in that it contains information of the most sensitive nature gathered from all sources available to the government and for which very few individuals have the necessary clearances for all the types of information it contains. Consequently, its handling must always meet these requirements."

> General **CHESTER CLIFTON**, senior military aide to President Kennedy, in a December 1961 memorandum

to the DCI and the Secretaries of State and Defense; in CIA's Historical Intelligence Collection.

"People were willing to work long hours and to come in at three o'clock in the morning because they knew damn well that what they produced was read personally by the President immediately upon its delivery to the White House."

> Former DDI **ROBERT AMORY** in a 1966 interview; cited in Weber, *Spymasters* (1999).

"In the Johnson administration [the PDB] frequently contained, in addition to the normal intelligence fare, rather scandalous descriptions of the private lives of certain world leaders, always avidly read by the President."

> **VICTOR MARCHETTI** and **JOHN MARKS**, *CIA and the Cult of Intelligence* (1974). Ah yes, the *Prurient Daily Brief.*

"[In January 1969] Kissinger proposed that the DCI change the publication time for the PDB from early morning to late afternoon, releasing the publication to him in the evening and to the President the following morning. This change, Kissinger admitted, would introduce a lag of 12 hours in the reporting time, but he was not disturbed that the PDB would be less current; he was more concerned that he have time to prepare his own comments on anything the President would see."

> Former DDI **JOHN HELGERSON**, *CIA Briefings* (1996). Helgerson describes a classic Washington situation wherein the imperatives of current intelligence are sacrificed for the exigencies of personality. The PDB long since has resumed its early morning publication.

"[In 1973] the National Intelligence Daily was born, and it became the journal with the smallest circulation (about 60), the largest reporting staff (the whole intelligence community), and the worst advertising in the world (none, since the entire con-

tent was highly classified) . . . it became the focus of my effort to present our intelligence better and produce it better."

> Former DCI **WILLIAM COLBY**, *Honorable Men* (1978). Colby mentioned only the NID because the existence of the PDB was classified into the 1980s.

"We should get the PDB to the Vice President so that he would know everything the President knew. We didn't want another situation like when Truman was unaware of the Manhattan project."

> Former DCI **WILLIAM COLBY** in 1993, recalling his decision to provide the PDB to Vice President Gerald Ford; quoted in Helgerson, *CIA Briefings* (1996).

"When [President Ford] and I were both in town, we would meet every morning. . . . The agenda was unvarying: we would discuss the President's daily intelligence brief, which I could be sure he would have read (unlike Nixon, who, deeply suspicious of the CIA, had frequently ignored it)."

> **HENRY KISSINGER**, *Years of Renewal* (1999).

"As every President since World War II, I depend on you as one of America's first lines of defense. Every morning, as a result of your efforts, an intelligence report is delivered to my desk which is complete, concise, perceptive, and responsible. . . . Let me express my personal gratitude for this fine work."

> President **GERALD FORD**'s remarks at the swearing-in of George H. W. Bush as DCI, 30 January 1976; quoted in CIA, *"Our First Line of Defense"* (1996).

"[Current intelligence] is a service to high-level officials that they invariably appreciate, and it is a way that all intelligence agencies use to capture the attention of the senior officials they want to serve. Policymakers do not always welcome something profound . . . but most of them can be hooked with something new—especially if they get it before their peers in other agencies."

> Former DDI **RAY CLINE**, *Secrets, Spies and Scholars* (1976).

"BE BRIEF. BE BLUNT. BE GONE."

> Sign on senior CIA official's desk as related by David Atlee Phillips, *The Night Watch* (1978). A fitting motto for those who prepare and deliver the PDB.

"Like most postwar presidents, Reagan began each day with the president's daily brief. . . . Despite suggestions to the contrary, Reagan did actually read the PDB."

> **CHRISTOPHER ANDREW**, *For the President's Eyes Only* (1995).

"As a rule, Reagan was a studious reader [of the PDB], going over each item deliberately and with considerable concentration. . . . Somewhat to our surprise, he showed no impatience with analysis that presented a different view."

> Former DDCI **RICHARD KERR** and **PETER DIXON DAVIS**, "Ronald Reagan and the President's Daily Brief," *Studies in Intelligence* (1997).

"The president routinely receives only one intelligence document that is not summarized or commented upon by someone outside the intelligence community: the President's Daily Brief."

> DDCI **ROBERT GATES**, *Washington Quarterly* (winter 1989).

"To be certain that your reports reach the president's eyes and ears without the intervention of a phalanx of aides and assistants is the ultimate reward. It is seldom achieved."

> Former DDI **R. JACK SMITH**, *The Unknown CIA* (1989).

"Current intelligence is journalism—with two differences. It is classified, and the target audiences seldom receive competing products."

> **ANGELO CODEVILLA**, *Informing Statecraft* (1992).

"Don't let anybody else tell you what the President wants or needs in the PDB—ask him."

> Former President **GEORGE H. W. BUSH** in 1993; quoted in Helgerson, *CIA Briefings* (1996).

"Every weekday morning, shortly after 6 a.m., a handful of CIA cars leaves the agency's Langley headquarters. They carry senior intelligence officers who hand deliver to President Clinton and four other top officials the President's Daily Brief, Washington's most exclusive publication."

> **WALTER PINCUS**, "PDB, the Only News Not Fit for Anyone Else to Read," *Washington Post*, 27 August 1994.

"Every morning I start my day with an intelligence report. The intelligence I receive informs just about every foreign policy decision we make. It's easy to take for granted, but we couldn't do without it."

> President **BILL CLINTON**, remarks at CIA Headquarters, 14 July 1995; quoted in CIA, *"Our First Line of Defense"* (1996).

"The *President's Daily Brief* [is] probably the world's smallest circulation, most highly classified, and—in some respects—best informed daily newspaper. . . . On average, about 60 percent of the items covered in the *President's Daily Brief* do not appear in the press at all."

> **CHRISTOPHER ANDREW**, foreword to John Helgerson, *CIA Briefings* (1996).

"The most important thing we do is what we say day after day."

DCI **GEORGE TENET** on the PDB, July 1999.

"For the policymaker, the PDB is necessary but not sufficient for understanding the world."

Senior U.S. administration official, July 1999.

"Analysts at the CIA ... often play the most crucial role in influencing U.S. policy. That's because they write the world's most expensive and exclusive newspaper: the President's Daily Brief."

Los Angeles Times, 21 July 2000.

"A 19th century delivery system carrying 20th century–quality analysis derived from 21st century collection systems."

Former DCI **ROBERT GATES** on the use of couriers in delivering intelligence; quoted in Studies in Intelligence (2000). Much of CIA's daily product is delivered by courier.

"I'm your customer. I see your product every morning at eight o'clock sharp, and it's always first-rate."

President **GEORGE W. BUSH**, remarks at CIA, 20 March 2001.

"I was sitting right there being briefed by my CIA briefer when the whole building shook."

Secretary of Defense **DONALD RUMSFELD** on where he was and what he was doing when terrorists struck the Pentagon on 11 September 2001, in an interview with Dan Rather on CBS, 9 October 2001.

"For the CIA, the PDB serves as a virtual umbilical cord linking the agency directly to the president and providing a symbol of its position as the nation's premier intelligence agency."

WALTER PINCUS, "Under Bush, the Briefing Gets Briefer," Washington Post, 24 May 2002.

D

- **Deception, Disinformation, & Propaganda**
- **Defectors**
- **Directors of Central Intelligence**
- **Domestic Activities**

DECEPTION, DISINFORMATION, & PROPAGANDA

The Literary Spy includes here relevant quotations that shed light on the sowing of darkness, that give insight into the unseen, that reveal truths about telling lies, and that give reliable information about unreliable data. The presumption behind these sorts of operations is that the ends often justify these means.

See also: Counterintelligence; Covert Action; Plausible Denial; Secrecy

"The Lord God said to the woman, 'What is this that you have done?' The woman said, 'The serpent beguiled me, and I ate.'"

> Genesis 3:13 (Revised Standard).

"Broken in war, set back by fate, the leaders
   of the Greek host, as years went by,
   contrived . . .
. . . a horse as big as a mountain.
They wove its sides with planks of fir,
   pretending
This was an offering [to the gods] for their
   safe return. . . . But inside

They packed, in secret, into the hollow sides
The fittest warriors; the belly's cavern,
Huge as it was, was filled with men in armor . . .
That day, our last, poor wretches, we were
   happy . . .
And the sky turned, and darkness
Came from the ocean, the great shade covering
   earth
And heaven, and the trickery of the Greeks.
Sprawling along the walls, the Trojans
   slumbered . . . the Greeks
Came out of the wooden womb. The air
   received them . . . they all
Came sliding down the rope . . . The watch
   was murdered,
The open doors welcome the rush of comrades,
They marshal the determined ranks for battle."

> **VIRGIL,** *The Aeneid* (1st century B.C.). The Trojan Horse is the ancient forefather of deceptions.

"All warfare is based on deception. Hence, when able to attack, we must seem unable; when using our forces, we must seem inactive; when we are near, we must make the enemy believe we are far away; when far away, we must make him believe

we are near. . . . O divine art of subtlety and secrecy! Through you we learn to be invisible,
through you inaudible, and hence we can hold the
enemy's fate in our hands."

   SUN TZU, *The Art of War* (6th century B.C.).

"Bread gained by deceit is sweet to a man, but
afterwards his mouth will be filled with gravel."

   Proverbs 20:17 (Revised Standard).

"One who has been able to gain the victory by
stratagem involves the enemy in ridicule as well
as disaster."

   ST. JOHN CHRYSOSTOM, *Treatise on the Priesthood*
   (c. 386).

"Though fraud in other activities be detestable,
in the management of war it is laudable and glori-
ous, and he who overcomes the enemy by fraud
is as much to be praised as he who does it by force."

   NICCOLÒ MACHIAVELLI, *The Art of War* (1520). At least
   as much—arguably more.

"Hide not thy poison with such sugar'd words."

   WILLIAM SHAKESPEARE, *King Henry VI, Part II* (1590),
   Act III, scene 2.

"I'll fill these dogged spies with false reports."

   WILLIAM SHAKESPEARE, *King John* (1596), Act IV,
   scene 1.

"Let every soldier hew him down a bough
And bear't before him: thereby shall we shadow
The number of our host and make discovery
Err in report of us."

   WILLIAM SHAKESPEARE, *Macbeth* (1606), Act V, scene 4.

"We are led to believe a lie,
When we see not through the eye."

   WILLIAM BLAKE, *Auguries of Innocence* (1803).

"We are deceiving our Enemies with false Opinions of our Numbers."

   General **GEORGE WASHINGTON** to the Continental
   Congress, early 1777; cited in Bakeless, *Turncoats, Traitors
   and Heroes* (1998). Bakeless notes that beginning in 1777,
   "when at last he had an organized military intelligence
   service with a widespread espionage network, George
   Washington, who proverbially 'could not tell a lie,' began
   to reveal an unexpected talent for ingenious and elaborate
   deceit." Bakeless calls this chapter "The Cherry Tree Hero
   Tells Some Whoppers."

"Keep it within the bounds of what may be thought
reasonable or probable."

   General **GEORGE WASHINGTON**, instruction on preparing disinformation for the enemy, 1779; cited in Bakeless,
   Turncoats, Traitors and Heroes (1998). The first rule of deception is to link it to some truth.

"Oh, what a tangled web we weave,
When first we practice to deceive!"

   Sir **WALTER SCOTT**, *Marmion* (1808).

"Words—so innocent and powerless as they are,
as standing in a dictionary—how potent for good
and evil they become, in the hands of one who
knows how to combine them!"

   NATHANIEL HAWTHORNE, 1847; quoted by propagandist and language maven William Safire, *New York Times
   Magazine*, 13 December 1998.

"I have discovered the art of deceiving diplomats.
I speak the truth, and they never believe me."

   Attributed to Italian statesman **CAMILLO DI CAVOUR**
   (1810–1861). Cute, but how did he know?

"Always mystify, mislead, and surprise the enemy."

General **THOMAS "STONEWALL" JACKSON**; quoted in Furse, *Information in War* (1895).

"If I can deceive my own friends, I can make certain of deceiving the enemy."

Attributed to General **THOMAS "STONEWALL" JACKSON**; cited in Heinl, *Dictionary of Military and Naval Quotations* (1966).

"Have not all been sent to deceive?"

President **ABRAHAM LINCOLN**, June 1862, questioning General George McClellan on reports concerning the movements of General Thomas "Stonewall" Jackson; quoted in Fishel, *Secret War for the Union* (1996). Lincoln's instincts were correct.

"Weak and hesitating men allow their bold and active enemies to make public opinion against them. Bold and active rulers make it on their side."

EDWARD BATES, President Lincoln's attorney general; quoted in Knott, *Secret and Sanctioned* (1996).

"We are bred up to feel it a disgrace even to succeed by falsehood; the word spy conveys something as repulsive as slave; we will keep hammering along with the conviction that honesty is the best policy, and that truth always wins in the long run. These pretty sentiments do well for a child's copybook, but a man who acts on them had better sheathe his sword forever."

Sir **GARNETT WOLSELEY**, *Soldier's Pocket-Book* (1869).

"Whatever is only almost true is quite false, and among the most dangerous of errors, because being so near truth, it is the more likely to lead astray."

Attributed to **HENRY WARD BEECHER** (1813–1887).

"The best liar is he who makes the smallest amount of lying go the longest way."

SAMUEL BUTLER, *The Way of All Flesh* (1903). He also said "Any fool can tell the truth, but it requires a man of some sense to know how to lie well."

"The state never has any use for truth as such, but only for truth which is useful to it, more precisely for anything useful to it, whether it be truth, half-truth, or error."

FRIEDRICH NIETZSCHE, *Schopenhauer as Teacher* (1874).

"There is nothing more deceptive than an obvious fact."

Sherlock Holmes in Sir **ARTHUR CONAN DOYLE**, "The Boscombe Valley Mystery" (1891).

"It would brighten my declining years to see a German cruiser navigating the Solent according to the mine-field plans which I have furnished."

Sherlock Holmes in Sir **ARTHUR CONAN DOYLE**, "His Last Bow" (1917). In this story Holmes is a double agent who renders Berlin's top spy in Britain impotent by giving him false information.

"I am increasingly convinced that there can be no more valuable propaganda . . . than graphic accounts of the Bolshevik outrages and futility, of the treacheries they have committed, and what ruin they have brought upon their country and the harm they have done to us and our fighting men."

WINSTON CHURCHILL as minister of munitions on fighting Soviet subversion in British factories, February 1918; quoted in Stafford, *Churchill and Secret Service* (1998).

"All kinds of Munchhausen tales can be spread about to confuse and baffle the truth."

WINSTON CHURCHILL, 1940; quoted in Stafford, *Churchill and Secret Service* (1998).

"What you have to remember about deceptions is that if they're to be successful, two things are imperative: First, the enemy must be kept totally in the dark about what you don't want him to know, and second, you must know everything he's thinking all the time, especially when he's confronted with what you want him to believe.... We were able to locate, early on, the entire German espionage network in Britain, eliminate parts of it and use others to feed Hitler disinformation. We were also able to learn Hitler's thinking about where and when the invasion would eventually come, play to his prejudices and hunches, and learn when and whether he took our bait. We were reading his mind all the time."

> Sir **F. H. HINSLEY**, historian of World War II British intelligence; quoted in the *Washington Post*, 31 May 1994.

"A judicious mixture of rumor and deception, with truth as bait, to foster disunity and confusion."

> **WILLIAM DONOVAN**'s description of OSS Morale Operations (covert propaganda); quoted in Russell, *The Secret War* (1981).

"Now that we are at war, foreign propaganda must be employed as a weapon of war. It must march with events. It is primarily an attack weapon.... In point of fact the use of propaganda is the arrow of initial penetration in conditioning and preparing the people and the territory in which invasion is contemplated."

> **WILLIAM DONOVAN**, then Coordinator of Information, to President Roosevelt, 4 March 1942; quoted in Troy, *Donovan and the CIA* (1981).

"An example of a successful [OSS] rumor: Mussolini had applied to Switzerland for asylum in case of an Allied invasion of Italy and was turned down. The rumor reached not only Italian troops defending their homeland but even the American minister in Bern, who cautiously warned State Department sources that 'this information be given careful protection.'"

> **ELIZABETH McINTOSH**, *Sisterhood of Spies* (1998).

"All depends on secrecy and speed. Secrecy can only be maintained by deception."

> **WINSTON CHURCHILL** to President Roosevelt, fall of 1942 before Operation TORCH, the Allied landings in North Africa; quoted in Stafford, *Churchill and Secret Service* (1998).

"You are a British Intelligence officer; you have an opposite number in the enemy Intelligence.... What you, as a Briton with a British background, think can be deduced from a document does not matter. It is what *your opposite number*, with his German knowledge and background, will think that matters—what construction *he* will put on the document. Therefore, if you want *him* to think such-and-such a thing, you must give him something which will make *him* (and not *you*) think it. But he may be suspicious and want confirmation; you must think out enquiries *he* will make (not what enquiries *you* would make) and give him the answers to those enquiries so as to satisfy him. In other words, you must remember that a German does not think and react as an Englishman does, and you must put yourself into his mind."

> **EWEN MONTAGU**, *The Man Who Never Was* (1954). Montagu masterminded the British deception involving a dead body—"Major Martin"—to deceive the Germans about the Allied invasion of Sicily in 1943. The code name for the operation was MINCEMEAT.

"The genuineness of the captured documents is above suspicion."

> German intelligence report of 13 May 1943 to Admiral Doenitz regarding documents found on "Major Martin" during the British deception operation MINCEMEAT; cited in Montagu, *The Man Who Never Was* (1954).

"'Mincemeat' swallowed rod, line and sinker by right people and from best information they look like acting on it."

> Message to **WINSTON CHURCHILL** in Washington, April 1943, confirming from ULTRA intercepts that the Nazis had fallen for the "Major Martin" deception later immortalized in Ewen Montagu's *The Man Who Never Was;* cited in Stafford, *Churchill and Secret Service* (1998).

"In wartime, truth is so precious that she should always be attended by a bodyguard of lies."

> **WINSTON CHURCHILL**, November 1943; quoted in Russell, *The Secret War* (1981). Churchill may have borrowed this line from Stalin.

"The lie must be consistent, both with the truth, as the enemy knows it, and with all other lies that have been told him. . . . The enemy's efforts to estimate our capabilities and intentions are continuous —and so must be our deception."

> British paper on deception provided to the Americans, September 1944; cited in Riebling, *Wedge: The Secret War Between the FBI and CIA* (1994).

"Diplomats and Intelligence agents, in my experience, are even bigger liars than journalists, and the historians who try to reconstruct the past out of their records are, for the most part, dealing in fantasy."

> Former SIS officer **MALCOLM MUGGERIDGE** in *Chronicles of Wasted Time: The Infernal Grove* (1973).

"To distract German attention from the real landing area in Normandy, Eisenhower's headquarters cooked up a complete cover-plan codenamed FORTITUDE. . . . Field Marshal Montgomery's radio messages were not broadcast from his actual location in the south of England, but were led by land line to a spoof headquarters near Dover and transmitted from there. Dummy ships were concentrated in the Cinque Ports to help the illusion. A very busy signals staff contrived, by sending out the right sort of dummy wireless traffic, to 'assemble' a fictitious 4th Army in Scotland. . . . FORTITUDE sought to let the Germans convince themselves of what they had always wanted to believe anyway—that the invaders would pour across the Channel at the narrowest point, from Dover to the Pas de Calais."

> **DAVID KAHN**, *The Codebreakers* (1996).

"The propagandist is a man who canalizes an already existing stream. In a land where there is no water, he digs in vain."

> **ALDOUS HUXLEY**, "Notes on Propaganda," *Harper's Magazine* (December 1936).

"In all deception . . . the ultimate doom is that the deceiver comes to believe his own deceits. . . . The worst feature of propaganda, advertising, or any form of organised lying, is that, try as one will, one comes to believe it; as press lords come to believe what they read in their own newspapers, and television producers what they see on the screen."

> Former SIS officer **MALCOLM MUGGERIDGE** in *Chronicles of Wasted Time: The Infernal Grove* (1973).

"Disinformation almost always works most effectively when it includes a basis of fact."

> **CHRISTOPHER ANDREW** and **VASILI MITROKHIN**, *The Sword and the Shield: The Mitrokhin Archive* (1999).

"Propaganda cannot control or decisively influence events within a country in a state of revolution."

> **WILLIAM GRIFFITH**, policy director for Radio Free Europe (covertly supported by CIA) in the 1950s; quoted in Puddington, *Broadcasting Freedom* (2000).

"The best English cooking is the best in the world."

> Fictional British agent and gourmand James Bond in **IAN FLEMING**, *Moonraker* (1955). Bond actually was serious.

"The Bible Designed to be Read as Literature."

> The hollowed-out book that James Bond used to carry his Walther PPK and holster in **IAN FLEMING**, *Goldfinger* (1959). Anglicanism *is* a rather large tent.

"[There is] no need for the Soviet Union to shift its weapons for the repulsion of aggression, for a retaliatory blow, to any other country, for instance Cuba. Our nuclear weapons are so powerful in their explosive force and the Soviet Union has so powerful rockets to carry these nuclear warheads, that there is no need to search for sites for them beyond the boundaries of the Soviet Union."

> Official Soviet statement of 11 September 1962; quoted in Hilsman, *To Move a Nation* (1967). The United States discovered Soviet ballistic missiles in Cuba on 15 October 1962.

"Often the very fear of deception has blinded an opponent to the real value of information which accidents or intelligence operations have placed in his hands. . . . If you suspect an enemy of constant trickery, then almost anything that happens can be taken as one of his tricks."

> Former DCI **ALLEN DULLES**, *The Craft of Intelligence* (1963). This often is the paranoid Achilles heel of counterintelligence—attributing anything that happens to one of the enemy's tricks.

"Don't give it to them all at once, make them work for it. Confuse them with detail, leave things out, go back on your tracks. Be testy, be cussed, be difficult. Drink like a fish; don't give way on the ideology, they won't trust that. They want to deal with a man they've bought; they want the clash of opposites, not some half-cocked convert. Above all, they want to deduce."

> Fictional British intelligence chief "Control" to a false British defector armed with disinformation to confuse a hostile service, in **JOHN LE CARRÉ** [David Cornwell], *The Spy Who Came in from the Cold* (1963).

"Do not believe everything you read in the newspapers. Penkovskiy is very much alive and was a double agent against the Americans."

> Soviet Ambassador to the U.N. **NIKOLAI FEDERENKO** speaking to a Western diplomat about Oleg Penkovskiy, the GRU colonel tried and convicted for spying for the United States and Great Britain, 27 May 1963; quoted in Schecter and Deriabin, *The Spy Who Saved the World* (1995). Federenko's statement was designed to mislead, as Penkovskiy was no double—his information made him the most valuable agent of the Cold War—and he was executed after his trial.

"We think that not only would the story be more valid, but also more dramatic if it sticks closer to the main facts and to Penkovskiy's own words."

> CIA memorandum to SIS, June 1963, arguing that maximum propaganda value would be derived from releasing the truth about Soviet GRU colonel Oleg Penkovskiy's motives for spying for the West. The British wanted to create the fiction that Penkovskiy had been a KGB officer. *The Penkovskiy Papers* subsequently were released for publication. Schecter and Deriabin, *The Spy Who Saved the World* (1995).

"Now a few words about misinformation. We have been given a special directive from the GRU leadership to spread, through our scientists, all sorts of provocative rumors and misinformation among foreign scientists and businessmen. This is done in the following way: Soviet scientists and engineers spread rumors among foreigners about various types of scientific work or construction work or about other major projects on which Soviet scientists are allegedly working at the present time, whereas in reality they are not even considering work on such projects. This makes the foreign scientists and their governments work seriously on expensive projects which are not of practical use, and they spend enormous sums of money on this."

OLEG PENKOVSKIY, *The Penkovskiy Papers* (1966).

"You gentlemen may pride yourselves on writing good French, grammatical French, but a Frenchman reading it would know it was not written by a Frenchman. I'll go further than that, gentlemen. Give a Frenchman a passage in English and tell him to render it into French, and a Frenchman will still be aware that all is not well when he reads it. You must have your French composed *ab initio* by a Frenchman, contenting yourselves with merely outlining what is to be said."

Master forger Doctor Claudius in **C. S. FORESTER**, *Hornblower During the Crisis* (1967).

"But let us not speak false words or engage in trickery. We don't steal your documents. You can deliberately leave them somewhere and try us out. Nor do we engage in eavesdropping and bugging. There is no use in those small tricks."

MAO ZEDONG to Henry Kissinger, February 1973; quoted in the *New York Times*, 10 January 1999.

"Against a closed-society target, simply providing information and news that the government wishes to keep from its people can have a significant effect. If, in addition, some clever disinformation can be inserted, then so much the better. The listeners, realizing that much of what they are hearing is true, tend to believe that all they are told is accurate."

VICTOR MARCHETTI and **JOHN MARKS**, *CIA and the Cult of Intelligence* (1974).

"Scores of agents are on the payrolls of the world's intelligence services precisely because they are disloyal and can be used as conduits of disinformation."

Former senior CIA operations officer **DAVID ATLEE PHILLIPS**, *The Night Watch* (1978). Scores? Sounds like . . . disinformation!

"You know, I've been working for the KGB for six years—and you're the most professional KGB officer I've ever met."

Latin American KGB asset to a Russian-speaking CIA officer posing as a KGB officer; quoted in Phillips, *The Night Watch* (1978). The CIA officer told the asset that his regular KGB contact was ill and learned much about KGB operations in that country.

"*Est summum nefas fallere:* deceit is gross impiety, my dear sir. . . . The necessary dissimulation, the disguise, the lack of candour, I may even say the deceit called for in such an undertaking would be mighty distasteful."

Fictional British spy Stephen Maturin turning down an offer from another British agent—unwitting of Maturin's real employment—to work for intelligence, in **PATRICK O'BRIAN**, *The Ionian Mission* (1981).

"On basic questions deception should not be possible unless it is facilitated by more than average incompetence on the part of the side trying to get the information."

WALTER LAQUEUR, *A World of Secrets* (1985). This hinges on what is meant by "average incompetence."

"[This book] is not a memoir or a chronicle of my stewardship as the Director of Central Intelligence. Above all, it is not an apology for errors I may have made."

Former DCI **STANSFIELD TURNER** in the introduction to his apologetic memoir chronicling his tenure as DCI, *Secrecy and Democracy* (1985).

"Someone had even claimed during the missile gap that a church tower in the Ukraine clothed an ICBM. Russia was the land of Grigori Potemkin, after all, and he had been a master of guile. Russia was a place where chess, a game of subterfuge and cunning (not to mention sacrifice), amounted to a national pastime. The Russians had even institutionalized deception, concealment and distortion, and given it a name: *maskirovka*."

WILLIAM E. BURROWS, *Deep Black* (1986).

"A small newspaper which no one knows (in France, India, or Japan), a newspaper which is subsidized by the KGB, publishes a small notice prepared by the KGB.... After this, this small article, which no one would have noticed, is spread throughout the world by TASS [the Soviet official press agency].... Thus it becomes material already having international importance."

Former KGB general **OLEG KALUGIN** in 1992; quoted in Levin, "Efficacy of Propaganda" (1999).

"Deception is the attempt to mislead an adversary's intelligence analysis concerning the political, military, or economic situation he faces and to induce him, on the basis of those errors, to act in a way that advances one's own interests rather than his."

ABRAM SHULSKY, *Silent Warfare* (1993).

"Covert propaganda can be black (well hidden) or gray (disseminated with a thin veil of cover). ... Gray propaganda hides its source from the uninitiated public, but not from sophisticated observers.... Propaganda is black when the source is false and well concealed, or when the information itself is false.... Inside societies where there is little freedom of information, it is next to im-

possible to check on rumors, and so it is not surprising that both opponents and proponents of the regimes employ black propaganda."

ROY GODSON, *Dirty Tricks or Trump Cards* (1995).

"We engage in deception to do our job, but we must never let deception become a way of life."

DCI **JOHN DEUTCH**, 1995; quoted in the *New York Times Magazine*, 3 December 2000.

"Probably the most successful Soviet 'active measure' during the early years of the Gorbachev era, promoted around the world by a mixture of covert action and overt propaganda, was the claim that the AIDS virus had been manufactured by the Pentagon during genetic engineering experiments at Fort Detrick in Maryland. In the first six months of 1987 alone, the story received major news coverage in over forty Third World countries.... [Later,] Gorbachev was bitterly critical of a State Department publication [that was] based on CIA and other intelligence reports, which gave pride of place to Soviet attempts to blame the Pentagon for the AIDS virus. Despite Gorbachev's denunciation of the report, however, Soviet press coverage of the AIDS story was abruptly halted in the autumn of 1987."

CHRISTOPHER ANDREW, *For the President's Eyes Only* (1995).

"The Iraqis [during the 1990–91 Gulf war] exhibited an accurate understanding of the limitations facing U.S. technical collection assets. Their concealment techniques included the construction of buildings within buildings ... deliberately making buildings designed for the same purposes look different, concealing water and power lines leading into buildings, hiding the value of a target by omitting security fences and guard facilities, burying key facilities underground, moving equipment at night, and controlling the emissions from facilities."

JOHN DIAMOND, "U.S. Imagery Intelligence," *National Security Studies Quarterly* (spring 1997).

"It's not a failure of the CIA. It's a matter of their intelligence being good, our deception being better."

Indian nuclear scientist **G. BALACHANDRAN** on India's nuclear tests; quoted in the *Washington Times*, 17 May 1997.

"We've never found anything that's been successfully hidden."

AMROM KATZ, pioneering designer of U.S. space reconnaissance systems; quoted in the *Washington Times*, 18 May 1997. An important tautology.

"The Americans were rookies. They never learned to lie as well as we."

Former KGB veteran **OLEG KALUGIN** on Cold War intelligence operations; quoted in the *Chicago Tribune*, 13 September 1999.

"If you are prepared to lie to protect people's lives, not to be too flip about it, but it had better be a good lie."

JODY POWELL, former White House press secretary during the Carter administration, on deceiving a U.S. journalist who had asked whether the White House was planning a rescue attempt of the hostages in Iran; quoted in the *New York Times*, 7 October 2001.

DEFECTORS

The Literary Spy considers it a tiresome truism that all defectors are in some way defective. Are not we all? The central issue is whether any of us, defector or not, in our human frailty managed to do the right thing, act in the right way, and join the right side.

See also: Counterintelligence; Espionage & Spies; Fighting the Cold War

"*Hostium beneficio.* The kindness of the enemy."

JULIUS CAESAR on intelligence obtained from defectors; quoted in Austin and Rankov, *Exploratio* (1995).

"We must always mistrust men who come with information from the enemy's camp, as they may have been purposely sent by him. Such men should be kept under the strictest observation, being located where they can see or hear nothing of what is going on, and should never be allowed to go away on the pretence of gathering further information."

British Colonel **GEORGE FURSE**, *Information in War* (1895).

"In the immediate postwar years, the United States had a policy of accepting as defectors those people who spontaneously left Communist territory. . . . CIA assumed responsibility for the custody of defectors in October 1947, in response to an urgent appeal from the Department of State. The role came to the Agency by default, since no other element of the US government had been designated to fill it, and it remained with CIA through precedent rather than through formal assignment."

CIA historian **ROBERTA KNAPP**, quotation in CIA's Historical Intelligence Collection.

"Sec. 8. Whenever the Director [of Central Intelligence], the Attorney General, and the Commissioner of Immigration shall determine that the entry of a particular alien into the United States for permanent residence is in the interest of national security or essential to the furtherance of the national intelligence mission, such alien and his immediate family shall be given entry into the United

States for permanent residence without regard to their inadmissibility under the immigration or any other laws and regulations, or to the failure to comply with such laws and regulations pertaining to admissibility."

The Central Intelligence Agency Act of 1949; reproduced in Warner, *CIA Under Truman* (1994).

"[In the late 1940s and early 1950s,] firsthand information on the USSR was so hard to come by that the lowest dogface private deserting from the Red Army was considered a valuable source and immediately flown out of Austria to a defector center in Germany."

Former CIA operations officer **WILLIAM HOOD**, *Mole* (1993).

"[Defectors] had to be handled carefully to note the stage at which their memory began to be supplemented by their imagination and their strong political views."

Former DCI **WILLIAM COLBY**, *Honorable Men* (1978).

"The profession of defector demands great patience. Very few are suitably qualified."

JOHN LE CARRÉ [David Cornwell], *The Spy Who Came in from the Cold* (1963).

"I do not claim that all so-called defectors have come to the West for ideological reasons. Some come because they have failed in their jobs; some because they fear a shake-up in the regime may mean a demotion or worse; some are lured by the physical attractions of the West, human or material. But there is a large band who have come over to us from Communist officialdom for highly ideological reasons. They have been revolted by life in the Communist world and yearn for something better. Hence, for these cases I use the term 'de-

fector' sparingly and then with apology. I prefer to call them 'volunteers.'"

Former DCI **ALLEN DULLES**, *The Craft of Intelligence* (1963).

"I've never seen a man who had a good relationship with his father becoming a defector and be disloyal to the regime."

CIA psychiatrist **ALAN STUDNER**; quoted in Schecter and Deriabin, *The Spy Who Saved the World* (1995). Perhaps the typical defector has a father who is a scoundrel.

"We must make people want to defect to us. Why do our people always defect to the West?"

KGB chief **YURI ANDROPOV** after the defection of KGB officer Oleg Lyalin to Britain in 1971; quoted in Kalugin, *The First Directorate* (1994). Andropov didn't know?

"One day, a Cuban ship was passing through the Bosporus into the Black Sea when a man leapt off his ship in the middle of the Bosporus and evaded the gunfire from the deck.... A Cuban lieutenant and missile officer, he was ... a defector of real value. With the approval of Turkish authorities, he was quickly moved to a location elsewhere in Europe for intensive debriefing. He provided substantial and highly valuable information that allowed us to construct countermeasures against [Soviet surface-to-air] missiles. He apparently knew the crucial mathematical equation for the intercept trajectory of one of them, but couldn't remember it. Days went by. A blackboard was set up in the apartment he was occupying, and one night he suddenly awoke, stumbled to the blackboard, and scribbled out an equation. It was correct."

Veteran CIA operations officer **DUANE CLARRIDGE**, *A Spy for All Seasons* (1997).

"Most defectors either become alcoholics or suffer mental illness or both. Once they've been milked for all they're worth to us they're thrown away like old rags."

PHILIP AGEE, *Inside the Company* (1975). A former CIA officer who "defected" to Cuba, Agee should know.

"You must remember that every defector has just committed emotional suicide."

Senior CIA official; quoted in Phillips, *The Night Watch* (1978). And, one hopes, has passed through to heaven.

"Very few of those who seek political asylum in the United States are treated as defectors. Within the U.S. government, the term 'defector' has a specific and narrowly defined meaning. An individual becomes a defector under our laws and regulations when his bona fides have been established and he has demonstrated his possession of significant secret information."

Former senior CIA official CORD MEYER, *Facing Reality* (1980).

"Defectors are the lifeblood of Western intelligence services. . . . [A defector] brings information to up-date your knowledge of the opposition agency, the nuts and bolts of his organization, his order of battle, training methods, strategy and tactics, and the relationship between his agency and the opposition government. If he is well-placed in his service, or if he has prepared for his defection, then he brings clues to the identity of opposition agents and moles in your country—almost every major counter-intelligence coup since the war in the United States, France, Britain, Germany, Scandinavia, and Australia has been sparked off by a defection."

PHILLIP KNIGHTLEY, *The Second Oldest Profession* (1988).

"The evaluation of defectors is always difficult, since the agent debriefing a defector has to allow for boasting, exaggeration, and the creation of new stories when the truth is used up. Above all, he has to take into account the possibility of a fake defector intentionally sowing disinformation, such as the allegation that there is a mole high up in the agency."

ROBIN W. WINKS, *Cloak and Gown* (1987).

"The more solid the information from a defector, the more you should not trust him, and the more you should suspect he has something to hide."

JAMES ANGLETON, longtime CIA counterintelligence chief, according to former DDI Ray Cline; quoted in Mangold, *Cold Warrior* (1991). A rather self-defeating approach. As always with Angleton, the truth simply could not win over his suspicions.

"The really interesting thing about [James] Bond is that he would be what I call the ideal defector. Because if the money was better, the booze freer and the women easier over there in Moscow, he'd be off like a shot. Bond, you see, is the ultimate prostitute."

JOHN LE CARRÉ [David Cornwell]; cited in Horning, *The Mystery Lovers' Book of Quotations* (1989). Le Carré must never have read the Bond of Ian Fleming's novels, who genuinely loved his country; this caricature better suits many of the Bond movies.

"All defectors should be treated at arm's length and made to earn their keep, and as little feedback as possible should ever be given them."

Former MI5 officer PETER WRIGHT; quoted in Mangold, *Cold Warrior* (1991).

"Though [defectors] have brought much information, they have never fingered a 'mole' within the CIA. This is either good news, or it is very bad news."

ANGELO CODEVILLA, *Informing Statecraft* (1992). It was bad news; CIA officer Aldrich Ames was arrested in 1994 after spying for Moscow for nine years.

"No one who spied for the Soviet Union at any period between the October Revolution and the eve of the Gorbachev era can now be confident that his or her secrets are still secure."

CHRISTOPHER ANDREW on the defection of Vasili Mitrokhin, a KGB officer who brought out six cases of notes compiled from KGB archives, in *The Sword and the Shield: The Mitrokhin Archive* (1999).

"The CIA has always had an institutional bias in favor of information coming from recruited agents rather than [from] volunteers and defectors."

Former DCI **R. JAMES WOOLSEY** in the *Wall Street Journal*, 18 October 2001.

DIRECTORS OF CENTRAL INTELLIGENCE

It must be the worst job in Washington: often ignored, hated by a few, ridiculed by some, feared by many, the object of misunderstanding by most. DCIs try loyally to serve presidents who themselves often do not understand intelligence, and DCIs' penchant for serving up bad news often puts them in the doghouse or even on the street. No, if one wants a cozy and secure job in Washington, the Literary Spy suggests a stab at journalism.

See also: Leadership; Politicization; Presidents & Intelligence; U.S. Intelligence "Community"

"There should be created a Central Intelligence Agency headed by a Director who should be ap-pointed or removed by the President on the recommendation of the National Intelligence Authority. The committee believes that in order to insure continuity the Director should be appointed for a long term of years, preferably not less than six."

Report of the interagency Lovett Committee to Secretary of War Robert Patterson, 3 November 1945; in *FRUS 1945–1950: Emergence of the Intelligence Establishment* (1996), document 42. On 22 January 1946, President Truman created the position of the DCI, who reported to the National Intelligence Authority, a proto-National Security Council comprising the Secretaries of War, State, and Navy. The National Security Act of 1947 brought both CIA and the NSC into being. The DCI, alas, didn't get his long tenure.

"[Secretary of War] Patterson inquired whether anyone knew of a good man for the important position of Director of [Central] Intelligence. Mr. Lovett said the only name he had heard mentioned was that of Allen Dulles who was generally regarded as highly competent in that field. He had organized the best job of the OSS in Switzerland."

Minutes of the meeting of the Secretaries of State, War, and Navy to discuss "The Central Intelligence Agency," 14 November 1945; in *FRUS 1945–1950: Emergence of the Intelligence Establishment* (1996), document 45.

"I think it desirable that the N.I.A. nominate and the President appoint the Director of the Central Intelligence Agency. It is recommended, however, that the Director be an Army, Naval or Marine officer for the following reasons:

(a) This will assure a non-political administration of the intelligence effort with unbiased and objective intelligence estimates.

(b) He will be subject to military discipline, continuing after retirement. He can be required to avoid publicity which is undesirable in the conduct of an intelligence agency.

The term of office should be for four years to assure continuity."

Admiral **CHESTER NIMITZ**, Chief of Naval Operations, memorandum to Secretary of the Navy James Forrestal, undated but probably late December 1945; in *FRUS 1945–1950: Emergence of the Intelligence Establishment* (1996), document 57. Nimitz is suggesting that civilians can't be trusted to be objective and discreet.

"As you know, my interest in this subject is wholly objective as I am not a candidate for the job of Director and couldn't accept it even if it were offered me."

Rear Admiral **SIDNEY SOUERS**, deputy director of Naval Intelligence, memorandum to Clark Clifford, 27 December 1945; in *FRUS 1945–1950: Emergence of the Intelligence Establishment* (1996), document 64. Within a month Souers was the first DCI.

"To note that the CIA under its first three directors was of no great importance is an understatement."

WALTER LAQUEUR, *A World of Secrets* (1985). The first two DCIs, who actually headed CIG before CIA came into being, were Rear Admiral Sidney Souers and Lieutenant General Hoyt Vandenberg. The third DCI, who was the first director of CIA, was Rear Admiral Roscoe Hillenkoetter.

"I want to go home."

DCI #1, Rear Admiral **SIDNEY SOUERS**, not long after his appointment in January 1946, to a question asked by a former OSS man, "So, what do you want to do?"; quoted in Riebling, *Wedge: The Secret War Between the FBI and CIA* (1994).

"To insure the most beneficial results in the Central Intelligence Group it is necessary that the Director be an officer to whom the specialists will look for leadership and guidance based on a thorough and comprehensive knowledge of this complex subject.... Lieutenant General [Hoyt] Vandenberg is 47 years of age, has a fine war record,

is regarded as an outstanding officer and is keenly interested in intelligence. His leadership in G-2 has been strong and determined. He has demonstrated his recognition of the necessity for the reorientation of the intelligence structure."

DCI **SIDNEY SOUERS**, memorandum of 7 May 1946 to the president's chief of staff, Admiral William Leahy, recommending his successor as DCI; in *FRUS 1945–1950: Emergence of the Intelligence Establishment* (1996), document 149.

"It seems to me that Lieutenant General [Hoyt] Vandenberg is the proper person for this position —he knows it from 'A to Z,' he is a diplomat and will be able to get along with the State and Navy, as well as the War Department, and if it will not completely cripple General Eisenhower I would like very much to have Lieutenant General Vandenberg assigned to serve as the Director of the Central Intelligence Group."

President **HARRY TRUMAN** to Secretary of War Robert Patterson, 16 May 1946; in *FRUS 1945–1950: Emergence of the Intelligence Establishment* (1996), document 152. It didn't completely cripple Eisenhower, and Vandenberg was sworn in the following month.

"Although [Lieutenant General Hoyt] Vandenberg had no long-term interest in the subject, he had very positive ideas about the proper role of the DCI and the CIA. He had a poor opinion of Souers' cautious, consultative approach . . . and was resolved not to follow it. . . . His instinct was to take command and issue orders. In this he was a reincarnation of General [William] Donovan. Indeed, he outdid Donovan, who had been more realistic. Vandenberg's simple conception was to build up the prospective CIA into an independent, entirely self-sufficient, national intelligence service."

CIA officer and historian **LUDWELL LEE MONTAGUE**, *General Walter Bedell Smith as Director of Central Intelligence* (1992).

"Hoyt Vandenberg was the personification of an Air Force general. Forty-seven years old, lean and handsome to the point of glamour, he was fresh from a brilliant wartime record in the Army Air Force. . . . When General Vandenberg took over CIG [in June 1946], he was determined to turn what many insiders still considered to be a fragile bureaucratic curiosity, manned by a hotchpotch of civilian and military personnel, into a national intelligence service. In July he created an Office of Research and Estimates (ORE) to provide the White House and other agencies with daily and weekly current intelligence summaries and analysis. The thunder of the State Department's furious objections was still shaking the walls when, without apparently pausing to catch his breath, Vandenberg simply absorbed the SSU, its responsibility for intelligence and counterintelligence abroad, its cadre of experienced personnel, foreign stations, and files into CIG."

> Former DCI **RICHARD HELMS**, *A Look over My Shoulder* (2003).

"Whoever takes the post of Director of Central Intelligence should make that his life work. . . . Appointment as Chief of Central Intelligence should be somewhat comparable to appointment to high judicial office, and should be equally free from interference due to political changes. In fact, the duties the Chief will have to perform will call for the judicial temperament in high degree. An appointee must gain that critical faculty which can only come of long experience and profound knowledge to enable him to separate the wheat from the chaff in the volume of information which will pass through his office."

> **ALLEN DULLES** (then a private citizen), statement submitted to the Senate Armed Services Committee, 25 April 1947, in consideration of the proposed National Security Act; in CIA's Historical Intelligence Collection. Why, Allen Dulles would be perfect for it.

"Since 1947 Directors of Central Intelligence . . . have had the responsibility of coordinating national intelligence collection and production without a full measure of the authority they needed to do so."

> **MICHAEL WARNER**, *Central Intelligence: Origin and Evolution* (2001).

"Rear Admiral Roscoe H. Hillenkoetter became Director of Central Intelligence on May 1, 1947. . . . [He] came to office with the advantage of becoming the first Director of Central Intelligence to serve as a statutory official; unlike his [two] predecessors, he would head an agency established by law and enjoying regular appropriations. At the same time, Hillenkoetter inherited most of the controversies that [DCI] General [Hoyt] Vandenberg had begun. . . . Vandenberg had been so energetic and aggressive and had served so briefly that most of the uproar he provoked was at full strength when Hillenkoetter took over."

> U.S. Department of State, *Foreign Relations of the United States, 1945–1950: Emergence of the Intelligence Establishment* (1996), introduction to "Hillenkoetter's Tenure as Director of Central Intelligence."

"Virtually every individual who has had occasion to deal with or to look into the activities of the Central Intelligence Agency has recognized that the system of rotating the director and the top staff personnel at frequent intervals has had disastrous consequences. . . . I am convinced that continuity of direction is essential for the Central Intelligence Agency not only for the reasons which make it desirable in any governmental department but also because secret intelligence and secret operations are the most highly specialized undertakings, and it is very harmful to be constantly educating a series of new chiefs and their immediate staffs."

CIA operations chief **FRANK WISNER**, memorandum to State Department Counselor Charles Bohlen, 15 April 1949; in *FRUS 1945–1950: Emergence of the Intelligence Establishment* (1996), document 381.

"[In 1950,] CIA lacked clout. The military and diplomatic people ignored our statutory authority . . . and the CIA leadership lacked the power to compel compliance. Our director was Rear Admiral Roscoe Hillenkoetter, a thoroughly decent, unpretentious man, but [only] a rear admiral. In the hierarchical maze of Washington, his authority scarcely extended beyond the front door."

Former DDI **R. JACK SMITH** on DCI #3, Hillenkoetter, in *The Unknown CIA* (1989). Former DCI Richard Helms noted that "Admiral Hillenkoetter's single star did not glow brightly enough for him to force the Pentagon's three star generals and admirals to comply with CIA's legislative charter." See Helms, *A Look over My Shoulder* (2003).

"It is symptomatic that when Truman called the NSC together in June 1950 to deal with the first real crisis of the era [the Korean War], [DCI Roscoe] Hillenkoetter was not present."

Former DDI **RAY CLINE**, *Secrets, Spies and Scholars* (1976).

"I expect the worst and I am sure I won't be disappointed."

General **WALTER BEDELL SMITH** on being nominated by President Truman as DCI, letter to John D. Hickerson, Assistant Secretary of State for U.N. Affairs, 23 August 1950; in Smith papers, Eisenhower Library, Abilene, Kansas. That same month, Smith told a senior FBI official, "I'm afraid I'm accepting a poisoned chalice." See Riebling, *Wedge: The Secret War Between the FBI and CIA* (1994).

"General Walter Bedell Smith . . . was a shrewd, dynamic man with broad experience and ab-

solutely no tolerance for fools. It was often said that he was the most even-tempered man in the world—he was always angry. . . . For the first time since [OSS director General William] Donovan, central intelligence was in the hands of a man with vision and drive, a man with the prestige persuasive to military commanders, ambassadors, and Congressmen, and finally, a man who had the full support of a President who wanted action."

Former DDI **RAY CLINE** on DCI #4 in *Secrets, Spies and Scholars* (1976).

"It's interesting to see all you fellows here. It'll be even more interesting to see how many of you are here a few months from now."

DCI **WALTER BEDELL SMITH** in his first staff meeting at CIA, according to the Agency's first legislative counsel, Walter Pforzheimer; quoted in *Studies in Intelligence* 10 (winter–spring 2001).

"An exacting, hard-hitting executive who brooked neither mediocrity nor ineptitude, a man who not only barked but bit."

Former DDI **R. JACK SMITH** on DCI Walter Bedell Smith, in *The Unknown CIA* (1989).

"[Walter Bedell Smith] put CIA on the map. If it hadn't been for Bedell, I don't think there would be a CIA today. He made it what it is: he firmly established it as an important element of government, both on the Hill with Congress and in the Executive Branch, particularly in the Defense Department."

Former CIA senior official **SAMUEL HALPERN** in a 1995 interview; in Weber, *Spymasters* (1999).

"The Director [of Central Intelligence] and his principal deputies and assistants are non-political appointees and, while the Director himself must undoubtedly be a man whom the Chief Executive is willing to accept . . . it is unlikely that you will ever have a Director whose status will change with changes in the Administration."

DCI **WALTER BEDELL SMITH** in late 1952 to junior CIA officers. Smith stepped down as DCI in the early weeks of the Eisenhower administration to become Undersecretary of State.

"It was very hard to have affection for General [Walter Bedell] Smith, because he was so frosty and chilly, but he was a very, very great man."

CIA's first legislative counsel, **WALTER PFORZHEIMER**; quoted in *Studies in Intelligence* 10 (winter–spring 2001).

"Here is one of the most peculiar types of operation any government can have, and it probably takes a strange kind of genius to run it."

President **DWIGHT EISENHOWER** on the leadership of Allen Dulles, DCI #5; quoted in Ranelagh, *The Agency* (1986).

"No other man left such a mark on the Agency. . . . Allen Dulles was unquestionably the 'Great White Case Officer' for all of CIA, spending at least three-fourths of his time and energy, I would judge, on clandestine collection and covert action tasks. . . . I suppose he spent less than 5 percent of his efforts on [analysis, and] often took a malicious delight in disregarding his higher-ranking advisers and siding with the junior analysts."

Former DDI **RAY CLINE**, *Secrets, Spies and Scholars* (1976).

"By golly, I am going to make a policy decision!"

DCI **ALLEN DULLES** upon deciding to release the text of Khrushchev's "secret speech"; quoted in Cline, *Secrets, Spies and Scholars* (1976).

"I'm not going to be able to change Allen. I have two alternatives, either to get rid of him . . . or keep him with his limitations. I'd rather have Allen as

my chief intelligence officer with his limitations than anyone else I know."

President **DWIGHT EISENHOWER** on DCI Dulles; quoted in Leary, *The Central Intelligence Agency* (1984).

"I thought that the one thing that could be most damaging to the Agency at the time of presidential change is that if you establish a precedent that when a new President . . . is in, change the Director [of Central Intelligence] and get somebody from the same party as the President. I've always felt that intelligence ought to be kept out of politics."

DCI **ALLEN DULLES** recalling when President-elect Kennedy asked him to stay on as DCI; quoted in Weber, *Spymasters* (1999). President Carter in 1977 replaced George H. W. Bush with Stansfield Turner, thereby establishing the precedent Dulles had feared.

"John McCone was exacting and direct to the point of brusqueness. . . . [National Estimates chief] Sherman Kent used to delight in asking senior CIA officers, 'What color are John McCone's eyes?' The answer was always some variant of 'ice-cold blue.' They were in fact dark brown. But it was true, his mind and persona were steely-blue eyed."

Former DDI **R. JACK SMITH** on DCI #6, John McCone, in *The Unknown CIA* (1989).

"[John McCone] is the only DCI who ever took his role of providing substantive intelligence analysis and estimates to the President as his first priority job, and the only one who considered his duties as coordinating supervisor of the whole intelligence community to be a more important responsibility than CIA's own clandestine and covert programs. . . . He hated being called a 'spymaster.'"

Former DDI **RAY CLINE**, *Secrets, Spies and Scholars* (1976).

"The best director the CIA ever had."

Former DCI **WILLIAM COLBY** on John McCone in *Honorable Men* (1978).

"I've been trying to get Johnson to sit down and read these papers. When I can't even get the President to read the summaries, it's time for me to leave."

DCI **JOHN McCONE** before resigning in April 1965; quoted in Powers, *The Man Who Kept the Secrets* (1979).

"The point need not be belabored. Admiral Raborn's background did not qualify him to direct CIA. He had no extensive service overseas; he knew little about foreign affairs and had little interest in international politics. He knew no more about intelligence methods and techniques than the average naval officer. . . . The saving grace during this period was that Lyndon Johnson had named Richard Helms as Raborn's deputy director."

Former DDI **R. JACK SMITH** on DCI #7, Vice Admiral William Raborn, in *The Unknown CIA* (1989).

"Vice Admiral William F. Raborn, Jr., a Naval Academy graduate, is the only DCI who stepped into office with no experience in intelligence. . . . Admiral Raborn's effort and hard work notwithstanding, it was clear that President Johnson had thrust him into the wrong job. To his credit, I never heard Red complain. . . . It was as easy as it was unfair to make fun of him, but it was impossible for me to dampen it down within the Agency."

Former DCI **RICHARD HELMS**, *A Look over My Shoulder* (2003).

"Who is this fellow Oligarchy anyway?"

Attributed to DCI **WILLIAM F. RABORN, JR.**, who allegedly asked the question during a briefing on a particular country's leadership; quoted in Ranelagh, *The Agency* (1986).

"Dulles ran a happy ship, McCone ran a tight ship, and Raborn runs a sinking ship."

CIA saying on the tenure of DCI William F. Raborn, Jr., possibly apocryphal; quoted in Jeffreys-Jones and Lownie, *North American Spies* (1991).

"The CIA rejected [DCI William F. Raborn, Jr.] the way a human body rejects a transplant."

THOMAS POWERS, *The Man Who Kept the Secrets* (1979).

"A sure-footed, cool professional, the very model of a new breed in American government service, the professional intelligence officer . . . Helms's leadership enabled CIA to become a unified, cohesive organization for the first time. . . . The year 1966 opened a golden era in CIA's history."

Former DDI **R. JACK SMITH** on DCI #8, Richard Helms, in *The Unknown CIA* (1989).

"Disciplined, meticulously fair and discreet, [Richard] Helms performed his duties with the total objectivity essential to an effective intelligence service. . . . No one is promoted through the ranks to Director of CIA who is not tempered in many battles; Helms was strong and wary. His urbanity was coupled with extraordinary tenacity; his smile did not always include his eyes. He had seen administrations come and go and he understood that in Washington knowledge was power. . . . At the same time I never knew him to misuse his knowledge or his power. He never forgot that his integrity guaranteed his effectiveness, that his best weapon with Presidents was a reputation for reliability."

HENRY KISSINGER, *White House Years* (1979). The Literary Spy noticed Kissinger in attendance at Helms's funeral on 20 November 2002.

"Asked for an example of Helms's characteristic utterance, three of his old friends came up with the same dry phrase: 'Let's get on with it.'"

THOMAS POWERS, *The Man Who Kept the Secrets* (1979).

"In 1971 a relatively unknown economist in the Bureau of the Budget, James Schlesinger, made a very sensible study of central intelligence. For his pains he was made Director of Central Intelligence."

Former DDI **RAY CLINE**, *Secrets, Spies and Scholars* (1976).

"This is a gentleman's club, and I am no gentleman."

Attributed to **JAMES SCHLESINGER** on his arrival at Langley as DCI #9 in 1973; quoted in Powers, *The Man Who Kept the Secrets* (1979).

"I can't take you through there. I don't think either one of us would emerge alive."

DCI **JAMES SCHLESINGER** to a visitor who had asked for a tour of the operations directorate's technical shop; quoted in Miller, *Spying for America* (1989). Schlesinger's purges and disdain for some of the old guard at CIA made him one of the most unpopular DCIs.

"It appeared to me that James Schlesinger, my successor as DCI, came to office with firm instructions from [President] Nixon: Jim was to shake up the Agency, trim it down, and rid it of what Nixon perceived to be the existing regime of anti-Nixon Georgetown dilettantes and free-range liberals. . . . During his brief tenure as DCI, Schlesinger moved to make changes. . . . It was in this period that some one thousand employees, a significant number of them from the operations element . . . were fired, retired, or caused to resign [in an] abrupt and unnecessarily callous dismissal."

Former DCI **RICHARD HELMS**, *A Look over My Shoulder* (2003).

"[DCI James] Schlesinger, for all his toughness, was a devoted family man who could enjoy such gentle pursuits as bird-watching. When he became Secretary of Defense in the spring of 1973 he left behind a CIA seething with resentment and rancor. But there was also a residue of admiration which remains today. Despite his tactics, his goals were sound and the results beneficial."

Former senior CIA operations officer **DAVID ATLEE PHILLIPS**, *The Night Watch* (1978). Faint praise indeed —he liked bird-watching and he meant well. Even so, this is the only good thing the Literary Spy has ever heard about Schlesinger from a former CIA officer.

"Fire everyone if necessary."

DCI **JAMES SCHLESINGER**, May 1973, to CIA operations chief William Colby after hearing news reports that Howard Hunt had used CIA equipment to break into the office of Daniel Ellsberg's psychiatrist; quoted in Colby, *Honorable Men* (1978).

"Nixon's revenge."

Informal CIA moniker for DCI James Schlesinger; cited in Riebling, *Wedge: The Secret War Between the FBI and CIA* (1994). Revenge for what? For refusing to go along with the Watergate cover-up.

"Had William Colby been born in the sixteenth century, his character and mindset might have led him into the Society of Jesus and a life as a Jesuit soldier of the Counter-Reformation. Having been born in the twentieth, he had joined the CIA and become a soldier of the Cold War. A need to serve and a desire to serve in secret were dominant traits in his personality."

NEIL SHEEHAN on DCI #10, William Colby, in *A Bright Shining Lie* (1988).

"Someone is supposed to have polled a group of ex-CIA officers as to which former DCI would they like to have at their side if they were stranded on an island. If there was an ample supply of good food and drink available, Allen Dulles was the overwhelming choice; if conditions smacked of danger, Richard Helms or William Colby won the nod."

> NATHAN MILLER, *Spying for America* (1989). That "someone" was former senior CIA operations officer David Atlee Phillips; see his *The Night Watch* (1978).

"Persons appointed to the position of Director of Central Intelligence should be individuals of stature, independence, and integrity. In making this appointment, consideration should be given to individuals from outside the career service of the CIA, although promotion from within should not be barred."

> Rockefeller Commission Report, June 1975; cited in Cline, *Secrets, Spies and Scholars* (1976).

"As presently defined, the DCI's job is burdensome in the extreme. He is to serve the roles of chief intelligence officer to the President, manager of community intelligence activities, and senior executive in the CIA. History has demonstrated that the job of the DCI as community manager and as head of the CIA are competing, not complementary roles."

> ANNE KARALEKAS, "The History of the Central Intelligence Agency" (prepared in 1975 for the Church Committee), in Leary, *The Central Intelligence Agency* (1984).

"[In November 1975] President Ford appointed a very able new DCI, Ambassador George Bush, a man with broad political experience, with good knowledge of foreign affairs, and with a reputation for personal integrity."

> Former DDI RAY CLINE on DCI #11, George Bush, in *Secrets, Spies and Scholars* (1976). Made a good President, too.

"Almost every friend I had in politics felt this would be the dead end, the absolute end of any politics in the future for me. And I kind of thought that maybe was true. That happily proved to be wrong."

> Former President GEORGE H. W. BUSH on his appointment as DCI in 1975; quoted in the *Houston Chronicle*, 22 April 1999.

"[George H. W. Bush] quickly proved by his performance that he was prepared to put politics aside and to devote all his considerable ability and enthusiasm to restoring the morale of an institution that had been battered enough by successive investigations. . . . He leaned over backward to protect the objectivity and independence of the Agency's estimates and to avoid slanting the results to fit some preconceived notion of what the President wanted to hear. On the other hand, his close relationship to Ford and the trust that the President obviously had in him gave Bush an access to the White House and an influence in the wider Washington bureaucracy that Colby had never enjoyed. Not only did morale improve as a result, but through Bush the Agency's views carried new weight and influence in the top reaches of the Ford administration."

> Former senior CIA official CORD MEYER, *Facing Reality* (1980).

"It's the best job in Washington."

> DCI GEORGE BUSH; quoted in Turner, *Secrecy and Democracy* (1985). Unfortunately, Turner didn't believe him.

"When George Bush was Director of Central Intelligence, he made a practice of letting analysts give presentations to high-level officials, up to and including the President. This may have reflected Bush's appreciation of the fact that he lacked the intelligence experience of such predecessors as Colby, Helms, and Dulles, but it also allowed the consumer to communicate directly with the analyst. In the give-and-take, the analyst would find out more about the specific concerns of the consumer and be better prepared to carry out the analysis. By most accounts, this practice also bolstered the morale of analysts, who believed they were making a meaningful contribution to policy."

BRUCE BERKOWITZ and ALLAN GOODMAN, *Strategic Intelligence* (1989).

"It is important to remember that no Director of Central Intelligence has ever approached the independence of [FBI director] J. Edgar Hoover. Almost all of the DCIs, in fact, lost the confidence of their Presidents and were fired or replaced."

THOMAS POWERS, *The Man Who Kept the Secrets* (1979).

"We talked for a few more minutes, and then the President turned to the Vice President and said he'd just narrowed the candidates to one. And my 31-year naval career flew out the window."

Admiral STANSFIELD TURNER on being asked by President Carter to be DCI #12 in 1977; quoted in the *New York Times*, 16 June 1985.

"Geoff, I've just left the Oval Office. I'm going to be the Chief Bean Counter!"

Admiral STANSFIELD TURNER telling his son in "code" over the telephone that he was President Carter's nominee to be DCI #12, in *Secrecy and Democracy* (1985).

"Carter's choice of DCI set an unhappy precedent. . . . For the first time, the DCI was dismissed simply because there was a change of administration. It has been assumed ever since that a newly elected president will automatically sack a DCI appointed by a president of the other political party."

CHRISTOPHER ANDREW, *For the President's Eyes Only* (1995). An assumption that has been stopped cold by the son of DCI George Bush.

"[Stansfield] Turner arrived at CIA leading with his chin and with a chip on his shoulder."

Former DCI ROBERT GATES, *From the Shadows* (1996).

"The admiral [DCI Stansfield Turner] always referred to his ward as 'the CIA,' instead of simply 'CIA,' as other directors had learned to do; it was a minor point that symbolized a major estrangement."

MARK RIEBLING, *Wedge: The Secret War Between the FBI and CIA* (1994).

"[Admiral Stansfield] Turner brought to the CIA the very qualities that many believed necessary in an Agency director: exceptional technical competence and the ability to manage an academic community."

RHODRI JEFFREYS-JONES, *The CIA and American Democracy* (1989). The "many" forgot about the ability to inspire.

"In my briefing sessions with [President Carter], I took him capacitors and resistors and stuff."

DCI STANSFIELD TURNER; quoted in Ranelagh, *The Agency* (1986). One compensates as one can.

"Ever since the [General William] Donovan days, it was a tradition that you stood up when the Director came into the room. That was a very clear indication of how you felt about him. But I remember once when [DCI Stansfield] Turner walked in. Nobody stood."

Former senior CIA official; quoted in Riebling, *Wedge: The Secret War Between the FBI and CIA* (1994).

"Of intelligence I had so little grip
That they offered me the Directorship.
With my brass-bound head of oak so stout,
I don't have to know what it's all about.
CHORUS: When he knows a whole ship
    from A to Z,
He surely can con the Agency.

"I know a man o' war from a bumboat raft,
But what kind of ship is called a trade-craft?
I never sailed a KUBARK, or spliced a PRQ,
And what's an esti-mate, I never had a clue.
CHORUS: He's stayed quite clueless so
    successfully
That he remains Director of the Agency.

"If anyone objects, I'll have him walk the plank;
If you don't think I mean it, just ask good old
    Hank.
I may run the ship aground if I keep on so,
But I don't care a fig; I'll be the CNO.
CHORUS: He'll be the CNO, so thinks he.
So why give a fig for the Agency?"

> Anonymous internal CIA doggerel protesting the leadership of DCI Stansfield Turner, November 1977; in CIA's Historical Intelligence Collection. In this Gilbert and Sullivan parody "Hank" is Enno Henry Knoche, deputy to the previous DCI, George Bush; Knoche was sacked after four months by Turner. Official Agency releases have identified KUBARK as a cryptonym meaning "CIA."

"It does not require special expertise in personnel or business management to conclude that an average tenure of less than three years is too short for optimal performance."

> WALTER LAQUEUR, *A World of Secrets* (1985). Laqueur spoke of the average length of service for DCIs from Sidney Souers (1946) to William Casey (1981–87). How much more he must lament the fact that CIA in the 1990s had five directors in six years.

"You understand, I call him Ron."

> DCI-designate WILLIAM CASEY interrupting a CIA briefing on the DCI's relationship with the president, December 1980; interview with senior CIA official Richard Lehman in *Studies in Intelligence* (summer 2000).

"I pass the test that says a man who isn't a socialist at 20 has no heart, and a man who is a socialist at 40 has no head."

> DCI #13 WILLIAM CASEY; quoted in the *Washington Post*, 7 May 1987.

"The president's chief intelligence officer must have ready access to the president if he is to carry out his mission effectively. Moreover, it must be comfortable access. Both men must feel easy, confident of the other's support. All DCIs want exactly this, but its achievement is more often desired than realized. It cannot be legislated or commanded. It is the product of personal chemistry and compatibility of mind."

> Former DDI R. JACK SMITH, *The Unknown CIA* (1989).

"No CIA director retained from one administration to the next is destined to succeed. All in this category were dismissed or felt obliged to resign. . . . The inescapable lesson from CIA history—albeit a lesson that neither Presidents nor DCIs are eager to draw explicitly—is that it works better when a new president appoints his own CIA director."

> Former DDI JOHN HELGERSON, *CIA Briefings* (1996).

"[William Casey] had not come to the CIA with the purpose of making it better, managing it more effectively, reforming it, or improving the quality of intelligence. . . . Bill Casey came to CIA primarily to wage war against the Soviet Union. . . . Without parallel in the history of postwar American intelligence, Bill Casey as DCI had his own foreign policy agenda and, as a Cabinet member, pursued that agenda vigorously and often in opposition to the Secretary of State."

Former DCI **ROBERT GATES**, *From the Shadows* (1996).

"Casey was an inappropriate choice. We would be having a Cabinet discussion of agriculture and there would be Casey. That shouldn't be—the DCI should not enter into policy discussions."

Former President and DCI **GEORGE H. W. BUSH** in 1993; quoted in Helgerson, *CIA Briefings* (1996).

"William Casey was the last great buccaneer from OSS."

Former CIA operations chief **CLAIR GEORGE** in congressional testimony, August 1987; cited in Riebling, *Wedge: The Secret War Between the FBI and CIA* (1994).

"The only man in government who doesn't need a secure telephone."

CIA folk saying about DCI **WILLIAM CASEY**, whose speech was nearly unintelligible and typically became even worse when speaking with journalists or congressmen.

"You know that country and western song, 'Take This Job and Shove It'?"

Acting DCI **ROBERT GATES**, asked by a reporter how he liked being President Reagan's nominee for DCI, February 1987; in Gates, *From the Shadows* (1996). Gates would have his chance later, as DCI #15, late in President George H. W. Bush's term.

"[William] Webster was a godsend to the Agency and to me. He had a huge reputation for integrity, honesty, and fidelity to the Constitution. After some twenty years as a federal judge and as FBI director, just as he was preparing to return to private life and a deserved opportunity to prosper, he put his reputation on the line for CIA. He

agreed, with CIA still under a shadow [from the Iran-Contra affair], to do another public service for his country and his President. Bill would later be criticized from time to time for his lack of expertise in foreign affairs and more—but none of that, in my view, amounted to a hill of beans compared to what he brought to CIA that May [of 1987]: leadership, the respect of Congress, and a sterling character."

Former DCI **ROBERT GATES** on DCI #14, in *From the Shadows* (1996).

"We could probably have overcome [William] Webster's ego, his lack of experience with foreign affairs, his small-town-America world perspective, and even his yuppier-than-thou arrogance. What we couldn't overcome was that he was a lawyer. . . . All his training as a lawyer and as a judge [told him] that you didn't do illegal things. He never could accept that this is exactly what the CIA does when it operates abroad. We break the laws of other countries. It's how we collect information. It's why we're in business. Webster had an insurmountable problem with the raison d'etre of the organization he was brought in to run."

Former senior CIA operations officer **DUANE CLAR-RIDGE**, *A Spy for All Seasons* (1997).

"Not to be liked."

Former DCI (#16) **R. JAMES WOOLSEY** on the DCI's job description; quoted in the *Washington Post*, 27 December 2001. Short, sweet, and true.

"Like William Webster before him, [John] Deutch demonstrated no real interest in supporting the CIA. . . . To the contrary, the more he attacked the [DO], the more the media and some in Congress applauded. Deutch was clearly using his time at the CIA and his attitude toward it to advance his own ambitions. He and Webster are unique among the CIA directors in this regard."

> Former senior CIA operations officer **DUANE CLAR-RIDGE**, *A Spy for All Seasons* (1997).

"It's a very hard job."

> **JOHN DEUTCH** at the end of his tenure as DCI #17; quoted in the *Washington Post*, 6 December 1996.

"George is a tremendously loyal and devoted public servant. The time I realized how devoted a deputy he was was in an extremely important meeting with important foreign dignitaries. He cleared the room to tell me I needed to zip up my fly."

> Former DCI **JOHN DEUTCH** after Acting Director George Tenet was nominated to succeed him; quoted in the *New York Times*, 20 March 1997.

"I served under five different DCIs from 1990–1998. You could not run a successful bowling alley with that kind of turnover, much less the nation's premier intelligence agency."

> Former CIA Inspector General **FRED HITZ** in *Insight Magazine*, 15 April 2002.

"Nobody who knew me when I was younger believed that I would ever be Director of CIA. I had the biggest mouth in town. No one would ever believe I could keep a secret. I want to tell you that I have learned my lessons. I'm very discreet now; I don't say anything to anybody."

> DCI #18 **GEORGE TENET** at Cardozo High School in New York, 11 June 1999.

"If President Jimmy Carter had taken up Mr. Bush on his offer to stay on as director of central intelligence during Mr. Carter's tenure, the dominos of American political history might have tumbled in quite a different way. Mr. Bush might never have

run for the Republican presidential nomination in 1980, he might never have been tapped to be Ronald Reagan's running mate, and his son might not be ... the 43rd president of the United States."

> **JAMES RISEN**, "Keeping CIA Chief Puts Pressure on Relationship," *New York Times*, 20 January 2001.

"Nobody wants to disappoint George Tenet. There's something about him."

> Senior Palestinian official in rare agreement with Israeli negotiators about DCI Tenet's role as American mediator in the Mideast; quoted in the *New York Times*, 16 June 2001.

"George Tenet, the Middle East diplomat who returns to Langley, Va., from time to time to warm the D.C.I.'s chair ..."

> **WILLIAM SAFIRE**, in the *New York Times*, 9 July 2001.

"We cannot be second-guessing our team, and I'm not going to. The nation's at war. We need to encourage Congress to frankly leave the man alone. [DCI George] Tenet's doing a good job. And if he's not, blame me, not him."

> President **GEORGE W. BUSH** to Republican congressmen, 27 September 2001; quoted in *Time*, 31 December 2001.

"The problem with being director of the CIA is you have to bat a thousand. If you bat .900 or .450, you're only remembered for the ones you missed."

> Former national security advisor **SAMUEL BERGER**; quoted in the *Baltimore Sun*, 6 February 2002.

"I was fortunate and indeed privileged to have our paths cross. I could have had no finer mentor, no better teacher, no wiser friend. Whatever the problem, I knew he had faced it. Whatever the challenge, I knew he had met it. And I always knew he was in my corner. In the toughest of times, it was his voice on my answering machine, his notes in the mail, or the phone call where he would simply say keep your head up—get on with it, always get on with it—because there is so much at stake."

DCI **GEORGE TENET**'s remarks at the memorial service for former DCI Richard Helms, 20 November 2002.

DOMESTIC ACTIVITIES

Whether a country's premier intelligence service involves itself in domestic operations, such as opening citizens' mail or spying on political dissidents, rather directly reflects that country's degree of democracy. To the Literary Spy, the American experience makes two things clear: first, that our country has not gone unsullied in this regard; and second, that always and everywhere there is a profound resistance to and distaste for those times when the line is crossed.

See also: FBI & Law Enforcement; Fighting the Cold War

"A fourth line of policy is that of endeavoring to get regular information about every man's sayings and doings. This entails a secret police."

ARISTOTLE (384–322 B.C.), *Politics,* Book V. Aristotle is describing how tyrannies preserve themselves.

"So they awaited their opportunity and sent agents to pose as upright men, and to catch him out in something he might say and so enable them to hand him over to the jurisdiction and authority of the governor."

Luke 20:20 (New Jerusalem).

"It is a strange desire to seek power and lose liberty."

FRANCIS BACON, *Of Great Place* (1601).

"Under cover of 'Liberty of speech,' 'Liberty of the press' and 'habeas corpus' they [the Confederacy] hoped to keep on foot amongst us a most efficient corps of spies, informers, suppliers, and aiders and abettors of their cause in a thousand ways."

President **ABRAHAM LINCOLN**; quoted in Andrew, *For the President's Eyes Only* (1995).

"Do not think that I seek forms of revolutionary justice; we are not now in need of justice. It is war now—face to face, a fight to the finish. Life or death! I propose, I demand, an organ for the revolutionary settlement of accounts with counter-revolutionaries."

FELIKS DZERZHINSKY addressing other members of Russia's new Bolshevik regime, 20 December 1918; quoted in Andrew and Gordievsky, *KGB* (1990). The regime responded by creating the Cheka, Soviet Russia's first secret police. Like all its successors, including the KGB, the Cheka's primary responsibility was internal security.

"To combat popular opposition to the war, [President] Wilson set up a Committee on Public Information, under George Creel. To arouse support for the war, the Creel Committee whipped up hatred of Germany and all things German. . . . Aroused to fury at an enemy 3,000 miles distant whom they could not strike at directly, civilians sought enemies within. . . . Men suspected of disloyalty were forced to kneel to kiss the flag. Supposedly responsible Red Cross leaders warned that German-Americans had infiltrated the Red Cross to put ground glass in bandages; while in humorless patriotic zeal sauerkraut was renamed 'liberty cabbage.' . . . Under the Espionage Act of

1917 and the Sedition law of 1918, more than 1,500 persons were arrested."

WILLIAM E. LEUCHTENBERG, *The Perils of Prosperity, 1914–32* (1958). Wilson was just one of several presidents who saw in domestic dissent foreign subversion. And doesn't the "liberty cabbage" prefigure "freedom fries"?

"The Red Scare reached its culmination with the so-called Palmer raids. [J. Edgar] Hoover instructed his undercover agents to call meetings of suspected organizations in thirty-three cities across the nation on the night of January 2, 1920, and then swooped down upon them. Mass arrests were made without warrants.... In Detroit, about eight hundred people were imprisoned for up to six days in a dark, windowless corridor.... In Newark, a man was arrested because he 'looked like a radical,' while another was seized when he stopped to inquire what was going on. Nationwide, the night's haul included more than four thousand suspected radicals and aliens, including the entire leadership of the communist movement."

NATHAN MILLER on Attorney General A. Mitchell Palmer's arrests and deportations of radicals and leftists during the Red Scare of 1919–20, in *Spying for America* (1989).

"Not for at least half a century, perhaps at no time in our history, had there been such a wholesale violation of civil liberties."

WILLIAM E. LEUCHTENBERG on the Red Scare of 1919–20, in *The Perils of Prosperity, 1914–32* (1958). Uh, Professor, are we forgetting two and a half centuries of slavery?

"There is no time to waste on hairsplitting over infringement of liberty."

The *Washington Post* approving the Palmer raids of January 1920; quoted in Miller, *Spying for America* (1989). Not the *Post*'s finest hour.

"There is always the possibility that a secret police may become a menace to free government and free institutions, because it carries with it the possibility of abuses of power which are not always quickly apprehended or understood.... It is important that its activities be strictly limited to the performance of those functions for which it was created and that its agents themselves not be above the law or beyond its reach.... When a police system passes beyond these limits, it is dangerous to the proper administration of justice and to human liberty, which it should be our first concern to cherish."

Attorney General **HARLAN FISKE STONE** in the *New York Times*, 10 May 1924; cited in U.S. Senate, *Final Report of the Senate Select Committee to Study Governmental Operations with respect to Intelligence Activities* [the Church Committee], Book II (April 1976). There is perhaps irony in the fact that Stone appointed J. Edgar Hoover acting director of the Justice Department's Bureau of Investigation, which later became the FBI.

"When we see the originality of malice, the ingenuity of aggression, which our enemy displays, we may certainly prepare ourselves for every kind of novel stratagem and every kind of brutal and treacherous manoeuvre."

WINSTON CHURCHILL, 1940, justifying to the House of Commons a massive domestic roundup of aliens and suspected fifth columnists by MI5; quoted in Stafford, *Churchill and Secret Service* (1998).

"The so-called democratic forms of government have serious drawbacks for a man in my position. It is impossible to arrest and detain people without absurd legal formalities."

Colonel Haki, fictional chief of the Turkish secret police, in **ERIC AMBLER**, *Journey into Fear* (1940).

"From hero to general, from general to politician, from politician to secret service agent, and thence to a thing that peers in at bedroom or bathroom windows, and thence to a toad, and finally to a snake—such is the progress of Satan."

C. S. LEWIS, *A Preface to Paradise Lost* (1942).

"I told [Budget Director Harold Smith] what my thinking was on the subject of intelligence activities and my misgivings about some of the fields of these activities. I again wanted to make one thing clear: 'I am very much against building up a Gestapo,' I told him."

Former President HARRY TRUMAN on his May 1945 deliberations regarding a central intelligence organization; in *Memoirs*, vol. I (1955).

"It seems to me that in the present troubled period in international affairs, accompanied as it is by an increase in subversive activity here at home, it is as necessary as it was in 1940 to take the investigative measures [i.e., wiretapping] referred to in President Roosevelt's memorandum."

Attorney General TOM CLARK to President Truman, 17 July 1946; quoted in Andrew, *For the President's Eyes Only* (1995). Truman replied, "I concur."

"The National Security Council hereby authorizes and directs that:

1. The Central Intelligence Agency shall be responsible for the exploitation on a highly selective basis, within the United States, of business concerns, other non-governmental organizations and individuals as sources of foreign intelligence information."

National Security Council, NSCID 7 ("Domestic Exploitation"), 12 February 1948; reproduced in Warner, *CIA Under Truman* (1994).

"There was . . . no way of knowing whether you were being watched at any given moment. How often, or on what system, the Thought Police plugged in on any individual wire was guesswork. It was even conceivable that they watched everybody all the time. But at any rate they could plug in your wire whenever they wanted to."

GEORGE ORWELL, *1984* (1949).

"In 1952 CIA had started a program of looking at the mail between the Soviet Union and the United States, and opening selected letters. Over the years this had grown into a major operation that was held in the deepest secrecy by the Office of Security, which did the work, and the Counterintelligence Staff, which received the products and passed them on to the FBI. . . . Two things bothered me about the project. First was that opening first-class mail was a direct violation of a criminal statute; I looked it up in the law library to make sure. And secondly, I could get nothing beyond vague generalities from the Counterintelligence Staff when I asked what the operation had actually accomplished of any value over the years. So [in 1974] it was terminated."

Former DCI WILLIAM COLBY, *Honorable Men* (1978).

"There's a few as do spy-work for the Chief and his Men."

One hobbit to another in J. R. R. TOLKIEN, *The Lord of the Rings: The Return of the King* (1955).

"It is such nonsense to have to waste time prosecuting the Communist Party [of the United States]. It couldn't be more feeble and less of a threat, and besides, its membership consists largely of FBI agents."

Attorney General ROBERT KENNEDY, January 1961; quoted in Andrew, *For the President's Eyes Only* (1995).

"[President Johnson] instructed the CIA to institute a program of surveillance of antiwar leaders to prove his suspicions that they were Communists operating on orders from foreign governments. This program, later institutionalized as Operation CHAOS, violated the CIA's charter."

GEORGE HERRING, *America's Longest War* (1986).

"Operation Chaos dated back to 1967 and the Johnson Administration. At the time, President Johnson was faced with a rapidly escalating antiwar movement . . . he ordered [DCI Richard] Helms to discover whether there was any foreign financing or manipulation behind the antiwar movement or behind any of the radical, dissident groups associated with it. . . . Helms was acutely conscious of the danger of seeming to involve the CIA in a domestic intelligence activity. . . . As a result his directives were plain: the purpose of the project was to identify foreign links to American dissidents, not to spy on the American dissidents themselves, and thus a proper Agency activity well within the CIA's statutory charter. [But it] led to the growth of an extensive exchange between the FBI and the CIA, and the buildup of substantial files on Americans. . . . And there were a few instances—actually only three in number—in which CIA agents, in their enthusiasm, reported on the activities of American dissidents while still in America."

Former DCI **WILLIAM COLBY**, *Honorable Men* (1978). After the terrorist attacks of September 11, it all seems fairly tame.

"[CIA has found] no evidence of any contact between the most prominent peace movement leaders and foreign embassies, either in the U.S. or abroad."

DCI **RICHARD HELMS**, memorandum to President Johnson, 15 November 1967; quoted in Jeffreys-Jones, *The CIA and American Democracy* (1989).

"Herewith is a survey of student assistance worldwide as requested by the President. In an effort to round out our discussion of this subject, we have included a section on American students. This is an area not within the charter of this Agency, so I need not emphasize how extremely sensitive this makes the paper. Should anyone learn of its existence, it would prove most embarrassing for all concerned."

DCI **RICHARD HELMS** to Henry Kissinger, 18 February 1969; quoted in Andrew, *For the President's Eyes Only* (1995).

"I found that the most remarkable thing about the list [of possible violations of CIA's charter, a list ordered by DCI James Schlesinger in 1973] was that it was not more serious, that it did not include more widespread dangers to the lives and liberties of our citizens—that, for example, the surveillance of Americans in the United States affected only employees or ex-employees of CIA and five newsmen suspected of receiving its leaked material, that the mail-intercept program involved essentially only the mail to and from the Soviet Union . . . that the domestic wire taps did stop in 1965, when the President so directed, and that Nixon had to set up the 'plumbers' in the White House because such activities would not be carried out by CIA."

Former DCI **WILLIAM COLBY**, *Honorable Men* (1978).

"Contrary to popular belief, the Nixon administration ordered fewer wiretaps per year for foreign intelligence and national security purposes than any of its predecessors since presidential authorizations had begun under Franklin Roosevelt."

CHRISTOPHER ANDREW, *For the President's Eyes Only* (1995).

"Who would have thought that it would someday be judged a crime to carry out the orders of the President of the United States?"

> Former DCI **RICHARD HELMS** in 1975; quoted in Miller, *Spying for America* (1989).

"The main result of Chaos and related operations [to find links between foreign communists and domestic dissent] was to collect huge amounts of useless intelligence, all of which had to be analyzed in a vain attempt to persuade a disbelieving president that it did not contain evidence of a vast international conspiracy."

> **CHRISTOPHER ANDREW**, *For the President's Eyes Only* (1995).

"For years and years I have approved opening mail and other similar operations, but no [longer]. It is becoming more and more dangerous and we are apt to get caught. I am not opposed to doing this. I'm not opposed to continuing the burglaries and the opening of mail and other similar activities, providing someone higher than myself approves of it. . . . But I'm not going to accept the responsibility myself anymore, even though I've done it for many years."

> FBI Director **J. EDGAR HOOVER** to President Nixon's ad hoc interagency intelligence committee, June 1970; quoted in Andrew, *For the President's Eyes Only* (1995).

"The KGB's most widely used methods of social control were the . . . immensely labor-intensive techniques of ubiquitous surveillance and intimidation. . . . The effort and resources employed to track down every author of an anonymous letter or seditious graffito criticizing the Soviet system frequently exceeded those devoted in the West to a major murder enquiry."

> **CHRISTOPHER ANDREW** and **VASILI MITROKHIN**, *The Sword and the Shield: The Mitrokhin Archive* (1999).

"No sane individual will oppose a regime that wants so badly to make the lives of its people better."

> KGB chief **YURI ANDROPOV**; quoted in Kalugin, *The First Directorate* (1994). This philosophy justified the Soviet practice of incarcerating dissidents in mental asylums.

"In America, tradition had trained few, if any, major talents in political espionage, deviltry or harassment. No trained corps of domestic partisan spies exists like the agents of the CIA, the G-men of the FBI, the accountants of the IRS. In operations of domestic malice, as in the operation of campaign intelligence, one recruits what one can get—usually remainder men from old campaigns, drifters, amateurs of such awkwardness, ineptness and silliness as must inevitably carry matters awry."

> **THEODORE WHITE**, *Breach of Faith: The Fall of Richard Nixon* (1975).

"Illegal CIA activity was entirely in domestic fields, often where the White House had pushed CIA into dubious enterprises, and they were not massive. . . . No stretch of the imagination turns them into the massive police-state activity initially conjured up [in 1946–47]. CIA has never come close to being an American Gestapo."

> Former DDI **RAY CLINE**, *Secrets, Spies and Scholars* (1976).

"The idea that the CIA could put a guy in jail without *habeas corpus* just scared the living daylights out of me. That kind of intelligence service is a threat to its own people."

> Former DCI **WILLIAM COLBY** commenting on CIA's hostile incarceration of defector Yuri Nosenko from 1964 to 1968 because of suspicions that Nosenko was a KGB plant; quoted in Mangold, *Cold Warrior* (1991). CIA eventually established Nosenko's bona fides.

"It was the CIA's refusal to become involved in the [Watergate] coverup that eventually made it unsustainable."

CHRISTOPHER ANDREW, *For the President's Eyes Only* (1995).

"Resolved, That Richard M. Nixon, President of the United States, is impeached for high crimes and misdemeanors.... On June 17, 1972, and prior thereto, agents of the Committee for the Re-election of the President committed unlawful entry of the headquarters of the Democratic National Committee in Washington, District of Columbia, for the purpose of securing political intelligence. Subsequent thereto, Richard M. Nixon, using the powers of his high office, engaged personally and through his subordinates and agents, in a course of conduct or plan designed to delay, impede, and obstruct the investigation of such unlawful entry; to cover up, conceal and protect those responsible; and to conceal the existence and scope of other unlawful covert activities. The means used to implement this course of conduct or plan included ... (6) endeavoring to misuse the Central Intelligence Agency, an agency of the United States."

Excerpt from the Articles of Impeachment voted by the House Committee on the Judiciary and submitted to the U.S. House of Representatives, 20 August 1974.

"The CIA, directly violating its charter, conducted a massive illegal domestic intelligence operation during the Nixon Administration against the antiwar movement and other dissident groups in the United States."

SEYMOUR HERSH, *New York Times*, 22 December 1974. Thus the public learned of CHAOS.

"Too many people have been spied upon by too many Government agencies, and too much information has been collected.... Groups and individuals have been harassed and disrupted because of their political views and their lifestyles. Investigations have been based upon vague standards whose breadth made excessive collection inevitable.... While the agencies often committed excesses in response to pressure from high officials in the Executive branch and Congress, they also occasionally initiated improper activities and then concealed them from officials whom they had a duty to inform."

U.S. Senate, *Final Report of the Senate Select Committee to Study Governmental Operations with respect to Intelligence Activities* [the Church Committee], Book II (April 1976).

"Much has been made of the alleged threats to American liberties from our own intelligence services. Some cases of stupidity and overzealousness have been distorted into a broad pattern of dangers to our liberties. I speak only of the Central Intelligence Agency in this connection. In the past thirty years some 76,000 men and women have passed through its ranks. None has been convicted or even indicted for threatening the freedoms of his fellow citizens. I submit that the record of the intelligence organizations compares favorably to that of most other government organizations. Biased reporting and propagandistic journalism have sometimes hidden that fact."

Former DDCI **VERNON WALTERS**, *Silent Missions* (1978).

"Only a radical fringe in our country really worries that our intelligence agencies may become another Gestapo, but the record of the CIA, the NSA, and Army intelligence in poking into American lives in the 1950s and 1960s cannot be ignored. If some DCI did abuse the combined powers of those agencies, it could cause untold damage to our citizens—and to our intelligence."

Former DCI **STANSFIELD TURNER**, *Secrecy and Democracy* (1985).

"In reality, and contrary to conventional wisdom, the CIA has no weapons with which to threaten our civil liberties. The FBI, not the CIA, has the power of arrest. The FBI, not the CIA, can work with federal and state prosecutors . . . the FBI also has the unique responsibility of carrying out, or supervising, all CI investigations in the U.S. . . . No other intelligence agency may hold files which relate to CI matters on any U.S. person not their employee. . . . The rule is: If Americans are to be investigated anywhere, the FBI will do it if possible. Within the U.S., only the FBI can conduct CI operations, period."

ANGELO CODEVILLA, *Informing Statecraft* (1992).

"A Clinton White House official asked the CIA in 1995 to provide intelligence on several U.S. citizens despite a presidential order banning the agency from distributing such information. . . . [An] NSC spokesman said that while it is illegal, with certain exceptions, for the CIA to spy on U.S. citizens or distribute intelligence about them, it is not illegal for the White House to ask the CIA for such information. . . . CIA attorneys say that the agency does not keep files on individual U.S. citizens. Under law, it can keep information that mentions U.S. citizens in other files gathered in the course of operations targeting foreign citizens, organizations, or governments."

JAMES RISEN, "Clinton Official Asked CIA for Intelligence on Citizens," *Los Angeles Times*, 19 December 1997.

"Collection inside the United States is the area where loosened constraints would have done the most to avert the September 11 attacks. . . . Compromises of individual privacy, through secret surveillance, monitoring of communications, and searches . . . is where pressing up to the constitutional limits offers the biggest payoff for counterterrorist intelligence. [These activities] need not threaten individuals unnecessarily, so long as careful measures are instituted to keep secret the irrelevant but embarrassing information that may inadvertently be acquired as a by-product of monitoring. Similarly, popular but unpersuasive arguments have been advanced against the sort of national identification card common in other democratic countries. The U.S. Constitution does not confer the right to be unidentified to the government. . . . Moreover, Americans should remember that many solid, humane democracies—the United Kingdom, France, and others—have far more permissive rules for gathering information on people than the United States has had, and their citizens seem to live with these rules without great unease."

RICHARD K. BETTS, "Fixing Intelligence," *Foreign Affairs* (January–February 2002).

"A free people have long had to decide where to plant the flag on that inevitable spectrum between security and liberty. We have always planted it close to liberty. We will keep it there."

NSA director **MICHAEL HAYDEN** addressing NSA employees; quoted in the *Baltimore Sun*, 19 April 2002.

- **Economic Intelligence**
- **Espionage & Spies**
- **Estimates**

ECONOMIC INTELLIGENCE

Since OSS days American intelligence has pursued information on foreign countries' industrial base, gross production, trade practices, adherence to economic agreements, strategic strengths and weaknesses—in short, all economic data of use to policymakers who make decisions that affect U.S. national security. The Literary Spy recalls that "economy" comes from Greek, referring to the management of a household, and good economic intelligence ultimately allows citizens to manage their households all the better.

See also: Covert Action; Espionage & Spies

"In late 1776 the first US intelligence agency, the Committee of Secret Correspondence of the Continental Congress, sent one William Carmichael to Europe, in the guise of a merchant, to report on a variety of economic topics of interest to the new government. . . . In a November 1776 secret dispatch from Amsterdam, Carmichael reported reassuringly that, 'You have been threatened that the Ukraine would supply Europe with tobacco. It must be long before that time can arrive. I have

seen some of its tobacco here, and the best of it is worse than the worst of our ground leaf.'"

PHILIP ZELIKOW, "American Economic Intelligence," in Jeffreys-Jones and Andrew, *Eternal Vigilance* (1997).

"The magnitude of what [Francis Cabot] Lowell achieved has few parallels, even in spy fiction. Few Americans recognize his name, but we are all indebted to this shrewd Yankee. By stealing Britain's most valuable secret, by analyzing it and quickly acting upon it, he brought the Industrial Revolution to New England. . . . There were plenty of prominent Americans trying to steal secrets from Britain. But none went so far as Lowell. He was after the Cartwright loom, the crown jewel of the British textile industry. . . . We still don't know how Lowell got the detailed plans for this tightly guarded machine, but the arrogance of the new lords of Britain's industry probably helped him. They tended to look down upon outsiders, especially the American rustics. Some . . . waived the rule stipulating that all plants be closed to foreigners. . . . British customs officers found nothing unusual because Lowell, who is credited by most historians with having a photographic memory, probably carried the blueprints in his head."

JOHN J. FIALKA, *Wilson Quarterly* (winter 1997).

"Having learned that several European nations were manufacturing smokeless gunpowder—said to be far superior to the black powder still being used in the United States—the War Department asked the du Pont family, America's leading powder makers, to obtain information about the process. Early in 1889, Alfred du Pont . . . arrived in Paris with a letter to French officials from Secretary of State James G. Blaine. . . . The French refused to make the process available to du Pont, but the young man picked up useful information. . . . Having heard that a Belgian firm, Coopal & Co., was also producing smokeless powder, young du Pont slipped over the frontier into Coopal's powder works as a laborer. Keeping his mouth shut and his eyes open, du Pont stole the secret for which he had come."

NATHAN MILLER, *Spying for America* (1989).

"The natural inquisitiveness of competitors is at once checkmated by a machine that enables you to keep all your documents, or at least their important parts, entirely secret."

1923 advertisement for a business cable security device manufactured by the Cipher Machine Corporation of Berlin; quoted in Russell, *The Secret War* (1981). The machine was the Enigma, the mainstay for Nazi Germany's communications security during World War II.

"How can I conduct the controversies on which the management of our finances depends unless I have the same knowledge of secret state affairs freely accessible to the officials of the Admiralty? The words 'monstrous' & 'intolerable' readily leap

to my mind. I prefer to bury them in the cooler word 'absurd.'"

WINSTON CHURCHILL, chancellor of the exchequer, protesting to Prime Minister Stanley Baldwin in 1925 that he needed access to British signals intelligence; quoted in Stafford, *Churchill and Secret Service* (1998).

"During the war Germany was chronically short of motor oil. . . . Refineries were vital for the Nazi war effort, and they were pinpointed as targets by Walter Levy, then a young analyst in the OSS and later a well-known petroleum expert. He calculated the exact location of refineries from the freight tariffs for petroleum products as published by the German railroads; once the refineries were located they became obvious targets for the Allied bombers."

WALTER LAQUEUR, *A World of Secrets* (1985).

"[The OSS economists'] group was able to show that only two manufacturers were involved in the production of German tank engines and that gear boxes were assembled in only two plants. With this information the new science of serial-number analysis left the laboratory and ushered the Economic Division into the real world of target selection in the air war over Europe."

BARRY KATZ, *Foreign Intelligence: Research and Analysis in OSS* (1989).

"Max Millikan, an economist from [MIT, and appointed chief of CIA's Office of Research and Reports in 1951], defined economic intelligence [as] more than a compilation of the target country's resources. It also included how the resources were used and what military establishments and social and political institutions they supported. He stressed that economic information becomes economic intelligence only when its relevance to national security is made clear."

CIA historian **ROBERTA KNAPP**; quotation in CIA's Historical Intelligence Collection.

"An Office of Research and Reports has been set up to provide coordinated intelligence, primarily on economic matters, as a service of common concern to interested Government agencies. Although accurate appraisal of an enemy's economic potential is a most important factor in estimating his military capabilities, this crucially-important task had previously been scattered among twenty-four separate agencies of the Government."

DCI **WALTER BEDELL SMITH**, memorandum to the National Security Council, 23 April 1952; reproduced in Warner, *CIA Under Truman* (1994).

"Our biggest problem was whether or not anybody would read our product."

CIA analyst on economic intelligence in the 1950s; quoted in Karalekas, "The History of the Central Intelligence Agency," in Leary, *The Central Intelligence Agency* (1984).

"Espionage of this modern sort, the use of scientific method by the powers to steal each other's secrets, with each theft impairs the robbed state's defences as thoroughly as if it had fought and been defeated."

REBECCA WEST, *The New Meaning of Treason* (1966).

"It was probably [its] economic expertise more than anything else that enabled CIA to get a handle on the military agencies and force them into effective coordination of substantive findings in NIEs [National Intelligence Estimates]."

Former DDI **RAY CLINE**, *Secrets, Spies and Scholars* (1976).

"The radars that guided the missiles fired from Soviet fighters were copied from blueprints of the radars on U.S. F-14, F-15, and F-18 fighters. The Soviets' space shuttle was created from documents carted away from NASA. The Soviet Ryad computer had been copied from the architecture of the IBM model 370 mainframe computer. In all, about 5,000 categories of Soviet military equipment entering its arsenals during the 1980s were products of the KGB's efforts; about 60 percent of the blueprints and other documents were taken either from the United States or its allies."

JOHN J. FIALKA, *Wilson Quarterly* (winter 1997).

"The assimilation of Western technology [from KGB espionage] is so broad that the U.S. and other Western nations are thus subsidizing the Soviet military buildup."

CIA report, "Soviet Acquisition of Western Technology," April 1982; cited in Fialka, *War by Other Means* (1997).

"There is no doubt that in the 1970s and 1980s more officers of the KGB and GRU, as well as of the intelligence services of Eastern Europe, were engaged in buying or stealing American technology than in any other task."

ANGELO CODEVILLA, *Informing Statecraft* (1992).

"The resources of a corporation—even a large one such as Corning—are no match for espionage activities that are sanctioned and supported by foreign governments."

Senior executive at Corning, Inc., in testimony to the U.S. Congress, April 1992; cited in Fialka, *War by Other Means* (1997).

"We steal secrets for our military preparedness. I don't see why we shouldn't stay economically competitive."

DCI **STANSFIELD TURNER**; quoted in Polmar and Allen, *Encyclopedia of Espionage* (1997).

"When Hitachi admitted in court that its employees tried to purchase stolen 'Adirondack' computer design workbooks from IBM, the judge in 1983 fined the company a whopping $10,000. The U.S. government did not blink an eye.... When it was disclosed that between the early 1970s and late 1980s the French DGSE had planted agents in Texas Instruments, IBM, and Corning and shared the purloined information with Comagnie des Machines Bull, the U.S. government merely sent a letter of diplomatic protest. Likewise, when Israeli intelligence officers stole valuable technological data from Illinois defense contractor Recon Optical, no penalties were imposed.... This state of affairs should be unsatisfactory."

PETER SCHWEIZER, "The Growth of Economic Espionage," *Foreign Affairs* (January–February 1996).

"I ordered that we begin collecting commercial intelligence in seven countries as a pilot project. Within a day a group of six top officials in the CIA came to my office to argue that helping business was not what the CIA had been created to do; it did not, in their view, further national security; it was not the kind of worthy cause for which they had signed up."

Former DCI **STANSFIELD TURNER**, *Secrecy and Democracy* (1985).

"We believe that Gorbachev's efforts at reviving the Soviet economy will produce no substantial improvement over the next five years."

Declassified National Intelligence Estimate, *Gorbachev's Economic Programs*, December 1988; in Fischer, ed., *At Cold War's End* (1999). Indeed, in just three years the Soviet economy would no longer exist.

"The spy of the future is less likely to resemble James Bond, whose chief assets were his fists, than the ... engineer who lives quietly down the street and never does anything more violent than turn a page of a manual or flick on his microcomputer."

Futurist **ALVIN TOFFLER**, *Powershift* (1990).

"In 1991, two men were spotted rifling through rubbish outside a private home in a suburb of Houston, Texas. An off-duty police officer took the number of their van, which was traced to the French consulate. The house belonged to an executive of Texas Instruments. A French representative explained that the men were collecting grass cuttings to fill a hole in the consulate garden."

MARK LLOYD, *Guinness Book of Espionage* (1994).

"I'm willing to die for my country, but not for General Motors."

CIA officer to DCI Robert Gates in 1992; quoted in *USA Today*, 23 August 1996.

"Economics is far from a new issue for the Intelligence Community. Contrary to the common perception, even in our earliest days we did not spend all of our time and energy worrying about Soviet throw weights or the pecking order of the Chinese Communist Party. Early on, we recognized the importance that economic trends and events could have on national security interests."

DCI **ROBERT GATES**, remarks to the Economic Club of Detroit, 13 April 1992; in Gates, *Speeches* (1993).

"Economic intelligence . . . can make individuals rich. But its effect on nations is marginal."

ANGELO CODEVILLA, *Informing Statecraft* (1992).

"In general . . . the contribution of intelligence sources to economic [intelligence] is small. Furthermore, the intelligence agencies cannot expect to attract the highest quality analysts [and] the freedom of academic life proves more attractive . . . even if the salaries are lower. In addition, multinational corporations, banks, and brokerage firms can easily outbid intelligence agencies for the services of highly qualified economists."

ABRAM SHULSKY, *Silent Warfare: Understanding the World of Intelligence* (1993).

"Let me be quite clear about this. The CIA is not going to be in the business that a number of our friends' and allies' intelligence services are in: spying on foreign corporations for the benefit of domestic business."

DCI **R. JAMES WOOLSEY**, remarks to the Economic Club of Chicago, 19 November 1993.

"In some countries the intelligence services have focused on developing a close relationship with private companies and quasi-private concerns. For many years these services have collected economic information and passed it directly to domestic businesses. . . . There are those who would argue that in order to level the playing field for American business, we need to conduct such operations and provide the fruits to U.S. companies. This, it is argued, is the only way to preserve the American competitive edge. . . . It is my view that the practice of industrial espionage is an unnecessary perversion of the intelligence process in a free country."

CIA Inspector General **FRED HITZ**, remarks to the French-American Chamber of Commerce, 11 April 1995. The French no doubt were comforted.

"We do not do industrial espionage. . . . There are places where economic intelligence makes sense. But it is not to provide commercial advantage to specific individuals or industries."

DCI **JOHN DEUTCH**, radio interview, 2 September 1995.

"We are military allies, but economic competitors. Therefore, industrial espionage, even among friends, is a normal action of an intelligence agency."

PIERRE MARION, former director of French intelligence; quoted in *National Defense* (October 1995). At least the French (what great friends, indeed) are forthright about it.

"The important stuff is garbled. And most of what you get is garbage. . . . If you are interested in Iraq's nuclear weapons program, you don't have many other choices for your information. But if you want to know what the Bundesbank is going to do next, or whether Brazil is thinking of devaluing its currency, there's a lot of competition. And it is hard for the agency to add value. . . . The best graduate students don't go there, and who can blame them? And yet, when you sit in a meeting, the views of the C.I.A. are often given more weight than the Council of Economic Advisors. Go figure."

Unidentified senior U.S. official on CIA economic intelligence; quoted in the *New York Times*, 15 October 1995.

"America has the most technical information of relevance. It is easily accessible. So naturally your country will receive the most attention from the intelligence services."

> **PIERRE MARION**, director of French intelligence under President François Mitterrand; quoted in Peter Schweizer, "The Growth of Economic Espionage," *Foreign Affairs* (January–February 1996). Naturellement.

"The state is not just responsible for law-making, it is in business as well. It is true that for some decades, the French state regulated the markets to some extent with its left hand while its right hand used the secret services to procure information for its own firms."

> **CLAUDE SILBERZAHN**, former chief of French intelligence; quoted by Agence France Presse, 10 January 1996.

"What makes it so difficult for American corporations is that they are not dealing with a competitor who is willing to use bribery or illegal means to obtain their trade secrets. They are dealing with a sophisticated intelligence service, in many cases a friendly intelligence service, [trying] to obtain, by all means possible, their secrets."

> FBI Director **LOUIS FREEH**, testimony to the House Judiciary Committee; quoted in the *Washington Post*, 10 May 1996.

"We have identified about a half dozen governments that we believe have extensively engaged in economic espionage as we define it. Those governments include France, Israel, China, Russia, Iran, and Cuba. Japan and a number of other countries engage in economic collection, but we believe their efforts are mostly legal and involve seeking openly available material or hiring well-placed consultants."

> CIA unclassified response to U.S. Senate inquiry, 10 May 1996; subsequently released by the Senate Select Committee on Intelligence.

"We are losing at a game of economic jujitsu in which Japan, which keeps its markets closed and does relatively little research within its largely closed university system, uses one of the U.S. system's main strengths—its openness—against it. ... While the fabled and probably fictitious 'missile gap' was used politically to galvanize U.S. concerns in the 1960s [*sic*] about the Soviet Union, the patently real 'intelligence gap' opened by the Japanese has caused no outcry."

> **JOHN J. FIALKA**, *Wilson Quarterly* (winter 1997).

"[Economic intelligence] is bad foreign policy and bad intelligence policy. There's enough real targets to go after out in the world, from terrorists to drug cartels to rogue states, without having to invent intelligence missions."

> **RICHARD HAASS** of the Brookings Institution; quoted in the *Wall Street Journal*, 11 March 1997.

"Why should products from nations who steal our ideas and mock our laws find their way onto the shelves at Wal-Marts?"

> **JOHN J. FIALKA**, *War by Other Means: Economic Espionage in America* (1997).

"I can say you very openly and very firmly that Russian intelligence activity against this country is much more active than it was in time of the former Soviet Union's existence. ... Russian spies here are conducting industrial espionage."

> Former Soviet GRU Colonel **STANISLAV LUNEV**, testimony to the Military R&D Subcommittee of the House National Security Committee, 4 August 1998.

"We do not spy on foreign countries for the economic gain of American companies. ... I'm not going to jeopardize the life of a man or a woman or a sensitive collection resource to go protect interests of companies to make money when they can do all this on their own. [But] if we find out that an American company is being robbed, cheated, or somebody is bribing and disenfranchising an American company, we will go to the Secretary of State or the Secretary of Commerce and say 'we have this information; you figure out how to deal with it.' So we play defense, but we don't play offense."

DCI **GEORGE TENET**, interview published by Reuters, 1 March 2000.

"With respect to allegations of industrial espionage, the notion that we collect intelligence to promote American business interests is simply wrong. We do not target foreign companies to support American business interests. If we did this, where would we draw the line? Which companies would we help? Corporate giants? The little guy? All of them? I think we would quickly get into a mess and would raise questions of whether we are being unfair to one or more of our own businesses."

DCI **GEORGE TENET**, testimony to Congress, April 2000.

ESPIONAGE & SPIES

The historical record suggests that espionage is one of the world's very oldest professions; the Literary Spy is all too aware of the numerous parallels between spies and prostitutes. History also clearly indicates that spying is ubiquitous in all human experience, that it is necessary for the exercise of proper statecraft, and that, unlike prostitution, its practice benefits a far wider circle of people than its direct practitioners.

See also: Collection; Counterintelligence; Treason & Betrayal

"You are spies. You have come to see the weakness of the land."

Joseph, governor of Egypt, to his brothers who have come from famine-plagued Canaan seeking to buy food; Genesis 42:8 (New Jerusalem). As Joseph intentionally kept his true identity a secret from his brothers, this first mention of espionage in the Bible illustrates how espionage and deception go hand in hand.

"And Joshua the son of Nun sent two men secretly from Shittim as spies, saying, 'Go, view the land, especially Jericho.' And they went, and came into the house of a harlot whose name was Rahab, and lodged there."

Joshua 2:1 (Revised Standard). SHITTIM would be a dandy code word for an espionage operation, wouldn't it?

"What enables the wise sovereign and the good general to strike and conquer, and achieve things beyond the reach of ordinary men, is foreknowledge. Now this foreknowledge cannot be elicited from spirits; it cannot be obtained inductively from experience, nor by any deductive calculation . . . the dispositions of the enemy are ascertainable through spies and spies alone."

SUN TZU, *The Art of War* (6th century B.C.).

"Of all the army's affairs, no relationship is closer than with spies; no rewards are more generous than those given to spies; no affairs are more secret than those pertaining to spies. . . . Be subtle! Be subtle! and use your spies for every kind of business."

SUN TZU, *The Art of War* (6th century B.C.).

"Our spies should be constantly abroad. We should spare no pains in tampering with their men, and giving encouragement to deserters. By these means we may get intelligence of their present or future designs."

FLAVIUS RENATUS, Roman strategist, 4th century A.D.; quoted in Polmar and Allen, *Encyclopedia of Espionage* (1997).

"From time immemorial the [Byzantine] government had maintained a large number of agents who used to travel about among our enemies. Thus, entering the kingdom of Persia, in the guise of merchants or in some other way, they would make detailed inquiries of all that was afoot, and on their return to this country were thus able to make a full report on all the enemy's secret plans to our government, who, forewarned and put upon its guard, was never taken by surprise.... But [the Emperor] Justinian would spend nothing; and, indeed, abolished the very name of secret agent from the [Byzantine] Empire, the result being, among many other disasters, the loss of Lazica to the enemy, when the [Byzantines] had not the remotest idea of where on earth the Persian king and his army were at the time."

PROCOPIUS, 6th-century Byzantine historian; cited in Dvornik, *Origins of Intelligence Services* (1974).

"To know our enemies minds, we'd rip their hearts;
Their papers, is more lawful."

WILLIAM SHAKESPEARE on stolen documents, *King Lear* (1606), Act IV, scene 6.

"In general it is necessary to pay spies well and not be miserly in that respect. A man who risks being hanged in our service merits being well paid."

FREDERICK THE GREAT, 1747; quoted in Heinl, *Dictionary of Military and Naval Quotations* (1966).

"SPY, a person hired to watch the actions, motions, etc. of another; particularly of what passes in a camp. When a spy is discovered he is hanged immediately."

Encyclopedia Britannica, 1771; cited in Phillips, *The Night Watch* (1978).

"It would be agreeable to Congress *to know the disposition of foreign powers toward us,* and we hope this object will engage your attention. We need not hint that *great circumspection and impenetrable secrecy* are necessary."

Committee of Secret Correspondence of the Continental Congress to an American spy in London, December 1775; quoted in Andrew, *For the President's Eyes Only* (1995).

"Secrecy respecting me on the part of the Gen[era]l is indispensible to my rendering him any services and ... is necessary to the preservation of my life ... instant death w[oul]d be my portion should a discovery be made."

Dr. **BENJAMIN CHURCH**, prominent member of the Massachusetts assembly and a spy for British General Gage, letter to Gage, 1775; quoted in Bakeless, *Turncoats, Traitors and Heroes* (1998). Church was discovered but not executed because the Continental Congress had not yet passed a law on treason.

"Resolved, That all persons not members of, nor owing allegiance to, any of the United States of America ... who shall be found lurking as spies in or about the fortifications or encampments of the armies of the United States ... shall suffer death, according to the law and usage of nations, by sentence of a court martial, or such other punishment as such court martial may direct."

Continental Congress, August 1776; cited in Knott, *Secret and Sanctioned* (1996).

"Every kind of service, necessary to the public good, becomes honorable by being necessary."

> **NATHAN HALE** to Yale classmate Captain William Hull before Hale's ill-fated mission to collect intelligence on British forces in New York, September 1776; quoted in Bakeless, *Turncoats, Traitors and Heroes* (1998). Hull had tried to dissuade Hale from his mission by saying that spying was disgraceful.

"I only regret that I have but one life to lose for my country."

> American spy **NATHAN HALE** before his hanging on 22 September 1776; cited in Heinl, *Dictionary of Military and Naval Quotations* (1966). John Bakeless, in *Turncoats, Traitors and Heroes* (1998), says that there is enough witness testimony to confirm the veracity of what many consider a myth. Christopher Andrew calls it a "pious but plausible" story.

"You must be well convinced, that it is indispensibly necessary to make use of these means to procure intelligence. The persons employed must bear the suspicion of being thought inimical, and it is not in their power to assert their innocence, because that would get abroad and destroy the confidence which the Enemy puts in them."

> **GEORGE WASHINGTON**, letter to Governor William Livingston of New Jersey asking for the release of Washington's spies who had been misapprehended as British agents, 20 January 1778; quoted in CIA, *"Our First Line of Defense"* (1996).

"Tappan, September 29th, 1780

Sir,

Your Excellency is doubtless already apprized of the manner in which I was taken and possibly of the serious light in which my Conduct is Considered and the rigorous determination that is impending. Under these Circumstances I have obtained General Washington's permission to send you this letter, the object of which is to remove from your Breast any Suspicion that I could imagine that I was bound by your Excellencys orders to expose myself to what has happened. The Events of coming within an Enemys post and of Changing my dress which led me to my present Situation were contrary to my own Intentions as they were to your Orders; and the circuitous route which I took to return was imposed (perhaps unavoidably) without alternative upon me. I am perfectly and tranquil in mind and prepared for any Fate to which an honest Zeal for my Kings service may have devoted me."

> British Major **JOHN ANDRÉ** to Sir Henry Clinton, 29 September 1780, in the Clinton Collection, Clements Library, University of Michigan. André was Benedict Arnold's case officer as Clinton's head of intelligence and was caught by the Americans in civilian attire after meeting with Arnold. André was hanged three days after he wrote this letter.

"I am reconciled to death but detest the mode. It will be but a moment's pang. I pray you bear witness that I met my fate like a brave man."

> British Major **JOHN ANDRÉ** before he was hanged by the Americans as a spy, 2 October 1780. André is interred at Westminster Abbey—one of only two known spies accorded that honor. Robert Hatch, *Major John André* (1986).

"We want an intelligent and prudent native, who will go to reside in N. Orleans as a secret correspondent for 1,000 dollars a year. He might do a little business, merely to cover his real office. Do point out such a one. Virginia ought to offer more loungers equal to this, and ready to do it, than any other state."

> Secretary of State **THOMAS JEFFERSON** to James Madison, 27 May 1793; cited in Sayle, "The Historical Underpinnings of the U.S. Intelligence Community," in *International Journal of Intelligence and Counterintelligence* (spring 1986). Virginia carries on the proud tradition, as home to CIA.

"One spy in the right place is worth 20,000 men in the field."

> Attributed to **NAPOLEON**.

"I have given you great sums of money for your services in the past. You may have another half million francs, but I cannot honor a spy."

> **NAPOLEON**, refusing his intelligence chief the Legion of Honor; quoted in Innes, *Book of Spies* (1966). Napoleon is also reputed to have said, "Gold is the only suitable reward for spies." See Polmar and Allen, *Encyclopedia of Espionage* (1997).

"The proper course to have adopted was to despatch an individual unknown to all parties; some intelligent, keen, silent, and observing man, of pleasing address and insinuating manners, who, concealing the object of his visit, would see and hear everything, and report it faithfully."

> Speaker of the House **HENRY CLAY** criticizing President James Monroe for sending well-known U.S. citizens on a well-publicized intelligence collection mission to South America, March 1818; quoted in Knott, *Secret and Sanctioned* (1996).

"Yes, such are their laws; the man who fights, and kills, and plunders, is honored; but he who serves his country as a spy, no matter how faithfully, no matter how honestly, lives to be reviled, or dies like the vilest criminal."

> Fictional Revolutionary War double agent Harvey Birch in **JAMES FENIMORE COOPER**, *The Spy* (1821). One of the very first American novels is a story about espionage conducted in the national interest.

"It is one of the dangerous characteristics of the sort of information supplied by secret agents that it becomes rarer and less explicit as the peril increases and the need for information becomes greater."

> **ALEXIS DE TOCQUEVILLE**; quoted in Heinl, *Dictionary of Military and Naval Quotations* (1966). A timeless truth of espionage.

"The spy is the greatest of soldiers. If he is the most detested by the enemy, it is only because he is the most feared."

> Attributed to **KING GEORGE V** (1865–1936).

"For anyone who is tired of life, the thrilling life of a spy should be the very finest recuperator."

> Sir **ROBERT BADEN-POWELL**, founder of the Boy Scouts; quoted in Andrew, *For the President's Eyes Only* (1995). Sure, if the stress doesn't kill you first.

"The first difficulty in espionage lies in finding reliable men; this is more difficult than one usually imagines, for we require men of intelligence and daring, on whom we can place a certain measure of dependence. We must disabuse ourselves of the idea that we can turn the first individual we come across into a trustworthy spy. . . . To turn spies to some account requires talent. The officer who employs them needs much ability to discover the most trusty ones; he must exercise great discernment in their selection. . . . Though we naturally despise them, we must not let this be seen; they all alike must be treated with fairness."

> British Colonel **GEORGE FURSE**, *Information in War* (1895). "We naturally despise them" no more. Such Victorian attitudes are neither helpful nor realistic.

"Our business is simple. All we have to do is to take note of a certain face pointed out by the officials, or to find it ourselves, gather information, make observations, give a report to the authorities, and let them do as they please. For all we care, they may flay people alive. Politics do not concern us."

> Tsarist Russian spy in **MAXIM GORKY**, *The Spy* (1908).

"The work appealed both to my sense of adventure and my sense of the ridiculous."

> **W. SOMERSET MAUGHAM**, SIS officer sent to Russia in the summer of 1917; quoted in Miller, *Spying for America* (1989). A good balance in this business.

"If you do well you'll get no thanks and if you get into trouble you'll get no help."

> Warning to **W. SOMERSET MAUGHAM**'s fictional spy Ashenden; cited in West, *Faber Book of Espionage* (1993).

"In Intelligence operations, money is an essential ingredient; even where other motives arise—as patriotism or ideological affiliations—money, however little, must be dropped in, like a touch of bitter in a mint julep, to validate the deal. Only when money has passed is the mystical union fully established; it's money that makes Intelligence go round."

> **MALCOLM MUGGERIDGE**, SIS officer during World War II, *Chronicles of Wasted Time: The Infernal Grove* (1973).

"My examination of the material has shown that [it] is of enormous and invaluable significance to our nation and our science. . . . It has made it possible to obtain important guidelines for our own scientific research, by-passing many extremely difficult phases in the development of this problem, learning new scientific and technical routes for its development, establishing three new areas for Soviet physics, and learning about the possibilities for using not only uranium-235 but also uranium-238."

> Soviet atomic bomb project chief **IGOR KURCHATOV**, to Soviet intelligence chief Lavrenti Beria, on the value of British atomic secrets stolen by Soviet spies, 7 March 1943; cited in Andrew and Mitrokhin, *The Mitrokhin Archive* (1999).

"The penetration of the MANHATTAN project was only the most spectacular part of a vast wartime expansion of Soviet scientific and technological espionage. S&T from the United States and Britain made a major contribution to the development of Soviet radar, radio technology, submarines, jet engines, aircraft and synthetic rubber, as well as nuclear weapons."

> **CHRISTOPHER ANDREW** and **VASILI MITROKHIN**, *The Sword and the Shield: The Mitrokhin Archive* (1999).

"The only thing is, treat me like a human being!"

> **PYOTR POPOV**, Soviet GRU major and CIA spy, to his CIA handlers, 1953; quoted in Andrew, *For the President's Eyes Only* (1995).

"Like lovers, spies cannot be taken for granted."

> Former CIA operations officer **WILLIAM HOOD**, *Mole* (1993).

"You can tell Mr. Dulles for me that there's a CIA cow grazing on the bank of the Volga."

> **PYOTR POPOV**, Soviet GRU major and CIA spy, 1953; quoted in Hood, *Mole* (1993). Popov spied for CIA out of his hatred of the Soviet system, but he accepted payment, which he used to improve his family's lot back on the farm.

"We didn't do it for the CIA; we did it through the CIA. We didn't do it for a medal or financial reward; we did it for our country."

> **BOHUSLAV PERUTKA**, a Czechoslovak citizen who reportedly spied on the Communist regime on behalf of the United States in the early 1950s; quoted in the *Los Angeles Times*, 17 July 1997.

"[In the 1950s] a distortion threatened to change the character of our work. The collectors with technical gadgets began to disparage the efforts of human collectors. The new cry from the gadgeteers was, 'Give us the money and leave it to us.' And, indeed, why take risks running spies when gadgets would tell you what you wanted to know? But therein lay a fallacy. And the debate over the elements of that fallacy is with us today and will inevitably crop up from time to time in the future. Why? Because gadgets cannot divine man's intentions."

> Former DCI **RICHARD HELMS**, remarks at an awards dinner, 24 May 1983; quoted in Ranelagh, *The Agency* (1986).

"My Dear Sir!

I request that you pass the following to the appropriate authorities of the United States of America. It is your good friend who is turning to you, a friend who has already become your soldier-warrior for the cause of Truth, for the ideals of a truly free world and of Democracy for Mankind. . . . I have at my disposal very important materials on many subjects of exceptionally great interest and importance to your government."

> Soviet GRU Colonel **OLEG PENKOVSKIY** in his letter making contact with CIA, August 1960; in Schecter and Deriabin, *The Spy Who Saved the World* (1995).

"I suppose I assume that when I'm given an unpleasant job in the Service the cause is a just one."

> Fictional spy James Bond in **IAN FLEMING**, *For Your Eyes Only* (1960).

"The great desire which I have carried in my soul . . . is to swear fealty to my Queen, Elizabeth II, and to the President of the United States, Mr. Kennedy, whom I am serving as their soldier."

> Soviet GRU Colonel **OLEG PENKOVSKIY**, agreeing to spy for the United States and Britain, April 1962; quoted in Andrew, *For the President's Eyes Only* (1995).

"[One] Oleg Penkovskiy is worth a hundred Ph.D.s."

> Former CIA operations officer **JOHN MAURY**, quoted in *Time*, 19 January 1981. Actually, at the current rate of exchange, taking into account severe academic depreciation, one sterling Penkovskiy is worth at least a thousand Ph.D.s, and the black market rate is dearer yet.

"Why spy? . . . For as long as rogues become leaders we shall spy. For as long as there are bullies and liars and madmen in the world, we shall spy. For as long as nations compete, and politicians deceive, and tyrants launch conquests, and consumers need resources, and the homeless look for land, and the hungry for food, and the rich for excess, your chosen profession is perfectly secure, I can assure you."

> **JOHN LE CARRÉ**'s character George Smiley in the novel *The Secret Pilgrim* (1991). A favorite quotation of DCI Robert Gates.

"Obscurity was his nature, as well as his profession. The byways of espionage are not populated by the brash and colorful adventurers of fiction. A man who, like Smiley, has lived and worked for years among his country's enemies learns only one prayer: that he may never, never be noticed."

> **JOHN LE CARRÉ** [David Cornwell], *A Murder of Quality* (1963).

"What do you think spies are: priests, saints, and martyrs? They're a squalid procession of vain fools, traitors too; yes, pansies, sadists and drunkards, people who play cowboys and Indians to brighten their rotten lives."

> **JOHN LE CARRÉ** [David Cornwell], *The Spy Who Came in from the Cold* (1963). Sounds like some writers.

"Espionage is not tainted with any 'legality.'"

> Former DCI **ALLEN DULLES**, explaining that espionage is inherently illegal wherever it is practiced, *The Craft of Intelligence* (1963).

"As motives, ideological and patriotic convictions stand at the top of the list. The ideological volunteer, if he is sincere, is a man whose loyalty you need rarely question, as you must always question the loyalties of people who work chiefly for money or out of a desire for adventure and intrigue. . . . In the upside-down world of espionage one also finds men driven by a desire for power, for self-importance, which they could not satisfy in normal employments."

> Former DCI **ALLEN DULLES**, *The Craft of Intelligence* (1963).

"Espionage is one of the toughest games played. An agent in the right place is hard to find, but when he is found he should be regarded as a pearl beyond price, like a good wife! Everything should be let go by the board rather than that he should be exposed. There are basic laws in that game and that is the first one."

> **DAVID NELLIGAN**, *The Spy in the Castle* (1968). Nelligan was an Irish spy against the British before 1922.

"I'm in the business of producing spies. If I'd wanted to produce widgets, I'd be in private industry."

> CIA operations officer **THEODORE SHACKLEY** to congressional staffer Gregory Treverton, 1975; quoted in Treverton, *Covert Action* (1987).

"Nobody recruits a Soviet—if they come over they recruit themselves."

> **PHILIP AGEE**, *Inside the Company* (1975). Agee, a Latin-American specialist, was guessing.

"The human sources collect the smallest volume of intelligence but generally it is the most difficult to obtain and the most useful when we do get it. It is in this area that the best information is acquired on the all-important subject of intentions."

> Former DDCI General **VERNON WALTERS**, *Silent Missions* (1978).

"The perfect operator in [intelligence] operations is the traditional gray man, so inconspicuous that he can never catch the waiter's eye in a restaurant."

> Former DCI **WILLIAM COLBY**, *Honorable Men* (1978).

"My only regret is that I was not able to cause more damage to the Soviet Union and render more service to France."

> Former KGB officer **VLADIMIR VETROV**, whom the Soviets imprisoned and executed in the early 1980s for spying for France; quoted in Andrew and Mitrokhin, *The Mitrokhin Archive* (1999).

"Like war, spying is a dirty business. Shed of its alleged glory, a soldier's job is to kill. Peel away the claptrap of espionage and the spy's job is to betray trust. The only justification a soldier or spy can have is the moral worth of the cause he represents."

> Former CIA operations officer **WILLIAM HOOD**, *Mole* (1993). The moral worth of the cause is the point of it all.

"It may take ten years for an agent to manoeuvre himself into a post where he has access to policy decisions. Temperamentally the Russians are prepared to wait that time. Temperamentally the Latins and the Anglo-Saxons find this waiting very hard."

> SIS official **JOHN BRUCE LOCKHART**, 1984; cited in West, *Faber Book of Espionage* (1993). And yet, who won the Cold War?

"Espionage must be solidly linked to analysis, because it exists only to provide support to the analysts."

> Former DCI **STANSFIELD TURNER**, *Secrecy and Democracy* (1985). True, but something many operators haven't understood.

"I will work with you. I am now placing my life in your hands. Please don't screw up."

> Soviet U.N. official **SERGEY FEDORENKO**, agreeing to work with CIA officer Aldrich Ames, who betrayed him to Moscow in 1985; quoted in Earley, *Confessions of a Spy* (1997).

"Some inner worm started to torment me; something has to be done. . . . Thus was born my plan of action. . . . I have chosen a course which does not permit one to move backward, and I have no intention of veering from this course."

> **ADOLF TOLKACHEV**, Soviet electronics expert, in 1979, explaining to CIA his reasons for spying for the United States; quoted in *Studies in Intelligence* 47/3 (2003). Tolkachev worked for CIA from 1979 until 1985, providing highly valuable and unique material on Soviet military equipment and R&D. The Soviets discovered his spying and executed him in 1986.

"To the public, 'HUMINT' [human intelligence] remains synonymous with 'spying' or clandestine activities, yet, in reality, overt collection operators such as State Department foreign service officers and military attachés still provide the bulk of HUMINT. Indeed, foreign service officers alone produce eight-tenths of all human reporting, according to some official accounts."

> **BRUCE BERKOWITZ** and **ALLAN GOODMAN**, *Strategic Intelligence* (1989). Quantity, it goes without saying, isn't quality.

"What I did was not spontaneous. It was deliberate. I thought about the price I might pay almost on an everyday basis. In the beginning I asked myself if I had the moral right to do this. I was a Pole. I understood that the Poles should be free and that the United States was the only country that might support the fight for freedom in Poland. . . . It was a dilemma, my moral dilemma, but I became convinced that I not only had the right, I had the moral obligation."

> **RYSZARD KUKLINSKI**, former Polish colonel who passed intelligence to the United States on Soviet and Warsaw Pact plans and capabilities from 1971 to 1981; in the *Washington Post Magazine*, 13 December 1992. After Kuklinski's death in February 2004, DCI George Tenet called him a "true hero of the Cold War to whom we all owe a debt of everlasting gratitude."

"The first Polish officer in NATO."

> **ZBIGNIEW BRZEZINKI**'s moniker for Ryszard Kuklinski, the Polish colonel who passed Warsaw Pact secrets to the United States for more than a decade; quoted in *Studies in Intelligence* 44/1 (2000).

"With expertise in the world of space, of microelectronics and of computer chips we can, and do, develop a remarkable capacity to obtain information which can thwart threats to our security. But there are places where the most sophisticated engineering feats can fall short, and where human reporting may be the only source to tip us off to impending threats. Moreover, even when we uncover with technical means news which could be disturbing or alarming, policymakers inevitably ask us two questions: 'Are you sure?' and 'Do you have a second source?' Human reporting . . . often can provide important corroboration for what we have otherwise picked up. In short: satellites can tip off spies, but spies can also tip off satellites."

> DCI **R. JAMES WOOLSEY** at a conference on "The Origins and Development of the CIA," sponsored by CIA's Center for the Study of Intelligence, March 1994.

"The most important thing to be said about espionage is that even though the take can occasionally be crucial, relatively little information comes from espionage, and very rarely is it decisive. . . . Given the end of the Cold War and the breakup of the Soviet Union, espionage is obviously something the United States can do without. The costs exceed any possible gain."

> Former State Department intelligence chief **ROGER HILSMAN**, *Foreign Affairs* (September–October 1995). Hilsman's was a fringe view then, even more so after September 11.

"There was . . . an evident shortage of spies, or 'human intelligence,' the most helpful kind to have and the hardest to gather."

> *Washington Post* editorial, 12 July 1996, charging that U.S. intelligence failed to warn of terrorist attacks to U.S. military personnel in Saudi Arabia. The *Post* wants more spies?

"This is an espionage organization . . . otherwise I don't know why we're here."

> DCI **GEORGE TENET**, quoted in the *Washington Post*, 22 July 1997.

"In any post I've ever been stationed, meeting and developing an individual is more often than not a very social business in which alcohol plays a major part. The trouble is you can't ply your target with alcohol while you sit there and take notes over iced tea. What you do is excuse yourself to go to the bathroom, go into the privacy of the stall, and write notes like crazy. Next morning you tend to your hangover, go to the office, and write up what you can decipher of your notes from the night before."

> Veteran CIA operations officer **DUANE CLARRIDGE**, *A Spy for All Seasons* (1997).

"We do espionage. That is the nature of what we do. We steal secrets."

> DCI **GEORGE TENET**, interview of 23 June 1998, in *Studies in Intelligence* 42/1 (1998).

"When people think of a spy, they think of James Bond. A good spy, however, is neither the loner nor the serious man in the corner of a room. A good spy is everybody's best friend. . . . It was rather easy to recruit Americans just by being friends with them."

> Former Soviet GRU Colonel **STANISLAV LUNEV**, testimony to the Military R&D Subcommittee of the House National Security Committee, 4 August 1998.

"At the end of the day, the human spy business is the way the human spy business was at the battle of Jericho many hundreds of years ago—human beings stealing secrets and giving those secrets to someone for gain, for advantage."

> CIA operations chief **JAMES PAVITT** in an interview with Reuters published 12 December 2000.

"Today, I have more spies stealing more secrets than at any other time in the history of CIA."

> CIA operations chief **JAMES PAVITT**, address at Duke University, 11 April 2002.

"Spies do not have any shelf life; they cannot be warehoused. Ninety-nine times out of a hundred, a spy is recruited for a specific assignment. . . . One of the benchmarks of a well-run [CIA] station is that it does not cling to spent spies. . . . Time spent attempting to retool a spy is better used in finding new sources."

> Former DCI **RICHARD HELMS**, *A Look over My Shoulder* (2003).

"We have spent the last seven years rebuilding our clandestine service. As Director of Central Intelligence, this has been my highest priority. . . . When you hear pundits say that we have no human intelligence capability—they don't know what they're talking about."

DCI **GEORGE TENET**, remarks at Georgetown University, 5 February 2004.

ESTIMATES

When the president of the United States, or his national security advisors, ask the U.S. intelligence community for its considered, official, predictive, and collective opinion on a vital intelligence matter, the result is an estimate. Estimates can change defense budgets, alarm the complacent, lull the paranoid, or, too often, have no effect at all. The Literary Spy knows the process to be a messy affair; enough metaphorical blood has been spilled over estimates that it's a wonder the various agencies still talk to each other. Rather like a family.

See also: Analysis & Analysts; Ignoring Bad News; U.S. Intelligence "Community"; Warning, Prediction, & Surprise

"And they told him, and said, We came into the land whither thou sentest us, and surely it floweth with milk and honey; and this is the fruit of it. Nevertheless, the people be strong that dwell in the land, and the cities are walled, and very great . . ."

Numbers 13:27–28 (King James). On the one hand . . . on the other hand . . .

"While the individual man is an insoluble puzzle, in the aggregate he becomes a mathematical certainty. You can, for example, never foretell what any one man will do, but you can say with precision what an average number will be up to. Individuals vary, but percentages remain constant."

Sherlock Holmes to Doctor Watson in Sir **ARTHUR CONAN DOYLE**, *The Sign of Four* (1890).

"You see, my dear Watson, it is not really difficult to construct a series of inferences, each dependent on its predecessor and each simple in itself. If, after doing so, one simply knocks out all the central inferences and presents one's audience with the starting-point and the conclusion, one may produce a startling, though possibly a meretricious, effect."

Sherlock Holmes in Sir **ARTHUR CONAN DOYLE**, "The Adventure of the Dancing Men" (1903).

"One forms provisional theories and waits for time or fuller knowledge to explode them. A bad habit . . . but human nature is weak."

Sherlock Holmes in Sir **ARTHUR CONAN DOYLE**, "The Adventure of the Sussex Vampire" (1924).

"No subject related to intelligence is more important than the professional art of making estimates."

Former DDI **RAY CLINE**, *Secrets, Spies and Scholars* (1976).

"Intelligence estimates are useless if produced in a vacuum. They are useful only when they assist directly in the formulation of foreign policy, or the conduct of foreign affairs. Any intelligence agency producing estimates must therefore be a part of some body performing those functions. . . . It has been suggested that a central agency producing national intelligence estimates could serve the President, the Secretaries of State, War and Navy. . . . That suggestion overlooks the fact that the Secretary of State is principally responsible for advising and assisting the President in the field of foreign affairs and for coordinating the activities of all governmental agencies in this field. It is therefore appropriate that the Department of State assume the responsibility for the production of any national intelligence estimates, with the advice and assistance of other governmental agencies."

> Paper prepared by the Secretary of State's staff, 15 November 1945; in *FRUS 1945–1950: Emergence of the Intelligence Establishment* (1996), document 46. The paper recommended that the Department of State oppose the creation of a central agency for the production of national estimates. The idea that a view independent of policymaking might be valuable was still new.

"The primary function of C.I.G. in the production of intelligence . . . will be the preparation and dissemination of definitive estimates of the capabilities and intentions of foreign countries as they affect the national security of the United States. [We need to assign] the best qualified and carefully selected personnel to this vital task."

> DCI **SIDNEY SOUERS** in June 1946 report on the Central Intelligence Group; reproduced in Warner, *CIA Under Truman* (1994).

"The first estimate on the USSR that the new central intelligence machinery tried to produce took two years to finish, from March 1946 to March 1948."

> Former DDI **RAY CLINE**, *Secrets, Spies and Scholars* (1976).

"The expert in an area of knowledge is expected to form judgments from his mastery of the facts and to express those judgments intelligently. It does not follow that in so doing he has arrived at the definitive judgment, that there can be no other besides his own. He certainly is not expected to be an expert in all fields of knowledge which may

have some association with his. Neither is the estimator supposed to know everything. But he is expected to subject the knowledge and the judgment of the expert to scrutiny and reflection and to correlate it with intelligence from other sources. It is the duty of the estimator to make the synthesis."

> **ARTHUR DARLING**, *The Central Intelligence Agency* (1990). Darling is describing the controversial position on estimates held by CIG/CIA in 1946–47—controversial because the military services held that a civilian agency had no right to pass judgment on their expert analyses regarding military intelligence. It's less of a problem today.

"Dissent published in a national intelligence paper should present a distinct difference of opinion on which CIA and the dissenting intelligence organization have found it impossible to agree."

> DCI **ROSCOE HILLENKOETTER** in September 1948 directive; quoted in Ranelagh, *The Agency* (1986).

"Intelligence does not claim infallibility for its prophecies. Intelligence merely holds that the answer which it gives is its most deeply and objectively based and carefully considered estimate."

> **SHERMAN KENT**, *Strategic Intelligence* (1949).

"A national intelligence report or estimate as assembled and produced by the Central Intelligence Agency should reflect the coordination of the best intelligence opinion, based on all available information."

> **ALLEN DULLES**, then a private citizen, in his 1949 report on CIA; quoted in Ranelagh, *The Agency* (1986).

"Legend has it that [DCI Walter Bedell] Smith offered [National Estimates chief William] Langer two hundred personnel slots, only for Langer to reply that he could make do with twenty-five."

BRUCE BERKOWITZ and **ALLAN GOODMAN**, *Strategic Intelligence* (1949). Former DDI Ray Cline says that Smith suggested an office of one thousand and that Langer gave Smith thirty names and said that was sufficient. See Cline, *Secrets, Spies and Scholars* (1976).

"Speculative knowledge [needed for estimates] is the rarest ingredient in the output of intelligence and is produced only by the most competent students this country possesses. It requires of its producers that they be masters of the subject matter, impartial in the presence of new evidence, ingenious in the development of research techniques, imaginative in their hypotheses, sharp in the analysis of their own predilections or prejudices, and skillful in the presentation of their conclusions. It requires of its producers the best in professional training, the highest intellectual integrity, and a very large amount of worldly wisdom. . . . It is that subtle form of knowledge which comes from a set of well-stocked and well-ordered brain cells."

SHERMAN KENT, *Strategic Intelligence* (1949).

"[Preparing a National Intelligence Estimate] is like writing a novel by assigning chapters to people with varying viewpoints and then trying to coordinate and revise the contributions into a consistent whole."

Former member of CIA's Office of National Estimates; quoted in Schecter and Deriabin, *The Spy Who Saved the World* (1995).

"No job I ever had in the intelligence business was more challenging and satisfying than writing the first draft of a national intelligence estimate. Let's say the subject was 'Likelihood of Imminent Arab-Israeli War.' Before you on your desk would be assembled all the intelligence the United States possessed on that subject, consisting of military attaché reports on the relative strengths of the opposing forces, U.S. Embassy analyses of concerns and goals of the rival governments, and agent reports of unusual military preparations and troop movements. These you would put together in a coherent account, fifteen to twenty-five pages long, that would tell your reader how things stood at present, what further developments would signal the imminent onset of war, and your best judgment as to when the tensions would boil over. Some of these pronouncements would rest on very thin ice. There is almost never enough firm intelligence to support a solid, definitive statement. If there were, there would be no need for an estimate; the threat would be self-evident. So, writing an estimate required some risk-taking, some chasm-jumping, and this was part of the challenge. The satisfying part came when your leaps across the unknown were accepted by your peers and superiors and presented to the president of the United States as the official position of the Central Intelligence Agency."

Former DDI **R. JACK SMITH**, *The Unknown CIA* (1989). Smith speaks of the 1950s; today, National Intelligence Estimates are less the "official" CIA position and more the consensus of the Intelligence Community.

"Estimating is what you do when you do not know."

SHERMAN KENT, "Estimates and Influence," *Foreign Service Journal* (April 1969).

"The estimates of the 1950s portray the Soviet Union as aggressive but unwilling to take foolish risks. . . . [CIA's] Office of National Estimates reassured American policymakers and planners that the USSR would not deliberately go to war unless it thought that its vital interests were at stake."

SCOTT KOCH, *Selected Estimates on the Soviet Union* (1993).

"We say there isn't going to be a war next year, but we say it in the most alarming way possible."

> CIA Office of National Estimates member **WILLIAM WRIGHT**; quoted in Powers, *The Man Who Kept the Secrets* (1979).

"The intelligence community, I am quite safe in saying, would be quite content if it were not called upon for such crystal-ball gazing."

> Former DCI **ALLEN DULLES**, *The Craft of Intelligence* (1963).

"Of all the different duties devolving on CIA as a result of the National Security Act's requirement that it 'correlate and evaluate' national security intelligence, the preparation of national estimates is the most difficult, the most sophisticated, and the most important. . . . When the answers are clear to questions about the future, there is no need for an estimate. The easy questions are never asked."

> Former DDI **RAY CLINE**, *Secrets, Spies and Scholars* (1976).

"It is no exaggeration to say that . . . there was rarely a day when I failed to give earnest study to reports of our progress [in ICBMs] and to estimates of Soviet capabilities."

> Former President **DWIGHT EISENHOWER** in his memoirs; cited in Andrew, *For the President's Eyes Only* (1995).

"The Eisenhower administration marked a golden era for national intelligence estimates. . . . Estimates had an acknowledged role, a designated place, in the process of formulating national policy and strategy. When policy papers were submitted to the National Security Council they were accompanied by an NIE that described and analyzed the potential threat—or opportunity—presented therein to U.S. security interests, analyzed its dynamics, and essayed some prediction as to the pace at which

it might proceed and its likely outcome. . . . It was a highly rational, precise, efficient system, [but it] gave way suddenly and without transition to the rollicking Kennedy style [that] resembled something like a pickup touch football game crossed with a Harvard seminar."

> Former DDI **R. JACK SMITH**, *The Unknown CIA* (1989).

"Circle now squared."

> DCI's Special Assistant on Vietnam **GEORGE CARVER** to DCI Richard Helms, reporting a compromise with the U.S. military on estimates of Vietcong strength, September 1967; quoted in Andrew, *For the President's Eyes Only* (1995).

"The mistake of the century. . . . [CIA] had sacrificed its integrity on the altar of public expediency."

> **GEORGE ALLEN**, deputy to Special Assistant on Vietnam George Carver, on CIA's compromise with the U.S. military on estimates of Vietcong strength; quoted in Andrew, *For the President's Eyes Only* (1995).

"Those goddam [Soviet] estimates of yours out of the Agency have been wrong for years, and they still are."

> President **RICHARD NIXON** in 1969, according to DCI Richard Helms; quoted in Andrew, *For the President's Eyes Only* (1995).

"Estimates tend to tell what the various intelligence agencies can agree upon rather than what the policymaker wants to know."

> Attributed, by CIA officers, to **HENRY KISSINGER**.

"[National Intelligence Estimates] are written jointly by as many of the intelligence agencies as have competence in a given subject . . . though the NIE process resembles the work of a committee, the final product is that of the DCI, whose opinion always prevails. It has to, or it would be one of committee compromise, too watered down to be of value. . . . If NIEs are worth the effort, it is because they force healthful interaction within the Intelligence Community, not so much because they produce useful material for policy-makers to read."

> Former DCI **STANSFIELD TURNER**, *Secrecy and Democracy* (1985).

"The Estimates are my Estimates. I'm a little bit looser about that when it comes to putting in other views. But they're my Estimates. I'm responsible for drawing the conclusions and presenting them. But I feel I have a concomitant obligation to the user to see that any well-substantiated alternative view is also laid on the table."

> DCI **WILLIAM CASEY**, October 1985; quoted in Ranelagh, *The Agency* (1986).

"No one has ever won a high-level policy debate by waving an NIE in the air and saying, 'But this is what the Estimate says!'"

> **BRUCE BERKOWITZ** and **ALLAN GOODMAN**, *Strategic Intelligence* (1989). No, the NIE-waving happens later.

"I am sick and tired with those in the political arena or, yes, in the media who do nothing but carp and criticize and second-guess the intelligence community of the United States. Measuring intentions . . . is an extraordinarily difficult task, and no one can expect every estimate to be 100 percent correct or 100 percent perfect."

> President and former DCI **GEORGE H. W. BUSH** in 1991; quoted in Andrew, *For the President's Eyes Only* (1995). How about 80–90 percent?

"Through INR State gets to participate in the intelligence community's most important products,

the National Estimates, and to influence matters far from its turf. Readers of 'the Estimates' often marvel at instances when the Director, Bureau of Intelligence and Research, Department of State takes a position with regard to abstruse matters of weapons technology about which State has no sources and which State officials are obviously unequipped to judge."

> **ANGELO CODEVILLA**, *Informing Statecraft* (1992). The intelligence chiefs of the military services used to make this same argument regarding CIA.

"'We believe' is probably the most common sentence starter in the National Estimates. . . . The second most common phrase in the Estimates is 'We have no evidence' or (its variant) 'We have no confirmed evidence.' That is longhand for 'no.' But since the Estimates often have very little evidence for *any* proposition, the difference between 'We believe' and 'We have no evidence' is subjective."

> **ANGELO CODEVILLA**, *Informing Statecraft* (1992). It's hard for us to believe that an often rancorous interagency process will allow the deliberate blurring of educated, evidence-based opinion and unsubstantiated speculation.

"It is precisely in long-term analysis of familiar subjects and broad trends where secret information tends to be less critical and government analysts are for the most part no better and often not as good as their counterparts in academia and the private sector. . . . The emphasis placed on such estimates should be reduced."

> Council on Foreign Relations, *Making Intelligence Smarter* (1996).

"Estimates are issued over the signature of the DCI in his capacity as the head of the US Intelligence Community and represent the coordinated views of the Community's member agencies. The final product bears the statement: *This National Intelligence Estimate represents the views of the Director of Central Intelligence with the advice and assistance of the US Intelligence Community.*"

BENJAMIN FISCHER, *At Cold War's End* (1999).

"There is unmistakable evidence that Saddam Hussein is working aggressively to develop nuclear weapons and will likely have nuclear weapons within the next five years. . . . We also should remember we have always underestimated the progress Saddam has made in development of weapons of mass destruction."

Senator **JAY ROCKEFELLER**, statement during Senate discussion supporting the resolution to authorize the use of force against Iraq, *Congressional Record*, 10 October 2002.

"As a student of this business, I know that intelligence estimates almost always underestimate capabilities. They rarely overestimate capabilities, in terms of time lines. The Soviet Union was supposed to have created an atomic weapon by 1955;

it was 1949. In 1991, we thought Iraq was years from the capability to enrich uranium and build nuclear weapons; it was a year from the capability to enrich uranium and build nuclear weapons. So time lines are always underestimated."

CONDOLEEZZA RICE, national security advisor to President George W. Bush; quoted in the *New Yorker* (14–21 October 2002).

"The President is under no obligation to accept any intelligence estimate at face value, nor is he required in any way to follow it. The President's responsibility is to act in the best interest of the country."

Former DCI **RICHARD HELMS**, *A Look over My Shoulder* (2003).

"Persons pretending to forecast the future shall be considered disorderly under Subdivision 3, Section 901 of the Criminal Code and liable to a fine of $250 and/or six months in prison."

New York State Code of Criminal Procedure, Sec. 899.

- **Fact versus Fiction**
- **Failures**
- **FBI & Law Enforcement**
- **Feedback & Tasking**
- **Fighting the Cold War**
- **Fronts**

FACT VERSUS FICTION

Storytellers and filmmakers have long found the world of intelligence irresistible as subject matter—for that world's perceived romance, adventure, intrigue, betrayal, and, yes, the sex, too. But like a physicist watching and even enjoying *Star Trek*, the Literary Spy knows the limitations and distortions that make up such storytelling and hopes that grown-ups will not mistake it for reality. In the hiring process for U.S. intelligence services, the Literary Spy would mandate that all applicants would be asked the following question: What two sources of information have had the most bearing on your knowledge of intelligence? (A) films; (B) spy novels; (C) newspaper articles and columns; (D) scholarly books and articles; (E) memoirs. Any candidate who answers with (A) or (B) would be politely shown the door.

See also: Intelligence & American Culture

"One of the greatest author-spies in history, Daniel Defoe, never wrote a word about espionage in his major novels. In the eyes of many, Defoe is accounted one of the professionals in the early history of British intelligence. He was not only a successful operative but later became the first chief of an orga-

nized British intelligence system, a fact which was not publicly known until many years after his death.... Try if you will to find even the slightest reference to spies or espionage in any of [his] books.... I cannot dispel the conviction altogether that he never did this because, having the inside view, he felt that for security reasons he could not give a true and full story of espionage as it was really practiced in his day, and, as a novelist Defoe was above inventing something at variance with his craft."

> Former DCI **ALLEN DULLES**, *The Craft of Intelligence* (1963).

"Every problem becomes very childish when once it is explained to you."

> Sherlock Holmes to Doctor Watson in Sir **ARTHUR CONAN DOYLE**, "The Adventure of the Dancing Men" (1903). The Sherlock Holmes stories are wonderful entertainment, full of wisdom about investigation and analysis, but in real life, of course, events do not happen in accordance with an author's predetermined outcome.

"This book is founded on my experiences in the [British] Intelligence Department during the last war, but rearranged for the purposes of fiction. Fact is a poor storyteller.... The work of an agent in the Intelligence Department is on the whole extremely monotonous. A lot of it is uncommonly useless. The material it offers for stories is scrappy and pointless; the author has himself to make it coherent, dramatic and probable."

> Former SIS officer **W. SOMERSET MAUGHAM** in the preface to his novel *Ashenden* (1927).

"If I didn't dramatise [this work] in some manner the reader would go to sleep. To write saleable stuff one must dramatise. Things don't happen in a dramatic fashion. There is therefore nothing to do but either dramatise or not write at all."

> American cryptologist **HERBERT YARDLEY** responding to criticism of his book *The American Black Chamber* (1931), an often fanciful account of U.S. codebreaking activities; quoted in Kahn, *The Codebreakers* (1996).

"In the high ranges of Secret Service work, the actual facts in many cases were in every respect equal to the most fantastic inventions of romance and melodrama. Tangle within tangle, plot and counter-plot, ruse and treachery, cross and double cross, true agent, false agent, double agent, gold and steel, the bomb, the dagger and the firing party were interwoven in many a texture so intricate as to be incredible and yet true."

> **WINSTON CHURCHILL**, 1932; cited in Stafford, *Churchill and Secret Service* (1998). Churchill's imagination, prodigious writing skills, and fascination with intelligence would have given him a fine career as a spy novelist or screenwriter—and thank heavens he didn't pursue such work.

"Look here, Blenkinsop, you're going to be invaluable to us. I ought to warn you, though, that our work doesn't consist entirely of meeting mysterious Polish countesses in old castles. Of course, we have our little dramas, but the greater part of the work is routine stuff. Card-indexing, filing, mak-

ing out lists, putting agents' reports into proper English."

> Fictional British intelligence chief to a new recruit in Sir **COMPTON MACKENZIE**'s spoof on intelligence, *Water on the Brain* (1933). Mackenzie's sendup was his response to the British government's suppression of his memoirs of his SIS work during World War I. Mackenzie later said, "It has indeed become impossible for me to devise any ludicrous situation the absurdity of which will not soon be surpassed by officialdom."

"*Water on the Brain*, which used to be almost impossible to procure in this country, was 'must' reading in the wartime OSS. It is actually a useful casebook of *do's* and *don'ts* in intelligence work. Chiefly *don'ts*. I recall that a Photostat copy of it was circulating in OSS and in great demand. There was a waiting list. Through some error on the part of the technicians who had photostated and bound the office copy, the pages had been set in the binding in reverse order, so that one had to read from back to front. Perhaps it was intentional, considering the nature of the contents."

> Former DCI **ALLEN DULLES** in his edited volume *Great Spy Stories from Fiction* (1969).

"I had rid myself long ago of any ideas that the Secret Service was the glamorous and exciting career of the novelists. I had yet to see any false beards or to encounter alluring adventuresses who would seduce me from my loyalties. My car was a Citroën, several years old, instead of a shining Bristol or Aston Martin. Although I had done some pistol practice on the range in London, I did not habitually carry a Beretta strapped to my armpit."

> SIS wartime officer **PHILIP JOHNS** describing his arrival in Lisbon as SIS station chief in 1941; cited in West, *Faber Book of Espionage* (1993).

"Reality hasn't the least obligation to be interesting."

> JORGE LUIS BORGES, *Death and the Compass* (1944). But every writer does.

"A little fact will sustain a lot of illusion."

> ERIC AMBLER, *Judgment on Deltchev* (1951).

"I listened, and it seemed more like a dime novel than a historical fact."

> President DWIGHT EISENHOWER, writing in his diary about the CIA debrief of Operation AJAX that restored the Shah of Iran to his throne in 1953; cited in Stafford, *Churchill and Secret Service* (1998).

"According to estimates from CIA officials who worked on the U-2 and the OXCART (SR-71 or Blackbird) project, over half of all UFO reports from the late 1950s through the 1960s were accounted for by manned reconnaissance flights (namely the U-2) over the United States. This led the Air Force to make misleading and deceptive statements to the public in order to allay public fears and to protect an extraordinarily sensitive national security project."

> CIA historian GERALD HAINES, "CIA's Role in the Study of UFOs, 1947–90," *Studies in Intelligence* (1997). Of course, that's what they *want* you to believe.

"People who know about spy systems do not write about them. People who do not know about them, or fancy that they know about them, do do some writing."

> CIA National Estimates chief SHERMAN KENT, 1951; quoted in Winks, *Cloak and Gown* (1987). And much of that writing *is* doo-doo.

"Spy fiction, however many shots ring out, is always neat and tidy; the facts of espionage are quite the opposite. It is abundant in loose ends, false starts, and in incidents that are never quite rounded off."

> Former SIS officer DAVID WALKER, 1957; cited in West, *Faber Book of Espionage* (1993).

"Not that it matters, but a great deal of the background to this story is accurate."

> IAN FLEMING, note to his James Bond novel *From Russia with Love* (1957). The major problem with the Bond stories, in the opinion of real intelligence officers, is that any correlation with accuracy seems coincidental. Not that it matters.

"These things don't happen in real life."

> James Bond in IAN FLEMING, *Thunderball* (1961). They don't until they do.

"Thank you very much for your note. . . . Please also thank your Chief for the splendidly gallant services he and his organization have always rendered on behalf of my good friend James Bond. . . . With kindest regards, Yours sincerely, Ian Fleming."

> Letter from IAN FLEMING, the creator of James Bond, to a member of DCI Allen Dulles's staff, 14 September 1961; in CIA's Historical Intelligence Collection.

"Bond. James Bond."

> Sean Connery in the 1962 film *Dr. No;* cited as the most famous movie line in history by *The Guinness Book of Film* (1998).

"James Bond in the real world of espionage wouldn't survive four minutes."

> H. KEITH MELTON, spy equipment connoisseur; quoted in *Smithsonian* (July 2001).

"I fear that James Bond in real life would have had a thick dossier in the Kremlin after his first exploit and would not have survived the second."

> Former DCI **ALLEN DULLES** in his edited volume *Great Spy Stories from Fiction* (1969).

"Most spy romances and thrillers are written for audiences who wish to be entertained rather than educated in the business of intelligence."

> Former DCI **ALLEN DULLES**, *The Craft of Intelligence* (1963). Most people, of course, *prefer* entertainment to education.

"In two and a half years of working with these men I have yet to meet a 007."

> President **LYNDON JOHNSON**, 30 June 1966, at the swearing-in of Richard Helms as DCI; cited in CIA, *"Our First Line of Defense"* (1996).

"It's depressing that the words 'secret agent' have become synonymous with 'sex maniac.'"

> "Sir" James Bond, played by David Niven, in the 1967 film and spy spoof *Casino Royale*. It's more depressing still that there's little truth behind it.

"Truth has a hard time once legends are established which appease our thirst for heroes and heroics."

> Former DCI **ALLEN DULLES**, foreword to his edited volume *Great True Spy Stories* (1968).

"The statesman, the diplomat, and the scientist may be the decisive figures in the real history of our time, but from the point of view of fiction they are colorless compared with the spy. . . . The spy has the muscle and the daring to take the place of the discarded hero of yore. . . . If it is a fact that a great many spy tales are not devoted to depicting the intelligence business as it really is practiced,

there is still no good reason why they cannot be good stories."

> Former DCI **ALLEN DULLES**, foreword to his edited volume *Great Spy Stories from Fiction* (1969).

"Every novelist has something in common with a spy; he watches, he overhears, he seeks motives and analyzes character."

> Former SIS officer and novelist **GRAHAM GREENE**, *A Sort of Life* (1971).

"A new organization of uncertain makeup, using the name 'Group of the Martyr Ebenezer Scrooge,' plans to sabotage the annual courier flight of the Government of the North Pole. Prime Minister and Chief Courier S. Claus has been notified and security precautions are being coordinated worldwide."

> Item in a White House "Weekly Situation Report on International Terrorism," 17 December 1974; cited by WashingtonTimes.com, 23 December 2003. This eight-page intelligence report, the rest of which contained genuine threat information, was recently declassified.

"[It is] the myths about intelligence—the cloak-and-dagger exploits—that have made it so hard to persuade the aficionados of spy fiction that the heart of intelligence work consists of properly evaluated information from all sources, however collected."

> Former DDI **RAY CLINE**, *Secrets, Spies and Scholars* (1976). The Literary Spy believes that the spy fiction buffs know this—and don't care.

"Writers of thrillers tend to gravitate to the Secret Service as surely as the mentally unstable become psychiatrists, or the impotent pornographers."

> Former SIS officer **MALCOLM MUGGERIDGE**, *Chronicles of Wasted Time: The Infernal Grove* (1973).

"Most books on the subject of intelligence operations are garbage."

Former DDI **RAY CLINE**, *Secrets, Spies and Scholars* (1976).

"[Former DCI Richard] Helms liked the standard spy stories in which secret agents are given impossible assignments and carry them out with the sort of neat dispatch so lacking in life. He enjoyed the novels of Ian Fleming [and] found a similar charm in the novels of E. Howard Hunt, who wrote more than forty thrillers, mostly under pseudonyms, after Helms gave him permission to do so in the 1960s. . . . But there was one spy novel Helms did not like—John le Carré's *The Spy Who Came in from the Cold,* a bitter and cynical story of violence, betrayal, and spiritual exhaustion. It was not just the violence Helms minded, but the betrayal, the mood of defeat, the meanness, the numb loneliness of a man for whom loyalty has become a joke. . . . Helms's son Dennis said his father didn't just dislike le Carré's book; he detested it."

THOMAS POWERS, *The Man Who Kept the Secrets* (1979). Helms may have mellowed; in his posthumously published autobiography, he characterized le Carré's early books as among "most of the better spy novels."

"Given le Carré's aim, it is not surprising that his spies fail, because in his somewhat Puritanical view of things spying is a misbegotten profession in an imperfect world. If people were good and nations decent, there would be no need for it. Which is quite true."

Former DCI **ALLEN DULLES** in his edited volume *Great Spy Stories from Fiction* (1969).

"This never happened to James Bond."

CIA officer and American hostage **WILLIAM DAUGH-ERTY** recalling his thoughts at being moved by his Iranian captors into a small steel cell; in *Studies in Intelligence* (spring 1998). In the 1969 film *On Her Majesty's Secret Service,* Bond says, "This never happened to the other fellow."

"Like its protagonists, the subject matter of the spy novel or film is enveloped in a shroud of secrecy inappropriate to other genres. In a realistic novel or film we can easily detect a false characterization, as we have some personal knowledge of how ordinary people behave, whether they be carpenters or physicians. With intelligence and espionage it is different."

WALTER LAQUEUR, *A World of Secrets* (1985). In other words, novelists or filmmakers can make up just about anything about the intelligence profession and people will tend to believe it.

"Writers are a subversive crowd, nothing if not traitors. The better the writer, the greater the betrayal tends to appear, a thing the secret community has learned the hard way, for I hear it is no longer quite so keen to have us aboard."

JOHN LE CARRÉ [David Cornwell] in 1986; cited in Polmar and Allen, *Encyclopedia of Espionage* (1997). Surely le Carré isn't surprised?

"*Nothing* I write is authentic."

JOHN LE CARRÉ [David Cornwell], who admits to "a few ineffectual but extremely formative years in British Intelligence"; quoted on CNN.com, 26 December 2000. At last, honesty.

"One of the main attractions of spy fiction is that [it] gives us not only a glimpse of the workings of the secret world, but also a picture which changes with the times and from generation to generation. It is this ability to adapt which ensures its continuation."

KATY FLETCHER, "Sense and Sensationalism in American Spy Fiction," in Jeffreys-Jones and Lownie, *North American Spies* (1991).

"Spy fiction is not so divorced from 'reality' as one might imagine."

> **RHODRI JEFFREYS-JONES** in Jeffreys-Jones and Lownie, *North American Spies* (1991). Jeffreys-Jones is a noted intelligence historian, but really, how would he know?

"The belief encouraged by many spy writers that Intelligence officers consist of moles, morons, shits and homosexuals makes the Intelligence job no easier."

> MI5 official (and spy novelist) **JOHN BINGHAM**; quoted in West, *Faber Book of Espionage* (1993).

"Hollywood and a few former intelligence operatives notwithstanding, the secret world bears little resemblance to the OK Corral. Spying is too productive an activity to be jeopardized by case officers turned gunslinger."

> Former CIA operations officer **WILLIAM HOOD**, *Mole* (1993).

"The satellites are good, but they're not that good."

> Former DCI **R. JAMES WOOLSEY** commenting on the movie *Patriot Games*, which depicted CIA officers observing real-time imagery of an attack on a terrorist training camp; quoted in *National Security Studies Quarterly* (spring 1997). Not yet, anyway.

"The first of many writers to liken espionage to chess coined one of the least apt analogies in literature. However fetching the notion that opposing intelligence chiefs are like chess-masters—pondering the black and white pieces and plotting tactics a dozen moves ahead—it is absurd. Worse, it ignores the real fascination of espionage. On the chessboard each piece is clearly visible and moves in a prescribed fashion. In victory and defeat, the white men remain indelibly white, the black resolutely black. There are no traitor pieces, no false knights, and even pawns never defect. Spy, counter-spy; agent, double agent; traitor, hero . . . spying is life turned all around."

> Former CIA operations officer **WILLIAM HOOD**, *Mole* (1993).

"[I decided] to commit literary iconoclasm: I would write a book in which the good guys and the bad guys were actually distinguishable from one another. I took a deep breath and further resolved that the good guys would be—the Americans! . . . And so I thought to attempt to write a book in which it was never left in doubt that the CIA, for all the complaints about its performance, is, when all is said and done, not persuasively likened to the KGB. . . . The point I sought to make, and continued to do so in subsequent novels, is that the CIA, whatever its failures, sought, during those long years in the struggle for the world, to advance the honorable alternative."

> **WILLIAM F. BUCKLEY, JR.**, on why he wrote the Blackford Oakes novels, in *The Right Word* (1996).

"The role of sex in espionage has always attracted more attention than it merited. American secret services have found that happy and well-adjusted family men and women make better agents than those who are sexually promiscuous, emotionally impaired, and susceptible to blackmail."

> **STAN TAYLOR** and **DANIEL SNOW**, "Cold War Spies," *Intelligence and National Security* (April 1997).

"The myth is that the United States has unlimited satellite resources providing real-time, minutely detailed coverage of any spot on Earth. That's Hollywood. The reality is that U.S. imagery assets are strained to their limits, with more demand being placed on them today than at any time in the last decade . . . the intelligence community often has to settle for one pass over an important target every few days."

> Former CIA officer **MILT BEARDEN** in the *Los Angeles Times*, 31 May 1998.

"It's like something from an Austin Powers episode, not a front-rank intelligence service."

> Canadian parliamentarian lamenting the loss of a top secret document of the Canadian Intelligence Security Service by an analyst who left the document in her car while watching a hockey game. Thieves broke into her car, stole her briefcase, and tossed it as worthless into a dumpster. Toronto's dumpsters were searched to no avail. *Boston Globe*, 18 November 1999.

"I suspect that CIA more than perhaps any institution in America has been subject to mythology and misinformation. The result of too many novels, too many television shows, too many conspiracy theorists, too many James Bond and Jack Ryan movies, at least one too many movies directed by Oliver Stone."

> Former DCI **ROBERT GATES**, conference on "US Intelligence and the End of the Cold War," Texas A&M University, 19 November 1999.

"I would never accept at face value the truth of a film. I would go out and read further."

> **OLIVER STONE**, director of at least one movie that suggests CIA murdered President John F. Kennedy; quoted in *USA Today*, 7 December 2001.

"We couldn't have won the Cold War without you."

> President **BILL CLINTON** declaring Sean Connery—filmdom's Agent 007—an honorary U.S. citizen, 5 December 1999. Depends on what the meaning of "we" is.

"I never saw a spy who carried a gun, apart from James Bond. No one ever tried to shoot me, nobody tried to machine-gun me, no American agent tried to take me away to the States."

> Retired KGB officer **MIKHAIL LYUBIMOV** explaining that espionage was not quite as romantic as he had thought; quoted in the *Philadelphia Inquirer*, 22 February 2001.

"Don [Adams] and I were recently invited to visit the CIA for an exhibit they had of gadgets from 'Get Smart,' 'I Spy,' 'The Man from U.N.C.L.E.,' the Bond movies, and so forth. And they said that during those years, the CIA actually did watch those shows and made some of those devices actually work."

> Television actress **BARBARA FELDON**, who played Agent 99 on the 1960s spy spoof *Get Smart*; quoted in "The old nostalgic TV trick," Knight-Ridder Newspapers, 31 March 2001. The main feature of the CIA exhibit was the shoe phone that actor Don Adams used as Maxwell Smart. Whether CIA replicated it will not be revealed outside of the Cone of Silence.

"We used to assign one of our officers to watch 'Mission: Impossible' every week because we'd always get the phone call the next morning, 'Can you guys do that?'"

> Retired CIA operations officer **TONY MENDEZ**; quoted in the *New York Times*, 4 December 2001.

"I don't know what fantasy people have about the CIA, but it looks like an ad agency with desks with dividers and computers with screen savers."

> Hollywood film producer **STRATTON LEOPOLD** on making *The Sum of All Fears* with CIA cooperation; quoted in the *New York Times*, 6 May 2001. And the screen savers are boring.

"If you believe the movies, the following is a pretty accurate rundown of a spy's daily schedule: Wake up with beautiful, satisfied woman nuzzling under your arm. Using judo, kill evil henchman hiding in closet. Go to casino. Order morning martini.

Play baccarat with nefarious leader of ACRONYM, an underground network of terrorists, thieves, and extortionists. Return to cabana. Discover that beautiful, satisfied woman has been murdered in a highly unusual fashion. Find beautiful, satisfied woman's standoffish but equally beautiful sister. Find ACRONYM headquarters. Snuff ACRONYM bid for world domination. Watch nefarious ACRONYM leader escape. Bed down with beautiful (and no longer standoffish) sister. Repeat."

> Film reviewer **DAVID BLEND** on America Online's website Moviefone.com, 14 June 2001. One can dream.

"There are a number of professions and jobs in which people do dangerous and important things for the country: the military, the FBI, the police, fire [departments], CIA, intelligence in general. Intelligence is the only one that has systematically, for the last 20 to 30 years, been portrayed by Hollywood and by television in a negative light."

> Former DCI **R. JAMES WOOLSEY**, interviewed on CNN, 31 August 2001.

"The acting job that we do is part of our workday world. It's very similar to the notion of role playing and acting in Hollywood. The difference is that [with Hollywood], when somebody says cut, you know they're talking about stopping the action. [But] for us, it could be your throat."

> CIA spokesman and former operations officer **CHASE BRANDON**, interviewed on CNN, 31 August 2001.

"If I were to have proposed a novel pre-Hanssen with a character like him in it, nobody would have bought it. Everyone would've said it's crazy."

> Spy novelist and former CIA officer **ROBERT ANDREWS** on the implausibility of real-life FBI agent Robert Hanssen, the staunchly anti-Communist and outwardly pious Roman Catholic arrested in 2001 for spying for Moscow; quoted in the *Washingtonian* (September 2001).

"Truth in art and truth in life are not the same."

> Former CIA operations officer and spy novelist **CHARLES McCARRY**; quoted in the *Washingtonian* (September 2001).

"After the Berlin Wall fell in 1989, it seemed that even before the dust had settled the obituary of the spy novel was being written. With the end of the Evil Empire, spies seemed obsolete. . . . All that has changed with Sept. 11. Once again America has real enemies and a great, ambient sense of anxiety that seems certain to produce a new age of espionage fiction."

> **JOSEPH FINDER**, "The Spy Novel Returns," *New York Times*, 25 November 2001.

"The difference between fiction and reality is that fiction makes sense."

> Novelist **TOM CLANCY**; interviewed in the *Washingtonian*, December 2001.

"[CIA] teams have even been sent to pick the brains of Hollywood scriptwriters who dream up far-fetched terror spectaculars. . . . The CIA has found evidence in seized al-Qaeda documents that bin Laden's operatives watch action-adventure movies for ideas."

> *Time* (8 July 2002). See? The Great Satan is good for something.

"The former intelligence officers [included in this anthology] share a certain literary perspective: sophisticated, cynical, and mordant. [They] write with a kind of cloaked anger, a belief that the world is a place where political power is maintained by means of treachery and betrayal, and, worse, that this gloomy fact of life has as much to do with elemental human nature as it does with the ambitions of states."

Spy novelist **ALAN FURST**, introduction to his edited volume *The Book of Spies: An Anthology of Literary Espionage* (2003). Furst is referring to Graham Greene, John le Carré, Somerset Maugham, and Charles McCarry.

"Best-sellers from William Le Queux, early in the [twentieth] century, to Ian Fleming, Len Deighton, and their less talented followers ignore the fact that the purpose behind the imagined hugger-mugger involved in secret intelligence collection is to keep national policymakers well enough informed to make sound decisions and to avoid catastrophic mistakes."

Former DCI **RICHARD HELMS**, *A Look over My Shoulder* (2003). Helms rightly points to intelligence analysis, not the sexy exploits of the operators, as "the heart of the matter" when it comes to the intelligence profession. But not even the Literary Spy wants to read stories about the production of important memoranda.

FAILURES

Intelligence serves the national interests of the state, and the high stakes involved mean that failure, as the saying goes, is not an option—or it shouldn't be. With high stakes, however, go the highest of expectations, and intelligence seems continually to fall short. More so than any other function of government, intelligence can fail in myriad ways. It can fail to warn, and it can simply fail to get its message across. It can fail at analysis, and it can fail to collect the right material. It can fail to keep operations secret, and it can fail at making operations successful. It can fail to catch spies, and it fails when it catches spies. With the specter of failure always haunting the intelligence profession, it's a wonder to the Literary Spy why anyone would want to join. But still the résumés come, thank heavens.

See also: Critics & Defenders; Estimates; Ignoring Bad News; Limits of Intelligence; Presidents & Intelligence; Successes; Warning, Prediction, & Surprise

"How dreadful it is when the right judge judges wrong!"

Greek poet **SOPHOCLES**, *Antigone* (c. 442 B.C.).

"I am more afraid of our own mistakes than of our enemies' designs."

PERICLES, speech to the Athenians, 432 B.C.; cited in Heinl, *Dictionary of Military and Naval Quotations* (1966).

"It is possible to fail in many ways . . . while to succeed is possible only in one way (for which reason also one is easy and the other difficult—to miss the mark [is] easy, to hit it difficult)."

ARISTOTLE, *Nichomachean Ethics* (c. 330 B.C.).

"What have appeared to be the most striking successes have often, if they are not rightly used, brought the most overwhelming disasters in their train, and conversely the most terrible calamities have, if bravely endured, actually turned out to benefit the sufferers."

POLYBIUS, *The Rise of the Roman Empire* (c. 200 B.C.); cited in Warner, *Central Intelligence* (2001).

"How I would hate the reputation of being clever at writing but stupid at everything else."

MONTAIGNE, *Essays* (1580).

"O, Where hath our intelligence been drunk? Where hath it slept?"

> King John upon hearing that a large French army is moving against England, in **WILLIAM SHAKESPEARE**, *King John* (1596), Act IV, scene 2.

"When sorrows come, they come not single spies, but in battalions."

> Claudius in **WILLIAM SHAKESPEARE**, *Hamlet* (1601), Act IV, scene 5.

"It is one thing to show a man that he is in error, and another to put him in possession of the truth."

> **JOHN LOCKE**, *An Essay Concerning Human Understanding* (1690).

"A man should never be ashamed to say he has been wrong, which is but saying in other words that he is wiser today than he was yesterday."

> **ALEXANDER POPE**, *Thoughts on Various Subjects* (1727).

"A spy from the enemy by his own full confession, apprehended last night, was executed [this] day at 11 o'clock in front of the Artillery Park."

> Entry in British General **WILLIAM HOWE**'s orderly book, marking the execution of American spy Nathan Hale, 22 September 1776; quoted in Miller, *Spying for America* (1989).

"Perhaps no mission in the history of American intelligence was more amateurishly conceived and carried out than [Nathan] Hale's.... The young officer was completely without experience in intelligence. He had no training, no contacts behind British lines, no cipher or code to hide any information he might be able to gather....Only a commander desperate for intelligence could have sent such a poorly prepared secret agent into the field."

> **NATHAN MILLER**, *Spying for America* (1989).

"The incomprehensible part about it all is that with this elaborate espionage network, operated by experts and staffed by brave and intelligent men, the information that was brought to [Union General George] McClellan was so disastrously wrong. Disastrously, because it made the Rebel armies appear more than twice as large as they really were and because McClellan believed it and acted on it. Pinkerton's spy system was well organized, bold, successful—and McClellan would have been infinitely better off if he had had no spy system whatever."

> **BRUCE CATTON** on Union intelligence, in *Mr. Lincoln's Army* (1951).

"For many years after the Second World War the U.S. Army, newly conscious of the importance of intelligence, had an intelligence school, situated at Fort Devens, Massachusetts. It is ironic that soldiers received intelligence training at a post named for the [Union] general who operated on the principle that the only reliable intelligence was what came down from higher headquarters. That error lies at the root of Charles Devens's action, or inaction, that led to the rout [at Chancellorsville]. ... General [Joseph] Hooker had created a competent intelligence service, but evidently he had failed to impress on his subordinate commanders the basic point that they were all part of an intelligence *system*."

> **EDWIN FISHEL**, *Secret War for the Union* (1996).

"To the thesis that good intelligence does not necessarily win battles, General [Joseph] Hooker [in June 1863] added the corollary that intelligence error does not always lose them. Chancellorsville, the battle engendered by a brilliant intelligence success, ended in inglorious defeat because of battlefield mistakes. Now intelligence error had a magnificent result: it put Hooker's army in the lead in what turned out to be a race for a crucial position on a fishhook-shaped ridge at Gettysburg."

EDWIN FISHEL, *Secret War for the Union* (1996). Hooker's fortuitous error was in thinking Lee's army was farther north than it really was, and this mistake may have helped win the battle, decide the war, and save the Union.

"'You don't know much,' said the Duchess, 'and that's a fact.'"

LEWIS CARROLL, *Alice's Adventures in Wonderland* (1865).

"Watson, if it should ever strike you that I am getting a little overconfident in my powers, or giving less pains to a case than it deserves, kindly whisper 'Norbury' in my ear, and I shall be infinitely obliged to you."

Sherlock Holmes in Sir **ARTHUR CONAN DOYLE**, "The Adventure of the Yellow Face" (1893). Norbury was the scene of one of Holmes's few failures—a case where his analysis was very far off—and he did not want Watson to let him forget it.

"Good, Watson, good! But not, if I may say so, quite good enough!"

Sherlock Holmes in Sir **ARTHUR CONAN DOYLE**, *The Valley of Fear* (1915). Holmes reminds Watson that logical, even astute analysis often is wrong and that in detective work, as in intelligence, "not quite good enough" usually is tantamount to total failure.

"The whole Intelligence service is starving for want of both money and brains."

WINSTON CHURCHILL, 1901, on the shortcomings of British intelligence during the Boer War; cited in Stafford, *Churchill and Secret Service* (1998).

"I am the best informed man in France, and at this moment I no longer know where the Germans are."

France's chief of military intelligence, just before the German offensive of March 1918; quoted in Polmar and Allen, *Encyclopedia of Espionage* (1997).

"We mustn't underestimate American blundering. I was with them when they blundered into Berlin in 1918."

Captain Renault, played by Claude Rains, in the 1942 film *Casablanca*.

"After such knowledge, what forgiveness?"

T. S. ELIOT, "Gerontion" (1920). This poem also is the source of the phrase "wilderness of mirrors," a metaphor that has become a cliché in intelligence (see "Counter-intelligence").

"The greatest curse upon us is the failure of our Intelligence Department. If we could only find out what He is really up to! Alas, alas, that knowledge, in itself so hateful and mawkish a thing, should yet be necessary for Power!"

Senior devil Screwtape in **C. S. LEWIS**, *The Screwtape Letters* (1961).

"In most fields of human endeavor allowances are made for difficulties and obstacles, failure may be counted as a step on the way to success, and even the unsuccessful effort may hope for recognition. Intelligence cannot count on this kind of sympathy; it is thought that to fail in intelligence is to fail utterly. To compound the problem, intelligence successes frequently remain unknown for a long time, whereas failures usually become known soon after they are recognized."

WALTER LAQUEUR, *A World of Secrets* (1985).

"Naval Intelligence places no credence in these rumours. Furthermore, based on known data regarding the present disposition and employment of Japanese naval and army forces, no move against

Pearl Harbor appears imminent or planned for the foreseeable future."

> U.S. naval intelligence assessment of rumors reported by the U.S. Embassy in Tokyo that Japan would attack Pearl Harbor if relations with the United States broke down; cited in Prange, *At Dawn We Slept* (1981).

"If any sudden aggressive action at all is planned, such action would be in the direction of further minor action against the South China coast or possibly directed towards seizure of additional bases in French Indo-China.... The number and equipment of Japanese troops and the organization of naval task forces indicate an amphibious expedition against either the Philippines, Thai or Kra Peninsula or possibly Borneo.... Strong indications point to an early Japanese advance against Thailand."

> U.S. naval intelligence assessments of possible Japanese aggression, from 2 July, 27 November, and 1 December 1941; cited in Richelson, *A Century of Spies* (1995).

"No matter what happens the U.S. Navy is not going to be caught napping."

> Secretary of the Navy **FRANK KNOX**, 4 December 1941; quoted in David McCullough, *Truman* (1992).

"There are always mitigating circumstances, but these do not count in the court of history. In the case of Pearl Harbor, there was no certainty about the direction of the main attack. No Japanese battleship had been sighted near Hawaii, which was thought to be an unlikely target in any case. As the result of intraservice and interservice rivalry—and also through incompetence—those on the spot were not informed in time about the general deterioration of the situation."

> **WALTER LAQUEUR**, *A World of Secrets* (1985).

"About eleven o'clock [on 7 December 1941]... a radio message from the Navy's strategic direction finder at Lualualei report[ed] an enemy aircraft carrier transmitting on bearing 357°.... The bearing reported was correct—the Japanese carrier was nearly due north—but all other information at CinCPac headquarters... indicated that Japanese surface activity was concentrated to the south.... As many direction finders in those days were unable to distinguish between the real and reciprocal bearings of a transmission, CinCPac directed Admiral William F. Halsey in the aircraft carrier *Enterprise* to search for the enemy to southward. The most important contribution of communications intelligence that day, therefore, sent Halsey at high speed directly away from the Japanese task force."

> **W. J. HOLMES**, *Double-Edged Secrets* (1979). Holmes, a naval intelligence officer, goes on to say, "It was a most fortunate error, for had Halsey steamed north and encountered six Japanese aircraft carriers, probably neither the *Enterprise* nor Halsey would have survived the first day of the war."

"*Shimatta* [we screwed up]."

> Japanese naval air commander Genda to a colleague upon realizing that Japan's intelligence had failed and that its invasion force for Midway had been ambushed by U.S. aircraft carriers, 4 June 1942; quoted in Prange, *Miracle at Midway* (1982).

"We have been caught napping!"

> **WINSTON CHURCHILL**, reacting to intelligence evidence that Nazi Germany had been able, contrary to the opinion of British scientific experts, to develop a liquid-fueled guided rocket—the V-2—to attack the British Isles; quoted in Keegan, *Intelligence in War* (2003). Keegan notes that British scientists, despite the successes of British aeronautical development (the Spitfire, for example), were far behind German rocket science: "They were like men from the age of the mechanical calculator striving to perceive the nature of the electronic computer."

"Intelligence makes no decisions. The mind-set of the people receiving the intelligence is more important than the intelligence itself."

> **STEPHEN AMBROSE**, *Citizen Soldiers* (1997), on why information in December 1944 pointing to a German offensive in the Ardennes—the beginning of the Battle of the Bulge—was disregarded.

"The Battle of the Bulge has long been cited as a failure of intelligence. It was not the intelligence that failed, however. The Bulge was a failure of evaluation."

> **DAVID KAHN**, *The Codebreakers* (1996).

"The cases of Pearl Harbor and the Battle of the Bulge, while in many respects quite different, have one thing in common: we did not make allowances for the enemy doing something which we regarded as totally unreasonable from his own point of view."

> Former DCI **ALLEN DULLES** in his edited volume *Great True Spy Stories* (1968).

"Germany lost the intelligence war. At every one of the strategic turning points of World War II, her intelligence failed. It underestimated Russia, blacked out before the North African invasion, awaited the Sicily landing in the Balkans, and fell for thinking the Normandy landing a feint."

> **DAVID KAHN**, *Hitler's Spies* (1978).

"Although the United States . . . was nothing if not accessible to foreign agents, both legal and covert, it was in another sense impenetrable to the Axis powers because of their own failure to comprehend the workings of democratic states. Both the Germans and the Japanese repeatedly underestimated the American polity—its tenacity and ingenuity, as well as its ability to organize, improvise, and produce. And these colossal failures of intelligence helped doom both states to ruinous defeat."

> **ELIOT COHEN** in Roy Godson, ed., *Intelligence Requirements for the 1990s* (1989).

"CIA does not believe that the USSR will change its support in the [U.N.] General Assembly from the Israelis to the Arabs."

> CIA's *Daily Summary*, 2 October 1948; reproduced in Kuhns, *Assessing the Soviet Threat* (1997).

"The earliest possible date by which the USSR might be expected to produce an atomic bomb is mid-1950 and the most probable date is mid-1953."

> CIA Intelligence Memorandum No. 225, "Estimate of Status of Atomic Warfare in the USSR," 20 September 1949; reproduced in Warner, *CIA Under Truman* (1994). What hurts especially about this assessment is that it was issued three weeks *after* the first Soviet atomic test, but days before its detection.

"President Truman's announcement on 23 September 1949 of the first Soviet nuclear explosion caught the US intelligence community in an embarrassing situation since, even though the fact of the Soviet achievement was no surprise, its timing upset all estimates. As of September 1949, the official coordinated statement on Soviet completion of an atomic weapon was to be found in an estimate that predicted three different dates for it—1958, 1955, and 'between 1950 and 1953.' The appearance in the same estimate of three dates for this accomplishment—all wrong—and the fact that none of them were accepted by all the departments constituted clear evidence of disarray in the intelligence community on this manifestly important subject."

> CIA historian **ROBERTA KNAPP**; in CIA's Historical Intelligence Collection.

"When intelligence errs there seems to be less tolerance of its error than there is for the error of other mistaken specialists. For example, when a dentist pulls out the wrong tooth or a lawyer loses a case, the client's reaction is not that he, himself could have done a better job, and that henceforth he will do his own dental and legal work. Yet in intelligence matters, pardonably wrong diagnosis and understandably inadequate presentation very often do arouse just such a reaction in the client."

SHERMAN KENT, *Strategic Intelligence* (1949).

"Failing U.S. military occupation and control, a non-communist regime on Taiwan probably will succumb to the Chinese communists by the end of 1950."

CIA estimate of 19 October 1949; cited in John Lewis Gaddis, *The Long Peace* (1987). This was a good one to get wrong.

"Despite [a recent] increase in North Korean military strength, the possibility of an invasion of South Korea is unlikely unless North Korean forces can develop a clear-cut superiority over the increasingly efficient South Korean Army."

CIA report "Korea: Troop Build Up," 13 January 1950, reproduced in Kuhns, *Assessing the Soviet Threat* (1997).

"Cogent political and military considerations make it unlikely that Chinese Communist forces will be directly and openly committed in Korea."

CIA's *Weekly Summary*, 15 September 1950; reproduced in Kuhns, *Assessing the Soviet Threat* (1997). CIA and the rest of the U.S. intelligence community continued to discount the possibility of direct Chinese intervention until it occurred in late November 1950.

"[DCI Walter Bedell] Smith wanted me to know ... that the CIA, being a new organization whose reputation had not yet been established, simply could not admit to other branches of Government —least of all to the highly competitive U.S. military intelligence services—its inability to collect intelligence on North Korea."

JOHN L. HART, CIA station chief in Seoul, 1952, when he suggested that CIA cease operations in Korea after learning that all its sources were working for the North; quoted in Andrew, *For the President's Eyes Only* (1995).

"The rather obvious truth [is] that with better intelligence support our nation might have avoided most of our present difficulties. Better intelligence might have put our leaders on notice as to the true character of the Communists, the men in the Kremlin, the men we were dealing with across the table at Yalta, Potsdam, and Teheran. Better intelligence might have given us a greater appreciation of the overall global character of the Chinese Communist movement in the early days of its development . . . and that, therefore, the choice in China was not between a Nationalist Government and something better, but between a Nationalist Government and something far, far worse."

Vice President RICHARD NIXON, remarks to new CIA officers, 10 February 1953; in CIA's Historical Intelligence Collection.

"Malenkov's key position in the Soviet Communist Party throughout the past fourteen years, his conspicuous and apparently planned elevation since 1948, his prominent role at and since the 19th Party Congress, and the accolade accorded him by Beria at Stalin's funeral suggest that there will be no immediate challenge to his position."

CIA estimate, *Probable Consequences of the Death of Stalin and of the Elevation of Malenkov to Leadership in the USSR*, 12 March 1953; cited in Koch, *Selected Estimates* (1993). Nikita Khrushchev replaced Malenkov as Party first secretary three days after this estimate was published.

"We believe that Soviet authority over the Satellite regimes will remain intact during the period of this estimate . . . and in the absence of general war popular dissatisfaction almost certainly will not develop beyond the stage of sporadic non-cooperation."

> CIA estimate, *Soviet Capabilities and Main Lines of Policy Through Mid-1959*, 7 June 1954; reproduced in Koch, *Selected Estimates* (1993). And then came the Hungarian Revolution of 1956.

"Beginning in February 1959 and extending through June 1960 an even dozen launches [of CORONA reconnaissance satellites] were attempted, with eight of the vehicles carrying cameras, and all of them were failures; no film capsules were recovered from orbit. Of the eight camera-carrying vehicles, four failed to achieve orbit, three experienced camera or film failures, and the eighth was not recovered because of a malfunction of the re-entry body spin rockets. . . . One might ask why the CORONA program officers persisted in the face of such adversity. The answer lay in the overwhelming intelligence needs of the period."

> **KENNETH GREER**, "Corona," in Ruffner, *CORONA* (1995).

"How could I have been so far off base? All my life I've known better than to depend on the experts. How could I have been so stupid, to let them go ahead?"

> President **JOHN F. KENNEDY** to Theodore Sorensen after the Bay of Pigs, 1961; quoted in Sorensen, *Kennedy* (1965).

"The President was pissed."

> DDCI **MARSHALL CARTER** after CIA admitted to President Kennedy that it did not know much about Soviet cruise missile capabilities; quoted in Andrew, *For the President's Eyes Only* (1995).

"The USSR could derive considerable military advantage from the establishment of Soviet medium and intermediate range ballistic missiles in Cuba, or from the establishment of a Soviet submarine base there. As between these two, the establishment of a submarine base would be the more likely. Either development, however, would be incompatible with Soviet practice to date and with Soviet policy as we presently estimate it. It would indicate a far greater willingness to increase the level of risk in US-Soviet relations than the USSR has displayed thus far."

> Special National Intelligence Estimate 85-3-62, *The Military Buildup in Cuba*, 19 September 1962; reproduced in McAuliffe, *Cuban Missile Crisis* (1992).

"The Soviets 'must know,' they 'probably realize,' they 'cannot possibly believe.' . . . Such words characterize all National Intelligence Estimates. One egregious example is the NIE of September 1962, bearing the signature of Sherman Kent himself, that refuted reports from agents in, and refugees from, Cuba about the presence of Soviet ballistic missiles on the island. Quite simply, reports of eye witnesses were overcome by beliefs about what the Soviets would and would not do, based exclusively on what the CIA analysts knew they themselves would do or would not do. But intelligence officers are paid to look outward, not inward. In this case they were watching something happen and saying, 'This can't be happening, because I wouldn't do it.'"

> **ANGELO CODEVILLA**, *Informing Statecraft* (1992).

"We believe that the near-total intelligence surprise experienced by the United States with respect to the introduction and deployment of Soviet strategic missiles in Cuba resulted in large part from a malfunction of the analytic process by which intelligence indicators are assessed and reported. . . . We believe that the manner in which the intelligence indicators were handled in the Cuba situation may well be the most serious flaw in our intelligence system, and one which, if uncorrected, could lead to the gravest consequences."

President's Foreign Intelligence Advisory Board, memorandum for the president, 4 February 1963; reproduced in McAuliffe, *Cuban Missile Crisis* (1992).

"I am returning the report of the President's Foreign Intelligence Advisory Board dated February 4th. . . . It should be noted that for two years the intelligence community had been surfeited with reports of 'missiles in Cuba,' all of which proved to be incorrect prior to those which we received on or about September 20th. Nevertheless, one can now readily conclude that greater emphasis should have been placed by the estimators on certain of [them]. . . . About 3,500 agent and refugee reports were analyzed in the preparation of my report to the [Board] and of this number, only eight in retrospect were considered as reasonably valid indicators of the deployment of offensive missiles in Cuba. I continue to feel that the intelligence community performed well."

DCI **JOHN McCONE**, memorandum for President Kennedy, 28 February 1963; reproduced in McAuliffe, *Cuban Missile Crisis* (1992).

"We believe that Communist progress has been blunted and the situation is improving. . . . Improvements which have occurred during the past year now indicate that the Viet Cong can be contained militarily and that further progress can be made in expanding the area of government control and in creating greater security in the countryside."

National Intelligence Estimate 53-63, *Prospects in South Vietnam*, April 1963. The first draft of this NIE had a different message: that the struggle in South Vietnam would be "protracted and costly" because of the gov-

ernment's ineptitude and Communist penetration of the country. See Harold Ford, *CIA and the Vietnam Policymakers* (1998).

"Intelligence officers have to face the fact that whenever a dramatic event occurs in the foreign relations field—an event for which the public may not have been prepared—one can usually count on the cry going up, 'Intelligence has failed again.'"

Former DCI **ALLEN DULLES**, *The Craft of Intelligence* (1963).

"The history of intelligence failures also includes the failure of believing false alarms."

Former State Department intelligence chief **ROGER HILSMAN**, *To Move a Nation* (1967).

"The Tet offensive was an intelligence failure in so far as we failed to anticipate the full scope and nature of the onslaught, and we wrongly assumed it would come at the end of the Tet holiday, rather than . . . three or four days earlier. The fact that we *had* predicted a massive offensive throughout South Vietnam on an unprecedented scale for late January [1968], however, and that American and Vietnamese commanders had been warned of its imminence and were planning to meet the anticipated offensive, is seldom noted."

GEORGE W. ALLEN, *None So Blind* (2001). Allen was one of CIA's top Vietnam analysts in the 1960s.

"During the early 1960s, the Intelligence Community took seriously Khrushchev's boast that ICBMs would be 'turned out like sausages' and, in the absence of confirmation from overhead photography, substantially overestimated the number of ballistic missiles that would be deployed. After the first overhead imagery became available, few ICBMs were found to be deployed and the Intelligence

Community's projections were scaled back accordingly. By then the Soviets had largely completed deployment of medium-range ballistic missiles opposite Europe and had solved the technical problems they had encountered with their early ICBMs. The Soviets were thus ready to begin a massive buildup in their ICBM force, which the NIEs published during the mid-1960s did not anticipate."

CIA report, "Intelligence Forecasts of Soviet Intercontinental Forces: An Evaluation of the Record," April 1989; reproduced in Haines and Leggett, *CIA's Analyses of the Soviet Union* (2001).

"Neither the president [Johnson] nor his secretary of defense [McNamara] grasped, until it was too late, that Hanoi was willing to endure greater pain than the United States could bring itself to inflict. . . . The major policy errors of the Vietnam War were due far less to lack of intelligence than to a failure to understand the nature of Vietnam."

CHRISTOPHER ANDREW, *For the President's Eyes Only* (1995).

"US intelligence, CIA Headquarters included, did little to prepare policymakers for the fact, scope, or significance of the Tet Offensive. . . . The CIA's field intelligence analysis prior to Tet was extremely good, but its alerting performance went largely for naught. In November and December 1967, Saigon Station sent in three major assessments, each of which warned that a powerful, nationwide enemy offensive was coming. . . . But the Saigon Station's assessments failed to shake the personal preconceptions of senior CIA and White House officials."

Former senior CIA official **HAROLD FORD**; quotation in CIA's Historical Intelligence Collection.

"Sorry about that, Chief."

Fictional U.S. agent Maxwell Smart, played by Don Adams in the 1960s TV comedy *Get Smart*. His other running gag line for failures was "Missed it by that much!"

"It's always darkest just before it gets pitch black."

Fictional U.S. agent Alexander Scott, played by Bill Cosby, in the 1960s TV drama *I Spy*.

"What the hell do those clowns do out there in Langley?"

President **RICHARD NIXON** upon hearing that CIA did not predict Lon Nol's 1970 coup against Prince Sihanouk; in *RN: The Memoirs of Richard Nixon* (1978).

"Of charges of intelligence failure, it should be remembered that the leader against whom [the Cambodian coup] was directed had a far greater incentive to know the truth in his country, and he failed to anticipate the plot."

HENRY KISSINGER on CIA's failure to predict Sihanouk's ouster, in *White House Years* (1979).

"One of the most significant failures in the history of American intelligence [occurred when] in the mid- to late 1960s and early 1970s, the Agency did not foresee [the] massive Soviet effort to match and then surpass the United States in strategic missile numbers and capabilities—and did not understand Soviet intentions."

Former DCI **ROBERT GATES**, *From the Shadows* (1996).

"Anyone who visited the Bar-Lev line left persuaded that no sensible military would want to attack it, especially the Egyptians. The Israelis were convinced that Egypt couldn't get through that line, and Washington believed them."

Former DCI **RICHARD HELMS**, discussing CIA's failure to predict the 1973 Yom Kippur War; quoted in Andrew, *For the President's Eyes Only* (1995).

"Every Israeli (and American) analysis before October 1973 agreed that Egypt and Syria lacked the military capability to regain their territory by force of arms; hence there would be no war. The Arab armies must lose; hence they would not attack. The premises were correct. The conclusions were not.... The day before war, the CIA reiterated its judgment of September 30 that Egypt did not appear to be preparing for war against Israel. Clearly, there was an intelligence failure, but misjudgment was not confined to the agencies. Every policymaker knew all the facts. The Israelis were monitoring the movement of every Egyptian and Syrian unit. The general plan of attack, especially of the Syrians, was fairly well understood. What no one believed —the consumers no more than the producers of intelligence—was that the Arabs would act upon it."

HENRY KISSINGER, *Years of Upheaval* (1982).

"The CIA station in Lisbon was so small, and so dependent upon the official Portuguese security service for information that very little was picked up."

CIA officials to congressional investigators regarding the surprise 1974 coup in Portugal; quoted in Andrew, *For the President's Eyes Only* (1995).

"We knew that they were fooling around with the nuclear stuff, but that they would go ahead and blow one seemed a little farfetched."

Former DCI **WILLIAM COLBY** recalling the lack of warning regarding India's 1974 nuclear test; quoted in Andrew, *For the President's Eyes Only* (1995).

"The Shah seems to have no health or political problems at present that will prevent him from being the dominant figure in Iran into and possibly throughout the 1980s."

CIA assessment on Iran, October 1977; cited in Richelson, *A Century of Spies* (1995). Actually, the Shah had both.

"Iran is not in a revolutionary or even a pre-revolutionary situation."

CIA assessment, August 1978; cited in Laqueur, *A World of Secrets* (1985). This is the most quoted example at internal CIA courses about intelligence failures.

"The failure to forecast the fall of the Shah [in 1979] was of far less significance than our mishandling of the report that a 'combat brigade' of Soviet troops was in Cuba. Had we predicted the Shah's fall from power even six or seven months ahead of time, there was little the United States could have done to prevent it. The reporting on the combat brigade, however, did play a direct part in scuttling the SALT II arms control treaty with the Soviet Union."

Former DCI **STANSFIELD TURNER**, *Secrecy and Democracy* (1985).

"In the best-known cases of intelligence failure, the most crucial mistakes have seldom been made by collectors of raw information, occasionally by professionals who produce finished analyses, but most often by the decision makers who consume the products of intelligence services. Policy premises constrict perception, and administrative workloads constrain reflection. Intelligence failure is political and psychological more often than organizational."

RICHARD K. BETTS, "Why Intelligence Failures Are Inevitable," *World Politics* (October 1978).

"There is no such thing as darkness; only a failure to see."

> Former SIS officer **MALCOLM MUGGERIDGE** in 1979; cited in *Touchstone* magazine (December 2003).

"It may be true that CIA spokesmen have been occasionally overeager in their claim that they never receive credit for their secret successes, but they are right in stating that the American people cannot forgive their mistakes."

> **RHODRI JEFFREYS-JONES**, *The CIA and American Democracy* (1989). The American people tend to be far more forgiving than certain historians.

"Scarred by forty years of Cold War, CIA assessments failed to keep pace with the sea-change in Soviet-American relations during the last two years of Reagan's presidency.... It was Gorbachev himself who did most to change Reagan's perception of the Soviet Union. The CIA struggled to keep up."

> **CHRISTOPHER ANDREW**, *For the President's Eyes Only* (1995).

"I learned more about the attempted coup in Panama from watching Cable News Network than from [DCI William] Webster's Central Intelligence Agency."

> **JOHN SUNUNU**, President George H. W. Bush's chief of staff; quoted in the *Washington Post*, 16 October 1989.

"The president put more faith in his own high-level Middle Eastern contacts than in the conclusions of his intelligence analysts."

> **CHRISTOPHER ANDREW** on why the administration of President George H. W. Bush downplayed warnings of an imminent Iraqi invasion of Kuwait; in *For the President's Eyes Only* (1995).

"There is a tendency for policymakers, after bungling an issue, to place the blame on an intelligence failure."

> Former DCI **JAMES SCHLESINGER** at the Council on Foreign Relations conference "The Future of the CIA," 18 February 1997, Washington, D.C.

"The operational record, though very strong—in fact, I would argue without peer in the world—was obviously far from perfect. We made significant mistakes in Central America, nearly all of them in Washington. We failed to dislodge Qadhafi in Libya. We were duped by double agents in Cuba and East Germany. We were penetrated with devastating effect at least twice by the Soviets, and suffered other counterintelligence and security failures. We never recruited a spy who gave us unique political information from inside the Kremlin, and we too often failed to penetrate the inner circle of Soviet surrogate leaders in Hanoi, Tripoli, Havana, Managua, and elsewhere. For too long, our support to US military operations was not as good as it should have been, plagued by bureaucratic rivalries and turf wars on both sides, and by a cultural gap that grew too wide after Vietnam.... No one can or will deny that there were lapses and failures and the Agency paid a high price for them. But in a shadow war that ranged across the globe, such failures were remarkably few and far between."

> Former DCI **ROBERT GATES**, "CIA and the Cold War," address at the University of Oklahoma, 12 September 1997.

"We had zero warning."

> U.S. administration official, quoted in various wire services, commenting on India's nuclear tests of 11 May 1998.

"It looks to me like this is a colossal failure of our intelligence-gathering system, perhaps the greatest failure in a decade."

> **RICHARD SHELBY**, Senate intelligence committee chairman, on the lack of warning for India's nuclear tests; quoted in the *Los Angeles Times*, 13 May 1998.

"Not to worry, says the administration. There will be no ballistic missile threat to the United States before 2010. How do they know? The CIA assures us. As it did about India."

> **CHARLES KRAUTHAMMER**, "Defenseless America," *Washington Post*, 22 May 1998.

"There are two certainties in the intelligence profession: the consequences of being wrong grow every day; and sooner or later you will be wrong."

> Senior CIA official **MARTIN PETERSEN** in *National Security Studies Quarterly* (spring 1999).

"It was a major error. I cannot minimize the significance of this.... Our ability to locate fixed targets is no better than our databases, and in this case the databases were wrong. Further, it is difficult, actually, it is impossible to keep current databases for cities around the globe. The databases are constructed to catalog targets, not non-targets."

> DCI **GEORGE TENET** explaining the targeting error that led to the May 1999 bombing of the Chinese Embassy in Belgrade, 22 July 1999.

"Don't make the same mistake once."

> Saying among CIA analysts, circa 2000.

"I think there has been a widespread assumption that the so-called intelligence failures, that is, the failure to produce or use intelligence well, have been the fault of the intelligence agencies.... Looking back on the history of the 20th century, I think

that it is now clear that intelligence failures were actually more a result of the inability of policy makers to make good use of intelligence, than [a failure of] collection of intelligence in the first place."

> **CHRISTOPHER ANDREW**, interviewed in the Italian online magazine *Per Aspera ad Veritatem* (May–August 2001). And then the twenty-first century dawned on 11 September 2001.

"For all its technological prowess and military might, the United States didn't see this coming. None of the vaunted intelligence tools at the nation's disposal gave any warning of the coming nightmare—a massively coordinated effort to hijack and crash at least four airliners at the same time. U.S. officials confirmed they had no reports that such attacks were imminent. Not from the CIA's networks of spies and informants. Not from the FBI's many counterintelligence agents. Not from the National Security Agency's telephone and computer taps. Not from the military's satellites or spy planes."

> Associated Press report, 11 September 2001.

"If we had a warning and missed it, that is a failure of intelligence, big time, [and] if we didn't have any inkling of this event ... that's a failure, too."

> Senator **RICHARD SHELBY**, vice-chairman of the Senate Select Committee on Intelligence; quoted in the *Washington Post*, 13 September 2001.

"[September 11th] was a systematic failure of the way this country protects itself. It's aviation security delegated to the airlines, who did a lousy job. It's a fighter aircraft deployment failure. It's a foreign intelligence collection failure. It's a domestic detection failure. It's a visa and immigration policy failure."

> Former DCI **R. JAMES WOOLSEY**; quoted in the *New York Times*, 30 December 2001.

"Postmortems of intelligence failures usually reveal that very bright analysts failed to predict the disaster in question, despite their great knowledge of the situation, or that they had warned that an eruption could happen but without any idea of when. In fact, expertise can get in the way of anticipating a radical departure from the norm, because the depth of expert knowledge of why and how things have gone as they have day after day for years naturally inclines the analyst to estimate that developments will continue along the same trajectory. It is always a safer bet to predict that the situation tomorrow will be like it has been for the past dozen years than to say it will change abruptly. And, of course, in the vast majority of cases predictions of continuity are absolutely correct; the trick is to figure out which case will be the exception to a powerful rule."

> **RICHARD K. BETTS**, "Fixing Intelligence," *Foreign Affairs* (January–February 2002). Professor Betts's observation reminds the Literary Spy of the old joke about the venerable British civil servant who informed the prime minister every year that there would not be a general war in Europe—turns out that in a career of half a century he was wrong only twice!

"September 11th . . . was not the result of the failure of attention and discipline and focus and consistent effort, and the American people need to understand that. . . . Intelligence will never give you 100 percent predictive capability on terrorist events . . . and the American people need to understand that, with the resources and authorities and priorities [they had], the men and women of the FBI and CIA performed heroically. Whatever shortcomings we may have, we owe it to the country to look at ourselves honestly and programmatically. But when people use the word 'failure'—'failure' means *no* focus, *no* attention, *no* discipline—and those [deficiencies] were not present in what either we or the FBI did here and around the world. . . .

We have disrupted numerous terrorist acts since September the 11th, and we will continue to do so with the FBI. And we welcome the committee's review. It is important for the American people. But how we paint it is equally important, because they need to know that there are competent men and women who risk their lives and undertake heroic risks to protect them."

> DCI **GEORGE TENET**, testimony before the Senate intelligence committee, 6 February 2002.

"Many factors went into creating the tragedy of 9/11. Lack of effort, interest, expertise or daring at the CIA, however, was not one of them."

> DCI **GEORGE TENET**, "The CIA and Sept. 11," *New York Post*, 13 February 2002.

"Intelligence fails because it is human, no stronger than the power of one mind to read another, to divine its intent, to know the enemy. Soldiers and spies—and now civilians—live with the terrible knowledge that while the enemy is out there, we may never see him coming."

> **TIM WEINER**, "Pearl Harbor as Prologue," *New York Times*, 8 September 2002.

"We now know more about the terror network behind [the 11 September 2001] attack—and the intelligence shortcomings that failed to stop it. . . . The CIA failed to share with the FBI crucial information about two hijackers the FBI was already watching. FBI higher-ups ignored a field agent's warnings about what looked like an influx of Osama bin Laden operatives into the nation's flight schools. The National Security Agency didn't even translate crucial intelligence about 9/11 until after it happened. And our military was reluctant to go after bin Laden in Afghanistan, claiming imprecise intelligence. These agencies weren't willfully negligent.

They failed to act on information because they operated amid an anti-terror mindset that wasn't serious."

> *Wall Street Journal* editorial, "The Limits of Hindsight," 28 July 2003.

"Before you complain too loud about intelligence failures, tell me what the stock market's going to do tomorrow. Go to the horse races, and you'll see a lot of people betting wrong—and that's a far more restricted set of possibilities than intelligence analysts face."

> **DAVID KAHN**; quoted in the *Baltimore Sun*, 8 February 2004.

FBI & LAW ENFORCEMENT

One of the great misunderstandings of the public about U.S. intelligence is that it is nearly synonymous with law enforcement. Increasingly, to be sure, you see them together, like salad dressing, but they remain as oil and vinegar. The challenges of our age—terrorism, international organized crime, narcotics trafficking—require both professions to cooperate even though there remain great differences in institutional culture and practice. We are all on the same side, the Literary Spy exhorts, serving and protecting the same public.

See also: Domestic Activities; Intelligence, the Missions of; Origins of Central Intelligence; Terrorism; Treason & Betrayal

"Intelligence and law enforcement simply do not mix."

> British naval intelligence officer **IAN FLEMING**, later the creator of James Bond, in a June 1941 memorandum; cited in *National Review*, 29 July 2002.

"We are not policemen. We are not concerned with sedition, secret meetings, sabotage, and betrayal. That is the province of the FBI."

> OSS Director **WILLIAM DONOVAN**, April 1942; quoted in Ranelagh, *The Agency* (1986).

"During World War II . . . an academic expert on Japan was once declared suspect by the FBI solely on the grounds of a report that he had a map of Japan on his wall. So he did. It was a *National Geographic* map, and in any event he was being hired [by the OSS] as an expert on Japan. [OSS Director] Donovan overruled the FBI and hired the man."

> **THOMAS POWERS**, *The Man Who Kept the Secrets* (1979). What's amazing is that Donovan was able to overrule the FBI.

"The Abwehr [Nazi intelligence] gets better treatment from the FBI than we do."

> OSS Director **WILLIAM DONOVAN**; quoted in Ranelagh, *The Agency* (1986).

"I feel very strongly that there is a need for the establishment and operation of a world-wide intelligence service. While I do not seek this responsibility for the Federal Bureau of Investigation, I do believe that upon the basis of our experience of the last five years we are well qualified to operate such a service in conjunction with parallel operations of the Military and Naval Intelligence. . . . I think that time is of the essence in reaching a decision upon this matter and, consequently, I urge that you personally take the matter up with Secretary of State Byrnes as soon as possible."

> FBI Director **J. EDGAR HOOVER**, memorandum to Attorney General Tom Clark, 29 August 1945; in *FRUS 1945–1950: Emergence of the Intelligence Establishment* (1996), document 5. Hoover's denial notwithstanding, he was indeed pushing for the FBI as the basis for a U.S. global intelligence service.

"The theory that police work and intelligence coverage cannot be combined has been entirely dispelled. . . . In fact, all police work specifically involves the gathering of information in the nature of intelligence. Extensive intelligence coverage must necessarily precede the arrest of the enemy agent in the United States and it is not possible to separate the gathering of intelligence from police functions. . . . A hazard in intelligence operation is the possibility of a charge being made that the organization is a 'Gestapo.' Also, a political agency which engages in intelligence operation may be called a 'political police.' Both charges are obnoxious to American citizens. The [FBI] set-up operating in the Western Hemisphere throughout the war has engaged in both police and intelligence activities and its record of protecting civil liberties has been highly praised even by the American Civil Liberties Union."

U.S. Attorney General **TOM CLARK**, memorandum to President Truman on "A Plan for U.S. Secret World-Wide Intelligence Coverage," October 1945; in *FRUS 1945–1950: Emergence of the Intelligence Establishment* (1996), document 17. Clark's proposal was that the FBI should be in charge of domestic law enforcement and foreign intelligence operations alike.

"Sec. 102 (d) (3). The [Central Intelligence] Agency shall have no police, subpena [*sic*], law-enforcement powers, or internal-security functions."

National Security Act of 1947, 26 July 1947; reproduced in Warner, *CIA Under Truman* (1994).

"[Our] liaison and cooperation attendant thereon with the Federal Bureau of Investigation have increased effectively over a considerable period of time. Obviously, the closest possible working relationship is not only highly desirable but also nec-

essary. . . . The Central Intelligence Agency feels that this liaison relationship at the present time is close, effective, and mutually advantageous."

DCI **ROSCOE HILLENKOETTER**, memorandum to the National Security Council's executive secretary, 27 December 1949; in *FRUS 1945–1950: Emergence of the Intelligence Establishment* (1996), document 407. Hillenkoetter was overstating the degree of cooperation at the time.

"The men of the FBI, with hardly an exception, were proud of their insularity, of having sprung from the grass roots. . . . They were therefore whisky-drinkers, with beer for light refreshment. By contrast, CIA men flaunted cosmopolitan postures. They would discuss absinthe and serve Burgundy at room temperature."

HAROLD "KIM" PHILBY, *My Secret War* (1968).

"The relationships between CIA on the one hand, and the Department of Justice—particularly the FBI, on the other, especially in connection with the defector problem, must be improved and clarified."

CIA General Counsel **LAURENCE HOUSTON** to DCI-nominee Walter Bedell Smith, 29 August 1950; reproduced in Warner, *CIA Under Truman* (1994).

"The Agency and the Bureau did not have what you would call connubial relations. . . . There was nothing we could do in the Agency to make Mr. Hoover happy about the fact that he didn't like the Agency in the first place. He didn't like its people in the second, and as far as he was concerned it was quite unnecessary."

Former DCI **RICHARD HELMS** on early CIA-FBI relations, at a conference on "Origins and Development of the CIA," sponsored by CIA's Center for the Study of Intelligence, March 1994.

"Does your boss really think he can send some bald-headed bastard in here to tell me how to run my business?"

> The volatile and eternally angry DCI **WALTER BEDELL SMITH** to the partially bald FBI liaison officer Sam Papich, regarding a sensitive counterintelligence issue; quoted in Helms, *A Look over My Shoulder* (2003).

"It's a joint CIA and FBI job. For God's sake don't step on the FBI's toes. Covered with corns. Good luck."

> James Bond's instructions on being dispatched to the United States by M, his spy chief, in **IAN FLEMING**, *Live and Let Die* (1954). Fleming knew the score.

"J. Edgar Hoover had been in office forty-two years when I was appointed director of Central Intelligence [in 1966]. . . . The day I first visited the FBI offices—as my grandmother would have said, 'to make my manners,' and to assure Hoover that CIA would continue to work closely with the FBI—Hoover greeted me cordially, and waved me to a chair directly in front of his desk. After a forty-five minute uninterrupted history of the FBI in peace and war, J. Edgar stood up. We shook hands, and he wished me well in my new job. As I recall it, I did not say a word during his monologue. Nor did Director Hoover mention anything that in any way concerned our respective professional concerns. It was after this bizarre session that I decided not to seek any further one-on-one meetings with him."

> Former DCI **RICHARD HELMS**, *A Look over My Shoulder* (2003).

"The Bureau's first inclination seems to be to arrest or deport foreign spies rather than to turn them, as the CIA tries to do, into double agents.

This fundamental difference in approach limits the degree of FBI-CIA cooperation in counterespionage and confirms the general view within the agency that FBI agents are rather unimaginative police-officer types, and thus incapable of mastering the intricacies of counterespionage work. (The FBI, on the other hand, tends to see CIA counterintelligence operators as dilettantes who are too clever for their own good.)"

> **VICTOR MARCHETTI** and **JOHN MARKS**, *CIA and the Cult of Intelligence* (1974).

"The man who excels at criminal investigation would be lost in intelligence. Instead of . . . clear cut black and white issues, intelligence is full of gray areas. In intelligence a man can investigate for years without getting any real results. A man who enjoys solving tantalizing and complex problems, who likes to experiment, could be bored stiff catching robbers and belongs in intelligence."

> Former FBI Assistant Director **WILLIAM C. SULLIVAN**, *The Bureau* (1979).

"Immediately discontinue all contact with the local CIA office."

> FBI Director **J. EDGAR HOOVER**, cable to FBI field offices, 2 March 1970; cited in Riebling, *Wedge: The Secret War Between the FBI and CIA* (1994). Hoover was peeved at CIA's refusal to identify an FBI agent who provided the Agency with information about a Czech émigré.

"We all know our intelligence product is not too good and never has been. You want the FBI to have as little to do jointly as possible with other members of the [intelligence] community. . . . You have always been hostile toward CIA despite the usual polite exchange of letters."

> Former FBI Assistant Director **WILLIAM C. SULLIVAN** to FBI Director J. Edgar Hoover, letter of 6 October 1971; reproduced in Sullivan, *The Bureau* (1979).

"Screw the CIA—let them do their own work! . . . We've got enough damned coordination in government now, too much in fact!"

Typical outburst of FBI Director **J. EDGAR HOOVER** regarding working with CIA, according to former Assistant Director William Sullivan; quoted in Riebling, *Wedge: The Secret War Between the FBI and CIA* (1994).

"The story that has yet to be told is how Saddam Hussein's terrorist teams were defeated during Desert Storm . . . due to the cooperation between FBI and the CIA."

Former DCI **WILLIAM WEBSTER** at the Council on Foreign Relations conference "The Future of the CIA," 18 February 1997, Washington, D.C.

"After more than fifty years of rivalry, Agency people are still perceived by FBI agents as intellectual, Ivy League, wine-drinking, pipe-smoking, international-relations types, sometimes aloof. The Bureau's people are regarded by CIA as cigar-smoking, beer-drinking, door-knocking cops. What kind of restructuring might overcome such stereotypical perceptions—especially when they are generally true?"

MARK RIEBLING, *Wedge: The Secret War Between the FBI and CIA* (1994).

"FBI agents are trained to think like bank guards. CIA officers are trained to think like bank robbers."

CIA operations officer **BURTON LEE GERBER**; quoted in Earley, *Confessions of a Spy* (1997).

"The goals of law enforcement and intelligence collection conflict. Law enforcement agencies collect information solely to put criminals in prison —a onetime, short-term goal; pay the informant, make a bust, go to trial with the informer as witness. Espionage is conducted for the long-term production of intelligence: recruit the agent, collect the information, hopefully for years or decades."

Former senior CIA operations officer **DUANE CLARRIDGE**, *A Spy for All Seasons* (1997).

"I think the Ames case was the jumping-off point in taking cooperation between the FBI and CIA seriously, because it proved that we could no longer tolerate petty bureaucratic jealousy and turf wars in dealing with threats to American security. We wanted people to understand that [when] it came to dealing with these transnational threats, the fortunes and efforts of both agencies would rise and fall together."

DCI **GEORGE TENET** referring to the case of Aldrich Ames, a CIA officer caught in 1994 after spying for Moscow for nine years; quoted in *Government Executive* (February 2001).

"More Americans have confidence in state and local police officers than they do in federal agents. Confidence level of 'a great deal' or 'quite a lot':

63% State police
59% Local police
38% FBI
29% CIA"

Gallup poll cited in *USA Today*, 5 July 2001. Apparently everyone connected with this poll failed to consider that CIA is not a law enforcement agency, has no police powers, and has less cause to be in this lineup than the Internal Revenue Service. This is a typical example of the irritating ignorance of the media regarding CIA.

"The simple and profound notion that spies should not be cops and cops should not be spies depended on the state-to-state nature of international relations during the Cold War. Gathering intelligence against the Soviet Union had little to do—except in espionage cases—with enforcing the law at home. International terrorism, however, sorely tests this premise. . . . Too dogmatic an insistence on separating intelligence and law enforcement can hinder both by keeping information too isolated within the government."

Washington Post editorial, "Spies and Cops," 25 September 2001.

"We should consider creating a new domestic security agency, like London's MI-5, take the counterintelligence and counterterrorism functions out of the F.B.I. and C.I.A., and create a new agency reporting to the attorney general, with no law enforcement functions. . . . I do not believe [that] law enforcement and intelligence work well together in a single agency. They have such competing functions. The missions are so different. They don't mix well. There's inherent tension between the two. It's like putting diplomacy under the War Department."

Former CIA general counsel **JEFFREY H. SMITH**; quoted in the *New York Times*, 8 September 2002.

FEEDBACK & TASKING

Tasking is what is asked of intelligence; feedback is the reaction to what intelligence provides, which provokes more tasking in a repetitive and crucial cycle. Without such guidance, intelligence flies blind. Intelligence organizations need direction from national leadership; in the field, spies need instructions from spy handlers. The needs are the same: what information must be collected first? What is the priority? And then: how am I doing? What can I do better? What's the value to you of the material I'm collecting at great risk? Without guidance, not only does intelligence fly blind, but its practitioners run the risk of losing faith in the mission, losing their morale, perhaps even losing their loyalty.

See also: Collection; Espionage & Spies; Presidents & Intelligence

"So the men Moses had sent to explore the land, who returned and made the whole community grumble against him by spreading a bad report about it—these men responsible for spreading the bad report about the land were struck down and died of a plague before the Lord."

Numbers 14:36 (New International). Now that's clear, unambiguous feedback.

"Hither, page, and stand by me,
If thou know'st it, telling;
Yonder peasant, who is he?
Where and what his dwelling?"

KING WENCESLAS of Bohemia (10th century), issuing specific collection tasking after seeing a poor man gathering winter fuel, in the Christmas carol "Good King Wenceslas" by John Mason Neale (1818–1866). The page's sources keep him remarkably well informed, for he answers, "Sire, he lives a good league hence, underneath the mountain; / Right against the forest fence, / By St. Agnes' fountain." Specific tasking usually yields specific answers.

"Hee was careful and liberall to obtain good Intelligence from all parts abroad. . . . Requiring likewise from his Ambassadors an Answere, in particular distinct Articles, respectively to his Questions."

FRANCIS BACON, *The Historie of the Raigne of King Henry the Seventh* (1622).

"Do not stick at expense to bring this to pass [to find willing spies], as I was never more uneasy than on account of my want of knowledge."

General **GEORGE WASHINGTON** to General George Clinton, 5 September 1776, urging establishment of a "Channel of information" to learn of British designs on New York; cited in Bakeless, *Turncoats, Traitors and Heroes*

(1998). Washington's desperation led to the misbegotten mission of Nathan Hale.

"You give me no instructions and not being a military man I can only trust to my untutored judgment as to what is of value."

Confederate spy **ROSE GREENHOW**, dispatch to Richmond from Washington, D.C., August 1861; quoted in Fishel, *Secret War for the Union* (1996). It's never wise to leave a collector to his or her own devices.

"[Spying] puts me to a great disadvantage and I do not wish to do it unless it is received welcomely."

ELIZABETH VAN LEW, Union spymaster in Richmond in 1864, to Union intelligence chief Colonel Sharpe; quoted in Fishel, *Secret War for the Union* (1996).

"Is there evidence of Russian propaganda? Are there active revolutionary groups of importance? Are revolutionary outbreaks likely to occur? If so, will they succeed? . . . It has been difficult in some instances in the reports already received to make out whether you are merely exposing the position which is presented to you, or whether you are actually in sympathy with that position. It would be most helpful if you will clearly distinguish between what is told to you and your valuation or criticism of it."

Future DCI **ALLEN DULLES**, while a U.S. diplomat in Paris, giving instructions to American observers sent into central Europe, letter of February 1919; quoted in Grose, *Gentleman Spy* (1995).

"You can send your 'source' from the German air force to his whore of a mother! This is not a 'source' but a disinformer. J. Stalin."

The Soviet dictator's feedback on a report from a Soviet spy in Berlin—who indeed was in the German air force—that the Nazis were planning to attack the USSR, 16 June 1941; cited in Andrew and Mitrokhin, *The Mitrokhin Archive* (1999). The Germans attacked on 22 June.

"Henceforth, we would like to have you make reports concerning vessels along the following lines. . . . The waters (of Pearl Harbor) are to be divided roughly into five sub-areas. . . . With regard to warships and aircraft carriers, we would like to have you report on those at anchor, tied up at wharves, buoys and in docks. Designate types and classes . . ."

Japanese Foreign Ministry cable to the consulate in Honolulu, 24 September 1941; cited in Prange, *At Dawn We Slept* (1981). The U.S. Army decrypted and translated this cable in early October, but neither the Army nor the U.S. Navy saw much significance in it.

"All [intelligence] from Bern these days is being discounted 100% by the War Department. . . . [Your material] disagrees with reports we have received from other sources and parts of it were months old. . . . Your information [is] now given a lower rating than any other source. This seems to indicate a need for using the greatest care in checking all your sources."

OSS Director **WILLIAM DONOVAN** to his station chief in Bern, Allen Dulles, in April 1943 and January 1944; quoted in Ranelagh, *The Agency* (1986). This didn't hurt Dulles's career.

"I have no doubt the high point of my career in intelligence came when I was called upon to answer a telephone request for the plural of 'epiglottis.'"

OSS analyst (and historian of revolutions) **CRANE BRINTON** to OSS analysis chief (and Harvard historian) William Langer, 22 January 1944; cited in Katz, *Foreign Intelligence: Research and Analysis in OSS* (1989). It's epiglottises or epiglotides.

"Dear Friend. Perhaps you remember my little son. His birthday is coming soon and I wanted to get him some of those clever Japanese toys with which the shops used to be full, but I can find none. I wonder if there might be some left in Berlin?"

> Postcard sent by **ALLEN DULLES**, OSS station chief in Bern, through a dummy Zurich address to a highly placed source in Nazi Germany; quoted in Grose, *Gentleman Spy* (1995). The source correctly surmised that U.S. intelligence was seeking Nazi information on Japanese political and military developments, which he delivered on his next visit to Dulles.

"For reasons I do not profess to understand . . . it appears easier to get out a 250-page epitome of what Europe will be like in 1986, to be delivered tomorrow at 8:30, [than] a 2-page summary of what you most want to know about the job you're doing."

> OSS official **SHERMAN KENT**, memorandum to the Europe-Africa Division of the Research and Analysis Branch, 4 July 1945; cited in Katz, *Foreign Intelligence: Research and Analysis in OSS* (1989).

"Intelligence often finds it impossible to get the sort of guidance which it must have to make its products useful."

> **SHERMAN KENT**, *Strategic Intelligence* (1949).

"Intelligence cannot serve if it does not know the doer's mind; it cannot serve if it has not his confidence; it cannot serve unless it can have the guidance any professional man must have from his client."

> **SHERMAN KENT**, *Strategic Intelligence* (1949).

"This is so you will know that your information is definitely reaching our leaders. . . . I can point out that in a number of the president's statements, exactly those thoughts which you suggested were mentioned by the president."

> CIA case officer **GEORGE KISEVALTER** to Soviet GRU Colonel (and CIA and SIS spy) Oleg Penkovskiy, 28 July 1961; quoted in Schecter and Deriabin, *The Spy Who*

Saved the World (1995). Kisevalter showed Penkovskiy President Kennedy's speech of 25 July on Berlin, in which Kennedy called Berlin "the great testing place of Western courage" and said "we cannot and will not permit the Communists to drive us out of Berlin."

"We are very much interested at this time in receiving concrete information as to military measures being undertaken by the USSR to convert Cuba into an offensive military base. In particular we would like to know if Cuba is to be provided with surface-to-surface missiles."

> Joint CIA-SIS letter to Soviet GRU Colonel Oleg Penkovskiy, September 1962; quoted in Schecter and Deriabin, *The Spy Who Saved the World* (1995).

"The Attorney General [was] also briefed. His initial comment was one four-letter word, off the record."

> DDI **RAY CLINE** on his briefing Robert Kennedy on 16 October 1962 that CIA had identified a ballistic missile site in Cuba, memorandum of 27 October 1962; reproduced in McAuliffe, *Cuban Missile Crisis* (1992).

"Shit."

> **ROBERT KENNEDY**'s reaction to hearing that the Soviets were putting missiles in Cuba, 16 October 1962, according to Richard Helms; quoted in Schecter and Deriabin, *The Spy Who Saved the World* (1995).

"Same old shit, isn't it?"

> President **LYNDON JOHNSON** commenting on CIA's assessment of rising Soviet influence in the Middle East, 1967; quoted in Powers, *The Man Who Kept the Secrets* (1979).

"Dick, I need a paper on Viet Nam, and I'll tell you what I want included in it."

> DCI **RICHARD HELMS** in a 1969 interview recalling a tasking from President Lyndon Johnson; cited in Weber, *Spymasters* (1999).

"Consumers are quick to criticize the intelligence services in general terms, while doing little to provide adequate guidance or detailed, constructive criticism."

WALTER LAQUEUR, *A World of Secrets* (1985).

"To Cy, Zbig, Stan: I am not satisfied with the quality of our political intelligence. Assess our assets and as soon as possible give me a report concerning our abilities in the most important areas of the world. Make a joint recommendation on what we should do to improve your ability to give me political information and advice. J. C."

President **JIMMY CARTER**, handwritten note to Secretary of State Cyrus Vance, National Security Advisor Zbigniew Brzezinski, and DCI Stansfield Turner, 11 November 1978; quoted in Turner, *Secrecy and Democracy* (1985).

"Unless we are responding to what our consumers want and need to know, then essentially we in the intelligence community are doing nothing more than spending a lot of money to build a very expensive library."

Senior intelligence official, quoted in Berkowitz and Goodman, *Strategic Intelligence* (1989).

"In a regrettable but immensely satisfying display of pique and immaturity, I bade farewell to Romania's security police with an uplifted middle finger from the doorway of Air Force Two."

ROBERT GATES, then a White House aide, after being harassed during an advance trip to Bucharest in 1975; in Gates, *From the Shadows* (1996). At least it was clear feedback.

"For many years, trying to get senior policy principals to attend meetings to discuss longer-range intelligence requirements has been an exercise in

frustration. Beyond the lack of help on requirements, the CIA gets little feedback on its longer-range work that might help improve its relevance to policymakers' needs. The CIA has been more aggressive in recent years in trying to engage policymakers on these matters, [but] such interest remains exceedingly, dangerously rare."

DDI **ROBERT GATES**, "The CIA and American Foreign Policy," *Foreign Affairs* (winter 1987–88).

"[President George H. W. Bush] regularly phoned analysts with questions and comments about their reports. No other president had provided so much of the feedback that analysts craved and for which they had in the past frequently felt starved."

CHRISTOPHER ANDREW, *For the President's Eyes Only* (1995).

FIGHTING THE COLD WAR

Intelligence helped to keep the Cold War cold by giving U.S. policymakers the information they needed about Soviet intentions and capabilities—as even former Soviet officials will admit. Moreover, intelligence allowed U.S. presidents a way to resist and challenge Soviet aggression and influence without mobilizing the Marines.

See also: Bay of Pigs; Collection; Covert Action; Fronts; Intelligence, the Missions of; Origins of Central Intelligence; Successes

"There is perhaps in every thing of any consequence, a secret history which it would be amusing to know, could we have it authentically communicated."

JAMES BOSWELL, *The Life of Samuel Johnson, LL.D.* (1791).

"There is no nobler fate than to be forgotten as the foe of a forgotten heresy and no better success than to become superfluous."

G. K. CHESTERTON, "Apologia," in *GKC as MC* (1929).

"Owing to the paucity of reliable data, it was actually easier for [OSS analysts] to produce hard estimates of the aggressive potential of the German enemy than of the defensive capabilities of the Soviet ally."

BARRY KATZ, *Foreign Intelligence: Research and Analysis in OSS* (1989).

"World War II had seen the United States encounter totalitarianism without real mastery of intelligence. It was followed immediately by a new world of permanent struggle with no clear limits."

Historian **JOHN RANELAGH** at a conference on "The Origins and Development of the CIA," sponsored by CIA's Center for the Study of Intelligence, March 1994.

"At the conclusion of hostilities in Russia, Russia will have neither the resources nor, as far as economic factors are concerned, the inclination to embark on adventurist foreign policies which, in the opinion of Soviet leaders, might involve the USSR in a conflict or a critical armaments race with the Western powers."

OSS analytic report, "Capabilities and Intentions of the USSR in the Postwar Period," 5 January 1945; cited in Katz, *Foreign Intelligence: Research and Analysis in OSS* (1989).

"There is an urgent need to develop the highest possible quality of intelligence on the U.S.S.R. in the shortest possible time."

DCI **SIDNEY SOUERS**, memorandum of 29 April 1946; in *FRUS 1945–1950: Emergence of the Intelligence Establishment* (1996), document 148.

"The Soviet Government anticipates an inevitable conflict with the capitalist world. . . . The Soviet Union will insist on exclusive domination of Europe east of the general line Stettin-Trieste. The Soviet Union will endeavor to extend its predominant influence to include all of Germany and Austria. . . . The Soviets will make a maximum effort to develop as quickly as possible such special weapons as guided missiles and the atomic bomb."

Opening lines of Central Intelligence Group report, "Soviet Foreign and Military Policy," 23 July 1946; reproduced in Kuhns, *Assessing the Soviet Threat* (1997). This report, known as ORE [Office of Reports and Estimates] 1, was the first "national estimate" produced by CIG.

"It is expected that when the present draft treaties are concluded, the entire western border of the USSR will be effectively flanked by a Soviet-controlled military bloc."

Central Intelligence Group's *Weekly Summary*, 23 August 1946; reproduced in Kuhns, *Assessing the Soviet Threat* (1997).

"In spite of the anti-Communist tenor of the Truman Doctrine, and in spite of the presence of anti-Communists in Congress, nobody mentioned the Soviet Union or its clandestine services in the congressional debate on the CIA provision of the National Security Act [of 1947]. . . . So the initial CIA did not have as one of its explicit guidelines the organization and sponsorship of programs to frustrate Soviet ambitions."

RHODRI JEFFREYS-JONES, *The CIA and American Democracy* (1989). Some things just went without saying.

"In the course of a few years, all of Eastern Europe was locked behind an Iron Curtain; Greece nearly fell to the Communists in a civil war; West Berlin was blockaded by Soviet armor; the Kuomintang was chased off mainland China; Hukbalahaps threatened the Philippines; South Korea was almost inundated by the North Korean army; and the Union of Soviet Socialist Republics exploded an atomic bomb. . . . In such circumstances the need for reliable intelligence was considered crucial. But the Soviet Union was vast, repressive, and obsessively secretive."

WILLIAM E. BURROWS, *Deep Black* (1986).

"Reliable information on what the Soviet military was building [was nil]. Out came an atomic bomb; a satellite called Sputnik suddenly appeared in the sky. Were they out-doing us or secretly getting ahead of us? Those were times when tightened sphincters were the order of the day."

Former DCI **RICHARD HELMS**, remarks at CIA's fiftieth anniversary ceremonies, 18 September 1997.

"Our initial approaches to intelligence collection in the USSR and Eastern Europe were heavily freighted with the high-priority requirement to provide what was called early warning. This was another manifestation of the Pearl Harbor syndrome—never again. The simple solution—seen ever so clearly by the intelligence consumers in Washington—was for CIA to establish agents in Moscow and in position to discover any Politburo plan for the Red Army to march to the English Channel. This was a logical requirement, but at the time the possibility of recruiting and running any such sources was as improbable as placing resident spies on the planet Mars."

Former DCI **RICHARD HELMS**, *A Look over My Shoulder* (2003). Mars will have to wait its turn.

"1. Among foreign powers, only the U.S.S.R. is capable of threatening the security of the United States.

2. The U.S.S.R. is presently incapable of military aggression outside of Europe and Asia, but is capable of overrunning most of continental Europe, the Near East, northern China, and Korea.

3. The U.S.S.R. is unlikely to resort to open military aggression in present circumstances. Its policy is to avoid war, to build up its war potential, and to extend its influence and control by political, economic, and psychological warfare against the United States.

4. The greatest danger to the security of the United States is the possibility of economic collapse in Western Europe and the consequent accession to power of Communist elements.

5. Stabilization and recovery in Europe and Asia would tend to redress the balance of power and thereby to restrain the U.S.S.R."

CIA report, "Review of the World Situation," 26 September 1947; reproduced in Kuhns, *Assessing the Soviet Threat* (1997). CIA had come into existence just eight days previously.

"I found the [CIA] assessments, particularly in the period 1946–1948, to be, generally speaking, remarkably good. I would commend particularly the realism and restraint shown in the judgments of Soviet military intentions and capabilities."

GEORGE KENNAN, October 1997, remarks to a CIA conference on the early Cold War, on recently declassified CIA assessments on the USSR.

"The current Soviet-Satellite meeting in Warsaw may have been called primarily to enable the eastern European powers to present a united answer to the London Conference on Germany. . . . CIA considers it probable that an "Eastern Union" will be formed, avowedly to protect the USSR and its

Satellites against aggression from a resurgent Germany sponsored by the West."

CIA *Daily Summary,* 24 June 1948; reproduced in Kuhns, *Assessing the Soviet Threat* (1997).

"The Cold War can be expected to continue undiminished in intensity."

CIA report on realignment within the Soviet leadership, 18 March 1949; reproduced in Kuhns, *Assessing the Soviet Threat* (1997).

"Whatever you do, just remember one thing—the Soviet Union is up to no good!"

The entirety of CIA's basic analytic training in 1949, according to senior CIA official **RICHARD LEHMAN**; quoted in DDCI John McLaughlin's remarks at a Princeton University conference on CIA's Cold War analysis of the USSR, March 1991.

"The USSR is unlikely deliberately to resort to direct military action during the next decade."

CIA memorandum, "Threats to the Security of the United States," 25 July 1949; reproduced in Kuhns, *Assessing the Soviet Threat* (1997).

"The basic objective of Soviet foreign policy is clearly the attainment of a Communist world under Soviet domination. In pursuit of this objective, the USSR regards the US as its major opponent and will wage against it a relentless, unceasing struggle *which promises success in terms of overall Soviet objectives.*"

CIA estimate on Soviet nuclear capabilities and intentions, 6 April 1950; reproduced in Kuhns, *Assessing the Soviet Threat* (1997). Emphasis in original.

"The Soviet rulers are simultaneously motivated by Marxist-Leninist-Stalinist doctrine and by considerations affecting the position of the Soviet Union as a world power. They have made clear that their long-term object is to establish World Communism under the domination of the Kremlin.... In the belief that their object cannot be fully attained without involvement in a general war against the Western Powers, the Soviet rulers may decide deliberately to provoke such a war at a moment when, in their opinion, the strength of the Soviet Union vis-à-vis the Western Powers is at its maximum. It is estimated that such a period exists now and will extend from the present through 1954 with its peak about halfway, i.e., 1952."

CIA estimate for President Truman, "Conclusions Regarding a Possible Soviet Decision to Precipitate Global War," 12 October 1950; reproduced in Warner, *CIA Under Truman* (1994).

"To comfort and encourage those now in bondage; to reassure them constantly of the West's steadfast concern for their plight; to keep alive and fortify among them the Western tradition of freedom and democracy; to hold up the prospect of a better future."

Goals for Radio Free Europe, memorandum of November 1950; quoted in Arch Puddington, *Broadcasting Freedom* (2000). Radio Free Europe, officially inaugurated on May Day 1951, was a CIA covert project until the 1970s.

"Imagery of the Soviet Union in the early days of the Cold War was so scarce that the British government authorities asked travelers for tourist photos they had taken when visiting Soviet bloc countries, and the U.S. Air Force sometimes depended on Tsarist-era maps and captured German reconnaissance photographs to plan bombing missions over the Soviet Union. Entire industrial cities had been built east of the Urals during the war on which the United States had no imagery."

BRUCE BERKOWITZ and **ALLAN GOODMAN**, *Strategic Intelligence* (1989).

"The Director [of Central Intelligence] . . . feels that operations have assumed such a very large size in comparison to our intelligence function that we have almost arrived at a stage where it is necessary to decide whether CIA will remain an intelligence agency or becomes a 'cold war department.' We have never had trouble with the Bureau of the Budget in asking for funds to conduct our intelligence work but the very large proposed budget for 1953, most of it for operations, may cause the Bureau of the Budget to scrutinize our activities very carefully."

Minutes of CIA staff conference, 22 October 1951; reproduced in Warner, *CIA Under Truman* (1994).

"Certainly Soviet policy challenges the intelligence officer to sharpen his wits. If we can rely upon the Toynbee theory that challenge provokes response in those civilizations which survive, we in the West should come out of this dilemma with the best intelligence services in the world. In any event, the situation calls for all the ingenuity of an organization such as the CIA which, as one of its major tasks, has the job of pulling together the evidence on Soviet capabilities and intentions."

ALLEN DULLES, speech in Boston, 16 November 1951; in CIA's Historical Intelligence Collection.

"We are working now in the most difficult era that intelligence has ever known. It was child's play to get intelligence during the war compared to getting intelligence today from behind the Iron Curtain."

DCI **ALLEN DULLES**, remarks at CIA course for new officers, 1953; in CIA's Historical Intelligence Collection.

"If I accept, as millions of other West Europeans do, that America is destined to be the mainstay of freedom in this mid-twentieth century world, it does not follow that American institutions are perfect, that Americans are invariably well-behaved, or that the American way of life is flawless. It only means that in one of the most terrible conflicts in human history, I have chosen my side, as all will have to choose, sooner or later."

Attributed to British writer (and SIS officer during World War II) **MALCOLM MUGGERIDGE**.

"There is no institution in the USSR that does not have in it an intelligence officer or agent of either the GRU or KGB. Furthermore, the majority of the personnel in Soviet embassies abroad are KGB and GRU employees. . . . The West is trying to accomplish some improvement of relations with the Soviet Union by diplomatic means. We do not even have diplomats, such as the West understands the term. We do all kinds of work except diplomatic."

Soviet GRU Colonel (and spy for CIA and SIS) **OLEG PEN-KOVSKIY**, in 1961; in Penkovskiy, *The Penkovskiy Papers* (1966).

"In applying the rule of force instead of law in international conduct, the Communists have left us little choice except to take counteraction of some nature to meet their aggressive moves. . . . And as we reach our decisions and chart our courses of action in meeting Communist secret aggression, the intelligence services with their special techniques have an important role to play, new to this generation perhaps but nonetheless highly important to the success of the enterprise."

Former DCI **ALLEN DULLES**, *The Craft of Intelligence* (1963).

"The United States was faced with hostile Communist nations that were determined, in Khrushchev's words, to 'bury' us, and knowing what those hostile nations were up to was vital to the survival of the United States. The Communists were also attempting to subvert weaker, developing countries all over the world with a lavish outlay of money, goods, and people, and there were occasions when a little counteraction in the field of covert political activity might make the difference between losing a country to Communist subversion or maintaining its independence. We had to have a CIA, and this particular one, in fact, had had great successes. . . . So long as the Communists themselves are openly antagonistic to the rest of the world, as they openly and avowedly are, and so long as they use the techniques of subversion to bring down governments, which they do and which they openly and avowedly advocate doing, then the countries to which they are so hostile have both a right and a duty to use the methods of secret intelligence to protect and defend themselves—where those methods are effective and appropriate and for which there is no effective and appropriate alternative."

ROGER HILSMAN, *To Move a Nation* (1967).

"To discover the exact dimensions of Communist activity in all the countries of the world and to counter and negate Communist political gains were two main tasks entrusted to the new CIA. . . . At that time no one questioned the morality of using CIA to conduct this covert part of the strategic contest. . . . There was an idealism and an urgency in all this that gave meaning to the lives of a generation of CIA officers and their many colleagues in the U.S. intelligence community."

Former DDI **RAY CLINE**, *Secrets, Spies and Scholars* (1976). It's too early to tell whether the fight against terrorism will similarly inspire a new generation of CIA officers.

"Just as advances in intelligence collection and analysis had helped to stabilize the Cold War in the mid-1950s, so in the early 1970s they made possible the first steps in controlling the nuclear arms race."

CHRISTOPHER ANDREW on intelligence verification of the SALT I and ABM treaties, *For the President's Eyes Only* (1995).

"Wish to advise that this will be final message from Saigon Station. . . . It has been a long fight and we have lost. . . . Those who fail to learn from history are forced to repeat it. Let us hope that we will not have another Vietnam experience and that we have learned our lesson. Saigon signing off."

Declassified final cable from CIA's Saigon station, April 1975.

"Soviet leaders themselves see their foreign policy as essentially revolutionary, resting on the expectation of fundamental change in the international system. . . . Soviet policy will continue to be competitive and assertive in most areas of engagement with the West."

National Intelligence Estimate, *Soviet Goals and Expectations*, mid-1978; reproduced in Steury, *Intentions and Capabilities* (1996).

"Your organizational discipline is for the purpose of imposing the will of one man . . . one ideology . . . on others. *Our* organization is defensive in nature. Its aim is to defeat your aggressive intentions. The acceptance of discipline in the one enterprise isn't the equivalent of the acceptance of discipline in the other enterprise. I accept the need for discipline. . . . But please, don't tell me that Goering following Hitler's orders is the equivalent of Montgomery following Churchill's orders. You begin by the dissimilarities between Churchill and Hitler."

> Fictional CIA officer Blackford Oakes explaining the facts of Cold War intelligence services to a Soviet intelligence officer in **WILLIAM F. BUCKLEY, JR.**, *Stained Glass* (1978).

"If we can't stop Soviet expansionism in a place like Nicaragua, where the hell can we?"

> DCI **WILLIAM CASEY**, March 1981; quoted in Andrew, *For the President's Eyes Only* (1995). Well, Grenada. Soon enough, Eastern Europe. Eventually, the Soviet Union.

"What would the CIA and SIS do without a KGB, and vice versa? . . . All have a direct interest in the continuation of the Cold War."

> **PHILLIP KNIGHTLEY**, *The Second Oldest Profession* (1988). This is a bit like saying that doctors are in favor of disease. Intelligence officers are relieved the Cold War is over but are too busy to rest on those laurels, thank you.

"I recall there were days when over 85 percent of our resources were on the Soviet target—and that focus is not likely to change. Yet we are also spending more time and resources collecting information on Third World countries . . . the proliferation of nuclear, chemical and biological weapons and the spread of ballistic missiles."

> DCI **WILLIAM WEBSTER**, remarks of 10 April 1989; in Webster, *1989 Speeches*.

"[CIA's] assessments of Gorbachev's economic policies and especially what really was happening—how little was happening economically—were, in retrospect, accurate and realistic. We understood better than Gorbachev the contradictions in his programs, their shortcomings, and the opposition within the bureaucracy."

> Former DCI **ROBERT GATES**, *From the Shadows* (1996).

"By 1990 there were more KGB employees in Moscow alone—47,000—than all of the CIA and FBI employees combined."

> Former KGB General **OLEG KALUGIN**, *The First Directorate* (1994).

"Economic crisis, independence aspirations and anti-communist forces are breaking down the Soviet Empire and system of governance."

> CIA assessment "The Soviet Cauldron," 25 April 1991; quoted in Gates, *From the Shadows* (1996). This prescient report was the work of CIA's premier Soviet expert George Kolt.

"I am confident that history will honor the 'cold warriors' of the Agency, of CIA: The men and women who struggled in the shadows, sent messages over the airwaves, smuggled forbidden books and magazines, all to help pierce the Iron Curtain. History will praise the secret strategies and operations, the personal valor and organizational excellence that gave our intelligence community success in its cold war mission."

> President **GEORGE H. W. BUSH**, remarks to OSS veterans, 23 October 1991; quoted in CIA, *"Our First Line of Defense"* (1996).

"In 1980—at the high point of our commitment of resources to the Cold War—only 58 percent of the Intelligence Community's resources were dedicated against the Soviet Union. The remainder—that is, over 40 percent—were dedicated to a range of issues that are of significance today: developments in the Third World, international arms sales, weapons proliferation, terrorism, global economic issues, international narcotics trafficking and a host of other concerns. . . . In short, the Intelligence

Community never was wholly preoccupied with the Soviet Union—far from it."

DCI **ROBERT GATES**, remarks of 11 May 1992; in Gates, *Speeches.*

"During the long decades of the Cold War, one of the reasons that 'containment' worked was that, while military forces trained and exercised and glowered at one another, US intelligence was in the trenches and at war—from Italy and France out of World War II to Afghanistan in the 1980s. Containment worked not just because the Soviet system was fundamentally flawed, but also because Soviet aggression and subversion were resisted— and that resistance was usually organized or supported by American intelligence."

DCI **ROBERT GATES**, remarks at the dedication of CIA's Berlin Wall Memorial, 18 December 1992; in *Studies in Intelligence* 36 (1992).

"What American intelligence contributed to the outcome [of the Cold War] was . . . the confidence that we knew what the Soviets were up to, and could afford to contain their forays while waiting for the deep change in attitude which George Kennan had predicted back in 1947."

THOMAS POWERS in the *New York Review of Books,* 13 May 1993.

"The mission of the CIA throughout [the Cold War] can best be captured by three verbs: to explain, to warn, and to spy."

DCI **R. JAMES WOOLSEY** at a conference on "The Origins and Development of the CIA," sponsored by CIA's Center for the Study of Intelligence, March 1994.

"The quarter of a trillion dollars spent on the NRO [National Reconnaissance Office] over the

past 35 years was by far the most productive investment America made during the Cold War."

JOHN PIKE, *The National Reconnaissance Office* (1994).

"Victory in the Cold War produced some disorientation in both Langley and the White House. To a greater extent than most other modern intelligence communities, that of the United States was a product of the Cold War. . . . The end of the Cold War thus produced greater uncertainty about the future role of foreign intelligence in the United States than in most other Western states."

CHRISTOPHER ANDREW, *For the President's Eyes Only* (1995). Andrew overstates the case.

"Some of [Gorbachev's] opponents would allege that he and his buddy Yakovlev had been CIA agents. They weren't, and it's a good thing: We could not possibly have guided him to engineer so successfully the destruction of the Soviet empire."

Former DCI **ROBERT GATES**, *From the Shadows* (1996).

"[It is necessary] to acknowledge the scale of the CIA's achievement. [Aldrich] Ames could betray so much . . . because the Americans had the Russians penetrated high, wide and handsome. They were winning the intelligence war hands down and have never received their rightful credit for it."

British journalist **ALAN JUDD**, *The Daily Telegraph*, 15 February 1997.

"During the Cold War, the CIA had the best knowledge of the Communist system and was able to provide the U.S. and allied governments with accurate information about the U.S.S.R. and the Warsaw Pact. Half the credit of the West's victory in the Cold War belongs to the agency."

Former KGB officer **OLEG GORDIEVSKY**, quoted in "The CIA Turns 50," *Wall Street Journal*, 17 September 1997.

"The CIA unquestionably was the major and most awesome tool of American foreign policy in the Cold War, and the judgment of history is that it succeeded beyond its wildest dreams."

AMOS PERLMUTTER, "Why the CIA Is Still Needed," *Washington Times*, 25 September 1997.

"Espionage was not really something exclusive and clandestine. It was actually the currency of the Cold War. Spies were the poor bloody infantry of the Cold War."

JOHN LE CARRÉ [David Cornwell], spy novelist and former MI5 officer, in *The Guardian*, 2 March 1999. Infantries, of course, win wars.

"It was all such fun during the cold war. But now, I wonder, what the hell is the point of it all?"

Veteran of British intelligence, quoted in the *Financial Times*, 3 October 1999. See below.

"I am pleased that our long, hard struggle has brought peace, freedom, and democracy not only to my country but to many other people as well."

Polish Colonel **RYSZARD KUKLINSKI** at a ceremony honoring those who died in the struggle for freedom during the Cold War, Texas A&M University, November 1999; quoted in *Studies in Intelligence* 44/1 (2000). Kuklinski, whom CIA officials have called "our second Penkovskiy," passed Warsaw Pact military secrets to the United States for more than a decade. Kuklinski's words remind us just what the point of it all was.

"[Radio Free Europe's] strategy, language, and short-term objectives would change during the course of the Cold War, just as American policy toward the Communist world would change. Yet no matter what doctrine predominated in Washington—liberation, gradualism, détente—RFE continued to fulfill its original mission as an instrument of anti-Communist diplomacy. Radio Free Europe, along with its sister organization, Radio Liberty, stood as the most visible institutions of official American anticommunism, and were arguably the most successful Cold War vehicles established by the American government."

ARCH PUDDINGTON, *Broadcasting Freedom* (2000). Radio Free Europe and Radio Liberty—RL broadcast to the people of the Soviet Union—were established covertly under CIA auspices.

"Closed or semi-closed societies have an inbuilt advantage over open societies in intelligence collection from human sources, because Western capitals invariably have much lower levels of security and surveillance than their counterparts in Communist and other authoritarian regimes. Equally, however, one-party states have an inherent disadvantage when it comes to intelligence analysis, since analysts usually fear to tell the Party hierarch what it does not want to hear."

CHRISTOPHER ANDREW and **VASILI MITROKHIN**, *The Sword and the Shield: The Mitrokhin Archive* (1999).

"The men and women of U.S. Intelligence are proud of the contributions they made to defending the security of the Free World during the Cold War. We believe that a careful study of our role in that great global struggle will show that, time and again, U.S. Intelligence provided American leaders with critical information and insights that saved American lives and advanced our most vital interests . . . for over four decades. An intelligence effort of such magnitude and fraught with such great risk and uncertainty was bound to have its flaws and failures, both operational and analytical. I believe, however, that the overall record is one of impressive accomplishment."

DCI **GEORGE TENET**, remarks at a Princeton University conference, "CIA's Analysis of the Soviet Union, 1947–1991," March 2001.

"The Cold War was mainly fought on the intelligence battlefield.... We gave as good as we got in the struggle with the Soviet Union, which never fielded a big new weapon system that caught American intelligence by surprise.... Exactly who won the counterintelligence war is still not quite clear; the Russians had an uncanny ability to recruit spies in the United States and at high levels in the governments of our allies, but it did them little good over the long haul, and our own feats of technical intelligence collection often reached deeper than even spies could go. The intelligence history of the Cold War is still unfolding, and a final verdict must wait."

THOMAS POWERS in the *Washington Post Book World*, 8 February 2004.

FRONTS

In intelligence, all is not what it seems.

See also: Covert Action; Fighting the Cold War; Plausible Denial

"[The] June 1950 meeting of the new Congress for Cultural Freedom (CCF) signaled the emergence of an activist anticommunist movement within the leftist Western intellectual community. ... The Congress's financial support came in large part from the CIA's International Organizations Division."

RICHARD GID POWERS, *Not Without Honor* (1995).

"There is something daring, even arrogant, in the notion of a country establishing a network of more than twenty radio stations with the ultimate goal of bringing down an entire system of government. Only in America could such an unusual enterprise

have been conceived and implemented, perhaps, indeed, only in an America secure in its power and brimming with confidence, as was the case in the immediate postwar era. Radio Free Europe owes its existence to some of the brightest lights of the early Cold War—men, such as Allen Dulles, George F. Kennan, and Gen. Lucius Clay, who ... were convinced that the Communist system was susceptible to an aggressive form of psychological warfare."

ARCH PUDDINGTON, preface to his *Broadcasting Freedom* (2000). RFE began as a CIA front, perhaps the most successful one ever.

"During the last days of Stalinism, the non-Communist trade-union movements and the non-Communist intellectuals [of the West] were under the most severe, unscrupulous and unrelenting pressure. For the United States government to have stood self-righteously aside at this point would have seemed to me far more shameful than to do what, in fact, it did—which was through intermediaries to provide some of these groups subsidies to help them do better what they were going to do anyway."

ARTHUR SCHLESINGER, JR., on CIA-funded groups; quoted in Powers, *Not Without Honor* (1995). A rare endorsement of covert action from Dr. Schlesinger.

"[DCI Allen] Dulles approved my appointment [in 1954] as chief of the International Organizations Division [with] a growing budget and a wide policy mandate under a new National Security Council directive to counter with covert action the political and propaganda offensive that the Soviets had launched through their control of a battery of international front organizations.... Over a period of fifteen years many American citizens and private voluntary organizations ... cooperated with the CIA in joint efforts to cope with the Soviet political offensive."

Former senior CIA official **CORD MEYER**, *Facing Reality* (1980).

"If you responded to the many appeals of Radio Free Europe on television, in magazines, even in buses and subways, then you became part of a CIA cover."

Journalist **MIKE WALLACE** in a 1967 CBS program on CIA; quoted in Arch Puddington, *Broadcasting Freedom* (2000). At the time, the president of CBS, Frank Stanton, was chairman of the Radio Free Europe Fund, which raised private funds for RFE.

"Radio Free Europe and Radio Liberty are public evidence of CIA covert action projects that were successful, served liberal democratic purposes, and never became the center of controversy as so many paramilitary projects did."

Former DDI **RAY CLINE**, *Secrets, Spies and Scholars* (1976).

"If we learn anything about events in our own country, it's from there."

ALEKSANDR SOLZHENITSYN on Radio Liberty, 1972; cited in the *Georgetown Journal of International Affairs* 1/1 (winter–spring 2000).

"As far as depots of 'untraceable arms,' airlines and other installations are concerned, one wonders how the CIA could accomplish the tasks required of it in Southeast Asia without such facilities."

Former CIA Executive Director **LYMAN KIRKPATRICK**; quoted in *U.S. News and World Report* (11 October 1971).

"CAT [Civil Air Transport], a CIA proprietary . . . supports covert and clandestine air operations by providing trained and experienced personnel, procurement of supplies and equipment through overt commercial channels, and the maintenance

of a fairly large inventory of transport and other type aircraft. . . . During the past ten years, [CAT] has had some notable achievements, including support of the Chinese Nationalist withdrawal from the mainland, air drop support to the French at Dien Bien Phu . . . air lifts of refugees from North Vietnam, more than 200 overflights of mainland China and Tibet . . ."

1961 CIA memorandum published in *The Pentagon Papers;* cited in Marchetti and Marks, *CIA and the Cult of Intelligence* (1974).

"The GRU and the KGB helped to fund just about every antiwar movement and organization in America and abroad. Funding was provided via undercover operatives or front organizations. These would fund another group that in turn would fund student organizations . . . the GRU and KGB had a larger budget for antiwar propaganda in the United States than [they] did for economic and military support of the Vietnamese."

STANISLAV LUNEV, former Soviet GRU colonel, *Through the Eyes of the Enemy* (1998).

"The vast majority of individuals and groups involved in the European peace movement in the early 1980s were sincere in their beliefs and had no connection with or particular sympathy for the Soviet Union. But that movement was the target of a Soviet campaign extending over a three-year period and involving a major effort to infiltrate, manipulate, and exploit it. Moscow indirectly and covertly provided propaganda themes, organizational expertise, coordination, and materials and financial resources. . . . The Soviets also sought to direct the focus of the West European peace movement by providing communist parties and front organizations with propaganda themes keyed to local concerns and U.S. and NATO policies."

Former DCI **ROBERT GATES**, *From the Shadows* (1996).

"Considerable work has been done to provide support for unofficial organizations in a number of countries abroad in their struggle against implementation of the American administration's militarist plans."

> Senior KGB official **VLADIMIR KRYUCHKOV**, report on "active measures" used to sway Western public opinion, February 1984; cited in Andrew and Mitrokhin, *The Mitrokhin Archive* (1999).

"Presenting works that were 'on the red censorship list,' it was our ministry of culture. Exposing absurd economic policies, it was our ministry of economics. Reacting to events promptly and pertinently, but above all truthfully, it was our ministry of information."

> **LECH WALESA**, Polish president and former anticommunist dissident, in a 1993 tribute to Radio Free Europe; quoted in Arch Puddington, *Broadcasting Freedom* (2000).

"The three operations that represented the most long-lived successes of the Agency's Cold War covert political action . . . achieved goals that went well beyond the optimistic objectives that decorate many initial operational proposals. To differing degrees, each gained foreign policy objectives which at the time could not have been achieved if openly supported by the United States. The scope of these programs encompassed a wide—often left-of-center—spectrum of Western political opinion. The net effect showed dramatic evidence of the strength of democracy in contrast to the false face the USSR was presenting through its front organizations in the West."

> Former DCI **RICHARD HELMS** on the Congress for Cultural Freedom and Radios Free Europe and Liberty, in *A Look over My Shoulder* (2003).

- **Ignoring Bad News**
- **Intelligence & American Culture**
- **Intelligence, Definitions of**
- **Intelligence, the Missions of**
- **Intercepts & Cryptology**

IGNORING BAD NEWS

This business of intelligence, like every human endeavor, is shot through with the very human shortcomings not only of its practitioners but of its customers. Intelligence officers are in the bad news business, and they must not expect national leaders to welcome such tidings with open arms. In extreme cases, the Literary Spy recommends messengers to expect to be shot.

See also: Failures; Feedback & Tasking; Objectivity; Politicization

"Nobody likes the man who brings bad news."
Greek poet **SOPHOCLES**, *Antigone* (442 B.C.).

"If I tell the truth, why do you not believe me?"
John 8:46 (Revised Standard).

"A wise chieftain never kills the Hun bearing bad news. Rather, the wise chieftain kills the Hun who fails to deliver bad news."
ATTILA THE HUN, as interpreted by Wess Roberts, *Leadership Secrets of Attila the Hun* (1985).

"Man prefers to believe what he prefers to be true."
FRANCIS BACON, *Novum Organum* (1620).

"Though it be honest, it is never good
To bring bad news: give to a gracious message
An host of tongues; but let ill tidings tell
Themselves when they be felt."
Cleopatra in **WILLIAM SHAKESPEARE**, *Antony and Cleopatra* (1607), Act II, scene 5.

"Four or five frigates will do the business without any military force."
LORD NORTH, on the American rebellion, to the House of Commons, 1774; quoted in Heinl, *Dictionary of Military and Naval Quotations* (1966). North misinterpreted the significance of the Boston Tea Party of December 1773.

"It is natural to man to indulge in the illusions of hope. We are apt to shut our eyes against a painful truth—and listen to the song of that siren, till she transforms us into beasts."
PATRICK HENRY, *Speech in the Virginia Convention* (March 1775).

"I tell you Wellington is a bad general, the English are bad soldiers; we will settle the matter by lunchtime."

> **NAPOLEON** on the morning of 18 June 1815, before the Battle of Waterloo; in Peter Tsouras, ed., *The Greenhill Dictionary of Military Quotations* (2000).

"[Union General Joseph] Hooker failed to put his intelligence to proper use. Prior to the devastating Confederate attack on his exposed right flank at Chancellorsville, the uneasy German troops in the area sent headquarters repeated warnings of rebel movements, but their reports were ignored by staff officers.... This failure to take prompt action on important intelligence resulted in another resounding Union defeat."

> **NATHAN MILLER**, *Spying for America* (1989).

"We are not interested in the possibilities of defeat."

> **QUEEN VICTORIA**, letter to A. J. Balfour, December 1899.

"It is an old maxim of mine that when you have excluded the impossible, whatever remains, however improbable, must be the truth."

> Sherlock Holmes in Sir **ARTHUR CONAN DOYLE**, "The Adventure of the Beryl Coronet" (1892).

"It is stupidity rather than courage to refuse to recognize danger when it is close upon you."

> Sherlock Holmes in Sir **ARTHUR CONAN DOYLE**, "The Adventure of the Final Problem" (1893).

"I didn't want to worry the poor dear Field Marshal."

> Aide to British Field Marshal Douglas Haig on why he did not pass intelligence pointing to a German counterattack after the Battle of Cambrai in November 1917; quoted in Knightley, *The Second Oldest Profession* (1988).

"The most costly of all follies is to believe passionately in the palpably not true."

> **H. L. MENCKEN**, *Prejudices* (1926).

"A war with Japan! ... I do not believe there is the slightest chance of it in our lifetime."

> **WINSTON CHURCHILL**, as chancellor of the exchequer, protesting in 1925 British Navy estimates justifying the development of naval bases in the Far East; quoted in Stafford, *Churchill and Secret Service* (1998).

"Colonel, I know that you are a good Intelligence officer and that you mean well. But if anything of this kind were happening, I, as Foreign Minister, would be the first to know about it. And bring us better news in the future."

> Czechoslovak Foreign Minister **FRANTISEK CHVAL-KOVSKY**, upon being informed that Germany planned to invade and occupy Czechoslovakia, 11 March 1938; quoted in Moravec, *Master of Spies* (1975). The Germans invaded on 15 March.

"It seems to me that Ministers run the most tremendous risks if they allow the information collected by the Intelligence Department ... to be sifted and coloured and reduced in consequence and importance, and if they ever get themselves into a mood of attaching weight only to those pieces of information which accord with their earnest and honourable desire that the peace of the world should remain unbroken."

> **WINSTON CHURCHILL** to the House of Commons, 13 April 1939; in Churchill, *The Gathering Storm* (1948).

"I cannot bring myself to believe that a real alliance between Russia and Germany is possible."

> Prime Minister **NEVILLE CHAMBERLAIN**, shrugging off intelligence of a pact between Moscow and Berlin, summer 1939; quoted in Richelson, *A Century of Spies* (1995). The Nazi-Soviet Nonaggression Pact was signed on 23 August 1939.

"Hitler is fully determined to make war upon and destroy the USSR as a raw materials and grain base."

> Soviet spy **RICHARD SORGE** on information from his contacts in the German Embassy in Tokyo, 2 May 1941; quoted in Richelson, *A Century of Spies* (1995). Sorge's warnings led Stalin to describe him as "a shit who has set himself up with some small factories and brothels in Japan."

"All of the military training in Germany in preparation for an attack on the Soviet Union is complete, and the strike may be expected at any time."

> Report from the senior Soviet intelligence officer in Berlin, **ALEKSANDR KOROTKOV**, relaying information from his two agent networks, 16 June 1941; cited in Andrew and Mitrokhin, *The Mitrokhin Archive* (1999). The KGB later counted more than one hundred warnings forwarded to Stalin by Soviet intelligence between 1 January and 21 June 1941. The Nazis attacked on 22 June.

"You can tell your source to fuck off."

> **JOSEPH STALIN** to his intelligence advisor on the report of a Soviet spy in Berlin that a German attack was imminent—five days before Germany attacked the USSR on 22 June 1941; quoted in Stafford, *Churchill and Secret Service* (1998).

"Stalin's reaction to the information he received about an impending German attack was a classic case of willful disregard of new evidence in order to preserve an already existing belief. . . . The countless warnings from the British, American, and other sources were seen as no more than clumsy attempts by the Western imperialists to embroil the Soviet Union in war. Information from reliable sources was submitted to Stalin by his intelligence chiefs, but they marked it 'doubtful,' for they knew that their boss had already made up his mind."

> **WALTER LAQUEUR**, *A World of Secrets* (1985).

"They don't have the ships for it."

> **ADOLF HITLER**, after being warned of the possibility of an Allied landing in North Africa, 1942; quoted in Dulles, *The Craft of Intelligence* (1963).

"CAUGHT CAUGHT CAUGHT."

> SOE radio operator **HUBURTUS LAUWERS**, trying to tell SOE headquarters in London that he had been caught by the Germans in 1942 and forced to transmit bogus messages from the Netherlands; quoted in Lloyd, *Guinness Book of Espionage* (1994). Even though Lauwers deliberately neglected to include in his radio messages the required security checks and even inserted coded warnings, SOE for two years considered his messages genuine.

"I'm too old a bunny to get excited about this."

> German Fifteenth Army commander General **HANS VON SALMUTH**, 5 June 1944, after his intelligence chief informed him at cards that the BBC had just broadcast the code message indicating an imminent Allied invasion. The message was "Wound my heart with a monotonous languor," broadcast in French. The general returned to his bridge game. In Kahn, *The Codebreakers* (1996).

"I wouldn't trouble myself about these if I were you."

> British Lieutenant General **FREDERICK BROWNING** to his intelligence officer who had brought him aerial photography indicating the presence of German armor in the Arnhem area, 16 September 1944; quoted in Cornelius Ryan, *A Bridge Too Far* (1974). The intelligence officer was right, and combined British-American airborne and ground assaults on Nazi-occupied Holland resulted in more Allied casualties than during the Normandy invasion.

"It is my personal opinion that this program is not sufficiently severe or damaging to the North Vietnamese to cause them to compromise their present policy. . . . I think what we are doing is starting on a track which, in all probability, will have limited effectiveness against guerrillas. . . . We can expect requirements for an ever-increasing commitment of U.S. personnel without materially improving the chance of victory. . . . In effect, we will find ourselves mired down in combat in the jungle in a military effort that we cannot win, and from which we will have extreme difficulty in extracting ourselves."

> JOHN McCONE, before resigning as DCI because his views were ignored, to President Johnson, 2 April 1965; quoted in Andrew, *For the President's Eyes Only* (1995) and in Ford, *CIA and the Vietnam Policymakers* (1998). Did he say "quagmire"?

"CIA was the bearer of bad tidings throughout the Vietnam War, and [its analysis] was not very happily received by any of the policymakers who tried to make the Vietnam intervention work. The intelligence was sound, but the policy was not firmly based on the evidence."

> Former DDI **RAY CLINE**, *Secrets, Spies and Scholars* (1976).

"Same old shit."

> President **LYNDON JOHNSON** to an aide on another, pessimistic CIA report on Vietnam; quoted in Miller, *Spying for America* (1989).

"[Lyndon] Johnson's memoirs contain no reference to intelligence analysis as being among the factors that influenced his thinking about Vietnam."

> **WALTER LAQUEUR**, *A World of Secrets* (1985).

"Our Vietnam experience should tell us that when the views of the Central Intelligence Agency—the preeminent national intelligence organization—are not given adequate consideration in the policy councils of government, flawed policy judgments are more likely to result and the chances of policy failure are raised accordingly."

> General **BRUCE PALMER, JR.**, *The 25-Year War* (1984).

"Defense Secretary Robert McNamara ... wanted us to analyze the success of the U.S. Air Force bombing program, code-named 'Rolling Thunder.' ... In two weeks we produced an intensive logistic analysis that demonstrated Rolling Thunder was not significantly slowing the flow [of arms] into South Vietnam. ... We finally determined that the North Vietnamese in the teeth of the U.S. bombing program had improved their capability for moving war materiel south *fivefold*. ... Which brings me to a baffling aspect of Robert McNamara. All things considered, I would have said that McNamara made the most intelligent use of CIA skills and resources of any high officer I have ever known. He asked the right questions to get searching, insightful answers. He respected our analysis and our objectivity even when most uncongenial to his own goals and undertakings. On most occasions before departing on one of his many trips to view the war in Vietnam firsthand he asked us for an update on our assessments of the situation. Armed with these he would set out, and several days later ... he would vent another of those incredibly optimistic statements about 'light at the end of the tunnel.'"

> Former DDI **R. JACK SMITH**, *The Unknown CIA* (1989).

"Peeing up a rope."

> DCI **RICHARD HELMS**, describing his lack of success in getting the White House to pay attention to the threat of a Soviet invasion of Czechoslovakia; quoted in Laqueur, *A World of Secrets* (1985).

"The situation is completely normal and will not develop into a war and there is no intention of turning it into a war."

> Israeli military intelligence chief **ELI ZEIRA**, dismissing indications in late September and early October of 1973 of a possible Egyptian-Syrian attack; quoted in Richelson,

A *Century of Spies* (1995). Egypt and Syria attacked on 6 October, Yom Kippur.

"[Intelligence consumers] are resistant to bad news; messengers bringing such news are no longer physically killed, as in ancient times, but the damage to their careers may be severe, if not fatal. . . . Much depends on the quality of the senior intelligence staff: if they are worthy of their responsible positions, they will not shield their superiors from inconvenient information. If, on the other hand, they lack sufficient backbone, or if the consumers are congenitally incapable of listening to unpleasant facts, it will not make any difference whether intelligence is organizationally close to, or remote from, the seats of power. It will be ignored anyway."

  WALTER LAQUEUR, *A World of Secrets* (1985).

"A special criticism by policymakers is that the CIA is too frequently a voice of doom and gloom. For policymakers who must try to find solutions to intractable problems or a way out of a no-win situation . . . the CIA's forebodings and pointing out of perils and dangers are of little help and may be highly irritating."

  DDI **ROBERT GATES**, "The CIA and American Foreign Policy," *Foreign Affairs* (winter 1987–88).

"As the arms [for hostages] deal [with Iran] went along, a central premise of supporters was that there was a 'moderate' faction in Tehran or an 'opposition' worth cultivating. This was the view of the Israelis and it was the view the NSC adopted. CIA's Iran experts thought differently [and] published analyses acknowledging a faction inside Iran that strictly in terms of internal affairs—especially economic policy—might be called moderate. But there was no such faction when it came

to the United States. Toward the United States, they were all radicals. This analysis was provided to [national security advisor] McFarlane and the NSC. They chose to believe the Israelis. The notion that there was no CIA intelligence on internal Iranian affairs is incorrect. The intelligence we had simply was inconvenient."

  Former DCI **ROBERT GATES**, *From the Shadows* (1996).

"I suspect I'm the only CIA officer to have had two Secretaries of State, a Secretary of Defense, and the General Secretary of the Soviet Communist Party all try at different times to get me fired."

  Former DCI **ROBERT GATES**, conference on "US Intelligence and the End of the Cold War," Texas A&M University, 19 November 1999.

"Don't shoot the messenger."

  DCI **WILLIAM WEBSTER** to President George H. W. Bush's national security advisor Brent Scowcroft when Scowcroft criticized CIA analysis that Boris Yeltsin was eclipsing Mikhail Gorbachev in the USSR, early 1991; quoted in Strobe Talbott and Michael Beschloss, *At the Highest Levels* (1993).

"Within the [Bush] administration, the CIA warnings were listened to, even believed. But they did not significantly affect US policy in large part, say administration officials, because it was not in the US interest to tilt support away from Gorbachev and toward the republics."

  KIRSTEN LUNDBERG, "CIA and the Fall of the Soviet Empire," *Studies in Intelligence* 39/3 (fall 1995). Lundberg writes case studies for Harvard University's Kennedy School of Government, and her work is a needed corrective for the myth that CIA failed to predict the USSR's demise.

"The Clinton Administration [in 1994] ignored powerful warnings of impending genocide, including a Central Intelligence Agency study saying half a million people could die if Rwanda exploded, former Administration officials and human rights experts said today."

New York Times, 26 March 1998.

"We keep telling them it won't work, but they keep ignoring us."

State Department intelligence officer on prospects for a peace settlement for Kosovo, February 1999.

"The warnings were there for President Clinton. For weeks before the NATO air campaign against Yugoslavia, sources said, CIA Director George J. Tenet had been forecasting that Serb-led Yugoslav forces might respond by accelerating their campaign of ethnic cleansing in the province of Kosovo —precisely the outcome that has unfolded over the past week."

"Advice Didn't Sway Clinton on Airstrikes," Washington Post, 1 April 1999.

"Within the medieval courts of Europe . . . one of the great problems was telling the ruler things which he did not want to hear. So, many of them had was what called the 'royal fool.' He was there to entertain the ruler, he had a kind of license to tell him uncomfortable truths. . . . It's absolutely essential, I think, that intelligence agencies should, to some extent, in modern democratic structures, be able to acquire the privilege of the medieval royal fool. That is to say, to tell policy makers what they do not want to hear."

CHRISTOPHER ANDREW, interview in the Italian online magazine Per Aspera ad Veritatem (May–August 2001).

INTELLIGENCE & AMERICAN CULTURE

With its long-standing distrust of standing armies, its insular tradition, and its historical antipathy to foreign entanglements, the United States could hardly have been expected to develop a culture that warmly embraces the intelligence profession—the Founding Fathers' practice of intelligence notwithstanding. As the sources in this section make clear, Americans have looked with disdain on intelligence and have questioned the very need for it. The Literary Spy thinks September 11 changed all that.

See also: Covert Action; Critics & Defenders; Domestic Activities; FBI & Law Enforcement; Presidents & Intelligence; U.S. Intelligence "Community"

"Spying is as American as George Washington and George Bush."

NORMAN POLMAR and THOMAS ALLEN, The Encyclopedia of Espionage (1997).

"Those committees [of correspondence] that linked together the various provincial legislatures after the suggestion of the Virginia burgesses in 1773 were designed in part to communicate the 'most early and authentic intelligence' of British innovations affecting the colonies. And networks of correspondence committees at local and county levels were set up . . . so that 'any intelligence of importance' could be 'quickly disseminated to the whole body of the people.'"

PAULINE MAIER, From Resistance to Revolution (1972).

"He is at this time transporting large armies of foreign mercenaries to compleat the works of death, desolation, and tyranny . . ."

Declaration of Independence, one of the "Facts . . . submitted to a candid world" documenting the British king's abuses of the American colonies. This passage was based on warning intelligence received from an American agent in London regarding George III's intent to send German mercenaries; see Sayle, "The Historical Underpinnings of the U.S. Intelligence Community," *International Journal of Intelligence and Counterintelligence* (spring 1986).

"Washington, Jefferson, and their successors engaged in a number of activities that in themselves are now condemned by critics of covert operations as alien to traditional American standards of conduct.... In the thirty-three years between the time Jefferson wrote the Declaration of Independence and the time he departed from the White House, the nascent American government had authorized an astounding variety of covert missions. In war and in peace, a series of American leaders had sanctioned operations involving espionage and deception, kidnapping, bribing foreign leaders, using the clergy and media for intelligence purposes, overthrowing a foreign government, and assisting insurgencies designed to remove hostile powers from the American continent."

STEPHEN KNOTT, *Secret and Sanctioned* (1996).

"After developing new defences on the Potomac river in 1866, Washington promptly revealed the details to the British authorities, even though the only country which had previously launched an attack up the Potomac was Britain (in the War of 1812)."

BRADLEY SMITH, "The American Road to Central Intelligence," in Jeffreys-Jones and Andrew, *Eternal Vigilance* (1997).

"Prior to World War I . . . intelligence activities were viewed as neither necessary nor serious concerns. The naive view prevailed that the major foreign powers of the day made little use of and had little use for intelligence. If this was the case, then the United States need not engage in such efforts. When World War I introduced America to mod-

ern warfare, it also provided an opportunity to examine the intelligence activities of the allies. The net effect was one of embarrassment."

U.S. Senate, *Final Report of the Senate Select Committee to Study Governmental Operations with respect to Intelligence Activities* [the Church Committee], Book VI, "The Evolution and Organization of the Federal Intelligence Function" (April 1976). It wasn't so embarrassing, however, that we did anything about it: only after World War II did the United States catch up with what every other country was doing.

"We should never send a spy to the Soviet Union. There is no weapon at once so disarming and effective in relations with the Communists as sheer honesty."

U.S. Ambassador to Moscow **WILLIAM BULLITT** to Secretary of State Cordell Hull, 20 April 1936; cited in Charles Bohlen, *Witness to History* (1973). Bohlen, himself ambassador to Moscow during the 1950s, wrote that Bullitt's advice "still made sense." Ah, détente.

"I could have walked into most of the government offices in Washington wearing a sandwich board saying 'Soviet spy on the prowl,' without attracting the least attention."

HEDE MASSING, an Austrian-born agent of the Soviet NKVD who spied in the United States during the mid- to late-1930s; quoted in Helms, *A Look over My Shoulder* (2003).

"The creation of any super-espionage military agency is both unnecessary and undesirable. It is alien to American tradition, and no glorified 'OGPU' secret police is needed or wanted here."

New York Times, 1 December 1938.

"It must be confessed that our Intelligence organization in 1940 was primitive and inadequate. It was timid, parochial, and operating strictly in the tradition of the Spanish-American War."

> U.S. diplomat **ROBERT MURPHY**; quoted in Warner, *The Office of Strategic Services* (2000).

"Another New Deal move right in the Hitler line."

> U.S. Representative **CLARE HOFFMAN**, Republican from Michigan, denouncing William Donovan's proposal for a postwar central intelligence organization, 2 February 1945; quoted in Riebling, *Wedge: The Secret War Between the FBI and CIA* (1994).

"Prior to the outbreak of the war, this nation had no foreign intelligence collection system worthy of the name. It appears to have been contrary to national policy to engage in clandestine intelligence or to maintain a foreign espionage system."

> Memorandum from the Lovett Committee to Secretary of War Robert Patterson, 3 November 1945; in *FRUS 1945–1950: Emergence of the Intelligence Establishment* (1996), document 42. The committee comprised several general officers who were intelligence specialists and was chaired by Assistant Secretary of War for Air Robert Lovett.

"[Before Pearl Harbor] there was something un-American about espionage and even about intelligence generally."

> DCI Lieutenant General **HOYT VANDENBERG** in Senate testimony on the National Security Act, April 1947; quoted in Ranelagh, *The Agency* (1986).

"It was largely the shackles which our prewar diplomacy placed on our peacetime intelligence that forces us to embark on a difficult total war without even elemental data on the enemy."

> **ELLIS ZACHARIAS**, *Secret Missions* (1946). Zacharias was a career intelligence officer for the U.S. Navy, specializing in Japan.

"In that day the totality of [our] government's intelligence resources was trifling. We knew almost

nothing about the tens of thousands of things we were going to have to learn about in a hurry."

> **SHERMAN KENT** on U.S. intelligence in 1941, in *Studies in Intelligence* (spring 1955). Kent led a division of OSS analysts during the war and later was chief of CIA's Office of National Estimates.

"There is no U.S. Secret Intelligence Service. Americans are inclined to refer to their 'S.I.S.,' but by this they mean the small and uncoordinated force of 'Special Agents' who travel abroad on behalf of one or another of the Governmental Departments. These 'Agents' are, for the most part, amateurs without special qualifications and without training in Observation. They have no special means of communication or other facilities and they seldom have clearer brief than 'to go and have a look.'"

> Admiral **JOHN GODFREY**, British chief of naval intelligence, July 1941; quoted in Andrew, *For the President's Eyes Only* (1995).

"Ever since John Winthrop set out to build a 'city on a hill' in Puritan Massachusetts, Americans had believed that their country was guided by uniquely high ethical principles. They regarded peacetime espionage, if they thought about it at all, as a corrupt outgrowth of Old World diplomacy, alien to the open and upright American way. It took two world wars and a cold war to persuade them otherwise."

> **CHRISTOPHER ANDREW**, *For the President's Eyes Only* (1995). It's telling that the most sober observers of U.S. intelligence history are, like Professor Andrew, British.

"All major powers except the United States have had for a long time past permanent worldwide intelligence services, reporting directly to the highest echelons of their Governments. Prior to the present war, the United States had no foreign secret intelligence service. It never has had and does not now have a coordinated intelligence system."

OSS Director **WILLIAM DONOVAN** to President Truman, 25 August 1945; quoted in Andrew, *For the President's Eyes Only* (1995).

"On July 26, 1947 . . . the President signed into law the National Security Act of 1947. . . . Never before had the country, through its constitutional procedures, accorded such formal recognition to the importance of intelligence both in peace and war. Never before had the country established an independent agency of government to give substance to the recognition. Never before had the country officially, albeit tacitly, authorized the conduct of foreign, peacetime espionage and counterespionage and 'such other' intelligence-related activities as the NSC might direct. It might also be claimed that never before had this or any country so publicly and candidly enacted a law on such a delicate subject."

THOMAS TROY, *Donovan and the CIA* (1981).

"The National Security Act of 1947 was deliberately cast in terms vague enough not to offend the elements of Congress and the public who might be shocked at the thought of the United States admitting that it was arming itself with a national intelligence service."

Former DCI **RICHARD HELMS**, *A Look over My Shoulder* (2003). Shocked at *having* a CIA, or *admitting* to it?

"Fifteen years of living in a troubled international world convinced Americans of the need for early, full, and accurate knowledge of the capabilities, vulnerabilities, and intentions of the great and small powers of the world. In 1947 no one doubted

the need for intelligence. The American people were certainly ready for CIA."

THOMAS TROY, *Donovan and the CIA* (1981).

"CIA became a basket of widely differing eggs. But eggs they are, nevertheless, and a basket they must have. This copious basket called Central Intelligence is a uniquely American concept. The arrangement has historic validity which includes our wartime experiences, our intimate observation of foreign practices in wartime and, last and most important, our governmental structure which dictates its being as it is. The more you try to change the composition of CIA the more obstinately do conditions force you back to the original concept of the CIA carry-all."

Brigadier General **JOHN MAGRUDER**, former SSU director, memorandum to Secretary of Defense Louis Johnson, 22 December 1949; in *FRUS 1945–1950: Emergence of the Intelligence Establishment* (1996), document 408. The "eggs" that Magruder says should naturally be assigned to one basket are the production of national intelligence, the collection of foreign intelligence by clandestine methods, covert operations, and counterespionage.

"Without [intelligence] you would have only your fears on which to plan your defense arrangements and your whole military establishment. Now if you're going to use nothing but fear and that's all you have, you're going to make us an armed camp. So this kind of knowledge is vital to us."

President **DWIGHT EISENHOWER**, approving the U-2 program in 1954; quoted in Paul Lasher, *Spy Flights of the Cold War* (1996).

"It should be emphasized that the national characteristics of American agents are such that they are often careless in their operations and they make poor conspirators. . . . The intelligence officer who knows the national traits of Americans should be able to establish rapport quickly with the agent and positively influence him. For example, knowing that Americans do not like discipline and are always demonstrating their independence, the intelligence officer must refrain from resorting to obvious pressure.... As we know, Americans are distinguished by their efficiency and resourcefulness. Therefore the intelligence officer must exhibit a high degree of precision and efficiency in working with American agents.... Americans have a great love of money and a desire for financial gain. This American trait can be exploited by paying an agent for his work in order to increase his personal interest in working for us. Payments must be prompt and equitable."

> Lecture by Soviet GRU instructor, 1961; quoted in Penkovskiy, *The Penkovskiy Papers* (1966).

"The United States, like every other government, must employ secret agents. But the United States cannot successfully conduct large secret conspiracies. It is impossible to keep them secret. It is impossible for everybody concerned, beginning with the President himself, to be sufficiently ruthless and unscrupulous. The American conscience is a reality. It will make hesitant and ineffectual, even if it does not prevent, an un-American policy. The ultimate reason why the Cuban affair was incompetent is that it was out of character, like a cow that tried to fly or a fish that tried to walk."

> **WALTER LIPPMANN**, "To Ourselves Be True," *Today and Tomorrow*, 9 May 1961. Did Lippmann ever meet Richard Nixon?

"Intelligence is probably the least understood and most misrepresented of the professions."

> Former DCI **ALLEN DULLES**, *The Craft of Intelligence* (1963). Rather like monasticism.

"Our mission, in the eyes of many thoughtful Americans, may appear to be in conflict with some of the traditions and ideals of our free society. It is difficult for me to agree with this view, but I respect it. It is quite another matter when some of our critics—taking advantage of the traditional silence of those engaged in intelligence—say things that are either vicious, or just plain silly."

> DCI **RICHARD HELMS**, address before the American Society of Newspaper Editors, Washington, D.C., 14 April 1971.

"At times Americans talk as if everything secret is evil."

> Former DDI **RAY CLINE**, *Secrets, Spies and Scholars* (1976).

"Every government is run by liars and nothing they say should be believed."

> Attributed to **I. F. STONE**, American journalist, 1973.

"Americans have always had an ambivalent attitude toward intelligence. When they feel threatened they want a lot of it, and when they don't, they tend to regard the whole thing as somewhat immoral.... We must recognize the importance for us of an effective American intelligence organization that can shed some light on the dark and troubled waters that lie ahead."

> Former DDCI **VERNON WALTERS**, *Silent Missions* (1978).

"In December 1974, the *New York Times* broke the story of domestic intelligence operations of the CIA; during the following year, the press, three governmental investigatory bodies, and sundry individuals competed and cooperated in revelations concerning U.S. intelligence and internal security agencies.... All [activities] were laid bare in what could only be viewed and was viewed by incredulous foreign officials and publics as a peculiarly virulent form of American madness."

SAMUEL P. HUNTINGTON, *American Politics: The Promise of Disharmony* (1981).

"America suffers from the 'parochialism of bigness'; precisely because it is a big country, it is quite possible to get along without ever mastering a foreign language, traveling abroad, or displaying much interest in the world beyond the oceans. . . . It is against this background that American failures to interpret events correctly in foreign lands must be viewed. Americans have probably been worse than others in tending to project their own standards and values onto the world outside, from the quality of plumbing to that of political institutions."

WALTER LAQUEUR, *A World of Secrets* (1985). Whether U.S. political institutions are superior is a matter of opinion, but can there be any doubt that our plumbing is unsurpassed?

"After I left CIA . . . I was unemployed. . . . And I was approached by the chairman of one of the largest corporations in America. 'We would like you to be on our Board of Directors, sir,' he said. Well, it interested me. And then there was a long, deathly silence. Nothing. Didn't hear from him. And then in comes a message. 'Well, our CEO and our Board feel that since you worked at CIA, maybe it wouldn't be good for you to come join our prestigious company.' The company went bankrupt a few years later, and I became President of the United States."

Former President and DCI **GEORGE H. W. BUSH**, address at CIA, 17 September 1997.

"In part, intelligence in the United States remains a vexing and complicated affair simply because it is not altogether clear whether the American people and their political elite have decided that

they really need and want a secret intelligence service. . . . The fact is that intelligence runs against the grain of American political culture."

WALTER LAQUEUR, *A World of Secrets* (1985).

"In the years immediately following the Second World War . . . our government felt itself justified in setting up facilities for clandestine defense operations. . . . As one of those who, at the time, favored the decision to set up such facilities, I regret today, in light of the experience of the intervening years, that the decision was taken. Operations of this nature are not in character for this country. They do not accord with its traditions or with its established procedures of government. The effort to conduct them involves dilemmas and situations of moral ambiguity in which the American statesman is deprived of principled guidance and loses a sense of what is fitting and what is not. Excessive secrecy, duplicity and clandestine skullduggery are simply not our dish. . . . One may say that to deny ourselves this species of capability is to accept a serious limitation on our ability to contend with forces now directed against us. Perhaps; but if so, it is a limitation with which we will have to live."

GEORGE KENNAN, "Morality and Foreign Policy," *Foreign Affairs* (winter 1985–86).

"American intelligence has always been characterized by huge expenditures of money and a dependence on quantity rather than quality."

JOHN RANELAGH, *The Agency* (1986).

"The activities in which we engage must be consistent with our foreign mission and our own laws, and they must reflect what the American people expect of us. We must find ways to get that message known and understood. The American public is very responsive when it believes that there is some order in this elusive world of cloak and dagger."

> DCI **WILLIAM WEBSTER**, remarks at the Intelligence Community Attorneys' Conference, Williamsburg, Virginia, 11 May 1988; in Webster, *1988 Speeches*.

"Americans still cling to the myth of innocence and forthright behavior as the only standard for their government even though their own personal and business lives often lack such innocence. . . . For the government of the United States to subvert citizens of another country into spying against their nation, or to skew an election in a foreign country by subsidizing anticommunist candidates, or to provide arms covertly to groups opposing antidemocratic forces—all this is somehow un-American and hard to accept as proper."

> Former DDI **R. JACK SMITH**, *The Unknown CIA* (1989).

"I believe most Americans understand the need to keep secrets. Where Americans want to be reassured is that the objectives make sense and that it's done effectively and responsibly. I don't think the American people object to [our] keeping secrets. They want us to make sure that our operations are consistent with American values and that they're carried out in a responsible way."

> DCI **JOHN DEUTCH**, testimony before the House intelligence committee, 19 December 1995.

"The American people don't trust government, and they particularly don't trust the CIA."

> Senator **BARBARA MIKULSKI**, Democrat from Maryland, during Senate hearings, 6 May 1997.

"For the CIA, the 'elite' status of the Directorate of Operations was a big PR problem. . . . In a democracy such as the United States, egalitarian sentiment runs strong and deep, and elitism in al-

most any form is suspect. For those who grew up believing that anyone could be president, it's not a big leap of logic to conclude that anyone should be able to become a case officer in the CIA."

> Former senior CIA operations officer **DUANE CLARRIDGE**, *A Spy for All Seasons* (1997).

"Intelligence is inevitably a profession in which certain American principles are going to be suspended to obtain the desired results."

> Former CIA operations officer **REUEL MARC GERECHT**, in *The New Republic* (13–20 September 1999).

"Our culture distrusts power and secrecy, and guess what I've got."

> Senior U.S. intelligence official, quoted on CNN, 12 April 2000.

"American society doesn't love its CIA, for the same reason that it doesn't always love its cops. We too often regard them as a threat to ourselves than [to] our enemies. Perhaps [the September 11 attacks] will make us rethink that. . . . But America, and especially the American news media, does not love the CIA. . . . As recently as two weeks ago, CBS's '60 Minutes' regaled us with the hoary old chestnut about how the CIA undermined the leftist government of Chile three decades ago. The effect of this media coverage, so solicitous to leftist governments, is to brand the CIA an antiprogressive agency that does Bad Things."

> **TOM CLANCY**, "First We Cripple the CIA, Then We Blame It," *Wall Street Journal*, 18 September 2001. Isn't undermining bad governments a Good Thing?

"It's fair to say that Americans have a schizophrenic attitude to their Central Intelligence Agency. At one level, thanks to Hollywood, it is shrouded in glamour and mystery. On the other hand, they tend to see it as incompetent and even dangerous. Now it has a clear mission and a chance for a full image makeover. . . . Now it has been given the money and the political support it needs. It just has to be successful."

> BBC Washington correspondent **TOM CARVER** on BBC News, 23 October 2001.

"I have absolutely no idea why Americans could have anything but a profound appreciation for what you do for us all."

> E-mail from Arizona to CIA's public website (www.cia .gov), responding to the death of CIA operations officer Mike Spann in Afghanistan, December 2001.

INTELLIGENCE, DEFINITIONS OF

Well, what is intelligence? Is it an activity, such as spying? Is it an institution—CIA or the KGB? Is it a product, like National Intelligence Estimates or the *President's Daily Brief*? Is it a process: tasking, collection, evaluation, dissemination, feedback? The Literary Spy says "yes."

See also: Intelligence, the Missions of

"To perceive things in the germ is intelligence."

> **LAO-TZU**, *Tao Teh Ching* (6th century B.C.).

"Intelligence . . . 7. Knowledge as to events, communicated by or obtained from one another; information, news, tidings . . . b. A piece of information or news . . . c. The obtaining of information; the agency for obtaining secret information; the staff of persons so employed, secret service . . . d. intelligence department, a department of the military or naval service whose object is to obtain informa-tion (esp. by means of secret service officers or a system of spies . . .)"

> *Oxford English Dictionary*, s.v. "Intelligence."

"Intelligence is the soul of public business."

> **DANIEL DEFOE**, "A Scheme for General Intelligence," 1704; cited in Haswell, *Spies and Spymasters* (1977).

"All the business of war, and indeed all the business of life, is to endeavour to find out what you don't know by what you do."

> Attributed to the **DUKE OF WELLINGTON**, 1828; quoted in Austin and Rankov, *Exploratio* (1995).

"All the knowledge which we have of the enemy and his country; therefore, in fact, the foundation of all our ideas and actions."

> **CARL VON CLAUSEWITZ**; cited by Furse, *Information in War* (1895).

"It is my business to know what other people don't know."

> Sherlock Holmes in Sir **ARTHUR CONAN DOYLE**, "The Adventure of the Blue Carbuncle" (1892).

"Strategic and national policy intelligence is that composite intelligence, interdepartmental in character, which is required by the President and other high officers and staffs to assist them in determining policies with respect to national planning and security in peace and in war and for the advancement of broad national policy."

> DCI **HOYT VANDENBERG**'s proposed definition of intelligence of concern to CIG, as approved by the National Intelligence Authority, with Secretary of State George Marshall presiding, 12 February 1947; in *FRUS 1945–1950: Emergence of the Intelligence Establishment* (1996), document 185.

"It has truthfully been said that intelligence is our first line of defense."

> **ALLEN DULLES**, then a private citizen, statement regarding the proposed National Security Act of 1947, submitted to the Senate Armed Services Committee, 25 April 1947, in CIA's Historical Intelligence Collection.

"Intelligence is a simple and self-evident thing. As an activity it is the pursuit of a certain kind of knowledge; as a phenomenon it is the resultant knowledge. . . . Intelligence work is in essence nothing more than the search for the single best answer. . . . Intelligence work remains the simple, natural endeavor to get the sort of knowledge upon which a successful course of action can be rested. And strategic intelligence, we might call the knowledge upon which our nation's foreign relations, in war and peace, must rest. If foreign policy is the shield of the republic, as Walter Lippmann has called it, then strategic intelligence is the thing that gets the shield to the right place at the right time. It is also the thing that stands ready to guide the sword."

> **SHERMAN KENT**, *Strategic Intelligence* (1949). The imagery here might make former Sovietologists nervous, as the sword and shield together made up the symbol of the Soviet secret police from 1917 through 1991.

"Intelligence is knowledge required for decision or action. . . . Intelligence is not the formulator of objectives; it is not the drafter of policy; it is not the maker of plans. . . . It performs a service function. Its job is to see that the doers are well informed; its job is to stand behind them with the book opened at the right page."

> **SHERMAN KENT**, *Strategic Intelligence* (1949).

"Our job [in intelligence] is to raise the level of debate."

> Attributed to **SHERMAN KENT**.

"Intelligence deals with all the things which should be known in advance of initiating a course of action."

> Hoover Commission Task Force on Intelligence Activities, 1955; quoted in Dulles, *The Craft of Intelligence* (1963).

"A distasteful but vital necessity."

> President **DWIGHT EISENHOWER** on intelligence, in the wake of the downing of the U-2 spyplane; quoted in the *New York Times*, 11 May 1960.

"Intelligence is information, not always available in the public domain, relating to the strength, resources, capabilities and intentions of a foreign country that can affect our lives and the safety and future of our people."

> Former DDCI **VERNON WALTERS**, *Silent Missions* (1978).

"'Intelligence' is an umbrella word covering a wide field of different activities and skills. . . . The five main areas of intelligence are as follows:

a) The laying down by governments of their information requirements and priorities.

b) The gathering of information, as required by the government, by overt, secret and technological methods.

c) Counter-intelligence and security.

d) Covert action: the extension of government policy by secret and nonattributable means.

e) The analysis and evaluation of all the information gathered."

> SIS official **JOHN BRUCE LOCKHART**, "Intelligence: A British View" (1984); cited in West, *Faber Book of Espionage* (1993).

"The heart of intelligence is getting at and faithfully representing the truth."

> DCI **WILLIAM WEBSTER**, remarks at Cornell Law School, 26 October 1989; in Webster, *1989 Speeches*.

"The Glory of God is intelligence."

> Slogan of Brigham Young University, Provo, Utah. CIA people also like the other slogan of BYU: "The World Is Our Campus."

"Intelligence is an instrument of conflict. It consists of words, numbers, images, suggestions, appraisals, incitements. It consists also of truths that enlighten or mislead, or of outright falsehoods. Because it is immaterial, intelligence cannot wound. But its use has led to the killing or saving of millions."

> **ANGELO CODEVILLA**, *Informing Statecraft* (1992).

"There is a difference between collecting information—there's a red coat, there's a red coat, there's a red coat—and intelligence, which is saying at the right time, 'The British are coming.'"

> DCI **JOHN DEUTCH**, address to the National Youth Leadership Forum in Washington, D.C., 16 February 1996.

"Intelligence is information not publicly available, or analysis based at least in part on such information, that has been prepared for policymakers or other actors inside the government. What makes intelligence unique is its use of information that is collected secretly and prepared in a timely manner to meet the needs of policymakers."

> Council on Foreign Relations, *Making Intelligence Smarter* (1996).

"Intelligence is information acquired by some people who need it, and by others for the sake of leaking it."

> Anonymous.

"Intelligence is always too much effort until suddenly it's not enough."

> Former DCI **WILLIAM WEBSTER**, interviewed on PBS, 20 October 1997.

"Intelligence is secret, state activity to understand or to influence foreign entities."

> CIA historian **MICHAEL WARNER**, "Wanted: A Definition of Intelligence," in *Studies in Intelligence* 46/3 (2002). This succinct definition is the "unified field theory" of intelligence, encompassing intelligence collection, analysis, counterintelligence, and covert action.

"By definition, intelligence deals with the unclear, the unknown, the deliberately hidden. What the enemies of the United States hope to deny, we work to reveal."

> DCI **GEORGE TENET**, remarks at Georgetown University, 5 February 2004.

INTELLIGENCE, THE MISSIONS OF

So, what's it all for? Why go to all this considerable trouble? Collecting intelligence through complex technical systems like satellites is hugely expensive. Running good spies risks international incidents if they are caught; running bad ones risks being misled if they are not caught. It's difficult to recruit the operations officers and the analysts with the right qualifications, especially in languages. So, why do it? The answer, submits the Literary Spy, ultimately is theological: it's at bottom a fallen world, like it or not, and intelligence—along with military power and diplomacy—helps the nation deal with the world as it is.

See also: Analysis & Analysts; Collection; Counterintelligence; Covert Action; People; Terrorism; Warning, Prediction, & Surprise

"One who knows the enemy and knows himself will not be endangered in a hundred engagements.

One who does not know the enemy but knows himself will sometimes be victorious, sometimes meet with defeat. One who knows neither the enemy nor himself will be defeated in every engagement."

SUN TZU, *The Art of War* (6th century B.C.).

"What is wisdom? To know the fact of suffering and its nature; to know the source of suffering; to know what constitutes the end of suffering; and to know what leads to the end of suffering."

The Teaching of Buddha (5th century B.C.). Knowledge that ultimately relieves suffering—that's the best kind of intelligence.

"He is best secure from dangers who is on his guard even when he seems safe."

PUBLILIUS SYRUS (c. 50 B.C.); cited in Heinl, *Dictionary of Military and Naval Quotations* (1966).

"And ye shall know the truth and the truth shall make you free."

John 8:32 (King James). Allen Dulles, who believed that this verse describes the mission of intelligence in a democracy, had it inscribed in the wall of CIA's main lobby.

"Peace hath her victories no less renowned than war."

JOHN MILTON, "To the Lord Generall Cromwell, May 1652"; quoted by former DCI Richard Helms in remarks at CIA, 7 June 1996.

"Every kind of service, necessary to the public good, becomes honorable by being necessary."

Attributed to **NATHAN HALE**; quoted in Colby, *Honorable Men* (1978).

"Accurate and comprehensive knowledge of foreign politics."

ALEXANDER HAMILTON on one of the prerequisites for the conduct of foreign policy, *The Federalist*, No. 75.

"Knowledge will forever govern ignorance, and a people who mean to be their own Governors must arm themselves with the power which knowledge gives."

JAMES MADISON, 1822; cited in U.S. Senate, *Alleged Assassination Plots* (1975).

"When everyone is dead the Great Game is finished. Not before."

RUDYARD KIPLING, *Kim* (1901).

"With the world in its present condition of extreme unrest and changing friendships and antagonisms . . . it is more than ever vital to us to have good and timely information."

British Minister for War and Air **WINSTON CHURCHILL**, March 1920, protesting in the Cabinet against budget reductions for MI5 and MI6; quoted in Stafford, *Churchill and Secret Service* (1998).

"I'm glad you've made up your mind to join us, Blenkinsop. You'll find the work fascinating even in peace time, and after all there's a jolly good chance of another war soon. A jolly good chance!"

Fictional British intelligence chief to a new recruit in Sir **COMPTON MACKENZIE**'s spoof on intelligence, *Water on the Brain* (1933).

"In an age of bullies, we cannot afford to be sissies."

WILLIAM DONOVAN, future director of OSS and considered the father of central intelligence, in November 1939; quoted in Troy, *Donovan and the CIA* (1981).

"There will always be espionage and there will always be counter-espionage. Though conditions may have altered, though difficulties may be greater, when war is raging, there will always be secrets which one side jealously guards and which the other will use every means to discover; there will always be men who from malice or for money will betray their kith and kin and there will always be men who, from love of adventure or a sense of duty, will risk a shameful death to secure information valuable to their country."

W. SOMERSET MAUGHAM, preface to the 1941 edition of his classic spy novel *Ashenden*.

"An adequate and orderly intelligence system will contribute to informed decisions."

OSS Director WILLIAM DONOVAN, arguing to President Roosevelt for a postwar centralized intelligence organization, 18 November 1944; quoted in Leary, *The Central Intelligence Agency* (1984).

"The primary functions of this organization [are] secret intelligence, counter-espionage, and the evaluation and synthesis of intelligence."

OSS Director WILLIAM DONOVAN to President Truman, 13 September 1945; reproduced in Warner, *CIA Under Truman* (1994).

"The practice of intensifying our intelligence activities *after* the outbreak of hostilities, while allowing them to languish during times of peace [is a] fundamentally wrong approach [that] inevitably leads to serious deficiencies in our entire national-security structure. The fact must be realized that intelligence is as important a function in peacetime as it is during war. The better a nation is prepared by its intelligence agencies for any eventualities in

times of real or nominal peace, the better chance it has to maintain that peace or to shorten the war."

ELLIS ZACHARIAS, *Secret Missions* (1946). Zacharias was a career intelligence officer for the U.S. Navy, specializing in Japan.

"The last thing we can afford to do today is to put our intelligence in chains. Its protective and informative role is indispensable in an era of unique and continuing danger."

Former DCI ALLEN DULLES, *The Craft of Intelligence* (1963).

"So long as governments conceal a part of their activities, other governments, if they wish to base their policy on full and correct information, must seek to penetrate the veil."

HUGH TREVOR-ROPER, veteran of both MI5 and SIS; cited in West, *Faber Book of Espionage* (1993).

"I have ordered the Central Intelligence Agency, early in this Administration, to mobilize its full resources to fight the international drug trade, a task, incidentally, in which it has performed superbly."

President RICHARD NIXON, remarks at the State Department, 18 September 1972; cited in CIA, *"Our First Line of Defense"* (1996).

"To operate without adequate and timely intelligence information will cripple our security in a world that is still hostile to our freedoms. Nor can we confine our intelligence to the question of whether there will be an imminent military attack. We also need information about the world's economy, about political and social trends, about food supply, population growth, and, certainly, about terrorism. To protect our security diplomatically, militarily, and economically, we must have a comprehensive intelligence capability."

President **GERALD FORD**, news conference of 17 February 1976; quoted in CIA, *"Our First Line of Defense"* (1996).

"Why do we need intelligence? We need it because our leaders are required to make their decisions in an entirely new framework of time and speed. We no longer can deliberate at great length about what we ought to do. Shrinking distances and time factors compel decision-making at a far faster rate than we have known in the past. The decisions are more complex and have more far-reaching consequences. Such decisions must be made on the basis of maximum knowledge of all the factors involved. Right decisions can only be made on the basis of the best possible information."

Former DDCI **VERNON WALTERS**, *Silent Missions* (1978). What was true more than a quarter-century ago is even more on the mark today.

"Intelligence services are as inevitable a part of modern states as armies, telephone and postal services, or a system for collecting taxes."

THOMAS POWERS, *The Man Who Kept the Secrets* (1979). On the bright side, they won't draft you, call you, send you junk mail, or audit you.

"Timely and accurate information about the activities, capabilities, plans, and intentions of foreign powers, organizations, and persons and their agents, is essential to the national security of the United States. All reasonable and lawful means must be used to ensure that the United States will receive the best intelligence available. . . . The United States intelligence effort shall provide the President and the National Security Council with the necessary information on which to base decisions concerning the conduct and development of foreign, defense, and economic policy, and the

protection of United States national interests from foreign security threats. All departments and agencies shall cooperate fully to fulfill this goal."

Executive Order 12333, *Governing Intelligence Activities*, 4 December 1981; cited in Leary, *The Central Intelligence Agency* (1984).

"To the present the CIA is an echo of its founders. Its job is not to find enemies, but to define them. Its theme is the substitution of intelligence for force."

JOHN RANELAGH, *The Agency* (1986). And, when force is necessary, to maximize it.

"An intelligence service thrives on threat. Its continued existence and its funding depend on its ability to convince its political masters that the nation is in danger and that intelligence is both a sword and a shield."

PHILLIP KNIGHTLEY, *The Second Oldest Profession* (1988). Knightley has it backward: when the nation is threatened, the "political masters" often lead the way on intelligence —that's how CIA was created, for example—and neither need nor appreciate convincing. They are the masters, after all, and generally are not dolts.

"Our world without the Cold War confrontation is a safer world, but it is no Garden of Eden. This is not the end of history. . . . We need a strong Intelligence Community to consolidate and extend freedom's gains against totalitarianism. We need intelligence to verify historic arms reduction accords. We need it to suppress terrorism and drug trafficking. And we must have intelligence to thwart anyone who tries to steal our technology or otherwise refuses to play by fair economic rules. We must have vigorous intelligence capabilities if we're to stop the proliferation of weapons of mass destruction. And so this is truly a life or death mission. . . . In sum, intelligence remains our basic national instrument for anticipating danger—military, political, and economic. Intelligence is and always will be our first line of defense. . . . I can certify to the American people with total confidence that we have the finest intelligence capability in the world. And we're going to strengthen it and we're going to see that we continue to have this as the guardian of the peace."

President **GEORGE H. W. BUSH**, remarks to CIA employees at CIA Headquarters, 12 November 1991.

"The most difficult task that falls to us in intelligence is to see the world as it is, not as we—or others—would wish it to be. . . . Some say we should avert our gaze and look only to domestic concerns—that the blood shed by Americans in two world wars, the sacrifices we made in Korea and Vietnam, and the more than two trillion American dollars spent to defeat Communism is enough. One can sympathize with the sentiment, but we must remember that repeatedly in this century Americans averted their eyes in the belief that remote events need not engage this country—how could an assassination in unknown Bosnia-Herzegovina touch us? Or the occupation of a little patch of ground called Sudetenland? Or a French defeat at a place called Dienbienphu? Or the return of an obscure cleric to Tehran? In truth, the world is even smaller today than earlier in this century. History is not over. It simply has been frozen and now is thawing with a vengeance Americans ignore at their peril."

DCI **ROBERT GATES**, address at CIA Headquarters, 4 December 1991; in Gates, *Speeches* (1993).

"The nation is at peace because we in intelligence are constantly at war."

DCI **ROBERT GATES**, remarks to CIA junior officers, 13 November 1992.

"The end product of intelligence is success in war."

ANGELO CODEVILLA, *Informing Statecraft* (1992).

"We must avoid the costly mistake of 1919, 1945, 1953, and 1975 in thinking that we could disengage from the world and of too quickly disarming ourselves—of letting our hopes and our weary impatience overshadow our judgment, good sense, and historical realism."

DCI **ROBERT GATES**, address to the Oklahoma Press Association, 21 February 1992; in Gates, *Speeches* (1993).

"Perhaps a day will dawn when tyrants can no longer threaten the liberty of any people, when the functions of all nations, however varied their ideologies, will be to enhance life, not to control it. If such a condition is possible, it is in a future too far distant to foresee. Until that safer, better day, the democracies will avoid disaster, and possibly total destruction, only by maintaining their defenses. Among the increasingly intricate arsenals across the world, intelligence is an essential weapon, perhaps the most important."

Sir **WILLIAM STEPHENSON** in his foreword to William Stevenson, *A Man Called Intrepid* (1976).

"Today, the leaders of American Intelligence are in a quandary. We hear demands from various quarters significantly to reduce the size and cost of U.S. intelligence in this post-Soviet world. And, yet, the demands for detailed, action-oriented information that policymakers, the military and Congress make upon us are growing, not slackening. These users of the world-spanning, constant flow of intelligence information twenty-four hours a day can't have it both ways."

DCI **ROBERT GATES**, remarks in Los Angeles, 15 December 1992; in Gates, *Speeches* (1993).

"The presidents of the twenty-first century, like their Cold War predecessors, will continue to find an enormously expensive global intelligence system both fallible and indispensable."

CHRISTOPHER ANDREW, *For the President's Eyes Only* (1995).

"We have evidence that a number of countries around the world are developing the doctrine, strategies and tools to conduct information attacks. . . . The electron is the ultimate precision-guided weapon. . . . I don't know whether we face an electronic Pearl Harbor, but we will have, I'm sure, some very unpleasant circumstances. . . . I'm certainly prepared to predict some very, very large and uncomfortable incidents in this area."

DCI JOHN DEUTCH, in Senate testimony, 25 June 1996.

"The need for an institution like the Central Intelligence Agency in today's multipolar world is at least as great as, if not greater than, it was during the cold-war era. In the past, intelligence was mainly an area of combat between the major developed powers, but with the rapid spread of weapons of mass destruction our potential foes have multiplied and become more diverse. Such challenging and threatening circumstances require that the CIA have at its disposal all appropriate capabilities to counteract them."

Former CIA operations chief RICHARD BISSELL, *Reflections of a Cold Warrior* (1996).

"Our ability to network has far outpaced our ability to protect ourselves against attack. We have a fundamental new danger in the cyber dimension."

NSA Director Lieutenant General KENNETH MINIHAN, USAF; quoted in *Aviation Week & Space Technology* (16 February 1997).

"The United States has the most robust economy, the biggest single market, the richest technological treasures, the most sprawling currency system, the largest free flow of information, the most powerful military, the most admired university system. . . . This America has become the chief target of the world's economic spies."

JOHN J. FIALKA, *War by Other Means: Economic Espionage in America* (1997).

"My sense of our mission is that it's enormously clear. It is to pursue the hardest targets that threaten American interests around the world. We are no longer in search of a mission. We know what the mission is, we know what the targets are."

DCI GEORGE TENET, press interview of 21 July 1997.

"To those who say we no longer need CIA, I say you are nuts. To those who want to dismantle CIA or put it under some other department, State Department or anybody else, you are nuts, too."

Former President GEORGE H. W. BUSH, address at CIA, 17 September 1997. Especially under State.

"No major state, in fact no state, can survive without information. Strategic, economic and political intelligence are fundamental to all modern states, especially to the only superpower—the United States. . . . Intelligence in democracies is as significant as the military is. You cannot abolish the military any more than you can bring an end to intelligence."

AMOS PERLMUTTER, "Why the CIA Is Still Needed," *Washington Times*, 25 September 1997.

"The flavor of the month."

DCI GEORGE TENET, on shifting U.S. foreign policy priorities requiring retargeting intelligence resources; quoted in the *Washington Post*, 25 May 1998.

"Let's be blunt about what we do. There is no dishonor in it. We steal secrets for a living. If we do not steal secrets for a living, then we ought to shut the doors and do something else for a living. That is at the core, along with the analytic arm of this agency, with why we were put in business. They are the equal of each other. There can be no skewing toward one or the other. They are both at the sharp end of the spear of the intelligence business. I do not know how else to tell people what we do."

> DCI **GEORGE TENET**, interview of 23 June 1998, in *Studies in Intelligence* 42/1 (1998).

"The CIA is beginning the biggest recruitment drive in its history to beef up clandestine operations [and] plans to reopen some of its overseas bureaus that were cut when the Soviet Union went out of business. This is a good thing. . . . The world of today argues in favor of enhancing this country's intelligence capabilities."

> *Boston Globe* editorial, 6 July 1998. Support from a nontraditional source.

"The hard truth is that America spies on China because it needs to be spied on. . . . If America, the only country ready and able to act as guardian, is to perform the task, it needs the sort of information that can be gathered only by aerial surveillance. . . . One day, there may be no need for any spy flights at all. But the stakes are too high, and China's commitment to the peaceful settlement of disputes too uncertain, for that day to be imminent."

> *The Economist*, "Carry on Spying," 21 April 2001.

"The mission of U.S. intelligence rests on a pillar of pure optimism: that seemingly ordinary men and women can do truly extraordinary things."

> DCI **GEORGE TENET**, address at Langley High School graduation, 14 June 2001. Pure optimism? Surely he meant clear-eyed realism.

"Intelligence = Information + Insight."

> Slogan on the website of Intellibridge, a business intelligence firm, June 2001.

"Someone's got to do the things that no one else wants to do."

> **JOHNNY "MIKE" SPANN**, CIA operations officer, as recalled by his family. Spann was the first U.S. combat death in Afghanistan during the war on terrorism, killed on 25 November 2001.

"It's guys like him that are keeping me and my family safe."

> E-mail from California to CIA's public website (www.cia.gov), responding to the death of CIA operations officer Mike Spann in Afghanistan, December 2001.

"An ounce of intelligence is worth a bucketful of trust."

> British writer **ANTHONY DANIELS** in *National Review*, 3 December 2001.

"Intelligence services should not be confused with the Boy Scouts."

> **WILLIAM HOOD**, former senior CIA operations officer; quoted in the *Washington Post Magazine*, 16 December 2001. This is similar to a saying attributed to Henry Kissinger, "Covert action should not be confused with missionary work." *See* Covert Action.

"The Central Intelligence Agency and the rest of the U.S. national-security apparatus work to preserve the rights of editorial writers in publications like the *New York Post* to say anything they want."

> DCI **GEORGE TENET** responding to a *Post* editorial, "Tenet Must Go"; in the *New York Post*, 13 February 2002.

"I always repeat that intelligence is a great civic duty. If you wish to protect our country and you want to use your resources, intellectual and otherwise, this is one of the best areas of human endeavor to do it. I want to encourage the young people . . . to join the intelligence service."

> Former KGB General **OLEG KALUGIN**; quoted in the *Washington Times*, 7 June 2002. Since he uttered those words, Kalugin has become a U.S. citizen, so we now know what he means when he says "our country."

"To Seek. To Know. To Forewarn."

> Motto of the Security Intelligence Division, Singapore's external intelligence service. A glance at a map of the island state confirms the need for this mission statement.

"I was, and still am, convinced that there is no greater threat to world peace than poorly informed or misinformed leaders and governments. . . . The first line of defense remains a competent intelligence service."

> Former DCI **RICHARD HELMS**, *A Look over My Shoulder* (2003).

"We are the eyes and ears of the nation and, at times, its hidden hand. We accomplish this mission by:

—Collecting information that matters.

—Providing relevant, timely, and objective all-source analysis.

—Conducting covert action at the direction of the President to preempt threats or achieve United States policy objectives."

> From a CIA mission statement poster, 2004.

INTERCEPTS & CRYPTOLOGY

The fact that humans communicate with each other by itself does not make us unique in creation—birds, dogs, whales, other primates, even ants and bees communicate. No, says the Literary Spy, what is unique to our species is the desire to conceal the meaning of one's own communications from unintended eyes and ears while going to great lengths to obtain and understand communications intended for someone else. Cryptology, as gentleman spymaster Allen Dulles explains below, is the general term for the profession of making and breaking codes—enabling such gentlemen to read other gentlemen's intercepted mail.

See also: Analysis & Analysts; Counterintelligence

"In a code, some word, symbol or group of symbols is substituted for a whole word or even for a group of words or a complete thought. . . . In a cipher, a symbol, such as a letter or number, stands for a single letter in a word. . . . In modern terminology, the word 'crypt,' meaning 'something hidden,' conveniently gets around the distinction between codes and ciphers since it refers to all methods of transforming 'plain text' or 'clear text' into symbols. The over-all term for the whole field is 'cryptology.' Under this broad heading we have two distinct areas. Cryptography has to do with making, devising, inventing or protecting codes and ciphers for the use of one's own government. Cryptanalysis, on the other hand, has to do with breaking codes and ciphers or 'decrypting' them. . . . And now, having confused the reader completely, we can get to the gist of the matter . . ."

> Former DCI **ALLEN DULLES**, *The Craft of Intelligence* (1963).

"King Belshazzar made a great feast for a thousand of his lords.... They drank wine, and praised the gods of gold and silver, bronze, iron, wood, and stone. Immediately the fingers of a man's hand appeared and wrote on the plaster of the wall of the king's palace ... and the king saw the hand as it wrote.... The king said to the wise men of Babylon, 'Whoever reads this writing, and shows me its interpretation, shall be clothed with purple, and have a chain of gold about his neck, and shall be the third ruler in the kingdom.' Then all the king's wise men came in, but they could not read the writing or make known to the king its interpretation."

> Daniel 5:1, 4–9 (Revised Standard). The prophet Daniel read the handwriting on the wall and told the king his days were numbered and his kingdom fated for division. According to cryptology historian David Kahn, this makes Daniel the first known cryptanalyst.

"A man is crazy who writes a secret in any other way than one which will conceal it from the vulgar."

> English monk ROGER BACON, 12th century; quoted in Kahn, *The Codebreakers* (1996).

"When you want to solve a message which you have received in code, begin first of all by counting the letters, and then count how many times each symbol is repeated.... When you see that one letter occurs in the message more often than the rest, then assume it is *alif* ..."

> 14th-century Arabic text, "Concerning the concealment of secret messages with letters," cited in Kahn, *The Codebreakers* (1996).

"Catherine de Medici had the blood of spies in her veins. When the palace at the Louvre was being constructed, she had tubes called *auriculaires* fitted into the walls, so she could listen from one room to conversations of her courtiers in the next. Hence the phrase: 'Walls have ears.'"

> BERNARD NEWMAN, *Epics of Espionage* (1950).

"A worthless cracking of the brain."

> French cryptologist BLAISE DE VIGENÈRE, on the efforts of cryptanalysts to break ciphers; quoted in Kahn, *The Codebreakers* (1996).

"The King hath note of all that they intend, By interceptions which they know not of."

> WILLIAM SHAKESPEARE, *King Henry the Fifth* (1600), Act II, scene 2. These words are engraved on a plaque at Bletchley Park, the manor house near London that housed British signals intelligence and codebreaking during World War II.

"The greatest Matters are many times carried in the weakest Cyphars."

> FRANCIS BACON, 1605; quoted in Kahn, *The Codebreakers* (1996).

"There's not a thing beneath the skies That can be hidden from your eyes ... How marvelous your skill, and bright, And how important your art's might! For with it provinces are gained, All princes' secrets ascertained."

> French poet BOISROBERT to 17th-century French cryptologist Antoine Rossignol; quoted in Kahn, *The Codebreakers* (1996).

"It is the Opinion of this House that it is not consistent with the public Safety, to ask the [Government's] Decypherers any Questions, which may tend to discover the Art or Mystery of Decyphering."

> English House of Lords, 1723; cited in Kahn, *The Codebreakers* (1996).

"But why a cipher between us, when official things go naturally to the Secretary of State, and things not political need no cipher. . . . There may be matters merely personal to ourselves, and which require the cover of a cipher more than any other character. This last purpose and others which we cannot foresee may render it convenient and advantageous to have at hand a mask for whatever may need it."

President **THOMAS JEFFERSON** to American envoy to Paris Robert Livingston, 18 April 1802; cited in Knott, *Secret and Sanctioned* (1996).

"Language merely serves to conceal one's thoughts."

Attributed to **TALLEYRAND** (1754–1838).

"It may well be doubted whether human ingenuity can construct an enigma of the kind which human ingenuity may not, by proper application, resolve."

EDGAR ALLAN POE, "The Gold-Bug" (1843).

"A certain document of the last importance has been purloined from the royal apartments. . . . I may venture so far as to say that the paper gives its holder a certain power in a certain quarter where such power is immensely valuable."

EDGAR ALLAN POE, "The Purloined Letter" (1845).

"Few false ideas have more firmly gripped the minds of so many intelligent men than the one that, if they just tried, they could invent a cipher that no one could break."

DAVID KAHN, *The Codebreakers* (1996).

"My mind rebels at stagnation. Give me problems, give me work, give me the most abstruse crypto-gram . . . and I am in my proper atmosphere. I can dispense then with artificial stimulants."

Sherlock Holmes, responding to Doctor Watson's remonstrations about his cocaine use, in Sir **ARTHUR CONAN DOYLE**, *The Sign of Four* (1890). So, cryptology replaces drug abuse!

"There is not a cipher system, however complicated, which cannot be unravelled; it will require more or less time, but in the end the key is always found."

British Colonel **GEORGE FURSE**, *Information in War* (1895).

"In 1901, when the French Navy began its first experiments with communication by radio telegraphy, the French carried out the tests in the Mediterranean rather than the Channel, presumably to lessen the possibility of eavesdropping by the Royal Navy. But not only did the British pick up the record of the French tests at a listening station on Gibraltar, HMS *Pyramis* closely tracked the French squadron and secured a complete record of the French messages. Apparently this was the first instance of radio intelligence interception."

BRADLEY SMITH, "The American Road to Central Intelligence," in Jeffreys-Jones and Andrew, *Eternal Vigilance* (1997).

"I am fairly familiar with all forms of secret writings, and am myself the author of a trifling monograph upon the subject, in which I analyze one hundred and sixty separate ciphers. . . . What one man can invent another can discover."

Sherlock Holmes in Sir **ARTHUR CONAN DOYLE**, "The Adventure of the Dancing Men" (1903).

"I dare say it may have come to your notice that if you walk into a post-office and demand to see the counterfoil of another man's message there may be some disinclination on the part of the officials to oblige you. There is so much red tape in these matters!"

Sherlock Holmes to Doctor Watson in Sir **ARTHUR CO-NAN DOYLE**, "The Adventure of the Missing Three-Quarter" (1904).

"When I was a young foreign service officer [in 1913] . . . our basic [encoding] system was based on a book code. . . . I spent thousands of worried hours over this book, which I have not seen for over forty years, but to this day I can still remember that we had six or seven words for 'period.' One was PIVIR and another was NINUD. . . . The theory then was—and it was a naive one—that if we had six or seven words it would confuse the enemy as to where we began and ended our sentences."

Former DCI **ALLEN DULLES**, *The Craft of Intelligence* (1963).

"Ring me up at fixed times. But talk in parables—for they all listen."

WINSTON CHURCHILL, note to his wife, July 1914; quoted in Stafford, *Churchill and Secret Service* (1998).

"At the beginning of September, 1914, the German light cruiser *Magdeburg* was wrecked in the Baltic. The body of a drowned German under-officer was picked up by the Russians a few hours later, and clasped in his bosom by arms rigid in death, were the cypher and signals books of the German Navy. . . . The Russians felt that as the leading naval Power, the British Admiralty ought to have these books."

WINSTON CHURCHILL, *The World Crisis* (1923). This incident is cited by David Kahn *(The Codebreakers)* as an "astounding windfall . . . perhaps the luckiest in the whole history of cryptology." The *Magdeburg* actually went aground in late August 1914.

"A gift more precious than a dozen Fabergé eggs."

Russian naval attaché to London, delivering to British authorities the captured German naval codebooks from the *Magdeburg*, October 1914; quoted in Stafford, *Churchill and Secret Service* (1998).

"An officer of the War Staff, preferably from the ID [Intelligence Division] should be selected to study all the decoded intercepts, not only current but past, and to compare them continually with what actually took place in order to penetrate the German mind and movements and make reports. . . . The officer selected is for the present to do no other work."

First Lord of the Admiralty **WINSTON CHURCHILL**, order of November 1914; quoted in Stafford, *Churchill and Secret Service* (1998).

"We intend to begin unrestricted submarine warfare on the first of February. We shall endeavor in spite of this to keep the United States neutral. In the event of this not succeeding, we will make Mexico a proposal of alliance on the following basis: Make war together, make peace together, generous financial support, and an understanding on our part that Mexico is to reconquer the lost territory in Texas, New Mexico, and Arizona."

The "Zimmermann telegram" from German Foreign Minister **ARTHUR ZIMMERMANN** to his ambassador in Mexico, intercepted in January 1917 by British intelligence and presented to Washington; cited in Miller, *Spying for America* (1989). We could have let California go.

"And so [with the Zimmermann telegram] it came about that Room 40's solution to an enemy message helped propel the United States into the First World War, enabling the Allies to win, and into world leadership. . . . No other single cryptanalysis has had such enormous consequences. Never before or since has so much turned upon the solution of a secret message. For those few moments in time, the codebreakers held history in the palm of their hand."

> **DAVID KAHN**, *The Codebreakers* (1996). Room 40 of the Admiralty building was the location for the codebreakers of British naval intelligence.

"The Intelligence that never fails."

> British Admiralty's term for intercepted communications during the First World War, possibly coined by First Lord Winston Churchill; cited in Stafford, *Churchill and Secret Service* (1998).

"This cipher is absolutely undecipherable."

> Plaintext of a cipher provided by the British government to test American cryptologist William Friedman, 1917; quoted in Kahn, *The Codebreakers* (1996). Friedman deciphered this and four other British messages in three hours. Silly Limeys.

"British cryptanalysts were [during World War I] entertained by the simplicity of U.S. codes and ciphers. . . . [President] Wilson and his wife spent 'many hours of many nights' laboriously encoding and decoding messages in a supposedly unbreakable cipher. . . . Room 40 [British codebreaking] doubtless found the few hours required to decrypt the top secret cables of the president of the United States unusually diverting. The great champion of open diplomacy was splendidly unaware of the degree to which he was practicing it himself."

> **CHRISTOPHER ANDREW**, *For the President's Eyes Only* (1995). Stupid Yanks.

"American diplomatic codes . . . were, from before World War I to the middle of World War II, as puny as those of many smaller nations. The United States must have been the laughingstock of every cryptanalyst in the world."

> **DAVID KAHN**, *The Codebreakers* (1996).

"Without exception the cheapest and most reliable form of Secret Service."

> British Foreign Secretary **GEORGE NATHANIAL** on the deciphering of intercepted messages; quoted in Richelson, *A Century of Spies* (1995). That was before supercomputers and satellites.

"Encode well or do not encode at all. In transmitting cleartext, you only give a piece of information to the enemy, and you know what it is; in encoding badly, you permit him to read all your correspondence and that of your friends."

> French cryptologist **MARCEL GIVERGE**, 1924; quoted in Kahn, *The Codebreakers* (1996).

"In the years I have been in office since [British codebreaking] began in the autumn of 1914 I have read every one of these [reports] and I attach more importance to them as a means of forming a true judgement of public policy in these spheres than to any other source of knowledge at the disposal of the State."

> **WINSTON CHURCHILL**, as chancellor of the exchequer, protesting to Prime Minister Stanley Baldwin when cut off from SIGINT reports, February 1925; quoted in Stafford, *Churchill and Secret Service* (1998).

"The Black Chamber, bolted, hidden, guarded, sees all, hears all. Though the blinds are drawn and the windows heavily curtained, its far-seeking eyes penetrate the secret conference chambers at Washington, Tokyo, London, Paris, Geneva, Rome. Its sensitive ears catch the faintest whisperings in the foreign capitals of the world."

> American cryptologist **HERBERT YARDLEY**'s overwrought description of the State Department codebreaking unit he headed from 1919 to 1929; cited in Kahn, *The Codebreakers* (1996).

"Gentlemen do not read each other's mail."

Secretary of State **HENRY STIMSON** explaining why he had shut down the department's codebreaking "Black Chamber" in 1929; in Henry Stimson and McGeorge Bundy, *On Active Service in Peace and War* (1947).

"This fine gesture will commend itself to all who are trying to develop the same standards of decency between Governments as exist between individuals."

Christian Science Monitor on Secretary of State Stimson's decision in 1929 to end U.S. codebreaking; cited in Miller, *Spying for America* (1989).

"When the fate of a nation and the lives of its soldiers are at stake, gentlemen do read each other's mail—if they can get their hands on it."

Former DCI **ALLEN DULLES**, *The Craft of Intelligence* (1963).

"What is extraordinary, positively intellectually heroic about the Polish effort [in the 1930s to crack the German cipher machine Enigma] is that it was done initially by the exercise of pure mathematics.... The Poles eventually designed a whole array of mechanical aids—some of which they passed to the British, some of which the British replicated independently, besides inventing others themselves —but their original attack, which allowed them to understand the logic of Enigma, was a work of pure mathematical reasoning. As it was done without any modern computing machines, but simply by pencil and paper, it must be regarded as one of the most remarkable mathematical exercises known to history."

JOHN KEEGAN, *Intelligence in War* (2003).

"With the outbreak of war, [German codebreaking] needed people and it made exceptions. Ottfried Deubner . . . was partly Jewish, but he was allowed to join and work on Italian cryptograms. . . . The Nazis made him an honorary Aryan."

DAVID KAHN, *The Codebreakers* (1996).

"The geese who laid the golden eggs—and never cackled."

WINSTON CHURCHILL, on Britain's SIGINT operations —especially ULTRA—during World War II; quoted in Russell, *The Secret War* (1981).

"The view that cryptology is black magic in itself springs ultimately from a superficial resemblance between cryptology and divination. Extracting an intelligible message from ciphertext seemed to be exactly the same thing as obtaining knowledge by examining . . . the length and intersections of lines in the hand, the entrails of sheep, the position of dregs in a teacup. In all of these, the wizardlike operator draws sense from grotesque, unfamiliar, and apparently meaningless signs. . . . People still think cryptanalysis mysterious. Book dealers still list cryptology under 'occult.' And in 1940 the United States conferred upon its Japanese diplomatic cryptanalyses the codename MAGIC."

DAVID KAHN, *The Codebreakers* (1996).

"The MAGIC group of cryptologists broke its first complete Japanese message in August 1940. Pearl Harbor was certainly one of the greatest intelligence failures in history, but that was not the fault of the intelligence collectors."

WALTER LAQUEUR, *A World of Secrets* (1985).

"This means war."

President **FRANKLIN ROOSEVELT** after reading the decrypted intercept from Japanese Prime Minister Togo to the embassy in Washington that scotched hope for continued negotiations, evening of 6 December 1941; cited in Prange, *At Dawn We Slept* (1981). FDR just didn't realize how soon it would come.

"[During World War II, the U.S.] Office of Censorship banned in advance the sending of whole classes of objects or kinds of messages. International chess games by mail were stopped. Crossword puzzles were extracted from letters, [and] so were newspaper clippings, which might have spelled out messages by dotting letters with secret ink.... Listing of students' grades was taboo. One letter containing knitting instructions was held up long enough for an examiner to knit a sweater.... Even lovers' X's, meant as kisses, were heartlessly deleted if censors thought they might be a code."

   DAVID KAHN, *The Codebreakers* (1996).

"Cracked cipher material was, indeed, as things turned out, the staple product of MI6, and provided the basis for most of its effective activities. The old procedures, like the setting up of agents, the suborning of informants, the sending of messages written in invisible ink ... all turned out to be largely cover for this other source; as one might keep some old-established business in rare books going in order to be able, under cover of it, to do a thriving trade in pornography and erotica. As 'C' [the chief of MI6] quickly saw, he never need fear criticism or cuts in his budget as long as he could drop in on the Prime Minister at breakfast time with some tasty item of Intelligence—the enemy's latest operational orders, say, or a full report of one of the meetings between Hitler and Mussolini immediately after it had happened—whose authenticity he could vouch for without being too particular as to its source."

   MALCOLM MUGGERIDGE, SIS officer during World War II, *Chronicles of Wasted Time: The Infernal Grove* (1973).

"The unprecedented measures taken to preserve the wartime Ultra secret ... derived from [Churchill's] acute sense of his own share of responsibility for revealing in 1927 that Soviet ciphers had been broken and for the subsequent inability of British codebreakers to decrypt Soviet diplomatic traffic."

   CHRISTOPHER ANDREW, in Jeffreys-Jones and Andrew, *Eternal Vigilance* (1997).

"This is good to know; in the future, they will also read what I want them to read."

   Italian Foreign Minister **GALEAZZO CIANO**, May 1941, after learning that Nazi Germany was decrypting Italy's dispatches; quoted in Kahn, *The Codebreakers* (1996).

"In contrast to American cryptanalysts, who were reading the vast majority of Japanese messages, including those in the cryptosystems of top-most security, the codebreakers of the Tokumu Han [Japan's naval cryptologic agency] failed almost completely in extracting usable knowledge from American messages.... Compared to the crystal-line precision of America's Midway intelligence, Japanese intelligence floundered in a miasma of vaporous generalities."

   DAVID KAHN, *The Codebreakers* (1996).

"[After 7 December 1941,] the demand for trained [cryptanalysts] greatly exceeded the supply. Admiral Bloch [naval commandant at Pearl Harbor] offered the band of the *California* as trainees.... The *California* was resting on the bottom of Pearl Harbor, her main deck under water. Her band had survived but their instruments had not, so they were among the technologically unemployed. Many of these musicians turned out to be such competent cryptanalysts after a short period of instruction that a theory was advanced that there must be a psychological connection between music and cryptanalysis."

   Former U.S. naval intelligence officer **W. J. HOLMES**, *Double-Edged Secrets* (1979).

"[In 1943] the Office of Strategic Services, America's new spy outfit, in a laudable attempt at espionage, penetrated the offices of the Japanese embassy in Portugal. . . . The Japanese discovered traces of the search, decided that their military attaché code might have been compromised, and changed it. The Allies, who had been comfortably reading the [Japanese] messages without benefit of espionage, still had not broken into the new code by the fall of 1944. Thus the attempt to gain information by cloak-and-dagger methods deprived the United States of intelligence that it had been obtaining by the traceless means of communications intelligence."

> **DAVID KAHN**, *The Codebreakers* (1996). Oops.

"Cryptanalysis was always a manic-depressive business. When we were reading the enemy's current secret messages, everyone was spurred to frantic effort. When darkness suddenly descended, everyone was plunged into correspondingly deep gloom. Each man feared in his bones that we would never again succeed in the long and difficult task of breaking a new code. . . . There was always danger that some key man would work himself into a nervous breakdown just when he was needed most."

> Former U.S. naval intelligence officer **W. J. HOLMES**, *Double-Edged Secrets* (1979).

"It's not necessary to be crazy to be a cryptanalyst, but it always helps."

> **JOSEPH ROCHEFORT**, eccentric Navy intelligence chief who led the unit that cracked the Japanese naval cipher before the Battle of Midway; quoted in Miller, *Spying for America* (1989). In the film *Midway*, Rochefort is played by Hal Holbrook.

"It [ULTRA] has simplified my task as commander enormously. It has saved thousands of British and American lives and, in no small way, contributed to the speed with which the enemy was routed and eventually agreed to surrender."

> General **DWIGHT EISENHOWER** to General Sir Stewart Menzies, chief of SIS, 12 July 1945; quoted in Andrew, *For the President's Eyes Only* (1995).

"The ULTRA intelligence provided to British and American commanders was, quite simply, the best in the history of warfare."

> **CHRISTOPHER ANDREW** and **VASILI MITROKHIN**, *The Sword and the Shield: The Mitrokhin Archive* (1999).

"It struck me at the time how often the art of undoing other people's cyphers was closely allied to a brain which could excel both in mathematics and music. It was rather frightening playing one's evening bridge with these men."

> **FRED WINTERBOTHAM**, in 1974, on the "backroom boys of Bletchley"—Britain's wartime codebreaking operation; cited in West, *Faber Book of Espionage* (1993).

"SIGINT . . . saved Europe from becoming the birthplace of nuclear warfare."

> **CHRISTOPHER ANDREW**, *For the President's Eyes Only* (1995).

"No spy could have furnished such top-grade information with such speed and accuracy—or had it accepted with equal trust."

> **NATHAN MILLER** on ULTRA, in *Spying for America* (1989).

"The young [Army] Air Force officer who shot down the plane carrying the Japanese fleet admiral Yamamoto received the highest decorations his country had to offer, but the men who provided him with the vital information that made possible his routine operation, the cryptanalysts working in their secret rooms, remain unrecognized and unrewarded. The ships and men who turned the tide of the Battle of Midway by intercepting and defeating a mighty Japanese invasion fleet received the nation's gratitude. Their names are carved in the war memorial erected to the heroes of America. But the quiet men and women whose unrecognized but spectacular work made such victories possible by reading Japanese codes and ciphers, remain anonymous and undecorated. It requires a true passion for anonymity to become wed to cryptography."

ELLIS ZACHARIAS, *Secret Missions* (1946). Zacharias was a career intelligence officer for the U.S. Navy, specializing in Japan.

"I am inclined to assume that there is at the bottom of the wish to break a code a continuation of the infantile desire to find out what is the secret of sexuality which the parents or the adult hide before the little boy."

Psychoanalyst THEODOR REIK, 1961; quoted in Kahn, *The Codebreakers* (1996). Did Reik ever do crossword puzzles?

"Fucked again!"

President JOHN F. KENNEDY after NSA intercepts showed Soviet nuclear testing soon after construction of the Berlin Wall; quoted in Andrew, *For the President's Eyes Only* (1995).

"The codebreaker isn't interested in the content of the message but in the solution of the code. He does not take a sneaking interest in the cryptogram but pride in its mastery. Cryptanalysis is not peeking through a keyhole. It is breaking down a door."

Psychiatrist JEPTHA MACFARLANE, 1964; quoted in Kahn, *The Codebreakers* (1996).

"We were able to overhear the communications of the Pentagon, the FBI, the State Department, the White House, the local police, and a host of other agencies. These communications all were broadcast on open, non-secure channels . . . a surprising amount of useful material was relayed over the airways."

Former KGB General OLEG KALUGIN on Soviet intercept operations in the Washington, D.C., area during the late 1960s, in *The First Directorate* (1994).

"One traitor in a main cryptographic centre can probably do his country more harm than in any other situation."

SIS official JOHN BRUCE LOCKHART, "Intelligence: A British View" (1984); cited in West, *Faber Book of Espionage* (1993).

"Electronic surveillance people are always entranced by their ability to intercept signals and want to do more, regardless of whether it's useful."

Former DCI STANSFIELD TURNER, *Secrecy and Democracy* (1985).

"The NSA is mandated to collect intelligence, not to analyze it. It must do enough analysis about what it has collected to decide what it should collect next. In intelligence jargon this level of analysis is termed 'processing.' Processing is regularly stretched by NSA into full-scale analysis. . . . Although the NSA has excellent analysts to do its processing, it does not have the full range of analytic talent needed for responsible analysis, nor all of the relevant data from the other collecting agencies needed for a comprehensive job. The NSA's analysis is bound to be biased in the direction of what signals intercepts tell, and is less likely to take account of photographic or human intelligence."

Former DCI STANSFIELD TURNER, *Secrecy and Democracy* (1985).

"An NSA listening post in Japan heard a Soviet fighter pilot say that he had fired a missile, then announce ... 'The target is destroyed.' ... Visibly angry and waving an intelligence report in his hand, [Secretary of State George] Shultz told a press conference [that] there was no possible doubt that the Soviet fighter pilot had identified KAL 007 as a civilian 747 and shot it down in cold blood. For the first time in State Department history a secretary of state was directly, and unmistakably, quoting SIGINT reports."

> **CHRISTOPHER ANDREW**, *For the President's Eyes Only* (1995). So much for gentlemen not reading each other's mail.

"The Cold War is characterized by battles not fought, lives not lost. That era was fought with mathematicians and cryptologists."

> NSA Director Lieutenant General **KENNETH MINIHAN**; quoted in the *Baltimore Sun*, 10 January 1998.

"We know that there are three things which are often associated with success in codebreaking: ability in chess, ability in music, and ability in mathematics."

> **DAVID KAHN** on the quality of Russian cryptanalysis; quoted in Polmar and Allen, *Encyclopedia of Espionage* (1997).

"It's nothing but an eight-story microphone plugged into the Politburo."

> U.S. Representative **RICHARD ARMEY** on the State Department's new embassy building in Moscow; quoted in *Time*, 20 April 1987.

"My association with NSA goes back many years. And over the years I've come to appreciate more and more the full value of SIGINT. As President and Commander in Chief, I can assure you, signals intelligence is a prime factor in the decisionmaking process by which we chart the course of this nation's foreign affairs."

> President **GEORGE H. W. BUSH**, during his May 1991 visit to the National Security Agency; quoted in Andrew, *For the President's Eyes Only* (1995). Andrew states that this was the first time a U.S. president had used the term "SIGINT" in public.

"In our time, a 'break' into the codes that protect the communications between the farflung parts of a military and diplomatic establishment is the equivalent not of one but of a thousand spies, all ideally placed, all secure, and all reporting instantaneously. ... To read an opponent's messages is to read his mind."

> **ANGELO CODEVILLA**, *Informing Statecraft* (1992).

"Reading a man's correspondence is not the same thing as reading his mind."

> Intelligence historian **PETER CALVOCORESSI**; quoted in Knightley, *The Second Oldest Profession* (1988). As we can't intercept brain waves, it's close enough.

"Cryptosystems today can be made unbreakable. ... This means that, although errors will occur that will occasionally enable the cryptanalyst to solve systems analytically, when systems are good enough and are properly used, they cannot be broken. The war of cryptographer against cryptanalyst has been won by the cryptographers."

> **DAVID KAHN**, *The Codebreakers* (1996).

"Codebreaking is often supposed to depend on little more than the cryptanalytic genius of brilliant mathematicians, nowadays assisted by huge networks of computers. In reality, most major twentieth-century codebreaking coups on which information is available have been assisted—sometimes crucially—by agent intelligence on code and cipher systems."

CHRISTOPHER ANDREW and **VASILI MITROKHIN**, *The Sword and the Shield: The Mitrokhin Archive* (1999).

"There may be perfect systems, but there are no perfect users."

Saying of cryptanalysts at the National Security Agency.

"Forty years ago there were 5,000 stand-alone computers, no fax machines, and not one cellular phone. Today there are over 180 million computers —most of them networked. There are roughly 14 million fax machines and 40 million cellphones, and those numbers continue to grow."

NSA Director Lieutenant General **MICHAEL HAYDEN** on the "needle in a haystack" problem that NSA faces in finding the crucial bit of intelligence to ward off another major terrorist attack; quoted in the *New York Times*, 8 September 2002.

• Journalists, Businessmen, & Clergy

The Literary Spy is a bit confused about contemporary bloviating in U.S. media, academic, and political circles against the imagined evils of employing certain professions in the practice of intelligence. While information from a journalist, for example, might be considered less reliable than most, when the stakes are high, it may have to do. In any case, we Americans have a rich history of pragmatism in these matters.

See also: Covert Action; Openness & Publicity; Plausible Denial

"To establish a free press . . . for the frequent publication of such pieces as may be of service to the cause of the United Colonies."

> Continental Congress, secret resolution of 26 February 1776, sending one Fleury Mesplat and his printing press to Canada; cited in Sayle, "The Historical Underpinnings of the U.S. Intelligence Community," *International Journal of Intelligence and Counterintelligence* (spring 1986). Sayle notes that one paper Mesplat founded, the *Montreal Gazette,* is still being published.

"Besides the humanity of affording them the benefit of your profession, it may in the conduct of a man of sense answer another valuable purpose.

And while it serves to prepare them for the other world, it will naturally lead to the intelligence we want in your inquiries into the condition of their spiritual concerns. You will therefore be pleased to take charge of this matter upon yourself, and when you have collected in the course of your attendance such information as they can give, you will transmit the whole to me."

> **GEORGE WASHINGTON** to the Reverend Alexander McWhorter, a military chaplain, regarding the final confession two British spies were to make before their executions, 12 October 1778; cited in Knott, *Secret and Sanctioned* (1996).

"I would imagine that with a little industry, he will be able to carry on his intelligence with greater security to himself and greater advantages to us, under cover of his usual business, than if he were to dedicate himself wholly to the giving of information. It may afford him opportunities of collecting intelligence, that he could not derive so well in any other manner."

> **GEORGE WASHINGTON** to Benjamin Tallmadge regarding the intelligence activities of merchant Robert Townsend, 24 September 1779; cited in Knott, *Secret and Sanctioned* (1996).

"The trust confided in you is one of great delicacy and importance. In performing the duties which it imposes, great prudence and caution will be required. You ought never to give the slightest intimation . . . that you are an agent of this Government."

> Secretary of State **JAMES BUCHANAN** to Moses Beach, 21 November 1846; quoted in Knott, *Secret and Sanctioned* (1996). Beach, the editor of *The Sun*, a New York newspaper, was sent by President Polk on a covert mission to Mexico to sway Roman Catholic clergy to support a peace agreement with the United States.

"While in Paris, you will study how, in conjunction with [U.S. Ambassador] Dayton, you can promote healthful opinions concerning the great cause in which our country is now engaged in arms."

> Secretary of State **WILLIAM SEWARD** to Roman Catholic Archbishop John Hughes of New York before the archbishop's trip to France in 1861; quoted in Knott, *Secret and Sanctioned* (1996). The U.S. government paid Archbishop Hughes more than five thousand dollars for his services to win support for President Lincoln's policies.

"As special agents we might employ commercial travellers. Not only would their business hide their employment, but they travel through many countries, they are forced by habit to accost many people, are not shy with strangers, have seen a good deal, and, as a rule, possess a good store of general information. . . . Brokers, commission agents, and contractors are good subjects for this business, as in the course of their occupations they see and hear much."

> British Colonel **GEORGE FURSE**, *Information in War* (1895).

"From 1894 to 1898, [British] secret funds were also paid to Reuters news agency, which supplied confidential reports from its correspondents and agreed to let the Foreign Office use the service to publish propaganda in foreign newspapers."

> **NORMAN POLMAR** and **THOMAS ALLEN**, *Encyclopedia of Espionage* (1997).

"When we talk of employing special agents, why should not the intelligence staff employ as such some war correspondent of well-known ability? It would be a matter of no little consequence to turn to account the great experience which these gentlemen have acquired by attending armies in the field and at manoeuvres, with the sole object of worming out information and interesting the public. They are all up to the dodges of their craft, and have considerable experience in feeling the pulse of public opinion. By subsidizing a foreign correspondent, it might be even possible to have a reporter within the enemy's lines."

> British Colonel **GEORGE FURSE**, *Information in War* (1895). CNN in Baghdad?

"Churchill told his mother [he] had been asked to collect information and statistics on various points, '& particularly as to the effect of the new bullet—its penetration and striking power.' . . . Before leaving he persuaded the *Daily Graphic* . . . to let him send regular reports from the scene of the insurrection."

> **MARTIN GILBERT**, *Churchill* (1991). At the age of twenty-one, Winston Churchill went to Cuba, where Spain was trying to quell a rebellion, with the aim of collecting intelligence for the British director of military intelligence while working as a journalist.

"The Press, Watson, is a most valuable institution if you only know how to use it."

> Sherlock Holmes in Sir **ARTHUR CONAN DOYLE**, "The Adventure of the Six Napoleons" (1904).

"I was assigned to MO [Morale Operations—OSS's disinformation branch] . . . mostly because of my newspaper experience. After spending three years in MO disguising the truth, slanting stories, and developing rumors, I had great difficulty writing a straight news story once the war was over."

ELIZABETH McINTOSH, *Sisterhood of Spies* (1998). They weren't hiring at the *New York Times*?

"[DCI] General [Hoyt] Vandenberg . . . stated that C.I.G. was now prepared to utilize, to the extent security permits, all American business concerns with connections abroad as valuable sources of foreign intelligence."

Minutes of the National Intelligence Authority, 25 September 1946; in *FRUS 1945–1950: Emergence of the Intelligence Establishment* (1996), document 169. At that meeting, the members of the NIA—the forerunner of the National Security Council—were the Secretaries of War and the Navy, the Acting Secretary of State, the DCI, and Admiral William Leahy, the personal representative of President Truman.

"Pursuant to the provisions of Section 102 of the National Security Act of 1947 . . . The Central Intelligence Agency shall be responsible for the exploitation, on a highly selective basis, within the United States of business concerns, other non-governmental organizations and individuals as sources of foreign intelligence information."

National Security Council Intelligence Directive No. 7, "Domestic Exploitation," 12 February 1948; in *FRUS 1945–1950: Emergence of the Intelligence Establishment* (1996), document 427.

"The cover of one [officer] was that of a journalist on the staff of a technical publication whose management was patriotic enough to allow the use of their name by CIA. . . . In dealing with him, I made clear that his work for the journal was his alone, and that I would have no voice in what he sub-

mitted to it, as CIA's mission was abroad, not in influencing what appeared in the American press. But as an inquiring reporter, he could go into circles and ask questions that would certainly not be appropriate for an embassy officer such as myself to do, and in the process he could spot likely candidates to help CIA's operations."

Former DCI **WILLIAM COLBY** describing the use of journalistic cover while posted in Scandinavia in the 1950s, in *Honorable Men* (1978).

"Our task is to expose the way of life in the capitalist world, and it is especially important to do so in relation to the United States."

Radio Moscow editor to KGB officer Oleg Kalugin, who in 1960 was assigned to New York under the cover of a Radio Moscow journalist; quoted in Kalugin, *The First Directorate* (1994). Kalugin writes that during the Cold War about two-thirds of Soviet foreign correspondents were working for the KGB.

"Up to 600 individuals are studying in the two ecclesiastical academies of the Moscow Patriarchate and the five ecclesiastical seminaries. These must be exploited in the interests of the KGB. We must infiltrate our people among the students of these ecclesiastical training establishments so that they will subsequently influence the state of affairs within the Russian Orthodox Church and exert influence on believers."

KGB directive, 1961; cited in Andrew and Mitrokhin, *The Mitrokhin Archive* (1999). A much higher judge awaits.

"The profession of journalism is in many ways an ideal training for espionage, and much journalism is in fact little more than spying."

BRIAN INNES, *The Book of Spies* (1966).

"One hundred percent of the [Russian] clergy were forced to cooperate to some extent with the

KGB and pass on some sort of information—otherwise they would have been deprived of the possibility to work in a parish."

Russian Orthodox priest **DMITRI DUDKO**; quoted in Andrew and Mitrokhin, *The Mitrokhin Archive* (1999). A senior KGB official, however, revealed before the breakup of the USSR that 15 to 20 percent of the clergy refused to work with the KGB.

"CIA has no secret paid or contractual relationship with any American clergyman or missionary. This practice will be continued as a matter of policy."

CIA announcement, February 1976; cited in U.S. Senate, *Final Report of the Senate Select Committee to Study Governmental Operations with respect to Intelligence Activities* [the Church Committee], Book I (April 1976).

"While I believe that any institution or organization has the right to take positions on domestic or foreign policy issues, I also believe each individual American has the right to cooperate with his government in its lawful pursuits. I submit this right should apply to academics, clergymen, businessmen, union members, newsmen, etc. The more groups we exclude from assisting the intelligence community, the poorer our intelligence will be. Surely, our values have been turned upside down, when cooperating with the CIA is viewed as unseemly or degrading."

Dissent of Senator **BARRY GOLDWATER** in U.S. Senate, *Final Report of the Senate Select Committee to Study Governmental Operations with respect to Intelligence Activities* [the Church Committee], Book I (April 1976).

"DCI George Bush announced in mid-1976 that CIA would no longer employ any person in the field of U.S. journalism. This self-denial stems from the view, publicized initially by the magazine *Ramparts* in 1967, that CIA used cover organizations and paid agents in them to corrupt the honest views of U.S. youth. In fact CIA used agents in these groups to collect information about Soviet propaganda efforts, to counter these efforts with objective information, and to sponsor the formation of U.S.-oriented organizations abroad."

Former DDI **RAY CLINE**, *Secrets, Spies and Scholars* (1976).

"At the present time, the Roman Catholic Church does not represent a threat. . . . Out of seventy bishops, good contacts are maintained with fifty. This makes it possible to bring influence to bear on the Catholic Church and to prevent undesirable moves."

General **CZESLAW KISZCZAK**, Poland's interior minister, to Soviet KGB chief Yuri Andropov, August 1981; cited in Andrew and Mitrokhin, *The Mitrokhin Archive* (1999). In fact, Kiszczak knew he was blowing smoke and later admitted that the Polish people considered the church, not the Communists, as the moral standard-bearer in Poland.

"One day Katharine Graham, publisher of the *Washington Post,* had someone call to see if the CIA would give her a briefing prior to a trip she was making to China. I was pleased to set up an unclassified briefing for her. . . . A few months later I met her at a cocktail party. After inquiring about her trip, I asked if she would come out to Langley again and have lunch with me and the people who had briefed her. I said we would be most interested in hearing about her trip and in learning whether our briefing seemed realistic in light of what she had seen. Seldom have I witnessed such shock and bewilderment. 'You know,' she said, 'I just couldn't do that.'"

Former DCI **STANSFIELD TURNER**, *Secrecy and Democracy* (1985). Of course not.

"There were two instances when media help was needed during my tenure and I gave my approval.

Once during the hostage crisis in Iran, we found a man who had a unique access and thought he could help resolve a problem. I didn't hesitate one minute in calling on him. Circumstances overtook the situation and we did not actually use him, but we were on the verge of doing so. Interestingly, I never found a newsman who denied that it might be desirable for us to use media people in such life-and-death situations. But somehow that did not reduce the press's ardor for a regulation or law prohibiting it. . . . Even if the CIA issued a regulation prohibiting the use of the media, few of our enemies or friends overseas would believe it was designed to do anything but mislead them."

> Former DCI **STANSFIELD TURNER**, *Secrecy and Democracy* (1985).

"As a writer and reporter I try to penetrate to the heart of the way the world works, and to describe what I see in the simplest and most direct way. That is what spies are supposed to do, so there is a neat fit."

> Reporter, editor, and spy novelist **DAVID IGNATIUS**; quoted in Jeffreys-Jones and Lownie, *North American Spies* (1991).

"Agency officials make a show of secrecy. But in fact, as any frequent visitor to Langley can observe, there is a steady traffic of favorite reporters in and out of CIA headquarters. . . . The record of journalists' private visits to Langley are voluminous, but the Privacy Act shields them from the Freedom of Information Act."

> **ANGELO CODEVILLA**, *Informing Statecraft* (1992).

"Newspaper reporters are trained to cultivate sources, check material against what is already held on file, and compile reports. . . . The attributes of the journalist and the process by which he de-velops a story are virtually identical to that of the intelligence professional."

> **NIGEL WEST**, *Faber Book of Espionage* (1993).

"Well, I'm not. No self-respecting journalist works for any government agency, particularly the CIA."

> **PETE EARLEY** to Aldrich Ames, under arrest for spying for Moscow, after Ames suggested that Earley might be working for CIA, July 1994; in Earley, *Confessions of a Spy* (1997).

"The priest's help in spotting a potential recruit is precisely the reason we in the KGB wanted agents inside the church."

> Former KGB officer **OLEG KALUGIN** on a Russian Orthodox priest's recruitment of a U.S. Army officer who passed U.S. military and NATO secrets to Moscow for twenty-five years, in Kalugin, *The First Directorate* (1994). The priest was made an archbishop, and in June 2000, the FBI arrested retired U.S. Army Colonel George Trofimoff for espionage.

"Clandestine operations for whatever purpose currently are circumscribed by a number of legal and policy constraints. These deserve review to avoid diminishing the potential contribution of this instrument. At a minimum, the Task Force recommended that a fresh look be taken at limits on the use of nonofficial 'covers' for hiding and protecting those involved in clandestine activities."

> Council on Foreign Relations, *Making Intelligence Smarter* (1996).

"Now we know why the Central Intelligence Agency, the National Security Agency, the Defense Intelligence Agency and all those other spook agencies that get $25 billion-plus from taxpayers every year can't bring down Saddam Hussein: They have not been able to use journalists or priests as part of their covert operations."

JIM HOAGLAND, "The CIA: No Cover for Failure," *Washington Post*, 22 February 1996.

"Obviously we don't want spies posing as journalists. If any of you are, please identify yourselves."

Secretary of State **MADELEINE ALBRIGHT** during a news conference after an FBI official told Congress that foreign spies posing as journalists have unescorted access to the State Department; quoted in the *Washington Post*, 12 May 2000. The State Department later dismissed the FBI warning.

"We cannot believe all of them are journalists. We are sure some of them are spies or military personnel from America and Britain."

QARI AHMEDULLAH, intelligence chief for Afghanistan's Taliban regime, on the three hundred foreign journalists reporting from northern Afghanistan; quoted in the *Washington Times*, 6 October 2001.

"In [CIA's] point of view, there may be higher values than the protection of journalists—and I'm not sure they're wrong. It may save many lives."

STEVEN AFTERGOOD of the Federation of American Scientists and frequent critic of CIA; quoted by Editor &Publisher.com, 7 December 2001. September 11 brought clarity to many things.

"There are more of them in Afghanistan than there are of us, and they are paid better."

CIA public affairs chief **BILL HARLOW**, asked why CNN rather than CIA was able to acquire an al-Qaeda video archive in Afghanistan; quoted in the *New York Times*, 19 August 2002.

L

- **Leadership**
- **Leaks**
- **Legislative Oversight**
- **Liaison**
- **Limits of Intelligence**

LEADERSHIP

The institutions of intelligence, like all large organizations, require managerial expertise to utilize a large workforce and wide array of physical resources (buildings, vehicles, satellites, computers, and databases). Good managers can be developed or imported from the outside world. More important for the success of intelligence, however, is leadership. Rather than simply manage resources, leaders lead men and women in difficult tasks, provide vision in adversity, and convey a sense of mission and uplift morale when intelligence is under attack both for what it does and for what it is. This sort of leadership requires a fundamental understanding of intelligence as well as of people, and it's much harder to import. The Literary Spy has seen too little of it. Above all that, the nation's top leadership won't benefit from intelligence unless it takes the time to learn something about it.

See also: Directors of Central Intelligence; Intelligence & American Culture; Origins of Central Intelligence; Presidents & Intelligence

"What enables the wise sovereign and the good general to strike and conquer, and achieve things beyond the reach of ordinary men, is foreknowledge."

    SUN TZU, *The Art of War* (6th century B.C.).

"Unless someone has the wisdom of a sage, he cannot use spies; unless he is benevolent and righteous, he cannot employ spies; unless he is subtle and perspicacious, he cannot perceive the substance in intelligence reports."

    SUN TZU, *The Art of War* (6th century B.C.). An interesting list of qualifications for DCI: wise, benevolent, righteous, subtle, perspicacious. Sounds like a combination of Allen Dulles, Richard Helms, and William Colby.

"The Lord said to Moses, 'Send men to spy out the land of Canaan . . . from each tribe of their fathers shall you send a man, every one a leader among them.' So Moses sent them . . . according to the command of the Lord, all of them men who were heads of the people of Israel."

    Numbers 13:1–3 (Revised Standard). The divine order: espionage properly done requires leadership.

"The Eye of the King."

Title for the intelligence chief in the Persian empire, 6th–5th centuries B.C.; cited in Dvornik, *Origins of Intelligence Services* (1974). "Eye of the King" sounds so much better than "Director of Central Intelligence."

"The Eye of the Caliph."

Title for the intelligence chief in the Arab Muslim empire, 10th century; cited in Dvornik, *Origins of Intelligence Services* (1974). The intelligence chief also ran the postal service.

"It is indispensable for a sovereign to obtain information on his subjects and his soldiers, on all which happens near him or in distant regions, and to know about everything which is occurring, be it of small or great importance. If he does not do so, this will prove a disgrace, a proof of his negligence and neglect of justice. . . . Sending out police agents and spies shows that the ruler is just, vigilant, and sagacious. If he behaves as I have indicated, his state will flourish."

NIZAM AL-MULK, vizier of the 11th-century Seljuk Sultan Malik Shah; cited in Dvornik, *Origins of Intelligence Services* (1974).

"Hee was careful and liberall to obtaine good Intelligence from all parts abroad."

FRANCIS BACON, *The Historie of the Raigne of King Henry the Seventh* (1622).

"Capital sport."

Captain MANSFIELD CUMMING, or "C," the first chief of Britain's MI6, on intelligence work; quoted in Richelson, *A Century of Spies* (1995).

"Der Führer! Der Führer!"

German official to Lord Halifax, who was arriving at Berchtesgaden for a talk with Adolf Hitler and, having mistaken Hitler for a footman, was handing Der Führer his hat and coat; cited in Andrew and Mitrokhin, *The Mitrokhin*

Archive (1999). Leadership analysis, properly done, anticipates the needs of political figures and helps prevent such embarrassments.

"[Winston] Churchill combined a creative strategic imagination drawn to the unorthodox with an unerring instinct for the importance of intelligence. . . . Amongst twentieth-century British politicians—indeed, all leaders of the major powers—Churchill is unique in consistently relishing and realising the potential for intelligence, in all its forms, in both peace and war."

DAVID STAFFORD, *Churchill and Secret Service* (1998).

"I think you had better tell all this to my intelligence staff. I don't go much for this sort of thing. You see, I just like fighting."

General GEORGE PATTON to a British intelligence officer briefing him on the ULTRA decrypts of German messages, 1942; quoted in Winterbotham, *Ultra Spy* (1989).

"Stalin . . . provides a textbook example of two diseases which afflict virtually all those who put their faith in espionage. He came to believe that information obtained secretly was always more valuable than information obtained openly and when secret information appeared to contradict his own assessment, he dismissed it out of hand as being wrong, a provocation, a plant."

PHILLIP KNIGHTLEY, *The Second Oldest Profession* (1988). What Stalin put his faith in was himself and his prejudices, not espionage properly conducted or intelligence honestly handled.

"The sort of guy who thought nothing of parachuting into France, blowing up a bridge, pissing in Luftwaffe gas tanks, then dancing on the roof of the St. Regis hotel with a German spy."

Film director JOHN FORD on his wartime boss, OSS Director William Donovan; quoted in Stafford, *Churchill and Secret Service* (1998).

"If Bill Donovan had been a Democrat, he'd be in my place today."

> Attributed to President **FRANKLIN ROOSEVELT**; quoted in Troy, *Donovan and the CIA* (1981).

"What a man! We have lost the last hero."

> President **DWIGHT EISENHOWER** in 1959 on hearing of William Donovan's death; quoted in Polmar and Allen, *Encyclopedia of Espionage* (1997). *The Last Hero* is the title of Anthony Cave Brown's 1982 biography of Donovan.

"William Donovan . . . would have been challenged to organize a dinner for four but ran a secret intelligence service willing to hazard any scheme, however harebrained it appeared to cooler eyes."

> **THOMAS POWERS** in the *New York Times Book Review*, 21 October 2001. Donovan, like all great men, had underlings to arrange his dinner parties.

"In recent years, between 1940 and 1945, our Naval Intelligence had no less than seven directors, while the British Navy changed its director of Naval Intelligence only once. Of the seven directors . . . only one was qualified to fill this particular job. Characteristically, his tenure was the shortest."

> **ELLIS ZACHARIAS**, *Secret Missions* (1946). Zacharias was a career intelligence officer for the U.S. Navy, specializing in Japan. He describes a situation similar to that regarding DCIs in the 1990s.

"My job is to hold an umbrella over you fellows and catch the crap so you can get on with your operating."

> CIA operations chief, and later DCI, **RICHARD HELMS**, to his operations officers; quoted in Phillips, *The Night Watch* (1978).

"You want information on a certain question, then the intelligence reports come in as so many snow-flakes. We also have our intelligence service and it is the same with them."

> **MAO ZEDONG** to Henry Kissinger, February 1973; quoted in the *New York Times*, 10 January 1999.

"Access to secret intelligence [is] one of the more potent aphrodisiacs of power."

> **DAVID STAFFORD**, *Churchill and Secret Service* (1998).

LEAKS

A leak is the unauthorized, deliberate release of classified information, and leaks get more attention and are more credibly received than the official dissemination of information. A leak is a lot sexier than a press release. As long as there is privileged information, there will be leakers of it—the small minds for whom inside knowledge is the only currency of power, and currency is valuable only if you can spend it occasionally.

See also: Compartmentation; Legislative Oversight; Openness & Publicity; Secrecy

"A tale-bearer revealeth secrets: but he that is of a faithful spirit concealeth the matter."

> Proverbs 11:13 (King James).

"If a secret piece of news is divulged by a spy before the time is ripe, he must be put to death together with the person to whom the secret was told."

> **SUN TZU**, *The Art of War* (6th century B.C.). Such practice applied today in Washington would mean a bloodbath.

"The Continental Congress established a number of precedents for the conduct of intelligence operations. They originated the first oaths pledging members and staff to secrecy. . . . Revolutionary propagandist Thomas Paine, serving as a clerk to one of the committees, earned the distinction of being one of the first government officials to be fired for leaking classified information."

> **NATHAN MILLER**, *Spying for America* (1989). Firing such a pain was simply common sense.

"Memorize this Group: '2222'—Code Lost."

> Cover of U.S. Army codebook, 1918; cited in Kahn, *The Codebreakers* (1996). Kahn reports that the codegroup for Code Lost was changed soon thereafter to DAM.

"My idea would be to hang a few of the offenders. . . . It would be a major saving of lives to do it."

> Major **FRANK BOORMAN**, U.S. Army radio intelligence chief in World War I, on careless communications; quoted in Kahn, *The Codebreakers* (1996).

"The disclosure of this breach of faith by the United States Government will doubtless serve as a valuable lesson for the future."

> Japanese official, 1931, on disclosures in Herbert Yardley's *The American Black Chamber* that U.S. cryptanalytic efforts had given Washington an advantage over Japan in the 1921 Washington Naval Conference; quoted in Kahn, *The Codebreakers* (1996).

"Navy Had Word of Jap Plan to Strike at Sea"

> *Chicago Tribune* headline, 7 June 1942, over article providing details about the U.S. Navy's ability to decrypt Japanese naval messages before the Battle of Midway; cited in Shulsky, *Silent Warfare* (1993). Despite the leak, the Japanese fortunately did not catch on.

"I should have much preferred to talk to you in person but I could not devise a method that would not be subject to press and radio reactions. . . . In brief the military dilemma is this: The most vital evidence in the Pearl Harbor matter consists of our intercepts of the Japanese diplomatic com-munications. . . . We have gone ahead with this business of deciphering their codes until we possess other codes, German as well as Japanese. . . . You will understand from the foregoing the utterly tragic consequences if the present political debates regarding Pearl Harbor disclose to the enemy, German or Jap, any suspicion of the vital sources of information we possess."

> General **GEORGE MARSHALL**, 27 September 1944, in a secret and personal letter to Governor Thomas E. Dewey of New York, the Republican nominee for president, adjuring Dewey not to refer publicly to U.S. codebreaking for political purposes; quoted in Kahn, *The Codebreakers* (1996).

"[President] Eisenhower considered much of the material [on space reconnaissance] so sensitive that he didn't even want the National Security Council to be informed of it for fear of leaks."

> **WILLIAM E. BURROWS**, *Deep Black* (1986).

"Hugh, do you have anyone in Cuba? Big things are about to happen. Better get someone there."

> Attorney General **ROBERT KENNEDY** to Time-Life's Hugh Sidey at a party three days before the Bay of Pigs invasion, April 1963; quoted in Thomas, *Robert Kennedy* (2000).

"What the press *never* does say is who the leaker is and why he wants the story leaked. Yet, more often than not, this is the more important story: that is to say, what policy wins if the one being disclosed loses, what individual, what bureau, and so on."

> **DANIEL PATRICK MOYNIHAN** in *Commentary* (March 1971).

"There is a strange levity, a strange weak irresponsibility, in playing with men's lives and a whole system of intelligence in this manner."

Fictional ship's doctor and spy Stephen Maturin on an intelligence leak in the British Admiralty in **PATRICK O'BRIAN**, *H.M.S. Surprise* (1973).

"There are more leaks here than in the men's room at Anheuser-Busch."

Senator **BARRY GOLDWATER** on whether Congress should increase its oversight of CIA; quoted in the *Washington Post*, 17 May 1978.

"Unfortunately, it was my experience that the most injurious leaks about intelligence came from the White House. . . . Sometimes the President's staff was so eager to use any information that would help his political position, they 'forgot' where it came from. Sometimes this was innocent; most of the time it was not."

Former DCI **STANSFIELD TURNER**, *Secrecy and Democracy* (1985).

"There aren't any budding authors in this room?"

President **GEORGE H. W. BUSH** before Oval Office meetings; quoted in *U.S. News and World Report* (25 June 2001).

"One has to appreciate the difference between a leak from the executive branch designed to enhance the implementation of policy (perhaps by sending a signal to a foreign government) and a leak from the legislative branch intended to veto or cripple a policy that a determined minority could not defeat through the formal processes of government."

STEPHEN KNOTT, *Secret and Sanctioned* (1996).

"We file crimes reports with the Attorney General every week about leaks, and we're never successful in litigating one."

Acting DCI **GEORGE TENET** in congressional testimony, 6 May 1997.

"We need people to consider these security agreements binding. It calls into question whether the agreement is worth much."

CIA General Counsel **MICHAEL O'NEIL** on alleged unauthorized disclosures concerning CIA activities in Iraq; quoted in the *Washington Post*, 19 July 1997.

"The executive branch leaks like a sieve. There's guilt everywhere, but . . . there are people all over this executive branch who have violated a trust. . . . We're doing the best we can with the FBI to find the people who are doing this, and when we do, we will fire them. . . . We have men and women all over the world who are putting their lives at risk every night to try and collect information. All of those capabilities are put at risk when people, really without regard for the consequences, throw real secrets out into the public domain and jeopardize our nation's interests. They shut down our ability to do our job. They make it impossible for us to protect Americans."

DCI **GEORGE TENET** in testimony before the Senate intelligence committee, 28 January 1998.

"It is not, of course, the press's job to protect government secrets. A newspaper's function is to present information, and leaks are central to that mission. . . . Asking journalists to denounce leaks because of their deleterious effects on the functioning of government is as hopeless as asking an airline to denounce jet fuel because of its impact on the environment."

BENJAMIN WITTES, "Why We Publish Leaks," *Washington Post*, 13 February 1998. The question is not whether the *Post* should "denounce" leaks—truly a red herring—but whether it will use leaks that put U.S. personnel in danger.

"Openness is something we believe in. But it is not anybody's inalienable right to share secret information. The problem is people believe they have some power from leaking classified information. People have lost their sense of discipline, and at the end of the day we will lose our ability to serve you because of that lack of discipline."

DCI **GEORGE TENET** in testimony before the Senate Armed Services Committee, 2 February 1999.

"I have nothing but contempt and anger for those who betray our trust by exposing the names of our sources. They are, in my view, the most insidious of traitors."

Former President and DCI **GEORGE H. W. BUSH** at CIA Headquarters, 26 April 1999.

"I regard them as dissidents and patriots."

Washington Times reporter **BILL GERTZ** on those who leak classified information to him; quoted in *Secrecy and Government Bulletin* (May 1999).

"The nature of the leaking that's going on in this town is unprecedented. It is compromising sources and methods. It is jeopardizing American security. . . . I would say to all of my colleagues in the executive branch that 95 percent of what leaks comes out of the executive branch, because some people believe they have some free right to disseminate this information."

DCI **GEORGE TENET** in testimony to the House intelligence committee, 22 July 1999.

"The fact is that leaking classified information has become one of the biggest threats to the survival of U.S. intelligence. When you ask the men and women in this community to put their lives on the line and spend the money and time they do to protect the American people, and I see that investment go down the drain and my officers' lives placed at risk because of frivolous Washington parlor games, I get damn mad."

DCI **GEORGE TENET**, interview in *USA Today*, 11 October 2000.

"Once, I had to plead with a major media executive to withhold one aspect of a forthcoming story in order to save an agent's life. I was successful—the executive was more of a patriot than the Central Intelligence Agency employee who had leaked the story—but I had to tell the executive a great deal about a very sensitive operation in order to win him over to my position."

Former DCI **R. JAMES WOOLSEY** in the *Wall Street Journal*, 3 November 2000.

"Why did he do it? In 25 years as a reporter, I've asked myself that question about hundreds of people who told me things they shouldn't have. 'Why people tell things to reporters is one of life's greatest mysteries,' I confided to a gathering of intelligence buffs 14 years ago. Someone from CIA's counterintelligence staff was in the audience, and he had my comment printed up as a poster—presumably as a warning to his fellow spooks to keep their mouths shut. But people talk—even when they know they shouldn't. And the fundamental reason, I have concluded over the years, is because they're human beings. They get lonely. . . . They want to share the details of what they're doing with people who are interested. And who is more interested and solicitous than a good reporter?"

Veteran journalist and spy novelist **DAVID IGNATIUS** in the *Washington Post*, 1 July 2001. Many reporters could have made successful careers as CIA case officers.

"We don't pretend to be neutral on this subject. Newspapers publish leaked material; our reporters solicit leaks. And some of the leaked material we publish is classified. But it is a mistake to imagine that all leaks of classified information are bad. . . . There have been times when the disclosure of irrationally or unjustifiably classified information has served the public."

> *Washington Post* editorial, 24 August 2001. Not *all* leaks are bad, and *there have been times* . . .

"They have an intercept of some information that includes people associated with bin Laden who acknowledged a couple of targets were hit."

> Senator **ORRIN HATCH** of Utah speaking to reporters after receiving a classified intelligence briefing on 11 September 2001, as reported by the *Chicago Tribune*, 14 September 2001. Hatch denied leaking classified information.

"It's now time to be extremely cautious about what we report. Please take great care to make sure that our broadcasts don't inadvertently pass along information that could prove helpful to those who would do harm to our citizens, our officials and our military. Let's be careful about reporting specifics of presidential travel, of security arrangements, of secret military plans, troop movements and the like."

> NBC News executive **BILL WHEATLEY** in a memorandum to staffers; cited in *USA Today*, 19 September 2001. About time, but what happens if ABC or CBS is going to run with a story?

"I want Congress to hear it loud and clear: It is unacceptable behavior to leak classified information when we have troops at risk."

> President **GEORGE W. BUSH** at the White House, 9 October 2001, as reported by ABC News.

"That's what I do for a living—I talk to people who prefer not to be identified. I'm not going to talk about this."

> **SEYMOUR HERSH**, showing greater security awareness than his sources; quoted in *Time* (4 February 2002).

"Note to insiders: Our address is 3600 New York Ave. NE, Washington, D.C. 20002."

> Invitation to leakers by *Washington Times* reporter **BILL GERTZ** in his "Inside the Ring" feature, 12 April 2002. Gertz also helpfully provides his e-mail address.

"Intercepted communications could be a more promising source of intelligence if it weren't for our national tendency to logorrhea about the subject. U.S. intelligence figured out in the late 1990s how to intercept bin Laden's satellite telephone conversations and then someone talked to the press about it: the source of course dried up. Recently there have been periodic press reports about how we have been able to intercept al Qaeda e-mail and other communications. (Hint to the blabbermouths in the government who have access to intercepts of terrorist communications: Members of al Qaeda read newspapers.)"

> Former DCI **R. JAMES WOOLSEY** in the *Wall Street Journal*, 21 May 2002. But probably not books of quotations, right?

"It's outrageous, it's inexcusable, and they ought to be in jail."

> Secretary of Defense **DONALD RUMSFELD** on Pentagon officials who leaked to the *New York Times* an alleged U.S. plan to attack Iraq; quoted in *USA Today*, 23 July 2002.

"Before [September 11th], I believed that I should vacuum up all the secrets I could and make them available on the Internet. Now, I have to first determine whether the material disclosed can be used by terrorists."

> **STEPHEN AFTERGOOD** of the Federation of American Scientists and perennial critic of CIA for its secrecy; quoted in the *Los Angeles Times*, 5 January 2003. Better late than never, but is the FAS qualified to decide what would help terrorists?

"As members of a profession that relies heavily on the willingness of government officials to defy their bosses and give the public vital information, we oppose 'leak investigations' in principle. But that does not mean there can never be a circumstance in which leaks are wrong—the disclosure of troop movements in wartime is a clear example."

> *New York Times* editorial, 2 October 2003. Two problems here: first, the view of the *Times* is that government workers should be able to decide for themselves, as against their "bosses," what is information "vital" for the public to know. Second, what the *Times* considers clearly a rare exception to this rule may well be inadequate.

LEGISLATIVE OVERSIGHT

Being a good student of democratic government, the Literary Spy accepts the need for congressional oversight. Even with its flaws, it sure beats the alternatives. The tendency of some politicians to reveal secrets, to posture for the press, and to play politics, however, can severely damage U.S. intelligence, as the congressional investigations of the 1970s demonstrated. The Literary Spy is not the first to reflect on the objective fact that standards for employment at U.S. intelligence agencies are much more stringent than those for election to the U.S. Congress.

See also: Budgets; Covert Action; Critics & Defenders; Intelligence & American Culture; Leaks; Presidents & Intelligence

"It would be agreeable to Congress *to know the disposition of foreign powers toward us,* and we hope this object will engage your attention. We need not hint that *great circumspection and impenetrable security are necessary.*"

> The Continental Congress's Committee of Secret Correspondence to an American spy in London, December 1775; cited in Andrew, *For the President's Eyes Only* (1995). The U.S. Congress has not always followed this tradition.

"It is somewhat ironic that at the beginning of the republic intelligence operations were conducted by the forebearer of today's Congress—the Continental Congress planned, directed, and carried out intelligence activities in support of the war effort. Secret committees of the Congress were formed for this purpose, and covert actions, use of secret writing, codes and ciphers, protection of sources, compartmentation, propaganda, and deception all were in the 'bag of tricks' used by these 'legislative intelligence officials.'"

> **JAMES VAN WAGENEN**, DIA chair, at the Joint Military Intelligence College, *Studies in Intelligence* 40 (1996).

"Communicate no other intelligence to Congress at large than what may be necessary to promote the common weal, not to gratify the curiosity of individuals."

> **JOHN JAY** to Robert Morris, October 1776; cited in Miller, *Spying for America* (1989). An early expression of the difference between an established "need to know" and the far more common "wanna know."

"The Secret Committee [should] take proper and effectual measures to procure a quantity of hard money, not less than 20,000 dollars, to be lodged in the hands of the commander in chief, for the purpose of secret services."

> Continental Congress, 27 November 1776; cited in Knott, *Secret and Sanctioned* (1996). Knott notes that this was

"the first American appropriation of funds for intelligence purposes."

"The crusading oversight bodies of the 1970s (Church committee and Pike committee) would have been appalled at the activities authorized by the Congress's founders. For example, [the Continental Congress] devised and implemented covert action operations, approved non-attributed black propaganda, and on learning of abuses in mail opening did not bring it to a halt. Rather, it issued firm instructions narrowing the scope of who was authorized to do so."

EDWARD F. SAYLE, "The Historical Underpinnings of the U.S. Intelligence Community," *International Journal of Intelligence and Counterintelligence* (spring 1986).

"There is as much intrigue in this state-house as in the Vatican, but as little secrecy as in a boarding school. It mortifies me on this occasion to reflect that the rules of Congress on the subject of secrecy, which are far too general and perhaps for that reason more frequently violated, restrain me from saying twenty things to you which have ceased to be private."

JOHN JAY, president of the Continental Congress, to George Washington, 26 April 1779; cited in Knott, *Secret and Sanctioned* (1996).

"If he still perseveres, I do not wish to be informed of any other Particulars."

JOHN JAY, president of the Continental Congress, to George Washington regarding the activities of a specific intelligence agent, 24 August 1779; cited in Knott, *Secret and Sanctioned* (1996).

"If men were angels, no government would be necessary. If angels were to govern men, neither external nor internal controls would be necessary. In framing a government which is to be adminis-

tered by men over men, the great difficulty lies in this: you must first enable the government to control the governed; and in the next place oblige it to control itself."

JAMES MADISON, *The Federalist*, No. 51. This Founding Father gives the basis for government in general as well as for legislative oversight of intelligence.

"There are cases where the most useful intelligence may be obtained, if the persons possessing it can be relieved from apprehensions of discovery. Those apprehensions will operate on those persons whether they are actuated by mercenary or friendly motives; and there doubtless are many of both descriptions who would rely on the secrecy of the President, and would not confide in that of the Senate, and still less in that of a largely popular assembly."

JOHN JAY, *The Federalist*, No. 64. A Founding Father argues for *not* telling the Congress everything.

"Decision, secrecy, and dispatch are incompatible with the genius of a body so variable and so numerous."

ALEXANDER HAMILTON on the House of Representatives, *The Federalist*, No. 75.

"It is essential the Executive should have half a million of secret service money. If the measure cannot be carried without it, the expenditure may be with the approbation of three members of each house of Congress. But 'twere better without this incumbrance."

ALEXANDER HAMILTON to Oliver Wolcott, Jr., 5 June 1798; cited in Knott, *Secret and Sanctioned* (1996).

"[Thomas] Jefferson believed that the president alone had the authority to make the difficult but often necessary decision to employ surreptitious means to further American interests abroad. Those seeking evidence of an alternative tradition in the American experience, one emphasizing strict congressional oversight of clandestine operations and an aversion to executive secrecy, will find an examination of the Jefferson presidency a discouraging experience."

STEPHEN KNOTT, *Secret and Sanctioned* (1996).

"It was given for all purposes to which a secret service fund should or could be applied to the public benefit. For Spies, if the gentleman pleases."

Senator **JOHN FORSYTH**, February 1831, revealing the nature of the president's secret contingency fund; quoted in Miller, *Spying for America* (1989).

"There is no doubt that [General William] Donovan deceived Congress when [in March 1945] he denied knowledge of the Communist links of . . . OSS personnel. [Moreover,] he concealed from Congress the extent of OSS dealings with the CPUSA [Communist Party of the United States]. If a senior intelligence official were to so mislead a congressional committee today, the deception would be regarded as worthy of a criminal charge."

HARVEY KLEHR et al., *The Secret World of American Communism* (1995).

"The final legacy of McCarthyism . . . was that it discredited the notion of congressional oversight and therefore contributed to much ignorance . . . about the true nature, significance, and quality of the Agency's intelligence work. . . . Had there been closer congressional supervision [in the 1950s], certain mistakes might have been avoided, and the CIA might have had a clearer idea of the restraints necessary to its long-term good name and success."

RHODRI JEFFREYS-JONES, *The CIA and American Democracy* (1989). Both the Congress and CIA have learned much in this regard.

"In the view of the general public, and of the Congress . . . a national intelligence service in those days was more or less a part and parcel of our overall defense establishment. Therefore, as our defense budget went sailing through Congress under the impact of the Soviet extension of power into Eastern Europe, Soviet probes into Iran and Greece, the Berlin blockade, and eventually the Korean War, the relatively modest CIA budget in effect got a free ride, buried as it was in the Defense and other budgets. When Directors [of Central Intelligence] appeared before the Congress, which they did only rarely, the main concern of the members was often to make sure we had what we needed to do our job."

CIA's legislative counsel on attitudes in the late 1940s and early 1950s; in Anne Karalekas, "The History of the Central Intelligence Agency," in Leary, *The Central Intelligence Agency* (1984). Walter Pforzheimer held the position during this period.

"There isn't a single member of this Senate that's so lowly that he can't make life unbearable for you fellows if he decides he wants to do it."

Senator **RICHARD RUSSELL** to a CIA official; quoted in Ranelagh, *The Agency* (1986). Lowly is as lowly does.

"[The Senate] trusted the director to give them an objective intelligence appraisal of what was going on around the world. That was the strength of our position, but it was also its weakness. Seldom could we get them to concentrate on what we were doing and why we were doing it. The House paid a lot more attention, particularly in the Appropriations Committee. . . . They knew our appropriations, line by line. Sure, they were hidden in the defense budget, but to get in they had to pass the committee. But we couldn't get the Senate interested."

LAURENCE HOUSTON, CIA's general counsel until 1973, on congressional oversight in the 1950s and early 1960s; quoted in Ranelagh, *The Agency* (1986).

"The difficulty in connection with asking questions and obtaining information is that we might obtain information which I personally would rather not have, unless it was essential for me as a Member of Congress to have it.... It is not a question of reluctance on the part of CIA officials to speak to us. Instead, it is a question of our reluctance, if you will, to seek information and knowledge on subjects which I personally as a Member of Congress and as a citizen would rather not have, unless I believed it to be my responsibility to have it because it might involve the lives of American citizens."

Senator **LEVERETT SALTONSTALL**, Republican from Massachusetts, in 1955 on CIA briefings to Congress; quoted in Ranelagh, *The Agency* (1986).

"Although knowledge of the U-2 [spyplane] project was a closely guarded secret within both the [Central Intelligence] Agency and the Eisenhower administration, DCI Dulles decided that a few key members of Congress should be told about the project. On 24 February 1956, Dulles met with Senators Leverett Saltonstall and Richard B. Russell, the ranking members of the Senate Armed Services Committee and its subcommittee on the CIA.... As a result of the senators' recommendation that the senior members of the House Appropriations Committee be briefed, Dulles later met with its ranking members, Representatives John Taber and Clarence Cannon. Official Congressional knowledge of the U-2 project remained confined to this small group for the next four years. The House Armed Services Committee and its

CIA subcommittee did not receive a CIA briefing on the U-2 project until after the loss of Francis Gary Powers's U-2 over the Soviet Union in May 1960."

GREGORY PEDLOW and **DONALD WELZENBACH**, *CIA and the U-2 Program* (1998).

"Before 1956 there were no formal subcommittees of Congress dealing with the CIA.... It is not just that the executive and the CIA did not want to tell Congress much; Congress also accepted the primacy of secrecy and did not want to know that much.... [It] was more interested in making sure the CIA had what it needed in the fight against communism than in overseeing its operations.... Watergate and Chile, coming on the heels of the war in Vietnam, changed all that."

GREGORY TREVERTON, *Covert Action* (1987).

"When the members of Congress got their noses into the private affairs of the President the setup ceased to function for the President."

Former President **HARRY TRUMAN** on congressional involvement in intelligence, letter of 11 April 1963; cited in Pisani, *CIA and the Marshall Plan* (1991).

"Dick, if I catch you trying to upset the Chilean election, I will get up on the Senate floor and blow the operation."

Senator **WILLIAM FULBRIGHT**, chairman of the U.S. Senate Foreign Relations Committee, to DCI Richard Helms, April 1969; quoted in Helms, *A Look over My Shoulder* (2003). Fulbright knew that CIA had assisted Chile's Christian Democrats in the 1964 election.

"One distinguished member apparently has never been quite clear on the difference between Libya, Lebanon, and Liberia.... [Another,] when shown a chart of various categories of covert action, reacted sharply and demanded to know, 'What the hell are you doing in covert parliamentary operations?' When it was explained that the box on the chart he was pointing to was 'paramilitary operations,' he was much reassured, remarking, 'The more of these, the better—just don't go fooling around with parliamentary stuff—you don't know enough about it.'"

> JOHN MAURY, senior CIA operations officer and legislative counsel in the 1970s, on the challenges of briefing certain members of Congress; cited in Ranelagh, *The Agency* (1986).

"Back in the 1950s and early 1960s, when I was on the House Appropriations Committee, no more than ten or twelve members of Congress were fully and regularly informed about the budget and the activities of the CIA. For eight years prior to January 1965, I was one of this group. By 1975, however, that number had swollen to between fifty and seventy-five. Inevitably, there were leaks."

> Former President GERALD FORD, *A Time to Heal* (1979).

"It was the senators and representatives themselves who [before the mid-1970s] voted against the various proposals to strengthen congressional oversight of the CIA."

> JOHN RANELAGH, *The Agency* (1986).

"Spying is spying. You have to make up your mind that you are going to have an intelligence agency and protect it as such, and shut your eyes and take what is coming."

> Senator JOHN STENNIS, Democrat from Mississippi, in 1971; quoted in Colby, *Honorable Men* (1978). The Literary Spy would argue for the "eyes wide open" approach.

"I submit that there is no federal agency of our government whose activities receive closer scrutiny and 'control' than the CIA."

> Former CIA Executive Director LYMAN KIRKPATRICK; quoted in *U.S. News and World Report* (11 October 1971).

"It is shameful for the American people to be so misled. There is no federal agency of our government whose activities receive less scrutiny and control than the CIA."

> Senator STUART SYMINGTON, Democrat from Missouri, 23 November 1971; quoted in Marchetti and Marks, *CIA and the Cult of Intelligence* (1974).

"In pre-Watergate days Congress and CIA had a strong and effective relationship. We could brief Congress candidly, confident that our intelligence would not be leaked to the press and thus to the world and to our adversaries. At that time, Congress operated under the discipline of a strong committee system, the committees headed by men of discretion and integrity. . . . What has seldom been realized by the press and public about the heated demands for closer, more open congressional control of CIA is that to a fair extent this was a revolt within the ranks of Congress against the discipline of its leadership."

> Former DDI R. JACK SMITH, *The Unknown CIA* (1989).

"I went up to the Hill and said, 'Mr. Chairman, I want to tell you about some of our programs.' To which the Senator quickly replied: 'No, no, my boy, don't tell me. Just go ahead and do it—but I don't want to know!'"

> DCI JAMES SCHLESINGER relating a 1973 meeting with Senator John Stennis, chairman of the intelligence subcommittee of the Senate Armed Services Committee; quoted in Jeffreys-Jones and Andrew, *Eternal Vigilance* (1997).

"It is a bit unsettling that 26 years after the passage of the National Security Act the scope of real Congressional oversight, as opposed to nominal Congressional oversight, remains unformed and uncertain."

Congressman **LUCIAN NEDZI** in 1973; quoted in Leary, *The Central Intelligence Agency* (1984).

"The months I spent with the Pike Committee [the House committee investigating U.S. intelligence in 1975] made my tour in Vietnam seem like a picnic. I would vastly prefer to fight the Viet Cong than deal with a polemical investigation by a Congressional committee."

CIA officer responsible for liaison with the House Select Committee on Intelligence (the Pike Committee); quotation in CIA's Historical Intelligence Collection.

"The CIA was subjected to the sort of scrutiny usually reserved for the intelligence agencies of nations conquered in war."

THOMAS POWERS on the congressional hearings of 1975, in *The Man Who Kept the Secrets* (1979).

"I recall only two instances in intelligence history in which the files of intelligence services were as thoroughly ransacked as those of the Agency during [the mid-1970s congressional] investigations."

Former DCI **RICHARD HELMS**, *A Look over My Shoulder* (2003). Helms cites the case of the Tsarist Russian files, thrown open by the Bolsheviks, and that of the Nazi services after World War II.

"As long as the CIA remains the President's loyal and personal tool to be used around the world at his and his top advisor's discretion, no President is likely, barring strong, unforeseen pressure, to insist that the agency's operations be brought under closer outside scrutiny."

VICTOR MARCHETTI and **JOHN MARKS**, *CIA and the Cult of Intelligence* (1974).

"We've got to dismantle the monster!"

Senator **FRED HARRIS**, Democrat from Oklahoma, regarding CIA, September 1975; quoted in Knott, *Secret and Sanctioned* (1996).

"The Committee finds that Congress has failed to provide the necessary statutory guidelines to ensure that intelligence agencies carry out their missions in accord with constitutional processes. Mechanisms for, and the practice of, congressional oversight have not been adequate."

U.S. Senate, *Final Report of the Select Committee to Study Governmental Operations with respect to Intelligence Activities* [the Church Committee], Book I (April 1976).

"It remains my opinion that Senator Church operated his committee at a level of self-serving hypocrisy unusual even for other run-of-the-mill presidential hopefuls."

Former DCI **RICHARD HELMS**, *A Look over My Shoulder* (2003).

"It would be a mistake to attempt to require that the Congress receive prior notification of *all* covert activities. . . . I believe that any attempt by the legislative branch to impose a strict prior notification requirement upon the Executive's foreign policy initiatives is neither feasible nor consistent with our constitutionally mandated separation of powers."

Senator **JOHN G. TOWER**, dissenting statement in U.S. Senate, *Final Report of the Senate Select Committee to Study Governmental Operations with respect to Intelligence Activities* [the Church Committee], Book II (April 1976). Tower was vice-chairman of the Select Committee.

"Had I tried to resist Congress [during its investigations in the 1970s], we would have been inundated by a flood of subpoenas and contempt citations. The information we would have tried to withhold would have been gotten out of us anyway. Only it would have been gotten out of us in the worst possible way—dragged out, raising all sorts of suspicions about what we were trying to hide and why, and what further hideous secrets were still being covered up. The sensations, the distortions and exaggerations, the misunderstandings, the utter lack of perspective on what was revealed were only starters to what would have happened in the other event, and the damage to the Agency would have been far greater."

> Former DCI **WILLIAM COLBY** on his disclosures to the Congress, in *Honorable Men* (1978). Colby's apologia is impossible to verify and thus remains a point of controversy among intelligence officers.

"[William] Casey was guilty of contempt of Congress from the day he was sworn in as DCI."

> Former DCI **ROBERT GATES**, *From the Shadows* (1996).

"It gets down to one, little, simple phrase: I am pissed off!"

> Senator **BARRY GOLDWATER** informing DCI William Casey that CIA had not adequately informed Congress of the mining of Nicaragua's harbors, letter of 9 April 1984; cited in Turner, *Secrecy and Democracy* (1985). Others say that Goldwater *had* been informed; he was just pissed off at not remembering.

"We briefed the Senate Intelligence Committee on the eighth and the thirteenth of March [1984], by which time several ships had already struck the mines. The Sandinistas had publicly complained that we'd mined their harbors. For goodness' sake —if the Sandinistas were whining and the contras were informing Lloyd's of London, how the hell can anyone believe we were trying to keep it a secret from Congress?"

> Former senior CIA operations officer **DUANE CLARRIDGE**, *A Spy for All Seasons* (1997).

"On intelligence and covert CIA operations it was reasonable for the Congress to establish special monitoring committees and mandate executive consultation with these committees, in secret, about specific operations. . . . This allowed Executive Branch flexibility but brought legislators at least marginally into the game. They could ask hard questions about operations they felt were wrong or simply stupid."

> **I. M. DESTLER, LESLIE GELB,** and **ANTHONY LAKE,** *Our Own Worst Enemy* (1984).

"The larger oversight role Congress demanded [in the 1970s and 1980s] was really just part of a general trend of a legislature that was becoming more active on most national security issues. . . . People may argue whether this legislative activism is a good fact or a bad fact, but it is nevertheless a fact."

> **BRUCE BERKOWITZ** and **ALLAN GOODMAN,** *Strategic Intelligence* (1989).

"An effective Congressional oversight is a crucial part of the blueprint for the essential CIA that the nation needs. . . . Accountability to the elected representatives of the people is a fundamental concept in the American political process. CIA has always been accountable to the President, but its relationship to Congress has been too vague and too little understood."

> Former DDI **RAY CLINE**, *Secrets, Spies and Scholars* (1976).

"There is a sense in the executive branch that the secrets belong to them and not to the Congress because intelligence belongs to the executive branch."

BERNARD McMAHON, staff director of the Senate Select Committee on Intelligence, October 1985; quoted in Ranelagh, *The Agency* (1986).

"If the oversight process is to work at all, it cannot do so on the front pages of American newspapers. The cost in compromise of sources, damaged morale and the effect on our overall capabilities is simply too high."

DCI **WILLIAM CASEY** in the *Washington Post,* 15 November 1985.

"Once one of the congressional committees on intelligence, when authorizing a new satellite, went so far as to specify the frequency on which it was to perform certain functions. That was ridiculous and dangerous."

Former DCI **STANSFIELD TURNER**, *Secrecy and Democracy* (1985).

"Virtually all CIA assessments go to the two congressional intelligence committees, so that many senators and representatives are often as well if not better informed about the CIA's information and assessments on a given subject than concerned policymakers. . . . Most specialists writing about the change in recent years in the balance of power between the executive and Congress on national security policy cite Watergate and Vietnam as primary causes. I believe there was a third principal factor: the obtaining, by Congress in the mid-1970s, of access to intelligence information essentially equal to that of the executive branch. . . . The end result is a strengthening of the congressional hand in policy debates and a great heightening of tensions between the CIA and the rest of the executive branch. . . . The CIA today finds itself in

a remarkable position, involuntarily poised nearly equidistant between the executive and legislative branches."

DDI **ROBERT GATES**, "The CIA and American Foreign Policy," *Foreign Affairs* (winter 1987–88).

"A Deputy Director of Central Intelligence has remarked that the CIA is already 'equidistant' between the president and the two Intelligence Committees of the Congress. Manifestly, this is an unconstitutional development, which all concerned with the integrity of the Constitution should oppose."

EUGENE V. ROSTOW in James Gaston, ed., *Grand Strategy and the Decisionmaking Process* (1992).

"I was on the [Senate] intelligence committee during the Reagan years. The CIA came up and briefed us on something they were going to do that I thought was wrong. . . . I asked for a secret session of the United States Senate. I demanded it. We had a secret session of the United States Senate. I stood up before my colleagues and I said, 'I just learned this is what the administration is going to do. It's against the interest of the United States of America in my view, and you should all know about it."

Senator **JOSEPH BIDEN** on *The NewsHour with Jim Lehrer,* PBS, 10 October 2001.

"I simply do not want to leave the Congress feeling by our answers that in some way the CIA has been disingenuous in dealing with them. I'd rather tell them we have an answer but we are not going to give it to them. And I'd rather fight it out on that level and sometimes lose than to give half an answer or say the question wasn't asked in the right way, because trust is absolutely vital in this relationship."

DCI **WILLIAM WEBSTER**, 13 April 1988, in *1988 Speeches*.

"There must be absolute truth in dealing with our oversight committees which act as surrogates for the American people . . . because unless we can find a system of oversight that builds rather than erodes trust and confidence, we are doomed to repeat some of the history that affects and occasionally hinders all secret organizations."

DCI **WILLIAM WEBSTER**, address to the Bar Association of St. Louis, 29 April 1988, in *1988 Speeches*.

"I firmly believe that the oversight responsibilities exercised by Congress are both necessary and beneficial. There must be a dependable system of oversight and accountability which builds, rather than erodes, trust between those who have the intelligence responsibility and those who are the elected representatives of the American people."

DCI **WILLIAM WEBSTER**, remarks at Georgetown University, 10 May 1988, in *1988 Speeches*.

"In dealing with the Congress there is no excuse for deception."

DCI **WILLIAM WEBSTER**, remarks to the District of Columbia Judicial Conference, 23 May 1988, in *1988 Speeches*.

"If the oversight system had not been established, then the intelligence community would have remained an anomaly in the government. Critics could reasonably argue that a secret intelligence community had no place in American democracy, or that the community was out of control. Once acceptable oversight mechanisms existed, these arguments were for the most part deflated."

BRUCE BERKOWITZ and **ALLAN GOODMAN**, *Strategic Intelligence* (1989).

"The resolutions establishing each Intelligence Committee provide that classified information and other information received by the committee in confidence may not be disclosed outside the committee other than in a closed session of the Senate or House of Representatives, respectively, unless the committee votes to release such information and such vote does not prompt an objection from the Executive Branch. Failure of members to abide by this restriction subjects them to investigation and, where appropriate, to referral to the Ethics Committee of each House for disciplinary action. In addition, the chairmen of each committee routinely advise their members that anyone who fails to protect such information will be asked to leave the committee. There have, in fact, been instances in which members have left the intelligence committees, either because of an infraction of security rules or because they were unwilling to remain bound by these limits on their actions. . . . Members of each committee receive access to classified information held by the committee by virtue of their elective office, i.e., they are not subjected to background investigations. . . . U.S. intelligence agencies are required by law to furnish to the oversight committees 'any information or material concerning intelligence activities . . . which is in their custody or control and which is requested by either of the intelligence committees in order to carry out its authorized responsibilities.' The law specifically provides that even information which reveals intelligence sources and methods shall not be denied the committees. In short, the committees, as a matter of law and principle, recognize no limitation on their access to information."

Senate Select Committee on Intelligence report "Legislative Oversight of Intelligence Activities," October 1994. The report goes on to say that, in practice, the committees do not seek to learn details about agents or collection operations because "no law can readily compel full access to information if intelligence agencies are convinced that such access will result in catastrophic disclosures of information on their sensitive sources and methods."

"Twenty years of congressional oversight of the intelligence community has led to the imposition of stultifying bureaucratic regulations that have transformed the CIA into a General Services Administration with Ph.Ds."

STEPHEN KNOTT, "Let Secret Agencies Stay Secret," *Washington Times*, 20 May 1996. Could GSA go toe-to-toe with the Taliban and al-Qaeda?

"As the situation now stands, one committee, in one branch of Congress, or even one committee member, can veto a secret presidential initiative."

STEPHEN KNOTT, *Secret and Sanctioned* (1996).

"The choice does not have to be between executive or legislative sovereignty over intelligence; the challenge is to tap into the best attributes of both branches in the service of the national security. The Congress brings to the table a strong sense of what the American people will support, plus a large amount of foreign policy expertise in its own right. It also provides a second opinion."

LOCH JOHNSON, "The CIA and the Question of Accountability," in Jeffreys-Jones and Andrews, *Eternal Vigilance* (1997). Potentially 535 second opinions.

"There is nothing wrong with congressional oversight. In fact, there is much to be said for it—provided that congressmen and their staff play by the rules of secrecy. . . . My problem with oversight is that the congressional staff are all wanna-be spies and demand access to all the secrets, yet none are trained or polygraphed—as are all employees of the CIA, NSA, and other intelligence agencies.

Some congressional staffers have tried and failed to get hired by these institutions; I would bet the farm that many could not sit for a counterintelligence polygraph without exhibiting deception."

Former senior CIA operations officer **DUANE CLARRIDGE**, *A Spy for All Seasons* (1997).

"Every once in a while, you hear some nutty congressman get up and say, well, we ought to put the money [for intelligence] in downtown Detroit or we ought to forget about intelligence, there are no enemies anymore. Well, heck with them."

Former President and DCI **GEORGE H. W. BUSH** giving them heck at a conference on the Cold War; quoted on CNN, 22 November 1999.

"I've never gone to one of those [intelligence] briefings where I couldn't turn on the TV or pick up a newspaper and get much better information. You get a lot more than you do from these jerks."

Senator **JOHN McCAIN**, Republican from Arizona, on CIA briefings of Congress; quoted on NBC's *Meet the Press*, 21 October 2001.

"Mr. Black will probably dissemble."

From a briefing book prepared by congressional staff for the joint House-Senate inquiry into the intelligence agencies and the September 11 attacks, referring to expected testimony by CIA officer Cofer Black, the former chief of the DCI's Counterterrorist Center; as reported in the *Washington Post*, 27 September 2002. This guidance was reported during the 26 September hearing by Senator Pat Roberts of Kansas.

"Dear Mr. Chairman,

I am grateful to Senator Roberts for revealing at this morning's hearing the attitude of the Joint Inquiry Staff regarding the testimony of CIA witnesses.

There can be no doubt about the meaning of the words Senator Roberts read. Your staff predicted to your members that one of the most senior and decorated officers of this Agency would not tell the truth. This suggestion is an affront not only to him but to every man and woman in the CIA.

The issue of how best to fight terrorism is a complex one, and reasonable people can disagree. It is clear to me, however, that some [of your] staff are acting not out of genuine disagreement but with bias, preconceived notions, and apparent animus.

Mr. Chairman, we have devoted considerable resources to providing an extraordinary amount of information and to answering your questions as fully and completely as possible—all while fighting a war.

I will not countenance our officers being accused of 'dissembling' by uninformed, anonymous staff.

I would appreciate hearing from you the steps you plan to take to eliminate the misguided efforts of the Joint Inquiry Staff to poison the atmosphere of what should be an exercise in objective and fair oversight.

Sincerely,

George J. Tenet"

Text in full of DCI **GEORGE TENET**'s letter to Senator Bob Graham, chairman of the Senate intelligence committee, 26 September 2002. Tenet is a former staff director of the Senate intelligence committee and has worked for Democrats and Republicans alike.

"Congressional oversight of intelligence is a key element in the effective functioning of the Intelligence Community (IC). When oversight has been capable and constructive, it has been a major asset to the IC. When degraded or misused, it has been an albatross around the neck of the intelligence agencies."

MARVIN C. OTT, "Partisanship and the Decline of Intelligence Oversight," *International Journal of Intelligence and Counterintelligence* (spring 2003).

"Congress is composed of members who keep their mouths shut and those who do not. More specifically, there will always be those in Congress who think they have a constitutional—not to say God-granted—right, without consultation with anyone, to expose any operation or activity of which they do not approve."

Former DCI **RICHARD HELMS**, *A Look over My Shoulder* (2003).

"I really fear these investigations, if they turn into witch-hunts. The worst thing that can happen is a demoralized CIA that's back on its heels, that thinks everybody is against them, that they have to hire lawyers [and] testify before Congress. If you're constantly pulling up the flowers to see if they're growing, you could do more harm than good with one of these investigations."

Newsweek editor **EVAN THOMAS** on *Inside Washington*, WUSA-TV, 7 February 2004.

LIAISON

Liaison is of little interest to spy novelists and is generally ignored in serious scholarly work on intelligence. Nonetheless, this unsung cooperation of foreign intelligence services—in wartime, during the Cold War, or while fighting terrorism; in joint operations, covert support, or sharing of analysis—is responsible for some of the greatest successes of U.S. intelligence. It also has been the source of huge headaches, and not just for our side.

See also: Intelligence & American Culture

"On your own intelligence rely not."

Proverbs 3:5 (New American).

"The US Army, while engaged in the great Indian Wars on the Western Plains, showed itself equally willing to cooperate with British authorities regarding information on the most formidable of Indian challenges, a British intelligence report on Sitting Bull being supplied to the Americans in the late 1870s."

> BRADLEY SMITH, "The American Road to Central Intelligence," in Jeffreys-Jones and Andrew, *Eternal Vigilance* (1997).

"If the picture was painted too darkly, elements in the United States would say that it is useless to help us, for such help would be wasted and thrown away. If too bright a picture was painted, then there might be a tendency to withhold assistance."

> WINSTON CHURCHILL to the British War Cabinet, considering sharing intelligence on German war aims with Washington in mid-1940; quoted in Stafford, *Churchill and Secret Service* (1998).

"Does J. Edgar think he's fighting on Bunker Hill against us Redcoats?"

> British intelligence official WILLIAM STEPHENSON, sent to establish an SIS presence in New York City in May 1940, on the FBI's hostility to "British spies"; quoted in Polmar and Allen, *Encyclopedia of Espionage* (1997).

"Are we going to throw all our secrets into the American lap? If so, I am against it. It would be much better to go slow, as we have far more to give than they."

> WINSTON CHURCHILL as Anglo-American intelligence sharing got under way in late 1940; quoted in Stafford, *Churchill and Secret Service* (1998).

"Once convinced [by the ULTRA intercepts that Hitler was set to invade the USSR], Churchill immediately decided to tell Stalin. He passed on the intelligence disguising it as 'information from a

trusted agent.' By making it personal, keeping it brief and ordering it to be delivered to Stalin personally, he hoped to increase its impact. But Stalin dismissed it as evidence of a Churchill plot to embroil him with Hitler and told [Foreign Minister Molotov to pass it on to the German ambassador in Moscow."

> DAVID STAFFORD, *Churchill and Secret Service* (1998).

"The Soviet Union's most striking intelligence successes during [World War II] were achieved not against its enemies but against its allies in the wartime Grand Alliance: Britain and the United States."

> CHRISTOPHER ANDREW and VASILI MITROKHIN, *The Sword and the Shield: The Mitrokhin Archive* (1999). With allies like these . . .

"They came among us, these aspiring American spy-masters, like innocent girls from a finishing-school anxious to learn the seasoned demi-mondaine ways of old practitioners—in this case, the legendary British Secret Service."

> MALCOLM MUGGERIDGE, SIS officer during World War II, in *Chronicles of Wasted Time: The Infernal Grove* (1973).

"The British are just as much the enemy as the Germans."

> An obviously hyperbolic OSS officer on wartime friction with British intelligence; quoted in Knightley, *The Second Oldest Profession* (1988).

"[Britain] suggests 'coordination' and 'agreement,' but as employed here the word 'coordination' means 'control' and 'agreement' means 'dependence.' . . . This attempt of the British, by reason of their physical control of territory and communication, to subordinate the American intelligence and counterintelligence service is shortsighted and dangerous to the ultimate interests of both countries."

> OSS Director General **WILLIAM DONOVAN**, appealing to the Joint Chiefs of Staff against the British SIS insistence on directing intelligence operations in Europe, September 1943; cited in Corey Ford, *Donovan of OSS* (1970).

"I had found in London that there existed [in SIS] a profound distrust of all USA covert intelligence. Their personnel were regarded as amateurish and lacking in security. This attitude is difficult if not impossible to understand in view of our own sad experiences with Philby, Burgess, and Maclean."

> SIS wartime officer **PHILIP JOHNS** on relations with OSS; cited in West, *Faber Book of Espionage* (1993). Of course, they weren't British experiences just yet.

"A rock of safety."

> **WINSTON CHURCHILL**'s term for the postwar intelligence relationship between Great Britain and the United States; quoted in Stafford, *Churchill and Secret Service* (1998).

"Whenever we want to subvert any place, we find that the British own an island within easy reach."

> CIA operations chief **FRANK WISNER** in 1948, according to British turncoat Harold "Kim" Philby, *My Silent War* (1968).

"That prostitute I put in my pocket."

> **IVAN AGAYANTS**, Soviet intelligence chief in Paris in the late 1940s, referring during a 1952 lecture in Moscow to his penetrations of French intelligence; quoted in Schecter and Deriabin, *The Spy Who Saved the World* (1995). Such information from Soviet defectors like Peter Deriabin led British and U.S. intelligence to the conclusion in the early 1960s that information shared with the French would become known to Soviet intelligence.

"Blame it on the CIA."

> FBI Director **J. EDGAR HOOVER** telling a senior FBI official in 1954 to lie to the Royal Canadian Mounted Police

about a ten-year delay in sharing Soviet intercepts; quoted in Sullivan, *The Bureau* (1979).

"There are moments of great luxury in the life of a secret agent. There are assignments on which he is required to act the part of a very rich man; occasions when he takes refuge in good living to efface the memory of danger and the shadow of death; and times when, as was now the case, he is a guest in the territory of an allied Secret Service. From the moment the BOAC Stratocruiser taxied up to the International Air Terminal at Idlewild, James Bond was treated like royalty."

> Opening lines from **IAN FLEMING**, *Live and Let Die* (1954).

"I don't like to do this to my friends, but I will G-2 them if I have to."

> President **DWIGHT EISENHOWER** ordering U-2 flights to monitor British and French military preparations in the Middle East before the Suez crisis of October 1956; quoted in Andrew, *For the President's Eyes Only* (1995). "G-2" is army jargon for "intelligence."

"You know what M is, independent old devil. He's never been happy about NATO security. Why, right in the SHAPE Intelligence Division there are not only a couple of Frenchmen and an Italian, but the head of their Counterintelligence and Security section is a German!"

> The SIS Paris station chief to James Bond in **IAN FLEMING**, "From a View to a Kill" (1959). The next line is, "Bond whistled."

"In the period 1952 to 1963 the Agency acquired most of its clandestine information through liaison arrangements with foreign governments.... Maintenance of liaison became an end in itself, against which independent collection operations were judged.... Often, a proposal for an independent operation was rejected because a Station Chief believed that if the operation were exposed, the host government's intelligence service would be offended."

ANNE KARALEKAS, "The History of the Central Intelligence Agency," in Leary, *The Central Intelligence Agency* (1984).

"We've teamed up with the CIA to cover the world."

M, James Bond's fictional boss and chief of British intelligence, in **IAN FLEMING**, *Thunderball* (1961).

"After Philby [the SIS officer who was a spy for Moscow], the special relationship was never to be the same again, and his treachery so poisoned the minds of some CIA officers that . . . they were never again able totally to trust even their closest colleagues."

PHILLIP KNIGHTLEY, *The Second Oldest Profession* (1988).

"One of the most gratifying features of recent work in intelligence, and one that is quite unique in its long history, has been the growing cooperation established between the American intelligence services and their counterparts throughout the Free World which make common cause with us as we face a common peril."

Former DCI **ALLEN DULLES**, *The Craft of Intelligence* (1963).

"We are engaged in espionage against every country in the world. And this includes our friends, the countries of the people's democracies. For, who knows, some fine day they may become our enemies. Look what happened with China!"

Soviet GRU Colonel **OLEG PENKOVSKIY**, *The Penkovskiy Papers* (1966).

"There are no friendly services."

Attributed to legendary CIA counterintelligence chief **JAMES ANGLETON**; cited in Powers, *The Man Who Kept the Secrets* (1979).

"My God, your service thinks of everything!"

Israeli intelligence officer to British liaison officer **NICHOLAS ELLIOT**; during a nude swimming party, the Mossad officer noticed that Elliot was circumcised. Quoted in Polmar and Allen, *Encyclopedia of Espionage* (1997).

"[The] proliferation of investigating bodies with overlapping jurisdictions, large staffs, and extensive authority to demand access to documents and to compel witnesses to testify raised serious questions of security in the minds of all foreign intelligence officials who had previously cooperated with the CIA in the exchange of information. The British were understandably anxious to have reassurance that the content and sourcing of whatever reports we received from them would be given iron-clad protection against deliberate leakage or inadvertent revelation in the course of the investigation. . . . Because of their fear that the rash of revelations in Washington might endanger their own sensitive sources, I did notice that their source descriptions became less specific and more opaque, but I do not believe they withheld any substantive information that was important to the common defense. They looked on the Agency as a friend suffering from a severe but temporary illness."

CORD MEYER, *Facing Reality* (1980). Meyer was CIA's station chief in London in 1975 while the U.S. Congress conducted investigations into U.S. intelligence activities.

"There is to be no direct participation. Give the Bulgarians whatever they need, show them how to use it, and send someone to Sofia to train their people. But that's all."

> KGB Chairman **YURI ANDROPOV**, responding to a Bulgarian request to help assassinate prominent émigré Georgi Markov, 1978; quoted in Andrew and Mitrokhin, *The Mitrokhin Archive* (1999). KGB technicians provided an umbrella gun that shot poison pellets, and Markov was killed with it while waiting for a bus in London.

"During most of its history, the CIA's Teheran station had been oriented toward maintaining friendly relations with SAVAK, the Iranian secret police, and the Shah in order to ensure favorable conditions for U.S. technical collection sites targeted at Soviet missile testing, the highest priority intelligence operation in the country. This was an interesting example of an operation that though designed to protect valuable operations actually undermined them, or at least contributed to their loss."

> **WALTER LAQUEUR**, *A World of Secrets* (1985).

"The Brits are first-rate at intelligence. And quite inept at security, paradoxical though that may sound."

> **WILLIAM F. BUCKLEY, JR.**, *High Jinx* (1986).

"It is in most parts of the world a primary duty of the British station chief to use his superior prestige and cunning to persuade his CIA colleague to join with him in joint Anglo-American operations for which he supplies the brains and the CIA colleague supplies the funds."

> Former CIA officer **MILES COPELAND**; quoted in Knightley, *The Second Oldest Profession* (1988).

"We were your friends. We wear a lot of your decorations on our breasts. We were said to have made a great contribution to your security. Now, in our hour of need, I assume that you will not deny us your help."

> East German spymaster **MARCUS WOLF**, appealing to Soviet leader Mikhail Gorbachev to insist on amnesty for East German security and intelligence officers as a condition for German reunification, 22 October 1990; cited in Andrew and Mitrokhin, *The Mitrokhin Archive* (1999). Gorbachev turned him down, suggesting that there is no honor among communists.

"Without allied intelligence [during Operation Desert Storm] we were nearly blind. Our extreme dependence on American sources of information . . . was flagrant, particularly in the initial phase. [The United States] provided, when and how it wanted, the essential information necessary for the conduct of the conflict."

> French Defense Minister **PIERRE JOXE**, arguing that France needed its own reconnaissance satellites, May 1991; quoted in Richelson, *A Century of Spies* (1995).

"The state of liaison between foreign intelligence services is a barometer of foreign relations—when foreign policy objectives coincide, intelligence liaison flourishes. . . . But no matter how close, or how special, a relationship, no intelligence service will ever refuse the opportunity to look over a liaison partner's shoulder and to peek at any cards he may be holding close to his chest."

> Former CIA operations officer **WILLIAM HOOD**, *Mole* (1993). Hood's analogy doesn't always hold. The intelligence liaison relationship with a particular country could well be far better than diplomatic relations and may even be the *only* productive relationship.

"When each country was asked to say what was their top priority security concern, I said 'Terrorism,' and the Namibian delegate said 'Cattle rustling.'"

> Former chief of MI5 Dame **STELLA RIMINGTON**, *Open Secret* (2001).

"Formal covert-action programs and liaison programs are the two ways that the C.I.A. can provide a foreign intelligence service with money, training, equipment and information. But unlike formal covert-action programs, liaison programs require no Presidential authorization and no notification of Senate and House intelligence committees. The reason, in part, is the fear that few foreign intelligence officials would cooperate with the C.I.A. if they knew Congress would be told."

TIM WEINER, "C.I.A.'s 'Liaison' Programs: The Cloak That Can Hide All," *New York Times*, 5 April 1995.

"Liaison is not explicitly spelled out in the theoretical approaches as regards intelligence. If one looks to the intelligence cycle paradigm, one will even discover that liaison has no fixed location in the cycle because . . . it is actually a mode of activity in every point in the intelligence cycle [and] shares this quality with counter-intelligence."

Dutch analysts BOB DE GRAAF and CEES WIEBES in Jeffreys-Jones and Andrew, *Eternal Vigilance* (1997).

"I had no more than a handful of officers whose educational credentials put them on an equal footing with their European counterparts. . . . Graduates of American universities whose biggest claims to fame are a lively social life and a successful football team often just don't have the intellectual horsepower to go head-to-head with graduates of major European universities."

Former senior CIA operations officer DUANE CLARRIDGE, *A Spy for All Seasons* (1997).

"The Israeli government has acknowledged that Pollard was indeed spying on its behalf but has refused—despite constant entreaties—to provide the United States with a complete list of the documents that were turned over to it."

SEYMOUR HERSH, "The Traitor: The Case Against Jonathan Pollard," *New Yorker* (18 January 1999). Pollard was the U.S. Navy employee convicted in 1986 of spying for Israel.

"The CIA believe that because their technology is so superior their analysis is always right. . . . That means that the CIA often do not listen to Europeans and they are forever getting things wrong."

PAUL BEAVER of Jane's Defense Group; quoted in *The Guardian*, 28 April 1999.

"We have allies who spy on us for technological and commercial reasons. And we have countries who we cooperate with, Russia is one, on some very important issues like terrorism, but they still spy on us and we on them for other purposes. That's just the nature of the world."

Former DCI R. JAMES WOOLSEY; quoted by Reuters, 25 December 1999.

"We live in Central Europe, and this gives us insights that people in Washington, Paris, or London do not have."

LASZLO KOVAR, Hungary's minister for civilian security services; quoted by Reuters, 24 January 2000.

"When truly vital interests are at stake, the blood of the English-speaking peoples is thicker than the water of the Channel. We don't mind sharing our military secrets with Her Majesty's Canadian subjects; but how many of us could honestly claim to feel the same about the Belgians? It is true that we Anglo-Saxons often seem to be acting in concert. But this is not, as the French believe, because we are subservient to the United States. It is rather that our shared constitutional heritage often makes us react to things in the same way."

> **DANIEL HANNAN**, British conservative member of the European Parliament, "I'm proud we're spying on Europe," *Daily Telegraph*, 25 February 2000.

"Yes, my continental European friends we have spied on you.... We have spied on you because you bribe. Your companies' products are often more costly, less technically advanced or both, than your American competitors'. As a result you bribe a lot. So complicit are your governments that in several European countries bribes still are tax-deductible.... Get serious, Europeans. Stop blaming us and reform your own statist economic policies. Then your companies can become more efficient and innovative, and they won't need to resort to bribery to compete. And then we won't need to spy on you."

> Former DCI **R. JAMES WOOLSEY**, "Why We Spy on Our Allies," *Wall Street Journal*, 17 March 2000.

"Although no one is a complete friend in the intelligence world, with Britain and America it is as close as it gets."

> Former DCI **R. JAMES WOOLSEY**; quoted in the *Economist* (10 February 2001).

"In an intelligence multilateral alliance, secrecy, so far as sources and methods are concerned, is as strong as its weakest link. This means, I think, that the future of intelligence collaboration is much more in bilateral relationships . . . than in multilateral ones, and it is an embarrassing and nonetheless significant fact that not all members of the European Union keep secrets as successfully as others."

> **CHRISTOPHER ANDREW**, interview in the Italian online magazine *Per Aspera ad Veritatem* (May–August 1991).

"Trust is not a quality generally associated with espionage. But in its battle against a threat that seems at once global, seamless, and suicidal, the American intelligence community is going to need extraordinary cooperation from a patchwork of foreign security services that sometimes seem more devoted to stonewalling or subverting each other than to engaging a common enemy."

> **EVAN THOMAS**, "Handbook for the New War," *Newsweek* (8 October 2001).

"Alongside military and diplomatic coalitions, [we have] a global coalition of intelligence services. From around the world, from our allies and our partners, we receive and share information. We plan operations together and together in many instances we take terrorists off the streets."

> CIA operations chief **JAMES PAVITT**, address at Duke University, 11 April 2002.

"The Directorate of Operations has many close and productive liaison relationships. To us, these are force multipliers, valuable extensions of our own activities. With the stakes as high as they are, I would be irresponsible not to use every legitimate resource at my command. But, fundamentally, for the spies we run, the secrets we steal, and the insights we develop about the world . . . we rely first and foremost on ourselves and our skills as intelligence professionals."

> CIA operations chief **JAMES PAVITT**, remarks to the American Bar Association's Committee on Law and National Security, 23 January 2003.

LIMITS OF INTELLIGENCE

The Literary Spy posits that, concerning intelligence, there are two kinds of people in the world: those who, on the one hand, look on the institutions and practitioners of intelligence and see unlimited or at least vast possibilities and powers; and those, on the other, who actually know something about the business.

See also: Critics & Defenders; Failures; Presidents & Intelligence; Warning, Prediction, & Surprise

"I have no data. I cannot tell."

> Sherlock Holmes in Sir **ARTHUR CONAN DOYLE**, "The Adventure of the Copper Beeches" (1892).

"We are divided from England by a ditch 37 kilometers wide and we are not even able to get to know what is happening there!"

> **ADOLF HITLER**, October 1941; quoted in Peter Fleming, *Operation Sea Lion* (1957).

"In the final analyses ... we are still to a large extent dependent upon 'the logic of the situation' and upon deductions from the pattern of Soviet behavior for our conclusions."

> Report of a joint ad hoc committee, comprising representatives from CIA, State Department, and the military branches, July 1948; reproduced in Haines and Leggett, *CIA's Analyses of the Soviet Union* (2001). The lack of good sources on Kremlin decisionmaking plagued the U.S. intelligence community for most of the Cold War.

"Intelligence is bound to make mistakes. Some of the questions it is required to answer demand a divine omniscience; others demand more painstaking work than can be accomplished in the time allotment; still others can be had only with the most elaborate sort of undercover preparations which have never been made. But let intelligence make a mistake or come up with an inadequate answer and all too often the reaction of the consumers is on the uncompromising and bitter side:

'I wouldn't ask those geniuses to tell me how many pints there were in a quart.'"

> **SHERMAN KENT**, *Strategic Intelligence* (1949). It's two.

"[The Director of Central Intelligence] is one of those jobs where one can never be right, as the American people expect the incumbent to predict with accuracy just what Stalin is likely to do three months from today at 5:30 a.m. and, of course, that is beyond the realm of human infallibility."

> **WALTER BEDELL SMITH**, before becoming DCI, August 1950; quoted in Jeffreys-Jones, *The CIA and American Democracy* (1989).

"The adequacy of intelligence on the Soviet bloc varies from firm and accurate in some categories to inadequate and practically nonexistent in others. We have no reliable inside intelligence on thinking in the Kremlin. Our estimates of Soviet long range plans and intentions are speculations drawn from inadequate evidence."

> CIA report, "Intelligence on the Soviet Bloc," March 1953; reproduced in Haines and Leggett, *CIA's Analyses of the Soviet Union* (2001).

"The President should be informed that this is not the greatest thing since peanut butter."

> DCI **JOHN McCONE** to McGeorge Bundy, President Johnson's national security advisor, on the efficacy of proposed covert operations to persuade Hanoi to stop subversive activities in South Vietnam, 7 January 1964; quoted in Ford, *CIA and the Vietnam Policymakers* (1998).

"It's easy to forget what intelligence consists of: luck and speculation. Here and there a windfall, here and there a scoop."

> **JOHN LE CARRÉ** [David Cornwell], *The Looking-Glass War* (1965). It's not so easy to forget that le Carré's intelligence is, well, fiction.

"The chances of providing warning of an ICBM attack designed to achieve maximum surprise would be virtually nil. Intelligence could almost certainly give no firm warning of an intention to attack. Intelligence is not likely to give warning of probable Soviet intent to attack until a few hours before the attack, if at all."

CIA estimate from 1966; quoted in Associated Press report of 23 December 1997.

"In a world of perfect information, there would be no uncertainties about the present and future intentions, capabilities, and activities of foreign powers. Information, however, is bound to be imperfect for the most part. Consequently, the intelligence community can at best reduce the uncertainties and construct plausible hypotheses about these factors on the basis of what continues to be partial and often conflicting evidence."

U.S. Senate, *Final Report of the Senate Select Committee to Study Governmental Operations with respect to Intelligence Activities* [the Church Committee], Book I (April 1976).

"It is ironic that whereas no reasonable person expects the Department of Health to stamp out disease altogether, or the Department of Agriculture to provide for good harvests every year, the various organs of intelligence are expected to be right every time."

WALTER LAQUEUR, *A World of Secrets* (1985).

"Sun Tzu, the sixth-century B.C. author of *The Art of War*, claimed that he who knows his adversary can win a hundred battles. But Sun Tzu's statement ought to be prefaced by 'other things being equal, or nearly equal.' The czarist regime is no longer in power in Russia, even though it had the most effective espionage organization of

its time. If Sun Tzu had been right, the French would not have been close to defeat in World War I and would not have been defeated in World War II, for the *Deuxime Bureau* was then second to none, and the Allies should have won World War II by 1943. . . . So unless a country has a more or less effective foreign policy, the quality of intelligence at its disposal is of little or no importance."

WALTER LAQUEUR, *A World of Secrets* (1985).

"Intelligence is an essential service, but only a service. It is an important element in the decision-making process, but only one element; its usefulness depends entirely on how it is used and guided."

WALTER LAQUEUR, *A World of Secrets* (1985).

"In part because of insufficient familiarity with intelligence work, too many policymakers arrive at their posts with an unrealistic expectation of what the CIA can do. When this expectation is disappointed, it often turns into skepticism that the agency can do much of anything. The apparent lack of CIA access to Soviet Politburo discussions, for example, leads some policymakers to question whether anything the agency says about Soviet intentions or politics has value, regardless of its other sources of intelligence. Similarly, the CIA has difficulty forecasting coups (which, of course, usually come as a surprise also to the targeted leader) or the results of difficult decisions not yet made by foreign governments."

DDI **ROBERT GATES**, "The CIA and American Foreign Policy," *Foreign Affairs* (winter 1987–88).

"One has to be realistic about the power of intelligence. Past experience suggests that intelligence information and judgments are ill-equipped for settling contentious disputes over policy."

BRUCE BERKOWITZ and **ALLAN GOODMAN**, *Strategic Intelligence* (1989).

"When high officials ejaculate 'Bad intelligence!' they are as often as not diverting attention from their own responsibilities. There is never enough intelligence to guarantee instant success at no cost and never enough to overcome entrenched prejudice."

ANGELO CODEVILLA, *Informing Statecraft* (1992).

"Presidents expect that, for what they spend on intelligence, the product should be able to predict coups, upheavals, riots, intentions, military moves, and the like with accuracy.... Presidents and their national security advisors usually are ill-informed about intelligence capabilities; therefore, they often have unrealistic expectations of what intelligence can do for them, especially when they hear about the genuinely extraordinary capabilities of U.S. intelligence for collecting and processing information."

Former DCI **ROBERT GATES**; quoted in Andrew, *For the President's Eyes Only* (1995).

"[U.S.] presidents have tended, more often than not, to take for granted their daily diet of all-source global intelligence. Indeed, they have frequently seemed disappointed by it.... Presidents' recurring disappointment with the intelligence they receive, however, has derived, at least in part, from their own exaggerated expectations. Good intelligence diminishes surprise, but even the best cannot possibly prevent it altogether.... Anxious to impress each incoming president with the sophistication of its product, the intelligence community was reluctant to emphasize its own limitations. It

was thus partly responsible for raising unrealistic expectations in the White House."

CHRISTOPHER ANDREW, *For the President's Eyes Only* (1995).

"There is an expectation that we have built a no-fault intelligence system. Intelligence is expected not only to tell you about the trends and to tell you about events and give you insight, but in each and every case to tell you the date, time, and place of an event. That will not happen."

DCI **GEORGE TENET**; quoted in the *New York Times*, 22 October 1998.

"Technical collection resources are finite. Not a day goes by here that I don't have to make a decision to 'uncover' something in order to cover something else."

DDI **JOHN McLAUGHLIN**, interview with CNN, 13 January 1999.

"It is understandable, but unrealistic, especially given our authorities and resources, to expect us to be perfect."

CIA spokesman **BILL HARLOW**; quoted in the *New York Times*, 30 December 2001.

"Surprise attacks often succeed despite the availability of warning indicators. This pattern leads many observers to blame derelict intelligence officials or irresponsible policymakers. The sad truth is that the fault lies more in natural organizational forces, and in the pure intractability of the problem, than in the skills of spies or statesmen ... intelligence can rarely be perfect and unambiguous."

RICHARD K. BETTS, "Fixing Intelligence," *Foreign Affairs* (January–February 2002).

"I wish I could promise perfection but cannot."

DCI **GEORGE TENET**, "The CIA and Sept. 11," the *New York Post*, 13 February 2002.

"Look at the Israelis. They've got one of the finest intelligence services in the world. They've got a very narrow target to focus on geographically and in terms of who their adversary is, and they still get hit repeatedly by suicide bombings."

Vice President **RICHARD CHENEY** on *Meet the Press*, NBC, 19 May 2002.

"Americans are a forgiving people. Knowing that their leaders will often have to make life-or-death judgments based on foggy and incomplete evidence, they will forgive Presidents for honest military or intelligence mistakes made in the aggressive protection of American life or liberty. What they will not forgive is a luxury . . . we cannot afford: waiting for perfect evidence, rather than the best intelligence at hand, to act."

Wall Street Journal editorial, "The Limits of Hindsight," 28 July 2003. The *WSJ* was referring to the failure to anticipate the 11 September 2001 attacks.

"Intelligence is imperfect. Sometimes it's wrong, sometimes it's right, sometimes it's over, sometimes it's under. But it's the best they can do."

Former DCI **R. JAMES WOOLSEY**, quoted in the *New York Times*, 10 November 2003.

"Intelligence services have never come close to possessing divine insight. . . . It is a serious mistake for any intelligence service ever to assume that it has achieved absolute wisdom."

Former DCI **RICHARD HELMS**, *A Look over My Shoulder* (2003).

"Knowledge of what the enemy can do and of what he intends is never enough to ensure security. . . . Foreknowledge is no protection against disaster. Even real-time intelligence is never real enough. Only force finally counts."

JOHN KEEGAN, *Intelligence in War* (2003).

"By all means let Congress explore why the CIA overestimated Saddam's WMD stockpiles this time around. But let's do so while recalling that the CIA had *underestimated* the progress of his nuclear, chemical, and biological programs before the first Gulf War. . . . Intelligence is as much art and judgment as it is science, and it is inherently uncertain. We elect Presidents and legislators to consider the evidence and then make difficult policy judgments that the voters can later hold them responsible for. . . . As intelligence failures go, we'd prefer one that worried too much about a threat than one that worried too little. The latter got us September 11."

Wall Street Journal editorial, "So Where's the WMD?" 28 January 2004.

"Blame James Bond or the Man from UNCLE. . . . We have been led by fictional spies and real-life satellite technology and some extraordinary espionage coups to think of intelligence as very nearly infallible."

MARTIN WALKER, "No Perfect Spy," Insightmag.com, 17 February 2004.

M

- **Military Attachés**
- **Military & Naval Intelligence**

MILITARY ATTACHÉS

The American officers who serve in U.S. embassies abroad—serving both as diplomats with official status and as intelligence officers who take risks—have earned the profound respect of the Literary Spy. Theirs is a hard job made more difficult by the tendency of military branches to consider such work as not particularly career-enhancing.

See also: Military & Naval Intelligence; People

"In 1887, the [U.S.] Army posted its first attachés, to Berlin, Paris, London, Vienna, and St. Petersburg. They were instructed to 'examine and report upon all matters of a military or technical character that may be of interest and value to any branch of the Department and the service in general.'"
   NATHAN MILLER, *Spying for America* (1989).

"I would never do any secret service work. My view is that the Military Attaché is the guest of the country to which he is accredited, and must only see and learn that which is permissible for a guest to investigate. Certainly he must keep his eyes and ears open and miss nothing, but secret service is not his business, and he should always refuse a hand in it."
   British military attaché, late 19th century; quoted in Richelson, *A Century of Spies* (1995). Victorian attitudes of fair play were not shared by Britain's adversaries during the Victorian era and certainly are not now.

"The military attachés, who now form part of the staff of diplomatic agencies abroad, have to watch and report on all military matters in foreign armies in peace and in war.... Their duty, however, is of a delicate nature, and requires considerable tact; for, being official agents of information, they are closely watched. Their task becomes more difficult as soon as there is some want of cordiality between the government that sends them and the one to which they are accredited. All this shows with what care the officers for this post should be selected; only those who have great prudence, a deep knowledge of the art of war, and a natural gift for observation are well adapted for it."
   British Colonel **GEORGE FURSE**, *Information in War* (1895).

"The mere fact that a man knew a foreign language was not positive proof that he would make a good attaché.... He should be a man with keen imagination, able to draw correct conclusions from very scanty evidence, courteous in manner, a man of the world (but not too worldly) and, in general, with sufficient intelligence to be a good mixer in all classes of society."

> Rear Admiral **ROGER WELLES**, U.S. naval intelligence director during World War I; cited in Polmar and Allen, *Encyclopedia of Espionage* (1997). Right—best not to have "too worldly" attachés.

"The US Army had military attachés in Rome, Berlin, and Tokyo in the 1920s and 1930s.... American officers watched the Fascists consolidate their rule in Italy, Hitler rearm Germany, and Japan begin its march of conquest in Asia. They sent thousands of reports on these developments to the Military Intelligence Division of the War Department.... Most reports languished forgotten in the files.... One reason may be the Army's attitude toward its attachés and their work. Officers went overseas with almost no training except in codes and rudimentary finances. Officially, the Army maintained that it chose only the best men and gave them superlative training. This position contrasted sharply with the attachés' experiences and recollections."

> CIA historian **SCOTT KOCH** in *Studies in Intelligence* (unclassified ed., 1995).

"Our Service Attachés are the backbone of the military collection effort. Their presence is particularly valuable in the countries behind the Iron Curtain where intelligence collection means are difficult to apply. The military information obtained from the Service Attachés ... is a major contribution to the accomplishment of the intelligence mission assigned by the National Security Council."

> DCI **ROSCOE HILLENKOETTER** to Secretary of Defense Louis Johnson, 17 February 1950; in *FRUS 1945–1950:*

Emergence of the Intelligence Establishment (1996), document 416.

MILITARY & NAVAL INTELLIGENCE

Only an ox or moron considers this category an oxymoron. Wanting one's army, navy, and air forces to have the best intelligence should go without saying, rather like asserting it is better, on balance, to drive a car with one's eyes open. But the Literary Spy would add that the military tends to interpret intelligence according to its particular point of view; if the services had had their way in 1945–47, intelligence today would be predominantly a military affair. The Literary Spy contends that there's prudent reason for civilian control.

See also: Leadership; Military Attachés; Origins of Central Intelligence; U.S. Intelligence "Community"

"If I know our troops can attack, but do not know the enemy cannot be attacked, it is only halfway to victory.... Knowing that the enemy can be attacked, and knowing that our army can effect the attack, but not knowing the terrain is not suitable for combat, is only halfway to victory.... Thus it is said that if you know the enemy and know yourself, your victory will not be imperiled. If you know Heaven and you know Earth, your victory will be complete."

> **SUN TZU**, *The Art of War* (6th century B.C.).

"Traditionally, the number-one means by which military forces obtain intelligence about the capacity and intention of opposing forces is to engage them."

> **ANGELO CODEVILLA**, *Informing Statecraft* (1992).

"Raising a host of a hundred thousand men and marching them great distances entails heavy loss on the people and a drain on the resources of the state. The daily expenditure will amount to a thousand ounces of silver.... Hostile armies may face each other for years, striving for victory that is decided in a single day. This being so, to remain in ignorance of the enemy's condition, simply because one grudges the outlay of a hundred ounces of silver in honors and emoluments, is the height of inhumanity."

   SUN TZU, *The Art of War* (6th century B.C.).

"There must be no more intimate relations in the whole army than those maintained with spies. No other relation should be more liberally rewarded. In no other relation should greater secrecy be preserved."

   SUN TZU, *The Art of War* (6th century B.C.).

"What king, going to make war against another king, does not sit down first and consider whether he is able with ten thousand to meet him who comes against him with twenty thousand?"

   Luke 14:31 (Revised Standard).

"One [Roman] roster dating from A.D. 219 makes reference to 15 *exploratores* [scouts] out of 721 men recorded."

   N. J. E. AUSTIN and **N. B. RANKOV**, *Exploratio* (1995).

"Never turn away freeman or slave, by day or night, though you may be sleeping or eating or bathing, if he says that he has news for you."

   Advice of an officer of the Byzantine imperial army, 10th century; cited in Dvornik, *Origins of Intelligence Services* (1974).

"Nothing is more worthy of the attention of a good general than the endeavor to penetrate the designs of the enemy."

   NICCOLÒ MACHIAVELLI, *Discourses* (1531).

"You ought to know that intelligence is the most powerful means to undertake brave designs, and to avoid great ruines: and it is the chiefest foundation upon which all generals do ground their actions."

   Pro-Cromwell General **GEORGE MONK**, *Observations Upon Military and Political Affairs* (1671).

"No war can be conducted successfully without early and good intelligence."

   JOHN CHURCHILL, First Duke of Marlborough (1650–1722); quoted in Keegan, *Intelligence in War* (2003).

"Where-ever their Army lies, it will be of the greatest advantage to us, to have spies among them."

   General **GEORGE WASHINGTON**, 1777; quoted in Bakeless, *Turncoats, Traitors and Heroes* (1998).

"I keep people constantly on Staten Island, who give me daily information of the operations of the enemy."

   General **GEORGE WASHINGTON**, report to the Continental Congress, 5 July 1777; cited in Polmar and Allen, *Encyclopedia of Espionage* (1997).

"If one could always be acquainted beforehand with the enemy's designs, one would always beat him with an inferior force."

   FREDERICK THE GREAT (1712–86); quoted in Furse, *Information in War* (1895).

"Marshall de Soubise is always followed by a hundred cooks; I am always preceded by a hundred spies. . . . The ratio of spies to cooks in my army is twenty to one."

FREDERICK THE GREAT (1712–86), explaining his victory over the French marshal in November 1757; quoted in Haswell, *Spies and Spymasters* (1977). Now there's food for thought.

"Many intelligence reports in war are contradictory; even more are false, and most are uncertain."

CARL VON CLAUSEWITZ, *On War* (1832). Not just in war.

"[During the Mexican War, General Winfield] Scott realized he needed swift and accurate intelligence. In the absence of reliable maps, he used engineer officers for special reconnaissance missions, thus giving future leaders such as Captain Robert E. Lee and lieutenants Pierre G. T. Beauregard, George G. Meade, and George B. McClellan a taste of intelligence work."

NATHAN MILLER, *Spying for America* (1989). Too bad it didn't take with McClellan.

"The gathering of knowledge by clandestine means was repulsive to the feelings of English Gentlemen."

Official British history of the Crimean War; cited in Haswell, *Spies and Spymasters* (1977). Nice Gentlemen finish Last.

"I warrant that the Light Brigade's G-2 was high on the list of survivors in the charge at Balaclava."

SHERMAN KENT, *Strategic Intelligence* (1949).

"Pinkerton's idea of military intelligence was to count the noses of the opposing troops and then to count them again to be sure the first figure was right."

Former DCI **ALLEN DULLES** on Union General George McClellan's spy chief in 1861–62, in *The Craft of Intelli-*

gence (1963). Allan Pinkerton's inflated figures suggest he added the two sums together.

"We were almost as ignorant of the enemy as if they had been in China."

Union General **DANIEL BUTTERFIELD** on U.S. military intelligence in late 1862; quoted in Miller, *Spying for America* (1989). Butterfield is best known as the creator of "Taps," which is played at every U.S. military funeral.

"The [Union Army's] Bureau of Military Information was not to be simply a new intelligence organ on the Pinkerton model. . . . By having [it] sort out and synthesize [the] jumble of information, [General Joseph] Hooker obtained a picture of the enemy's situation as coherent and complete as the supply of information permitted. This was an innovation: Hooker [in February 1863] invented a process and a product now called all-source intelligence. . . . His all-source intelligence operation was decades ahead of its time; it passed from the scene with the end of the Civil War, not to be reinvented until the Second World War."

EDWIN FISHEL, *Secret War for the Union* (1996).

"It is better to lose men than to be without knowledge of the enemy."

Union General **JOSEPH HOOKER**, June 1863; quoted in Fishel, *Secret War for the Union* (1996).

"In the great game that is now being played, everything in the way of advantage depends upon which side gets the best information."

Colonel **GEORGE SHARPE**, chief of the U.S. Army's Bureau of Military Information, to a spy in Gettysburg, 29 June 1863; cited in Fishel, *Secret War for the Union* (1996).

"The best generals have always valued detailed knowledge of topography, almost above any other sort of intelligence."

JOHN KEEGAN on Confederate General Thomas "Stonewall" Jackson's Shenandoah Valley operations in 1862–63, in *Intelligence in War* (2003).

"In the 1880s the first peacetime military and naval intelligence organizations were created in the United States. . . . The Army unit was known as the Military Information Division and came under the Adjutant General's Office. The Navy's Office of Intelligence belonged to the Bureau of Navigation."

Former DCI **ALLEN DULLES**, *The Craft of Intelligence* (1963). The navy seemed a bit lost at sea regarding intelligence.

"A good deal of a nuisance to us as it is continually pestering us for assistance and information."

U.S. naval intelligence chief Commander **CHARLES DAVIS**, 1890, on army intelligence; cited in Miller, *Spying for America* (1989).

"For [intelligence work] we need officers who have talent, certain natural gifts, and a fair amount of experience. Only officials who have been trained in the intricacies of the detective service are of any good in unravelling a mysterious crime. . . . The same applies to the intelligence officers: they must be carefully trained; they must learn the exact description of information which will be most useful to their general; they must be made familiar with the various means by which it can be obtained; and they must be taught by what system of reasoning, and by what comparison of conflicting particulars it becomes possible to distinguish true from false reports."

British Colonel **GEORGE FURSE**, *Information in War* (1895).

"The brainy go to the engineers, the brave to the infantry, the deaf to the artillery, and the stupid to intelligence."

U.S. Army adage; cited in Miller, *Spying for America* (1989).

"The Chief of the Office of Naval Intelligence has got to be the man on whom we rely for initiating strategic work."

THEODORE ROOSEVELT, December 1897; quoted in Andrew, *For the President's Eyes Only* (1995).

"There are three kinds of intelligence: human, animal, and naval."

U.S. Navy adage; cited in Miller, *Spying for America* (1989).

"If there was one Department on which money could be spent with advantage it was the Intelligence Department. . . . We wanted an Army based on economy; it should be an Army of efficiency, and it should be an Army of elasticity, so that comparatively small regular units in time of peace might be expanded into a great and powerful Army in time of war. For that expansion nothing was more needed than an efficient and well-staffed Intelligence Department."

WINSTON CHURCHILL in 1903; cited in Stafford, *Churchill and Secret Service* (1998).

"You are not expected to take anything with you in the field that would reveal your identity or in any way show that you are an agent of the government. . . . Discovery would be greatly to the prejudice of your military reputation."

U.S. Army orders to an intelligence officer posted to Latin America ostensibly for language training, circa 1905; cited in Miller, *Spying for America* (1989).

"Strong suspicions prevailed in the army commands regarding the possibility and the usefulness of espionage in mobile operations. This went so far that one army commander, on the advance through Belgium, left the Intelligence Officer behind in Liege as needless ballast."

> Memoirs of Colonel **WALTER NICOLAI**, Germany's military intelligence chief in World War I; cited in Haswell, *Spies and Spymasters* (1977).

"Remember, if they get you, we never heard of you."

> U.S. Army General **FREDERICK FUNSTON**, commanding U.S. troops on the Mexican border in 1916, to his intelligence officer sent into Mexico; quoted in Miller, *Spying for America* (1989).

"The High Contracting Parties undertake in no way to conceal from each other the condition of such of their industries as are capable of being adapted for war-like purposes or the scale of their armaments and agree that there shall be full and frank interchange of information as to their military and naval programs."

> **WOODROW WILSON**, Covenant of the League of Nations, 1919; cited in Andrew, *For the President's Eyes Only* (1995). This sort of agreement puts peaceful nations, who don't need restraint, at the mercy of aggressive ones, who sign with no intention of complying.

"[In 1920] the whole Far Eastern section of ONI (the Office of Naval Intelligence) occupied just one room, holding one officer and one stenographer. ONI itself comprised a handful of officers and a few yeomen, filing the occasional reports of naval attachés about naval appropriations of the countries to which they were attached, a few notes on vessels building or projected, most of them clipped from local newspapers, and descriptions of parties given in honor of some visiting American celebrity. The last-named usually represented the most illuminating and comprehensive of these so-called intelligence reports."

> Captain **ELLIS ZACHARIAS**, U.S. Navy, *Secret Missions: The Story of an Intelligence Officer* (1946). ONI sent Zacharias to Japan in 1920 to study its language and culture.

"Three years and six months after my departure from Washington, I was back again in the Navy Department standing in the familiar office of the director of Naval Intelligence. . . . The director listened to my report with gentlemanly boredom and evident condescension and then suddenly closed the discussion without any indication of a follow-up job for me. I soon found out that no one had given it the slightest thought. It was not in the routine. I had spent three years studying a forbidding language, penetrating the mind of a strange people, gathering data of vital importance, participating in secret missions—and now it was my turn for sea duty."

> Captain **ELLIS ZACHARIAS**, U.S. Navy, *Secret Missions: The Story of an Intelligence Officer* (1946).

"Most of the divisional commanders were cold, almost hostile, to their Intelligence officers. One could see their point. They were in no position to give intelligent orders in a field of which they knew nothing. And seldom having received any worthwhile information they tended to underestimate Intelligence as a weapon and to regard those who specialized in it as useless drones, wasting government's time while being showered in privileges."

> **FRANTISEK MORAVEC** on the state of Czechoslovakia's military intelligence in 1929; in *Master of Spies: The Memoirs of General Frantisek Moravec* (1975).

"[President Benes] listened to my views with condescending indulgence as soon as they touched the political field, an attitude I have since found customary with professional politicians toward professional soldiers. He felt that politics was his domain and I was not supposed to understand."

> **FRANTISEK MORAVEC** while chief of Czechoslovak military intelligence in 1937; in *Master of Spies: The Memoirs of General Frantisek Moravec* (1975).

"In some battleships . . . the most important duty assigned to new combat intelligence officers was keeping track of ship's laundry when the ship was in port."

> **W. J. HOLMES**, former U.S. naval intelligence officer, describing the situation in 1940; in *Double-Edged Secrets* (1979).

"Capt. Dean Rusk, a future Secretary of State, was recalled to the U.S. Army's military intelligence unit, G-2, in Washington, D.C., two months before the attack on Pearl Harbor and directed to organize a new geographical section covering the region from Afghanistan through the Indian subcontinent, Burma, Ceylon, Malaya, Australia, New Zealand, and the British Pacific islands. Searching for research materials in the army office, he found a single file drawer containing: one volume of *Murray's Handbook* for travelers to India and Ceylon, marked 'Confidential' because it was the only copy in Washington; clippings from the *New York Times* dating back to World War I; and one 1925 military attaché's report from London on the British Army in India."

> **RALPH WEBER**, ed., *Spymasters* (1999), from the introduction.

"I have studied the enemy all my life. I have read the memoirs of his generals and his leaders. I have even read his philosophers and listened to his music. I have studied in detail the account of every one of his damned battles. I know exactly how he will react under any given set of circumstances,

and he hasn't the slightest idea of what I'm going to do. So when the time comes, I'm going to whip the hell out of him."

> General **GEORGE PATTON**, *War As I Knew It* (1947).

"He does not have to look like an officer—only like a staff officer."

> **EWEN MONTAGU**, *The Man Who Never Was* (1954). Montagu was speaking to another British officer about the dead body the British planned to use in deceiving the Germans about the Allied invasion of Sicily in 1943 —an operation appropriately named MINCEMEAT.

"It should be insisted upon that, in times of peace, however great may be the reduction in certain other military departments, a comprehensive military intelligence organization must be carefully preserved and supported so its fruits will be always available for the nation's interests."

> U.S. Army intelligence chief General **GEORGE STRONG**, May 1943; quoted in Troy, *Donovan and the CIA* (1981). Strong was an ardent opponent of OSS and civilians in intelligence.

"Overestimates of enemy losses are dangerous. They are apt to lead commanders into making unsound tactical decisions. . . . [Commanders at sea,] working under great stress and with limited opportunity to observe, frequently believed that they saw and heard things that did not happen. One of the most thankless, but necessary, tasks of intelligence units [in the Pacific war] was the deflation of inflated battle reports."

> Former U.S. naval intelligence officer **W. J. HOLMES**, *Double-Edged Secrets* (1979).

"Complete merger of the intelligence services of the State, War, and Navy Departments is not considered feasible or desirable since each of these departments requires operating intelligence which is of no value or interest to the others and in the acquisition and processing of which peculiar abilities and background knowledge are indispensable."

> Fleet Admiral **E. J. KING**, memorandum to Navy Secretary James Forrestal, 12 October 1945; in *FRUS 1945–1950: Emergence of the Intelligence Establishment* (1996), document 27.

"Prior to the war we had little more [intelligence] than what a military attaché could learn at dinner, more or less, over the coffee cups. . . . We should know as much as possible about the intent, as well as the military capabilities, of every country in the world. We must know the facts for our own defense."

> General **GEORGE C. MARSHALL** in testimony before the Senate Military Affairs Committee, 18 October 1945; quoted in Troy, *Donovan and the CIA* (1981).

"The lack of trained and experienced intelligence officers in both military services has been an important contributing factor to the unsatisfactory situation. It is important to note that there has never been any serious effort to make intelligence a career activity. Officers who were undoubtedly competent in the combat arms or services, but who had had no intelligence training, were from time to time pressed into service in intelligence roles. The natural tendency was for them to seek to return to their own basic branch at the first opportunity. Changes among the top personnel were frequent. During the war there were in succession four Assistant Chiefs of Staff, G-2, eight Assistant Chiefs of Air Staff-2 and five heads of the Office of Naval Intelligence."

> Report of the Lovett Committee on "War Department Intelligence Activities" to Secretary of War Robert Patterson, 3 November 1945; in *FRUS 1945–1950: Emergence of the Intelligence Establishment* (1996), document 42.

"Military intelligence officers . . . are always subordinate to the operations staff and rarely make full careers in intelligence; indeed, most seek transfer to the operations branch, in the all too understandable hope of becoming masters rather than servants."

> **JOHN KEEGAN**, *Intelligence in War* (2003).

"The fluidity and momentum inherent in the immediate situation render an abrupt change in the present balance readily possible."

> U.S. Air Force dissent to CIA estimate ORE 22-48, *Possibility of Direct Soviet Military Action During 1948*, 2 April 1948; cited in Darling, *The Central Intelligence Agency* (1990). The services, especially during the early years of the Cold War, tended to focus on what *might* happen rather than what was *likely* to happen.

"The Assistant Chief of Staff, G-2, dissents with the subject paper. . . . The threat of Soviet aggression is minimized [in the estimate] to the point where dissemination of the paper and its use for planning purposes could seriously affect the security of the United States."

> U.S. Army dissent to CIA estimate on Soviet military capabilities and intentions, 6 April 1950; reproduced in Kuhns, *Assessing the Soviet Threat* (1997).

"Allowing any military service, but particularly the Air Force, to compose its shopping list for weapons based on a threat assessment that came from intelligence it alone collected, processed, and interpreted was absolutely untenable as far as Eisenhower was concerned. . . . Eisenhower was at that moment feeling the effects of the bomber gap, which the Air Force was using to pry more funding out of Congress. And the gap had only been created in the first place, Eisenhower was convinced, because of faulty Air Force intelligence."

WILLIAM E. BURROWS on President Eisenhower's decision that CIA would develop the U-2 spyplane, in *Deep Black* (1986).

"[The] victory in the bomber gap controversy instilled in CIA analysts something of a crusading zeal in challenging the figures of the military services in future estimates."

CIA historian **ROBERTA KNAPP**, quotation in CIA's Historical Intelligence Collection.

"In retrospect, it is easy to criticize and to postulate that the Missile Gap affair would not have occurred if the NIE in 1959 had been left to the Army, or that the estimates of the 1960s would have been more accurate had the national estimate just been left to Air Force analysts. Yet . . . it is only in retrospect that we know what the best bias would have been."

BRUCE BERKOWITZ and **ALLAN GOODMAN**, *Strategic Intelligence* (1989).

"My first priority as DDI was to pull together the several groups in the Agency who were working on military intelligence. . . . This was considered a bold stroke. By long-standing custom and, for a time, mutual consent, military affairs was held to be the exclusive province of the armed services. Military intelligence was thought to be too specialized, too arcane for mere civilians. . . . Unfortunately for that concept, the military services throughout the 1950s and 1960s had consistently displayed an inability to make objective, dispassionate judgments regarding the strategic threat, with the Air Force leading the rest in flagrant disregard for impartial assessment."

Former DDI **R. JACK SMITH**, *The Unknown CIA* (1989).

"To lack intelligence is to be in the ring blindfolded."

General **D. M. SHOUP**, U.S. Marine Corps, 1960; quoted in Heinl, *Dictionary of Military and Naval Quotations* (1966).

"From 1961 to 1970, no fewer than six major studies were commissioned by the federal government to probe redundancy within the military intelligence community. All concluded that, despite the establishment of the DIA, the defense intelligence community performed neither effectively nor efficiently. . . . [DIA] was created to consolidate the intelligence activities of the three armed services, [but] it in fact resulted in the growth of the individual service intelligence operations."

PATRICK MESCALL, "The Birth of the Defense Intelligence Agency," in Jeffreys-Jones and Lownie, *North American Spies* (1991).

"Military intelligence analysts, being human, cannot see the future. They do their jobs if they describe the setting in which the future will occur (the scenery, the cast, the props), and they are excellent if they do this from the point of view of the enemy. But if the commander asks the intelligence analyst to predict what the enemy *will* do, he takes the analyst into an area where the commander himself has more to say than any intelligence officer. This is because how the enemy actually performs depends in part on what one's own side actually does."

ANGELO CODEVILLA, *Informing Statecraft* (1992). One of the paradoxes of intelligence analysis.

"CIA analysts . . . have created and fed the myth that military intelligence agencies consistently produced bloated, self-serving intelligence, and that only by feeding these deliberate Pentagon distortions through the cool medium of CIA could the nation get honest military intelligence."

> Former DIA Director Lieutenant General **DANIEL GRA-HAM**, U.S. Air Force (retired), in 1976; quoted in Andrew, *For the President's Eyes Only* (1995). The distortions probably weren't deliberate.

"In my view, only if the service intelligence organizations are disbanded permanently is there hope for measurably improving the DIA's capabilities. There is no serious need for those four separate organizations that the DIA could not fill."

> Former DCI **STANSFIELD TURNER**, *Secrecy and Democracy* (1985). Another CIA propagandist.

"Military analysts have a prime obligation to defense—and hence to 'worst-case analysis.' In the CIA and INR, on the other hand, there may be an anti-military reflex at work, the feeling that DIA 'exaggerations' have to be resisted."

> **WALTER LAQUEUR**, *A World of Secrets* (1985). But don't they?

"Both the INR and the CIA expected the DIA to exaggerate the Soviet Union's military strength and intentions. I do not mean to imply that the DIA deliberately distorted the facts. But when data about whether the Soviets had a particular military capability were inconclusive, the DIA would always credit them with having it. Or when we knew that the Soviets had a certain capability but did not know how good it was, the DIA would 'mirror-image' it; that is, they would assume that the Soviets' capability was just as good as ours. One way or another, just by calling all the shots on the high side, the DIA would usually come up with a more menacing view of Soviet military potential than did the nonmilitary agencies. Both the

CIA and the INR tended to exaggerate in the other direction in order to compensate."

> Former DCI **STANSFIELD TURNER**, *Secrecy and Democracy* (1985).

"Inevitably, the DIA must be understood in contrast to [the CIA]. The first impression one receives after taking the George Washington Parkway from the CIA's wooded domain overlooking the Potomac to the new DIA building on the tidal flats of the Anacostia is that one has come down in class. Everything about the people seems lower, from rank and pay to pretenses. Clothing changes from wool or cotton to synthetics. When occasionally a DIA civilian, or a retiring military officer, is offered a job at CIA he is regarded as having made a major step up."

> **ANGELO CODEVILLA**, *Informing Statecraft* (1992). Yet another CIA propagandist.

"Potentially the most dangerous intelligence failures [of the Gulf war with Iraq] were the errors of tactical battle damage assessment (BDA). Military intelligence officers in [General] Schwarzkopf's command greatly exaggerated the amount of Iraqi tanks, armored personnel carriers, and artillery destroyed before the ground offensive began. Both DIA and CIA analysts in Washington believed that the BDA was giving the White House and the Pentagon misleading assessments of the achievements of the air campaign. . . . Schwarzkopf defended the BDA produced by his command and took deep offense at the skepticism of Washington. . . . His army G-2, however, later accepted that much of the criticism was justified. The number of Iraqi vessels reported sunk eventually amounted to three times the size of the Iraqi navy.

The total number of claimed Scud kills was probably wrong by a similar order of magnitude."

CHRISTOPHER ANDREW, *For the President's Eyes Only* (1995).

"Military intelligence analysis at the national level, where the Director of Central Intelligence comes eyeball to eyeball with the needs of the President and the Congress, is too important to be left to the military."

Former DDI **BRUCE CLARKE**, July 1997; quotation in CIA's Historical Intelligence Collection.

"Writing intelligence reports is like having intercourse with an elephant. There is very little pleasure to be derived from it; you are very likely to be squashed; and there will be no result for two years."

An "unknown military sage" via British intelligence writer Nigel West.

"I am military intelligence and I am always out front . . . always."

Plaque at a memorial at NSA.

"We have a saying in the Army that the first two or three reports from the scouts are always wrong."

General **TOMMY FRANKS**, U.S. Central Command; quoted on ABCNEWS.com, 22 December 2001.

"Intelligence in war, however good, does not point out unerringly the path to victory. Victory is an elusive prize, bought with blood rather than brains. Intelligence is the handmaiden, not the mistress, of the warrior. . . . Intelligence, while generally necessary, is not a sufficient means to victory. Decision in war is always the result of a fight, and in combat willpower always counts for more than foreknowledge. Let those who disagree show otherwise."

JOHN KEEGAN, *Intelligence in War* (2003). Not even the most enthusiastic proponent of intelligence would defend the strawman thesis that Keegan attacks in his otherwise excellent book.

Nut Cases & Conspiracies

NUT CASES & CONSPIRACIES

There will always be the sanity-challenged or reality-deficient who see nothing but evil, complex, all-encompassing machinations in the secret but honest work of U.S. intelligence services. The Literary Spy advises: the course of human events is better explained by idiocy than by conspiracy, by stumbling than by planning, by accident than by design.

See also: Critics & Defenders; Intelligence & American Culture

"There are always some lunatics about. It would be a dull world without them."
>   Sherlock Holmes in Sir **ARTHUR CONAN DOYLE**, "The Adventure of the Three Gables" (1926).

"Our asylums are full of people who think they're Napoleon—or God."
>   James Bond, played by Sean Connery, in the 1962 film *Dr. No.*

"The reader would be amazed to know how many psychopaths and people with grudges and pet foibles and phobias manage to make connections with intelligence services all over the world and to tie them in knots. . . . The intelligence service is vulnerable because of its standing need for information and because of the unpredictability of the quarter from which it might come."
>   Former DCI **ALLEN DULLES**, *The Craft of Intelligence* (1963).

"Something about a secret intelligence agency attracts an endless stream of letters, cards, telegrams, phone calls, and personal visits from deranged, possibly dangerous, or merely daffy citizens. . . . One disturbed gentleman from Buffalo claimed the Communists had kidnapped him, cut open his head, removed his brains, and substituted a radio. . . . He asked CIA to remove the radio and replace the brains. . . . A New York correspondent informed us that Rudolph Hess, from his cell in Spandau [prison], was controlling ten leading Southern segregationists by long-distance hypnotism."
>   **DAVID R. McLEAN**, "Cranks, Nuts, and Screwballs," *Studies in Intelligence* 9 (summer 1965).

"Within any intelligence service, more time than most people realize is spent separating valid information from false information invented and offered by fakers and cranks.... I have seen instances during and after World War II in which informants, under pressure and possessed of lively imaginations, have spun out incredible tales of enemy plots which had to be taken seriously, at least for the moment.... This sort of thing can cause a great deal of turmoil and we sometimes wondered, after the air had been cleared, whether it was the enemy who had sent us these nut cases in order to waste our time and tie us in knots."

Former DCI **ALLEN DULLES**, ed., *Great Spy Stories from Fiction* (1969). Sounds a lot like the case of a prominent Soviet defector, but that's another story.

"To CIA Investigation Department: Please investigate these allegations. A number of years ago, certain powerful investors in Columbus, Ohio contrived a plan to blow up Wall Street in New York, blame it on an Islamic sneak attack or the Chinese, then move Wall Street to Columbus, Ohio. They plotted to have a British nuclear missile fall off track and slam into the hill top, clean up the mess then expand downtown Columbus into the hill top area. These people have also caused a war between political prisoners and the CIA as a pretext to get rid of the CIA."

Geoffrey, who lives in Columbus, a frequent faxer to CIA in 1995–96. Curious, that bit about the "Islamic sneak attack" on New York . . .

"Dear Director Deutch: I am possessed by several CIA spirits. The spirits are very intelligent and well informed. One has taken control of my body for a hidden agenda. I appear to be normal except the spirits are crippling me. As a result, I have a crippling disability with defined CIA purpose and goals that were not originally mine. I have been contacting the Director of the FBI to deliver me from the CIA spiritual dilemma."

Alan, from Pennsylvania. Neither Alan nor the FBI director is cleared for this particular program.

"Please mature and consult me openly! I am demanding 'massive damages and truth.' Who is the organizer of this insane conspiracy? which has forced our precious earth off its axis. Please cease tricking me & poisoning my sacred body. Also = where's all my children? & my C.I.A. badge. I am demanding your agency's abolishment."

Mary, letter to CIA. Mary, you're on to us.

"I am unemployed at present and I cannot implement my plans in favor of the C.I.A. I need financial support from the C.I.A. to continue my plans. I don't consider myself professional but I can do something significant as a counter-measure on escalating propaganda and disinformation against the C.I.A. I don't even have my own typewriter and fax machine. The C.I.A. can provide me with all the things I need."

Ruben, from New Jersey. We suggested to Ruben that he try NSA.

"To CIA. Sometimes I'll try to second guess the anti-Christ. He'll send in the Nazis, to destroy our Star Fleet Command and at the same time attack us with the Russians & anyone else who has it in for us. His next invasion from outer space will finish us off. We'll need a defense shield around the earth to protect us all. Here are a few more equations for geoplanetary force fields & disintegrators. This should keep the invaders off our world thanks to the C.I.A."

Frequent faxer and amateur physicist Geoffrey, from Ohio. Geoffrey's detailed equations are forwarded to CIA scientists on the infinitesimally small chance he's on to something.

"Since 1944 the entire contents of Plaintiff's mind have been present in the mind of everyone else. Since this phenomenon became manifest in wartime, and since Plaintiff was then in military service, the Office of Strategic Service (OSS), whose mission and operations were transferred to the Central Intelligence Agency (CIA) upon its formation in 1947, was designated to investigate this hitherto unheard-of fluke and to curtail, or if possible eliminate, its disquieting effect upon the populace. Since then, Plaintiff has been confined to an invisible 'bubble' as the subject of this CIA project. Any rational justification for this confinement and 'treatment,' however, has long since disappeared."

> Complaint filed against CIA in a U.S. court, 1997. Gosh, the dates seem right . . .

"The CIA has satellites that read the pulses and patterns of the human brain, and it translates these readings into words and sentences using thermo imaging."

> Yet another complaint filed against CIA in a U.S. court, 1997. That's how the Literary Spy compiled this book!

"Once contracted, conspiracy theory is an incurable condition."

> **CHRISTOPHER ANDREW**, in Jeffrey-Jones and Andrew, *Eternal Vigilance* (1997).

"The assertion that the CIA played any role in the death of Princess Diana is ludicrous."

> CIA spokesman **TOM CRISPELL** on allegations that the car crash that killed Diana Spencer was engineered by British and U.S. intelligence; Reuters, 29 April 1998.

"A Libyan prosecutor on Wednesday ordered the arrest of nine American officials allegedly behind the 1986 bombing of two Libyan cities. . . . Among those on the list is the late William Casey, the former director of the CIA. . . . The prosecutor said if Libya failed to secure their arrest, 'it will resort to [the U.N.] Security Council to get the accused.'"

> Associated Press report, 30 December 1998.

"Naturally, there's the 'CIA did it' theory, with speculation that the spy agency tampered with the plane for unspecified reasons dating back to President Kennedy's Bay of Pigs invasion of Cuba."

> *Washington Times*, 22 July 1999, on Internet discussions of the death of John F. Kennedy, Jr., in the crash of a small airplane he was piloting.

"What I would like to have from you is some type of evidence that I'm no threat to national security. And if you have opened a file on me, please let me know I still have the 14th amendment. I do have tremendous respect for the CIA, and I wish I could qualify to serve and protect the constitution."

> A Nebraskan, letter to CIA, July 1999. You aren't. You do. You can't.

"I wouldn't be surprised if the hairy hand of the CIA and some of its veteran hatchers of plots against Cuba were behind this cold front. I wouldn't be surprised if in 50 years time when they declassify things, it will show there was a plan to send these cold fronts to ruin the summit."

> Cuban Foreign Minister **FELIPE PEREZ-ROQUE**, blaming CIA for the bad weather at the start of the Ibero-American Summit in Havana; Reuters, 15 November 1999. The Literary Spy, as humorist Dave Barry would say, swears he's not making this stuff up.

"Years ago, William Webster, then the director of the CIA, wanted to date me. We never did date, but my girls were convinced that if I married him he'd implant homing devices in them, and they'd never be able to have sex again."

> Country music star **NAOMI JUDD**, interview in the *Ladies Home Journal* (May 2000). The latest homing devices are guaranteed not to interfere with sex.

"Never attribute to a conspiracy that which can be explained by incompetence."

> Secretary of Defense **DONALD RUMSFELD** in the *Wall Street Journal*, 29 January 2001. This is similar to an axiom of the late Professor John P. Roche of Tufts University: "Whenever an event can be explained either by conspiracy or by idiocy, choose idiocy."

"We understand his grief and tremendous sense of loss but any suggestion that the CIA spied on Dodi Fayed or Princess Diana or has knowledge of any plot to murder them or had anything to do with this tragic accident is totally unfounded."

> CIA spokesman **MARK MANSFIELD** on continuing allegations by Dodi Fayed's father that a U.S.-British intelligence conspiracy did the couple in; quoted by Reuters, 30 August 2001. If the conspiracy theory were true, this quotation would have appeared under "Liaison."

"The CIA has done this to justify its crusades against Muslims."

> **SAMIUL HAQ**, leader of Pakistan's radical Jamiat-e Ulema Islam party, on the massacre of Christians in a church in eastern Pakistan; quoted in the *Washington Times*, 29 October 2001.

"We know there were numerous warnings of the events to come on September 11th. . . . What did this administration know and when did it know it, about the events of September 11th? Who else knew, and why did they not warn the innocent people of New York who were needlessly murdered? . . . What do they have to hide?"

> U.S. Representative **CYNTHIA McKINNEY** suggesting in an interview with a Berkeley, California, radio station

that the Bush administration had foreknowledge of the September 11 terrorist attacks; quoted in the *Washington Post*, 12 April 2002. McKinney was defeated in her next election . . . in a primary. Coincidence?

"It sounds like he might have been standing too close to the gong all those years."

> CIA spokesman **TOM CRISPELL** regarding the claim of former TV executive Chuck Barris, creator of *The Gong Show*, that Barris had served as an undercover CIA assassin; quoted in the *Washington Post*, 15 January 2003.

"Have you ever heard the CIA acknowledge someone was an assassin? Believe what you want."

> Former TV executive and *Gong Show* creator **CHUCK BARRIS** reacting to CIA denials that he ever was an Agency employee; quoted in the *Washington Post*, 15 January 2003. Barris asserts in his "unauthorized autobiography" *Confessions of a Dangerous Mind* that he was a CIA assassin even while creating and producing what in the 1960s and 1970s was considered dreck (but which, compared with today's "reality" programming, seems upbeat and thoughtful). In any case, Mr. Barris, we'll believe you're a nut case.

"Indonesians could not possibly have built such a powerful bomb. The CIA was behind it all."

> **ABU BAKAR BASHIR**, Indonesian Muslim cleric and spiritual leader of the extremist group Jemaah Islamiyah, on the terrorist bombing in Bali that killed two hundred people on 12 October 2002; quoted in the *Java Post*, 2 February 2004.

"P.S. If you don't take appropriate action, I'll write to the President and tell him you're chicken."

> Closing of 1964 letter to CIA; in David R. McLean, "Cranks, Nuts, and Screwballs," *Studies in Intelligence* 9 (summer 1965).

- **Objectivity**
- **Openness & Publicity**
- **Open Sources**
- **Origins of Central Intelligence**
- **Overhead & Imagery**

OBJECTIVITY

The Literary Spy believes that objectivity relates to intelligence as humility does to a virtuous life—it is absolutely central. With objectivity as the guiding principle of an intelligence service, there's at least a chance that policymakers can be influenced to make the right decisions. A lack of objectivity, however, results in skewed analysis and, even worse, the loss of credibility that means a service's voice no longer matters even when it's right. Without objectivity, moreover, the wrong things get collected, which means that the wrong things are analyzed; operations, fueled by wishful thinking instead of sober calculation, go awry; and the service might even tend to overlook evidence of traitors in its midst. The Literary Spy offers this heresy: in the absence of objectivity, it might even be better not to have an intelligence service at all.

See also: Analysis & Analysts; Estimates; Military & Naval Intelligence; Policy Role; Politicization

"The first law for the historian is that he shall never dare utter an untruth. The second is that he shall suppress nothing that is true. Moreover, there shall be no suspicion of partiality in his writing, or of malice."

> **CICERO** (106–43 B.C.), *De Oratore*. It is more important that these maxims be observed by U.S. intelligence analysts than by historians.

"There is nothing so powerful as the truth—and often nothing so strange."

> **DANIEL WEBSTER**, *Argument on the Murder of Captain White* (1830).

"There are no whole truths; all truths are half truths. It is trying to treat them as whole truths that plays the devil."

> English mathematician and philosopher **ALFRED NORTH WHITEHEAD**, *Dialogues* (1953).

"It is a capital mistake to theorise before one has data. Insensibly one begins to twist facts to suit theories, instead of theories to suit facts."

> Sherlock Holmes to Doctor Watson in Sir **ARTHUR CONAN DOYLE**, "A Scandal in Bohemia" (1891). In Conan Doyle's novel *The Valley of Fear* (1915) Holmes declares, "The temptation to form premature theories upon insufficient data is the bane of our profession."

"We approached the case, you remember, with an absolutely blank mind, which is always an advantage. We had formed no theories. We were simply there to observe and to draw inferences from our observations."

Sherlock Holmes in Sir **ARTHUR CONAN DOYLE**, "The Adventure of the Cardboard Box" (1893). In "The Adventure of the Greek Interpreter" (1893) Holmes tells Doctor Watson, "All things should be seen exactly as they are."

"I can discover facts, Watson, but I cannot change them."

Sherlock Holmes in Sir **ARTHUR CONAN DOYLE**, "The Problem of Thor Bridge" (1922).

"*Cynic*, n. A blackguard whose faulty vision sees things as they are, not as they ought to be."

AMBROSE BIERCE, *The Devil's Dictionary* (1911). Most CIA analysts are cynics.

"The great thing is to get the true picture, whatever it is."

WINSTON CHURCHILL, November 1940; cited in Heinl, *Dictionary of Military and Naval Quotations* (1966).

"Since the nature of the work requires it to have status it should be independent of any Department of the Government (since it is obliged to serve all and must be free of the natural bias of an operating Department)."

OSS Director **WILLIAM DONOVAN**, "Establishment of a Centralized United States Foreign Intelligence System," 25 August 1945; cited in Troy, *Donovan and the CIA* (1981).

"In the writing of reports, one is expected to turn out thoroughly objective and neutral intelligence. There should be no personal pronouns, no wisecracks, no slang or clichés, and care should be taken about the use of color words such as 'reactionary,' 'progressive,' 'left or right,' etc."

OSS analyst **ARTHUR SCHLESINGER, JR.**, on standards of objectivity in OSS intelligence reports; cited in Katz, *Foreign Intelligence: Research and Analysis in OSS* (1989). The writing of history is another matter entirely.

"The [central intelligence] agency itself should be completely denied any policy-making function, in order that its objectivity may be preserved and that it may not succumb to the inevitable temptation to tailor its reports to support a policy in which it has an interest. It should be apparent that this danger will be more readily avoided if the central intelligence agency does not find itself part of a single policy forming department."

Brigadier General **JOHN MAGRUDER**, SSU director, memorandum on "Intelligence Matters" to the Assistant Secretary of War for Air, October 1945; in *FRUS 1945–1950: Emergence of the Intelligence Establishment* (1996), document 34.

"The evaluation of information is not an exact science and every safeguard should be imposed to prevent any one department from having the opportunity to interpret information in such a way as to make it seem to support previously accepted policies or preconceived opinions."

Rear Admiral **SIDNEY SOUERS** (before his appointment as the first DCI), letter to presidential aide Clark Clifford, 27 December 1945; reproduced in Warner, *CIA Under Truman* (1994).

"Intelligence must be close enough to policy, plans, and operations to have the greatest amount of guidance, and must not be so close that it loses its objectivity and integrity of judgment."

SHERMAN KENT, *Strategic Intelligence* (1949).

"Duplication is inevitable and desirable inasmuch as CIA examines these documents from the standpoint of national security whereas each of the other intelligence agencies examines them from the standpoint of departmental responsibilities. . . . The services have a tendency to reflect their own interests in their intelligence estimates. For this reason, CIA strives to maintain in its estimates an objective, balanced view, and to keep U.S. national security, rather than departmental interests, as the dominant consideration."

> DCI **ROSCOE HILLENKOETTER**, in a 1950 letter to President Truman; quoted in Ranelagh, *The Agency* (1986).

"Once we have a satisfactory definition of truth, the definition of falsity is simple."

> **GEORGE CARVER**, *Aesthetics and the Problem of Meaning* (1952); cited in Winks, *Cloak and Gown* (1987). Carver went from philosophy student at Yale and Oxford to analyst at CIA and eventually became the DCI's special assistant on Vietnam.

"In 1953, [DCI] Dulles took a dramatic stand against Senator Joseph McCarthy, and his action contributed significantly to the Agency's reputation as a liberal institution. At a time when the State Department and even the military services were cowering before McCarthy's preposterous charges and attempting to appease the Wisconsin Senator, Dulles openly challenged McCarthy's attacks on the Agency . . . and demanded that McCarthy make available to him any evidence of Communist influence or subversion in the Agency. Within a month, McCarthy backed off. The episode had an important impact on agency morale and on the public's perception of the CIA. As virtually the only government agency that had successfully resisted McCarthy's allegations and intrusions, the CIA was identified as an organization that fostered free and independent thinking."

> **ANNE KARALEKAS**, "The History of the Central Intelligence Agency," in Leary, *The Central Intelligence Agency* (1984).

"I believe it is the utmost importance to maintain the principle of non-political objectivity in the Central Intelligence function. . . . It is essential that in the course of our work neither the Agency nor its personnel becomes identified with partisan politics, and it is the duty of all personnel to keep out of political controversies."

> DCI **ALLEN DULLES**, letter to Sherman Adams, assistant to President Eisenhower, 5 April 1957; quotation in CIA's Historical Intelligence Collection.

"I was taking a position that there were Soviet offensive missiles in Cuba and the whole Kennedy administration was opposing me, all Democrats. Here I was the sole Republican with a very different view. I had a devil of a time to persuade the President and his brother, Bobby Kennedy, that I was not the source of information to a Republican Senator."

> Former DCI **JOHN McCONE** in 1988, explaining how he was the lone voice in the Kennedy administration who believed in 1962 that the Soviets would try to put strategic missiles into Cuba; quoted in Schecter and Deriabin, *The Spy Who Saved the World* (1995).

"I grant that we are all creatures of prejudice, including CIA officials, but by entrusting intelligence coordination to our central intelligence service, which is excluded from policymaking and is married to no particular military hardware, we can avoid, to the greatest possible extent, the bending of facts obtained through intelligence to suit a particular occupational viewpoint."

> Former DCI **ALLEN DULLES**, *The Craft of Intelligence* (1963).

"The CIA was the bearer of bad tidings throughout the Vietnam War, and was not very happily received by any of the policymakers who tried to make the Vietnam intervention work."

Former DDI **RAY CLINE**, *Secrets, Spies and Scholars* (1976).

"Let me tell you about these intelligence guys. When I was growing up in Texas, we had a cow named Bessie. I'd go out early and milk her. I'd get her in the stanchion, seat myself and squeeze out a pail of fresh milk. One day, I'd worked hard and gotten a full pail of milk, but I wasn't paying attention, and old Bessie swung her shit-smeared tail through that bucket of milk. Now, you know, that's what these intelligence guys do. You work hard and get a good program or policy going, and they swing a shit-smeared tail through it."

Attributed to President **LYNDON JOHNSON**; in Andrew, *For the President's Eyes Only* (1995). Note that LBJ says he "wasn't paying attention."

"Everyone agrees that your analysts are the only honest guys in town, and we need to know the truth."

McGEORGE BUNDY, assistant to President Johnson; quoted in Cline, *Secrets, Spies and Scholars* (1976).

"Only mystics, clowns, and artists, in my experience, ever speak the truth."

MALCOLM MUGGERIDGE, former SIS officer; quoted in Hunter, ed., *The Very Best of Malcolm Muggeridge* (1998).

"Let things be such that if our policy-making master is to disregard our knowledge and wisdom, he will never do so because our work was inaccurate, incomplete, or patently biased."

SHERMAN KENT in 1968; quoted in Polmar and Allen, *Encyclopedia of Espionage* (1997).

"There was [in 1969–70] uncertainty about the status of Soviet MIRV [multiple independently targetable reentry vehicle] development, and some American proponents of MIRVs went to considerable lengths to overstate and play upon those uncertainties and fears about possible Soviet MIRVs. Secretary of Defense Laird pushed the matter publicly, and Kissinger put unusually brazen pressure on Director of Central Intelligence Richard M. Helms and the intelligence community to alter a draft national intelligence estimate to support Laird's position that the Soviet SS-9 [ICBM] had a MIRV capability. The pressure, however, was ignored . . . the estimate was not changed."

RAYMOND GARTHOFF, *Detente and Confrontation* (1985).

"The same objectivity which makes us useful to our government and our country leaves us uncomfortably aware of our ambiguous place in it."

DCI **RICHARD HELMS**, address to the American Society of Newspaper Editors, Washington, D.C., 14 April 1971.

"This organization, the CIA, has a distinguished record of being bipartisan in character. It is a highly professional group. It will remain that in this Administration."

President **RICHARD NIXON**, remarks at the swearing in of Lieutenant General Robert Cushman as DDCI in May 1969; quoted in CIA, *"Our First Line of Defense"* (1996). Nixon didn't mean it.

"Our judgments had no more value, indeed less, than that of the most junior analyst on Henry Kissinger's staff. . . . After a decade of demonstrated competence and dispassionate objectivity, we were suddenly seen as partisan and biased."

Former DDI **R. JACK SMITH**, on CIA analysts' relationship with the Nixon administration, in *The Unknown CIA* (1989).

"As important as it is for analysis to remain free of any influence of policy-makers, I found that the CIA's approach was frequently carried to extremes. Sometimes doing the best work possible was placed ahead of meeting deadlines. The result was analyses that were not always timely or directly relevant to the needs of policy-makers."

> Former DCI **STANSFIELD TURNER**, *Secrecy and Democracy* (1985).

"Objectivity is the only virtue that really counts."

> Former DDI **RAY CLINE** on analysis, in *Secrets, Spies and Scholars* (1976).

"I have never seasoned a truth with the sauce of a lie in order to digest it more easily."

> **MARGUERITE YOURCENAR**, Belgian novelist; quoted in the *New York Times*, 5 May 1980.

"Although in the abstract objectivity may be the most desirable quality in intelligence analysis, objective judgments are frequently not what senior officials want to hear about their policies. In most cases, Presidents are inclined to look to the judgments of individuals they know and trust. Whether or not a DCI is included among them is the President's choice."

> **ANNE KARALEKAS**, "The History of the Central Intelligence Agency," in Leary, *The Central Intelligence Agency* (1984).

"[The DCI] is the only one of the President's advisers who has even a chance of presenting unbiased intelligence to him."

> Former DCI **STANSFIELD TURNER**, *Secrecy and Democracy* (1985).

"The next Director of the Central Intelligence Agency . . . will be told repeatedly by virtually everyone in policy positions at the Agency that the CIA is a highly professional, non-political agency that produces 'objective' intelligence. Those assertions are arrant nonsense."

> Transition team working for Ronald Reagan, Working Paper on Intelligence, November 1980; quoted in Ranelagh, *The Agency* (1986).

"The goal of our intelligence analysts can be nothing short of the truth, even when that truth is unpleasant or unpopular. I have asked for honest, objective analysis, and I shall expect nothing less. When there is disagreement, as there often is, on the difficult questions of our time, I expect those honest differences of view to be fully expressed."

> President **RONALD REAGAN**, 4 December 1981; quoted in CIA, *"Our First Line of Defense"* (1996).

"Far from kowtowing to policymakers, there is sometimes a strong impulse on the part of intelligence officers to show that a policy or decision is misguided or wrong, to poke an analytical finger in the policy eye. Policymakers know this and understandably resent it."

> DDI **ROBERT GATES**, "The CIA and American Foreign Policy," *Foreign Affairs* (winter 1987–88).

"Intelligence agencies that permit analysts to reach conclusions that politicians want to hear as opposed to those they must hear, governments that endanger the necessary political and ideological neutrality on which intelligence best thrives by placing those agencies under political appointees, betray civic responsibility."

> **ROBIN W. WINKS**, *Cloak and Gown: Scholars in the Secret War, 1939–1961* (1987).

"Policymakers have always liked intelligence that supported what they want to do, and they often try to influence the analysis to buttress the conclusions they want to reach. They ask carefully phrased questions; they sometimes withhold information; they broaden or narrow the issue; on rare occasions they even try to intimidate. The pressures can be enormous. This is where the integrity of intelligence officers, bolstered by a natural tendency to resist pressure and an often adversarial bureaucratic relationship, comes into play to protect the independence of the agency's assessment."

> DDI **ROBERT GATES**, "The CIA and American Foreign Policy," *Foreign Affairs* (winter 1987–88).

"Unless we have an objective view of the world, seeing it unadorned and free of clichés and stereotyped ideas, all claims about the effectiveness of our foreign policy operations will be nothing but empty words."

> KGB chief **VLADIMIR KRYUCHKOV** to KGB officers of the First Chief Directorate (responsible for foreign intelligence), October 1988; quoted in Andrew and Mitrokhin, *The Mitrokhin Archive* (1999). Like a stopped clock, Kryuchkov got it right only this once; the KGB never freed itself from bias and sycophancy and thereby helped render Soviet diplomacy ineffective.

"Our intelligence estimates are provided for the use of policymakers. They can be used in whole or in part. They can be ignored, torn up, or thrown away, but they may not be changed."

> DCI **WILLIAM WEBSTER**, remarks of 13 April 1988, in *1988 Speeches*.

"It is essential that the director of Central Intelligence be an official who is prepared to present a president with unpleasant information. When the director is a loyalist more than an analyst, an enforcer of the president's ideology rather than a skeptical and independent figure, the result can be disastrous, as was the case with William Casey and the Reagan administration's policies in Central America."

> **ANTHONY LAKE**, *Somoza Falling* (1989).

"The reason I like to get [intelligence] from you folks is that I know you tell it like you see it. . . . You have no policy axe to grind and you are absolutely discreet."

> President **GEORGE H. W. BUSH** to DDI John Helgerson; quoted by Helgerson in CIA, *Symposium* (1994).

"I think elements of the Agency were kind of fearless [in their analyses of the USSR in 1990–91]. They did not tell policymakers what they wanted to hear. . . . You've got to have somebody who doesn't care what the president thinks of them."

> Former NSC staffer **NICHOLAS BURNS**; quoted in *Studies in Intelligence* 39/3 (fall 1995).

"One of the most important functions of intelligence is not to ease the job of policymakers but to complicate it, to tell them things they do not want to hear."

> Council on Foreign Relations, *Making Intelligence Smarter* (1996).

"Being Director of Central Intelligence is a skunk-at-the-garden-party job. You're always telling people things they don't want to hear—sometimes that their policies aren't working."

> Former DCI **R. JAMES WOOLSEY**; quoted in the *New York Times*, 9 December 1996.

"There is no room for either politics or partisanship in the way the intelligence community performs its functions."

> DCI **GEORGE TENET**; quoted by the Associated Press, 16 January 2001.

"CIA's most important responsibility is to present the President with the best possible data on which decisions can be made. The unvarnished intelligence . . . must be presented accurately, no matter whether the material supports the incumbent administration's policy or not."

Former DCI **RICHARD HELMS**, *A Look over My Shoulder* (2003).

"Let me take one of the explanations most commonly given [for CIA's assessment that Iraq had weapons of mass destruction]: Analysts were pressured to reach conclusions that would fit the political agenda of one or another administration. I deeply think that is a wrong explanation. . . . I had innumerable analysts who came to me in apology [saying] that the world that we were finding was not the world that they had thought existed and that they had estimated. . . . And never—not in a single case—was the explanation, 'I was pressured to do this.' . . . I did not come across a single one that felt it had been, in the military term, 'inappropriate command influence' that led them to take that position. It was not that. It was the honest difficulty based on the intelligence we had—the information that had been collected that led the analysts to that conclusion."

Former top U.S. weapons inspector **DAVID KAY**, testimony to the Senate Armed Services Committee, 28 January 2004.

"We will always call it as we see it. . . . As intelligence professionals, we go where the information takes us. We fear no fact or finding, whether it bears us out or not. Because we work for high goals —the protection of the American people—we must be judged by high standards. . . . But as all these reviews [of CIA's Iraq intelligence] are underway, we must take care. We cannot afford an en-

vironment to develop where analysts are afraid to make a call, where judgments are held back because analysts fear they will be wrong. Their work and these judgments make vital contributions to our nation's security. . . . We constantly learn and improve. And at no time will we allow our integrity or our willingness to make the tough calls be compromised."

DCI **GEORGE TENET**, remarks at Georgetown University, 5 February 2004.

OPENNESS & PUBLICITY

Only in a quotation book on intelligence from an American perspective does such a category make any sense, for intelligence in the United States, in all of human history, is uniquely open to public scrutiny. What CIA now discloses about itself (go ahead, try www.cia.gov) is astounding and probably invaluable to foreign services, and it would be inexplicable to American spymasters of previous generations. The American people can learn more about CIA than citizens of any other country can learn about their intelligence services. And this is a Good Thing.

See also: Budgets; Critics & Defenders; Intelligence & American Culture; Open Sources; Secrecy

"For nothing is hidden but it will be made clear, nothing secret but it will be made known and brought to light."

Luke 8:17 (New Jerusalem).

"How we shall ever win this war I cannot tell. . . . Mr Congreve invents a military rocket with vast potentialities—we instantly inform the world, like a hen that has laid an egg, thus throwing away all the effect of surprise. The worthy Mr Snodgrass finds out a way of rendering old ships serviceable in a short time and at little expense: without a moment's pause we publish his method in all the papers, together with drawings, lest some particular should escape our enemy's comprehension."

Fictional British spy Dr. Stephen Maturin lamenting Britain's openness on the eve of its 1810 invasion of Ile de France in **PATRICK O'BRIAN**, *The Mauritius Command* (1977).

"Four hostile newspapers are more to be feared than a thousand bayonets."

NAPOLEON; cited in Heinl, *Dictionary of Military and Naval Quotations* (1966).

"I say in giving intelligence to the enemy, in sowing discord and discontents in an army, these men fulfill all the conditions of spies. . . . Napoleon himself would have been defeated by a free press."

Union General **WILLIAM T. SHERMAN** on Northern reporters; quoted in Andrew, *For the President's Eyes Only* (1995).

"I will never again command an army in America if we must carry along paid spies. I will banish myself to some foreign country first."

Union General **WILLIAM T. SHERMAN**, letter to his wife, on reporters following his campaign, February 1863; cited in Heinl, *Dictionary of Military and Naval Quotations* (1966).

"My dear fellow, what do the public, the great unobservant public, who could hardly tell a weaver by his tooth or a compositor by his left thumb, care about the finer shades of analysis and deduction!"

Sherlock Holmes to Doctor Watson in Sir **ARTHUR CONAN DOYLE**, "The Adventure of the Copper Beeches" (1892).

"We can well believe that, inspired by a true spirit of patriotism, the editors of newspapers will accept any restriction placed on them in the way of publishing news which may in any way be detrimental to our army."

British Colonel **GEORGE FURSE**, *Information in War* (1895). Maybe in Britain.

"Spies are of no use nowadays. Their profession is over. The newspapers do their work instead."

OSCAR WILDE, *An Ideal Husband* (1895).

"It is not a lie not to tell a person that which he is not entitled to know."

ROBERT LANSING, President Wilson's Secretary of State; quoted in Winks, *Cloak and Gown* (1987).

"If we are going to do secret intelligence, we should not advertise the fact, nor should we set up an agency with pretentious titles. I think the term 'Central Intelligence Agency' is both misleading and dangerous. That is why I favor a 'Secretariat' . . . instead of a Central Intelligence Agency, and an unpretentious title for the executive head of it."

ALFRED McCORMACK, special assistant to the Secretary of State for Intelligence and Research, to the Bureau of the Budget Director Harold Smith, 10 January 1946; in *FRUS 1945–1950: Emergence of the Intelligence Establishment* (1996), document 70.

"In principle, all publicity is undesirable."

A Report to the National Security Council by the Secretaries of State and Defense on the Central Intelligence Agency (NSC 50), 1 July 1949; reproduced in Warner, *CIA Under Truman* (1994).

"The Director [of Central Intelligence, General Walter Bedell Smith], citing the case of a correspondent who had obtained a story concerning CIA, asked [whether] it were not possible to keep this story from being published or, if published, to have it so written that it would show no connection with the Agency. Colonel Grogan [the DCI's assistant] replied that this could be done and added that, in general, arrangements to stop a story could be made in individual cases. General Smith remarked that when news correspondents request information regarding some story that they might have, involving CIA, they should be told nothing. He added that in rare cases, however, it might be necessary to go to the top man of a news organization in order to kill a story. Colonel Grogan warned against off-the-record remarks. Regarding this, the Director stated that it is safe to make remarks 'off-the-record' only when there is complete censorship, which we do not have in this country."

> Minutes of CIA staff conference, 27 October 1952; reproduced in Warner, *CIA Under Truman* (1994).

"I am the head of the silent service and cannot advertise my wares. Sometimes, I admit, this is a bit irksome. For major reasons of policy, however, public relations must be sacrificed to the security of our operations."

> DCI **ALLEN DULLES**, speech to the Advertising Council, 19 September 1957.

"We took the position that the national interest came before the story."

> *Washington Post* reporter **CHALMERS ROBERTS** on why he and other reporters chose not to use information they had in the late 1950s on CIA's U-2 spyplane; quoted in Marchetti and Marks, *CIA and the Cult of Intelligence* (1975). How . . . quaint.

"We started moving in [to CIA's new headquarters building] in 1961, and there were big signs [saying] 'To CIA.' [DCI] Dulles was at the White House for a meeting sometime before the building was finished, and President Kennedy said to him,

'Mr. Dulles, do you really think you should have signs to your building? It doesn't seem consistent with the character of your organization.' Mr. Dulles said, 'Oh, Mr. President, we've got to have [them]. If we didn't have the signs, they probably could not get the building built; the workers wouldn't find their way.' He sort of laughed and left. A week or two passed, and Mr. Dulles was over at the White House for another meeting, [and the President said] 'Allen, I really think you ought to take those signs down at the CIA building. They attract attention, and your Agency is one that shouldn't attract attention.' [And Dulles said,] 'If we take the signs down, it would probably cause more comment than not.' So another day passed, and [operations chief] Richard Bissell got a phone call, and a very familiar voice said, 'Who in the hell do I have to talk to to get those signs down?' They were down the next day."

> Former CIA Executive Director **LYMAN KIRKPATRICK** in a 1967 interview; cited in Weber, *Spymasters* (1999).

"It is well to remember that what is told to the public also gets to the enemy. . . . [But] certain information must be given out if public confidence in the intelligence mission is to be strengthened and if the profession of the intelligence officer is to be understood."

> Former DCI **ALLEN DULLES**, *The Craft of Intelligence* (1963).

"'No comment' . . . for years has been, and I believe properly, the stock reply when the press calls on the CIA for information."

> Former DCI **ALLEN DULLES**, *The Craft of Intelligence* (1963).

"In my own experience in planning intelligence operations, I always considered, first, how the operation could be kept secret from the opponent and, second, how it could be kept from the press. Often the priority is reversed."

Former DCI **ALLEN DULLES**, *The Craft of Intelligence* (1963).

"[CIA] discovered at the end of 1963 that ... crop failure brought Soviet economic growth to a halt that year—to less than 2 percent—and completely torpedoed Khrushchev's boasts of overtaking the U.S. economy. President Johnson was delighted by this good news and instructed the CIA to release the data.... It was decided to hold the first press conference ever convened in CIA Headquarters Building in Langley.... Very few straight news stories emerged, however. Many reporters wrote colorful stories about being escorted through the security barriers at Langley and being escorted to the bathrooms. The worst coverage was in the *New York Times,* which [stated] in effect that CIA was conducting psychological warfare against the USSR by releasing dubious statistics on the economy.... It was an incredible performance."

Former DDI **RAY CLINE**, *Secrets, Spies and Scholars* (1976).

"I think there's a tradition that the CIA is a silent service, and it's a good one. I think the silence ought to begin with me."

CIA operations chief **RICHARD HELMS** on his appointment as DCI in 1966; quoted in Ranelagh, *The Agency* (1986). Helms also famously said, "I will never write a book," a quotation recently remembered by several retired CIA officers and Agency historians who were marking the posthumous publication of Helms's autobiography (with William Hood), *A Look over My Shoulder: A Life in the Central Intelligence Agency* (2003). The man, as expected, still kept the secrets.

"[In the 1970s] CIA, it seemed obvious to me, was in very real danger of ultimately being crippled as an effective weapon in the defense of the nation's security if not in fact threatened with being destroyed outright—unless something was done to reverse this trend. And that something, in my view, was to lift as much as possible that thick cloak of secrecy that had traditionally veiled the Agency and its operations from the scrutiny—and more important, the understanding—of the public at large."

Former DCI **WILLIAM COLBY**, *Honorable Men* (1978). The Colby approach remains a matter of debate within CIA.

"[DCI] Colby's 'passive' public relations program ... had its shortcomings.... A Hollywood company requested exterior shots on the grounds of the CIA for a film—a request granted, I'm told, when a California legislator leaned on the Director. The Bell Telephone Company would have insisted on the right to review the script, but CIA did not. The result was *Scorpio,* with Burt Lancaster cast as the CIA agent who assassinated people at the drop of a cloak."

Former senior CIA operations officer **DAVID ATLEE PHILLIPS**, *The Night Watch* (1978).

"Bill, do you really have to present all this material to us? We realize that there are secrets that you fellows need to keep and so nobody here is going to take it amiss if you feel that there are some questions you can't answer quite as fully as you seem to feel you have to."

Vice President **NELSON ROCKEFELLER**, chairman of President Ford's commission investigating CIA involvement in domestic activities, to DCI Colby; quoted in Colby, *Honorable Men* (1978).

"It is epistemologically impossible to determine what a journalist actually knows to be true as distinguished from what he merely suspects might be true."

EDWARD JAY EPSTEIN, *Commentary* (October 1978). Unless you first assume that he's lying.

"The legal requirement to satisfy inquiries under the Freedom of Information Act is further eroding security. . . . FOIA is good legislation if it results in someone learning from the Department of Transportation or the Department of the Interior or [from] elsewhere information the American public has a right to know. But it is used as a device to ferret out information about intelligence and security operations, and I think that is bad and ought to be changed. I realize that I am opening myself up to criticism about the public's right to know, but the public's right to know is the Russians' right to know; it is everybody else's right to know."

Former DCI **RICHARD HELMS** in a 1978 interview with David Frost; cited in Weber, *Spymasters* (1999).

"Whereas former secret agents in Britain tend to defect to the Russians, in America former secret agents tend to defect to their publishers."

DAVID FROST during a 1978 interview with former DCI Richard Helms; cited in Weber, *Spymasters* (1999).

"The media's . . . alternately tawdry, sloppy, and/or demonic portrayals of intelligence operations in recent years help to explain the public's mood surrounding the investigations of the intelligence community that occurred in the 1970s."

WALTER LAQUEUR, *A World of Secrets* (1985).

"I sometimes had the feeling reading the Church Committee reports that the public knows more about the inner workings of the CIA's Clandestine

Service than it does about the Department of Health and Human Services."

Newsweek editor **EVAN THOMAS** on the 1975 U.S. Senate investigation of intelligence activities, in *Studies in Intelligence* (summer 1995).

"The published findings of the Senate and House committees [investigating CIA in the mid-1970s] weighed some twenty pounds. My impression was that these hundreds of thousands of words were more useful to the KGB and some of our other adversaries than to the American taxpayers footing the bill."

Former DCI **RICHARD HELMS**, *A Look over My Shoulder* (2003).

"As many academicians prefer to denounce the existence of intelligence agencies from a distance rather than come to terms with them, the public, except for the sector that seeks sensations, is likely to discount even accurate accounts, or to think that an author has himself been part of that community, or has compromised normal scholarly canons, in order to gain access to materials; or to think of the field as akin to writing of crime from the inside: unclean."

Yale historian **ROBIN W. WINKS** on the challenges of writing intelligence history, in *Cloak and Gown: Scholars in the Secret War, 1939–1961* (1987). Winks doesn't let intelligence off the hook; he also says, "Historians traditionally rely on documentation, and the intelligence field is based on the denial, the falsifying, and the destruction of documentation."

"I was appalled by the irresponsible reporting, the twisting of evidence, the blatant use of unfounded assumption, and the lack of perspective, historical or otherwise. I knew for a fact that CIA analysts who turned in such sloppy, loosey-goosey work would have been fired. . . . Soon the American press . . . began to treat as an established fact that CIA had over twenty-five years set itself up as an independent body, answerable in no way to Congress, the White House, or American traditions of truth and fair play, and had undertaken through malice or whim, or both, to assassinate national leaders far and wide, to topple the governments of small countries at random, to tap telephones and open the mail of U.S. citizens, and for the hell of it, to administer drugs to unsuspecting persons and observe the result."

> Former DDI **R. JACK SMITH** on *Washington Post* coverage of CIA, in *The Unknown CIA* (1989).

"A new phenomenon, I believe, is the thirst for notoriety that leads some to paint the defenders of their country as the worst threats to its freedoms. The men and women who serve America on the silent battlefield of intelligence have neither the forum nor the means to rebut these slanders."

> Former DDCI General **VERNON WALTERS**, *Silent Missions* (1978).

"The CIA must build, not assume, public support, and it can do this only by informing the public of the nature of its activities and accepting the public's control over them. . . . A public informed of the CIA's accomplishments and capabilities will support it. A public aware of its true mission and the limits of its authority will accept it. A public that understands the issues and problems involving intelligence and its role in the American government will debate and decide them. A public convinced of the CIA's value will help protect its true secrets."

> Former DCI **WILLIAM COLBY**, *Honorable Men* (1978).

"On October 1, 1978, in a speech at Cape Canaveral, Florida, President Carter acknowledged that the United States had been using space satellites to conduct photographic reconnaissance. . . . It was the president's intent that U.S. representatives and legislative supporters of SALT be able to talk about their use in assuring the United States that the Soviets were not cheating on the provisions of the treaty."

> **JEFFREY RICHELSON**, *United States Strategic Reconnaissance* (1983) and *America's Secret Eyes* (1990).

"Destroying the mystique of the CIA is in itself a psychological handicap."

> **HENRY KISSINGER** in the *Washington Post*, 26 February 1979.

"Every word in this manuscript is classified."

> Initial CIA security review of the manuscript of former CIA operations officer William Hood's memoir, which eventually was published in 1982 as *Mole* and became recognized as a great espionage classic. Even "and" and "the," apparently. Hood related his experience to Agency officers in April 2003.

"The dangers of placing faith in documentary records was pointed out by one particular retired Head of Station who told me that much of the information in his Station's Registry was pure fiction."

> British intelligence historian **NIGEL WEST** in 1983; cited in Polmar and Allen, *Encyclopedia of Espionage* (1997).

"I want a no-profile agency."

> DCI **WILLIAM CASEY**, quoted in the *Washington Post*, 29 April 1983. Too late.

"I believe that the American people should be informed about [overhead] reconnaissance systems. It would make it much easier for our political leaders to justify a number of important military and foreign policy initiatives if people really knew what our adversaries around the world are doing."

> Former NRO Director **HANS MARK** in 1985; quoted in Richelson, *America's Secret Eyes* (1990).

"The story of James Angleton as chief of Counter-Intelligence cannot be told now, at least not well, and perhaps never. . . . To tell the story the historian would need to have unfettered access to the archives of the British, French, Italian, Israeli, and Russian intelligence services, as well as the American and, quite probably, others. No such historian will ever exist. The scholar lacks access, assets, penetration, sources, contacts—the entire array of resources by which a professional intelligence officer may, after much time, great expenditure of money, and with the support of his government, obtain an intelligence story. Angleton both tests and proves Sherman Kent's dictum: while much can be learned that is presumed to be irretrievable, one cannot learn enough to tell in the end precisely how interesting, how significant, how true what one does know may be."

> **ROBIN W. WINKS** on the intelligence historian's dilemma in *Cloak and Gown: Scholars in the Secret War, 1939–1961* (1987). Angleton was CIA's CI chief from 1954 to 1974. Of intelligence history more generally, Winks says, "If the truth were known hundreds of books now on the shelves would be reclassified from history to fiction. But the truth is not known."

"One of the ways we are accountable is through the press. . . . Our policy with the media—as it is with the Congress—is to be both candid and responsive. . . . We cannot build the capability [to inform policymakers objectively] without confidentiality, the protection of our sources and methods. You do the same. We will help you when we can, but when we don't it's not because we don't want

to. It's because we can't. . . . We are all serving the cause of freedom in a better and safer world."

> DCI **WILLIAM WEBSTER**, remarks to the American Society of Newspaper Editors, 11 April 1988, in *1988 Speeches*.

"I firmly believe the government has a right, and an obligation, to keep certain information secret. . . . We live in a dirty and dangerous world. There are some things the general public does not need to know and shouldn't."

> **KATHARINE GRAHAM**, chairman of the board of the *Washington Post*, remarks at CIA Headquarters, 16 November 1988; reprinted in *Studies in Intelligence* (winter 1988). Did she ever tell this to the staff of the *Post*?

"The Freedom of Information Act worked wonders with the Federal Bureau of Investigation. . . . It worked less well with the Central Intelligence Agency."

> **PHILLIP KNIGHTLEY**, *The Second Oldest Profession* (1988), in his Acknowledgments.

"In spite of the occasional slings and arrows of outrageous publicity, more people than ever before are interested in intelligence work. . . . Applications are coming in at the rate of one thousand per month."

> DCI **WILLIAM WEBSTER**, remarks of 10 April 1989, in *1989 Speeches*.

"Information about intelligence activities will never be as readily available as some civil libertarians would like nor as restricted as some intelligence professionals might like, but the openness of the U.S. intelligence community is extraordinary among nations."

> **BRUCE BERKOWITZ** and **ALLAN GOODMAN**, *Strategic Intelligence* (1989).

"The British secret services have been held in high esteem all over the world by those who are interested in such matters. How do we maintain that esteem? Of course, partly by secrecy, but partly by allowing the different successes to be known after an appropriate time."

> **JULIAN ARMORY**, member of Parliament and former SIS officer, in the House of Commons, 24 January 1989; quoted in West, *Faber Book of Espionage* (1993).

"The world's ultimate oxymoron."

> **TED KOPPEL** to CIA Director of Public Affairs William Baker on the term "director of public affairs" for any intelligence organization; quoted in *Studies in Intelligence* (spring 1990).

"One who never volunteers anything to the press, who always says 'no comment' in response to a question, and who just minds his own business."

> CIA operations officer on the ideal CIA spokesman to CIA Director of Public Affairs William Baker; quoted in *Studies in Intelligence* (spring 1990).

"Building a reconnaissance satellite obviously requires one to know the maximum focal length or antenna size that will fit on a satellite intended to be launched from a particular booster or to collect a particular type of data. But such details are no more critical to a public discussion of intelligence than, say, the precise specifications of a thermonuclear weapon are critical to a discussion of arms control."

> **BRUCE BERKOWITZ** and **ALLAN GOODMAN**, *Strategic Intelligence* (1989).

"What date are we going to start the ground attack? Where are our forces most vulnerable to attack? If there is one thing you don't want Saddam Hussein to know, what would that be?"

> *Saturday Night Live* "reporters" asking questions in a "General Schwarzkopf press briefing" skit on the NBC program during the Gulf war, 1991.

"We are under no illusions that CIA, whatever the level of its efforts, will be able to win recognition as an 'open' institution."

> DCI **ROBERT GATES**, address to the Oklahoma Press Association, 21 February 1992; in *Speeches* (1993).

"Few realize that CIA was the world's first publicly acknowledged intelligence service—and it remains perhaps the only one that is based on the rule of law."

> DCI **ROBERT GATES**, remarks to the American Law Institute, 15 May 1992; in *Speeches* (1993).

"It is very difficult now to remember that in Britain, which had a very exaggerated notion of official secrecy, all Governments, up to and including that of Margaret Thatcher, in the 1980s, agreed that we could not even officially admit that we had a foreign intelligence service. So it was not until the Queen's speech of 1992 that the British Government actually admitted [it]."

> **CHRISTOPHER ANDREW**, interview in the Italian online journal *Per Aspera ad Veritatem* (May–August 2001).

"After World War II, we were ahead of the Soviets in nuclear technology and about even with them in electronics. We maintained a closed system for nuclear design while designing electronics in the open. Their systems were closed in both regards. After 40 years, we are at parity in nuclear science, whereas, thanks to our open system in the study of electronics, we are decades ahead of the Russians."

> Dr. **EDWARD TELLER** speaking to Department of Energy personnel in the early 1990s; quoted in *Forbes ASAP* (7 October 2002).

"There is no question that we must continue to protect intelligence sources and methods. But there is no reason why we cannot describe to the American people what it is we do, what our priorities are, our process for producing intelligence and providing it to policymakers and the Congress, and the way in which we are organized to do that."

> DCI **ROBERT GATES**, remarks to the Association of Former Intelligence Officers of Boston, Massachusetts, 14 November 1992; in *Speeches* (1993).

"It is an unpalatable irony that the two senior SIS officers to betray their country [Kim Philby and George Blake] received substantial royalties from British publishers for their memoirs, while [others] who all served their country faithfully were to be harassed through the courts for attempting to do the same thing."

> **NIGEL WEST**, in *Faber Book of Espionage* (1993).

"The first purpose of the intelligence community isn't to enable scholars to write better history."

> **RICHARD BETTS** of Columbia University at a CIA-sponsored conference on teaching intelligence; in CIA, *Symposium* (1994).

"I am not particularly interested in being enormously visible as Director of Central Intelligence to the press."

> DCI **JOHN DEUTCH** in a meeting with CIA employees, 11 May 1995.

"I would never knowingly publish a story that I thought would get somebody killed. There are certain basic human standards that even the press can obey."

> *New York Times* reporter **TIM WEINER**, whose beat includes CIA, remarks at a conference in Washington, D.C., October 1995.

"Not everything a government is doing, or even just thinking about and discussing, should be disclosed—that would be the end of skillful, subtly designed action. Publicity is the enemy of intellectual honesty, objectivity, and decisiveness."

> Former CIA operations chief **RICHARD BISSELL**, *Reflections of a Cold Warrior* (1996). The Bay of Pigs operation, which Bissell oversaw, reflected few of these things.

"I have never seen a greater gap between what an agency is actually doing and what the public perception is of that agency. . . . There is a lot of very good work that goes on in that agency that the American public would be proud of if only they knew about it."

> DCI-nominee **ANTHONY LAKE** in Senate confirmation hearings, 12 March 1997.

"In the annals of international spookery, has there ever been a cadre of spies that has been so thoroughly exposed as the Central Intelligence Agency? The revelations have become a kind of burlesque show: as the trappings of secrecy fall away, the nation gets a peek at everything that was supposed to be private."

> Television reviewer **WALTER GOODMAN** in the *New York Times*, 31 March 1997.

"According to the dictionary definition, 'redact' means to edit, revise, and prepare for publication. In CIA parlance, 'redact' means to delete key words and phrases, to censor sometimes beyond recognition. . . . In an especially chilling moment, one troglodyte from the Directorate of Operations referred to the Executive Order [on declassification] as that 'silly old law.'"

> **GEORGE C. HERRING**, "My Years with the CIA," *Organization of American Historians Newsletter* (May 1997). Herring is describing his experiences as a member of CIA's Historical Review Panel, a body of outside historians hired in part to deal with troglodytism.

"[Declassification] is very challenging work. We have to be painstaking. We have to have double and triple checks to be absolutely certain we are not compromising valuable sources and methods, even when the records are 40 or 50 years old. And that's why it takes so long. We don't want to release something that's going to create a problem for some brave source. We can't unilaterally release information that would reflect on another government. There are also some very complicated foreign policy sensitivities."

> **BRIAN LATELL**, director of CIA's Center for the Study of Intelligence; quoted in the *New York Times*, 20 May 1997.

"I request a copy of every document relating to the CIA."

> Freedom of Information Act request, 1997. Fortunately, FoIA requires that requesters limit the scope of the request to documents that are "reasonably described."

"No other nation's foreign intelligence agency has voluntarily released as much information about its past as has the Central Intelligence Agency. And within the limits imposed upon me by law not to jeopardize intelligence sources or methods, impinge on our liaison relations with other countries, or interfere with our ability to carry out the Agency's mission, we will build upon that record in the years ahead."

> DCI **GEORGE TENET**, statement on declassification, May 1998.

"When you work for a largely secret organization, you get used to being misunderstood fairly often by the public."

> DCI **GEORGE TENET**, "What 'New' Role for the C.I.A.?" *New York Times*, 27 October 1998.

"A child in the dark will imagine things—creepy, scary things. So it is with a nation kept in the dark. The obsession with secrecy has bred a population vulnerable to conspiracy theories and sinister imaginings. Who can blame those who believe the CIA was complicit in the assassination of JFK or responsible for introducing crack cocaine into South-Central L.A.? People were constantly asking me if I was afraid for my life while I was working on my CIA book, so little did they trust their own government."

> Journalist **TED GUP**, author of a book on CIA officers killed in the line of duty, in *Newsweek* (9 October 2000).

"I don't wake up every morning asking how many documents we declassified today, but I've got as many people working on declassification as on counterterrorism."

> DCI **GEORGE TENET**, interview in *USA Today*, 11 October 2000. And that was a problem, as it turned out.

"Intelligence agencies are usually laid open to public view only when a nation is defeated in war and its conquerors are able to ransack its archives."

> CIA historian **MICHAEL WARNER**, Introduction to *The Office of Strategic Services* (2000).

"I think a DCI should keep a low profile. The only reason the media would want me to appear [on talk shows] is to figure out how to drive wedges between the intelligence community and policymakers, and I'm not going to let that happen."

DCI **GEORGE TENET** on why he declines to appear on Sunday talk shows, in *USA Today*, 11 October 2000.

"Declassification is not easy. There are no shortcuts. It takes experienced, knowledgeable people . . . going over it page by page, line by line. There is no alternative. A mistake can put a life in danger or jeopardize a bilateral relationship integral to our country's security. Despite the difficulties involved in the declassification process, no other nation's foreign intelligence agency has voluntarily released as much information about its past as has the Central Intelligence Agency."

DCI **GEORGE TENET**, remarks at Princeton University, 8 March 2001. But it's never enough.

"I thought it would be sensible to let the hounds see the fox."

Sir **STEPHEN LANDER**, director of Britain's MI5, at a rare public appearance; quoted in the *Economist* (31 March 2001).

"The American people aren't told much about your labors. In fact, you might be the only federal agency where not making the newspapers or network news qualifies as good news."

President **GEORGE W. BUSH**, remarks at CIA, 20 March 2001.

"If they appear to be interested in accuracy, if they do not misportray the role of the agency, and we can do so without interfering with our mission,

we will consider providing assistance. We will decide on a case-by-case basis."

CIA public affairs chief **BILL HARLOW** on the Agency's cooperation with television and film producers; quoted in the *New York Times*, 6 May 2001.

"So far as official [British] government policy is concerned, the British security and intelligence services, MI5 and MI6, do not exist. Enemy agents are found under gooseberry bushes and intelligence is brought by the storks."

Sir **MICHAEL HOWARD**, professor of history at Oxford; quoted by Christopher Andrew in the *Times* (London), 17 September 2001. Clever sources and methods.

"President Bush has approved a secret effort to strengthen a diverse array of groups opposing the Taliban rulers of Afghanistan, administration officials said today."

"Bush Approves Covert Aid for Taliban Foes," *New York Times*, 1 October 2001. This sort of thing gives new and strange meanings to the words "secret" and "covert."

"We knew our son was in a bad situation, but he was not confirmed dead. . . . When I asked everyone to please don't put this on the news, please, you don't have to say he was in the CIA. . . . Everyone was getting on the news media and the papers and saying 'Mike Spann was a CIA operative.' And if those folks over there had been able to receive those transmissions, I feel like they would have shot him if they hadn't already shot him. . . . People need to realize that there's a time for everything. You can wait sometimes and sometimes . . . you need to shut up. . . . I probably feel a little angry about that because I felt like I wasn't getting any help from some of the news media . . . because they were doing things and saying things on TV and on the radio and in the newspapers that were putting his life at risk."

> JOHNNY SPANN, father of fallen CIA officer Mike Spann, who was killed in Afghanistan on 25 November 2001 during an uprising of Taliban prisoners he was interrogating; press conference of 28 November 2001. "Sometimes you need to shut up" should be taught in journalism school.

"The job of the government is not to make reporters' jobs easier. They don't have to do that. They have other things to do than to maximize the amount of information that reporters get. The most unattractive aspect of reporting is when reporters whine and complain about how they're not getting enough information."

> FRED BARNES, editor of the *Weekly Standard;* on "Media Matters," WETA-TV, Washington, D.C., 21 March 2002.

"Journalists' sources are protected by custom if not by law, yet a secret agent whose reports are of national importance and whose life and the well-being of his family may be at stake is considered fair game for the media."

> Former DCI RICHARD HELMS, *A Look over My Shoulder* (2003).

OPEN SOURCES

Sometimes the best information, like Poe's purloined letter, is right there out in the open, hidden like a tree in a vast forest. Even so, the openness of these open sources—and the fact that they're usually cost-free or nearly so—makes it hard to convince intelligence consumers that the information from them is often worth more than that acquired dearly and through highly classified means. The trick is to find the important stuff among the dreck, which puts a premium on the expertise of analysts who are suffering from information and metaphoric overload: to separate the wheat from the chaff and find the needle in the haystack, it's necessary to drink from a fire hose with a straw.

See also: Academia; Analysis & Analysts; Openness & Publicity

"Contrive to send us in regular succession some of the best London, French, and Dutch newspapers, with any valuable political publications that may concern North America."

> Continental Congress, Committee of Secret Correspondence, to an agent in Europe, 21 December 1776; cited in Sayle, "The Historical Underpinnings of the U.S. Intelligence Community," in *International Journal of Intelligence and Counterintelligence* (spring 1986).

"If it is true that the better diplomats are to be found among the Russians than among the most advanced peoples, the reason is that our press informs the Russians about every plan that is proposed and every event that occurs among us. Instead of prudently concealing our weaknesses we reveal them every morning with passion, while the Byzantine policy of the Russians, at work in the shadows, is careful to hide what they are thinking and doing and fearing. We go forward in the light of day; they advance under cover. We are blinded by the ignorance in which they leave us; they are enlightened by our candor. We are weakened by rumor; they are strengthened by secrecy. And there you have the secret of their cleverness."

> Marquis ASTOLPHE DE CUSTINE, *Letters from Russia, 1839* (1843).

"We have no need of spies. We have the *Times.*"

> Tsar NICHOLAS I during the Crimean War; quoted in Haswell, *Spies and Spymasters* (1977).

"You are aware of the great amount of valuable information obtained by us through the medium of the enterprising journals of the North, and we may derive profit from their example by unremitting and judicious reserve in communications for the Southern journals."

> Confederate Secretary of War **LEROY WALKER** to Southern newspapermen, 1861; quoted in Fishel, *Secret War for the Union* (1996).

"From them we learned not only of all arrivals, but also of assignments to brigades and divisions, and, by tabulating these, we always knew quite accurately the strength of the enemy's army."

> Confederate officer on the value of Northern newspapers during the Civil War; quoted in Miller, *Spying for America* (1989). Lot of good it did.

"The chief of my secret service department would have willingly paid $1,000 for such information."

> Union General **JOSEPH HOOKER** to Secretary of War Edwin Stanton, following the April 1863 publication in the *Washington Morning Chronicle* of a report on the composition and overall strength of the Federal army; quoted in Fishel, *Secret War for the Union* (1996).

"Whatever may be the result of the military operations about Vicksburg, their interest will soon be eclipsed by greater events elsewhere. Within the next fortnight the campaign of 1863 will be pretty well decided. The most important movement of the war will probably be made in that time."

> *Richmond Examiner* editorial, May 1863, an item that helped Union intelligence chief Colonel George Sharpe conclude that Lee's army was commencing a long march to the northwest; cited in Fishel, *Secret War for the Union* (1996).

"At all times, but more so in time of war, newspapers contain a considerable fund of information, and from a diligent perusal of them many things may be learnt. . . . In peace certain particulars which the general reader would pass over as being of no interest, turn out of great consequence to such as know how to draw useful inferences from them, and when many of these items are put together they may reveal matters of considerable importance."

> British Colonel **GEORGE FURSE**, *Information in War* (1895).

"After the [Spanish-American] war began [it was discovered] that one major War Department secret report on the Philippines had actually just been copied from the *Encyclopedia Britannica*."

> **BRADLEY SMITH**, "The American Road to Central Intelligence," in Jeffreys-Jones and Andrew, *Eternal Vigilance* (1997). Ah, but did Madrid *know* we had the *Encyclopedia*?

"The world is full of obvious things which nobody by any chance observes."

> Sherlock Holmes in Sir **ARTHUR CONAN DOYLE**, *The Hound of the Baskervilles* (1901).

"Our information regarding the famine in Russia is from Bolshevist sources, and while I am not very confident as to the accuracy of these sources, I don't think there can be the slightest doubt as to the extent of the catastrophe. We are sending on to the Department regularly Bolshevist radio messages which are filled with figures and statistics of the famine."

> State Department official (and future DCI) **ALLEN DULLES**, letter from the U.S. legation in Constantinople to the U.S. Commerce Department, 21 August 1921; original in Hoover Institution archives, Stanford University.

"If you read the *New York Times*, the *Washington Post*, and the *Boston Globe*, you don't need to go to college."

> **MOE BERG**, legendary major league baseball player, lawyer, intellectual, and OSS operative; quoted in Nicholas Dawi-

doff, *The Catcher Was a Spy* (1994). Berg, who had two Ivy League degrees and had studied at the Sorbonne, read as many as a dozen newspapers daily.

"Such information as published by your paper, if true, would furnish any real or potential enemy a valuable basis to predicate their operations."

> Rear Admiral **CLAUDE BLOCH**, commandant of the Fourteenth Naval District in Hawaii, complaining to the *Honolulu Star-Bulletin* about its coverage of U.S. Pacific Fleet movements, 4 March 1941; cited in Prange, *At Dawn We Slept* (1981). Japanese consulate personnel used newspaper accounts and their own observations between February and December 1941 to establish patterns of ship movements—including the useful conclusion that most ships were in Pearl Harbor on Sunday mornings (as indeed they were on 7 December 1941).

"In February 1941 an intelligence unit was created for collecting open source data of a particularly useful kind. This intelligence unit proved so useful in providing information to government officials who covered foreign affairs that it has been in operation ever since. The Federal Communications Commission, at the suggestion of the State Department, established a Foreign Broadcast Monitoring Service to record broadcasts of foreign origin, translate speeches and news items, and report the important findings to other agencies. . . . Its name was settled upon later as the 'Foreign Broadcast Information Service' (FBIS) and it eventually ended up as a 'service of common concern' managed by CIA."

> Former DDI **RAY CLINE**, *Secrets, Spies and Scholars* (1976).

"There is no reliable majority among the American people at present in favor of Roosevelt's policy and of entry into the war."

> German Foreign Minister **JOACHIM VON RIBBENTROP** to Adolf Hitler, August 1941; quoted in Levin, "Efficacy of Propaganda" (1999). Ribbentrop based his analysis

on American public polling that showed that only one in five Americans favored going to war to help Britain.

"Japanese radio intensifies still further its defiant, hostile tone; in contrast to its behavior during earlier periods of tension, Radio Tokyo makes no peace appeals. Comment on the United States is bitter and increased."

> First analytic report of the Foreign Broadcast Monitoring Service (later FBIS), 6 December 1941; cited in *Studies in Intelligence* 45/3 (2001).

"The overwhelming majority of basic intelligence data is obtained by open observation, by studying reference books, consulting libraries, reading the newspapers of foreign countries, listening to their radios, interviewing bona fide travelers. . . . Approximately 95 per cent of our peacetime intelligence comes to us from open sources: from books published abroad; from the reports of observing travelers; from newspaper articles or surveys in professional magazines; from foreign radio broadcasts and similar sources. An additional 4 per cent comes from semi-open sources: reports of naval attachés or informants who gather their data in the normal pursuit of their everyday business. Only 1 per cent, and often less than that, is derived from truly secret sources: agent reports and the information obtained from certain confidants and contacts. There is very little these confidential agents can tell that is not accessible to an alert analyst who knows what he is looking for and knows how to find it in open sources."

> **ELLIS ZACHARIAS**, *Secret Missions* (1946). Zacharias was a career intelligence officer for the U.S. Navy, specializing in Japan.

"Pursuant to the provisions of Section 102 of the National Security Act of 1947 . . . the Director of Central Intelligence shall conduct all Federal monitoring of foreign propaganda and press broadcasts required for the collection of intelligence information to meet the needs of all Departments and Agencies in connection with the National Security."

> National Security Council Intelligence Directive No. 6, 12 December 1947; in *FRUS 1945–1950: Emergence of the Intelligence Establishment* (1996), document 424.

"That extremely important surveillance organization known as the Foreign Broadcast Information Branch [*sic*] is established [to] pick up the most significant programs; the home office transcribes them, translates (and sometimes abstracts them), reproduces them, and sends them around to officers of the government."

> **SHERMAN KENT**, *Strategic Intelligence* (1949).

"It is essential not to lose any time in building the uranium bomb."

> Soviet physicist **G. N. FLYOROV** in a letter to Stalin, May 1942; cited in Andrew and Gordievsky, *KGB* (1990). Flyorov had been monitoring British and American scientific journals and, noting a dramatic drop in the articles on nuclear fission, had concluded—correctly—that such research had become secret and that the U.S. atomic bomb program was under way. The first Soviet atomic bomb was tested in August 1949.

"Of the things our state must know about other states some 90 percent may be discovered through overt means."

> **SHERMAN KENT** in 1951; quoted in Winks, *Cloak and Gown* (1987). Kent later revised his estimate upward to 95 percent. It's safe to say that intelligence analysts believe that a higher overt/covert ratio exists than do clandestine or technical collection officers.

"FBIS got its first 'scoop' in December 1941, when it reported Italy's declaration of war against the United States ahead of the wire services. Then,

during the 1962 Cuban Missile Crisis, FBIS provided President Kennedy with the first news of the Soviet decision to withdraw missiles from Cuba. And in 1967 FBIS provided Washington with the first report that war had broken out between Egypt and Israel. . . . Throughout its history, [FBIS] has been right there—close to the action—giving us an understanding of world dramas as they unfold."

> DCI **WILLIAM WEBSTER**, remarks for FBIS's fiftieth anniversary, 26 February 1991; in *1991 Speeches*.

"Even a novel or a play may contain useful information about the state of a nation."

> Former DCI **ALLEN DULLES**, *The Craft of Intelligence* (1963).

"More can be deduced by an intelligent study of public sources than by any number of 'reliable' but unintelligent 'agents' listening at keyholes or swapping drinks at bars."

> **HUGH TREVOR-ROPER**, veteran of both MI5 and SIS, in 1968; cited in West, *Faber Book of Espionage* (1993).

"In general, we tend to undervalue unclassified information. For example, because the public speeches of Saddam Hussein and other dictators are often florid and mendacious, we tend to ignore them and not subject them to serious analysis. In this case, at least, that was a mistake."

> **PAUL WOLFOWITZ**, Undersecretary of Defense for Policy, 1989–93; quoted in *Studies in Intelligence* (spring 1995).

"The CIA is reluctant to acknowledge how much it relies upon open sources. Some officials fear that Congress will not appropriate money for experts who 'just read the newspapers.' But all agencies performing economic intelligence must admit the obvious: the world economy functions on the basis of publicly available information. In general, the CIA does more to aggregate and interpret open-source literature than any other government agency. . . . To say, as some do, that this task is little more than 'reading the newspapers' is like saying that the US Navy's multibillion dollar acoustic signal processing technology just 'listens to the ocean.'"

> **PHILIP ZELIKOW**, "American Economic Intelligence," in Jeffreys-Jones and Andrew, *Eternal Vigilance* (1997).

"Let's say you're looking at Iraq and you've got a history of top scientists working there. You notice that so-and-so hasn't published for three years and is currently working in a baby milk factory. It's the old story of 'listening to silence.' You infer that either the man's suddenly become stupid, or there's a black project working there."

> Open source database expert **RICHARD CLAVENS**; quoted in Fialka, *War by Other Means* (1997).

"So much of what the CIA learns is collected from newspaper clippings that the director of the agency should be called the Pastemaster General."

> Columnist **WESLEY PRUDEN** in the *Washington Times*, 27 November 2001.

"Making a case for avoiding open source intelligence is a bit like saying that the air is filled with carcinogens and other harmful substances and that it would be better not to breathe."

> **ARTHUR HULNICK**, "Expanding Open Source Intelligence," paper presented at the International Studies Association convention, New Orleans, March 2002.

ORIGINS OF CENTRAL INTELLIGENCE

Before CIA was created in 1947, U.S. intelligence was fragmented by function and by institution. The relatively late development of a centralized American system

of intelligence brought the United States in line with the practice of most other countries in human history. Nevertheless, it was a close thing—and the Literary Spy is aware that some still rue its success.

See also: Covert Action; FBI & Law Enforcement; Fighting the Cold War; Intelligence & American Culture; Intelligence, the Missions of; Redundancy Redundancy; U.S. Intelligence "Community"

"There must naturally be a connection between the Military Intelligence Department and the Foreign Office. On the subject of general policy the latter receives from its diplomatic agents abroad much useful information relating to military matters, which cannot but be most useful to the former; whilst the officers of the Intelligence Department, being specialists, can always supply the Foreign Office with their views on the probable military effect which may result from passing events."

> British Colonel **GEORGE FURSE**, *Information in War* (1895).

"Leaving the acquisition of intelligence simply to the discretion of a number of individuals, without any central guide to direct their efforts in the most profitable manner, does not appear the best plan; acting thus we are liable to waste our exertions in a wrong direction."

> British Colonel **GEORGE FURSE**, *Information in War* (1895).

"[The Bureau of Investigation and the Secret Service] are willing to report to the State Department but not [to] each other."

> Secretary of State **ROBERT LANSING** to President Woodrow Wilson, April 1917; quoted in Andrew, *For the President's Eyes Only* (1995).

"The lessons to America are clear as day. We must not be caught napping with no adequate national Intelligence organization. The several Federal bureaus should be welded into one, and that one should be eternally and comprehensively vigilant."

New York Police Commissioner **ARTHUR WOODS**, 1919; quoted in *Studies in Intelligence* 46/1 (2002).

"File this."

Army intelligence chief Colonel **STANLEY FORD**, responding to a proposal from civilian John Gade on establishing "some sort of a central Intelligence Agency, reporting directly to [President] Hoover," May 1929; quoted in Troy, *Donovan and the CIA* (1981).

"In great confidence O.N.I. [Office of Naval Intelligence] tells me there is considerable reason to believe that there is a movement afoot, fostered by Col. Donovan, to establish a super agency controlling all intelligence. This would mean that such an agency, no doubt under Col. Donovan, would collect, collate and possibly evaluate all military intelligence that we now gather from foreign countries. From the point of view of the War Department, such a move would appear to be very disadvantageous, if not calamitous."

U.S. Army intelligence chief General **SHERMAN MILES** to General George Marshall, 8 April 1941; cited in Troy, *Donovan and the CIA* (1981).

"[Donovan's] concept presupposed a multi-faceted organization which would collect information, conduct research and analysis, coordinate information, print and broadcast propaganda, mount special operations, inspire guerrilla action, and send commandos into battle. The program was, at one and the same time, commonplace and unusual, academic and operational, overt and covert,

peaceful and forceful, legal and illegal. Donovan's task [was] unprecedented in American history."

THOMAS TROY, *Donovan and the CIA* (1981). But very much precedented in world history.

"The military and naval intelligence services have gone into the field of undercover intelligence to a limited extent. In view of the appointment of the Coordinator of Information and the work which is understood the President desires him to undertake, it is believed that the undercover intelligence of the two services should be consolidated under the Coordinator of Information. The reasons for this are that an undercover intelligence service is much more effective if under one head rather than three, and that a civilian agency, such as the Coordinator of Information, has a distinct advantage over any military or naval agency in the administration of such a service."

General **SHERMAN MILES** to Secretary of War Henry Stimson, 5 September 1941; quoted in Cline, *Secrets, Spies and Scholars* (1976). The Coordinator of Information was the small agency headed by William Donovan in 1941–42 that was the immediate predecessor of the Office of Strategic Services.

"It was nobody's particular and exclusive business to study all intelligence material and come up with an estimate. Nobody got anything but excerpts and driblets."

SAMUEL ELIOT MORISON on the intelligence situation that contributed to the Pearl Harbor debacle, in *The Two-Ocean War* (1963).

"With virtually no precedent, virtually no model to build upon, Donovan really did set out to build this thing [OSS] from scratch. There was no sense of how to do it right, how to do it wrong, simply because it hadn't been done before."

Historian **BARRY KATZ**, remarks at a conference on "The Origins and Development of the CIA," CIA report of March 1995.

"The precise name—'Central Intelligence Agency' —appeared for the first time in March 1942. Then, the Marine commandant proposed the establishment of such an agency at Pearl Harbor to serve as a 'clearing house' for the 'Advanced Joint Intelligence Centers' which at the same time he was proposing be established throughout the Pacific."

THOMAS TROY, *Donovan and the CIA* (1981).

"There seemed to be no coordination. Because everybody was bent upon doing his own intelligence work, duplication abounded in virtually every government agency. The Navy for the time being had its ONI, but the Office of Communications was also doing its own independent intelligence work and passing it directly to the Commander in Chief. The Army had G-2, with the Secretary of War just about to set up still another intelligence agency under his own jurisdiction and independent of G-2. There were intelligence organizations at the headquarters of theater commanders which maintained an independent attitude, unmindful of the needs of Washington. The Office of Strategic Services was trying its wings. The Treasury Department, Commerce Department, State Department, Office of Censorship, and several other agencies were busily engaged in intelligence work; and the first thing the newly established Office of War Information did was to establish its own intelligence service."

ELLIS ZACHARIAS on the state of U.S. intelligence when he became deputy director of naval intelligence in 1942, in *Secret Missions* (1946). Zacharias's experience turned him into a champion of centralized intelligence.

"A new and somewhat cumbersome and possibly dangerous organization."

U.S. Army intelligence chief General **GEORGE STRONG** to President Franklin Roosevelt's advisor Harry Hopkins on "Proposed Establishment of a Central Intelligence Service," 13 December 1944; cited in Troy, *Donovan and the CIA* (1981).

"The [proposal] is unsound and dangerous. If approved, it would provide for a monstrous, inefficient and expensive organization, capable of paralyzing military and naval intelligence, and dangerous to the national government."

U.S. Army intelligence policy paper, commenting on a Joint Staff proposal to create a "Central Intelligence Agency," 21 December 1944; cited in Troy, *Donovan and the CIA* (1981).

"At the end of this war, there simply must be a consolidation of Foreign Intelligence between State and War and the Navy."

President **FRANKLIN ROOSEVELT**, January 1945; quoted in Andrew, *For the President's Eyes Only* (1995).

"Apropos of your memorandum of November 18, 1944, relative to the establishment of a central intelligence agency, I should appreciate your calling together the chiefs of the foreign intelligence and internal security units in the various executive agencies, so that a consensus of opinion can be secured. It appears to me that all of the ten executive departments, as well as the Foreign Economic Administration, and the Federal Communications Commission have a direct interest in the proposed venture. They should all be asked to contribute their suggestions to the proposed centralized intelligence service."

President **FRANKLIN ROOSEVELT** to William Donovan, 5 April 1945 (one week before Roosevelt's death); cited in CIA, *"Our First Line of Defense"* (1996).

"With Roosevelt's death the first, indispensable prerequisite of a true central intelligence system also perished—Presidential understanding of the concept and the Chief Executive's trust in the man who would put the concept into practice."

Former DDI **RAY CLINE**, *Secrets, Spies and Scholars* (1976).

"I considered it very important to this country to have a sound, well-organized intelligence system, both in the present and in the future. . . . Plans needed to be made but it was imperative that we refrain from rushing into something that would produce harmful and unnecessary rivalries among the various intelligence agencies."

Former President **HARRY TRUMAN** on his position in April 1945 regarding a central intelligence organization, in *Memoirs*, vol. I (1955).

"One thing is certain. The notion that CIA was created in response to the Cold War is totally false. The need for a central intelligence authority was clearly perceived long before the postwar ambitions and hostility of the Soviet Union were recognized. Even before the Japanese surrender, the advent of the atomic bomb sharpened insiders' conviction that the United States could never again risk another Pearl Harbor."

Former DCI **RICHARD HELMS**, *A Look over My Shoulder* (2003).

"It must be clear that any government intelligence service outside the Post Office Department must operate through the Post Office Department and recognize the absolute jurisdiction of the Department."

Postmaster General **FRANK WALKER** to OSS Director Donovan, April 1945; quoted in Darling, *The Central Intelligence Agency* (1990). Huh?

"The central intelligence service which you propose . . . seems to me most inadvisable. . . . For a proper system of coordination, I do not believe it either necessary or advisable to establish an independent agency or budget."

Secretary of War **HENRY STIMSON** to General William Donovan, 1 May 1945; in CIA Historical Intelligence Collection.

"Judged on the basis of contemporary evidence, Truman's thought on intelligence was, in the spring and summer of 1945, far removed from the sophisticated concepts of the experienced General Donovan. Truman had barely gotten beyond discontent with the existing situation, tended to confuse intelligence and information, and also tended to equate 'espionage' with 'gestapo.'"

THOMAS TROY, *Donovan and the CIA* (1981). These are hard concepts.

"Prior to the present war, the United States had no foreign secret intelligence service. It never has had and does not now have a coordinated intelligence system."

WILLIAM DONOVAN to President Truman, 25 August 1945; cited in Andrew, *For the President's Eyes Only* (1995).

"In our Government today there is no permanent agency to take over the functions which OSS will have ceased to perform. These functions while carried on incident to the war are in reality essential in the effective discharge by this nation of its responsibilities in the organization and maintenance of peace."

WILLIAM DONOVAN to Budget Director Harold Smith on hearing that the Office of Strategic Services would be disbanded, 25 August 1945; cited in Troy, *Donovan and the CIA* (1981).

"The end of hostilities has tended to emphasize the importance of proceeding without further delay to set up a central intelligence system . . . failure to provide such a system might bring national disaster."

Joint Chiefs of Staff to President Truman, September 1945; reproduced in Warner, *CIA Under Truman* (1994).

"I understand that there has been talk of attempting to allocate different segments of [OSS] to different departments. This would be an absurd and unsatisfactory thing to do. The organization was set up as an entity, every function supporting and supplementing the other. It's time for us to grow up, Sam, and realize that the new responsibilities we have assumed require an adequate intelligence system."

OSS Director **WILLIAM DONOVAN** to President Truman's special counsel Samuel Rosenman, 4 September 1945; in *FRUS 1945–1950: Emergence of the Intelligence Establishment* (1996), document 6.

"I understand that it has been, or will be, suggested to you that certain of the primary functions of this organization, more particularly, secret intelligence, counter-espionage, and the evaluation and synthesis of intelligence—that these functions be severed and transferred to separate agencies. I hope that in the national interest, and in your own interest as Chief Executive, that you will not permit this to be done. Whatever agency has the duty of intelligence should have it as a complete whole. To do so otherwise would be to add chaos to existing confusion in the intelligence field. The various functions that have been integrated are the essential functions in intelligence. One is dependent on the other."

OSS Director **WILLIAM DONOVAN** to President Truman, 13 September 1945; reproduced in Warner, *CIA Under Truman* (1994). Despite Donovan's advice, Truman that

same month ordered OSS abolished, only to recognize the need to establish CIG the following year.

"I have today directed, by Executive order, that the activities of the Research and Analysis Branch and the Presentation Branch of the Office of Strategic Services be transferred to the State Department. This transfer . . . represents the beginning of a coordinated system of foreign intelligence within the permanent framework of the Government."

President **HARRY TRUMAN** to William Donovan, 20 September 1945; reproduced in Warner, *CIA Under Truman* (1994).

"Truman's order [to disband OSS] was a 'Solomon's solution,' dividing the baby in half."

Former DDI **RAY CLINE**, *Secrets, Spies and Scholars* (1976).

"I consider this whole subject of intelligence to be one of the most far-reaching problems of interdepartmental coordination that we currently face. My own gloomy opinion is that it will not be solved in an orderly fashion and that we will go through the usual two, three or more reorganization stages —God bless bureaucracy!"

Budget Director **HAROLD SMITH**, memorandum to presidential advisor Samuel Rosenman, 10 January 1946; Harry S. Truman Library, Papers of Samuel I. Rosenman.

"It is my desire, and I hereby direct, that all Federal foreign intelligence activities be planned, developed and coordinated so as to assure the most effective accomplishment of the intelligence mission related to national security."

President **HARRY TRUMAN** to the Secretaries of State, War, and the Navy on the establishment of the National Intelligence Authority (forerunner to the National Security Council) and of the Director of Central Intelligence, 22 January 1946; reproduced in Warner, *CIA Under Truman* (1994).

"[Truman's directive of 22 January 1946] created a headless body and a bodiless head! It created a 'Central Intelligence Group' to work 'under the direction of a Director of Central Intelligence.' The CIG was not 'headed' by the DCI; nor was the DCI the 'head' of the CIG.... [The DCI] directed the work of the people who were assigned to him, but they were not his people to hire, train, assign, reassign, direct, supervise, retire, or fire; they were simply on loan to him.... It was a State and Budget Bureau concept."

THOMAS TROY, *Donovan and the CIA* (1981).

"A good debating society but a poor administering instrument."

Former OSS Director **WILLIAM DONOVAN** on the new CIG, March 1946; quoted in Riebling, *Wedge: The Secret War Between the FBI and CIA* (1994).

"Essentially a facade of centrality covering up the usual departmental fragmentation and inefficiency."

Former DDI **RAY CLINE** on CIG in *Secrets, Spies and Scholars* (1976).

"Before 1946 such information as the President needed was being collected in several different places in the government.... I have often thought that if there had been something like co-ordination of information in the government it would have been more difficult, if not impossible, for the Japanese to succeed in the sneak attack at Pearl Harbor.... On becoming President, I found that the needed intelligence information was not co-ordinated in any one place."

Former President **HARRY TRUMAN**, *Memoirs*, vol. II (1956).

"How can there be any efficient organization with such a setup?"

Former OSS Director **WILLIAM DONOVAN** to Senator Chan Gurney, 7 May 1947, on proposed legislation establishing a CIA; cited in Troy, *Donovan and the CIA* (1981). Donovan criticized the proposed CIA for its dependence on the military services and its subordination to the NSC.

"In the past, the State Department, the Army, and the Navy have incessantly disagreed with respect to intelligence, which has certainly facilitated the Bureau's position and our domination of the intelligence picture. The concentration, however, of all these intelligence functions, including the research and analysis formerly performed by various agencies, into one strong, central group would place the Bureau at a great disadvantage and would probably mean that we would be overshadowed in this field."

Internal FBI memorandum of 21 June 1946; in *FRUS 1945–1950: Emergence of the Intelligence Establishment* (1996), document 157. There was never any doubt where the FBI stood on the matter of central intelligence.

"Congress passed the National Security Act on 26 July 1947 and President Truman immediately signed it into law. The act gave America something new in the annals of intelligence history; no other nation had structured its foreign intelligence establishment in quite the same way. CIA would be an independent, central agency, but not a controlling one.... Under this regime, DCIs were faced with contradictory mandates: they *could* coordinate intelligence, but they *must not* control it. ... Because of this tendency to emphasize coordination instead of control, CIA never quite became the integrator of US intelligence that its presidential and congressional parents had envisioned. ... This ambiguity is likely to endure for the same reasons it arose in the first place: no one can agree on what should replace it."

MICHAEL WARNER, *Central Intelligence: Origin and Evolution* (2001).

"As far as our intelligence production is concerned, the Central Intelligence Agency is basically an assembly plant for information produced by collaborating organizations of the Government, and its final product is necessarily dependent upon the quality of the contributions of these collaborating organizations."

DCI **WALTER BEDELL SMITH**, memorandum to NSC, 23 April 1952; reproduced in Warner, *CIA Under Truman* (1994).

OVERHEAD & IMAGERY

The impulse is natural even to young children and is as old as man's imagination—to get as high as possible in order to see more. From mountaintops to kites, balloons to supersonic aircraft, and finally to satellites, man's eyes have been raised ever higher—and at progressively greater expense. The Literary Spy is certain that the national investment in getting high, man, has been worthwhile.

See also: Analysis & Analysts; Collection; Military & Naval Intelligence

"A man trusts his ears less than his eyes."

HERODOTUS, *Histories* (5th century B.C.).

"Man must rise above the earth—to the top of the atmosphere and beyond—for only then will he fully understand the world in which he lives."

SOCRATES (470–399 B.C.); quoted in Brugioni, *From Balloons to Blackbirds* (1993).

"'Tis pleasant through the loopholes of retreat To peep at such a world; to see the stir Of the great Babel, and not feel the crowd."

WILLIAM COWPER, "The Winter Evening" (1785).

"*Voir c'est savoir*—To see is to know."

Motto of the U.S. Air Force's 363rd Tactical Reconnaissance Wing; cited in Burrows, *Deep Black* (1986).

"The idea of getting high enough for a good view of the enemy has always been irresistible. Military commanders have therefore sent observers into the sky in a variety of contraptions for centuries so they could spy on the opposition. Chinese and Japanese folklore mention the use of spotters who either went up in baskets suspended from giant kites or else were strapped right onto them."

WILLIAM E. BURROWS, *Deep Black* (1986). They probably had a hard time getting life insurance.

"To the President of the United States:

This point of observation commands an area nearly fifty miles in diameter. The city, with its girdle of encampments, presents a superb scene. I take pleasure in sending you this first dispatch ever telegraphed from an aerial station, and in acknowledging indebtedness to your encouragement, for the opportunity of demonstrating the availability of the science of aeronautics in the military service of the country. Yours respectfully, T. S. C. Lowe"

Cable to President Abraham Lincoln from a captive balloon manned by **THADDEUS LOWE** over Washington, D.C., 18 June 1861; quoted in Andrew, *For the President's Eyes Only* (1995).

"Balloons can be usefully employed when it is a great object to ascertain what the enemy is doing. By this means we raise an officer to a considerable altitude, from which point of vantage he can get a clear view of the enemy's position. Of course we here refer only to captive balloons, in which case there is seldom any difficulty in keeping up communication."

British Colonel **GEORGE FURSE**, *Information in War* (1895).

"We saw that the aeroplane would give eyes to armies, and the armies with the most eyes would win the war."

ORVILLE WRIGHT; cited in the *Chicago Tribune*, 25 November 2001.

"By World War I airplanes had so established themselves in reconnaissance, an activity traditionally undertaken by cavalry, that air units were even given cavalry names: squadrons."

WILLIAM E. BURROWS, *Deep Black* (1986).

"One flight over the lines gave me a much clearer impression of how the armies were laid out than any amount of traveling around on the ground."

General **BILLY MITCHELL** in his World War I memoirs; cited by Russell Weigley, *The American Way of War* (1973).

"The nation with the best photo interpreters will win the next war."

General **WERNER VON FRITSCH**, chief of the German General Staff, in 1938; quoted in Brugioni, *From Balloons to Blackbirds* (1993). Von Fritsch was wrong; it was the countries with the best SIGINT that won World War II.

"The photographs one brings back are submitted to stereoscopic analysis, as organisms are examined under a microscope; the interpreters of these photographs work exactly like bacteriologists. They seek on the vulnerable body of France traces of the virus which devours her. One can die from the effects of these enemy strongholds and depots and convoys which, under the lens, appear like tiny bacilli."

ANTOINE DE SAINT-EXUPÉRY, French reconnaissance pilot and author of *The Little Prince;* quoted in Burrows, *Deep Black* (1986).

"Aerial photos give crisp, hard information, like the dawn after long darkness."

ARTHUR LUNDAHL, chief of CIA's imagery interpretation center during the Cuban missile crisis; quoted in *Studies in Intelligence* (winter 1992).

"It appears that no air reconnaissance is being conducted by the fleet air arm."

Final sentence of the last message sent to Tokyo by the Japanese consulate in Honolulu, evening of 6 December 1941; cited in Prange, *At Dawn We Slept* (1981).

"In the late 1940s, the US Air Force and Navy began trying to obtain aerial photography of the Soviet Union. The main Air Force effort involved Boeing RB-47 aircraft equipped with cameras and other 'ferret' equipment. . . . One RB-47 aircraft even managed to fly 450 miles inland and photograph the city of Igarka in Siberia."

GREGORY PEDLOW and **DONALD WELZENBACH**, *CIA and the U-2 Program* (1998).

"Over forty U.S. aircraft . . . were lost on intelligence-gathering missions by the end of the 1940s as they flew up and down the Berlin corridors, prowled along the Kremlin's vast frontier, or actually made penetrations—some of them hundreds of miles deep—into Soviet airspace with camera shutters clicking and radio receivers and recorders turned on. . . . Much of the problem was due to the fact that the United States had no airplane specifically designed for reconnaissance."

WILLIAM E. BURROWS, *Deep Black* (1986).

"One day, I had forty-seven airplanes flying all over Russia."

A U.S. Air Force general on reconnaissance flights in the late 1940s; quoted in Miller, *Spying for America* (1989).

"The national intelligence establishment made do with what it had, and in 1947 it had balloons as well as airplanes. . . . [As] part of a program to be code-named Moby Dick . . . large balloons were developed by the Office of Naval Research (ONR); the high-altitude cameras were provided by the Air Force; and the project was one of the first to be sponsored by the Central Intelligence Agency. . . . [The balloons] were launched from Western Europe to drift over the Soviet Union, where their cameras recorded whatever the vagaries of the wind and the absence of clouds permitted. . . . Even those that successfully completed the transcontinental voyage often yielded photographs whose contents were unintelligible. Moby Dick was a singularly unsuccessful way to collect intelligence. The fact that such a haphazard scheme was tried at all is a measure of the desperation with which Washington wanted photo coverage of the Soviet Union."

WILLIAM E. BURROWS, *Deep Black* (1986).

"The British were also working on high-altitude reconnaissance aircraft. . . . Sometime during the first half of 1953, the RAF employed a high-altitude Canberra on a daring overflight of the Soviet Union to photograph the missile test range at Kapustin Yar. Because of advanced warning from either radar or agents inside of British intelligence, the overflight did not catch the Soviet Union by surprise. Soviet fighters damaged and nearly shot down the Canberra."

GREGORY PEDLOW and DONALD WELZENBACH, *CIA and the U-2 Program* (1998).

"The CL-282 design [Lockheed's plan for what became the U-2] was presented to the commander of the Strategic Air Command (SAC), Gen. Curtis E. LeMay, in early April [1954]. . . . General LeMay stood up halfway through the briefing, took the cigar out of his mouth, and told the briefers that, if he wanted high-altitude photographs, he would put cameras in his B-36 bombers and added that he was not interested in a plane that had no wheels or guns. The general then left the room, remarking that the whole business was a waste of his time."

GREGORY PEDLOW and DONALD WELZENBACH, *CIA and the U-2 Program* (1998). "No wheels" refers to the early design that lacked wheeled landing gear. The U-2 eventually had wheels but was never armed.

"As I look into our future intelligence requirements, it is clear to me that the Nation will be forced to call more and more upon air photographic and electronic reconnaissance. . . . In no other way does it appear to me that we can be assured of obtaining the valid intelligence concerning many vital matters upon which major decisions will have to be based. Accordingly, I recommend that no effort be spared in the development and acquisition of the specialized aircraft and operational capabilities necessary for such operations."

DCI ALLEN DULLES to General Nathan Twining, Air Force chief of staff, 18 October 1954; in CIA's Historical Intelligence Collection.

"Well, boys, I believe the country needs this information, and I'm going to approve it. But I'll tell you one thing. Some day one of these machines is going to be caught, and then we'll have a storm."

President DWIGHT EISENHOWER approving the U-2 project, November 1954; quoted in Andrew, *For the President's Eyes Only* (1995). Who knew Ike was psychic?

"Before [CIA's spyplane] could actually take to the air, it needed an Air Force designator. [In July 1955, Air Force] officers looked through the aircraft designator handbook to see what the options were. They decided they could not call the project aircraft a bomber, fighter, or transport plane, and they did not want anyone to know that the new plane was for reconnaissance, so [they] decided it should come under the utility aircraft category. At the time, there were only two utility aircraft on the books, a U-1 and a U-3."

> **GREGORY PEDLOW** and **DONALD WELZENBACH**, *CIA and the U-2 Program* (1998).

"Eisenhower's scepticism of the missile gap was based on hard evidence. He had been charmed and convinced of the powers of the U-2 when the CIA gave him a photograph of himself playing golf at Augusta, taken from 70,000 ft. He could even discern the golfball."

> **MARTIN WALKER**, *The Cold War* (1993).

"I'll give it one shot. Then if they don't accept it, we'll fly the U-2."

> President **DWIGHT EISENHOWER** regarding his "Open Skies" proposal to Moscow that the United States and the USSR should open their airspaces to reconnaissance aircraft from the other country; quoted in Pedlow and Welzenbach, *CIA and the U-2 Program* (1998).

"High-altitude testing of the U-2 soon led to an unexpected side effect—a tremendous increase in reports of unidentified flying objects. In the mid-1950s, most commercial airliners flew at altitudes between 10,000 and 20,000 feet, and military aircraft like the B-47s and B-57s operated at altitudes below 40,000 feet. Consequently, once U-2s started flying at altitudes above 60,000 feet, air-traffic controllers began receiving increasing numbers of UFO reports. . . . No one believed

manned flight was possible above 60,000 feet, so no one expected to see an object so high in the sky. Not only did the airline pilots report their sightings to air-traffic controllers, but they and ground-based personnel also wrote letters to the Air Force unit at Wright [Base] in Dayton charged with investigating such phenomena. This, in turn, led to the Air Force's Operation BLUE BOOK [which] attempted to explain such sightings by linking them to natural phenomena. BLUE BOOK investigators regularly called on the [CIA] in Washington to check reported UFO sightings against U-2 flight logs. This enabled the investigators to eliminate the majority of the UFO reports, although they could not reveal to the letter writers the true cause of the UFO sightings. U-2 and later OX-CART [CIA's A-12, the predecessor of the SR-71] flights accounted for more than one-half of all UFO reports during the late 1950s and most of the 1960s."

> **GREGORY PEDLOW** and **DONALD WELZENBACH**, *CIA and the U-2 Program* (1998).

"On most missions [U-2] pilots had virtually no freedom to deviate from their assigned course. . . . Nevertheless, one of the rare occasions when a pilot left his pre-established route proved to yield among the richest intelligence finds of the entire program, the discovery of Tyuratam in Russia, the first test site for full-scale intercontinental ballistic missiles. In June 1957, three months before the launching of Sputnik, a U-2 pilot flying over Kazakhstan spotted something in the distance that caught his attention. Departing from his course, he stumbled on the crown jewel of Soviet space technology, whose existence had not even been suspected. . . . One of the ironies of history is that months before the launching of Sputnik, an event that would shake American self-confidence, the

United States was flying with impunity above this most secret of Soviet military locations."

Former senior CIA official—and U-2 project officer—**RICHARD BISSELL**, *Reflections of a Cold Warrior* (1996).

"I take full responsibility for approving all the various programs undertaken by our government to secure and evaluate military intelligence. It was in the prosecution of one of these intelligence programs that the widely publicized U-2 incident occurred. . . . It must be remembered that over a long period, these flights had given us information of the greatest importance to national security. In fact, their success has been nothing short of remarkable."

President **DWIGHT EISENHOWER**, statement of 25 May 1960; cited in CIA, *"Our First Line of Defense"* (1996).

"Five years ago, before the beginning of the U-2 program . . . half knowledge of the Soviet Union and uncertainty of its true power position posed tremendous problems for the United States. We were faced with the constant risk of exposing ourselves to enemy attack or of needlessly expending a great deal of money and effort on misdirected military preparations of our own. . . . Our knowledge of Soviet military preparations, however, resulting from the overflight program, has given us an ability to discount or call the bluffs of the Soviets with confidence. We have been able to conclude that Soviet statements were more rhetorical than threatening and that our courses of action could be carried through without serious risk of war and without Soviet interference."

DCI **ALLEN DULLES**, "Accomplishments of the U-2 Program," memorandum of 27 May 1960; quoted in Pedlow and Welzenbach, *CIA and the U-2 Program* (1998).

"[The U-2] provided proof that the horrors of the alleged 'bomber gap' and the later 'missile gap' were nothing more than imaginative creations of irresponsibility."

DWIGHT EISENHOWER in his memoirs; quoted in Andrew, *For the President's Eyes Only* (1995).

"The U-2 thus saved the American taxpayers tens of billions of dollars and spared the world a major escalation in the nuclear arms race."

CHRISTOPHER ANDREW, *For the President's Eyes Only* (1995).

"After CIA's U-2 was shot down in the USSR in May 1960, we set in motion an arrangement for furnishing U-2s to the Republic of China Air Force and training their best pilots to fly them. . . . Many of the fliers lost their lives on flights over the mainland, but when they got in trouble the Chinese pilots destroyed their airplanes and themselves rather than let the Communists learn anything from their capture."

Former DDI **RAY CLINE**, *Secrets, Spies and Scholars* (1976).

"The very day that [U-2 pilot] Francis Gary Powers was standing in the dock in Moscow taking his sentence was the very first successful day the [CORONA spy] satellite was flying over Moscow taking pictures from above."

ARTHUR LUNDAHL, chief of CIA's National Photographic Interpretation Center; quoted in Bissell, *Reflections of a Cold Warrior* (1996).

"We gained more than 1 million square miles of coverage of the Soviet Union—more coverage in one capsule than the combined four years of U-2 coverage."

Legendary CIA imagery analyst **DINO BRUGIONI** on the results of the first successful CORONA *(Discoverer)* satellite mission in August 1960; quoted in Andrew, *For the President's Eyes Only* (1995).

"Although the superbly detailed photographs taken from [space] could not show what foreign policymakers were thinking or discussing among themselves, the data on foreign *capabilities* were outstanding. A good agent in the right place can be expected to produce intelligence that cannot be duplicated by any amount of overhead photography, but no spy can hope to reveal the mass of data that were such easy pickings for the unmanned satellites. The fact that this material could be produced without any compelling diplomatic or political bothers is also a significant advantage. Outer space and other technical legerdemain costs millions. Espionage was—at least in those days—dirt cheap. Both activities are essential, and the one can be counted upon to nourish the other. There remains an obvious management problem in maintaining a balance between the two."

> Former DCI **RICHARD HELMS**, *A Look over My Shoulder* (2003).

"Taking photos . . . from outer space, the disturbances and turbulence are far away. The atmosphere is much more transparent from without than from underneath. . . . Pick up a piece of wax paper. Hold it in front of your face and you see only a blur. Hold it on a piece of newsprint, and it is perfectly transparent. You have such the situation here."

> **WERNHER VON BRAUN**, speech in October 1956; quoted in Shulsky, *Silent Warfare* (1993).

"Not high enough."

> U-2 pilot **FRANCIS GARY POWERS**, when asked by his son, "How high were you flying, Dad?" referring to his shootdown over the USSR on 1 May 1960; quoted in the *Boston Globe*, 3 June 2001.

"When Gagarin made his flight [in April 1961], it was said officially that there was not a single camera in his sputnik. This was nothing but a big lie. There was a whole system of cameras with different lenses for taking pictures. . . . Our people in the General Staff felt very uncomfortable when they learned that the Americans had launched a satellite which would fly over the territory of the USSR. They denounced this as a spy satellite. They believe that this satellite can make photographs, which frightens them."

> Soviet GRU Colonel **OLEG PENKOVSKIY**, who was spying for CIA and SIS, in 1961; in *The Penkovskiy Papers* (1966). In this case, the Soviet General Staff were entirely correct.

"New information, providing a much firmer base for estimates on Soviet long range ballistic missiles, has caused a sharp downward revision in our estimate of present Soviet ICBM strength. . . . We now estimate that the present Soviet ICBM strength is in the range of 10–25 launchers from which missiles can be fired against the US, and that this force level will not increase markedly during the months immediately ahead."

> National Intelligence Estimate 11-8/1-61, 21 September 1961; reproduced in Ruffner, *CORONA* (1995). The "new information" was satellite imagery, and it refuted the idea of the "missile gap." By comparison, a mid-1959 NIE had estimated that the Soviets probably would have 140 to 200 ICBMs by mid-1961; see Steury, *Intentions* (1996).

"Presidential Assistant McGeorge Bundy, appearing on ABC-TV's *Issues and Answers* on Sunday, October 14 [1962], denied that the Soviets had any offensive weapons in Cuba just as a U-2 was taking the first pictures of them."

> **ROGER HILSMAN**, former chief of State Department's Bureau of Intelligence and Research, *To Move a Nation* (1967).

"Mr. President, I am as sure of this as a photo interpreter can be sure of anything."

> **ARTHUR LUNDAHL**, director of CIA's National Photographic Interpretation Center, after President Kennedy asked him if he was sure that U-2 imagery indicated Soviet missile sites in Cuba; quoted in Miller, *Spying for America* (1989).

"Experts arrived with their charts and pointers and told us that if we looked carefully, we could see there was a missile base being constructed in a field near San Christobal, Cuba. I, for one, had to take their word for it. I examined the pictures carefully, and what I saw appeared to be no more than the clearing of a field for a farm or the basement of a house. I was relieved to hear later that this was the same reaction of virtually everyone at the meeting, including President Kennedy. Even a few days later, when more work had taken place at the site, he remarked that it looked like a football field."

> **ROBERT KENNEDY**, *Thirteen Days* (1969).

"Baseball fields, perhaps?"

> KGB official **GEORGI BOLSHAKOV**, shown the U-2's photos of Cuban missile sites and asked what he thought they showed; quoted in Polmar and Allen, *Encyclopedia of Espionage* (1997). At that point Bolshakov was an informal intermediary between Soviet Premier Nikita Khrushchev and the Kennedy White House.

"After [the Cuban missile crisis,] I asked both [National Security Advisor McGeorge] Bundy and [Robert] Kennedy if they would tell me how much that single evaluated piece of photographic evidence was worth, and they each said it fully justified all that CIA had cost the country in all its preceding years."

> Former DDI **RAY CLINE**, *Secrets, Spies and Scholars* (1976). But no forward credit?

"*C'est formidable! C'est formidable!*"

> French President **CHARLES DE GAULLE**, when informed that the U-2 photographs of the Cuban missile sites he was reviewing were taken from an altitude of fourteen miles; quoted in Andrew, *For the President's Eyes Only* (1995).

"The OXCART is an even better example [than the U-2] of the technological advances generated by CIA's reconnaissance program. Although the OXCART was designed almost 30 years ago and first flown in 1962, *its speed and altitude have never been equaled*. The development of this aircraft also led to the use of new materials in aircraft construction. . . . The tremendous technological achievement represented by the OXCART ultimately led to the aircraft's demise by inspiring the Air Force to purchase its own version of the aircraft. The government could not afford to maintain two such similar reconnaissance programs. The elimination of the Agency's OXCART program did not, however, spell the end of the usefulness of the world's most advanced aircraft; its offspring, the SR-71, is still in service."

> **GREGORY PEDLOW** and **DONALD WELZENBACH**, *CIA and the U-2 Program* (1998); emphasis added. The codename OXCART refers to the program that developed CIA's A-12 aircraft. This declassified version of a 1992 CIA classified study undermines the oft-heard claim that the Air Force's SR-71, now retired from service, is the world's highest and fastest aircraft.

"You cannot take pictures of what happens in the dark or under cover or what takes place inside somebody's head. For those things we still need agents or some other method of intelligence collection. Everything else, however, that is outside in the light of day lies open to inspection if a good enough camera can be put above it."

> Former DDI **RAY CLINE**, *Secrets, Spies and Scholars* (1976).

"Photo interpretation has to do with making assumptions based on association and orders of probability. . . . The successful interpretation of imagery—analyzing what a photograph or other imagery shows and trying to predict the consequences of that event—is dependent upon the fact that all command organizations, foremost among them the military, follow sets of narrowly defined, carefully established procedures without appreciable variation. That is to say, all military organizations follow rigid patterns in the type and numbers of equipment used, training, support, and operational practices. In other words, all armies and navies 'go by the book.' Without such a book, there would be chaos, a situation dreaded by generals and admirals. But when the 'book' is learned by the other side, it can be used to interpret the meaning of what is taking place."

WILLIAM E. BURROWS, *Deep Black* (1986).

"The totality of CORONA's contributions to U.S. intelligence holdings on denied areas and to the U.S. space program in general is virtually unmeasurable. Its progress was marked by a series of notable firsts: the first to recover objects from orbit, the first to deliver intelligence information from a satellite, the first to produce stereoscopic satellite photography, the first to employ multiple re-entry vehicles, and the first satellite reconnaissance program to pass the 100-mission mark. . . . CORONA explored and conquered the technological unknowns of space reconnaissance, lifted the curtain of secrecy that screened developments within the Soviet Union and Communist China, and opened the way for the even more sophisticated follow-on reconnaissance systems. . . . [CORONA] had made it possible for the President in office to react more wisely to crucial international situations when armed with the knowledge provided. . . . Conversely, it can be said that without the intelligence which this program furnished, we might have misguidedly been pressured into a World War III."

KENNETH GREER, "Corona," in Ruffner, *CORONA* (1995).

"Strategic reconnaissance aircraft have many advantages, even in the space age. Unlike satellites, which are prisoners of orbits that cannot vary a great deal . . . aircraft can change speed abruptly, fly in any direction, drop under the clouds with their cameras, return to a target area as often as necessary, and even loiter until an intelligence-gathering opportunity ripens."

WILLIAM E. BURROWS, *Deep Black* (1986). Did Burrows ever meet Francis Gary Powers?

"On the basis of new overhead photography, we are now convinced that the previously suspect facility at Lop Nor in Western China is a nuclear test site which could be ready for use in about two months."

Special National Intelligence Estimate 13-4-64, 26 August 1964; reproduced in Ruffner, *CORONA* (1995). The first Chinese nuclear test was on 14 October 1964.

"I wouldn't want to be quoted on this, but we've spent 35 or 40 billion dollars on the space program. And if nothing else had come out of it except the knowledge we've gained from space photography, it would be worth ten times what the whole program has cost. Because tonight we know how many missiles the enemy has and, it turned out, our guesses were way off. We were doing things we didn't need to do. We were building things we didn't need to build. We were harboring fears we didn't need to harbor."

President **LYNDON JOHNSON**, speaking in Nashville, 16 March 1967; quoted in Richelson, *America's Secret Eyes* (1990).

"A total of 245 probably destroyed aircraft are observed at airfields in 3 Arab countries—201 in Egypt, 26 in Jordan, and 18 in Syria."

> CIA National Photographic Interpretation Center report for 17–22 June 1967; reproduced in Ruffner, *CORONA* (1995). Satellite imagery in 1967 was of little help to U.S. policymakers concerned about the Six-Day War, but it certainly chronicled the reason for the Israeli victory.

"The KH-4B system represents an important breakthrough for national resources exploration. The economic and political impact of this cannot be overstated. While world-wide demand increases dramatically for minerals and fossil fuels (those resources in fixed supply), our ability to locate and harvest these hidden deposits lags far behind. . . . Exploration from space provides an enlarged perspective, a previously unattainable synoptic view of the earth. Though the geologists' discipline is a study of the earth, until now he has never seen it. With his vision broadened from this space perspective, he is enabled to search for oil provinces instead of oil fields and mineral districts instead of mineral deposits. The barrier of inaccessibility has been broken."

> CIA contract report, "KH-4B System Capability: Appraisal of Geologic Value for Mineral Exploration," March 1971; reproduced in Ruffner, *CORONA* (1995).

"You cannot photograph an intention."

> Attributed to DCI **JAMES SCHLESINGER**; in Knightley, *The Second Oldest Profession* (1988).

"Here I was, the head of the whole Intelligence Community of the United States, and I couldn't produce a few pictures of a Mickey Mouse War."

> Former DCI **STANSFIELD TURNER** on his frustration trying to acquire specific overhead imagery requested by President Carter; in *Secrecy and Democracy* (1985).

"Critics of [intelligence] bureaucracy would cite [Turner's frustration] as a typical case of recalcitrant, unresponsive behavior. Yet, in reality, the agencies responsible for satellite imagery regularly provide thousands of images that meet the requirements of consumers across the national security community—a remarkable feat. . . . Yet consider the consequences if the agency responsible for satellite imagery had to respond regularly to the off-the-cuff requests of high-level customers such as the President."

> **BRUCE BERKOWITZ** and **ALLAN GOODMAN**, *Strategic Intelligence* (1989).

"We are approaching a time when we will be able to survey almost any point on the earth's surface with some sensor, and probably more than one. . . . One way or another, we should soon be able to keep track of most activities on the surface of the earth, day or night, good weather or bad."

> Former DCI **STANSFIELD TURNER**, *Secrecy and Democracy* (1985). That's turned out about as true as the predictions of the "paperless office."

"The total tab for technical intelligence collection in the decade of the 1980s is impossible to come by with accuracy, but most informed observers put the figure at close to $50 billion. Allowing for inflation, that is almost twice what it cost to land men on the moon."

> **WILLIAM E. BURROWS**, *Deep Black* (1986). And worth every dime.

"The quarter of a trillion dollars spent on the NRO [National Reconnaissance Office] over the past 35 years was by far the most productive investment America made during the Cold War."

> **JOHN PIKE**, *National Reconnaissance Office* (1994).

"We are operating at the frontiers of technology, and no one really knew how much things would cost when we started."

> Former senior NRO official, quoted in Burrows, *Deep Black* (1986).

"It's nice to see it from the ground."

> **ROBERT GATES**, on his first visit to Moscow, 1989; quoted in Richelson, *America's Secret Eyes* (1990).

"The failure to disseminate much of the remarkable imagery available within the theater of operations was one of the major intelligence failures of operations Desert Shield and Desert Storm."

> **CHRISTOPHER ANDREW**, *For the President's Eyes Only* (1995).

"HUMINT—the use of agents to gather intelligence—is necessary, its advocates claim, because cameras cannot read minds, guess intentions, or even see through the roofs of buildings.... This is true. On the other hand, no reconnaissance camera has ever lied for purposes of expediency or because it worked for the opposition, had a lapse of memory or became confused."

> **WILLIAM E. BURROWS**, *Deep Black* (1986). But they *are* lied to and *do* break.

"National reconnaissance systems that track the movement of tanks through the desert can, at the same time, track the movement of the desert itself, see the sand closing in on formerly productive fields or hillsides laid bare by deforestation and erosion. Satellite systems allow us to quickly assess the magnitude and severity of damage.... We have long used satellite imagery to estimate crop size

in North Korea and elsewhere. This allowed us to forecast shortages that might lead to instability."

> DCI **JOHN DEUTCH**, remarks to the World Affairs Council of Los Angeles, 25 July 1996.

"These days satellites tip off spies, and spies tip off satellites."

> Former DCI **R. JAMES WOOLSEY** at the Council of Foreign Relations conference on "The Future of the CIA," 18 February 1997, Washington, D.C.

"U.S. space reconnaissance and surveillance in the twenty-first century and beyond will have a mission that is extraordinarily complex.... They will be responsible for seeing and hearing everything of importance to the national security everywhere on earth and in space, day and night, regardless of the weather. And they will be expected to send their intelligence not only to the agencies and departments in Washington ... but directly down to military units in the field as well."

> **WILLIAM E. BURROWS**, *Deep Black* (1986).

"Satellite reconnaissance is the one form of espionage that is essentially sanctioned in the world community, or at least by the United States and Russia.... There is something about the violation of 'space space' that is less odious to target states than the violation of 'air space.'"

> **JOHN DIAMOND**, in *National Security Studies Quarterly* (spring 1997).

"Everyone knows about our satellites. There is even a Web site where you can plug in your longitude and latitude and you will be told the exact time that U.S. intelligence satellites will pass over."

> Congressional intelligence specialist, quoted in the *Washington Post*, 14 May 1998.

"So many things I would have done, but clouds
   got in my way.
I've looked at clouds from both sides now . . ."

Unofficial anthem of imagery analysts; from **JONI MITCH-
ELL**'s 1967 hit song "Both Sides Now."

- **People**
- **Plausible Denial**
- **Policy Role**
- **Politicization**
- **Prescriptions**
- **Presidents & Intelligence**

PEOPLE

What sort of people make the best intelligence officers? The Literary Spy's answer is: all kinds, provided they wish to serve, are willing to take risks, and can be trusted. A sense of humor is not required, but it should be.

See also: Academia; Analysis & Analysts, Espionage & Spies; Intelligence & American Culture; Recruiting

"Your spy must be a man of keen intellect, though in outward appearance a fool; of shabby exterior, but with a will of iron. He must be active, robust, endowed with physical strength and courage: thoroughly accustomed to all sorts of dirty work, able to endure hunger and cold, and to put up with shame and ignominy."
    SUN TZU, *The Art of War* (6th century B.C.).

"[Union General Philip Sheridan's spies] were a peculiar combination of intelligence operatives, communications experts, counterespionage men, and sluggers.... The biggest part of their job was to keep Sheridan at all times up to date on the enemy's strength, movements, and dispositions.

If captured, of course, they could expect nothing better than to be hanged to the nearest tree, and they always ran a fair chance of being potted by Yankee outposts, since they did look like Rebels. They tended to be an informal and individualistic lot."
    BRUCE CATTON, *A Stillness at Appomattox* (1953).

"The officers best qualified for the intelligence service are those who possess a deep knowledge of human nature, which is the result of much reflection, who are very observant, who are gifted with a very retentive memory and a calculating turn of mind, who have the knack of worming themselves into the confidence of their fellows, and can beguile them to speak, who have by study acquired an insight into all the ruses an enemy is likely to employ, and who are familiar with all the means which can be turned to account in ferreting out information. The sharp man of action, who can quickly grasp the truth, and loses no time in letting his report reach its destination, is the best officer for this kind of duty."
    British Colonel **GEORGE FURSE**, *Information in War* (1895).

"From time to time, God causes men to be born . . . with a lust to go abroad at the risk of their lives and discover news. . . . These souls are very few."

RUDYARD KIPLING, *Kim* (1901).

"For men of sober, solid sense, Commend to
  me 'Intelligence.'
They never babble, never gush; The motto of
  their Corps is 'Hush.'
Their Badge, a Spyglass and a Pen. They're all
  the most strong and silent men. . . .
They always speak with bated breath; (Undue
  verbosity spells DEATH).
So inarticulate are some, That they are almost
  deaf and dumb.
In little Offices they stay, And natter quietly all
  day.
They're all distinguished-looking chaps, Much
  bent with poring over Maps
To see if Shaikhs are playing tricks, in P.a.5 or
  Q.b.6.
So Secret are their inner lives, That should they
  ever meet their wives
They just say 'Ah' with close-set lips, And bow
  obliquely from the hips.
(Why this should be, I cannot say, Perhaps
  because they're built that way.)"

"Intelligence" from Flight Lieutenant **A. E. VAUTIER**, RAF, *Rhymes of Iraq* (Baghdad, 1927).

"I doubt if there was one man among the professionals of SIS [in the 1930s] who had read *Mein Kampf*, or more than one who had read any of the works of Marx."

HUGH TREVOR-ROPER, veteran of both MI5 and SIS, in 1968; cited in West, *Faber Book of Espionage* (1993). The "one" who had read Marx presumably was Harold "Kim" Philby, who headed SIS counterespionage while serving as a Soviet spy.

"In our work boldness, daring, risk, and great audacity must be combined with great prudence."

YAN BERZIN, chief of GRU from 1924 to 1938; quoted in Penkovskiy, *The Penkovskiy Papers* (1966). Especially prudence, if you're working for a madman; Stalin had Berzin arrested and executed in 1939.

"Consider the life of an Intelligence man's wife. Either he tells her what his job is, or he doesn't. If he does, she will never know another peaceful moment as long as she lives, because there's no end to our war—that is, if she cares for him. If she doesn't, she may talk, and then he'd have to shoot her. Suppose he doesn't tell her. He says instead that he's an insurance agent, or a traveller in pig food, or an inspector of nuisances, which last is nearer the truth than most of us get in this life. He tells her he's going to Bristol to see a man about a drain, but you can bet your boots that some dear school-friend of hers will write and tell her that he was seen last Wednesday strolling along the promenade at Felixstowe with a dazzling blonde, after which he will spend the next twenty years of his life giving lucid and convincing explanations, and she won't believe any of 'em. No, we don't marry on our job, Bill. Pass the beer."

MANNING COLE, *Drink to Yesterday* (1940). Fortunately, it's not as bad as novels make it out to be.

"During the Second World War many more people discovered that those responsible for Secret Intelligence do, in very fact, as often as not behave like characters created by the Marx brothers. *Duck Soup,* for instance, appealed to me as a film of stark realism."

Former SIS officer Sir **COMPTON MACKENZIE** in the preface to his comic novel on intelligence, *Water on the Brain* (1954).

"Intelligence work necessarily involves . . . cheating, lying and betraying, which is why it has deleterious an effect on the character. I never met anyone professionally engaged in it whom I should care to trust in any capacity."

MALCOLM MUGGERIDGE, SIS officer during World War II, in *Chronicles of Wasted Time: The Infernal Grove* (1973). He says much the same thing about journalists.

"After the Battle of Midway, it required some time to collate conflicting [intelligence] to reach the firm conclusion that four Japanese aircraft carriers and one heavy cruiser had been sent to the bottom by American carrier planes. I remember crossing them off the order-of-battle list. [One officer] looked at the abbreviated list and remarked, 'It makes you feel kind of sad, doesn't it?' I knew then that I had a true intelligence officer working for me. [He] was more familiar with the names, characteristics, and organization of Japanese ships than he was with the ships of his own navy. The best intelligence officers come to identify more or less with the enemy's organization, and strive to think as the enemy does."

Former U.S. naval intelligence officer **W. J. HOLMES**, *Double-Edged Secrets* (1979). As long as this habit of mind doesn't lead him actually to *work* for the enemy.

"[OSS director William Donovan] knew the world, having traveled widely. He understood people. He had a flair for the unusual and for the dangerous, tempered with judgment. In short, he had the qualities to be desired in an intelligence officer."

Former DCI **ALLEN DULLES**, *The Craft of Intelligence* (1963).

"I'd rather have a young lieutenant with guts enough to disobey an order than a colonel too regimented to think and act for himself."

OSS Director **WILLIAM DONOVAN**; quoted in Ranelagh, *The Agency* (1986).

"I believe [OSS Director William] Donovan's greatest legacy to American Intelligence was that he brought talented people from all walks of life into the national security business: people like prominent Harvard historian William Langer, jazz musician Miles Copeland, filmmaker John Ford, baseball player Moe Berg, and future chef Julia Child."

DCI **ROBERT GATES**, remarks to the Center for the Study of the Presidency, 21 March 1992, in *Speeches* (1993).

"I knew nothing [about cooking]. I just enjoyed every time we went to a Chinese restaurant. All I did was eat. I had no culinary skills whatsoever."

Former OSS staffer **JULIA CHILD**; quoted in the *Chicago Tribune*, 21 July 1997.

"We had all kinds of egomaniacs and crazies."

GEOFFREY JONES, president of the Veterans of the OSS; quoted in Nicholas Dawidoff, *The Catcher Was a Spy* (1994).

"There were men who did careful, scholarly work; men who did sensationally dangerous work; and men who did absolutely nothing except travel around the world on a high priority at government expense."

STEWART ALSOP on his OSS experience; quoted in Miller, *Spying for America* (1989).

"A high proportion of young Agency people had taken heavy personal risks during the war. They knew horror. Espionage and operations to keep

[the] peace seemed an infinitely preferable alternative. . . . The elite and wealthy families that sprinkled Donovan's OSS lent their gloss to the CIA, taking the curse off secrecy. Traditionally, intelligence services tend to be in the hands of oddballs—the necessary paranoia of the profession pushes toward this—but by placing intelligence in the hands of people with a solid stake in the republic, the creators of the Agency averted such oddballism."

JOHN RANELAGH at a conference on "The Origins and Development of the CIA," sponsored by CIA's Center for the Study of Intelligence, March 1994. Not entirely.

"The greatest collection of individualists, international rolling stones, and slightly batty geniuses ever gathered together in one organization."

A wartime journalist's description of the men and women of the Foreign Broadcast Information Service in Helena Huntington Smith, "It Pays to Listen," *Colliers*, January 1943; cited in *Studies in Intelligence* 45/3 (2001).

"Men who only a few months before had been peaceful private citizens, newspaper publishers, lawyers, insurance salesmen, bankers, writers, radio commentators were now rapidly becoming ingenious and even brilliant intelligence officers."

ELLIS ZACHARIAS, on his arrival as deputy director of U.S. naval intelligence in 1942, in *Secret Missions* (1946).

"To create an effective Central Intelligence Agency, we must have in the key positions men who are prepared to make this a life work, not a mere casual occupation. They must find their reward primarily in the work itself, and in the service they render their Government, rather than in public acclaim."

ALLEN DULLES, then a private citizen, statement submitted to the Senate Armed Service Committee, 25 April 1947, in CIA Historical Intelligence Collection. The Senate was considering the proposed National Security Act of 1947.

"Joining the CIA back in 1950 was a highly esteemed, indeed a rather glamorous and fashionable and certainly a most patriotic thing to do. In those days the Agency was considered the vanguard of the fight for democracy and it attracted what nowadays we would call the best and the brightest, the politically liberal young men and women from the finest Ivy League campuses and with the most impeccable social and establishment backgrounds."

Former DCI **WILLIAM COLBY**, *Honorable Men* (1978).

"Continuity of high caliber personnel, possessing specialized training and experience, is essential for the conduct of the Agency's activities. Accordingly, plans for a career service within the Central Intelligence Agency are being worked out and the first groups of prospective junior career officers are in training. . . . Meanwhile, one of the Agency's continuing problems will be the difficulty of securing adequately qualified personnel, particularly for senior positions."

DCI **WALTER BEDELL SMITH**, memorandum to the National Security Council, 23 April 1952; reproduced in Warner, *CIA Under Truman* (1994).

"Intelligence is more than just an occupation, more than a livelihood, more than just another phase of government work. . . . People work at it until they are numb, because they love it, because it is their life, and because the rewards are the rewards of professional accomplishment."

SHERMAN KENT, chief of CIA's Office of National Estimates, "The Need for an Intelligence Literature," *Studies in Intelligence* (spring 1955).

"Just a civil servant."

> James Bond, on being asked what he does for a living, in **IAN FLEMING**, *Diamonds Are Forever* (1956).

"From the day of its founding, the CIA has operated on the assumption that the majority of its employees are interested in a career and need and deserve the same guarantees and benefits which they would receive if in the Foreign Service or in the military. In turn, the CIA expects most of its career employees to enter its service with the intention of durable association."

> Former DCI **ALLEN DULLES**, *The Craft of Intelligence* (1963).

"I have found that good fishermen tend to make good intelligence officers. The fisherman's preparation for the catch, his consideration of the weather, the light, the currents, the depth of the water, the right bait or fly to use, the time of day to fish, the spot he chooses and the patience he shows are all part of the art and essential to success."

> Former DCI **ALLEN DULLES**, *The Craft of Intelligence* (1963).

"If he was concerned about the morale of the Central Intelligence Agency and that was the reason for coming he'd better not come. On the other hand, if there was anything wrong with the President's morale and he wanted a little lift we'd be very glad to have him."

> DCI **JOHN McCONE** relating to CIA employees his conversation with President Lyndon Johnson, who was concerned that CIA had a morale problem, 1964; in CIA's Historical Intelligence Collection.

"In Kinshasa in the early morning hours of 28 May 1966, three armed Congolese men broke into the house of a CIA representative. The daughter of our representative, then age 14, was alone in the house. When it became apparent that the men would kill her parents, she was able to reason with the men in their own language, Lingala. She is credited with saving the lives of her family and was awarded the Agency's medal for bravery."

> **WALTER PFORZHEIMER**, anecdote for DCI Colby, CIA's Historical Intelligence Collection.

"You have to be a bit of a villain for that sort of work."

> MI5 official **WILLIAM SKARDON** commenting on the work of SIS; quoted in Knightley, *The Second Oldest Profession* (1988).

"I'll have a shower and a shave, and once again I will be your alert, clean-cut, government-issue Captain Marvel."

> Fictional U.S. agent **KELLY ROBINSON**, played by Robert Culp, in the 1960s TV series *I Spy*.

"I have met dozens of men who are moved and motivated by the highest and most patriotic and dedicated purposes—men who are specialists in economics, and political science, and history, and geography, and physics, and many other fields where logic and analysis are crucial to the decisions that the President of their country is called to make. Through my experience with these men I have learned that their most significant triumphs come not in the secrets passed in the dark but in patient reading, hour after hour, of highly technical periodicals. In a real sense they are America's professional students; they are unsung, just as they are invaluable."

> President **LYNDON JOHNSON** at the swearing-in of Richard Helms as DCI; cited in CIA, *"Our First Line of Defense"* (1996). Too bad LBJ didn't trust these "professional students" about Vietnam.

"Despite the new tools which science is now putting into the hands of the intelligence collector, it is still the human competence to operate the tools and to interpret the product which remains the decisive element in the intelligence equation today."

Former DCI **ALLEN DULLES**, foreword to his edited volume *Great True Spy Stories* (1968).

"The nation must to a degree take it on faith that we too are honorable men devoted to her service."

DCI **RICHARD HELMS**, address to the American Society of Newspaper Editors, 14 April 1971.

"The CIA is not a threat to our liberties and never has been. It is composed of dedicated officers of extremely high standards of integrity and patriotism. Should anyone attempt to subvert the agency to purposes that would threaten our society, it would be members of CIA who would be the first to sound the alarm."

Former State Department intelligence chief **ROGER HILSMAN,** *To Move a Nation* (1967).

"In an essay not included in this book my father had said that, in addition to being right most of the time, a good Intelligence officer must also have two other qualities to help him sublimate the ugly aspects of his calling: a deep love of country and an unshakable belief in his principles. To be a master of spies, a man must be above all a master of himself and must be convinced of the intrinsic goodness of his cause."

HANYI MORAVEC DISHER in the foreword to the memoirs of her father, who had been chief of Czechoslovak military intelligence before the Communist takeover; see Frantisek Moravec, *Master of Spies* (1975).

"People who are suitable as special agents . . . are 20 to 45 years old. Persons from aristocratic and bourgeois-conservative circles are of no interest. . . . People who adhere strictly to church dogma and rules are not suitable, nor are people with a tendency toward alcoholism, drug addiction, and sexual deviations."

KGB 13th Department file; cited in Andrew and Mitrokhin, *The Mitrokhin Archive* (1999).

"The best part of being a CIA officer is that you never get bored for long."

PHILIP AGEE, *Inside the Company* (1975).

"The most complex lesson I had to learn . . . was how to live the double life. And I have to say that there was an enormous temptation to not even try. Considering the importance and all-consuming nature of the work I was doing at the Agency; considering the missionary zeal, sense of elitism and marvelous camaraderie among my colleagues there; considering above all that I was strictly forbidden to talk about what I was doing with anyone outside the Agency . . . considering all this, one can see how it would have been easy to drop out of [the real] world and immerse myself exclusively in the cloak-and-dagger life. And some of my colleagues at the Agency did just that. Socially as well as professionally they cliqued together, forming a sealed fraternity. They ate together at their own special favorite restaurants; they partied together almost only among themselves; their families drifted to each other, so their defenses did not always have to be up. In this way they increasingly separated themselves from the ordinary world and developed a rather skewed view of that world. Their own delicate life became the proper norm, and they looked down on the life of the rest of the citizenry. And out of this grew what was later named—and condemned—as the 'cult' of intelligence, an inbred, distorted, elitist view of intelligence that held it to be above the normal processes of society, with its own rationale and justification, beyond the restraints of the Constitution, which applied to everything and everyone else."

> Former DCI **WILLIAM COLBY**, *Honorable Men* (1978). Former DCI Richard Helms did not recognize the culture Colby described; see *A Look over My Shoulder* (2003).

"Those [CIA officers] who must depend on cover to conduct their business abroad are obliged to continue the cover at home. A routine life is not possible for them even when living in the Washington area. They must pretend to be somewhere else when a creditor or visitor from out of town telephones them at the office at Langley on an 'outside' line. . . . If troubled they may not select their own psychiatrist, but instead must visit one cleared and approved by CIA. They—and their families—must lie constantly. They cannot tell the truth to bankers, neighbors, lodge brothers, or delivery boys. I even lied to the Boy Scouts of America when filling out an application paper to be a Scoutmaster. They must lead a double life at home so that cover will be intact when next they are assigned overseas. It is a vexing existence."

> Former senior CIA operations officer **DAVID ATLEE PHILLIPS**, *The Night Watch* (1978).

"Perhaps the most fascinating aspect of my career has been meeting the people who fight for us on the invisible battlefield of intelligence, a battlefield that is quiet but never still. My own experience with those I met in the intelligence services of the Armed Forces was a truly rewarding one. These were splendid men and women serving with devotion and integrity. I count myself lucky to have worked with such people for nearly thirty years. . . . I would speak too of the men and women who served in the Central Intelligence Agency during my tenure as deputy director or acting director. I have never known a finer group of Americans. They live by the same principles and beliefs as their fellow countrymen. I am as proud of my association with them as I am of my service in the Army. They stood steadfast as a rock under a barrage of lies, slander and innuendo without parallel in American history. Their sturdy courage helped bring the agency through the almost mortal storm that rocked it. It survived because of them."

> Former DDCI General **VERNON WALTERS**, *Silent Missions* (1978).

"Who are these CIA people, after all? They are the men and women living next door, down the street, or across town—these are normal Americans who have gone through an extraordinary experience to get into the Agency in the first place. . . . These are people serving this country very well and very loyally and very patriotically, in some cases under very difficult circumstances. But too often they are reviled and cast as second-class citizens. If this is the way the public wants to deal with its intelligence professionals, then we ought to disband the Agency and go back to the way we were before World War II. Otherwise, it is up to the citizens of this country, the Congress, and the President to support these people and to support them adequately, or else there is no reason to expect them to do these kinds of dirty jobs. It isn't fair, it isn't right, and it won't work."

> Former DCI **RICHARD HELMS** in a 1978 interview with David Frost; cited in Weber, *Spymasters* (1999).

"OK, so what?"

> CIA officer and American hostage **WILLIAM DAUGHERTY** to his Iranian captors after being confronted with a State Department cable that blew his cover; in *Studies in Intelligence* (spring 1998).

"Intelligence performance depends on those who perform it, their ability, competence, and experience. The idea that the quality of intelligence can somehow be improved beyond the level of its producers is a dangerous delusion. . . . In the long run, ignorant people will not be consistently lucky, nor will competent individuals be consistently wrong."

WALTER LAQUEUR, *A World of Secrets* (1985).

"You can't spend your life bribing people, seducing people into committing treason, betraying their own movements, sometimes betraying their own families—and that's the nice-guy stuff—and come away a healthy, whole person whatever your rationales are. You can't go through your entire career with a plausible denial to your own conscience."

Former CIA officer JOHN STOCKWELL; quoted in Knightley, *The Second Oldest Profession* (1988).

"If I ever have to run another organization with bad morale, I hope that it will be just like the CIA. I've never noticed any letdown in performance, no matter what the state of morale."

Former DCI (and bad morale expert) STANSFIELD TURNER, *Secrecy and Democracy* (1985).

"Our machines, our systems, and our satellites are the wonders of the age. But intelligence is preeminently an affair of people. It is the caliber of men and women of American intelligence—their creativity, determination, brilliance, and courage —that spells the difference between success and failure. . . . People to whom fame and fortune are not a necessary part of their lives, but who can find in this difficult work an avenue to pursue their highest aspirations for a safer and better world."

DCI WILLIAM WEBSTER, 19 September 1988, in *1988 Speeches*. Fortune is not even an option.

"In a world where dictators can openly bludgeon their opposition in the streets, where terrorists bully nations and individuals are hunted by zealots, intelligence provides our best, and often our only, defense. Such defense is not without its cost. . . . This service today is a reminder of what we have paid. . . . Let us reflect on this legacy, and let us resolve to keep alive and vital the dedication, the wisdom, and the strength of purpose that is represented by each of these stars."

DCI WILLIAM WEBSTER, remarks at the CIA memorial ceremony, 31 May 1989, in *1989 Speeches*. Stars etched into a wall in the main lobby of CIA Headquarters represent those who have died in the line of duty.

"Ponder the circumstances of our work:

Many intelligence officers serve in inhospitable climates and dangerous places—some of them outside of Washington.

Intelligence officers work incredible hours under enormous pressure and stress, both in Washington and elsewhere.

Intelligence officers and their families face many difficulties and sacrifices because of their chosen path, from the hardships of living abroad to lost holidays and missed family gatherings here at home.

But the intangible compensations are unparalleled.

In this new age, American Intelligence still preserves and protects the nation.

Intelligence officers are trusted—as no others in this government or elsewhere—with extraordinary responsibilities. From those who manage multi-billion dollar programs and services to those who hold the lives of agents and even the future of other governments in their hands, to those who tell presidents, members of Congress, cabinet secretaries and flag officers unpopular things or unwelcome news.

Their integrity, dedication, loyalty, sacrifice and skill are repaid many times over with friendships of a lifetime, pride, unique experiences, and the certainty that they have served their country well."

DCI **ROBERT GATES**, remarks to U.S. Air Force intelligence officers, 17 December 1992, in *Speeches* (1993).

"It is not entirely true that when an intelligence officer 'smells the flowers' he looks around for a coffin. But the nature of our business, in both operations and analysis, makes of us great skeptics and pessimists."

Former DCI **ROBERT GATES**, *From the Shadows* (1996).

"My philosophy of leadership boils down to one idea: 'People come first.' Leadership does not require complicated theories, flow charts, or behavioral models, or memos. It flows from the heart. There will be times when you will have to ask a lot from your people. That's the reality of the intelligence profession. But if you take care of them, listen to them, be frank with them, and, above all, involve them—they will astound you with what they can do."

DCI **GEORGE TENET**, address to senior CIA officials, 17 July 1997.

"I was saddled with an overabundance of yuppie spies who cared more about their retirement plan and health insurance benefits than about protecting democracy. For them, CIA was just a job."

Former senior CIA operations officer **DUANE CLARRIDGE**, *A Spy for All Seasons* (1997).

"Most CIA officers and decision makers, although they use historical analogies every day, are basically ahistorical. They believe they have no time or need for history."

CIA chief historian **GERALD HAINES**; in Jeffreys-Jones and Andrew, *Eternal Vigilance* (1997).

"You never sit at the head table, you never get singled out, but you are there for the love of country."

Former President **GEORGE H. W. BUSH** to CIA employees, 26 April 1999.

"If you want to find the [CIA] spies in an American embassy, look for the ones who don't speak the language."

Former State Department officer in Moscow; quoted in the *New York Review of Books*, 23 September 1999.

"We're ready to bleed for our country, but the bureaucrats won't let us."

CIA employee after the Red Cross ended bimonthly blood collection drives at CIA because of new FDA rules that donors provide true names and travel histories; quoted in *U.S. News and World Report* (11 September 2000).

"The analytical people have to be as good as the best academics in the country. The scientific people have to be as good as the best scientists and engineers. And the operations people have to be clever, brave, shrewd, and willing to live a life in which often even members of their own family don't know what they do for a living. It's tough, important work. For the overseas people, often dangerous work."

Former DCI **R. JAMES WOOLSEY** interviewed on CNN, 31 August 2001.

"It's important for America to realize that there are men and women who are spending hours on the task of making sure our country remains free: Men and women of the CIA who are sleeping on the floor, eating cold pizza, calling their kids on the phone, saying, 'Well, I won't be able to tuck you in tonight,' because they love America. . . . And I want to thank you for what you're doing."

President **GEORGE W. BUSH**, remarks at CIA Headquarters, 26 September 2001.

"I was honoured to know that this courageous man was working to make the world safer for myself and all of us. To me he was the very best kind of hero, comparable to the firefighters who went into the [World Trade Center]. . . . I and the civilized world are very grateful for his work, and sad for his sacrifice. . . . Thank you and God bless that honourable man."

E-mail from Britain to CIA's public website (www.cia.gov), responding to the death of CIA operations officer Mike Spann in Afghanistan, December 2001.

"Base rates of diagnosable mental health problems are significantly lower for [CIA] employees than they are for comparable age groups in the general population."

CIA staff psychologist in the Agency's Mental Health Division; quoted in the American Psychological Association's *Monitor on Psychology* (April 2002). The key word here is *diagnosable*.

"Secret intelligence is not for the fainthearted."

Former DCI **RICHARD HELMS**, *A Look over My Shoulder* (2003).

"I came here today . . . to tell the American people that they must know that they are served by dedicated, courageous professionals. It is evident on the battlefields of Afghanistan and Iraq. It is evident by their work against proliferators. And it is evident by the fact that well over two-thirds of al-Qaida's leaders can no longer hurt the American

people. We are a community that some thought would not be needed at the end of the Cold War."

DCI **GEORGE TENET**, remarks at Georgetown University, 5 February 2004.

PLAUSIBLE DENIAL

If covert action is conducting foreign policy without saying so, then it follows that there must be ways to maintain the pretense of noninvolvement. The Literary Spy sees the term "plausible denial" used in various senses when a covert action becomes known or otherwise goes bad, from protecting the head of state from responsibility to abdicating responsibility over men in the field. Some of these denials are more noble than others.

See also: Bay of Pigs; Covert Action; Fighting the Cold War; Secrecy

"Ah, this thou shouldst have done,
And not spoken on 't! In me 'tis villainy;
In thee 't had been good service . . .
Repent that e'er thy tongue
Hath so betray'd thine act: being done
    unknown,
I should have found it afterwards well done;
But must condemn it now."

Pompey, in **WILLIAM SHAKESPEARE**, *Anthony and Cleopatra*, Act II, scene vii.

"Above all, do not get into any trouble; for I suppose you know that, if anything happened to you, it would be of no use to talk of your mission. We should be obliged to know nothing about you, for ambassadors are the only avowed spies."

> Instructions to the famed lover and spy **JACQUES CASA-NOVA** in *The Memoirs of Jacques Casanova;* cited in Dulles, *Great True Spy Stories* (1968).

"If . . . retaliation is necessary let another mode be chose. Let under actors be employed and let the authority by which it is done be wrapt in obscurity and doubt. . . . Let not the Commander in Chief considered as the first and most respectable character among us come forward in person and be the avowed author of an act at which every humane feeling revolts. . . . Appoint some obscure agents to perform the ceremony."

> **ALEXANDER HAMILTON** to General Henry Knox on General George Washington's plan to execute a British prisoner in retaliation for the execution of an American officer captured by the British; cited in Knott, *Secret and Sanctioned* (1996). Washington did not carry out the plan.

"If I accustom a servant to tell a lie for *me*, have I not reason to apprehend that he will tell many lies for *himself*?"

> **SAMUEL JOHNSON**; quoted in Boswell, *Life of Samuel Johnson* (1791).

"It is important, that these instructions are shown to them of your own mere will, & begging at the same time that it may not be known to us—but in such a manner as to induce the belief that it must be kept a profound secret from your own government, as on that event, it would destroy you. When you have read this P.S. and my private letter you will burn them both . . . these might be stolen from you & made a handle against this government."

> President **ANDREW JACKSON**, letter instructing envoy Anthony Butler to show Mexican authorities his general instructions to demonstrate that they make no mention of the acquisition of Texas, October 1829; cited in Knott, *Secret and Sanctioned* (1996). Butler's secret mission was to bribe Mexican officials to part with Texas.

"Such a mission as he promises I think promises good, if it were free from difficulties, which I fear it can not be. First, he can not go with any government authority whatever. This is absolute and imperative. Secondly, if he goes without authority, he takes a great deal of personal risk—he may be condemned, and executed as a spy."

> President **ABRAHAM LINCOLN** on the sending of a Union colonel who was also a Methodist minister into Confederate territory to make contact with the Southern Methodist Church, 28 May 1863; quoted in Knott, *Secret and Sanctioned* (1996).

"We of the Game are beyond protection. If we die, we die. Our names are blotted from the book."

> **RUDYARD KIPLING**, *Kim* (1901). Agent E27 is explaining the facts of life in the Great Game to the aspiring agent Kim.

"If you do well you'll get no thanks and if you get into trouble you'll get no help. Does that suit you?"

> Fictional British spy chief R in **W. SOMERSET MAUGHAM**, *Ashenden* (1927). Ashenden answers, "Perfectly." Maugham was an SIS officer in World War I.

"You can count on us for all help and aid possible, unless you are caught. Then, we agree, we have never heard of you."

> **JAMES R. MURPHY**, chief assistant of William Donovan, then Coordinator of Information, to a COI agent bound for Europe, early 1942; quoted in Riebling, *Wedge: The Secret War Between the FBI and CIA* (1994).

"The State Department has not opposed putting secret intelligence under a central agency, but it would oppose it if the central agency were directly under the President, because such operations might compromise the President."

> State Department memorandum of 10 January 1946; in *FRUS 1945–1950: Emergence of the Intelligence Establishment* (1996), attachment to document 70.

"Covert operations are understood to be all activities ... conducted or sponsored by this Government against hostile foreign states or groups or in support of friendly powers or groups but which are so planned and executed that any US Government responsibility for them is not evident to unauthorized persons and that if uncovered the US Government can plausibly disclaim any responsibility for them."

> National Security Council directive 10/2, June 1948; reproduced in Warner, *CIA Under Truman* (1994).

"As Secretary of Defense, I recognize the importance of covert foreign operations under present world conditions. ... I believe [it] must be emphasized as this organization for covert operations develops [that] the organization must assume autonomous responsibility and be so effectively obscured as to assure that neither the President nor the Secretaries of State or Defense will be placed in a position of having to answer publicly for its activities."

> Secretary of Defense **LOUIS JOHNSON** to DCI Roscoe Hillenkoetter, 6 October 1949; in *FRUS 1945–1950: Emergence of the Intelligence Establishment* (1996), document 312.

"It is the policy of the United States not to intervene in the internal affairs of other nations."

> U.S. State Department press release in response to reports of U.S. assistance to Guatemalan rebels, 30 January 1954; cited in Treverton, *Covert Action* (1987).

"I want this whole thing to be a civilian operation. If uniformed personnel of the armed services of the United States fly over Russia, it is an act of war —legally—and I don't want any part of it."

> President **DWIGHT EISENHOWER** deciding on CIA rather than Air Force control of the U-2 program, 1955; quoted in Pedlow and Welzenbach, *CIA and the U-2 Program* (1998).

"Unannounced U.S. foreign policy will from time to time be conveyed to [Radio Free Europe]. ... In most instances, guidance on unannounced U.S. policy will relate to objectives which can be undertaken by RFE as an unattributable radio, but which would be inadvisable or inappropriate positions to be taken by an official organ or spokesman of the U.S. Government."

> U.S. State Department policy paper for Radio Free Europe, which was funded covertly by CIA, 1957; reprinted in Puddington, *Broadcasting Freedom* (2000).

"A NASA U-2 research plane, being flown in Turkey on a joint NASA-USAF Air Weather Service mission, apparently went down in the Lake Van, Turkey area at about 9:00 a.m. (3:00 a.m. E.D.T.), Sunday, May 1."

> NASA cover story for the missing CIA U-2 flight piloted by Francis Gary Powers, 3 May 1960; cited in Andrew, *For the President's Eyes Only* (1995).

"For the executive to have taken the position that a subordinate of his had exercised authority on his own to mount and carry forward such an enterprise as the U-2 operation without higher sanction ... would have been an intolerable position to take."

> Former DCI **ALLEN DULLES** explaining why plausible denial was abandoned after the U-2 incident of May 1960, in *The Craft of Intelligence* (1963).

"The great problem is leakage and breach of security. Everyone must be prepared to swear he has not heard of it. ... Our hand should not show in anything that is done."

> President **DWIGHT EISENHOWER** on the initiation of covert action against Fidel Castro; quoted in Andrew, *For the President's Eyes Only* (1995).

"In the case of an operation of high sensitivity of the sort that we are discussing [i.e., assassination plots against Castro], there was a further objective . . . to protect the President. And, therefore, the way in which I believe that [DCI] Allen Dulles would have attempted to do that was to have indicated to the two successive Presidents the general objective of the operation that was contemplated, to make that sufficiently clear so that the President —either President Eisenhower or President Kennedy—could have ordered the termination of the operation, but to give the President as little information about it as possible beyond an understanding of its general purpose. Such an approach to the President would have had as its purpose to leave him in the position to deny knowledge of the operation if it should surface."

> Former senior CIA operations officer **RICHARD BISSELL** in Senate testimony; quoted in U.S. Senate, *Alleged Assassination Plots* (1975).

"The [Bay of Pigs] project had lost its covert nature by November 1960. As it continued to grow, operational security became more and more diluted. For more than three months before the invasion the American press was reporting, often with some accuracy, on the recruiting and training of Cubans. Such massive preparations could only be laid to the U.S. The agency's name was freely linked with these activities. Plausible denial was a pathetic illusion."

> CIA Inspector General **LYMAN KIRKPATRICK**'s report on the Bay of Pigs operation, October 1961; quoted in the *New York Times*, 22 February 1998.

"This better not be another Francis Gary Powers. Those Americans better be dead."

> Attorney General **ROBERT KENNEDY** on hearing that American pilots had been shot down during the Bay of Pigs invasion; quoted in Evan Thomas, *Robert Kennedy*

(2000). RFK's wish was granted; all four American pilots had been killed.

"The most effective way to have organized operations against the Castro regime, even if they would have been carried out exclusively by Cubans, would have been to do so perfectly openly, on the largest scale and with the best equipment feasible. Practically every departure from this pattern of behavior imposed operational difficulties and reduced effectiveness. . . . The operation was not so much beyond the Agency's capability as it was beyond the scope of activities judged to be acceptably deniable."

> CIA operations directorate report "An Analysis of the Cuban Operation," 18 January 1962, now declassified.

"As my father always told me, 'never write it down.'"

> Attorney General **ROBERT KENNEDY** to DCI John McCone, 2 May 1962; cited in Evan Thomas, *Robert Kennedy* (2000). The Kennedy secret.

"In all cases of this kind [i.e., covert action] . . . I have always felt the Director [of Central Intelligence] should naturally assume full responsibility for anything his Agency has done, and wherever he could shield or protect the President in any way, he should do it. Some people say, well, you ought always to deny these things, and they said that after the U-2 and they said it again after the Bay of Pigs. Well, no Director of the Central Intelligence Agency can really control that. He stands there ready at any time to take any responsibility that the President wants him to take, to resign if the situation calls for it, but at any rate to take any responsibility that he can."

> Former DCI **ALLEN DULLES** in a 1964 interview; cited in Weber, *Spymasters* (1999).

"I asked you not to tell me that!"

Running gag line of fictional U.S. agent Maxwell Smart, played by Don Adams, in the 1960s television comedy *Get Smart*.

"I think that any of us would have found it very difficult to discuss assassinations with a President of the U.S. I just think we all had the feeling that we're hired out to keep those things out of the Oval Office."

Former DCI **RICHARD HELMS** in 1975 testimony before the Senate committee investigating intelligence [the Church Committee]; quoted in Treverton, *Covert Action* (1987).

"Because of the emphasis I put on the crucial importance of protecting national security, I can understand how highly motivated individuals could have felt justified in engaging in specific activities that I would have disapproved of had they been brought to my attention."

RICHARD NIXON, on the Ellsberg break-in; quoted in Andrew, *For the President's Eyes Only* (1995).

"As always, should you or any of your IMF [Impossible Missions Force] be caught or killed, the Secretary will disavow any knowledge of your actions. This tape will self-destruct in five seconds. Good luck."

Tape-recorded instructions in every episode of television's *Mission Impossible*, 1966–73.

"One of the advantages a secret agency like the CIA provides to a President is the unique pretext of being able to disclaim responsibility for its actions. Thus, a President can direct or approve high-risk clandestine operations . . . without openly accepting the consequences of these decisions. If the clandestine operations are successful—good. If they fail or backfire, then usually all the President and his staff need do to avoid culpability is to blame the CIA."

VICTOR MARCHETTI and **JOHN MARKS**, *CIA and the Cult of Intelligence* (1974).

"It is part of the CIA director's job to be the fall guy for the President."

HARRY ROSITZKE, *CIA's Secret Operations* (1977).

"The concept of 'plausible denial' had an undeniable flavor of wishful thinking about it."

Former CIA operations officer **WILLIAM HOOD**, *Mole* (1993).

"Two presidents, when I was Director, told me in almost identical words, 'Okay, but don't get caught.'"

Former DCI **RICHARD HELMS** in remarks at CIA, 7 June 1996.

"Non-attribution to the United States for covert operations was the original and principal purpose of the so-called doctrine of 'plausible denial.' . . . This concept, designed to protect the United States and its operatives from the consequences of disclosures, has been expanded to mask decisions of the President and his senior staff members. A further consequence of the expansion of this doctrine is that subordinates, in an effort to permit their superiors to 'plausibly deny' operations, fail to fully inform them about those operations. . . . 'Plausible denial' can also lead to the use of euphemism and circumlocution, which are designed to allow the President and other senior officials to deny knowledge of an operation should it be disclosed. The converse may also occur; a President could communicate his desire for a sensitive operation in an indirect, circumlocutious manner. An additional possibility is that the President may, in fact, not be fully and accurately informed about a sensitive operation because he failed to receive the 'circumlocutious' message."

U.S. Senate, *Alleged Assassination Plots Involving Foreign Leaders: Interim Report of the Senate Select Committee to Study Governmental Operations with respect to Intelligence Activities* [the Church Committee] (November 1975).

"The President must sign and present to the intelligence oversight committees of Congress a document known as a presidential finding. In addition to describing each planned covert action operation in detail, each finding is to include a certification that the President has determined that the operation was necessary. At this point, 'plausible denial' went straight out the window. Today, only the boldest chief executive would deny knowledge of a document which he has signed and presented to both houses of Congress. . . . Today, the spoiled detritus of every failed covert action initiative is flushed directly onto the President's lap."

Former DCI **RICHARD HELMS**, *A Look over My Shoulder* (2003). Eewww . . .

POLICY ROLE

Policymaking, like the production of laws and sausages, is not for the squeamish. The Literary Spy is not squeamish but is forever grateful for a policy rotation which made clear that less thought goes into much policy than one would either suppose or hope. Busy policymakers rely on intelligence, but they are apt to blame it if it does not support policy. Intelligence exists to help policymakers, but professional commitment requires intelligence to stand aloof and not become the parroting servant of policy. It will always be a difficult relationship.

See also: Leadership; Objectivity; Politicization; Presidents & Intelligence

"The aim of the intelligence staff on service is to acquire all the information which may be useful to the general commanding. . . . The staff would be descending into a matter which is quite beyond their province were they to try and influence his decision by a too forward submission of their views."

British Colonel **GEORGE FURSE**, *Information in War* (1895).

"[Winston] Churchill understood that intelligence is far too important to be left to the professionals. His insistence on seeing the raw material provided a constant reminder that policy came first, and that intelligence was not an end in itself and did not belong to those who produced it. It was a commodity, to be deployed or withheld for purposes only he as leader could decide."

DAVID STAFFORD, *Churchill and Secret Service* (1998).

"International steps of some sort should be taken, without undue delay, to see what really legitimate grievances Germany has. . . . If there are genuine cases for self-determination [of Sudeten Germans], they should be established and remedied. . . . It may be argued that this would be giving in to Germany, strengthening Hitler's position and encouraging him to go to extremes. Better, however, that realities be faced and that wrongs, if they do exist, be righted, than leave it to Hitler to do the righting in his own way and time."

SIS memorandum to Prime Minister **NEVILLE CHAMBERLAIN** advocating a policy of appeasement, 18 September 1939; cited in Richelson, *A Century of Spies* (1995). This is an astounding example of policy advocacy by an intelligence service. Not only that, it was stupid policy.

"Whether an intelligence organization is located in Washington or Moscow, in the twentieth century or the second, its success depends on its ability to separate analysis from policy advocacy and from action: with the best will in the world, it is difficult to give a fair hearing to reports that undermine policies and actions to which one is committed."

RHODRI JEFFREYS-JONES, *The CIA and American Democracy* (1989).

"You are supposed to tell us what the Japanese are going to do, and I will then decide whether it is good or bad and act accordingly."

U.S. Pacific Fleet commander Admiral **CHESTER NIMITZ** to his communications intelligence chief Commander Joseph Rochefort, early 1942; quoted in Prange, *Miracle at Midway* (1982).

"Strictly impartial, designed to inform rather than to persuade, they should avoid all recommendations, whether explicit or veiled."

OSS guide to writing intelligence reports; cited in Katz, *Foreign Intelligence: Research and Analysis in OSS* (1989).

"[Secretary of War Robert] Patterson said that one of the principal reasons why he favors a separate central intelligence agency, outside all three Departments, is that he feels strongly that the collection of intelligence must be divorced from policy making."

Minutes of Meeting of Acting Secretary of State Dean Acheson, Secretary of War Robert Patterson, and Acting Secretary of the Navy John Sullivan, 26 December 1945; in *FRUS 1945–1950: Emergence of the Intelligence Establishment* (1996), document 61. And not just collection.

"It was agreed that the Director [of Central Intelligence] should take no part in the decisions of the [National Security] Council as this was a policy making body, and it had long been agreed that Central Intelligence should not be involved in policy making. . . . General Vandenberg [Army G-2 in the War Department, later DCI #2] stated that

he was strongly opposed to the Central Intelligence Agency or its director participating in policy decisions on any matter."

CIG legislative counsel **WALTER PFORZHEIMER**, memorandum for the record, 28 January 1947; reproduced in Warner, *CIA Under Truman* (1994).

"But for the proper judging of the situation in any foreign country it is important that information should be processed by an agency whose duty it is to weigh facts, and to draw conclusions from those facts, without having either the facts or the conclusions warped by the inevitable and even proper prejudices of the men whose duty it is to determine policy and who, having once determined a policy, are too likely to be blind to any facts which might tend to prove the policy to be faulty. The Central Intelligence Agency should have nothing to do with policy. It should try to get at the hard facts on which others must determine policy."

ALLEN DULLES, then a private citizen, statement to the Senate Armed Service Committee, 25 April 1947; in CIA Historical Intelligence Collection. The Senate was considering the National Security Act of 1947.

"No covert psychological operations will be undertaken unless they are fully consistent with the foreign policy and objectives of the United States Government."

DCI **ROSCOE HILLENKOETTER**, memorandum of 22 March 1948; reproduced in Warner, *CIA Under Truman* (1994).

"The fundamental hostility of the Soviet Government to the United States and its formidable military power require, in common prudence, that the United States be prepared for the eventuality of war with the USSR."

CIA estimate "Threats to the Security of the United States," 28 September 1948; reproduced in Kuhns, *Assessing the*

Soviet Threat (1997). Even an anodyne policy statement such as this is unusual.

"The intelligence officer must always keep in mind that he is not making policy; that is up to others. In the preparations of his estimates he is a fact finder. Once he exceeds that role, he becomes useless as an intelligence officer."

> **ALLEN DULLES**, then a private citizen, speech in Boston, 16 November 1951; in CIA's Historical Intelligence Collection.

"This is a policy matter, and not my job."

> Saying of DCI **ALLEN DULLES**; quoted in Laqueur, *A World of Secrets* (1985).

"If we allow ourselves to be influenced in our estimates by political or other considerations [then] we are failing in our work. Politics plays no role in this Agency. Anybody that wants to get into politics actively or to have any political activity had better leave, right away quick, because I won't tolerate that. . . . We're going to keep this Agency out of politics, as far as I'm concerned, and we're going to keep politics out of our estimating."

> DCI **ALLEN DULLES**, internal remarks to new CIA officers, 1953; in CIA's Historical Intelligence Collection.

"The objectives for an affirmative foreign policy can be attained only by the support which policy makers receive from you. I speak now as a member of the administration and as a member of the National Security Council, which is the greatest consumer of your product, to emphasize that knowledge of the facts is essential if we are to make the right decisions. Essentially that is why we have to have intelligence."

> Vice President **RICHARD NIXON**, remarks to new CIA officers, 10 February 1953; in CIA's Historical Intelligence Collection.

"Our analysis leads us to believe that if the US military posture develops as presently planned, the USSR will in 1961 have its most favorable opportunity to gain a decided military, political, and psychological advantage over the United States by the rapid development of operational ICBMs."

> National Intelligence Estimate 11–8–59, *Soviet Capabilities for Strategic Attack through Mid-1964*, 9 February 1960. According to a former DDI, this estimate "came as close as the US intelligence community ever did to a net assessment," that is, a comprehensive review that includes U.S. capabilities and policies. See Helgerson, *CIA Briefings* (1996).

"[DCI] John McCone . . . was a man who believed that he had two hats: one hat was running the Agency, and the other hat was as one of the President's policymakers. But he was the only one at the Agency who felt that way."

> Former DCI **RICHARD HELMS** in a 1981 interview; cited in Weber, *Spymasters* (1999). And, other than William Casey, apparently the only DCI who felt that way.

"We have worked very closely together in the National Security Council in the last two months attempting to meet the problems we faced in South Viet-Nam. I can find nothing, and I have looked through the record very carefully over the last nine months, and I could go back further, to indicate that the CIA has done anything but support policy. It does not create policy; it attempts to execute it in those areas where it has competence and responsibility."

> President **JOHN F. KENNEDY**, news conference of 9 October 1963; cited in CIA, *"Our First Line of Defense"* (1996). Apparently JFK didn't think McCone was a policymaker, either.

"In accepting [an intelligence] assignment in Saigon [in 1964], I had mistakenly assumed that from that vantage point my analysis of the situation might be more effectively heard in policy deliberations than if I remained in Washington. For years I had been told that my views were not as credible as those expressed by authorities in the field. . . . As it turned out, being in Saigon had no effect on the credence given to my analysis. It seems that the message itself was the problem, not the messenger. . . . Some people I met with suggested that in Saigon I was probably 'too close to the trees to be able to see the forest.' Only in Washington, I was told, could one see the big picture. I have since concluded that there is *no* ideal vantage point for the intelligence officer."

> GEORGE W. ALLEN, *None So Blind* (2001). Allen was a thirty-year veteran of U.S. intelligence, an analyst who specialized in Vietnam.

"The figure of [Vietnamese Communist] combat strength and particularly of guerrillas must take a steady and significant downward trend as I am convinced this reflects true enemy status."

> Intelligence chief of the U.S. Military Assistance Command Vietnam, in a 15 August 1967 memorandum outlining how MACV would assess enemy numbers; cited in Allen, *None So Blind* (2001). Reality, in other words, should follow belief.

"There is a natural tension between intelligence and policy, and the task of the former is to present as a basis for the decisions of policymakers as realistic as possible a view of forces and conditions in the external environment. Political leaders often find the picture presented less than congenial. . . . Thus, a DCI who does his job well will more often than not be the bearer of bad news, or at least will make things seem disagreeable, complicated, and uncertain. . . . When intelligence people are told, as happened in recent years, that they were ex-

pected to get on the team, then a sound intelligence-policy relationship has in effect broken down."

> Senior CIA official JOHN HUIZENGA, January 1976; cited in U.S. Senate, *Final Report of the Senate Select Committee to Study Governmental Operations with respect to Intelligence Activities* [the Church Committee], Book I (April 1976).

"It is the Director [of Central Intelligence] on whom the President relies to supply early warning; it is to the Director that the Assistant [to the President for National Security Affairs] first turns to learn the facts in a crisis and for analysis of events. And since decisions turn on the perception of the consequences of actions, the CIA assessment can almost amount to a policy recommendation."

> HENRY KISSINGER, *White House Years* (1979). Almost. Policymakers often see policy recommendations in an intelligence report even if the suggestion would come as a surprise to the intelligence officers who produced the report.

"Intelligence always has a policy effect, no matter what you say to a policy maker. . . . You can't divorce intelligence from policy. The only thing you can do is what I did, which was to try not to get into the actual policymaking process by trying to influence it one way or another."

> Former DCI RICHARD HELMS in a 1983 interview; in Ranelagh, *The Agency* (1986).

"Without parallel in the history of postwar American intelligence, Bill Casey as DCI had his own foreign policy agenda and, as a Cabinet member, pursued that agenda vigorously and often in opposition to the Secretary of State. . . . In meetings, he would sometimes offer his own views of a situation overseas without being explicit that they were his personal views and not necessarily shared by CIA's experts or others in the intelligence community. A President is not well-served if his DCI cannot offer views different than those of the intelligence community's analysts, but the DCI should be very clear to distinguish between the two. Casey rarely was. . . . All in all, there was no line between policy advocacy and intelligence for Bill Casey."

Former DCI **ROBERT GATES**, *From the Shadows* (1996).

"I am not a policymaker and CIA is not engaged in policymaking."

DCI **WILLIAM WEBSTER**, remarks in Phoenix, Arizona, 15 January 1988, in *1988 Speeches*.

"The CIA does not have a foreign policy. To the extent that we are engaged in activities to implement a foreign policy, it is the foreign policy of the United States."

DCI **WILLIAM WEBSTER**, remarks in Washington, D.C., 23 March 1988, in *1988 Speeches*.

"Policymakers can use intelligence well only if they keep an open mind about intelligence assessments, established policies, the identification of friends and foes, and definitions of national interest."

NATHAN MILLER, *Spying for America* (1989).

"I take the position that intelligence officers are not in the policy business. To underscore this, I asked not to serve in the Cabinet. When I go to National Security Council meetings, I argue the intelligence, not the policy. And I only intervene when the policymakers are obviously ignoring or twisting the intelligence that we have given them."

DCI **WILLIAM WEBSTER**, remarks in Ithaca, New York, 26 October 1989, in *1989 Speeches*.

"The problem mysteries pose to the intelligence analyst is that government officials often expect

answers to them, when no answer is possible and the analyst has to say so. In truth, the analyst's best response—though often impolitic—is to help the intelligence consumer reframe the question so that some useful information can be provided."

BRUCE BERKOWITZ and **ALLAN GOODMAN**, *Strategic Intelligence* (1989).

"Contrary to the view of those who are apprehensive over a close relationship between policymakers and intelligence, it is not close enough. More interaction, feedback, and direction as to strategy, priorities, and requirements are critical to better performance. This can be accomplished without jeopardizing the independence and integrity of intelligence assessments and judgments."

DDCI **ROBERT GATES**, *Washington Quarterly* (winter 1989).

"Our job in intelligence is not that of the ship's captain—the policymaker. It's more like the ship's navigator. We have to identify the rocks and the shoals, identify alternate courses for the ship to take and try to look out beyond the horizon and see what's out there."

DCI **WILLIAM WEBSTER**, remarks in Columbia, Missouri, 27 April 1990, in *1990 Speeches*. Webster served as a naval officer in the Pacific during World War II.

"I think that looking for big strategic answers from the Intelligence Community is actually the wrong use [of it]. I think where they're best is at the tactical level. If you ask me, did I need the Intelligence Community to know that the Soviet Union was collapsing and that Gorbachev was trying to put a finger in the dike, but that in fact the dike was coming at him and Eastern Europe was exploding? No, I could read that in the *New York Times*. . . . What they're very good at doing is watching with a real worm's eye view. They can tell you it looks like the threat to move airborne forces into Lithuania to enforce the draft is credible. And they can marry that up with hard-core military intelligence.... What you need help with is, 'This is going to happen today,' so we're not caught in the position of announcing a summit tomorrow, and the next day they invade Lithuania. That's where intelligence is helpful."

> Former NSC staff director **CONDOLEEZZA RICE** on her experience with intelligence in 1989–91; quoted in *Studies in Intelligence* 39/3 (fall 1995).

"In their heart of hearts the analysts [at CIA] think they are more expert at policy than the policymakers [and that] their profoundest obligation is not so much to draw pictures of the outside world as it truly is, but rather by drawing pictures of the outside world to help bring about good policy in Washington."

> **ANGELO CODEVILLA**, *Informing Statecraft* (1992). Codevilla was a staffer on the Senate intelligence committee and has never been an intelligence analyst. It's not clear that he knows any analysts.

"CIA's rationale for existence is to provide 'policy support.' But on a day-to-day basis, most analysts are given scant sense that their work is relevant to policy. They get little or no feedback from policy makers and seldom have contact with policy officials.... Analysts are concerned not with the policy audience, but the readership among their peers in the intelligence community and with fulfilling their quota of reports and assessments. Despite an elaborate 'requirements' process, most of the topics that analysts address are selected by the DI itself. It is the proverbial 'self-licking ice cream cone.'"

> **MARVIN OTT** in the *Wall Street Journal*, 23 December 1992.

"The intelligence producer's job is to eschew manipulation, and to put the proverbial monkey of responsibility for deciding about ambiguities and relevance clearly where it belongs: on the action officer. Both the intelligence officer, who chooses and analyzes the facts, and the action officer, who decides what to do, have their own separate specialty. But for each to perform his own well, both must become intellectual partners."

> **ANGELO CODEVILLA**, *Informing Statecraft* (1992).

"My job is to protect foreign policy.... The point is that intelligence serves diplomacy.... How do we find a diplomatic opportunity? How do we make it part of a strategy? How do we use these facts to make our diplomacy more effective? ... We're trying to shape the intelligence community so it serves the State Department's needs."

> **TOBY GATI**, Assistant Secretary of State for Intelligence and Research; quoted in *Foreign Service Journal* (February 1996).

"Policymakers carry their own [intelligence estimates] around in their heads.... They can be especially reluctant to accept new images of reality on the say-so of midlevel officers from across the Potomac."

> Former senior CIA official **HAROLD FORD**, "Calling the Sino-Soviet Split," *Studies in Intelligence* 41/4 (1997).

"A good day is when we prevent one bad policy decision from being made."

> Senior State Department intelligence official when asked what INR does, February 1999.

"The intelligence function is unique in that it focuses on reality, the way the world is. Almost everyone else in the national security structure is focused on changing that reality through policy. If policy makers are to succeed, they need an intelligence community that is focused on the factors that will determine the success or failure of that policy, not on forecasting whether they will succeed."

> Senior CIA analyst **MARTIN PETERSEN**, "What We Should Demand from Intelligence," *National Security Studies Quarterly* (spring 1999).

"If you are not close enough to policy action to risk crashing, you are probably not close enough to be taken seriously."

> Axiom coined by CIA's Balkan Task Force, the Agency's primary analytic effort on the Balkans in the 1990s.

"There are no policy failures. There are only policy successes and intelligence failures."

> Senior State Department official quoted "only half in jest" in Petersen, "What We Should Demand from Intelligence," *National Security Studies Quarterly* (spring 1999).

"In the mind of the policymaker, there's no policy that's so bad that intelligence can ruin it. To the intelligence professional, there's no policy so good that intelligence can't devastate it."

> National Security Council official to CIA officers, July 1999.

"One of the most dangerous things a policymaker can do is to act as his own intelligence analyst.... The quality of intelligence a policymaker can expect is a function of the questions he asks. And analysts will kill for a decent question."

> White House official with intelligence responsibilities to CIA officers, July 1999.

"The most difficult task the foreign affairs policymaker faces is making decisions in an environment of ambiguity and inadequate information. The role of intelligence is to narrow the range of un-

certainty within which a decision must be made. What really matters is not how well the intelligence community predicts particular events but its ability to spot, track, and interpret trends and patterns."

> **BRENT SCOWCROFT**, former national security affairs advisor to President George H. W. Bush, letter to the *Washington Post*, 12 January 2000.

"I hear people in the Intelligence Community saying [DCI George Tenet] should just tell the President what he won't and can't do. Well, I can tell you that's not the kind of conversation with a President that you would seek. I can only say most of us look on his position with great sympathy."

> Former DCI **RICHARD HELMS** on the CIA's reluctant role as a broker between Israeli and Palestinian security forces; quoted in the *New York Times*, 13 November 2000.

"While the Director of Central Intelligence must not offer policy advice, he needs to be present in the small meetings at which the crucial decisions are made. He must be the one to make sure all the players have the same information and that the facts on the table are the best available, not just those supporting one position or another."

> Former DCI **ROBERT GATES** in the *Wall Street Journal*, 23 January 2001.

"Intelligence officers can be at the mercy—I use that word carefully—of policymakers. Policymakers may not always listen to what is being said, but they are quite ready to blame their failures, or foul ups, on faulty intelligence. Intelligence and the Intelligence Community are the handiest of scapegoats."

> Former DCI **JAMES SCHLESINGER**, remarks at a Princeton University conference, March 2001.

"Very little research so far has been done on the way in which policy makers use and have used intelligence. We know far more about how intelligence agencies have collected and analysed intelligence than on how policy makers have used it. ... The biggest failure in Western intelligence during the 20th century was in the relationship between intelligence and policy makers."

CHRISTOPHER ANDREW, interview in the Italian online journal *Per Aspera ad Veritatem* (May–August 2001).

"I think one of the keys to having the whole system work is managing that relationship between the intelligence community on the one hand, and the policymaker on the other. The intelligence community can have the best intelligence in the world, the finest collection, the best analysis. And if nobody in the White House ever hears about it, it's absolutely worthless. And by the same token, [the analysts] have to expect that they have to defend their analysis. They've got to be able to withstand the kind of questioning that goes with a good interchange back and forth. It's got to be a two-way street. You've got to be able to say to the analysts, well, wait a minute, why did you conclude that? Or what are your underlying assumptions? And I do a lot of that. And I see that very much as part of my job. You don't simply take what the community produces and say, oh, okay, this is gospel. It's rarely gospel."

Vice President RICHARD CHENEY, interview with *USA Today* and the *Los Angeles Times*, 18 January 2004.

POLITICIZATION

The Literary Spy remembers one fine day when a member of the policymaking community called to complain about an intelligence report that contradicted what she had been told by a foreign official—and what she des-

perately wanted to believe was true. For all her influence, for all her threats, that report was not recalled. Eventually she was recalled to civilian life, and the intelligence professionals breathed more easily. Sometimes it's far more difficult to avoid the temptation of telling the policymaker what he wants to hear.

See also: Ignoring Bad News; Objectivity; Policy Role

"But now you seek to kill me, a man who had told you the truth."

John 8:40 (Revised Standard).

"If you give me six lines written by the hand of the most honest of men, I will find something in them which will hang him."

Attributed to CARDINAL RICHELIEU, French prelate and statesman (1585–1642).

"Ignorance is less remote from truth than prejudice."

Attributed to DENIS DIDEROT, French philosopher (1713–1784).

"A truth that's told with bad intent,
Beats all the lies you can invent."

WILLIAM BLAKE, *Auguries of Innocence* (1803).

"The estimate was founded upon all information then in my possession ... and was made large, as intimated to you at the time, so as to be sure and cover the entire number of the Enemy that our army was to meet."

ALLAN PINKERTON to Union General George McClellan, November 1861, referring to the report on Confederate strength Pinkerton had given to McClellan, who had already begun his notorious inflation of enemy forces facing him; cited in Fishel, *Secret War for the Union* (1996). Even if the politicization is admitted to the consumer, as it was here, it is still politicized intelligence.

"We get accurate information, but [General Joseph] Hooker will not use it and insults all who differ from him in opinion."

> Bureau of Information, Union Army, May 1863; quoted in Andrew, *For the President's Eyes Only* (1995).

"It is of the first importance not to allow your judgment to be biased by personal qualities."

> Sherlock Holmes to Doctor Watson in Sir **ARTHUR CONAN DOYLE**, *The Sign of Four* (1890).

"Convictions are more dangerous enemies of truth than lies."

> **FRIEDRICH NIETZSCHE**, *Human, All Too Human* (1878).

"You have made it impossible for my plan of campaign to be carried out. I will see to it that you do not receive any promotion in the army in the future."

> Secretary of War **RUSSELL ALGER** to U.S. Army intelligence chief Colonel Arthur Wagner, who was asked by the White House for a report on Cuba in 1898 and had recommended postponing a U.S. invasion until winter due to tropical weather and disease; cited in Haswell, *Spies and Spymasters* (1977).

"Truth is sacred; and if you tell the truth too often nobody will believe it."

> **G. K. CHESTERTON** in the *Illustrated London News*, 24 February 1906.

"For the most part we do not first see and then define, we define first and then see."

> **WALTER LIPPMANN**, *Public Opinion* (1922).

"Give me the facts, Ashley, and I will twist them the way I want to suit my argument."

> **WINSTON CHURCHILL** to an Oxford historian assisting him during the 1930s on a biography of the first Duke of Marlborough; quoted in Stafford, *Churchill and Secret Service* (1998).

"Hitler is reasonable and sees your point of view as long as you put it to him properly."

> Admiral **WILHELM CANARIS**, chief of the Abwehr (Nazi Germany's military intelligence organization); quoted in Russell, *The Secret War* (1981).

"It might be a good thing if Captain Talbot went to sea as soon as possible."

> **WINSTON CHURCHILL**, April 1940, shortly before firing Arthur Talbot, the chief of the British antisubmarine division who had been circulating intelligence contradicting Churchill's upbeat announcements regarding the war against the U-boats; quoted in Stafford, *Churchill and Secret Service* (1998). Stafford describes Talbot as "an officer who rigorously abstained from wishful thinking" —the kind policymakers often wish would get "on the team."

"I again insist on recalling and punishing our ambassador to Berlin, Dekanozov, who keeps bombarding me with 'reports' on Hitler's alleged preparations to attack the USSR. He has reported that this attack will start tomorrow. . . . But I and my people, Iosif Vissarionovich, have firmly embedded in our memory your wise conclusion: Hitler is not going to attack us in 1941."

> NKVD chief **LAVRENTI BERIA** to Stalin, 21 June 1941; cited in Andrew and Mitrokhin, *The Mitrokhin Archive* (1999). Hitler, in fact, attacked the following day. Andrew notes that the Soviet intelligence officers excelled at surviving through sycophancy.

"When intelligence producers realize that there is no sense in forwarding to a consumer knowledge which does not correspond to his preconceptions, then intelligence is through. At this point there is no intelligence and the consumer is out on his own with no more to guide him than the indications of the tea leaf and the crystal ball."

> **SHERMAN KENT**, *Strategic Intelligence* (1949). Kent does not allow for a consumer who can recognize and dismiss bad intelligence.

"We are all capable of believing things which we know to be untrue, and then, when we are finally proved wrong, impudently twisting the facts so as to show that we were right. Intellectually, it is possible to carry on this process for an indefinite time; the only check on it is that sooner or later a false belief bumps up against the solid reality, usually on a battlefield."

> **GEORGE ORWELL** after World War II; quoted in the *London Financial Times*, 13 May 2003.

"Just as prejudice has no place in intelligence, neither has politics. Facts are neither Republican nor Democratic. And if the fearless reporting of the facts to the policy makers is colored with the prejudice pro or con of existing politics of government or of any political party, the intelligence has lost its integrity and its usefulness."

> **ALLEN DULLES**, then a private citizen, speech in Boston, 16 November 1951; in CIA's Historical Intelligence Collection. The Cold War showed that facts often are partisan.

"The determination of policy is not the function of intelligence, although some . . . may try to influence policymaking by biasing their information. This is one of the greatest mistakes an intelligence organization can make."

> **WILLIAM FISHER**; cited in *Studies in Intelligence* (winter 1986). Wise words, considering the source: Fisher was a Soviet intelligence officer better known as "Colonel Rudolf Abel," who was sent to the United States to estab-

lish a spy ring and whom the FBI arrested in 1957. Fisher was exchanged for the U-2 pilot Francis Gary Powers in 1962.

"Wishful intelligence, the desire to please or reassure the recipient, was the most dangerous commodity in the whole realm of secret information."

> **IAN FLEMING** in the James Bond novel *Thunderball* (1961).

"[CIA must] show *indisputable evidence* that Castro-types are in charge. This cannot *just* be a statement. [DCI William] Raborn must have *pictures, names,* a full *dossier.*"

> Presidential aide **JACK VALENTI** to Lyndon Johnson on justifying the U.S. invasion of the Dominican Republic, April 1965; quoted in Jeffreys-Jones, *The CIA and American Democracy* (1989).

"CIA military analysts were skeptical of the actuality of the [Tonkin Gulf] attack. . . . To my surprise the White House decided, without consulting CIA, that the attack was a reality and that it justified expanding the U.S. war effort. . . . We, of course, had seen the report but had discounted it heavily because we had found the source previously unreliable. To CIA, it proved nothing."

> Former DDI **R. JACK SMITH**, *The Unknown CIA* (1989).

"America failed in Vietnam not because intelligence was lacking, or wrong, but because it was not in accord with what its consumers wanted to believe. . . . When this occurs—when political and ideological factors dominate the decision-making process—there is little the intelligence community can do except to stay on course."

> **GEORGE W. ALLEN**, *None So Blind* (2001). Allen was a thirty-year veteran of U.S. intelligence, an analyst who specialized in Vietnam.

"Within a year of becoming KGB chairman, [Yuri] Andropov was submitting distorted intelligence assessments to the Politburo designed to strengthen its resolve to crush the Prague Spring [reform movement in Czechoslovakia] by armed force. His obsession with Western attempts to promote ideological sabotage in the Soviet Bloc made him unwilling to consider any evidence which suggested otherwise. In 1968 the [KGB] Centre destroyed classified US documents obtained by the Washington residency which showed that neither the CIA nor any other American agency was manipulating the reformers of the Prague Spring."

> **CHRISTOPHER ANDREW** and **VASILI MITROKHIN**, *The Sword and the Shield: The Mitrokhin Archive* (1999). That's called "mirror-imaging." Andropov believed it because that's what *he* would do.

"All lies and jest;
Still a man hears what he wants to hear
And disregards the rest."

> **PAUL SIMON**, "The Boxer," from Simon and Garfunkel's 1970 album *Bridge over Troubled Water*.

"When intelligence producers have a general feeling that they are working in a hostile climate, what really happens is not so much that they tailor the product to please, although that's not been unknown, but more likely, they avoid the treatment of difficult issues."

> **JOHN HUIZENGA**, chief of CIA's Office of National Estimates, in 1976; quoted in Andrew, *For the President's Eyes Only* (1995).

"Kissinger disregarded analytical intelligence except for what was convenient for use by Kissinger's own small personal staff in support of Nixon-Kissinger policies. . . . Crucial intelligence was often suppressed to insure that only Nixon and Kissinger had the full body of information on which to make broad judgments."

> Former DDI **RAY CLINE**, *Secrets, Spies and Scholars* (1976).

"It was the CIA's refusal to become involved with the [Watergate] cover-up that eventually made it unsustainable."

> **CHRISTOPHER ANDREW**, *For the President's Eyes Only* (1995).

"The man is a shit."

> Former DCI **RICHARD HELMS** when asked his opinion of Richard Nixon, who tried to involve CIA in the Watergate cover-up and then sacked Helms when he refused to comply; quoted in Andrew, *For the President's Eyes Only* (1995).

"The trouble with you fellows is that you're not on the team."

> Unnamed assistant of DCI James Schlesinger speaking to the chief of CIA's Office of National Estimates; quoted in Ranelagh, *The Agency* (1986).

"There is a tendency in some analysts to regard disagreement from above as an attempt to coerce their thinking or limit their freedom."

> Former DDCI General **VERNON WALTERS**, *Silent Missions* (1978). Occasionally politicization really is in the eyes of the beholder.

"Far from being the hawkish band of international adventurers so facilely portrayed by its critics, the Agency usually erred on the side of the interpretation fashionable in the Washington Establishment. In my experience the CIA developed rationales for inaction much more frequently than for daring thrusts. Its analysts were only too aware that no one has ever been penalized for not having foreseen an opportunity, but that many careers have been blighted for not predicting a risk."

HENRY KISSINGER, *White House Years* (1979).

"Would a politicized Agency have disclosed in the middle of the SALT II debates that the Soviets had a brigade in Cuba? Would a politicized Agency have undercut an Administration policy on Korea by revealing a build-up of North Korean military forces? Would a politicized Agency in the middle of a debate on the Panama Canal Treaty have disclosed that some of Trujillo's relatives were dealing in drugs? Would a politicized Agency have published some of the unclassified studies we have published in the last couple of years, some of which have not been very popular with the policy makers?"

DCI **STANSFIELD TURNER** in remarks to CIA employees, 1979; in CIA's Historical Intelligence Collection.

"In order to please our superiors, we sent in falsified and biased information, acting on the principle 'Blame everything on the Americans, and everything will be OK.' That's not intelligence, it's self-deception!"

Soviet intelligence officer, early 1980s; quoted in Andrew and Mitrokhin, *The Mitrokhin File* (1999).

"Pressures . . . on the DCI to make intelligence support policy are not unusual, but they are almost always blatant [*sic*]. That's because they have to come from someone without authority over the DCI. His only boss is the President. If a President ever pressured a DCI to bias his intelligence reports, the DCI would have no option other than to resign. Pressures on the DCI by outsiders, then, have to be those of persuasion, not threat. . . . Policy-makers exert such pressures because they are

eager not to have some intelligence report floating around that can be used to torpedo their programs or policies."

Former DCI **STANSFIELD TURNER**, *Secrecy and Democracy* (1985).

"If one's analysis or prose seems to be ignored, is not used, or is 'butchered' (edited), a martyr's role at the hands of 'political trimmers' or because of 'political pressure' is far more congenial than acknowledgment (private or public) that the prose or analysis in question might have been turgid, poorly written, ill thought-out, irrelevant, or simply unconvincing to equally knowledgeable peers or superiors."

WALTER LAQUEUR, *A World of Secrets* (1985).

"Policy makers are power seekers, and they will always use intelligence for what they want and need."

JOHN RANELAGH, *The Agency* (1986).

"It has been my experience over the years that the usual response of a policymaker to intelligence with which he disagrees or which he finds unpalatable is to ignore it; sometimes he will characterize it as incomplete, too narrowly focused or incompetent (and sometimes rightly so); and occasionally he will charge that it is 'cooked'—that it reflects a CIA bias. In my 21 years in intelligence, I have never heard a policymaker (or anyone else for that matter) characterize as biased or cooked a CIA assessment with which he agreed. . . . Some CIA analyses are better than others; some intelligence experts are better than others; estimates sometimes alleged to be politicized or biased usually are not at all—sometimes they were just not very well done. But unevenness of quality should not be confused with politicization."

> DDI **ROBERT GATES**, "The CIA and American Foreign Policy," *Foreign Affairs* (winter 1987–88).

"If the policy-intelligence relationship is to work, there must be mutual respect, trust, civility, and also a certain distance. Intelligence people must provide honest and best judgments and avoid intrusion on policymaking or attempts to influence it. Policymakers must assume the integrity of the intelligence provided and avoid attempts to get materials suited to their tastes."

> Senior CIA official **JOHN HUIZENGA**; quoted in Berkowitz and Goodman, *Strategic Intelligence* (1989).

"When policy biases intelligence, it is less often because of pressure than because an analyst decides on his own not to press a case that seems too out of step with current thinking."

> **BRUCE BERKOWITZ** and **ALLAN GOODMAN**, *Strategic Intelligence* (1989).

"Politicization is a serious matter, and it has no place at CIA or in the Intelligence Community. . . . In no instance should we alter our judgments to make a product more palatable to a policymaker."

> DCI **ROBERT GATES**, speech to CIA analysts, 16 March 1992; in *Speeches* (1993).

"Ultimately . . . the only safeguards [against politicization] are the backbones of the chiefs of the intelligence services and their willingness and ability to protect analysts from outside pressure."

> **ABRAM SHULSKY**, *Silent Warfare* (1993).

"Politicization cannot be reasonably defined to mean providing support to the policymaking pro-

cess, because that is why intelligence analysis exists in the first place."

> **JACK DAVIS** in *Studies in Intelligence* (fall 1995).

"The need to protect intelligence from political pressure and parochialism is a powerful argument for maintaining a strong, centralized capability and not leaving decisions affecting important intelligence-related questions solely to the policymaking departments. . . . Unlike [in] business, the customer is not always right."

> Council on Foreign Relations, *Making Intelligence Smarter* (1996).

"You have to advise the President impartially and objectively. That becomes particularly tricky when you have to portray a policy as not being a success and you've got the President sneaking up to you and asking, 'Aren't you on the team?'"

> Former DCI **RICHARD HELMS**; quoted in the *New York Times*, 10 March 1997.

"Be attentive to those who seek the truth. Beware of those who have found it."

> Heard in a CIA leadership course, 2001.

"The president of the United States would never tolerate anything other than our most honest judgment. Our credibility and integrity are our most precious commodities. We will not let anyone tell us what conclusions to reach."

> DCI **GEORGE TENET** responding to allegations that CIA analysts were being pressured by senior Bush administration officials to find links between Iraq and the al-Qaeda terrorist group; quoted in the *Los Angeles Times*, 11 October 2002.

"It's a disgrace that the case for war [against Iraq] seems to have been based on shoddy intelligence, hyped intelligence, and even false intelligence."

    Senator **EDWARD KENNEDY**; quoted on ABC's *World News Tonight*, 15 July 2003.

"The invasion and conquest of Iraq by the United States last spring was the result of what is probably the least ambiguous case of the misreading of secret intelligence information in American history. . . . Left on their own the analysts would have walked gingerly all around the mystery of Iraq's nuclear program, couching their findings in well-hedged paragraphs full of that special verb form we might call the intelligence conditional—things that may, might, or could be the case. We can be sure it was not the analysts who leaped to conclusions."

    THOMAS POWERS, "The Vanishing Case for War," *New York Review of Books*, 4 December 2003.

"What has happened was more than a failure of intelligence. It was the result of manipulation of the intelligence to justify a decision to go to war."

    Senator **EDWARD KENNEDY** during a hearing conducted by the Senate's Armed Services Committee, 29 January 2004.

PRESCRIPTIONS

The Literary Spy is skeptical of many ideas that seem never to go away: universal health care, collectivist politics, and intelligence reform. The need for intelligence stems from the irrefutable fact that the world is imperfect—yet it seems everyone wants to write a prescription that will make intelligence work perfectly. It ain't gonna happen.

See also: Critics & Defenders; Failures; Limits of Intelligence; Origins of Central Intelligence; U.S. Intelligence "Community"

"The textbooks agree, of course, that we should only believe reliable intelligence, and should never cease to be suspicious, but what is the use of such feeble maxims? They belong to the wisdom which for want of anything better scribblers of systems and compendia resort to when they run out of ideas."

    CARL VON CLAUSEWITZ, *On War* (1832).

"CIA should be guided by one high overriding principle—it should stay out of primary substantive work. CIA will have to staff up on a few men of highest professional competence in appropriate fields of study. It will have to have some outstanding economists and political scientists, some international relations specialists, some specialists in the military art. . . . But as little as possible should this staff get into the creative substantive work. . . . As soon as CIA departs from this principle, as soon as it gets into substantive work and itself makes descriptive or evaluative studies, it is in trouble. For when it does this, it becomes little more than a fifth major research and surveillance outfit."

    SHERMAN KENT, *Strategic Intelligence* (1949). Kent, head of CIA's Board of National Estimates, believed the Agency should do little more than serve as the staff of the BNE. But even before Kent's book was published, CIA under NSC direction was "into substantive work," and as a result CIA today is the primary rather than the fifth wheel of intelligence that Kent forecast.

"The position of Director of Central Intelligence should be elevated by legislation to Cabinet level [and] have broad supervisory control over all intelligence agencies, including an independent, new, purely analytical and estimative intelligence agency to be established by Congressional legislation. It might be called the Central Institute of Foreign Affairs Research (CIFAR). It should consolidate the work of the main analytical staffs now in CIA, State, and Defense. . . . The Central Intelligence Agency, with the famous acronym that has become a worldwide public relations liability, would cease to exist. The DCI, the analysts in CIFAR, and the various collection agencies would have replaced it."

> Former DDI **RAY CLINE**, *Secrets, Spies and Scholars* (1976). Centralizing the now competitive analysis that exists in the Intelligence Community, however, would not guarantee that U.S. intelligence would CIFARther or better than it does today. Besides, CIA is a pretty good brand name these days.

"Observers who see notorious intelligence failures as egregious often infer that disasters can be avoided by perfecting norms and procedures for analysis and argumentation. This belief is illusory. Intelligence can be improved marginally, but not radically, by altering the analytic system. . . . The use of intelligence depends less on the bureaucracy than on the intellects and inclinations of the authorities above it."

> **RICHARD K. BETTS**, "Why Intelligence Failures Are Inevitable," *World Politics* (October 1978).

"The two jobs, head of the CIA and head of the Intelligence Community, conflict. . . . The solution is to have a Director of National Intelligence and a separate Director of the CIA."

> Former DCI **STANSFIELD TURNER**, *Secrecy and Democracy* (1985).

"There have been periodic attempts to improve intelligence; most of them have had no positive

effect. . . . It has at least become clear which approaches do not work. This goes above all for attempts at organizational reform."

> **WALTER LAQUEUR**, *A World of Secrets* (1985).

"No panaceas, no new laws, no sudden breakthroughs in technology will provide better intelligence. Prosaic measures provide the best hope for genuine improvement: recruitment of promising individuals, systematic training, a constant search for improved collection and analysis, an upgrading of the quality and independence of senior staff."

> **NATHAN MILLER**, *Spying for America* (1989). A strikingly similar passage is found in Laqueur, *A World of Secrets* (1985).

"Operational problems are not solved with reorganizational fixes—only good people and good management can do that."

> **HAYDEN PEAKE**, curator of CIA's Historical Intelligence Collection.

"In the long run, governments get the intelligence they deserve."

> **ANGELO CODEVILLA**, *Informing Statecraft* (1992).

"The most important reform that could be made to the current system would be the elimination of the [congressional] intelligence committees and the restoration of the system that existed from 1947 to 1974."

> **STEPHEN KNOTT**, *Secret and Sanctioned* (1996).

"Could it not be that the time has come at this 50th anniversary to take a hard look at the numbers of people employed by the Central Intelligence Agency. . . . A serious case can be made for sharpening the focus on important targets and by reducing the number of hands, or layers if you like, through which every operational decision or analytical disagreement must pass. This is no plea for the quick-fix department. But excellence in performance is the prerogative of comparatively few human beings.... It is not numbers of people who will produce good intelligence and prevent another Pearl Harbor. It is quality, teamwork, leadership."

> Former DCI **RICHARD HELMS**, remarks at CIA's fiftieth anniversary ceremonies, 18 September 1997.

"There is simply no instant cure for what ails the intelligence community. They have simply failed to develop the necessary expertise and access to those parts of the world that most need watching."

> **RICHARD PERLE**, former Pentagon official in the Reagan administration; quoted in the *Wall Street Journal*, 25 September 2001.

"What will the nation's intelligence services have to change to fight this war? The short answer is: almost everything."

> **TIM WEINER** in the *New York Times*, 7 October 2001.

"A lot must, can, and will be done to shore up U.S. intelligence collection and analysis.... There is no shortage of proposals and initiatives to shake the system up. There is, however, a shortage of perspective on the limitations we can expect from improved performance.... The only thing worse than business as usual would be naive assumptions about what reform can accomplish.... The crying need for intelligence reorganization is no recent discovery. It is a perennial lament, amplified every time intelligence stumbles. The community has undergone several major reorganizations and innumerable lesser ones over the past half-century. No one ever stays satisfied with reorganization because it never seems to do the trick—if the trick is to prevent intelligence failure. There is little reason to believe, therefore, that the next reform will do much better than previous ones."

> **RICHARD BETTS**, "Fixing Intelligence," *Foreign Affairs* (January–February 2002).

"It's important for us to avoid a situation in which we spend so much time moving the boxes around on the chart and redrawing wiring diagrams that we lose sight of our basic requirements and missions.... [Instead,] you put good people in those jobs, give them clear direction and then hold them accountable for their performance, and I think that's probably more important than whatever reporting arrangements we have inside in the community itself."

> Vice President **RICHARD CHENEY**; quoted in the *Washington Post*, 9 April 2002.

"The failure to prevent Sept. 11 was not a failure of intelligence or coordination. It was a failure of imagination. Even if all the raw intelligence signals had been shared among the F.B.I., the C.I.A. and the White House, I'm convinced that there was no one there who would have put them all together, who could have imagined evil on the scale Osama bin Laden did.... Imagining evil of this magnitude simply does not come naturally to the American character.... We need an 'Office of Evil,' whose job would be to constantly sift all intelligence data and imagine what the most twisted mind might be up to."

> **THOMAS FRIEDMAN**, "A Failure to Imagine," *New York Times*, 19 May 2002. There would be a lot of volunteers for such an office.

PRESIDENTS & INTELLIGENCE

Intelligence agencies in most countries are servants exclusively of the executive, and therein lies the potential for abuse. U.S. presidents have had to contend with limitations of intelligence, bad publicity, and the encroachment of Congress on the process and product of intelligence, but by and large U.S. intelligence still serves primarily the president.

See also: Current Intelligence; Directors of Central Intelligence; Leadership; Plausible Denial; "Rogue Elephant"

"Everything, in a manner, depends upon obtaining intelligence."

> **GEORGE WASHINGTON**, to General William Heath, 5 September 1776; quoted in Miller, *Spying for America* (1989).

"The necessity of procuring good intelligence is apparent & need not be further urged—All that remains for me to add is, that you keep the whole matter as secret as possible. For upon Secrecy, Success depends in Most Enterprizes of the kind, and for want of it, they are generally defeated."

> **GEORGE WASHINGTON** to Colonel Elias Dayton, 26 July 1777; cited in Helgerson, *CIA Briefings* (1996). When President Kennedy visited CIA in January 1961 he saw this letter on display and asked for a copy of it. He later wrote to DCI Allen Dulles, "The letter is both a fine memento of my visit with you and a continuing reminder of the role of intelligence in national policy."

"[The Revolutionary War] was one time in our history when the U.S. Intelligence Service encountered no difficulty whatsoever in getting its finding accepted, correctly interpreted, and given due weight by the government's Executive Branch. There is much to be said for an intelligence operation which is run by the commander-in-chief himself."

> Former DCI **ALLEN DULLES** in his edited volume *Great True Spy Stories* (1968). Was Dulles, the DCI at the time of the Bay of Pigs, speaking with tongue firmly in cheek?

"The [Constitutional] Convention have done well . . . in so disposing of the making of treaties that although the President must, in forming them, act by the advice and consent of the Senate, yet he will be able to manage the business of intelligence in such a manner as prudence may suggest."

> **JOHN JAY**, *The Federalist*, No. 64.

"Jefferson had requested funding for [the Lewis and Clark] mission in a secret message to Congress on January 18, 1803. However, planning for the mission had been under way throughout 1802 as Jefferson began taking steps for acquiring at least part of the Louisiana Territory from France, which would be ceded it by Spain. Jefferson's carefully crafted rationale for the expedition, delivered in his message to Congress, emphasized its commercial and scientific benefits while excluding any reference to territorial designs or strategic considerations. . . . The selection of William Clark for the mission is revealing, for Clark was a veteran military-intelligence officer who had conducted a detailed reconnaissance of Spanish fortifications along the Ohio River in 1795. . . . As the two explorers made their way through the new territory . . . Clark charted locations for proposed American forts, some two-thirds of which were built in response to his recommendations. The Lewis and Clark mission was a success on many fronts, not the least of which was the strategic intelligence it provided for military planners to secure the area."

> **STEPHEN KNOTT**, *Secret and Sanctioned* (1996).

"That the whole of the enemy is concentrating on Richmond, I think, cannot be known to you or me."

President **ABRAHAM LINCOLN** responding to General George McClellan's complaint that "the whole of the enemy is concentrating everything" on the Confederate capital, May 1862; quoted in Fishel, *Secret War for the Union* (1996). It's important that a president be willing to express skepticism about intelligence.

"Let me testify to this, my fellow citizens, I not only did not know it until we got into this war, but I did not believe it when I was told that it was true, that Germany was not the only country that maintained a secret service. Every country in Europe maintained it . . . and the only difference between the German secret service and the other secret services was that the German secret service found out more than the others did!"

President **WOODROW WILSON**, speech of 5 September 1919; quoted in Andrew, *For the President's Eyes Only* (1995). The former president of Princeton University, the only U.S. president with a Ph.D., did not realize that European countries spied on each other.

"No postwar president has been nearly as ignorant of intelligence as Truman was when he succeeded FDR. Yet it was his administration, more than any other, that shaped today's intelligence community."

CHRISTOPHER ANDREW, *For the President's Eyes Only* (1995).

"I referred briefly to the Office of Strategic Services. . . . The President again commented that he has in mind a broad intelligence service attached to the President's office. He stated that we should recommend the dissolution of Donovan's outfit [OSS] even if Donovan did not like it."

Budget Director **HAROLD SMITH** on his 13 September 1945 meeting with President Truman; cited in Troy, *Donovan and the CIA* (1981).

"Truman contributed little, if anything, to the theory and structure of CIA. . . . In the circumstances he did no more, and probably less, than Roosevelt would have done. . . . Truman deserves some credit but not as much as he has given himself."

THOMAS TROY, *Donovan and the CIA* (1981).

"The President ought to have a source of information that covers the whole world and the only way to get it is to have an intelligence agency of his own which will keep him informed of what goes on."

Former President **HARRY TRUMAN** to former DCI Allen Dulles, letter of 6 November 1963; quoted in Pisani, *CIA and the Marshall Plan* (1991).

"There were so many things I did not know when I became President."

President **HARRY TRUMAN** to DCI Walter Bedell Smith, saying he wanted the 1952 presidential candidates—General Dwight Eisenhower and Governor Adlai Stevenson—briefed by CIA on foreign affairs, summer 1952. Truman thus began a CIA tradition that continues to this day. See Helgerson, *CIA Briefings* (1996).

"We have the Central Intelligence Agency . . . this agency puts the information of vital importance to the President in his hands. . . . You are the organization, you are the intelligence arm that keeps the Executive informed so he can make decisions that always will be in the public interest for his own country, hoping always that it will save the free world from involvement with the totalitarian countries in an all-out war—a terrible thing to contemplate. Those of you who are deep in the Central Intelligence Agency know what goes on around the world—know what is necessary for the President to know every morning. . . . I came over here to tell you how appreciative I am of the service which I received as the Chief Executive of the greatest nation in the history of the world. . . . I am extremely thankful to you. I think it is good that some of you have found out just exactly what a tremendous organization Intelligence has to be in this day and age. You can't run the government without it. Keep up the good work."

> President **HARRY TRUMAN**, transcript of remarks to officials of CIA and other government agencies, 21 November 1952; reproduced in Warner, *CIA Under Truman* (1994).

"[CIA is] an efficient and permanent arm of the Government's national security structure. . . . No President ever had such a wealth of vital information made available to him in such a useful manner as I have received through CIA."

> President **HARRY TRUMAN** in letter to DCI Walter Bedell Smith, December 1952; cited in Ranelagh, *The Agency* (1986).

"To the Central Intelligence Agency, a necessity to the President of the United States, from one who knows.

Harry S Truman
June 9, 1964"

> President **HARRY TRUMAN**'s inscription on his photograph displayed at CIA Headquarters.

"In war nothing is more important to a commander than the facts concerning the strength, dispositions, and intentions of his opponent, and the proper interpretation of those facts. In peacetime the necessary facts are of a different nature. They deal with conditions, resources, requirements, and attitudes prevailing in the world. They and their correct interpretation are essential to the development of policy to further our long-term national security and best interests. To provide information

of this kind is the task of the organization of which you are a part. No task could be more important."

> President **DWIGHT EISENHOWER**, remarks at the laying of the cornerstone for the new CIA Headquarters building, 3 November 1959; cited in CIA, *"Our First Line of Defense"* (1996).

"As I think you know, I wish you and your associates in the Central Intelligence Agency well in the tremendously important job you do for our country. Upon the work of your organization there is an almost frightening responsibility; I know all members of the CIA will continue to do the best they can for all of us."

> President **DWIGHT EISENHOWER**, letter to DCI Allen Dulles, 18 January 1961; cited in CIA, *"Our First Line of Defense"* (1996).

"For: The Central Intelligence Agency
An indispensable organization to our country.
Dwight D. Eisenhower"

> President **DWIGHT EISENHOWER**'s inscription on his photograph displayed at CIA Headquarters.

"If someone comes in to tell me this or that about the minimum wage bill, I have no hesitation in overruling them. But you always assume that the military and intelligence people have some secret skill not available to ordinary mortals."

> President **JOHN F. KENNEDY** after the Bay of Pigs, according to Arthur Schlesinger; cited in Andrew, *For the President's Eyes Only* (1995). Hard to believe, that stunning Kennedy naïveté.

"In the course of the past months I have had occasion to again observe the extraordinary accomplishments of our intelligence community, and I have been singularly impressed with the overall professional excellence, selfless devotion to duty, resourcefulness and initiative manifested in the work of this group. The fact that we had timely and accurate information, skillfully analyzed and clearly presented, to guide us in our judgments during the [Cuban missile] crisis is, I believe, the greatest tribute to the effectiveness of these individuals and agencies. The magnitude of their contribution can be measured, in part, by the fact that the peace was sustained during a most critical time."

> President **JOHN F. KENNEDY**, letter to DCI John McCone, 9 January 1963; cited in CIA, *"Our First Line of Defense"* (1996).

"CIA could not have had a better friend in a President than John F. Kennedy. He understood the Agency and used it effectively, exploiting its intellectual abilities to help him analyze a complex world and its paramilitary and covert political talents to react to it."

> Former DCI **WILLIAM COLBY**, *Honorable Men* (1978).

"For: the Central Intelligence Agency—with esteem

John F. Kennedy."

> President **JOHN F. KENNEDY**'s inscription on his photograph displayed at CIA Headquarters. According to former CIA senior official Lyman Kirkpatrick, when Kennedy wrote these words one of his aides remarked, "Mr. President, if you write that to CIA, you've got to do it for the rest of the government." The president is said to have answered, "Well, maybe I don't hold the rest of the government in esteem!" Kirkpatrick interview cited in Weber, *Spymasters* (1999).

"[DCI John] McCone one time pushed me forward at the Cabinet table to show the new President [Johnson] a photograph of a Vietnamese installation. But it was clear that the President did not want to examine it the way Kennedy would have done, and his only reaction was to caution me sharply to be careful not to spill coffee onto his lap."

> Former DCI **WILLIAM COLBY**, *Honorable Men* (1978).

"I know you are not a man to rest on laurels of the past—and we really don't have many laurels in the intelligence field."

> President **LYNDON JOHNSON**, draft letter (never sent) to DCI William Raborn, 27 July 1965; cited in Jeffreys-Jones, *The CIA and American Democracy* (1989).

"You know it is my hope that we can continue to build and strengthen the effectiveness of the Agency, making full utilization of the imaginative talent assembled in the organization. . . . Our intelligence must be unquestionably the best in the world. You have my full support to do so [*sic*]."

> President **LYNDON JOHNSON**, letter to DCI William Raborn, 29 July 1965; cited in CIA, *"Our First Line of Defense"* (1996). Much better.

"I'm sick and tired of [DCI] John McCone's tugging at my shirttails. If I want to see you, Raborn, I'll telephone you!"

> President **LYNDON JOHNSON** at his first session with DCI William Raborn (who replaced McCone), according to CIA Executive Director Lawrence White; quoted in Helms, *A Look over My Shoulder* (2003).

"To the Central Intelligence Agency with appreciation."

> President **LYNDON JOHNSON**'s inscription on his photograph displayed at CIA Headquarters. Johnson didn't really mean it.

"The CIA is made up of boys whose families sent them to Princeton but wouldn't let them into the family brokerage business."

> President **LYNDON JOHNSON**; cited in *Simpson's Contemporary Quotations* (1988).

"I do not believe that [President Johnson] had the faintest idea how the Central Intelligence Agency was organized, or how the Intelligence Community was organized. He expected me to produce the goods."

> DCI **RICHARD HELMS** in a 1969 interview; cited in Weber, *Spymasters* (1999).

"No DCI during the Agency's early decades was able to replicate on a continuing basis the relationship that [Walter] Bedell Smith had established with Truman. During the early Johnson years, John McCone attempted to restart regular briefings of the President, but the President became impatient and ended them before long. The third DCI to serve under Johnson, Richard Helms, saw that an alternative approach was needed and managed to establish an excellent relationship with the President. . . . But even Helms could not sustain his access or influence with Nixon. During Nixon's years in office, the relationship between the President and the CIA reached the lowest point in the Agency's history."

> Former DDI **JOHN HELGERSON**, *CIA Briefings* (1996).

"Aware of CIA's failure to forecast accurately Soviet missile deployments in the 1960s, [President] Nixon disdained its assessments, believing the Agency had been wrong or, worse, 'soft' in its estimates. . . . Nixon saw the Agency as politically liberal."

> Former DCI **ROBERT GATES**, *From the Shadows* (1996).

"From the very beginning of the Nixon administration, Nixon was criticizing Agency estimates. . . . He would make nasty remarks about this and say this obviously had to be sharpened up. The Agency had to understand it was to do a better job and so on. . . . It was bound to be a rocky period with Richard Nixon as President, given the fact that he held the Agency responsible for his defeat in 1960. And he never forgot that and he had a barb out for the Agency all the time because he really believed, and I think he believes to this day, that that 'Missile Gap' question was the responsibility of the Agency and that it did him in."

> Former DCI **RICHARD HELMS** in 1982; quoted in Helgerson, *CIA Briefings* (1996).

"Let me interject a word for that much maligned agency. As I have often said, in the field of intelligence we always find that the failures are those that are publicized. Its successes, by definition, must always be secret, and in this area there are many successes and particularly ones for which this agency can be very proud."

> President **RICHARD NIXON**, remarks on CIA's twenty-fifth anniversary, 18 September 1972; cited in CIA, *"Our First Line of Defense"* (1996). Much maligned by whom?

"Helms has got to go. Get rid of the clowns—cut personnel 40 percent. Its info worthless."

> Presidential aide **H. R. HALDEMAN**'s September 1972 notes on Nixon's goals for his second term; quoted in Helms, *A Look over My Shoulder* (2003). These notes were among Nixon White House documents released in 1998.

"What use are they? They've got 40,000 people over there reading newspapers."

> President **RICHARD NIXON** on CIA; quoted in Miller, *Spying for America* (1989). Not all at the same time.

"To the Central Intelligence Agency, a vital aid in the defense of freedom."

> President **RICHARD NIXON**'s inscription on his photograph displayed at CIA Headquarters.

"There's something I've had to learn to understand. I've had to learn to understand Presidents."

> DCI **RICHARD HELMS**; quoted in Miller, *Spying for America* (1989).

"I have one president at a time. I only work for you."

> DCI **RICHARD HELMS** to President Nixon; quoted in Nixon, *RN: Memoirs of Richard Nixon* (1978).

"A move of surpassing pettiness."

> **HENRY KISSINGER** on Richard Nixon's dismissal of Richard Helms as DCI in February 1973, two months before Helms reached mandatory retirement age; foreword to Helms, *A Look over My Shoulder* (2003).

"Nixon seemed perpetually cranky in his relations with CIA. . . . What he wanted from CIA was intelligence reports and estimates most likely to support his foreign policy and domestic positions. In effect, he wanted a claque underwriting and applauding his policies. . . . Nixon showed little interest in an independent intelligence service."

> Former DCI **RICHARD HELMS**, *A Look over My Shoulder* (2003).

"Let me speak frankly to some in this chamber and perhaps to some not in this chamber. The Central Intelligence Agency has been of maximum importance to Presidents before me. The CIA has been of maximum importance to me. The Central Intelligence Agency and its associated intelligence organizations could be of maximum importance to some of you in this audience who might be President at some later date."

> President **GERALD FORD**, address before the Congress, 10 April 1975; cited in CIA, *"Our First Line of Defense"* (1996). That's right: the Maximum Importance Agency. In any case, Congress at the time was not listening.

"No power has yet been found to force Presidents of the United States to pay attention on a continuing basis to people and papers when confidence has been lost in the originator."

> Former DCI **RICHARD HELMS** in Senate testimony, 1975.

"As conflict and rivalry persist in the world, our United States intelligence capabilities must be the best in the world. . . . Without effective intelligence capability, the United States stands blindfolded and hobbled."

> President **GERALD FORD**, State of the Union address, 19 January 1976.

"As Americans we must not and will not tolerate actions by our government which will abridge the rights of our citizens. At the same time we must maintain a strong and effective intelligence capability in the United States. I will not be a party to the dismantling of the CIA or other intelligence agencies."

> President **GERALD FORD**, 17 February 1976; in Ford, *A Time to Heal* (1979). Perhaps Ford could have offered up DIA?

"To the Central Intelligence Agency—in peace there is no substitute for intelligence."

> President **GERALD FORD**'s inscription on his photograph displayed at CIA Headquarters. Wartime, too.

"Intelligence has been the province of the President. It has informed his decisions and furthered his purposes. Intelligence information has been seen as largely belonging to the President, as being his to classify or declassify, his to withhold or share. The instruments of U.S. intelligence have been the Presidents' to use and sometimes to abuse. The President is the only elected official in the chain of command over the United States intelligence community. It is to him the Constitution and the Congress have granted authority to carry out intelligence activities. It is the President who is ultimately accountable to the Congress and the American people."

U.S. Senate, *Final Report of the Senate Select Committee to Study Governmental Operations with respect to Intelligence Activities* [the Church Committee], Book I (April 1976).

"American Presidents are strong-willed men. They wouldn't get there if they weren't. If they don't have an intelligence service they will create their own. It might not be very big, and not very good, and they might have to reach into the loony bin to find the people to run it. But they will have one."

Senior CIA official, 1976; quoted in Phillips, *The Night Watch* (1978).

"Our system of government, in spite of Vietnam, Cambodia, CIA, Watergate, is still the best system of government on earth."

Presidential candidate **JIMMY CARTER** in debating President Gerald Ford, 1976; cited in *The Columbia World of Quotations* (1996). Despite CIA. Thanks.

"We have got to have a good intelligence system in order to protect the security of our country. . . . And if we should ever be in danger in time of crisis, it's too late to build up an adequate intelligence community, including our worldwide system of information."

President **JIMMY CARTER**, remarks at the State Department, 24 February 1977; cited in CIA, *"Our First Line of Defense"* (1996).

"The Agency is often criticized, 'Well, you did what the President wanted.' What [else] is the Agency for? It is part of the President's bag of

tools, if you like, and if he and proper authorities have decided that something has to be done, then the Agency is bound to try to do it. We would have a very strange government indeed in this country if everybody with an independent view of foreign policy decided he was free to take or not take the President's instructions according to his own likes and beliefs."

Former DCI **RICHARD HELMS** in a 1978 interview with David Frost; cited in Weber, *Spymasters* (1999).

"I've told many groups that one of the most pleasant surprises that I have had as President of our country has been the quality of the work done by the Central Intelligence Agency, and I want to thank you for that."

President **JIMMY CARTER** at CIA Headquarters, 16 August 1978; quoted in Andrew, *For the President's Eyes Only* (1995).

"I am impressed with the professionalism and responsiveness of the CIA. I think if all Americans knew what I know, there would be an alleviation of concern."

President **JIMMY CARTER**'s inscription on his photograph displayed at CIA Headquarters. No other president, in his CIA inscription, uses the first person singular; Carter's has three.

"We sometimes referred to [President Carter] as the nation's chief grammarian. He even corrected CIA's *President's Daily Brief*."

Former DCI **ROBERT GATES**, *From the Shadows* (1996).

"The President is the sun in the CIA's solar system. . . . If the President does not trust or value the Agency's product, then the paper it produces will cease to have weight in government councils and it might as well unplug its copiers, because it is only talking to itself. The first duty of the DCI, then, not by statute but as a matter of practical reality, is to win the trust, the confidence, and the ear of the President."

THOMAS POWERS, *The Man Who Kept the Secrets* (1979).

"Our national interests are critically dependent on a strong and effective intelligence capability. We will not shortchange the intelligence capabilities needed to assure our national security."

President **JIMMY CARTER**, State of the Union address, 21 January 1980.

"Whether you work in Langley or a faraway nation, whether your tasks are in operations or analysis sections, it is upon your intellect and integrity, your wit and intuition that the fate of freedom rests for millions of your countrymen and for many millions more all around the globe. You are the tripwire across which the forces of repression and tyranny must stumble in their quest for global domination. You, the men and women of the CIA, are the eyes and ears of the free world."

President **RONALD REAGAN**, 23 June 1982; cited in CIA, *"Our First Line of Defense"* (1996).

"The United States cannot survive in the modern world without a vigorous intelligence agency, capable of acting swiftly and in secret."

President **RONALD REAGAN** at the swearing-in of William Webster as DCI; cited in CIA, *"Our First Line of Defense"* (1996).

"My KGB handler must be trying to reach me."

President **RONALD REAGAN** after his hearing aid acted up during an intelligence briefing, November 1985; quoted in Gates, *From the Shadows* (1996).

"With Appreciation & Very Best Wishes."

President **RONALD REAGAN**'s inscription on his photograph displayed at CIA Headquarters.

"Reagan's preparations . . . included astrological as well as intelligence briefings. . . . [Nancy Reagan] played a part not only in scheduling all four of Reagan's summit meetings with Gorbachev on astrologically auspicious days, but also in providing horoscopes of the Soviet leader that purported to reveal secrets of his character and probable behavior. The president, it appears, took this nonsense seriously. His sources of information on the Soviet Union thus ranged from high-tech intelligence to ancient superstition."

CHRISTOPHER ANDREW, *For the President's Eyes Only* (1995).

"A search of presidential memoirs and those of principal assistants over the past 30 years or so turns up remarkably little discussion or perspective on the role played by directors of central intelligence (DCIs) or intelligence information in presidential decision making on foreign affairs. What little commentary there has been . . . is nearly uniformly critical."

DDCI **ROBERT GATES**, *Washington Quarterly* (winter 1989).

"It is this author's impression that most presidents often attach as much—if not more—credibility to the views of family, friends, and private contacts as they do to those of executive agencies. . . . Despite the mystique of intelligence for the public, for most presidents it is just one of a number of sources of information. Intelligence reporting must compete for the president's time and attention, and that competition is intense."

DDCI **ROBERT GATES**, *Washington Quarterly* (winter 1989).

"I am absolutely convinced that we have the finest intelligence service in the world. It is second to none. And as President of the United States of America I intend to keep it that way, to support it, to strengthen it, and to honor those who serve with such selfless dedication."

> President and former DCI **GEORGE H. W. BUSH**, remarks to OSS veterans, 23 October 1991; cited in CIA, *"Our First Line of Defense"* (1996).

"To the CIA, an indispensable Agency—especially the men and women who serve with dedication & distinction."

> President **GEORGE H. W. BUSH**'s inscription on his photograph displayed at CIA Headquarters.

"The decline of covert action in the U.S. government . . . is due to a lack of capacity on the part of presidents to formulate policies and to force opponents to oppose them on the merits. Presidents have themselves chosen covert action as half-measures when they have been unwilling to force the issue."

> **ANGELO CODEVILLA**, *Informing Statecraft* (1992).

"Over the past two centuries only four American presidents—Washington, Eisenhower, Kennedy (briefly) and [George H. W.] Bush—have shown a real flair for intelligence."

> **CHRISTOPHER ANDREW**, *For the President's Eyes Only* (1995).

"I left here 22 years ago. . . . CIA became part of my heartbeat back then, and it's never gone away."

> Former President **GEORGE H. W. BUSH** at a ceremony renaming CIA Headquarters the George Bush Center for Intelligence, 26 April 1999.

"CIA is a uniquely presidential organization. Virtually every time it has gotten in trouble, it has been for carrying out some action ordered by a President—from Nicaragua to Iran. Yet few Presidents have anything good to say about CIA or the intelligence they received. How come?"

> Former DCI **ROBERT GATES**, *From the Shadows* (1996). Because it got into trouble, Bob.

"I believe making deep cuts in intelligence during peacetime is comparable to canceling your health insurance when you're feeling fine."

> President **BILL CLINTON**, remarks at CIA Headquarters, 14 July 1995. Fortunately, CIA is no HMO.

"To the Central Intelligence Agency—with respect and appreciation for the work you do for the United States."

> President **BILL CLINTON**'s inscription on his photograph displayed at CIA Headquarters.

"I made repeated attempts to see [President Bill] Clinton privately to take up a whole range of issues and was unsuccessful. . . . I didn't have a bad relationship with him, I just had no relationship."

> Former DCI **R. JAMES WOOLSEY**; quoted in *National Review* (17 December 2001) and in the *Washington Post*, 27 December 2001.

"There is no substitute for direct access to the President."

> Former DDI **JOHN HELGERSON**, *CIA Briefings* (1996).

"For all their unhappiness and complaining, Presidents keep CIA around for two simple reasons. First, the unending river of information . . . the politicians' mother's milk of factual, accurate information. Second, Presidents also always want to retain the option of covert action. . . . Presidents always turn to the only governmental organization that can operate in [the] world of ambiguity and shadows: CIA. In the real world, if CIA were to disappear, Presidents would create some entity to take its place. And one, to be sure, not as constrained by Congress and the law."

Former DCI **ROBERT GATES**, *From the Shadows* (1996).

"Our experience with a number of [presidential] administrations was that they started with the expectation that intelligence could solve every problem, or that it could not do anything right, and then moved to the opposite view. Then they settled down and vacillated from one extreme to the other."

Former DDCI **RICHARD KERR** and presidential briefer Peter Dixon Davis, "Ronald Reagan and the President's Daily Brief," *Studies in Intelligence* 41 (1997). Not comforting.

"You can never say no to a president."

DCI **GEORGE TENET**; quoted in the *Washington Post*, 25 May 1998.

"One informed official described a private moment at the Wye peace summit when George Tenet, the C.I.A. director, warned the President [Clinton] that Pollard's release would enrage and demoralize the intelligence community. What he got back, the official told me, was 'Nah, don't worry about it. It'll blow over.'"

SEYMOUR HERSH, "The Traitor: The Case Against Jonathan Pollard," *New Yorker* (18 January 1999).

"Through intelligence the president and his advisors gain their understanding of what may be possible."

Senior CIA analyst **MARTIN PETERSEN**, "What We Should Demand from Intelligence," *National Security Studies Quarterly* (spring 1999).

"Thanks to American intelligence, every American President from Lyndon Johnson through George

[H. W.] Bush made policy toward the Soviet Union knowing that economic problems in the Soviet Union provided the United States with increasing leverage and advantage."

Former DCI **ROBERT GATES**, conference on "US Intelligence and the End of the Cold War," Texas A&M University, 19 November 1999.

"To the men & women of the CIA: Thanks for your service to our country, with respect and admiration, George Bush."

President-elect **GEORGE W. BUSH**, inscription on the first PDB he received, 6 December 2000.

"In retrospect, the world of 1976 looks staid and static compared to the revolutions of change that characterize our times. But what hasn't changed, what isn't different is the fact that sound intelligence is still critically important to America's national security. The challenges are new, but we still need your work to help us meet them. The opportunities are new, but we need your help to take advantage of them. But perhaps most of all, in a world where change itself seems to be the only constant, we need your help to anticipate change and to shape it in a way that favors freedom."

President **GEORGE W. BUSH**, remarks at CIA, 20 March 2001. The new Bush Intelligence Doctrine: anticipate change and help shape it.

"Those stories about my intellectual capacity do get under my skin. You know for a while I even thought my staff believed it. There on my schedule first thing every morning, it said 'Intelligence Briefing.'"

President **GEORGE W. BUSH** at the Gridiron Club dinner; quoted in *National Review* (16 April 2001).

"George and I have been spending a lot of quality time together. There's a reason: I've got a lot of confidence in him, and I've got a lot of confidence in the CIA."

President **GEORGE W. BUSH** speaking to DCI George Tenet and CIA employees at CIA Headquarters, 25 September 2001.

"The regulations, rules, and practices under which the DCI labors are as clearly established as those of other government agencies and departments. . . . A DCI who, on his own, ignores or violates these boundaries should expect no more consideration than might be given the chief of any other federal agency or department. However obvious, this is a less than useful guide come crunch time, when a president orders his DCI to step out-of-bounds. If, after reminding the President of the Agency's charter restrictions and suggesting any appropriate alternatives, the President remains insistent, what is the DCI to do? He is neither a policymaker nor a judicial officer. Has he the authority to refuse to accept a questionable order on a foreign policy question of obvious national importance? If the President's directive cannot be deflected, the DCI's responses range from acceptance to outright refusal and presumably resignation."

Former DCI **RICHARD HELMS**, *A Look over My Shoulder* (2003).

"Here is an observation on the presidency in the twenty-first century. Except for George Bush the elder, who served for some twelve months as director of Central Intelligence, no American president in a hundred years has had but a slight idea of how clandestine operations are conceived and run. What presidents do know about secret intelligence seems most often to come from high-spirited movies, novels, press coverage, and, occasionally, bits of Washington 'insider' gossip. Nothing wrong with that, except that none of it—and rarely any nonfiction—gives the slightest idea of the dreary routines and the vast amount of time involved in establishing a sound covert action or espionage operation."

Former DCI **RICHARD HELMS**, *A Look over My Shoulder* (2003).

"In theory the director of the CIA can and should reach his own independent judgment; but in fact no director of central intelligence can disagree with the White House and keep his job for long. . . . Presidents can fire directors they don't like, and the CIA has no other customer. The big mistakes all come when presidents don't listen, or let it be known what they want to hear. The CIA is as serious, as prudent, as honest as the presidents for whom it works—never more. Directors deliver what is wanted, or depart. . . . It is not that all CIA directors are slaves and toadies; but if they don't establish a close working relationship with the White House, someone else soon gets the chance."

THOMAS POWERS, "The Vanishing Case for War," *New York Review of Books*, 4 December 2003. Powers here is uncharacteristically off base: DCIs often disagree with the White House; CIA does have other customers (albeit none as important as the president); and CIA often is more serious, more prudent, and more honest about intelligence issues than the sitting president (e.g., Johnson and Nixon).

- **Recruiting**
- **Redundancy Redundancy**
- **"Rogue Elephant"**

RECRUITING

Intelligence services seek—and tend to get—the most talented people the nation can provide. Democracies have it especially hard: the best people have to be persuaded, as there are a host of other opportunities for them, and because democracies often view their intelligence services with disdain or contempt.

See also: Academia; Intelligence & American Culture; Intelligence, the Missions of; People

"I told you to leave no stone unturned in your recruiting. I did not expect you to take me quite so literally."

> **WINSTON CHURCHILL** to Alastair Denniston, chief of Britain's Government Code and Cypher School, after seeing the rumpled, eccentrically clothed staff of codebreakers; quoted in Russell, *The Secret War* (1981).

"[OSS Director William] Donovan lifted intelligence out of its military rut, where it had little prestige and little dynamism, and made it a career for adventurous, broad-minded civilians. This tradition carried down to CIA, which regularly re-cruited some of the most able graduates from U.S. universities to learn the intelligence business."

> Former DDI **RAY CLINE**, *Secrets, Spies and Scholars* (1976).

"Lieut. Commander Ian Fleming of British Naval Intelligence . . . advised [OSS Director William] Donovan to pick men in their forties and fifties, possessing 'absolute discretion, sobriety, devotion to duty, languages and wide experience.' But such staid advice did not suit Wild Bill. He preferred younger men, rakehells who were 'calculatingly reckless, of disciplined daring and trained for aggressive action.'"

> **FRANCIS RUSSELL**, *The Secret War* (1981).

"An intelligence service in a free society is not only an institution in a democracy in that it is the creation of the Congress and subordinated to the executive; it also mirrors in its membership the society which it serves. . . . If CIA recruitment fails to equip the Agency with the best minds to keep the country's intelligence ahead of all its adversaries [then] we are not properly taking advantage of the unique opportunities this country affords."

> Former DCI **ALLEN DULLES**, *The Craft of Intelligence* (1963).

"If one attempt in fifty is successful, your efforts won't have been wasted."

> British turncoat and KGB spy **HAROLD "KIM" PHILBY** to KGB officer Oleg Kalugin, who was trying to recruit CIA officers to spy for Moscow; quoted in Kalugin, *The First Directorate* (1994).

"[By 1981,] the recruitment process for [CIA's] clandestine service had led to new officers looking very much like the people who recruited them— white, mostly Anglo-Saxon; middle and upper class; liberal arts college graduates.... Few were non-Caucasians. Few women. Few ethnics, even of recent European background. In other words, not even as much diversity as there was among those who had helped create CIA and the clandestine service in the late 1940s."

> Former DCI **ROBERT GATES**, *From the Shadows* (1996).

"We are looking for risk takers but not risk seekers, people who are dedicated and responsive to our law and our discipline, people who understand and play by the rules."

> DCI **WILLIAM WEBSTER**, 13 April 1988, in *1988 Speeches*.

"At CIA, we are constantly amazed at the quality of people we are able to recruit. When we ask them why, the answers almost always focus on the opportunity to do something truly meaningful, to make a contribution."

> DCI **ROBERT GATES**, remarks of 4 April 1992, in *Speeches* (1993).

"Exceptional powers of communication and persuasion will make you adept at talking your way into situations with the opportunity for gathering useful information, as well as the resourcefulness to extract yourself from less promising circumstances."

> MI5 want ad in the London *Guardian;* cited in *U.S. News and World Report* (2 June 1997).

"The Ultimate Overseas Experience: For the extraordinary individual who wants more than a job, this is a way of life that will challenge the deepest resources of your intelligence, self-reliance and responsibility. It demands an adventurous spirit ... a forceful personality ... superior intellectual ability ... toughness of mind ... and the highest degree of integrity. It takes special skills and professional discipline to produce results. You will need to deal with fast-moving, ambiguous and unstructured situations that will test your resourcefulness to the utmost."

> CIA employment ad for the Clandestine Service, *Chicago Tribune*, 19 October 1997; ellipses in the original.

"Wanted—25-year-old Asian-American woman with M.B.A. and working knowledge of automatic weapons, expert in computer programming, fluent in Turkic and Uzbek. Middling salary, long hours, utter anonymity. Call the C.I.A.—please."

> **TIM WEINER** describing a hypothetical employment ad for today's CIA, "You Spy? Let's Talk," *New York Times*, 8 June 1997.

"You took apart the family radio at age six. We should talk."

> A real CIA employment ad seeking computer experts and engineers; *Boston Globe*, 18 October 1998.

"The Mossad is opening up. Not to everyone. Not to many. Maybe to you."

> The Israeli service's first employment ad, August 2000.

"Virtually any job you can imagine is available within the CIA, plus some you can't imagine."

CIA recruitment ad, *Fortune* (March 2001).

"American intelligence will need to rebuild its own ability to engage in old-fashioned espionage. But can it recruit a new generation, one that has never known real war, real fear, real danger? Will college seniors in New York and New Haven spurn J. P. Morgan, Chase and Microsoft, taking it on faith that serving their country in anonymity is as important as making a bundle on war-scarred Wall Street? Will they pose as junior diplomats in Dushanbe for the same money they would make managing a Pizza Hut?"

TIM WEINER, "To Fight in the Shadows, Get Better Eyes," *New York Times*, 7 October 2001. Let's hope so.

"For over 100 years Arab-Americans have served the nation. Today we need you more than ever. ... Your heritage is Arab-American. Your citizenship is All-American."

CIA employment ads, in the *Washington Post*, 19 January 2003 and 9 March 2003.

"[In Chinese] Happy New Year! [In English] Staying true to our global focus, the Central Intelligence Agency welcomes the Chinese New Year and its celebration of rejuvenation and renewal. Just as the Year of the Ram is centered on a strong and clear motivation for peace, harmony, and tranquility during challenging times, we are equally intent on our mission to safeguard America and its people. ... Why work for a company when you can serve the nation?"

CIA employment ad targeting Chinese-Americans; reproduced in the *Washington Times*, 3 February 2003.

"The Central Intelligence Agency is seeking locksmiths to work with the best minds in the country while performing a mission critical to our nation."

Job posting on CIA's website, as reported by Reuters, 23 June 2003. Sometimes intelligence has specific needs.

"I am an Applied Scientist [and] an Inventor of over 20 devices and systems, including ... Portable Nuclear Powered Engine. ... The Transistorized Plastic Paper Computer. ... The Artificial Womb. ... The Resurrection Burial Tomb. ... A Disposable Space Ship. ... US Patents issued or pending."

From a résumé received by CIA recruiters, December 2003. The Internet, which this gentleman does not claim to have invented, has made this sort of thing more frequent.

REDUNDANCY REDUNDANCY

It's the old story: a man with one watch is absolutely certain what time it is; a man with several is never really quite sure. As an argument for having more than one intelligence agency, the Literary Spy would add: the man with several watches has better insurance against failure than the man with only one.

See also: Origins of Central Intelligence; U.S. Intelligence "Community"

"You are the third person who has brought me the same information."

PAUL REVERE to a boy bringing him news that the British were on the move from Boston, 16 April 1775; quoted in Bakeless, *Turncoats, Traitors and Heroes* (1998).

"Prudence enjoins the employment of several spies. ... As we are never sure that a spy is not in the enemy's pay, or, if voluntarily offers his services, that he is not deputed by him, sending more than one spy for the same information tends to make things doubly sure."

British Colonel **GEORGE FURSE**, *Information in War* (1895).

"General Vandenberg [the DCI] . . . said that what he believed to be essential coordination to reduce duplication had been retarded by an uncertainty as to the directive authority of the Director of Central Intelligence."

Minutes of the National Intelligence Authority (the short-lived predecessor to the NSC), 12 February 1947; reproduced in Warner, *CIA Under Truman* (1994).

"People who shout duplication at the first sign of similarity in two functions and who try to freeze one of them out on the ground of extravagance often cost the government dearly in the long run."

SHERMAN KENT, *Strategic Intelligence* (1949).

"Duplication is inevitable and desirable inasmuch as CIA examines these documents from the standpoint of national security whereas each of the other intelligence agencies examines them from the standpoint of departmental responsibilities. . . . The services have a tendency to reflect their own interests in their intelligence estimates. For this reason, CIA strives to maintain in its estimates an objective, balanced view, and to keep U.S. national security, rather than departmental interests, as the dominant consideration."

DCI **ROSCOE HILLENKOETTER** in a 1950 letter to President Truman; quoted in Ranelagh, *The Agency* (1986).

"There is, of course, always the possibility that two such powerful and well-financed agencies as CIA and DIA will become rivals and competitors.

Some of this could be healthy; too much of it could be both expensive and dangerous."

Former DCI **ALLEN DULLES**, *The Craft of Intelligence* (1963).

"Many wonder if there is not some duplication within the [intelligence] community. There is. What is essential is that this duplication not reach wasteful or destructive proportions. A certain amount of duplication held within reasonable limits can provide additional perspective. I have always been able to get a far better picture by looking through binoculars than through a telescope."

Former DDCI General **VERNON WALTERS**, *Silent Missions* (1978).

"There are no grounds to support the notion that intelligence competition is more expensive than an intelligence monopoly; even if this were the case, it would be worth the cost."

WALTER LAQUEUR, *A World of Secrets* (1985).

"One of our main tasks is to keep CIA honest."

Assistant Secretary of State for Intelligence and Research **TOBY GATI**; quoted in *Foreign Service Journal*, February 1996. In the same interview she says the intelligence community should "serve the State Department's needs." *See* Policy Role.

"Competitive analysis of controversial questions can also help guard against politicization. . . . Competitive or redundant analysis needs to be carried out and conveyed to policymakers in those areas where being wrong can have major consequences."

Council on Foreign Relations, *Making Intelligence Smarter* (1996).

"The [U.S.] intelligence services are an absurd parody of American government, which delights in fomenting competition."

The Economist, 28 March 1997.

"The DCI, in his capacity as head of the Intelligence Community, is charged with eliminating waste and unnecessary duplication within the Intelligence Community."

DCI GEORGE TENET, DCI Directive 1/1, "The Authorities and Responsibilities of the Director of Central Intelligence as Head of the US Intelligence Community," 19 November 1998; reproduced in Warner, Central Intelligence (2001). How about another look at DIA?

"I've always felt that in intelligence gathering . . . what you need is multiple sources of information . . . to be dependent upon a single source or a single line or a single viewpoint is not a great idea."

Secretary of Defense DONALD RUMSFELD; quoted in the Washington Post, 9 April 2002.

"ROGUE ELEPHANT"

The idea that U.S. intelligence is out of control—the famous "rogue elephant" epithet coined by a U.S. senator decades ago—is both tiresome and amusing to the Literary Spy. The notion makes for interesting spy novels and films but has little connection with the reality that our intelligence agencies are populated by good-willed Americans who, like other Americans, are law-abiding fathers and mothers, community leaders, churchgoers, and voters who rather like the Constitution, our federal system, even the Congress.

See also: Assassination; Covert Action; Legislative Oversight; Presidents & Intelligence

"CIA has never carried out any action of a political nature, given any support of any nature to any persons, potentates or movements, political or otherwise, without appropriate approval at a high political level in our government outside the CIA."

Former DCI ALLEN DULLES, The Craft of Intelligence (1963).

"Political leverage is power. Information is power. Secrecy is power. Speed in communications is power. Ability is power. And the sheer number of people is power. CIA had all these."

Former State Department intelligence chief ROGER HILSMAN, To Move a Nation (1967). Still does, although the political leverage is way overstated.

"Mongoose [the Kennedy administration's covert effort to get rid of Castro] was not some bizarre fringe activity by a government agency that barely captured the attention of a busy president. On the contrary, at the beginning of 1962, it was [Kennedy's] chief—and most expensive—foreign policy initiative."

CHRISTOPHER ANDREW, For the President's Eyes Only (1995).

"There was never, to my knowledge, any foundation for the charge of free wheeling by the CIA."

Undersecretary of State U. ALEXIS JOHNSON, member of President Kennedy's "Special Group" overseeing covert action; quoted in Andrew, For the President's Eyes Only (1995).

"[In 1962] the Kennedy administration directed the Agency to provide covert support to [Chile's] Christian Democratic Party. . . . The Agency did not initiate the policy of covert intervention in Chile but rather acted as an executive agent in carrying out the decisions reached at the highest level of the American government, as it was required to do under the National Security Act of 1947. What was done in Chile, for better or for worse, was the responsibility of successive American Presidents —Kennedy, Johnson, and Nixon. The myth that the Agency was rampaging like 'a rogue elephant' out of control in the activities that it undertook in Chile does not stand up in the light of the historical record."

Former senior CIA official **CORD MEYER**, *Facing Reality* (1980).

"I can just assure you flatly that the CIA has not carried out independent activities but has operated under close control of the Director of Central Intelligence, operating with the cooperation of the National Security Council and under my instructions. So I think that while the CIA may have made mistakes, as we all do, on different occasions, and has had many successes which may go unheralded, in my opinion in this case it is unfair to charge them as they have been charged. I think they have done a good job."

President **JOHN F. KENNEDY**, 9 October 1963; cited in CIA, *"Our First Line of Defense"* (1996).

"The notion that the CIA engages in any paramilitary or political activity on its own authority is so transparently false that only repeated press references to 'CIA wars' make any comment necessary. To refer [for example] to U.S. clandestine support of the Laotian resistance to North Vietnam's military invasion as 'CIA's war' is as absurd as calling the war in South Vietnam the 'Pentagon's war against North Vietnam.'"

Former DCI **RICHARD HELMS**, *A Look over My Shoulder* (2003).

"In deciding on covert intervention . . . most presidents have not been captives of organizations they

did not understand or processes they could not control. Far from it. More often they put pressure on the CIA rather than vice versa."

GREGORY TREVERTON, *Covert Action* (1987).

"Everybody should realize that the policies of the CIA are not set by the Agency. They operate under instructions."

Senator **STUART SYMINGTON**, February 1967; quoted in Jeffreys-Jones, *The CIA and American Democracy* (1989).

"Beyond a certain point the secret agent, whether spy, secret propagandist, or guerrilla warrior cannot be controlled. To set loose expensive networks of secret agents is to open a Pandora's box of potential blunders, misfortunes, and uncontrollable events. To pack off a secret agent with a satchel of money to intervene, say, in a Brazilian election, and expect to maintain tight operational control of him is a dubious expectation."

HARRY HOWE RANSOM, *The Intelligence Establishment* (1970).

"The CIA does not on its own choose to overthrow distasteful governments or determine which dictatorial regimes to support [but] act[s] primarily when called upon by the Executive."

VICTOR MARCHETTI and **JOHN MARKS**, *CIA and the Cult of Intelligence* (1974). This from CIA critics.

"The agency may have been behaving like a rogue elephant on the rampage."

Senator **FRANK CHURCH** describing CIA at a press conference, 19 July 1975. At the end of its investigation— the most in-depth in the Agency's history—the Church Committee concluded that at no time did CIA act as a "rogue elephant." See U.S. Senate, *Final Report of the Senate Select Committee to Study Governmental Operations with respect to Intelligence Activities* [the Church Committee] (April 1976).

"Ever since the intelligence investigations of the Church and Pike [congressional] committees popularized the theme in television, films, and print, the American intelligence services have been portrayed as fanatical Cold Warriors not amenable to political control and ever eager to risk American assets in pursuit of frequently maniacal schemes. If such a CIA ever existed, it was in hiding throughout the Nixon and Ford periods."

HENRY KISSINGER, *Years of Renewal* (1999). Still in hiding.

"It is clearly untrue that the CIA had operated in defiance of or independently of White House instructions; [Senator] Church soon began to look very foolish for having made the statement [that CIA may have been a 'rogue elephant']. . . . [It also] alienated the vast majority of CIA employees and veterans, encouraging them to close ranks against congressional meddling and even to ally with Church's foes."

RHODRI JEFFREYS-JONES, *The CIA and American Democracy* (1989). While not disagreeing with this British scholar's conclusion about Frank Church, the Literary Spy still wonders how he managed to poll the opinions not only of "the vast majority of CIA employees" but also of CIA veterans.

"It is inconceivable that a secret intelligence arm of the government has to comply with all the overt orders of the government."

CIA counterintelligence chief JAMES ANGLETON in September 1975 during Senate testimony; quoted in Mangold, *Cold Warrior* (1991). When a senator later quoted this back to Angleton and asked whether the quotation was accurate, Angleton cryptically replied, "Well, if it is accurate, it should not have been said."

"I have stated before and I believe today that the CIA [during the Kennedy administration] was a highly disciplined organization, fully under the control of senior officials of the government. . . . I know of no major action taken by CIA during the time I was in the government that was not properly authorized by senior officials."

Former Secretary of Defense ROBERT McNAMARA responding in Senate testimony to Senator Frank Church's question whether "CIA was a rogue elephant rampaging out of control, over which no effective direction was given in this matter of assassination [plots against Castro]"; in U.S. Senate, *Alleged Assassination Plots* (1975). McNamara's failure to blame CIA or to express outrage at the assassination plots suggests to some that senior officials of the Kennedy administration knew exactly what CIA was doing.

"All the evidence in hand suggests that the CIA, far from being out of control, has been utterly responsive to the instructions of the President and the Assistant to the President for National Security Affairs."

Report by the House Committee on Intelligence (the Pike Committee), 1977; cited in Andrew, *For the President's Eyes Only* (1995).

"With today's supervision, and with the command structure trying to keep things straight, the people in CIA know what they should do and what they should not do—as distinct from the fifties, in which there were no particular rules. If CIA people today are told to violate their limits, or if they are tempted to violate those limits, one of the junior officers will surely raise that question and tell the command structure, and, if not satisfied there, he will tell the Congress, and, if not satisfied there, he will tell the press, and that is the way you control it."

Former DCI WILLIAM COLBY, January 1978 interview with *Der Spiegel*; quoted in Jeffreys-Jones and Andrew, *Eternal Vigilance* (1997).

"It was almost like a rogue elephant, doing what it wanted to."

House Intelligence Committee Chairman **EDWARD BOLAND** on CIA in Central America; quoted in the *Washington Post*, 6 August 1983.

"The CIA today is not out of control. If anything, the agency has been made fearful and timid by years of scandal and congressional investigations."

Newsweek editor **EVAN THOMAS**, in the *Washington Post*, 9 March 1997.

"In all [its] activities the C.I.A. has not been a rogue elephant. It has been carrying out the wishes of the highest American authorities. But the existence of the C.I.A., operating in secret, allowed those authorities to act as if they knew nothing of the torments inflicted on other people in what we deemed to be our interest."

ANTHONY LEWIS in the *New York Times*, 25 April 1997.

"I would like to ask America: What is your definition and criteria for what is a rogue? And then I would like to apply America's action of the CIA in the past 50 years to that criteria. And will the real rogue nation stand up?"

LOUIS FARRAKHAN during a trip to Iraq; quoted by Reuters, 12 December 1997.

"Unbeknownst to an awful lot of Americans, the CIA follows our instructions."

Senator **BOB KERREY** in the *Los Angeles Times*, 15 May 1998.

- **Secrecy**
- **Subcultures in CIA**
- **Successes**

SECRECY

Contrary to popular opinion, American intelligence officers generally do not regard secrecy as an end in itself. Some do, unfortunately, but they are anomalies. Most intelligence practitioners know that the Congress gave the Director of Central Intelligence the responsibility for protecting intelligence "sources and methods." This duty implies that secrets are justified if, by the telling of them, sources—people giving us information—would be arrested and very possibly killed, and methods—the various ways we collect intelligence—would be compromised and perhaps turned against us. Without these conditions, the Literary Spy admits, it is hard to justify secrecy. But there is one more justification, and it gets no play in the debate over secrecy: often the persistence of a secret is the result of a promise made. It is often the case that the secrets we keep remain secrets simply because we promised to keep them, and that incurs—believe it or not—a moral obligation. And practically speaking, why should anyone believe our promises if we're known not to keep them?

See also: Budgets; Compartmentation; Covert Action; Intelligence & American Culture; Leaks; Legislative Oversight; Openness & Publicity; Plausible Denial; Treason & Betrayal

"O divine art of subtlety and secrecy! Through you we learn to be invisible, through you inaudible; and hence hold the enemy's fate in our hands."
SUN TZU, *The Art of War* (6th century B.C.).

"I said, 'I will guard my ways,
that I may not sin with my tongue;
I will bridle my mouth,
so long as the wicked are in my presence.'"
Psalm 39:1 (Revised Standard). This psalm was read as British submarine officers launched a dead body, "Major Martin," into the sea off the Spanish coast to deceive the Nazis about the planned invasion of Sicily in 1943. See Montagu, *The Man Who Never Was* (1954).

"For God will bring every deed into judgment, with every secret thing, whether good or evil."
Ecclesiastes 12:13 (Revised Standard).

"The business asketh silent secrecy."

WILLIAM SHAKESPEARE, *King Henry VI, Part II* (1590), Act I, scene 2. Here, the business is treachery and betrayal.

"The life of spies is to know, not to be known."

English poet **GEORGE HERBERT**, *Jacula Prudentum* (1651).

"Secrets are edged tools,
That must be kept from children
and from fools."

English poet **JOHN DRYDEN**, *Annus Mirabilis* (1667).

"On May 10, 1776, the Committee of Secret Correspondence was directed to lay its proceedings before [the Continental] Congress but obtained permission to withhold the names of secret agents. Secret journals were kept in which intelligence and foreign relations matters were recorded, and access to them was severely restricted."

NATHAN MILLER, *Spying for America* (1989). Secrecy, in other words, is as American as the American Revolution.

"I do solemnly swear, that I will not directly or indirectly divulge any manner or thing which shall come to my knowledge as (clerk, secretary) of the board of War and Ordnance for the United Colonies. . . . So help me God."

Continental Congress, secrecy oath for government employees, 12 June 1776; cited in Sayle, "The Historical Underpinnings of the U.S. Intelligence Community," in *International Journal of Intelligence and Counterintelligence* (spring 1986).

"We agree in opinion that it is our indispensable duty to keep it a secret, even from Congress. . . .

We find, by fatal experience, the Congress consists of too many members to keep secrets."

BENJAMIN FRANKLIN and **ROBERT MORRIS**, members of the Continental Congress's Committee of Secret Correspondence, 1 October 1776; cited in Sayle, "The Historical Underpinnings of the U.S. Intelligence Community," in *International Journal of Intelligence and Counterintelligence* (spring 1986). Some would say that this revolutionary tradition lives on.

"There are some secrets, on the keeping of which so depends, oftentimes, the salvation of an Army: Secrets which cannot, at least ought not to, be intrusted to paper; nay, which none but the Commander in Chief at the time, should be acquainted with."

GEORGE WASHINGTON to Patrick Henry, 24 February 1777; cited in Knott, *Secret and Sanctioned* (1996).

"All that remains for me to add is, that you keep the whole matter as secret as possible. For upon Secrecy, success depends in most Enterprizes of the kind, & for want of it, they are generally defeated, however well planned."

GEORGE WASHINGTON to Colonel Elias Dayton, 26 July 1777; cited in Andrew, *For the President's Eyes Only* (1995).

"His name and business should be kept profoundly secret, otherwise we not only lose the benefits desired from it, but may subject him to some unhappy fate."

GEORGE WASHINGTON to his chief of intelligence, Benjamin Tallmadge, regarding one of Tallmadge's spies, 27 June 1779; in the Sir Henry Clinton collection, Clements Library, University of Michigan. The first rule of espionage is: protect your sources.

"One day General Washington had spent the night at the home of a revolutionary sympathizer and, as he was leaving, the sympathizer's wife said to him, 'Oh General, where do you ride tonight?' And he leaned down in the saddle and said, 'Madame, can you keep a secret?' And she said, 'Of course.' And he said, 'So can I. Good day, Madame' —and rode on."

Lieutenant General **VERNON WALTERS**, remarks in Pittsburgh while he was Deputy Director of Central Intelligence (1972–76).

"Perfect *secrecy* and immediate *dispatch* are sometimes requisite. There are cases where the most useful intelligence may be obtained, if the persons possessing it can be relieved from apprehensions of discovery."

JOHN JAY, *The Federalist*, No. 64.

"Three may keep a secret, if two of them are dead. . . . If you would keep your secret from an enemy, tell it not to a friend."

BENJAMIN FRANKLIN, *Poor Richard's Almanac* for 1735 and 1741.

"Where secrecy or mystery begins vice and roguery are not far off."

SAMUEL JOHNSON; quoted in P. J. Smallwood, *The Johnson Quotation Book* (1989).

"If a subaltern should only venture to ask you what is it o'clock? you must not inform him, in order to show that you are fit to be entrusted with secrets."

FRANCIS GROSE, *Advice to the Officers of the British Army* (1782).

"The experience of every nation on earth has demonstrated that emergencies may arise in which it becomes absolutely necessary for the public good to make expenditures the very object of which would be defeated by publicity. . . . In no nation is the application of such sums ever made public. In time of war or impending danger the situation of the country may make it necessary to employ individuals for the purpose of obtaining information or rendering other important services who could never be prevailed upon to act if they entertained the least apprehension that their names or their agency would in any contingency be divulged. So it may often become necessary to incur an expenditure for an object highly useful to the country. . . . But this object might be altogether defeated by the intrigues of other powers if our purposes were to be made known by the exhibition of the original papers and vouchers to the accounting officers of the Treasury. It would be easy to specify other cases which may occur in the history of a great nation, in its intercourse with other nations, wherein it might become absolutely necessary to incur expenditures for objects which could never be accomplished if it were suspected in advance that the items of expenditure and the agencies employed would be made public."

President **JAMES POLK** refusing the request of the House of Representatives for accounting records of the President's Secret Service fund, 20 April 1846; cited in CIA, *"Our First Line of Defense"* (1996).

"The service stipulated by the contract was a secret service; the information sought was to be obtained clandestinely, and was to be communicated privately; the employment and the service were to be equally concealed. Both employer and agent must have understood that the lips of the other were to be for ever sealed. . . . This condition . . . is implied in all secret employments of the government in time of war, or upon matters affecting our foreign relations."

Supreme Court Justice **STEPHEN FIELD** writing the court's opinion in *Totten, Administrator, v. United States* (1875), establishing that, because of the breach of secrecy involved, secret agents may not sue the government over their contracts. See Knott, *Secret and Sanctioned* (1996).

"We have said that it is a great point not to compromise a spy.... A trustworthy spy who furnishes us with valuable news has a claim to our consideration on this point."

British Colonel **GEORGE FURSE**, *Information in War* (1895).

"It would be absolutely intolerable if ex-police officers and ex-agents of the secret service were to be allowed, after they retired, without fear of consequence to publish secrets.... It is far easier for them to invent ... fairy tales in many cases than to give authentic facts."

WINSTON CHURCHILL, speech in the House of Commons, April 1910; cited in Stafford, *Churchill and Secret Service* (1998). And many do.

"America's oldest classified documents date back to 1917, and contain information about the use of invisible ink by German spies in World War I. Locked away in the bowels of the National Archives, the government refuses to make them public, but won't say why."

Christian Science Monitor, 27 November 1998.

"The age and availability of information about the science of secret ink does not diminish the value of keeping secret the particular formulas and methods at issue here."

U.S. government lawyers asking a federal judge to dismiss a suit that seeks to force the government to divulge its oldest secrets; cited in the *Washington Post*, 8 June 2001. In February 2002 a federal court agreed with CIA lawyers that the formulas for invisible ink still were useful for spies and should be kept secret.

"The abolition of secret diplomacy is the primary condition of an honorable, popular, really democratic foreign policy."

LEON TROTSKY, Soviet Russia's first People's Commissar for Foreign Affairs; quoted in Andrew and Gordievsky, *KGB* (1990). Despite Trotsky's pious comments, Soviet foreign policy was not honorable, popular, or democratic in the slightest.

"What we cannot speak about we must pass over in silence."

LUDWIG WITTGENSTEIN, *Tractacus Logico-philosophicus* (1919).

"Telling us that we had been recommended as good men, he handed us a Bible and we repeated after him: 'I ... solemnly swear by Almighty God that I will faithfully perform the duties assigned to me as a member of His Majesty's secret service: that I will obey implicitly those placed over me: that I shall never betray such service or anything connected with it even after I have left it. If I should fail to keep this oath in every particular I realise that vengeance will pursue me to the ends of the earth. So help me God."

DAVID NELLIGAN, *The Spy in the Castle* (1968). Nelligan, despite his oath, was an Irish spy against the British before 1922.

"If this operation is not kept a secret, then it will fail."

Japanese Vice Admiral **CHUICHI NAGUMO** on the planned attack on Pearl Harbor, September 1941; quoted in Prange, *At Dawn We Slept* (1981). It was, and it didn't.

"Almost a complete blank of information on the Carriers today ... It is evident that carrier traffic is at a low ebb."

Report of Commander **JOSEPH ROCHEFORT**, chief of naval communications intelligence at Pearl Harbor, 2 December 1941; cited in Prange, *At Dawn We Slept* (1981).

At the time of his report, six Japanese aircraft carriers were nearing striking distance of Pearl Harbor. Rochefort had drawn the wrong conclusion from the lack of information, as the Japanese had intended with their radio silence.

"Operations in which large numbers of men may lose their lives ought not to be described by code-words which imply a boastful and overconfident sentiment, such as 'Triumphant,' or, conversely, which are calculated to invest the plan with an air of despondency, such as 'Woebetide' [or] 'Jaundice.' They ought not to be names of a frivolous character.... After all, the world is wide, and intelligent thought will readily supply an unlimited number of well-sounding names which do not suggest the character of the operation or disparage it in any way and do not enable some widow or mother to say that her son was killed in an operation called 'Bunnyhug' or 'Ballyhoo.'"

WINSTON CHURCHILL to British military chiefs of staff, 8 August 1943; cited in Churchill, *Closing the Ring* (1951). Churchill personally chose the names for the invasions of North Africa (TORCH) and Europe (OVERLORD); see Kahn, *The Codebreakers* (1996).

"The great story of the solution of the Enigma machine and its effects on World War II remained a tightly held secret for almost 30 years.... The tens of thousands of people involved in the work remained utterly silent about it for decades—probably the best example of general security in history."

DAVID KAHN, *The Codebreakers* (1996).

"Secrecy is as essential to intelligence as vestments and incense to a Mass or darkness to a spiritualist séance and must at all times be maintained, quite irrespective of whether or not it serves any purpose."

MALCOLM MUGGERIDGE, SIS officer during World War II, *Chronicles of Wasted Time: The Infernal Grove* (1973).

"This might be a good place to insert a provision to provide an 'Official Secrets Act,' in the case of all employees of the Agency as well as all government employees of any department who make any unauthorized disclosure or who are responsible therefor in the case of any information or documents coming into their possession and originating with the Central Intelligence Agency."

Comments of ALLEN DULLES, then a private citizen, on a draft "CIG Enabling Act"—what eventually became the provisions of the National Security Act of 1947 that created CIA—as recorded in a memorandum from CIG legislative liaison Walter Pforzheimer to DDCI Colonel Edwin Wright, 5 March 1947; in *FRUS 1945–1950: Emergence of the Intelligence Establishment* (1996), document 208.

"Sec. 102 (d) (3). The Director of Central Intelligence shall be responsible for protecting intelligence sources and methods from unauthorized disclosure."

National Security Act of 1947 (S. 758), 26 July 1947; reproduced in Warner, *CIA Under Truman* (1994).

"Secrets are a burden. That's why some people are so anxious to have somebody else carry them."

Anonymous.

"Sec. 7 ... [The Central Intelligence] Agency shall be exempted from the provisions of [any laws] which require the publication or disclosure of the organization, functions, names, official titles, salaries, or numbers of personnel employed by the Agency."

The Central Intelligence Agency Act of 1949 (H.R. 2663), 20 June 1949; reproduced in Warner, *CIA Under Truman* (1994).

"Security is like armor. You can pile on the armor until the man inside is absolutely safe and absolutely useless. Both producers and consumers of intelligence have their secrets, and in safeguarding them they can so insulate themselves that they are unable to serve their reasons for being."

SHERMAN KENT, *Strategic Intelligence* (1949).

"Whether it be treason or not, it does the United States just as much harm for military secrets to be made known to potential enemies through open publication, as it does for military secrets to be given to an enemy through the clandestine operation of spies.... I do not believe that the best solution can be reached by adopting the approach based on the theory that everyone has a right to know our military secrets and related information affecting the national security."

President **HARRY TRUMAN**, press conference of 4 October 1951; cited in CIA, *"Our First Line of Defense"* (1996).

"Some of them are not fit to be trusted with secrets of this kind."

Former British Prime Minister **CLEMENT ATTLEE** on why he concealed the British atomic bomb project from his cabinet; quoted in Andrew and Mitrokhin, *The Mitrokhin Archive* (1999). Attlee also did not bother to inform Parliament. Andrew says that, thanks to Soviet espionage, "Stalin had been far better briefed on the construction of the bomb than most British ministers." The first British nuclear device was exploded off the Australian coast in October 1952.

"We all think our own secrets are the only ones that matter.... Other people's secrets are never quite as important as one's own."

James Bond in **IAN FLEMING**, *Goldfinger* (1959).

"We never allude to N by his name.... Of course, in one way it doesn't matter in my room at the War Office. But it's against the principles of the Secret Service. You do it once in private, and then before you know where you are you'll go and do it in the middle of Piccadilly. After all, the whole point of the Secret Service is that it should be secret.... Of course I wouldn't go so far as to say that the secrecy was *more* important than the service, but it's every bit *as* important."

Fictional British intelligence chief to a new recruit in Sir **COMPTON MACKENZIE**'s spoof on intelligence, *Water on the Brain* (1959).

"What we were, never was. What we did, never happened."

Advice to fictional spy Matt Helm in **DONALD HAMILTON**, *Death of a Citizen* (1960).

"It takes a very strong head to keep secrets for years, and not go slightly mad. It isn't wise to be advised by anyone slightly mad."

C. P. SNOW, *Science and Government* (1961).

"Those things we've been worrying about in Cuba are there."

DDI **RAY CLINE** informing McGeorge Bundy, President Kennedy's national security advisor, on a nonsecure telephone line that Soviet missiles had been detected in Cuba, 15 October 1962; quoted in Richelson, *A Century of Spies* (1995). No one listening in would have thought Cline was talking about cigars.

"One of my own guiding principles in intelligence work when I was Director of Central Intelligence was to use every human means to preserve the secrecy and security of [intelligence] activities, but only those where this was essential, and not to make a mystery of what is a matter of common knowledge or obvious to friend and foe alike."

Former DCI **ALLEN DULLES**, *The Craft of Intelligence* (1963).

"Vandenberg [Air Force Base] was excellent as a launch site [for the CORONA satellite program] from many standpoints, but it had one feature that posed a severe handicap to screening the actual launches from unwanted observation: the heavily traveled Southern Pacific railroad passes through it. . . . Throughout its existence [1960–72], the CORONA program at Vandenberg was plagued by having to time the launches to occur during one of the intervals between passing trains."

KENNETH GREER, "Corona," in Ruffner, *CORONA* (1995).

"Too much secrecy can be self-defeating. . . . When we try to make a mystery out of everything related to intelligence, we tend to dissipate our effort to maintain the security of operations where secrecy is essential to success. . . . We often fail to make the vital distinction between the types of operation that should be secret and those which, by their very nature, are not and cannot be kept secret."

Former DCI ALLEN DULLES, *The Craft of Intelligence* (1963). A veiled reference, perhaps, to the not-very-secret Bay of Pigs operation.

"Secrecy means secret from inception to eternity."

Attributed to senior CIA official LYMAN KIRKPATRICK; quoted in Powers, *The Man Who Kept the Secrets* (1979).

"Intelligence has come a long way since the good old days when everything could be shoved under the rug of silence."

Former DCI ALLEN DULLES, *The Craft of Intelligence* (1963). Good old days?

"Once a secret society establishes itself within an open society, there is no end to the hideous mistrust it must cause."

REBECCA WEST, *The New Meaning of Treason* (1966). West here was referring to the work of Communists seeking to undermine democracies.

"Secrecy in this work is essential. Achievements and triumphs can seldom be advertised. Shortcomings and failures often are advertised. The rewards can never come in public acclaim, only in the quiet satisfaction of getting on with the job and trying to do well the work that needs to be done in the interests of your nation."

President LYNDON JOHNSON on presenting the National Security Medal to DCI William Raborn, 17 August 1966; cited in CIA, *"Our First Line of Defense"* (1996).

"There are those who feel that candour is all and that the international situation would be ideal if only we invited the neighbours to come in and look in the cupboards, but they should reflect that had we been as steadily robbed by Hitler's spies [as we have by Communist ones] we could not have won the Second World War and those of our fellow citizens who are Jewish would not be with us today. If any generation should be cautious about staking our lives on human innocence, it is ours."

REBECCA WEST, *The New Meaning of Treason* (1966).

"The real problem of CIA, the inherent tension in conducting secret intelligence in a free society, remains. Secrecy and deception will always create problems in a free society. . . . A reputation for openness, respect for others, and idealism is one of our greatest political assets. But openness, respect for others, and idealism are inconsistent with the deviousness and intrigue of secret service techniques."

Former State Department intelligence chief ROGER HILSMAN, *To Move a Nation* (1967).

"The undersigned has been informed that Radio Free Europe is a project of the CIA and that the CIA provides funds for the operation of the organization. The undersigned has now been officially informed. If he divulges this information to a third party, he becomes liable for a fine and punishment not to exceed 10,000 dollars and ten years in prison."

> Secrecy agreement required of "witting" staff members of Radio Free Europe; cited in Puddington, *Broadcasting Freedom* (2000). RFE was a CIA covert project nearly from its inception in 1950 until 1971, after which time funding was provided openly by the Congress.

"Not all official secrets need protection; but some do. The date of a surprise military operation; the details of a vital technical process; the *arcana imperii* of any political system; the identity of an agent who can supply such facts; the list of secret codes which are read—these are secrets which are rightly protected by one side, and rightly sought out by the other, in the contests of international power politics, which do not cease because some literary men are virtuous."

> **HUGH TREVOR-ROPER**, veteran of both MI5 and SIS, in 1968; cited in West, *Faber Book of Espionage* (1993).

"The primary purpose of secrecy (initially, keeping information from the foreign governments against which operations were being run) became [in the 1960s] keeping it from Americans in or out of government who might object to the policy implications of the activity."

> **ANGELO CODEVILLA**, *Informing Statecraft* (1992).

"Secrecy . . . has become a god in this country, and those people who have secrets travel in a kind of fraternity . . . and they will not speak to anyone else."

> Senator **WILLIAM FULBRIGHT**, November 1971; quoted in Marchetti and Marks, *CIA and the Cult of Intelligence* (1974).

"We're going to take the President's clearances away."

> Senior State Department official **U. ALEXIS JOHNSON** after President Nixon unintentionally revealed U.S. SIGINT capability during a press conference; quoted in Andrew, *For the President's Eyes Only* (1995).

"Secrecy and a free, democratic government don't mix."

> Former President **HARRY TRUMAN**; quoted in Merle Miller, *Plain Speaking* (1974). This from the man who presided over the creation of CIA.

"You get so used to lying that after a while it's hard to remember what the truth is."

> **PHILIP AGEE**, *Inside the Company* (1975). Agee has long had that problem.

"Secrecy has been a tragic conceit. Inevitably, the truth prevails, and policies pursued on the premise that they could be plausibly denied, in the end damage America's reputation and the faith of her people in their government."

> U.S. Senate, *Final Report of the Senate Select Committee to Study Governmental Operations with respect to Intelligence Activities* [the Church Committee], Book I (April 1976).

"Only the purist could argue that the obvious benefits of secret intelligence should be completely sacrificed on the altar of total openness in government operations."

> Former DDI **RAY CLINE**, *Secrets, Spies and Scholars* (1976). In democracies, we have lots of purists.

"The Committee finds that the operation of an extensive and necessarily secret intelligence system places severe strains on the nation's constitutional government. The Committee is convinced, however, that the competing demands of secrecy and the requirements of the democratic process —our Constitution and our laws—can be reconciled. The need to protect secrets must be balanced with the assurance that secrecy is not used as a means to hide the abuse of power or the failures and mistakes of policy. Means must and can be provided for lawful disclosure of unneeded or unlawful secrets."

U.S. Senate, *Final Report of the Senate Select Committee to Study Governmental Operations with respect to Intelligence Activities* [the Church Committee], Book I (April 1976).

"When Frank Snepp, a former CIA officer, published *Decent Interval,* a book about the fall of Saigon, the Carter administration prosecuted and convicted him on the ground that he had violated his CIA contract by failing to submit his manuscript for clearance. No classified information was involved; no allegation was made of injury to national security; no one denied that Snepp's book was of value to the concerned citizen and the future historian."

ARTHUR SCHLESINGER, JR., *The Cycles of American History* (1986). Schlesinger appears to believe that people should be free not to do what they have promised to do—the "CIA contract" was actually the personal oath required of every employee: no promise, no job, your choice.

"The habits and language of clandestinity can intoxicate even its own practitioners."

Former DCI WILLIAM COLBY, *Honorable Men* (1978).

"CIA people are cynical in most ways, but their belief in secrets is almost metaphysical. In their bones they believe they know the answer to that ancient paradox of epistemology which asks: If a tree falls in the forest without witnesses, is there any sound? The CIA would say no."

THOMAS POWERS, *The Man Who Kept the Secrets* (1979). Powers, uncharacteristically, misses the point. Secrets have power, but the metaphysics enters in the promise not to reveal them.

"The current [classification] system's pervasiveness and often arbitrary nature have had a numbing effect and has therefore become counterproductive. So many documents are classified top secret and higher that the designations tend to be shrugged off and even ridiculed. To classify almost everything is to classify almost nothing."

WILLIAM E. BURROWS, *Deep Black* (1986).

"[In the mid-1970s] CIA still represented a mystery to most Congressmen and most citizens. The secrecy in which CIA had enveloped its work, necessary to protect clandestine sources but grossly excessive for the majority of CIA employees and activities, backfired. In the post-Watergate climate, the nearly total lack of confidence in government institutions, combined with the sensational way in which the journalistic media and the Congress exposed CIA to the public, nearly destroyed its effectiveness at home and abroad. It will take a long time to restore the confidence of the American people in an agency so essential to this nation's survival in a disorderly, often hostile international environment. Only then will it be possible to restore the morale of intelligence officers, to reassure friendly foreign nations they can share secrets with the United States, and to rebuild the agent relationships that feed the central analytical intelligence machine in Washington."

Former DDI RAY CLINE, *Secrets, Spies and Scholars* (1976).

"The fundamental issue faced by the Committee in its investigation was how the requirements of American democracy can be properly balanced in intelligence matters against the need for secrecy. Secrecy is essential for the success of many intelligence activities. At the same time, secrecy contributed to many of the abuses, excesses and inefficiencies uncovered by the Committee. Secrecy also makes it difficult to establish a public consensus for the future conduct of certain intelligence operations."

U.S. Senate, *Final Report of the Select Committee to Study Governmental Operations with respect to Intelligence Activities* [the Church Committee], Book I (April 1976).

"There are certain matters that you take to the tomb."

Former CIA counterintelligence chief **JAMES ANGLETON**, in 1976; quoted in Winks, *Cloak and Gown* (1987).

"The first rule in keeping secrets is nothing on paper: paper can be lost or stolen or simply inherited by the wrong people; if you really want to keep something secret, don't write it down."

THOMAS POWERS, *The Man Who Kept the Secrets* (1979).

"It is one thing to argue that a government that consistently misleads its people has effectively lost its legitimacy and should be replaced. But it is preposterous to demand that governments should always tell the truth, as if that single moral value everywhere and forever transcended other values. An individual may legitimately decide to act this way, even at the cost of life, but governments are not free to choose this 'ethic of ultimate ends.'"

WALTER LAQUEUR, *A World of Secrets* (1985).

"Our intelligence activities cannot be put back under the cloak of near-total secrecy that existed in the thirty years immediately following World War II. . . . Secret agencies within democratic governments are anachronisms; because popular controls break down when citizens cannot know everything their government is doing."

Former DCI **STANSFIELD TURNER**, *Secrecy and Democracy* (1985). Everything?

"Whereas there are criminal laws in the United States likely to send a Department of Agriculture employee to prison for up to ten years if he revealed advance information about next year's soybean crop, defense secrets are not protected in a similar way."

WALTER LAQUEUR, *A World of Secrets* (1985).

"[We are] rightly regarded as a candid and open people who pride ourselves on a free society. And yet our secret services, our spies and intelligence agencies—from Nathan Hale to Midway, from OSS to CIA—have not written just a striking, stirring chapter in our history but have often provided the key to victory in war and the preservation of our freedom during an uneasy peace."

President **RONALD REAGAN**, remarks to OSS veterans, 29 May 1986; cited in CIA, *"Our First Line of Defense"* (1996).

"In 1987 . . . the U.S. Air Force asked its civilian employees with security clearances to sign an agreement calling on them not to discuss or publish classified information *and information that could be classified in the future.* Thus to the concept of classified information was added the bizarre idea of 'classifiable' information—ordinary data that *someday* might undergo a transformation into secret data. The Air Force branded those reluctant to sign the agreement as lacking in 'personal commitment to protect classified information.'"

NORMAN POLMAR and **THOMAS ALLEN**, *Encyclopedia of Espionage* (1997). The Air Force later backed away from this shocking measure to protect "future secrets."

"It would be impossible to conduct clandestine activities—either to collect information or to carry out covert activity—without secrecy. If we cannot protect our sources, we will not get information that we need. If we cannot protect the sensitive methods by which we collect the information, both in terms of individuals on the ground and satellites in space, we will cease to have the means of collecting information."

DCI **WILLIAM WEBSTER**, remarks to CIA retirees, 8 February 1988; in *1988 Speeches*.

"An agency whose servants are obliged for ever to keep everything secret will never develop an objective view of the world. It will see everything around it through a miasma of suspicion and therefore proffer unwarranted observations and conclusions."

AUBREY JONES, SIS veteran, in 1988; cited in West, *Faber Book of Espionage* (1993).

"These meetings were so secret our secretaries weren't allowed to put them on our calendars because all we needed was a story that the administration was making contingency plans for the breakup of the Soviet Union, and our Soviet policy was dead."

CONDOLEEZZA RICE, Soviet director on the National Security Council during the administration of President George H. W. Bush, on the interagency committee she chaired; quoted in *Studies in Intelligence* 39/3 (fall 1995).

"Governments should do secretly abroad only such things as they could profitably defend at home."

ANGELO CODEVILLA, *Informing Statecraft* (1992).

"Washington has a long, dishonorable history of mistaking secrecy for patriotism and misusing the cover of national security to shield abuses of power and amoral policies. The C.I.A. is the most skilled practitioner of these undemocratic arts.... There is a place and time for secrecy. Matters diplomatic and military often need to be protected, and many intelligence activities cannot be conducted in the open. But instead of maintaining a reasonable use of secrecy, the C.I.A. has concealed almost all of its business from the public and much of it from the Congress."

New York Times editorial "The Secrecy Infection," 5 April 1995. The *New York Times*, of course, knows best what is a "reasonable use of secrecy."

"If you want a secret respected, see that it's respectable in the first place."

Senator **DANIEL PATRICK MOYNIHAN**, address at the Department of State, 4 March 1996.

"It is my conviction, based on some 70 years of experience . . . that the need by our government for *secret* intelligence about affairs elsewhere in the world has been vastly overrated. I would say that something upward of 95 percent of what we need to know could be very well obtained by the careful and competent study of perfectly legitimate sources of information open and available to us in the rich library and archival holdings of this country."

GEORGE KENNAN in the *New York Times*, 18 May 1997. It's the other 5 percent that will kill us.

"Secrecy is a form of government regulation [in which] government tells you what you may know. Secrecy is the normal weapon of bureaucracy."

Senator **DANIEL PATRICK MOYNIHAN**, on *The Charlie Rose Show*, PBS, 4 November 1998.

"Don't spill the beans, pardner, the steaks are too high. No classified talk."

> Sign in NSA cafeteria, as reported by Reuters, 23 September 2000. NSA is such a hoot.

"When somebody accuses a clandestine services officer of being preoccupied with security, 99 times out of 100 it's because he's got the burden of responsibility of somebody else's life on his hands."

> Former DCI **ROBERT GATES**, on CBS, 12 November 2000.

"This is secret. This can't be the second half of a sentence that begins, 'Honey, you won't believe what happened to me at work today.'"

> NSA director **MICHAEL HAYDEN** relating what he told NSA employees over closed-circuit television when NSA's computer system went down for three days in January 2000, on *60 Minutes II*, CBS, 13 February 2001.

"Any sources and methods of intelligence will remain guarded [and] secret. My administration will not talk about how we gather intelligence, if we gather intelligence, and what the intelligence says. That's for the protection of the American people."

> President **GEORGE W. BUSH**; quoted in the *New York Times*, 14 September 2001.

"War requires secrecy; an intelligence war requires even greater secrecy. No one, the media included, should begrudge the administration its necessary secrecy."

> **BOB WOODWARD** in the *Washington Post*, 25 October 2001. Woodward?!

"Why, you might ask, would [intelligence] spending figures from a half-century ago, when the agency was in its cradle, still be sensitive? The government contends that releasing such numbers would compromise 'intelligence sources and methods.' And it is litigating to keep them under wraps. . . . So Americans will soon see the ends to which the CIA is prepared to go to keep data of this sort under wraps. What conceivable reason could the government have for withholding? . . . Will Mr. Tenet really put his name on a declaration swearing that the budget numbers from the Truman administration must remain classified? If so, he will only draw attention to the nonsense of the classification system."

> *Washington Post* editorial, "Central Intelligence Test," 2 October 2002.

"No. It would compromise sources and methods."

> An "Information Review Officer" in the U.S. intelligence community denying a proposed official release of information acknowledging that the German army, *in August 1914*, exploited Russian radio transmissions made in the clear before the Battle of Tannenberg. This "secret" is well-documented in various historical works.

"Just say no."

> A Nancy Reagan poster in the office of another U.S. intelligence "Information Review Officer."

"No amount of secrecy tinkering can be counted on to contain the circle of compromise in any long-lasting secret activity involving numbers of people and extensive funding."

> Former DCI **RICHARD HELMS**, *A Look over My Shoulder* (2003).

SUBCULTURES IN CIA

Much of CIA's history has been animated by a fundamental internal dichotomy that has existed since OSS times. On the one side, there are the operators—the case officers, the clandestine collectors, the spymasters, the DO. On the other, there are the analysts—the thinkers and scholars, the synthesizers of "all-source" intelligence, the estimators, the DI. The stereotypes of years past were cruel: DO types were called glad-handing, manipulative cowboys with more crazy ideas than brains; DI types were considered overeducated eggheads driving desks and careless about security. Today, the two sides work closely together, understanding and appreciating each other. Mostly.

See also: Academia; Analysis & Analysts; Bay of Pigs; Covert Action; Espionage & Spies; People

"The separation of the [OSS] research and analysis scholars from the clandestine operatives encouraged and exacerbated the growth of two 'cultures' within the intelligence profession, cultures severely compartmented from each other and often hostile to or contemptuous of each other—a condition that has plagued and complicated intelligence work to this day."

Former DCI **WILLIAM COLBY**, *Honorable Men* (1978).

"The mild-mannered scholars and scientists who undertook OSS studies were known as the Choirboys . . . while the field agents came to be characterized as Cowboys because of their wild exploits."

FRANCIS RUSSELL, *The Secret War* (1981).

"All intelligence information collected by the Office of Special Operations will be put in useable form, graded as to source and reliability, and delivered as spot information to the Office of Research and Evaluation or to other departments and agencies when appropriate. The Office of Special Operations will carry out no research and evaluation functions other than those pertaining to

counterintelligence and to the grading of source and reliability."

DCI **HOYT VANDENBERG** in October 1946 directive; reproduced in Warner, *CIA Under Truman* (1994).

"An intellectual partnership between scholars and spies is the best formula for successful intelligence collection and evaluation. . . . [But] I have always felt it violated a cardinal rule of sound intelligence organization in allowing the same unit to conduct intelligence operations and then evaluate the results."

Former DDI **RAY CLINE**, *Secrets, Spies and Scholars* (1976).

"[In 1956] the denizens of the DDP [the operations directorate] lived on the other side of the Lincoln Memorial from the DDI [the analytic directorate] elements of the CIA. Their home was a dismal row of World War II temporary buildings labeled J, K, and L, now destroyed, but then stretching the whole length of the reflecting pool from 17th to 23rd Streets. There was not a great deal of intercourse between the two areas."

Former DDI **RAY CLINE**, *The CIA Under Reagan, Bush, and Casey* (1981).

"In the first ten to fifteen years the division between the separate offices was almost water-tight and sometimes hostile. Clandestine service officers often regarded the analysts as walking sieves, leaking hard-won espionage reports from every pore. The analysts responded by characterizing the 'spooks' as reckless blunderers who were paranoid about secrecy, especially as it pertained to their reports, which, in the view of the analysts, were often trivial and second- or third-rate compared to State Department reporting or the intercepted communications of the National Security Agency."

Former DDI **R. JACK SMITH**, *The Unknown CIA* (1989).

"Since 1948 . . . the Central Intelligence Agency has been shared by three distinct types of personality: the spy runners, the analysts, and the political operators. For the most part, they have been cool toward one another, skeptical within the bounds of politeness; but occasionally civility is strained, differences grow acerbic, and conflicts of style and outlook erupt into something very like open warfare, with all the incestuous bitterness of an argument in the family."

THOMAS POWERS, *The Man Who Kept the Secrets* (1979).

"You never know who the enemy is. The enemy is the Defense Department. The enemy is the State Department. The enemy is the DDI."

Former DDI **RAY CLINE** quoting from a CIA Clandestine Service lecture on security that he attended in 1957; cited in Weber, *Spymasters* (1999). At the time, "DDI" referred to the entire Directorate of Intelligence, not just the Deputy Director for Intelligence, which Cline became in 1962.

"[In the 1960s,] armed guards and turnstiles separated the analytical and operational sides of the Agency, and you could not go back and forth without a special marker on your security badge."

Former DCI **ROBERT GATES**, *From the Shadows* (1996). The armed guards, needless to say, were not there to protect the analysts.

"Something has to give in an organization which attempts to combine such opposite kinds of activity [as analysis and covert action], and what usually resulted was that truly clandestine practices were compromised while perfectly legal scholarly analysis was clothed in an atmosphere of secrecy that was unnecessary, frequently counterproductive, and in the long run damaging to the role of independent and objective evaluation for which CIA was designed."

Former DDI **RAY CLINE**, *Secrets, Spies and Scholars* (1976).

"Cloak-and-dagger work encouraged vigorous storytelling and advocacy—it contrasted with analytical work that frequently remained top secret long after the event and was invariably dull to all but the experts."

RHODRI JEFFREYS-JONES, *The CIA and American Democracy* (1989).

"A man who is more interested in intellectual pursuits than in people, in observation and thought than in action, will make a better 'analyst' than an 'operator.'"

Former DCI **ALLEN DULLES**, *The Craft of Intelligence* (1963).

"Your analyst is trying to abstract general frameworks of ideas out of any issue he's studying so as to predict what's going to happen next and see patterns of past and future situations, whereas the operator has some such framework in his mind, [but] the operator's job is not to tinker with the subtlety of the framework but to manipulate people and events. . . . So the personality of a good operator will normally be a hands-on manipulator of people. . . . It is a distinction between the end product, which is for the analyst a coherent and articulate set of concepts, and for the operator either data or events taking place that you can report on and describe. So one is more analytical and one is more descriptive; one is more thoughtful and the other more manipulative."

Former DDI **RAY CLINE** in a 1983 interview; cited in Weber, *Spymasters* (1999). These stereotypes can go too far: there are cerebral operators and manipulative analysts.

"I suggested that a weekend discussion be organized among all the working-level Agency officers who were concerned about Indonesia. We gathered political, military, economic, biographic and geographic experts and mixed them together with clandestine operators, who had lived and worked in that part of the world, and with technical and scientific personnel. To me, the startling thing was that most had never before met any of the others."

Former DCI **WILLIAM COLBY**, *Honorable Men* (1978).

"There is nothing more irritating in this job than finding out that this directorate has been denied the information needed to do its job. . . . We have given considerable deference to the DO in terms of our use of information drawn from their operational traffic on the Contras, probably too much deference. . . . We can no longer go down this track with one hand tied behind us."

CIA Deputy Director for Intelligence **ROBERT GATES** complaining to the Deputy Director for Operations, 3 February 1984; cited in Gates, *From the Shadows* (1996).

"The division of CIA into analytic, espionage, and scientific branches is based on the historic evolution of the Agency and administrative convenience rather than on considerations of operational effectiveness. Each branch has its own culture and folklore, its own problems, and its own internal loyalties, which are often stronger than its loyalty to the whole organization."

Former DCI **STANSFIELD TURNER**, *Secrecy and Democracy* (1985).

"Operations and intelligence officers are now located together in certain CIA offices. The stated objective of such a 'partnership' between the Agency's 'DO' and 'DI' sides is to improve cooperation between the two, an unobjectionable goal.

. . . But this stratagem is a decidedly bad one [as it] greatly increases the opportunities for a mole like Aldrich Ames to destroy whole intelligence networks."

FRANK GAFFNEY, JR., in the *Washington Times*, 3 January 1995.

"You must reverse [DCI R. James] Woolsey's decision to merge the directorates of operations and intelligence, which gives clandestine operations more attention than they deserve and runs the risk of politicizing intelligence analysis. . . . The two directorates are different organizations and must be kept apart."

MELVIN GOODMAN, "A memo to the next director," *Christian Science Monitor*, 24 January 1995. Mel missed the mark: Woolsey just got the directorates to work together better. The cultures are such that a merger would fail disastrously.

"Nearly 50 years since the creation of the C.I.A., the agency's operations directorate retains an insular, arrogant culture that breeds a dangerous contempt for democratic principles and accountability."

New York Times editorial, 8 December 1996.

"The Directorate of Operations . . . has always 'marched' for the president, no matter what his political party. On the other hand the Directorate of Science and Technology, which is involved in large and expensive programs, usually of a technical nature, has a very different focus, and Congress controls its funding. The president is a beneficiary of its intelligence collection, but the implementation of its programs, the success thereof, and thus its officers' promotions depend on congressional financial largess. No wonder then that officers largely brought up in this directorate . . . develop an almost symbiotic relationship with Congress, in stark contrast with [the DO], which is beholden to Congress for little."

> Former senior CIA operations officer **DUANE CLAR-RIDGE**, *A Spy for All Seasons* (1997).

"Generally speaking, operators make bad analysts. We are different kinds of people. Operators are actors, doers, movers and shakers; we are quick, maybe a little impulsive, maybe a little 'cowboy.' Our best times are away from our desks. We love the street. Research and analysis is really not our thing—and when we have tried to do it, we have not been good at it. True analysts are different. They love it. They are more cerebral, patient, and sedentary. They find things we could not. They write better."

> Former CIA operations officer and counterintelligence chief **JAMES M. OLSEN** in *Studies in Intelligence* 45/3 (2001).

SUCCESSES

The question "How successful is intelligence?" the Literary Spy proposes, is a lot closer to the question "How successful is Harvard?" than "How successful is IBM?" The metrics of intelligence success are as elusive as those for education and are not the same as the metrics of business success, for all our appropriation of corporate terms such as "product" and "consumer." It is well nigh impossible to measure the insight and understanding intelligence provides on a daily basis. More than one U.S. policymaker have said that intelligence's true value lies not in its predictive success but in its expanding their knowledge base. Even so, there are some specific successes the Literary Spy can point to that are both significant and unclassified—not that they will satisfy those looking for success one can measure.

See also: Failures; Fighting the Cold War; Intelligence, the Missions of; Warning, Prediction, & Surprise

"The credit [for the U.S. naval victory at the Battle of Midway] must be given to [Pacific Fleet commander-in-chief Admiral Chester] Nimitz. Not only did he accept the intelligence picture but he acted upon it at once."

> Rear Admiral **RAYMOND SPRUANCE**, who was able to ambush a superior Japanese fleet attacking Midway Island because U.S. Navy codebreakers could read Japanese naval messages; quoted in Prange, *Miracle at Midway* (1982).

"Even though the current French offensive in northern Indochina appears to have limited objectives, the campaign will probably not be successful in forcing the Vietnam Republic to negotiate on French terms.... The French expectation that the Vietnam Government would be willing to negotiate on French terms ignores the hatred and contempt felt for the French by most of the population of northern Indochina.... None of the political figures advanced by the French ... as alternatives to President Ho and the Vietnam Republic can command enough popular support to weaken the Vietnam Republic."

> CIA report "Prospects for French Success in Indochinese Campaign," 24 October 1947; reproduced in Kuhns, *Assessing the Soviet Threat* (1997).

"The USSR ... cannot expect the US and the other Western powers to evacuate the city [of Berlin] voluntarily. The USSR, therefore, will probably use every means short of armed force to compel these powers to leave the city. These devices may include additional obstruction to transport and travel to and within the city."

DCI **ROSCOE HILLENKOETTER**, memorandum to President Truman, 22 December 1947; reproduced in Kuhns, *Assessing the Soviet Threat* (1997). The Berlin blockade began six months later.

"The USSR has been organizing a North Korean army, clandestinely trained by Soviet advisers and equipped with Soviet weapons. The 'draft provisional constitution'... anticipates eventual incorporation of all Korea into the 'People's Republic of Korea' and goes so far as to specify Seoul, capital of the present US zone, as the future capital of a united Korea."

CIA report "Soviet Expansionism in Korea," 20 February 1948; reproduced in Kuhns, *Assessing the Soviet Threat* (1997).

"We have been directed to estimate the likelihood of a Soviet resort to direct military action during 1948.... The preponderance of available evidence and of considerations derived from the 'logic of the situation' supports the conclusion that the USSR will not resort to direct military action during 1948."

Report by a Joint Ad Hoc Committee, comprising representatives from CIA, State Department, and the military branches, responding to U.S. military leaders' fears of a surprise attack by the USSR, 30 March 1948; reproduced in Haines and Leggett, *CIA's Analyses of the Soviet Union* (2001). One of the more important missions of U.S. intelligence during the Cold War was predicting what was likely *not* to happen.

"Communist military forces are capable during the summer months of 1949 of destroying all semblance of unity in the National Government of China.... The US cannot reverse or significantly influence this course of events."

CIA report "Probable Developments in China," 16 June 1949; reproduced in Kuhns, *Assessing the Soviet Threat* (1997).

"I have always viewed this as one of the major intelligence coups of my tour of duty in intelligence."

Former DCI **ALLEN DULLES** on CIA's acquisition of the text of Soviet Premier Nikita Khrushchev's "secret speech" in 1956, in *The Craft of Intelligence* (1963).

"The differences between Peiping and Moscow are so basic and are so much a product of the different situations and problems in the two countries that any genuine resolution of the fundamental differences is unlikely."

National Intelligence Estimate, *Communist China*, 6 December 1960; in *Foreign Relations of the United States, 1958–1960*, vol. 19: *China*. CIA was ahead of the rest of the intelligence community in predicting the Sino-Soviet split.

"Given the inherent difficulties of espionage and the special circumstances, the laboriousness and risk in recruiting agents, the time lag in communicating secretly with an agent once recruited, the risk of a U-2 being shot down and the possible restrictions this might impose on our best source of information, the frustrations of cloud cover, the elaborate security precautions taken by the Soviets, their efforts at deception—given all these difficulties, it is probably something to be proud of that the missiles were discovered as early as they were. In sum, Cuba in 1962, it seems to me, must be marked down as a victory for American intelligence —and a victory of a very high order.... The most important fact in the whole intelligence story is that the missiles were discovered before they were operational—and long enough before to permit the United States Government to assess the situation, develop a policy, and launch on a course of action."

Former State Department intelligence chief **ROGER HILSMAN**, *To Move a Nation* (1967).

"An extraordinarily successful predictive analysis by CIA enabled the United States to make a formal statement on the imminence of China's first nuclear explosion shortly before it occurred in October 1964."

Former DDI **RAY CLINE**, *Secrets, Spies and Scholars* (1976).

"On balance, the [Central Intelligence] Agency did a good job in assessing the situation in Southeast Asia during the 1965–74 period. . . . First, the Agency, in evaluating the effectiveness of U.S. air attacks, consistently concluded that the attacks did not reduce North Vietnam's logistic capabilities to sustain the war, that North Vietnam could afford to take the punishment, [and] that Hanoi's will was not shaken. . . . Second, with respect to North Vietnam's ability to wage a prolonged war, the Agency consistently estimated that Hanoi would continue to base its strategy on a war of attrition. . . . Finally, as South Vietnam's fortunes waned and U.S. support faltered in late 1973 and in 1974, the Agency consistently warned that the South Vietnamese situation was becoming parlous and that the North Vietnamese would exploit their military advantage to gain their long-sought final victory."

General **BRUCE PALMER, JR.**, *The 25-Year War* (1984).

"The most pointless—and damaging—disclosures [from the congressional investigations of the 1970s] concerned technical intelligence. Of these, the revelation that American submarines were tapping Soviet underwater cables was the most out-rageous. It destroyed the indispensable source which enabled our intelligence analysts to read the results of Soviet long-range missile tests. . . . Other egregious examples of damaging technical disclosures concerned the Glomar Explorer . . . a ship specially designed to raise a sunken Soviet submarine from the ocean floor. Various communications intercepts, such as our ability to listen to some of the Soviet leaders' telephone conversations, were also pointlessly disclosed. These revelations involved intelligence successes, not failures, and carried not the slightest implication of abuse of authority."

HENRY KISSINGER, *Years of Renewal* (1999).

"The Soviet economy faces serious strains in the decade ahead. . . . In the past, rapid growth enabled Moscow simultaneously to pursue three key objectives: catching up with the US militarily; steadily expanding the industrial base; and meeting at least minimal consumer expectations for improved living conditions and welfare. Reduced growth, as is foreshadowed over the next decade, will make pursuit of these objectives much more difficult, and [will] pose hard choices for the leadership. . . . Soviet responses to these challenges could be further complicated by the fact that leadership changes will almost surely take place during the coming period. Even a confident new leadership would have difficulties in coming to grips with the problems ahead."

CIA report "Soviet Economic Problems and Prospects," July 1977; reproduced in Haines and Leggett, *CIA's Analyses of the Soviet Union* (2001). This report, coming eight years before Mikhail Gorbachev's rise to power, is prescient.

"The USSR's invasion of Afghanistan in December 1979 provided a rare opportunity to test the efficacy of the US warning system in situations involving substantial movements of the Soviets' armed forces outside their borders.... [U.S.] analysts were unable to forecast precisely the timing or the size of the Soviets' move, but gave warning at least 10 days beforehand that the USSR was prepared to invade."

U.S. Intelligence Community report, October 1980; reproduced in Haines and Leggett, *CIA's Analyses of the Soviet Union* (2001).

"The large phased-array radar (LPAR) located near Krasnoyarsk, USSR has been an ABM Treaty issue since it was first detected in July 1983 because of its inland, rather than peripheral, siting. Responding to US demands about its inconsistency with the ABM Treaty, the Soviets have repeatedly argued that the radar is for satellite detection and tracking. Our analyses indicate ... that the primary mission of this radar is ballistic missile detection and tracking."

CIA report "The Krasnoyarsk Radar: Closing the Final Gap in Coverage for Ballistic Missile Early Warning," 19 June 1986; reproduced in Haines and Leggett, *CIA's Analyses of the Soviet Union* (2001). Moscow finally admitted, after the breakup of the USSR, that the Krasnoyarsk LPAR had been built to detect and track ballistic missiles.

"In late 1987, the [Central Intelligence] Agency was warning about growing ethnic conflict in the USSR ... that the potential was growing for ethnic crises in different republics to combine and produce an overall crisis of central control in the non-Russian republics."

Former DCI **ROBERT GATES**, conference on "US Intelligence and the End of the Cold War," Texas A&M University, 19 November 1999.

"Should a sharp polarization of the [Soviet] leadership prevent it from acting resolutely to deal with a growing crisis, the prospects would increase for a conservative coup involving a minority of Polit-buro members supported by elements of the military and the KGB."

CIA assessment, January 1989; cited in *Studies in Intelligence* 39/3 (fall 1995).

"As deputy national security adviser in the White House, in the spring of 1989 I was inundated by the CIA with information on the accelerating domestic crisis in the U.S.S.R. In July, prompted by this intelligence, I obtained President Bush's approval to establish inside the White House a top-secret, very select interagency task force to begin contingency planning for the collapse of the Soviet Union. In short, based on CIA's warnings, our government began planning for the collapse of the Soviet Union more than two years before it happened. This was just one of CIA's great successes—unpublicized and contrary to current conventional wisdom."

Former DCI **ROBERT GATES**, quoted in the *Wall Street Journal*, 17 September 1997.

"[Soviet President Mikhail] Gorbachev has started a conflict without a visible program and with scant prospect of long-term success. He will not easily escape the predicament for which he is largely responsible, and he may become its principal casualty."

CIA's *National Intelligence Daily*, 24 January 1991; cited in Strobe Talbott and Michael Beschloss, *At the Highest Levels* (1993).

"The USSR is in the midst of a revolution that probably will sweep the Communist Party from power and reshape the country within the five-year time frame of this Estimate."

Opening lines of National Intelligence Estimate, *Implications of Alternative Soviet Futures*, June 1991; in Fischer, *At Cold War's End* (1999). Much within.

"Economic crisis, independence aspirations and anti-communist forces are breaking down the Soviet Empire and system of governance."

> CIA assessment "The Soviet Cauldron," April 1991; cited in Andrew, *For the President's Eyes Only* (1995). This prescient paper was the work of CIA's top Soviet analyst, George Kolt.

"With or without Gorbachev, with or without a putsch, the most likely prospect for the end of this decade, if not earlier, is a Soviet Union transformed into some independent states and a confederation of the remaining republics, including Russia."

> CIA assessment "The Soviet Cauldron," April 1991; cited in *Studies in Intelligence* 39/3 (fall 1995).

"There is an increasing danger that the [Soviet] traditionalists will want to provoke a situation that will justify the use of force to restore order."

> CIA's *President's Daily Brief*, 17 August 1991, just before the attempted coup against Soviet President Mikhail Gorbachev; cited in Strobe Talbott and Michael Beschloss, *At the Highest Levels* (1993).

"In the field of intelligence, the opportunities for success are so spectacular and so important that there is only the possibility of total failure or total success. The risks are very high, but people must have the courage to take chances."

> Former CIA chief of operations **RICHARD BISSELL**, *Reflections of a Cold Warrior* (1996).

"When we were having our greatest successes . . . on the intelligence front, no one knew about them. That's the nature of intelligence success."

> Former senator and chairman of the Senate intelligence committee **DAVID BOREN**; quoted in the *Washington Times*, 3 January 2002.

"The Central Intelligence Agency predicted more than three years ago that increased international air travel, trade, and tourism would dramatically increase the spread of infectious diseases around the world, and that governments might try to hide the outbreaks for fear of economic losses. While not predicting with specificity the outbreak of a coronavirus like SARS, [the report said] 'The next major infectious disease threat to the United States may be, like HIV, a previously unrecognized pathogen. . . . Some countries hide or understate their infectious disease problems for reasons of international prestige and fear of economic losses.'"

> *Boston Globe*, "Forethoughts on a Threat," 27 April 2003.

"The American people must know just how reliable American intelligence is on the threats that confront our nation. Let's talk about Libya, where a sitting regime has volunteered to dismantle its weapons of mass destruction programs. This was an intelligence success. . . . Only through intelligence did we know each of the major programs Libya had going. . . . We learned all this through the powerful combination of technical intelligence, careful and painstaking analytic work, operational daring, and, yes, the classic kind of human intelligence that people have led you to believe that we no longer have."

> DCI **GEORGE TENET**, remarks at Georgetown University, 5 February 2004.

T

- **Terrorism**
- **Timeliness**
- **Traitors in Their Own Words**
- **Treason & Betrayal**

TERRORISM

The Literary Spy finds a bit tiring the truism that terrorism is a brand new object of intelligence. During the Cold War the possibility of getting nuked, unlikely as it turned out to be, was nonetheless fairly terrifying. The very real enslavement of nations by tyrannical, anti-human ideologues was a form of institutionalized terror. The present fight against terrorism, of course, has much that is new: unfamiliar and stateless faces and names, diabolically creative methods of mass murder, a unique global environment. At bottom, however, it's the same fight: totalitarianism is terrorism come to power, and terrorists are would-be totalitarians.

See also: FBI & Law Enforcement; Intelligence, the Missions of; Unsavory Characters; Warning, Prediction, & Surprise

"I will have such revenges . . . I will do such
    things,—
What they are, yet I know not; but they shall be
The terrors of the earth."

> Lear in **WILLIAM SHAKESPEARE**, *King Lear* (1606), Act II, scene 4.

"I proposed to shoot against the Americans arrows dipt in the matter of the small pox, and so conquer them by their known terror of that disorder."

> British Major **ROBERT DONKIN**, *Military Collections and Remarks* (1777); cited in the *Washington Post*, 13 December 2001.

"What is one to say to an act of destructive ferocity so absurd as to be incomprehensible, inexplicable, almost unthinkable; in fact, mad? Madness alone is truly terrifying. . . . The attack must have all the shocking senselessness of gratuitous blasphemy."

> Mr. Vladimir, fictional spymaster of an unnamed foreign power, ordering the bombing of Greenwich Observatory in **JOSEPH CONRAD**, *The Secret Agent* (1907).

"Our job is to get him and when we've got him to shoot him. . . . I've not yet made up my mind whether the best men for this kind of job are those who do it with passion or those who keep their heads. Some of them are filled with hatred for the people we're up against and when we down them it gives them a sort of satisfaction like satisfying a personal grudge."

Fictional British spy chief R on dealing with a terrorist in **W. SOMERSET MAUGHAM**, *Ashenden* (1927). Maugham was an SIS officer in World War I.

"Foreign and domestic civil intelligence are inseparable and constitute one field of operation. . . . In order to cope with the activities of various subversive agents in the United States with speed and dispatch, it is entirely evident that their activities must be followed throughout the various countries by one intelligence agency of the United States Government."

U.S. Attorney General **TOM CLARK**, memorandum to President Truman on "A Plan for U.S. Secret World-Wide Intelligence Coverage," October 1945; in *FRUS 1945– 1950: Emergence of the Intelligence Establishment* (1996), document 17. Clark's proposal was that the FBI should be in charge both of domestic law enforcement and foreign intelligence operations.

"As a rule of thumb, one learns more about a terrorist group by looking at its victims than at its manifestos."

WALTER LAQUEUR, *Terrorism Reader* (1978).

"The Soviets are deeply engaged in support of revolutionary violence worldwide. Such involvement is a basic tenet of Soviet policy, pursued in the interests of weakening unfriendly societies, destabilizing hostile regimes, and advancing Soviet interests. . . . Whether terrorist tactics are used in the course of revolutionary violence is largely a matter of indifference to the Soviets, who have no scruples against them. The Soviet attitude is determined by whether those tactics advance or harm Soviet interests in the particular circumstances. Revolutionary groups that employ terrorist tactics are simply one of the many instru-

ments of Soviet foreign policy. . . . With respect to Soviet policy toward nihilistic, purely terrorist groups, available evidence remains thin and in some respects contradictory."

Special National Intelligence Estimate, *Soviet Support for International Terrorism and Revolutionary Violence*, May 1981; reproduced in Haines and Leggett, *CIA's Analyses of the Soviet Union* (2001).

"In confronting the challenge of international terrorism, the first step is to call things by their proper names, to see clearly and say plainly who the terrorists are, what goals they seek, and which governments support them. What the terrorist does is kill, maim, kidnap, and torture. His or her victims may be children in the schoolroom, innocent travelers on airplanes, businessmen returning home from work, political leaders. . . . The terrorist's victims may have no particular political identity, or they may be political symbols, like Aldo Moro or, perhaps, Pope John Paul II. They may be kidnapped and held for ransom, maimed, or simply blown to bits. One defining characteristic of the terrorist is his choice of method: the terrorist chooses violence as the instrument of first resort."

DCI **WILLIAM CASEY**, "The International Linkages— What Do We Know?" in Uri Ra'anan et al., *Hydra of Carnage* (1986).

"The words, 'One man's terrorist is another man's freedom fighter,' from a national intelligence estimate in 1979, express . . . the most concise symbol of philosophic and moral illiteracy that one could imagine. In the minds of the officials who carry such words in their very bones, the differences between a Jonas Savimbi and an Idi Amin, between the Khmer Rouge and the Khmer People's Liberation Front, between the Sandinistas, the Contras, and Salvador's Farabundo Marti Front, indeed the differences between Gorbachev and Solzhenitsyn, are matters of taste: a dilettante's distinction of distractingly empty thought processes."

> Senator **MALCOLM WALLOP**, "The Role of Congress," in Uri Ra'anan et al., *Hydra of Carnage* (1986).

"The [1983] papal assassination attempt would dog CIA for years. The criticism came from every direction. Some accused us of trying to cover up the Soviet role, though why we—and especially [DCI William] Casey—would do such a thing I never grasped. Others, then and later, would claim that we were trying too hard to pin the blame on the Soviets. [But we] were agnostic about who was behind the crime, much to the impatience of some senators.... The truth was we really didn't know."

> Former DCI **ROBERT GATES**, *From the Shadows* (1996).

"On December 27 [1985] twenty people, five of them Americans, were killed in simultaneous terrorist attacks at Rome and Vienna airports.... Soon afterward the CIA set up a new Counter-Terrorism Center, in which, for the first time, analysts and operations officers worked side by side, together with representatives of NSA and other sections of the intelligence community."

> **CHRISTOPHER ANDREW**, *For the President's Eyes Only* (1995).

"As you have violated our land and our honor, we will violate everything, even your children."

> Note carried by one of the Abu Nidal terrorists who perpetrated the December 1985 massacre at the Fiumicino Airport in Rome; cited in Clarridge, *A Spy for All Seasons* (1997).

"From my experience at the FBI and now at the CIA, I can say that this country is indeed well equipped to deal with international terrorist activities that may be imported to the United States.

No one can say that such activities will not occur, but I believe that our special capabilities, including very good intelligence, will in many cases prevent terrorism from succeeding."

> DCI **WILLIAM WEBSTER**, 22 March 1988, in *1988 Speeches*.

"Unless we find absolute evidence of a conspiracy to commit an illegal act, law enforcement will end up reacting to terrorist acts after the event."

> Former FBI assistant director **OLIVER "BUCK" REVELL**; quoted in Riebling, *Wedge: The Secret War Between the FBI and CIA* (1994).

"The story that has yet to be told is how Saddam Hussein's terrorist teams were defeated during Desert Storm ... due to the cooperation between the FBI and the CIA."

> Former DCI **WILLIAM WEBSTER** at the Council on Foreign Relations conference "The Future of the CIA," 18 February 1997, Washington, D.C.

"Our overriding recommendation is to give the threat of terrorism with weapons of mass destruction the highest priority in U.S. national security policy. Of the threats that could inflict major damage to the U.S., such terrorism is the threat for which we are least prepared."

> Former NIC chairman **JOSEPH NYE** and former DCI **R. JAMES WOOLSEY** in the *Los Angeles Times*, 3 June 1997. After September 11, Woolsey said, "I wish I didn't feel so much like a prophet"; quoted in the *Washington Post*, 27 December 2001.

"No successful counterterrorism strategy is possible unless our leaders accept that the United States cannot insulate itself from the rest of humankind, cannot treat the rest of the world as a part-time emergency or a political football, and cannot abdicate the responsibilities and costs and sacrifices of global leadership."

Former DCI **ROBERT GATES** in the *New York Times*, 16 August 1998.

"You can harden an embassy. You can increase security for airports. You can increase security for military installations. But if you increase your intelligence you cover them all."

Senator **JON KYL**; quoted in the *Defense Daily*, 2 September 1998.

"In the future I think the great burden of intelligence work will be counter-terrorist, from wherever the terrorist threat comes. . . . I don't think there is a case for saying [intelligence services] should not exist anymore. We expect them to find out who is going to blow us up next and if they don't do it we say they are inefficient but we don't say that we should abolish them."

JOHN LE CARRÉ [David Cornwell], spy novelist and former MI5 officer, in *The Guardian*, 2 March 1999.

"Today, Americans must realize that ours is a world without front lines. That the continental United States—and not just our embassies and forces abroad—is itself susceptible to attack. And that the potential method of assault goes well beyond a terrorist with a truck full of conventional explosives. Whether we like it or not, our global leadership has made us a lightning rod for the disaffected and the disappointed. . . . When you take the sheer number and variety of people out in the world who would do harm to our country, its interests, or its allies . . . you will understand why we in the intelligence community believe the chances for unpleasant, even deadly, surprise are

greater now than at any time since the end of the Second World War."

DCI **GEORGE TENET** in a speech delivered at the Town Hall of Los Angeles, 7 December 2000. Too little attention has been given to this prescient speech among those crying "intelligence failure."

"I can walk into any diplomatic reception, anywhere in the world, and get belly-to-belly with targets, if you will, of the traditional ilk—a fellow diplomat from a country of concern to us. How do I walk into a camp in Afghanistan? How do I walk into a small cell that consists of no more than ten people in some country where we no longer have a diplomatic presence? Well, the answer is: through extraordinary, thoughtful, operational initiative, which is what we're doing. I do not accept as a tenet that we can only serve up a disruptive purpose. We must disrupt terrorism, but we also need to spot, assess, develop, and recruit people who are penetrations of terrorist organizations so we know what they're planning. That's a big, big order."

CIA operations chief **JAMES PAVITT** in an interview with Reuters published on 12 December 2000.

"Is counterterrorism a law enforcement or an intelligence mission? The answer is 'yes.'"

JOHN MacGAFFIN, former CIA operations officer and FBI consultant; quoted in *Government Executive* (February 2001).

"I can guarantee you that the millennium operation was an example where the cooperative counterterrorism system now in place was directly responsible for saving hundreds, and possibly even thousands, of American lives. Several tons of explosives were confiscated, as were well-designed plans with specific targets identified to kill the maximum number of Americans in as bloody and high-profile fashion as possible for the sake of the CNN cameras. This was an operation designed to shock the United States away from its geopolitical goals in the Middle East."

A senior CIA counterterrorism expert; quoted in *Government Executive* (February 2001).

"On orders from Director of Central Intelligence George J. Tenet, the CIA played an unusually high-profile role in supporting Scottish prosecutors in the Pan Am 103 case, providing dozens of secret operations cables and a foreign informer as a witness for the first time in a foreign court case. But the CIA's most important contribution in helping secure the conviction of a Libyan intelligence officer . . . may have come a decade ago when a CIA engineer was able to identify the timer that detonated a bomb aboard the 747 jetliner carrying 259 people."

VERNON LOEB, "A New Witness for the Prosecution," *Washington Post*, 4 February 2001.

"This is a time for all of us to come together, to bring all our talents to bear in a steely determination to do what we are called to do—protect our fellow citizens. It is our turn again to step up to a challenge, and to meet it as we meet all challenges: with commitment and courage. Put some spirit in your step, square your shoulders, focus your eyes. We have a job to do."

DCI **GEORGE TENET** in his message to CIA employees the day after the World Trade Center and Pentagon attacks, 12 September 2001.

"It is clear now, as it was on December 7th, 1941, that the United States is at war. The question is: with whom?"

Former DCI **R. JAMES WOOLSEY**; quoted in the *Washington Post*, 12 September 2001.

"Let's roll."

Unofficial slogan of CIA's Counterterrorist Center, in honor of a passenger on United flight 93 on 11 September, who said this to his wife in a cell phone conversation before joining a passenger revolt that apparently caused the hijacked jet to crash into an empty field in Pennsylvania.

"To us belongs the mission of unmasking the authors and sponsors of this evil. . . . The road ahead will be neither short nor easy. Yet it is one we must take without hesitation. Indeed, we have already taken the first steps, as a nation and as an agency. Part of our response can be seen around you: the task forces, the heightened tempo of our global operations, the surge in support and security. But there is a crucial part that cannot be seen: the determination that is cut into our hearts, the resolve that is burned into our minds."

DCI **GEORGE TENET** in his message to CIA employees on the National Day of Prayer and Remembrance, 14 September 2001.

"There is no such thing as 100 per cent intelligence, particularly in the field of counter-terrorism. What you get are snippets of intelligence, which you have to piece together. You are very lucky if you get intelligence about when, where and how."

Dame **STELLA RIMINGTON**, former head of MI5; quoted in the *Times* (London), 17 September 2001.

"The tragedy is at the moment that the single most important weapon for the United States of America is intelligence. It's the single most important weapon in this particular war, unlike other wars where it was overwhelming force or air force or something."

Senator **JOHN F. KERRY**, on *Face the Nation* with Bob Schieffer, CBS, 23 September 2001.

"Central Intelligence Agency,

I am a dentist. I am not a madman or a sadist. . . . I am volunteering my services for the interrogation of anybody you choose. . . . No person could withstand the dental pain I am capable of delivering. I will take any lie detector test and pass any background check. I will leave my job and go anywhere you would like. . . . I will be happy to talk with anyone about anything I can do for your agency."

> Résumé submitted to CIA, one of hundreds received daily in the wake of the 11 September attacks, and one of the most memorable. Lest this confirms malicious suspicions about both the dental and the intelligence professions, the reader can be assured that, despite the patriotic intent, this doctor was not hired.

"You can't penetrate a six-man [terrorist] cell when they're brothers and cousins—no matter how much Urdu you know."

> Senior CIA official, quoted by Seymour Hersh in the *New Yorker* (8 October 2001).

"The United States is combating terrorism with a rickety structure built a half century ago to contain global communism."

> **EVAN THOMAS**, "Handbook for the New War," *Newsweek* (8 October 2001).

"It's hard for your nice, suburban shopping-mall bred American to understand that some of the real threats, particularly in the terrorist area, are from people who actually believe in something. They believe in something enough to die for it. They'll go out and commit suicide with a bomb on them, which makes them very dangerous. How do you stop that, by tapping phones? (laughs) Probably the best way to stop it is by penetrating the organization, which is made up of people who aren't very nice."

> Former CIA counterintelligence chief **PAUL REDMOND** on the Discovery Channel's *Deadline Discovery*, 19 October 2001.

"Posing the question, 'Should we use the war against terrorism to get Saddam?' is parallel to asking, 'Should we, as of December 7, 1941, use the war against fascism to get Hitler?' . . . Give war a chance."

> Former DCI **R. JAMES WOOLSEY**; quoted in the *Washington Post*, 27 December 2001.

"The awful truth is that even the best intelligence systems will have big failures. The terrorists that intelligence must uncover and track are not inert objects; they are living, conniving strategists. They, too, fail frequently and are sometimes caught before they can strike. But once in a while they will inevitably get through."

> **RICHARD K. BETTS**, "Fixing Intelligence," *Foreign Affairs* (January–February 2002).

"How to use a code, security of operations, security plan, intelligence, intelligence gathering, surveillance, methods of communication, methods of opening envelopes, persuasion, planning for intelligence operations, recruitment, managing assets, choosing an asset."

> Al-Qaeda intelligence training topics from student jihadi notebooks found in a terrorist training camp south of Kabul; cited in the *New York Times*, 17 March 2002.

"It's like Elvis."

> Unidentified U.S. official on the 200 to 300 daily intelligence reports of a bin Laden sighting; quoted in *USA Today*, 12 April 2002.

"Victory in the new war on terror will depend little on the awesome American capacity to destroy the works of man, so evident in the first Gulf War, and depend much on outwitting a clandestine enemy who travels light and moves in secret. . . . But victory won't come from big intelligence, the kind Americans are best at—gathering so much information and acting on it in so timely a manner that the terrorists will be nailed as soon as they step out the door. Winning this contest requires an older kind of intelligence: the kind that grows out of deep knowledge of place, language, culture and people, and then getting the basic question right—knowing what the locals want to do on their own and putting that first."

THOMAS POWERS in the *Washington Post Book World*, 8 February 2004.

"The al-Qaeda leadership structure we charted after September 11 is seriously damaged—but the group remains as committed as ever to attacking the U.S. homeland. But as we continue the battle against al-Qaeda, we must overcome a movement —a global movement infected by al-Qaeda's radical agenda. In this battle we are moving forward in our knowledge of the enemy—his plans, capabilities, and intentions. And what we've learned continues to validate my deepest concern: that this enemy remains intent on obtaining, and using, catastrophic weapons. . . . Over the past 18 months, we have killed or captured key al-Qaeda leaders in every significant operational area. . . . We are creating large and growing gaps in the al-Qaeda hierarchy. And, unquestionably, brining these key operators to ground disrupted plots that would otherwise have killed Americans. . . . So we have made notable strides. But do not misunderstand me. I am not suggesting al-Qaeda is defeated. It is not. We are still at war. . . . Even catastrophic

attacks on the scale of 11 September remain within al-Qaeda's reach. Make no mistake: these plots are hatched abroad, but they target U.S. soil or that of our allies."

DCI **GEORGE TENET**, annual testimony on global threats before the Senate Select Committee on Intelligence, 24 February 2004.

"Thanks be to God, al-Qaeda remains on the battleground of the holy war, raising the banner of Islam in the face of the Zionist-Crusader campaign against the Islamic community. . . . Bush, fortify your defenses and intensify your security measures because the Muslim nation, which sent brigades to New York and Washington, has decided to send you one brigade after another, carrying death and seeking Paradise."

AYMAN AL-ZAWAHIRI, al-Qaeda leader under Osama bin Laden; broadcast quoted in the *New York Times*, 25 February 2004.

TIMELINESS

The Literary Spy once heard a policymaker (and dedicated consumer of intelligence) complain that a certain intelligence analysis was very nearly perfect: it was insightful, provocative, told him things he didn't know, was well argued and yet succinct. The problem? It arrived on his desk the day after decisions were made— decisions that involved U.S. military movements. Despite its considerable virtues, that report had not zero impact, but negative impact, as its arrival after the train had left the station only annoyed some important customers.

See also: Analysis & Analysts; Warning, Prediction, & Surprise

"Who knows what is sufficient time to make effective use of the news—that is as good a definition of 'real-time' intelligence, the gold standard of modern information practice, as is possible."

JOHN KEEGAN, *Intelligence in War* (2003).

"It is a fine thing to have immediate intelligence of everything, in order to attend to it as quickly as possible."

XENOPHON, *Cyropaedia* (4th century B.C.), on the Persians' use of a system of messengers on horseback; quoted in Dvornik, *Origins of Intelligence Services* (1974). It is these messengers that the Greek historian Herodotus (5th century B.C.) said were "stayed neither by snow nor rain nor heat nor darkness from accomplishing their appointed course with all speed"; cited in Dvornik. The Persians valued intelligence more than a public mail system.

"Hell is truth seen too late."

THOMAS HOBBES (1588–1679); quoted by Johnson, *Enemies of Society* (1977). Johnson's corollary is "Survival is falsehood detected in time."

"From our present position the intelligence is so long getting to hand that it is of no use by the time it reaches me."

General GEORGE WASHINGTON to his intelligence officer Major Benjamin Tallmadge, 1778; quoted in Dulles, *Great True Spy Stories* (1968).

"The good effect of Intelligence may be lost if it is not speedily transmitted."

General GEORGE WASHINGTON to Major Benjamin Tallmadge, 30 April 1781; cited in Knott, *Secret and Sanctioned* (1996).

"In view of the present situation, the presence in port of warships, airplane carriers, and cruisers is of utmost importance. Hereafter, to the utmost of your ability, let me know day by day. Wire me in

each case whether or not there are . . . balloons above Pearl Harbor [and] whether or not the warships are provided with antimine nets."

Japanese Foreign Ministry to Consul General at Honolulu, 2 December 1941; cited in Prange, *At Dawn We Slept* (1981). The message was intercepted by the U.S. Navy on 2 December but was not mailed to Washington until 11 December and was not translated until the 30th.

"At the present time there are no signs of barrage balloon equipment. In addition, it is difficult to imagine that they have actually any. . . . I imagine in all probability there is considerable opportunity left to take advantage for a surprise attack against these places. In my opinion the battleships do not have torpedo nets."

Japanese consulate in Honolulu to Tokyo, 6 December 1941; cited in Prange, *At Dawn We Slept* (1981). The U.S. Army did not decrypt and translate this cable until 8 December.

"It's a good thing that you got me started on this."

President FRANKLIN ROOSEVELT to William Donovan, at 2 A.M. on 8 December 1941; quoted in Polmar and Allen, *The Encyclopedia of Espionage* (1997). Donovan had persuaded Roosevelt to establish an executive intelligence organization, the Office of the Coordinator of Information, the previous July. As head of COI, Donovan the following year saw it become OSS.

"R&A's [OSS's Research and Analysis unit] first major act was to prepare, on two weeks' notice, complete area handbooks for the U.S. forces that invaded North Africa at the end of 1942."

ANGELO CODEVILLA, *Informing Statecraft* (1992).

"[On June 30, 1942] U-158 went on the air to report to [German Admiral Karl] Doenitz that he had nothing to report. [U.S. Navy direction-finding stations] plotted his position as latitude 33 degrees north, longitude 67 degrees 30 minutes west. This information raced through channels until it reached Lieutenant Richard E. Schreder, U.S.N., flying an antisubmarine patrol out of Bermuda. Ten miles from the plotted position he found the U-158 loafing on the surface, its crew sunbathing. One of Schreder's depth charges landed on the submarine's superstructure as it was trying to dive. It went down all right, but it never came up."

   DAVID KAHN, *The Codebreakers* (1996).

"Our Intelligence had played a vital part. The size and performance of the weapon, and the intended scale of the attack, were known to us in excellent time. This enabled our fighters to make ready. The launching sites and the storage caverns were found, enabling our bombers to delay the attack and mitigate its violence. Every known means of getting information was employed, and it was pieced together with great skill. To all our sources, many of whom worked amid deadly danger, and some of whom will be for ever unknown to us, I pay my tribute."

   WINSTON CHURCHILL on the British response to the German V-1 flying bomb campaign of the summer of 1944, in *Triumph and Tragedy* (1953).

"ORE 1 was produced by one man over a weekend to meet an unanticipated and urgent requirement."

   CIA official **LUDWELL MONTAGUE** on the first report of the newly created Central Intelligence Group, ORE 1, "Soviet Foreign and Military Policy," 23 July 1946; quoted in Jeffreys-Jones and Andrew, *Eternal Vigilance* (1997).

"If I need some material fast or an idea fast, CIA is the place to go. The State Department [approach] is four or five days to answer a simple yes or no."

   President **JOHN F. KENNEDY**; quoted in Andrew, *For the President's Eyes Only* (1995).

"I don't know of any single instance where intelligence was more immediately valuable than at this time."

   Former DCI **RICHARD HELMS** on the information provided by GRU officer Oleg Penkovskiy, which gave President Kennedy three extra days to formulate a response to the placement of Soviet missiles in Cuba; quoted in Schecter and Deriabin, *The Spy Who Saved the World* (1995).

"In October 1962, after the first photographs from the U-2 reconnaissance aircraft had confirmed the presence of Soviet ballistic missiles in Cuba, President John F. Kennedy had all the substantive knowledge he would ever have on the Soviet missile presence there. Yet Kennedy delayed the decision to confront the Cuban missile situation until he got close-up photographs. These additional photos not only cost the life of one pilot, but also a week's time. . . . Had the Soviets readied their missiles to fire, the U.S. might well have found the better pictures a poor substitute for timelier action based on poorer ones."

   ANGELO CODEVILLA, *Informing Statecraft* (1992).

"I'm leaving in 45 minutes to go brief the President of the United States, and I don't really know what I'm going to say yet."

   CIA senior analyst preparing to brief President George H. W. Bush the day before the Berlin Wall came down in November 1989; quoted in the *Washington Post*, 23 December 1999.

"In the CIA world nobody waits because everyone is on time, or has been kidnapped."

   WILLIAM F. BUCKLEY, JR., *Tucker's Last Stand* (1990). In the fictional CIA world, maybe.

"We just don't have an immediately responsive intelligence capability that will give the theater commander near real-time information that he personally needs to make a decision."

> General **NORMAN SCHWARZKOPF** in Senate testimony after the 1991 Gulf war with Iraq.

"A U.S. intelligence satellite took photographs of Muslim men held at gunpoint in open fields [in Bosnia] on 13 July 1995, but no one in Washington looked at the pictures for three weeks. In the meantime, a U-2 flight took pictures showing evidence of mass graves at the same site. When the matter was finally brought to President Clinton's attention on 4 August 1996, the victims were already dead and buried."

> **JOHN DIAMOND** in *National Security Studies Quarterly* (spring 1997).

"I alternate between being impressed with what intelligence can do, and depressed at how slow it can be."

> **MADELEINE ALBRIGHT**, U.S. ambassador to the United Nations, on intelligence support for war crimes investigations in the former Yugoslavia; quoted in the *New York Review of Books* (9 May 1996).

"The match is about to begin. . . . Tomorrow is zero hour."

> Arabic language messages intercepted by NSA on 10 September 2001 but not translated until 12 September; cited in the *Washington Post*, 20 June 2002.

TRAITORS IN THEIR OWN WORDS

The Literary Spy observes that traitors have a great deal in common with rapists and child molesters: both groups are overwhelmingly male, often grew up in dysfunctional families, and invariably come up with the most astonishing rationalizations for their behavior, as the reader will see. Another parallel: only a few end up coming to their senses, feeling remorse, and by so doing perhaps saving their souls.

See also: Counterintelligence; Espionage; Fighting the Cold War; Intelligence & American Culture; Treason & Betrayal

"If I point out a plan of cooperation by which [British general Sir Henry Clinton] shall possess himself of West Point, the Garrison, etc., etc., etc., twenty thousand pounds Sterling I think will be a cheap purchase for an object of so much importance."

> American General **BENEDICT ARNOLD**, commander of the fort at West Point, New York, to British Major John André in an enciphered letter of 15 July 1780; Sir Henry Clinton papers, Clements Library, University of Michigan.

"In the mid-1930s it seemed to me and to many of my contemporaries that the Communist Party and Russia constituted the only firm bulwark against fascism. . . . I was persuaded by Guy Burgess that I could best serve the cause of antifascism by joining him in his work for the Russians."

> **ANTHONY BLUNT**, the "Fourth Man" in Britain's Cambridge spy ring (of which Burgess was also a member), 1979; quoted in Andrew and Gordievsky, *KGB* (1990).

"It's like being a lavatory attendant; it stinks but someone has to do it."

> **DONALD MACLEAN**, British diplomat and member of the Cambridge spy ring, on spying for the Soviets; quoted in Andrew and Gordievsky, *KGB* (1990). The major difference is this: cleaning toilets is honorable work.

"Well, it's given me great pleasure to pass on the names of every MI5 officer to the Russians!"

> **ANTHONY BLUNT**, MI5 officer and Soviet spy, to an MI5 colleague during an unguarded moment, 1945;

quoted in Andrew and Gordievsky, *KGB* (1990). The colleague didn't follow up.

"The whole affair was extremely painful to me and I only embarked on it because I felt this was a contribution I could make to the safety of mankind."

British nuclear physicist **ALLAN MAY** admitting in 1946 that he had passed atomic bomb secrets to Moscow; quoted in Polmar and Allen, *Encyclopedia of Espionage* (1997).

"I used my Marxian philosophy to establish in my mind two separate compartments."

British physicist and traitor **KLAUS FUCHS** explaining how he could take an oath of allegiance to the British crown and still betray atomic secrets to the USSR; quoted in Dulles, *The Craft of Intelligence* (1963).

"It was always my intention, when I had helped the Russians to take over everything, to get up and tell them what is wrong with their own system."

British physicist and traitor **KLAUS FUCHS**; quoted in Robert Chadwell Williams, *Klaus Fuchs, Atom Spy* (1987). But, Klaus, once the Russians run everything, there is no alternative system, and certainly no getting up and telling them what they're doing wrong.

"We are the first victims of American fascism."

JULIUS and **ETHEL ROSENBERG** in a letter released on the day of their execution for espionage, 19 June 1953; cited in *Simpson's Contemporary Quotations* (1988).

"Suddenly I felt an upsurge of indignation and I wanted my interrogators and everyone else to know that I had acted out of conviction, out of a belief in Communism, and not under duress or for financial gain. This feeling was so strong that without thinking what I was doing I burst out, 'No, nobody tortured me! No, nobody blackmailed me! I myself approached the Soviets and offered my services to them of my own accord!'"

Former SIS officer and turncoat **GEORGE BLAKE** recounting his 1961 confession to MI5; quoted in West, *Faber Book of Espionage* (1993).

"All through my career, I have been a straight penetration agent working in the Soviet interest. . . . My connection with SIS must be seen against my total prior commitment to the Soviet Union which I regarded then, as I do now, the inner fortress of the world movement."

HAROLD "KIM" PHILBY, *My Secret War* (1968). Too bad Philby didn't live to see the demise of the "inner fortress" and the "world movement" alike.

"To betray you must first belong. I never belonged."

HAROLD "KIM" PHILBY in 1967; quoted in Knightley, *The Second Oldest Profession* (1988).

"I considered, and still consider now, that by this work I also served my own English people."

HAROLD "KIM" PHILBY, in 1980; quoted in Knightley, *The Second Oldest Profession* (1988). Philby "never belonged," but he says he "served" the English people. Which is it?

"I'm a naval officer. I'd like to make some money and I'll give you some genuine stuff in return."

JOHN A. WALKER, JR., chief warrant officer in the U.S. Navy, upon entering the Soviet embassy in 1967; quoted in Andrew, *The Mitrokhin File* (1999). Walker's spy ring —he recruited his brother and his son—passed naval communications codes to the Soviets until 1985.

"I have decided to name all the names and organizations connected with CIA operations and to reconstruct as accurately as possible the events in which I participated. I have also decided to seek ways of getting useful information on the CIA to revolutionary organizations that could use it to defend themselves better."

PHILIP AGEE, *Inside the Company* (1975).

"A spy is someone who regularly gets secret material, passes it on, takes orders, and gets paid for it. I have never been paid."

Canadian academic and ex-NATO official **HUGH HAMBLETON**, who was arrested in 1982 and sentenced to ten years in prison; quoted in Andrew, *The Mitrokhin File* (1999). Actually, Hambleton's KGB file shows he was four for four, having been paid $18,000 in the late 1970s.

"If I had access to a secret, color it gone."

JOHN A. WALKER, JR., the U.S. naval officer arrested in 1985 for espionage; quoted in Miller, *Spying for America* (1989).

"There was this piece of paper. I thought it might be worth $25,000. I took the avenue of least resistance. I didn't have the foggiest idea of how to rob a bank."

THOMAS PATRICK CAVANAUGH, the Northrup employee convicted in 1985 of trying to pass radar technology to the KGB; quoted in Taylor and Snow, "Cold War Spies," *Intelligence and National Security* (April 1997).

"Thanks for catching me before this got out of hand. . . . You caught me red-handed. . . . I'm going to be a model prisoner. . . . How much time do you think I'll get?"

Airman 1st class **BRUCE OTT** babbling to FBI agents upon his arrest in January 1986; quoted in Polmar and Allen, *Encyclopedia of Espionage* (1997). Ott was trying to sell information on the SR-71 Blackbird spyplane, and he got twenty-five years.

"I wasn't enjoying myself. I wanted to start somewhere else."

U.S. Army intelligence officer **MICHAEL PERI**, convicted in 1989 of passing classified information to East Germany; quoted in Polmar and Allen, *Encyclopedia of Espio-*

nage (1997). Peri got twenty-five years—now that's a change of scenery.

"I would love to say that I did what I did out of some moral outrage over our country's acts of imperialism or as a political statement or out of anger toward the CIA or even a love for the Soviet Union. But the sad truth is that I did what I did because of money and I can't get away from that."

Former CIA officer and turncoat **ALDRICH AMES**; quoted in Pete Earley, *Confessions of a Spy* (1997). Rare candor from Ames.

"In hindsight, my financial situation was not really as desperate as I had remembered. I could have gotten some guidance, but instead I convinced myself that I was in this huge hole and didn't have any choice but to do what I did. . . . The truth is that things weren't really that desperate, even though I convinced myself that they were. That says something about me. You see, I really didn't have to do what I did. I didn't!"

Former CIA officer and turncoat **ALDRICH AMES**; quoted in Pete Earley, *Confessions of a Spy* (1997).

"KGB is for me."

Slogan on sweatshirt worn by a smiling **HAROLD NICHOLSON**, then a CIA operations officer and traitor; photograph on a counterintelligence poster at CIA, March 2003. Nicholson is now in a federal penitentiary, where the dress code is not so cute.

"I reasoned I was doing this for my children—to make up for putting my country's needs above my family's needs and for failing to keep my marriage together for having done so."

Former CIA operations officer **HAROLD NICHOLSON** after being sentenced to twenty-four years in prison for spying for Moscow; quoted in the *Washington Post,* 6 June 1997. The reaction of U.S. Attorney Helen Fahey: "Where was Mr. Nicholson's concern for his children when he decided to spy? There is no question he did it for the money, but he was making more than $70,000 a year, and his children were hardly in danger of going without. What's more, an awful lot of people get divorced and don't spy for the Russians."

"I'm glad it's over."

NSA analyst **DAVID SHELDON BOONE** when arrested in October 1998 for espionage; quoted in the *Washington Post*, 27 February 1999. Boone was convicted and sentenced to twenty-four years in prison.

"I did what I did not to make money but to help prevent the defeat of a new system which had, at great cost, given ordinary people food and fares which they could afford, a good education and a health service. . . . In general, I do not agree with spying against one's country."

MELITA NORWOOD, an eighty-seven-year-old London woman who admitted to spying for Moscow from the 1940s through the early 1970s while a secretary for Britain's nuclear weapons research project; quoted in the *New York Times*, 13 September 1999. Treason for health care! Why did the USSR's spies never seem to know anything true about the USSR?

"I felt it would be better for humanity if the Communist system prevailed, that it would put an end to war. . . . I justified it in my mind by believing that I was helping, in a small way, in building a new society, in which there would be equality, social justice, no longer any war, no longer any national conflict. That was my dream . . . obviously it has failed. It has not been possible to build that society. . . . The reason I have worked out for myself is that a Communist society is in a way a perfect society, and we are not perfect people. . . . People have to change a great deal still."

Former British SIS officer and Soviet spy **GEORGE BLAKE**, interviewed on the PBS series *Red Files*, 1999. The murderous nature of communist regimes, which try to change people through gulags and secret police in order to attain the perfect society, eludes Blake.

"Deciding whether to trust or credit a person is always an uncertain risk, and in a variety of situations, a bad, lazy or just unlucky decision about a person can result not only in serious problems for the organization and its purposes, but in career-damaging blame for the unfortunate decision maker."

Convicted turncoat and former CIA officer **ALDRICH AMES**, letter from his cell at the Allenwood Federal Penitentiary to Stephen Aftergood of the Federation of American Scientists, November 2000; cited on the FAS website. Ames, you see, was not at fault; it was those who trusted him.

"I'm not an American in here."

Retired U.S. Army Colonel **GEORGE TROFIMOFF**, tapping his chest while speaking to what he thought were Russian intelligence officers; quoted in the *Miami Herald*, 21 June 2000. The "Russians" were FBI agents, and in June 2000 the FBI arrested Trofimoff for spying for Moscow.

"I have come about as close as I ever want to sacrificing myself to help you. . . . One might propose that I am either insanely brave or quite insane. I'd answer neither. I'd say, insanely loyal. . . . I decided on this course when I was 14 years old. I'd read Philby's book. . . . I have proven inveterately loyal and willing to take grave risks which even could cause my death. . . . I ask you to help me survive."

FBI affidavit citing alleged communications in March and November 2000 between FBI counterintelligence expert **ROBERT HANSSEN** and Russian intelligence officers; cited in the *New York Times*, 22 February 2001. Hanssen was charged with spying for Moscow for fifteen years.

"What took you so long?"

FBI officer **ROBERT HANSSEN** after being arrested by the FBI for passing secrets to Moscow, 18 February 2001; quoted in the *Washington Post Magazine* (6 January 2002).

"[FBI security] was pathetic. What I did was criminal, but it's criminal negligence. . . . Security was lax. . . . The only thing that possibly could have uncovered my espionage activities was a complete investigation of my financial positions and deposits to bank accounts. If I had been a more malevolent spy than I was, they would have had a very difficult time finding me. I could have been a devastating spy, I think, but I didn't want to be a devastating spy. I wanted to get a little money and to get out of it. . . . There is no way I can justify what I have done. It's criminal and deceitful and wrong and sinful."

> Former FBI officer and Russian spy **ROBERT HANSSEN** in a Justice Department panel report; quoted in the *New York Times* and in the *Washington Post,* 5 April 2002. If he had wanted to, he could have been a much more dangerous spy and not been caught.

"The only thing I missed was whipped cream, because I have a passion for whipped cream."

> Aging turncoat **GEORGE BLAKE** on living in Russia since he escaped from a British prison in 1966; quoted in Reuters, 14 May 2003.

TREASON & BETRAYAL

The Literary Spy does not suffer the canard that CIA and the KGB during the Cold War were engaged in exactly the same activity—namely, inducing the other's citizens to betray their country. No one should be confused: betraying the USSR and all it stood for was an act of courage in the service of humanity; betraying the United States—the best earthly hope for justice and peace, for all its shortcomings—was and remains an affront to reason and charity.

See also: Counterintelligence; Espionage; Fighting the Cold War; Intelligence & American Culture; Traitors in Their Own Words

"It may be that there is among you a man or woman, or a family or tribe, whose heart is already turning away from the Lord our God to serve the gods of those nations. It may be that there is among you a root sprouting poisonous and bitter growth."

> Deuteronomy 29:17–18 (Revised Standard).

"My companion stretched out his hand against his friends, he violated his covenant.
His speech was smoother than butter, but war was in his heart;
his words were softer than oil, yet they were drawn swords."

> Psalm 55 [54 LXX]:20–23 (Revised Standard).

"Trust no neighbor,
put no confidence in a friend;
do not open your mouth to the wife who shares your bed.
For . . . a person's enemies come from within the household itself."

> Prophecy of Micah (8th century B.C.) 7:5, 6 (Jerusalem Bible).

"The greatest crimes are committed not out of necessity, but from excess."

> **ARISTOTLE** (384–322 B.C.), *Politics,* Book II.

"A nation can survive its fools and even the ambitious. But it cannot survive treason from within. An enemy at the gates is less formidable, for he is known and he carries his banners openly against the city. But the traitor moves among those within the gates freely, his sly whispers rustling through all the alleys, heard in the very halls of government itself. For the traitor appears no traitor; he speaks in the accents familiar to his victims, and he wears their face and their garments and he appeals to the baseness that lies deep in the hearts of all men. He rots the soul of a nation; he works secretly and unknown in the night to undermine the pillars of a city; he infects the body politic so that it can no longer resist. A murderer is less to be feared. The traitor is the carrier of the plague."

> CICERO (106–43 B.C.) speaking to the Roman Senate, as recorded by Sallust in *The Catiline War* (c. 40 B.C.). This quotation is a favorite of CIA counterintelligence officers.

"And a man's foes shall be they of his own household."

> Matthew 10:36 (King James).

"If a man do levy war against our Lord the King in his realm or be adherent to the King's enemies in his realm, giving them aid and comfort in the realm or elsewhere."

> Statute of Edward III defining treason, 1351; cited in West, *The New Meaning of Treason* (1966).

"For Wales? Why, Richard, it profits a man nothing to give his soul for the whole world . . . but for Wales—?"

> THOMAS MORE (1478–1535) to his betrayer Richard Rich, who was paid for his perjury with Welsh revenues, in Robert Bolt's 1962 play *A Man for All Seasons*.

"*Protectio trahit subjectionem, et subjectio protectionem.* Protection draws allegiance, and allegiance draws protection."

> English jurist Sir EDWARD COKE, *Third Institute* (1644), citing the legal maxim that citizens enjoying the protection of the crown are obliged to maintain allegiance to it.

"This was the unkindest cut of all;
For when the noble Caesar saw [Brutus] stab,
Ingratitude, more strong than traitors' arms,
Quite vanquish'd him: then burst his mighty
   heart . . . great Caesar fell.
O, what a fall was there my countrymen!
Then I, and you, and all of us fell down,
Whilst bloody treason flourish'd over us."

> Mark Antony in WILLIAM SHAKESPEARE, *Julius Caesar* (1599), Act III, scene 2.

"France hath [in England] found out
A nest of hollow bosoms, which he fills
With treacherous crowns: and three corrupt
   men . . .
Have for the gilt of France (O guilt, indeed!)
Confirmed conspiracy . . ."

> WILLIAM SHAKESPEARE, *King Henry V* (1600), end of Act I.

"God quit you in his mercy! Hear your
   sentence.
You have conspired against our royal person,
Join'd with an enemy proclaim'd and from
   his coffers
Received the golden earnest of our death;
Wherein you would have sold your king to
   slaughter,
His princes and his peers to servitude,
His subjects to oppression and contempt
And his whole kingdom into desolation.
Touching our person seek we no revenge;
But we our kingdom's safety must so tender,
Whose ruin you have sought, that to her laws
We do deliver you. Get you therefore hence,
Poor miserable wretches, to your death:

The taste whereof, God of his mercy give
You patience to endure, and true repentance
Of all your dear offences! Bear them hence."

> King Henry to the traitors Cambridge, Scroop, and Grey in **WILLIAM SHAKESPEARE**, *King Henry V* (1600), Act II, scene 2.

"May he dream treason, and believe, that he
Meant to perform it, and confess, and die,
And no record tell why:
His sons, which none of his may be,
Inherit nothing but infamy."

> **JOHN DONNE**, "The Curse" (c. 1600).

"...[T]hough those that are betray'd
Do feel the treason sharply, yet the traitor
Stands in worse case of woe."

> **WILLIAM SHAKESPEARE**, *Cymbeline* (1609), Act III, scene 4.

"Treason doth never prosper: what's the
    reason?
For if it prosper, none dare call it treason."

> Sir **JOHN HARRINGTON**, *Of Treason* (1618).

"The treason past, the traitor is no longer needed."

> Spanish playwright **PEDRO CALDERÓN DE LA BARCA**, *Life Is a Dream* (1637).

"Though I love the treason, I hate the traitor."

> **SAMUEL PEPYS**, *Diary* entry for 7 March 1667 (Old Style).

"If this be treason, make the most of it."

> **PATRICK HENRY** speaking against the Stamp Act in the Virginia legislature, 1765; cited in Samuel Eliot Morison, *The Oxford History of the American People* (1965).

"I well remember, that I argued with my self, if a Man will risque his life in a Cause, he must be Friend to that cause; & I never suspected him after, till He was charged with being a Traytor."

> **PAUL REVERE** recalling how Dr. Benjamin Church had showed him bloodstained clothing the day after the Lexington battle; quoted in Bakeless, *Turncoats, Traitors and Heroes* (1998). Church was not at Lexington and had told his story to cover his activity as a British spy.

"The unhappy fate of *Thomas Hickey*, executed this day for mutiny, sedition, and treachery, the General hopes will be a warning to every soldier in the Army to avoid those crimes, and all others, so disgraceful to the character of a soldier, and pernicious to his country, whose pay he receives and bread he eats."

> General **GEORGE WASHINGTON**'s orders of the day for 28 June 1776, when a former member of his guard was hanged before 20,000 Continental troops; cited in Bakeless, *Turncoats, Traitors and Heroes* (1998). Hickey was found guilty of conspiring to kidnap or kill Washington.

"Surely a more active, a more spirited and more sensible officer fills no department of the army."

> General **GEORGE WASHINGTON** on Benedict Arnold before his treason; quoted in Miller, *Spying for America* (1989).

"Money is this man's god, and to get enough of it he would sacrifice his country."

> Prescient broadside against **BENEDICT ARNOLD**, published in April 1777 by a former Continental officer; cited in Bakeless, *Turncoats, Traitors and Heroes* (1998).

"We... assure him that in the very instance of receiving the Tidings or good offices we expect from him, our liberality will be evinced, that in case any partial but important blow shou'd by his means be Struck or aimed, upon the Strength of just and pointed information & cooperation, rewards equal or least to what what Such Service can be estimated at, will be given, But Shou'd the Abilities and Zeal of that able and enterprizing gentleman amount to the seizing of an Obnoxious band of men, to the delivering into our power or enabling us to attack to advantage by judicious assistance compleatly to defeat our enemy a numerous body, then wou[l]d the generosity of the nation exceed even his own most Sanguine hopes."

> British Major **JOHN ANDRÉ** to Joseph Stansbury, 10 May 1779, on the recompense that Benedict Arnold could expect for his treason. André was Sir Henry Clinton's chief of intelligence, and Stansbury was the go-between for Arnold. Sir Henry Clinton papers, Clements Library, University of Michigan.

"Treason, of the blackest dye, was yesterday discovered! General Arnold, who commanded at West Point, lost to every sentiment of honor, of public and private obligation, was about to deliver that important post into the hands of the enemy. Such an event would have given the American cause a deadly wound, if not a fatal stab. Happily, the treason has been timely discovered to prevent the fatal misfortune. The providential train of circumstances which led to it affords the most convincing proof that the liberties of America are the object of divine protection."

> General **NATHANIEL GREENE**, general order to the Continental Army on Benedict Arnold's treason, 26 September 1780; cited in Gorton Carruth and Eugene Ehrlich, *American Quotations* (1994).

"The personal bitterness of General Washington toward the traitor [Benedict] Arnold was without parallel in the life of that magnanimous man. Though the commander-in-chief had to approve many death sentences, Arnold was the only man he ever really wanted to hang. So savage was his

resentment that Lafayette, marching south against Arnold's Tories, carried positive orders: the traitor, if captured, would go instantly to the gallows."

> **JOHN BAKELESS**, *Turncoats, Traitors and Heroes* (1998). Washington tried several times to get the British to hand over Arnold but was refused. There were at least four schemes to kidnap Arnold, and Washington initiated one plot and perhaps the rest, but Arnold eluded him.

"Treason against the United States, shall consist only in levying war against them, or in adhering to their enemies, giving them aid and comfort."

> Constitution of the United States of America, Article III, section 3.

"The authorised maxims and practices of war are the satire of human nature. They countenance almost every species of seduction as well as violence; and the General that can make most traitors in the army of the adversary is frequently most applauded."

> **ALEXANDER HAMILTON** to John Laurens, 11 October 1789; cited in Knott, *Secret and Sanctioned* (1996).

"The unsuccessful strugglers against tyranny, have been the chief martyrs of treason laws in all countries. . . . We should not wish, then, to give up to the executioner, the patriot who fails and flees to us."

> Secretary of State **THOMAS JEFFERSON**, instructions to his negotiators regarding a treaty with Spain, April 1792; cited in Knott, *Secret and Sanctioned* (1996).

"I would sooner die a thousand deaths than betray a friend or be false to duty."

> Confederate courier Private **SAM DAVIS** when offered his freedom for information about Confederate forces; quoted in Polmar and Allen, *Encyclopedia of Espionage* (1997). Davis gave no information and was hanged as a spy in November 1863.

"Intelligence of all kind is to be obtained with money.... That an underpaid official, possibly burthened with a numerous family, or having a difficulty in making both ends meet, should have been tempted to betray his trust by the prospect of gaining a considerable sum of money does not astonish one very much. What, however, is really surprising is to find officers of high rank involved in a disgraceful transaction of this nature."

British Colonel **GEORGE FURSE**, *Information in War* (1895).

"How do your learn [your information]? By playing the imposter and winning your way into an unsuspecting confidence. To you friendship is a tool and honour a convenience. You cheat in every breath you draw. And what a man gives you in his innocence may bring him to the gallows. By God! I'd rather slit throats on a highway for a purse or two than cozen men to their death by such arts as yours."

Fictional Jacobite Scot to an English spy in **JOHN BUCHAN**, *The Path of the King* (1920).

"'Love of country!' There's a curious phrase. Love of a particular patch of earth? Scarcely. Put a German down in a field in Northern France, tell him that it is Hanover, and he cannot contradict you. Love of fellow-countrymen? Surely not. A man will like some of them and dislike others. Love of the country's culture? The men who know most of their countries' cultures are usually the most intelligent and the least patriotic. Love of the country's government? But governments are usually disliked by the people they govern. Love of country, we see, is merely a sloppy mysticism based on ignorance and fear."

Fictional German spy Moeller trying to induce an Englishman to treason in **ERIC AMBLER**, *Journey into Fear* (1940).

"I consider your crime a crime worse than murder. ... By your betrayal, you have undoubtedly altered the course of history to the disadvantage of our country.... It is not in my power, Julius and Ethel Rosenberg, to forgive you. Only the Lord can find mercy for what you have done.... You are hereby sentenced to the punishment of death."

Judge **IRVING R. KAUFMAN**, 5 April 1951, sentencing convicted Soviet spies Julius and Ethel Rosenberg; cited in Virginia Carmichael, *Framing History: The Rosenberg Story and the Cold War* (1993). The Rosenbergs were executed in the electric chair at the Sing Sing federal prison in New York on 19 June 1953.

"The Rosenberg case still haunts American history, reminding us of the injustice that can be done when a nation gets caught up in hysteria."

New York Times editorial, "Remembering the Rosenbergs," 19 June 2003.

"Despite all the evidence, the Rosenbergs' most fervent supporters are once again trying ... to reopen the case to promote the idea of the couple's essential innocence and moral heroism.... Let us not be mistaken. Julius and Ethel Rosenberg did show courage and commitment—on behalf of Josef Stalin, one of the last century's most brutal and vile dictators.... Let us be clear. Julius and Ethel Rosenberg and the members of their spy network were Soviet—not American—patriots who betrayed their own country for an illusion. They acted with courage and strength on behalf of a corrupt and evil cause."

Historian **RONALD RADOSH** in the *Los Angeles Times*, 19 June 2003.

"No task was too hard for him; no hours too long. He gained the reputation of one who would always take over a tangled skein from a colleague who was sick, or going on leave, or simply less zealous. In this way he was able to manoevre himself into the hidden places that were of the most interest to the NKVD."

> British diplomat **ROBERT CECIL** on his traitorous colleague Donald Maclean, who spied for Moscow from the late 1930s until he fled Britain in May 1951; quoted in Polmar and Allen, *Encyclopedia of Espionage* (1997).

"Guy Burgess . . . gave me a feeling, such as I have never had from anyone else, of being morally afflicted in some way. His very physical presence was, to me, malodorous and sinister, as though he had some consuming illness. . . . The impression fit in well enough with his subsequent adventures."

> Former SIS officer **MALCOLM MUGGERIDGE** on meeting Guy Burgess, Soviet spy in the Cambridge ring, during the London blitz; in *Chronicles of Wasted Time: The Infernal Grove* (1973). Memo to counterintelligence: traitors *stink*.

"The psychotic will very readily take sides against his own country. He is as if commanded by Heaven to be a prop for any neighboring power which desires to swallow up his fatherland. He hates the people around him, because he hates the real world."

> **REBECCA WEST**; quoted in the *New York Times Magazine*, 19 August 1951. The Soviets, in their paranoiac suppression of dissent, would declare dissidents psychotics and would incarcerate them in mental hospitals.

"I hate the idea of causes, and if I had to choose between betraying my country and betraying my friend, I hope I should have the guts to betray my country."

> **E. M. FORSTER**, *Two Cheers for Democracy* (1951). That choice is a cause of sorts, too, a curious one that considers betraying one's country something utterly disconnected from the betrayal of friends, family, neighbors, co-workers, the local grocer, the postman, etc., etc.

"[With the 1961 conviction of British civil servant Harry Houghton, who passed naval technology to the Soviets,] we were stumped by a new situation. Now the insignificant human being and the unimpressive material object could inflict crucial danger on Britain. . . . The only way that Houghton, a homekeeping native mediocrity, could have been a menace in the past would have been for him to pretend to be someone of greater importance. . . . He could not conceivably have been a peril to the English defences against the Armada, nor to Nelson's fleet. . . . But today there are millions of people as commonplace as Houghton who, by their employment in certain factories or offices, have access to documents which can deliver us over to death. . . . What is new is that the small fry also have the power of betrayal, having now access to secrets which can be betrayed and are worth betraying. Science, adding to our armoury, continually demands more mechanics and more clerks, and with every demand makes the problem of security more difficult to solve."

> **REBECCA WEST**, *The New Meaning of Treason* (1966).

"You cannot leave to a scientist the discretion of what should be classified."

> Federal District Judge **TERRY J. HATTER** at the sentencing of Peter H. Lee, a Department of Energy scientist who pleaded guilty in 1998 to passing classified information to Beijing; quoted in the *New York Times*, 13 March 1999.

"When you betray somebody else, you also betray yourself."

> **ISAAC BASHEVIS SINGER**, interviewed in the *New York Times Magazine*, 3 December 1978.

"I, Oleg Vladimirovich PENKOVSKIY, Colonel in the Soviet Army, do hereby on this 21st day of April in the year 1961, offer my services totally and unreservedly to the Governments of the United States of America and Great Britain. I undertake to serve these Governments loyally and faithfully and to carry out to the best of my ability the orders transmitted to me by the representatives of these Governments.... Henceforth I consider myself to be a soldier of the free world fighting for the cause of humanity as a whole and for the freeing from tyrannical rule of the people of my homeland Russia."

Soviet GRU Colonel **OLEG PENKOVSKIY** agreeing to spy for the United States and the United Kingdom; in Schecter and Deriabin, *The Spy Who Saved the World* (1995).

"Cheats, liars and criminals may resist every blandishment while respectable gentlemen have been moved to appalling treasons by watery cabbage in a departmental canteen."

JOHN LE CARRÉ [David Cornwell], *The Spy Who Came in from the Cold* (1963).

"Blackmail based on the threatened exposure of illicit sexual acts is a powerful instrument when applied to men of certain nationalities, not so when applied to others.... I will refrain here from naming those countries which fall into the one category or the other."

Former DCI **ALLEN DULLES**, *The Craft of Intelligence* (1963). This is regrettably less true today in the West.

"A good agent is one whose vital statistics are the following: he works, for example, in a military department and holds a middle-ranking but key position giving him access to information; he doesn't aspire to higher office, has a chip on his shoulder about being a failure; he drinks (an expensive habit);

he has a weakness for the fair sex (which is also not cheap); he is critical of his own government."

KGB officer **KONON MOLODY**, who, under the name Gordon Lonsdale, ran agents in the West in the 1950s and 1960s; cited in Andrew and Gordievsky, *KGB* (1990).

"The Soviets will search out the misfits and the disgruntled, people in trouble, people with grievances and frustrated ambitions, with unhappy domestic lives—neurotics, homosexuals and alcoholics. Such people sometimes need only a slight nudge, or a slight inducement to fall into the practice of treason."

Former DCI **ALLEN DULLES**, *The Craft of Intelligence* (1963).

"A private grievance is never so dangerous as when it can be identified with a matter of principle."

British historian **J. M. THOMPSON**; quoted in Schecter and Deriabin, *The Spy Who Saved the World* (1995).

"The traitor's offense is that he conspires against the liberty of his fellow countrymen to choose their way of life."

REBECCA WEST, *The New Meaning of Treason* (1966).

"A man who will take it upon himself to betray his government because he is uniquely convinced that he is right and they are wrong is by definition unbalanced, although he may also be a martyr."

EDWARD CRANKSHAW, foreword to Oleg Penkovskiy, *The Penkovskiy Papers* (1966).

"The ideological traitor ... is most often a dedicated zealot whose deeds of betrayal are in his own eyes not really violations of an ethical code but actions in the cause of humanity.... Those who worship only at the altar of History tend to regard all means of serving it as admissible."

SIDNEY HOOK, introduction to Rebecca West, *The New Meaning of Treason* (1966).

"Who among us has not committed treason to something or someone more important than a country?"

GRAHAM GREENE, novelist and former SIS officer, in his apologetic introduction to British traitor and Soviet spy Harold "Kim" Philby's *My Secret War* (1968). It evidently did not occur to Greene that treason to a country *is* treason to what it stands for, which can be much higher and more important indeed.

"I liked [Philby]. I've often asked myself what I would have done if I'd discovered he was a secret agent at the time. . . . I think, perhaps, if in a drunken moment he had slipped a hint, I would have given him twenty-four hours to get clear and then reported him."

GRAHAM GREENE after Harold "Kim" Philby was exposed; quoted in Polmar and Allen, *Encyclopedia of Espionage* (1997).

"You choose your side once and for all—of course, it may be the wrong side. Only history can tell that."

GRAHAM GREENE in his novel *The Confidential Agent* (1939); cited by Harold "Kim" Philby by way of explanation for Philby's decision to "stick it out" as a spy for the USSR despite the excesses of Stalinism. History has made it abundantly clear Philby chose the wrong side. Philby, *My Secret War* (1968).

"[Philby had] an ability to inspire loyalty and even affection in his staff. He was one of those people who were instinctively liked but more rarely understood. . . . Outwardly he was a kindly man. Inwardly he must have been cold, calculating and

cruel—traits which he cleverly concealed from his friends and colleagues."

NICHOLAS ELLIOT, SIS colleague of the turncoat Harold "Kim" Philby, *Never Judge a Man by His Umbrella* (1991).

"Donald Maclean, Guy Burgess, Kim Philby, Anthony Blunt, John Cairncross and their hangers-on were elegant young men of good family, educated at expensive schools and leading colleges, who had been seduced by the warped logic of Marxism to become Soviet agents before they joined the British Foreign Office or intelligence services. . . . The Cambridge spies were not only traitors; they were also, in different but closely similar ways, monsters of egotism. No wonder that they remained for so long objects of fascination to the prurient."

JOHN KEEGAN, *Intelligence in War* (2003).

"There is no place on earth for this traitor and spy who sold out his motherland."

Soviet prosecutor recommending the death sentence for Oleg Penkovskiy, the GRU colonel who spied for the United States and Great Britain, 11 May 1963; quoted in Schecter and Deriabin, *The Spy Who Saved the World* (1995). Penkovskiy was executed five days later.

"Treason is a charge invented by winners as an excuse for hanging the losers."

Quip by the character **BENJAMIN FRANKLIN** in the musical *1776* (1972). The line may say more about the early 1970s than it does about Franklin, who probably never said it.

"England, so tolerant of eccentricity, has hated two species: traitors, and people unkind to animals."

WILLIAM F. BUCKLEY, JR., *Saving the Queen* (1976). The latter more than the former.

"Betrayal, in one form or another, is at the very heart of the world of intelligence."

THOMAS POWERS, *The Man Who Kept the Secrets* (1979).

"That is what is at the core of the intelligence officer's world—betraying another person's trust in you."

Former CIA operations officer and Soviet spy **ALDRICH AMES**; quoted in Earley, *Confessions of a Spy* (1997). Most U.S. intelligence officers would disagree: intelligence is more a matter of keeping promises.

"We could have read all correspondence between U.S. naval headquarters and your subs across the world. We could have delivered a pre-emptive strike."

Former KGB general **OLEG KALUGIN** on the damage to U.S. security from the treason of naval officer John Walker, who spied for Moscow from the late 1960s until 1985; quoted in *U.S. News and World Report* (3 February 2003).

"The suspicion or actual evidence that your own intelligence service has a traitor within the house is the most miserable event that can happen to a service. All secret intelligence services have been through this trauma. It destroys morale, upsets judgements, destroys personal relationships, and gravely threatens inter-allied confidence."

SIS official **JOHN BRUCE LOCKHART**, 1984; quoted in West, *Faber Book of Espionage* (1993).

"History is so full of high-level intelligence officials who actually worked for the other side that one is forced to conclude that whether or not top intelligence jobs *attract* the disloyal, they surely offer *incentives* to disloyalty."

ANGELO CODEVILLA, *Informing Statecraft* (1992).

"[Aldrich] Ames was, and is, a malignant betrayer of his country, who killed a number of people who helped the United States and the West win the Cold War. He killed them just as surely as if he pulled the trigger of a revolver put to their heads in the basement of the Lubyanka prison—the classic method of KGB execution. They, our agents in the Cold War against the Soviet Union, risked their lives, helped keep you free, and died because this warped, murdering traitor wanted a bigger house and a Jaguar."

DCI **R. JAMES WOOLSEY**, address at the Center for Strategic and International Studies, Washington, D.C., 18 July 1994.

"We knew that CIA always eyed a prospective recruit carefully . . . our adversaries would study one of our officers for months before deciding to approach him. They would ask the same questions we asked. Does this man have financial problems? Does he have a mistress? Is he drinking heavily? Did he lose a briefcase with documents? Is his wife sleeping with a Great Dane?"

Former KGB general **OLEG KALUGIN**, *The First Directorate* (1994). The last question refers to a case Kalugin relates in which a Soviet officer was vulnerable to foreign recruitment because it turned out his wife, in fact, was . . . ohnevermind.

"When recruiting agents, case officers are guided by the factors most likely to motivate people to become spies. These can be summed up by the acronym MICE—money, ideology, compromise, and ego."

H. KEITH MELTON, *The Ultimate Spy Book* (1996).

"As communism and the Soviet bloc began to come apart, our side expected that KGB agents, having lost their moral and political raison d'être, would begin to offer themselves to the CIA in large numbers. That happened. What we did not anticipate, however, was that the same phenomenon would affect a number of our own operatives. . . . When the excitement and intrigue of subverting the monolithic, closed and threatening Soviet system ended, a few of the gung-ho performers turned to the only equally satisfying and more dangerous alternative—betrayal of their own country."

> **JAY TAYLOR**, former Deputy Assistant Secretary of State for Intelligence and Research, in the *Washington Post*, 22 December 1996.

"Ames is in nothing like gulag."

> Russian arms control expert **VLADIMIR POTASHOV**, who spent seven years in the Russian gulag after his betrayal by Aldrich Ames; quoted in the *Chicago Tribune*, 7 March 1997.

"Although the Ames case may be big at the moment, it will simply take its place with some of the more serious ones that the Allies had since World War II."

> Former DCI **RICHARD HELMS** at a conference on "The Origins and Development of the CIA," sponsored by CIA's Center for the Study of Intelligence, March 1994.

"[Aldrich Ames] is a humanitarian. How did he hurt your country? He didn't betray any of your secrets, he simply told us who were the traitors in our midst. I consider him a very fine fellow."

> **VIKTOR CHERKASHIN**, the KGB official who handled Ames; quoted in Earley, *Confessions of a Spy* (1997).

"I knew the people I identified would be arrested and put in prison. [Ames] knew the people he identified would be arrested and shot. That is one of the differences between us."

> **OLEG GORDIEVSKY**, the former KGB chief in London who spied for SIS; quoted in Earley, *Confessions of a Spy* (1997). Gordievsky was one of the few agents betrayed

by Ames who eluded execution when he was spirited out of Moscow while under KGB surveillance.

"Ames is a monumental embarrassment. . . . Let's not make it complicated. Ames is simply a common murderer, who did so for money. He had no fig leaf of real or imagined ideological identification with the Soviet Union or Russia, unlike the Rosenbergs, [Morris] Cohen, and others. Ames should have been executed not because he is a traitor, but because he is guilty of murder."

> Former senior CIA operations officer **DUANE CLARRIDGE**, *A Spy for All Seasons* (1997).

"Clyde Lee Conrad was . . . perhaps the most damaging case in US history, even more damaging than Rick Ames. Ames gave up CIA assets and information on the KGB; Conrad, during the 10 years he worked for Warsaw Pact intelligence services, gave up everything: military operations plans, communications, order of battle information and weapons data. If NATO and the US had gone to war with the Warsaw Pact during this time, we would have lost."

> Former CIA counterintelligence chief **PAUL REDMOND** on the U.S. Army sergeant who spied for Czechoslovakia and Hungary from 1975 to 1985.

"Nearly all motivations [for treason] can be grouped into four categories—money, ideology, ingratiation, and disgruntlement. . . . Our data reveal that financial gain has been the primary motivation in 55.4 percent of all cases of Cold War espionage, by far the single most prevalent motive."

> **STAN TAYLOR AND DANIEL SNOW**, "Cold War Spies," *Intelligence and National Security* (April 1997).

"Tomorrow's traitors are more likely to be driven to betray not from ideological convictions but from whining complaints about poor pension provisions or underfunded performance-related pay."

ANDREW ROBERTS in the *Sunday Times* (London), 25 May 1997.

"They go to church every Sunday—if that means anything."

Neighbor of FBI agent **ROBERT HANSSEN**, arrested on charges of spying for Moscow for fifteen years; quoted by the Associated Press, 20 February 2001. In this case, it did not.

"Never go home at night without worrying where the mole is."

Former DCI **RICHARD HELMS** to Robert Gates when Gates became DCI; quoted by Gates in the *New York Times,* 23 February 2001.

"Bob Hanssen is a very kind, thoughtful, intelligent person with some tremendous problems who did some terrible things. People are not either good or bad, evil or benign. Most of us, like Bob Hanssen, are mixtures."

Psychiatrist **ALEN SALERIAN** on the former FBI agent who spied for Moscow; quoted in the *Washington Post,* 3 July 2001. Actually, the fallen nature of the world leaves almost all of us "mixtures." But most of us do not end up betraying country, spouse, children, and employer.

"Treason reflects man's renunciation of his humanity."

SADDAM HUSSEIN in a broadcast to Iraqi military commanders; quoted in the *Washington Times,* 3 February 2003.

U

- **United Nations**
- **Unsavory Characters**
- **U.S. Intelligence "Community"**

UNITED NATIONS

No matter what one thinks of the United Nations—stepping-stone to peaceful world government, feckless debating society that should be disbanded, or something in between—it stands to reason that the U.N., like any organization, needs reliable information. The Literary Spy professes realism about the U.N.: inasmuch as it can help the United States advance its global interests—interests that are the world's best hope for freedom and justice—the U.N. has its uses, and to that degree, and no further, U.S. intelligence can and should help.

See also: Weapons of Mass Destruction

"How under the sun they expect to function without it, I can't imagine and am sure they will have to come to it in the end."

> Former U.S. Army intelligence chief **RALPH VAN DEMAN** in 1917 on the need for the new League of Nations to have its own international intelligence service; cited in Miller, *Spying for America* (1989).

"The CIA was formed in the immediate wake of the United Nations and with the support of people

conditioned by their own activities in the UN sphere. . . . An important probability [is] that the formation of the CIA in 1947 was an assertion of national sovereignty at a time when it could be seen to be under challenge not just from the USSR and Britain, but from the United Nations as well."

> **RHODRI JEFFREYS-JONES**, in Jeffreys-Jones and Andrew, *Eternal Vigilance* (1997).

"In early 1985 [CIA studied] the Soviet presence at the United Nations. One of our analysts tracked every one of the eight hundred Soviet nationals assigned to the UN and showed how they reported directly to Soviet diplomatic missions and were part of an organization managed by the Soviet Foreign Ministry, intelligence services, and the Central Committee of the Communist Party. The [CIA] argued persuasively that about one-fourth of the Soviets in the UN Secretariat were intelligence officers."

> Former DCI **ROBERT GATES**, *From the Shadows* (1996). This assessment is consistent with the testimony of former Soviet intelligence officers.

"An insult to the intelligence of the [Security] Council."

> U.S. Ambassador to the United Nations **MADELEINE ALBRIGHT** on Iraq's claim that U.N. inspectors were conducting intelligence activities; quoted in the *New York Times*, 13 June 1996.

"United States officials said today that American spies had worked undercover on teams of United Nations arms inspectors ferreting out secret Iraqi weapons programs."

> *New York Times*, 7 January 1999.

"We are not an espionage service, a spy organization. We want intelligence from member governments, but it must be a one-way street. We will tell them what we are interested in."

> **HANS BLIX**, chief U.N. weapons inspector, insisting that his inspection teams will not provide intelligence to the United States or other nations; quoted in the *Los Angeles Times*, 23 October 2002.

"We worked with the [U.N.] inspectors [in Iraq], giving them leads, helping them fight Saddam's deception strategy of 'cheat and retreat.'"

> DCI **GEORGE TENET**, remarks at Georgetown University, 5 February 2004.

UNSAVORY CHARACTERS

In this section the Literary Spy advances the not very trenchant idea that the best sources of information about bad things are often the worst sort of people. Though logically banal, this obvious idea is difficult to understand for many well-meaning humanitarians, members of Congress, and journalists.

See also: Covert Action; Espionage; Fighting the Cold War; Terrorism

"When Joshua dispatched two case officers to Jericho, it didn't matter that the agent they recruited there to establish a safe house was a prostitute."

> Former DCI **R. JAMES WOOLSEY**; quoted in the *Los Angeles Times*, 22 September 1996.

"They say best men are moulded out of faults;
And, for the most, become much more the
  better
For being a little bad."

> **WILLIAM SHAKESPEARE**, *Measure for Measure* (1604), Act V, scene 1. The ones who are at least a little bad make the better sources.

"Ambiguous characters."

> **GEORGE WASHINGTON**'s term for those people— such as black marketeers—he regretted it was necessary to employ for intelligence work; see Knott, *Secret and Sanctioned* (1996).

"With the approval of President Polk and Secretary of War William Marcy, General Winfield Scott [during the Mexican War] created the Mexican Spy Company, composed of 'contraguerrillas' or 'contrabandistas'—native Mexicans, many of whom were bandits acting as insurgents for the U.S. Army. . . . Approximately two hundred bandits were recruited to assist the American military, many of whom had been 'liberated' from Mexican jails and asked to reward their liberators by providing them with intelligence services."

> **STEPHEN KNOTT**, *Secret and Sanctioned* (1996).

"We must bear in mind that we shall have to deal with individuals whose ideas, principles, and manner of acting are entirely at variance with our notions; with whom to excel in astuteness and deception is a commendable ambition. We shall have to treat with men whose life is full of trickery and

intrigue, who can assume such an amicable attitude, and make such a show of favourable dispositions, as will often mislead the most wary. . . .
When we are precluded from obtaining information by any other means, we must discard all
question of morality. We must overcome our feelings of repugnance . . . because it is imposed on
us by sheer necessity."

British Colonel **GEORGE FURSE**, *Information in War* (1895).

"**I**'d put Stalin on the OSS payroll if I thought it
would help us defeat Hitler."

OSS director **WILLIAM DONOVAN**; quoted in Russell,
The Secret War (1981). Or Stalinists, as it transpired.

"**W**e were more interested in his power than in
his morals. We did not expect to find this SS General a Sunday School teacher."

ALLEN DULLES, then OSS station chief in Bern, on his
contact in March 1945 with Nazi SS General Karl Wolff
regarding the surrender of German forces in Italy; quoted
in Grose, *Gentleman Spy* (1994).

"**T**here are few archbishops in espionage. He's
on our side and that's all that matters. Besides,
one needn't ask him to one's club."

ALLEN DULLES on working with senior Nazi intelligence
officer Reinhard Gehlen; quoted in Miller, *Spying for
America* (1989).

"**Y**ou give us information on which decisions
affecting the course of history are made. Your product must be as perfect as is humanly possible—
though the material you must work with is far from
perfect."

President **LYNDON JOHNSON** on CIA's twentieth anniversary, 18 September 1967; cited in CIA; *"Our First Line
of Defense"* (1996).

"**W**hat evil thing have you done today?"

Admonition on identification card for the evil T.H.R.U.S.H.
organization, from the 1960s U.S. television spy series
The Man from U.N.C.L.E. Okay, U.N.C.L.E. stands for
United Network Command for Law and Enforcement
(yes, so technically it's not intelligence). T.H.R.U.S.H.
originally didn't mean anything but later was dubbed
the Technical Hierarchy for the Removal of Undesirables
and the Subjugation of Humanity. In Arabic, "al-Qaeda."

"**G**entlemanly behaviour can put any who practise
it in intelligence at a disadvantage."

SIS scientific chief **R. V. JONES** in 1978; cited in West,
Faber Book of Espionage (1993).

"**I**t is a sad fact of life that at no point in the Cold
War were there many democratic governments in
the Third World. As a result, during the global
struggle against the Soviet Union, CIA (and the
United States more broadly) ended up with some
strange and unsavory bedfellows. Most you
wouldn't bring home to Mom."

Former DCI **ROBERT GATES**, *From the Shadows* (1996).

"**I**t is true that the information needed to detect
and foil terrorist plots or nuclear blackmail is not
always available from people with clean hands.
But there should be a flat prohibition on the recruitment of criminals and thugs except in cases
vital to American national security."

New York Times editorial, 18 August 1996. "Not *always*
available"? And which "terrorist plots or nuclear blackmail" are *not* "vital to American national security"?

"**T**he queasiness that so many Americans have
about having foreign bad guys on the CIA's payroll
is understandable—but it is wildly inconsistent.
No one objects when the FBI pays Mafia informants generously for leads, and the less said about
the Drug Enforcement Agency's informants, the

better. In the intelligence business, you need the help of criminals to catch criminals. If the CIA is so fortunate as to snag an informant inside Hezbollah, he's going to be a ruthless terrorist, or else he's not going to be there. The same goes for sources, or potential sources, inside Saddam Hussein's circle; or in the presidential palace in North Korea. They'll all be human-rights violators, perhaps environmental polluters, too."

> JOSEPH FINDER, "Hiring Bad Guys," *Los Angeles Times*, 22 September 1996. They probably abuse animals, too.

"There will be those who say the CIA should not employ anybody who might be a criminal. This would be naïve. . . . In the jargon of intelligence, what the CIA is doing is simply good tradecraft. It is weighing value for risk—something every organization should do, not just the clandestine service of the CIA."

> *Boston Globe* editorial, 6 March 1997. A viewpoint unusual for the *Globe*.

"[CIA] refuses to recognize that the 'friends' it acquired during the Cold War are now the principal enemies of the policies of democracy and human rights."

> Former State Department official RICHARD NUCCIO; quoted in *The Nation* (19 May 1997).

"No one seriously disputes that [CIA] should collect secret intelligence on terrorism, proliferation of weapons of mass destruction, narcotics, and international crime. . . . The perpetrators of [these] activities are a collection of dangerous, wicked individuals, groups, and nation-states. The handwringers claim that by collecting information on these targets, one perforce becomes 'one of the bad guys.' This is absurd. But you do have to deal with undesirables to penetrate the organizations or states involved to obtain information. Mother Teresa, for all her wisdom, unfortunately doesn't have it. . . . You can't have it both ways."

> Former senior CIA operations officer DUANE CLARRIDGE, *A Spy for All Seasons* (1997).

"Everybody wants to do the intelligence business according to antiseptic procedures. Unfortunately, the people who usually have helpful intelligence aren't people you'd want to have your daughter marry. They don't seem to have a problem with the DEA and FBI dealing with scumbags, but Americans expect CIA operatives to confine themselves to contacts with Boy Scouts."

> Former senior CIA operations officer DUANE CLARRIDGE; quoted in *Insight* (17 August 1998).

"Bad folks are the folks we need to penetrate bad organizations."

> Former Senator SAM NUNN, Democrat from Georgia; quoted in the *Wall Street Journal*, 13 September 2001.

"If you are trying to recruit inside Hezbollah or Osama bin Laden's organization, there is nobody in there but human rights violators."

> Former DCI R. JAMES WOOLSEY; quoted in the *Washington Times*, 13 September 2001.

"To be able to penetrate [terrorist] organizations, you need to have on the payroll some very unsavory characters if, in fact, you're going to be able to learn all that needs to be learned in order to forestall these kinds of activities. It is a mean, nasty, dangerous, dirty business out there, and we have to operate in that arena. . . . If you're going to deal only with officially approved, certified good guys, you're not going to find out what the bad guys are doing."

Vice President **RICHARD CHENEY** on NBC's *Meet the Press*, 16 September 2001.

"When does the end justify the means in spying on terrorists? And just exactly what does 'unsavory' mean? . . . Few Americans would have opposed using 'unsavory' foreign agents to learn about plans for the Sept. 11 attacks. And yet, how far does the US want to go in paying such agents again and again, perhaps supporting their evil deeds elsewhere? . . . US spies cannot operate in an 'all rules are off' environment without eroding America's moral standing against the use of terror."

Christian Science Monitor editorial, 18 September 2001.

"Look, we recruited assholes. I handled bad guys. But we don't recruit people from the Little Sisters of the Poor—they don't *know* anything."

Former CIA operations officer; quoted in **SEYMOUR HERSH**, "What Went Wrong: The CIA and the Failure of American Intelligence," the *New Yorker* (8 October 2001).

"I don't think that saying the agency did outrageous things in Chile and the Bay of Pigs disqualifies me from saying the agency needs good intelligence. . . . It's a tough world. You have to rely on unsavory people."

SEYMOUR HERSH; quoted in *The Nation* (31 December 2001). Not sure to whom Hersh is referring.

"There is no principle in the espionage canon more important than that an intelligence service must know—or at the least continuously strive to know—exactly with whom it is dealing."

Former DCI **RICHARD HELMS**, *A Look over My Shoulder* (2003).

U.S. INTELLIGENCE "COMMUNITY"

The Literary Spy here puts quotation marks around "Community" because the various agencies that compose U.S. intelligence seem more like the squabbling states of the Articles of Confederation than the more centralized and efficient entity under the U.S. Constitution. Still, for all their problems in cooperation and communication, U.S. intelligence agencies are better off in this regard than those of almost any other country.

See also: FBI & Law Enforcement; Military & Naval Intelligence; Origins of Central Intelligence; Prescriptions

"In carrying out your newly assigned duties as DCI, it is my wish that you serve as the government's principal foreign intelligence officer, and as such that you undertake as part of your responsibility, the coordination and effective guidance of the total U.S. foreign intelligence effort. As the government's principal intelligence officer, you will assure the proper coordination, correlation, and evaluation of intelligence from all sources and its prompt dissemination to me and to other recipients as appropriate. . . . I shall expect you to delegate to your principal deputy, as you may deem necessary, so much of the direction of the detailed operation of the Agency as may be required to permit you to carry out your primary task as DCI."

President **JOHN F. KENNEDY** to DCI John McCone, 16 January 1962; cited in Leary, *The Central Intelligence Agency* (1984).

"There are some advantages to having the kind of centralized intelligence setup which CIA represents. Without this centralization, for example, there would be continuous disasters in the field of clandestine collection activities. Competing intelligence services would inevitably stumble over each other with ridiculous and dangerous consequences. Without this centralization, intelligence priorities would be developed by each individual service and department, instead of by the whole of the United States Government. . . . Finally, without this centralization CIA would not have been able to bring about the truly *national* intelligence estimates that it has . . . in which all the different services and departments have educated each other. And the alternative would have been competing estimates that would have torn policy asunder."

ROGER HILSMAN, *To Move a Nation* (1967).

"Clearly, the CIA is not the hub, nor is its Director the head, of the vast U.S. intelligence community."

VICTOR MARCHETTI and **JOHN MARKS**, *CIA and the Cult of Intelligence* (1974).

"The United States is further today from having truly centralized intelligence collection or analysis than it has been since Pearl Harbor."

ALLAN GOODMAN, "Dateline Langley: Fixing the Intelligence Mess," *Foreign Policy* (winter 1984–85).

"The authors of the National Security Act of 1947 empowered the DCI to control the dissemination of all information collected by all collection agencies. The authors did not want another Pearl Harbor, [but] they hedged their bet. They created a tension by stipulating that departmental intelligence agencies would have the right to disseminate 'departmental' intelligence. They intended that the departmental organizations, like the NSA, would be free to work on matters of departmental concern and to share their conclusions within their departments. It was not intended that such agencies send their analyses to the White House or anywhere else outside their departments. What's

needed is clarification: Is the dissemination by the collection agencies to be controlled by the DCI or [by] the Secretary of Defense?"

Former DCI **STANSFIELD TURNER**, *Secrecy and Democracy* (1985). Depends on whom you ask.

"'Intelligence community' has always been an unduly cozy phrase. Not only does it imply a degree of happy cooperation among the various bodies charged with obtaining and analyzing intelligence when cooperation has not been the invariable norm, but it also suggests a concert of purpose and interest that simply does not exist."

ROBIN W. WINKS, *Cloak and Gown: Scholars in the Secret War, 1939–1961* (1987).

"Intelligence planning in the U.S. intelligence community often resembles, ironic as it may seem, management practices in the Soviet Union: planning is highly centralized; planners are supposed to respond to the needs of the consumers but are in fact insulated from them; and there is often little connection between satisfying the needs of an intelligence consumer and being rewarded for one's efforts. . . . [Likewise,] intelligence consumers are often left dissatisfied with the intelligence product they receive, and a good amount of intelligence production in the United States appears to go unread. . . . Overly rigid, centralized intelligence planning has some of the same shortcomings as does centralized economic planning: it may seem like a rational way to distribute resources in an optimal fashion, but over the long run it stifles the creativity an intelligence organization requires."

BRUCE BERKOWITZ and **ALLAN GOODMAN**, *Strategic Intelligence* (1989).

"During the Gulf War, I almost needed three different in-boxes for the bomb damage assessments from CIA, DIA, and CENTCOM."

> RICHARD HAASS, chief of State Department's policy planning staff, at a CIA symposium on DI analysis, 8 November 2002. Haass was NSC director for the Mideast from 1989 to 1993.

"It is not too gross an exaggeration that when considering any given threat DIA will overestimate, CIA will underestimate, and INR will blame the U.S. for it."

> ANGELO CODEVILLA, *Informing Statecraft* (1992).

"Our stuff is better [than CIA's]. I'm partisan, but I think our stuff is better because it's written by individuals, not groups. It doesn't have to be cleared."

> Assistant Secretary of State for Intelligence and Research TOBY GATI; quoted in *Foreign Service Journal* (February 1996).

"The organization and leadership of the intelligence community is a structural oddity. It is something of a holding company, with the DCI more 'first among equals' than someone with true executive authority. He is the principal adviser to the president on matters of intelligence, but his relations with the heads of other key intelligence organizations are more that of a colleague than a boss. As a result, the primary tool available to the DCI is persuasion."

> Council on Foreign Relations, *Making Intelligence Smarter* (1996).

"Today's model for intelligence—how it is organized and how it operates—is an artifact from an earlier age. Even the name 'Central Intelligence Agency' is reminiscent of the New Deal era, when large, powerful national bureaucracies were the accepted way of getting things done efficiently. When the CIA was established, the notion of a centralized bureaucracy for producing information was at least as plausible as, say, a centralized bureaucracy for economic planning."

> BRUCE BERKOWITZ, "Information Age Intelligence," *Foreign Policy* (summer 1996).

"CIA is the small teat on the very large udder of the intelligence community. If a tsunami rolled over it today we wouldn't miss it."

> WILLIAM ODOM, former NSA director, quoted in *Insight* (17 August 1998).

"After five decades of helter-skelter growth, the system is unwieldy and disjointed. There are no less than 13 different intelligence agencies affiliated with five different cabinet departments. Any company that was organized that way—with overlapping divisions, ambiguous lines of authority and no cohesive strategy—would go out of business. In the intelligence world, it's business as usual."

> *New York Times* editorial, "The Spy Puzzle," 4 November 2001.

"There is always tension between State, Defense, the national security advisor and the CIA, and this is creative tension. We each bring different perspectives and we bring different constituencies to the process."

> Secretary of State COLIN POWELL on CNN's *Larry King Live*, 26 November 2001.

"Early reports on the formation of the Office of Homeland Security indicated that the new director, Tom Ridge, will be responsible for coordinating all of the agencies in the intelligence community. This is odd, because that was precisely the function for which the office of Director of Central Intelligence was created in the National Security Act of 1947."

RICHARD K. BETTS, "Fixing Intelligence," *Foreign Affairs* (January–February 2002).

"I want one dog to kick, but when it comes to intelligence, I have to go down to the pound!"

Attributed to Secretary of Defense **DONALD RUMSFELD**; in Washingtonpost.com, 15 July 2002.

W

- Warning, Prediction, & Surprise
- Weapons of Mass Destruction
- Women

WARNING, PREDICTION, & SURPRISE

Many people—not just Congressmen and journalists—seem to think that U.S. intelligence should be able to predict or warn of events with a high degree of accuracy and precision alike (getting the details right not only on what will happen but when). To them, failure to bat somewhere near 1.000 indicates scandalous incompetence and warrants the rolling of heads and massive reorganizations. The Literary Spy responds with the reminder that the myth of the omniscient spymaster, like that of Santa Claus, is a juvenile fantasy. U.S. intelligence officers are uncommonly learned, dedicated, and accomplished, but they necessarily retain their frail and fallible humanity. Besides, wouldn't anyone very good at predictions prefer to be rich?

See also: Analysis & Analysts; Critics & Defenders; Current Intelligence; Estimates; Failures; Ignoring Bad News; Limits of Intelligence; Successes; Timeliness

"What is called 'foreknowledge' cannot be elicited from spirits, nor from gods, nor by analogy with past events, nor from calculations. It must be obtained from men who know the enemy situation."
   SUN TZU, *The Art of War* (6th century B.C.).

"Let none say, 'it cannot happen here.'"
   SOPHOCLES, *Ajax* (5th century B.C.). He also said (in *Acrisius*), "To him who is in fear, everything rustles."

"War, as the saying goes, is full of false alarms."
   ARISTOTLE, *Nichomachean Ethics* (c. 340 B.C.).

"In the beginning the world was so made that certain signs come before certain events."
   CICERO, *Divinatione* (1st century B.C.).

"Behold, an angel of the Lord appeared to Joseph in a dream and said, 'Rise, take the child and his mother, and flee to Egypt, and remain there until I tell you; for Herod is about to search for the child, to destroy him.' And he rose and took the child and his mother by night, and departed to Egypt."
   Matthew 2:13–14 (Revised Standard).

"In [4th-century] Britain there was a special [Roman] force known as the *Areani* whose purpose was to 'range over long distances' in order to provide advance warning of trouble threatening among the tribes neighboring the frontier."

N. J. E. AUSTIN and **N. B. RANKOV**, *Exploratio* (1995).

"There is less danger in fearing too much than too little."

Sir **FRANCIS WALSINGHAM** (1532–1590), intelligence chief for Queen Elizabeth I; cited in *U.S. News and World Report* (27 January 2003).

"The French, advis'd by good intelligence
Of this most dreadful preparation,
Shake in their fear; and with pale policy
Seek to divert the English purposes."

WILLIAM SHAKESPEARE, *King Henry V* (1600), end of Act I.

"This bodes some strange eruption to our
   state . . .
If thou art privy to thy country's fate,
which, happily, foreknowing may avoid,
   O speak!"

Soldier in **WILLIAM SHAKESPEARE**, *Hamlet* (1601) to the ghost of the late King of Denmark, Act I, scene 1.

"Say from whence
You owe this strange intelligence."

Macbeth after hearing the witches' prophecy that he would be king, in **WILLIAM SHAKESPEARE**, *Macbeth* (1606), Act I, scene 2.

"It is pardonable to be defeated, but never to be surprised."

Variously attributed to Frederick the Great, Napoleon, the U.S. Cavalry, and others.

"Often do the spirits
Of great events stride on before the events,
And in today already walks tomorrow."

SAMUEL TAYLOR COLERIDGE, *Wallenstein* (1800).

". . . [I]f the British march
By land or sea from the town tonight,
Hang a lantern aloft in the belfry arch
Of the North Church tower as a signal light—
One if by land, two if by sea,
And I on the opposite shore will be,
Ready to ride and spread the alarm."

HENRY WADSWORTH LONGFELLOW, "Paul Revere's Ride," from *Tales of a Wayside Inn* (1863).

"Every intelligence agrees that General Howe now, no doubt with his whole force, is immediately to take the field in quest of this army."

General **JOHN ARMSTRONG** of the Continental Army, 29 November 1777, regarding the excellent spy network the Americans worked against the British in Philadelphia; cited in Bakeless, *Turncoats, Traitors and Heroes* (1998).

"The ideal reasoner would, when he has once been shown a single fact in all its bearings, deduce from it not only all the chain of events which led up to it, but also all the results which would follow from it. . . . The observer who has thoroughly understood one link in series of incidents, should be able to accurately state all the other ones, both before and after."

Sherlock Holmes in Sir **ARTHUR CONAN DOYLE**, "The Five Orange Pips" (1891). The key words here are "in all its bearings" and "thoroughly." In real life, of course, it's deucedly difficult.

"'Is there any other point to which you would wish to draw my attention?'

[Sherlock Holmes:] 'To the curious incident of the dog in the night-time.'

'The dog did nothing in the night-time.'
'That was the curious incident.'"

Sir **ARTHUR CONAN DOYLE**, "The Adventure of Silver Blaze" (1892). Here Holmes points to the absence of an expected event—in this case, the dog that did not bark —as a positive warning.

"Don't ever prophesy. For if you prophesy wrong, nobody will forget it; and if you prophesy right, nobody will remember it."

Humorist **JOSH BILLINGS** [Henry Wheeler Shaw], *Affurisms* (1865).

"We never sleep."

Slogan of **ALLAN PINKERTON**'s National Detective Agency, founded in 1850 and still doing business as Securitas Security Services USA.

"Am I surrounded by dolts? Why have I never been told that we have no spies in England?"

KAISER WILHELM on learning that his First Army was surprised by British troops at Mons, August 1914; quoted in Haswell, *Spies and Spymasters* (1977).

"If you do not think about the future, you cannot have one."

English novelist and Nobel Prize winner **JOHN GALSWORTHY**, *Swan Song* (1928).

"Those who knew most were least scared."

WINSTON CHURCHILL on the wartime value of intelligence; quoted in Stafford, *Churchill and Secret Service* (1998).

"The security of the U.S. Pacific Fleet while in Pearl Harbor, of the Pearl Harbor Naval Base itself, has been under renewed study by the Navy Department and forces afloat for the past several weeks. This reexamination has been, in part, prompted by the increased gravity of the situation with re-spect to Japan, and by reports from abroad of successful bombing and torpedo plane attacks on ships while in bases. If war eventuates with Japan, it is believed easily possible that hostilities would be initiated by a surprise attack upon the Fleet or the Naval Base at Pearl Harbor."

Secretary of the Navy **FRANK KNOX**, letter to Secretary of War Henry Stimson, 24 January 1941; cited in Prange, *At Dawn We Slept* (1981). Knox went on to say that the possibilities of a "major disaster to the fleet of naval base warrant taking every step, as rapidly as can be done, that will increase the joint readiness of the Army and Navy to withstand a raid of the character mentioned above." The naval authorities in Pearl Harbor received Knox's letter on 5 February 1941.

"National sanity would dictate against such an event, but Japanese sanity cannot be measured by our own standards of logic. . . . Japan's resort to measures which might make war with the United States inevitable may come with dramatic and dangerous suddenness."

U.S. Ambassador to Tokyo **JOSEPH GREW**, cable to State Department, 3 November 1941; cited in Prange, *At Dawn We Slept* (1981).

"As relations between Japan and the United States are most critical, make your ships in harbor report irregular, but at a rate of twice a week. Although you are no doubt aware, please take extra care to maintain secrecy."

Japanese Foreign Ministry cable to the consulate in Honolulu, 15 November 1941; cited in Prange, *At Dawn We Slept* (1981). The U.S. Navy finished decrypting and translating this message on 3 December 1941.

"This dispatch is to be considered a war warning. Negotiations with Japan looking toward stabilization in the Pacific have ceased and an aggressive move is expected within the next few days."

U.S. Navy communication to Pacific commands, 27 November 1941; cited in *Studies in Intelligence* 44/2 (2000).

"We have been receiving reports from you on ship movements, but in the future will you also report even when there are no movements."

> Japanese Foreign Ministry cable to the consulate in Honolulu, 29 November 1941; cited in Prange, *At Dawn We Slept* (1981). The U.S. Navy had decrypted and translated this message by 5 December 1941.

"Army and Navy Intelligence officers in Washington [before the Pearl Harbor attack] were somewhat in the position of a woman with a sick child trying to take instructions from a doctor over the telephone while the neighbors are shouting contrary advice in her ear, dogs are barking, children screaming, and trucks roaring by the house. The noise overwhelmed the message."

> **SAMUEL ELIOT MORISON**, *The Two-Ocean War* (1963).

"Japan is the most vulnerable nation in the world to attack and blockade. She is without natural resources. Four years of war already have left deep scars. She has a navy, but no air arm to support it."

> *Honolulu Advertiser* editorial, 3 December 1941; cited in Prange, *At Dawn We Slept* (1981).

"What a target that would make!"

> Lieutenant General **WALTER SHORT**, commander of the U.S. Army in Honolulu, to his intelligence chief while driving by Pearl Harbor on the evening of 6 December 1941; cited in Prange, *At Dawn We Slept* (1981).

"It is probable that the capability of the U.S.S.R. to develop weapons based on atomic energy will be limited to the possible development of an atomic bomb to the stage of production at some time between 1950 and 1953."

> Central Intelligence Group, *Soviet Capabilities for the Development and Production of Certain Types of Weapons and Equipment*, 31 October 1946; reproduced in Kuhns, *Assessing the Soviet Threat* (1997). This CIG report illustrates

how CIA's immediate predecessor was concerned about a "nuclear Pearl Harbor."

"I remember the rage I used to feel when a prediction went awry. I could have shouted . . . 'Behave, damn you, behave as you ought!' Eventually I realized that the subjects were always right. It was I who was wrong. I had made a bad prediction."

> Behavioral psychologist **B. F. SKINNER**, *Walden Two* (1948).

"The substantive problem [of warning] may emerge as a result of the reflections of a man employed to do nothing but anticipate problems. In actual fact, the intelligence business employs all too few of such men. . . . A Pearl Harbor disaster is to be ascribed in no small measure to the absence of some unpleasant and insistent person, who, knowing of the growing animus of Japan, kept asking when is the attack coming, where is it coming, and how is it coming?"

> **SHERMAN KENT**, *Strategic Intelligence* (1949).

"The northern Korean regime is . . . capable, in pursuit of its major external aim of extending control over southern Korea, of continuing and increasing its support of the present program of propaganda, infiltration, sabotage, subversion, and guerrilla warfare against southern Korea. . . . At the same time the capability of the northern Korean armed forces for both short- and long-term overt military operations is being firmly developed . . . as presently constituted and supported, [they] have a capability for attaining limited objectives in short-term military operations against southern Korea, including the capture of Seoul."

> CIA estimate *Current Capabilities of the Northern Korean Regime*, 19 June 1950; reproduced in Kuhns, *Assessing the Soviet Threat* (1997). The North Koreans invaded the South

five days after this report was published. CIA, however, had not given a clear warning.

"In cooperation with the Department of Defense, there has been established the Interdepartmental Watch Committee. Its function is to provide constant and periodic review of indications of possible enemy action. The Central Intelligence Agency also maintains a twenty-four hour watch on behalf of the Agency. . . . [However,] despite the utmost vigilance, despite watch committees, and all of the other mechanics for the prompt evaluation and transmission of intelligence, there is no real assurance that, in the event of sudden undeclared hostilities, certain advance warning can be provided."

DCI **WALTER BEDELL SMITH**, memorandum to the National Security Council, 23 April 1952; reproduced in Warner, *CIA Under Truman* (1994).

"We *must* find ways to increase the number of hard facts upon which our intelligence estimates are based, to provide better strategic warning, to minimize surprise in the kind of attack, and to reduce the danger of gross overestimation or gross underestimation of the threat. To this end, we recommend the adoption of a vigorous program for the extensive use, in many intelligence procedures, of the most advanced knowledge in science and technology."

Killian Committee, commissioned by President Eisenhower to investigate the possibility of a surprise attack, report of 14 February 1955; cited in Polmar and Allen, *Encyclopedia of Espionage* (1997). The report confirmed Eisenhower's views on gathering strategic intelligence: he had already approved the U-2, and the following year it began flying over the Soviet Union.

"You can only predict things after they have happened."

EUGENE IONESCO, *Rhinoceros* (1960).

"At this morning's private session, despite the violence and inaccuracy of Mr. Khrushchev's statements, I replied to him in the following terms . . . the position of the United States was made clear with respect to the distasteful necessity of espionage activities in a world where nations distrust each other's intentions. We pointed out that these activities had no aggressive intent but rather were to assure the safety of the United States and the free world against surprise attack by a power which boasts of its ability to devastate the United States and other countries by missiles armed with atomic warheads."

President **DWIGHT EISENHOWER**, statement at the Paris Summit, 16 May 1960; quoted in CIA, *"Our First Line of Defense"* (1996). CIA's U-2 had been shot down over the USSR on 1 May. Khrushchev no doubt loved Ike's reference to "the free world."

"Intelligence bought the time [Kennedy] needed."

CIA operations chief, later DCI, **RICHARD HELMS**, on the Cuban missile crisis; quoted in Andrew, *For the President's Eyes Only* (1995).

"Successful warning is essentially a two-fold process; if warning is to be effective, not only must the alert be given, but the consumer of intelligence must accept the fact that he has in fact been warned."

DCI **JOHN McCONE** in 1962; quotation in CIA's Historical Intelligence Collection.

"I'm so tired of listening to McCone say he was right, I never want to hear it again."

McGEORGE BUNDY, President Kennedy's national security advisor; quoted in Jeffreys-Jones, *The CIA and American Democracy* (1989). DCI McCone, contrary to everyone in the Kennedy administration and to CIA estimates, believed in August and September 1962 that the USSR would try to place strategic missiles in Cuba. This quotation shows they don't like it when you're right, either.

"Quite simply, it is hard to predict an irrational, or unsound, or simply unique initiative by another party."

RAYMOND GARTHOFF, *Reflections of the Cuban Missile Crisis* (1987).

"Surprise, when it happens to a government, is likely to be a complicated, diffuse, bureaucratic thing. It includes neglect of responsibility, but also responsibility so poorly defined or so ambiguously delegated that action gets lost. It includes gaps in intelligence, but also intelligence that, like a string of pearls too precious to wear, is too sensitive to give to those who need it. It includes the alarm that fails to work, but also the alarm that has gone off so often it has been disconnected. It includes the unalert workman, but also the one who knows he'll be chewed out by his superior if he gets higher authority out of bed. It includes the contingencies that occur to no one, but also that everyone assumes somebody else is taking care of. It includes straightforward procrastination, but also decisions protracted by internal disagreement. It includes, in addition, the inability of individual human beings to rise to the occasion until they are sure it is an occasion—which is usually too late."

THOMAS E. SCHELLING, foreword to Roberta Wohlstetter, *Pearl Harbor: Warning and Decision* (1962).

"Since World War II the methods and systems for obtaining military intelligence and, what is more important, evaluating it and seeing that the proper people get it, have been vastly improved. But let us not forget that we were surprised by the North Koreans in June 1950; surprised when China entered the war later that year; surprised in 1961 by discovery of the attempt to overthrow Castro in Cuba; surprised by the building of the East Berlin wall. In a tense international situation . . .

it is important not only to gather intelligence but to see that the right people get it, and to have it evaluated intelligently. It is vital to ascertain not only the capabilities of a potential enemy but his intentions."

SAMUEL ELIOT MORISON, *The Two-Ocean War* (1963).

"Human experience largely consists of
   surprises
Superseding surmises."

OGDEN NASH; cited in Heinl, *Dictionary of Military and Naval Quotations* (1966).

"Any coup d'etat I have heard about isn't going to happen."

Attributed to **SHERMAN KENT**, chief of CIA's Office of National Estimates.

"To warn of everything is to warn of nothing."

Saying among CIA's warning staff.

"You warned me—but you did not persuade me."

Saying attributed to former Secretary of State **HENRY KISSINGER**; another favorite of the CIA warning staff.

"I think the one game that is played in intelligence agencies after an event is to look around for the one report that predicted it, and I guarantee you, you can find it. There is always one report somewhere that predicts an event is going to happen. It may be lost in a hundred that predict it won't . . . but, after a particular event, you can always find one report."

DCI **WILLIAM COLBY**, remarks at CIA, 1975.

"Ring the gong for me."

DCI **RICHARD HELMS**'s frequent admonition to new CIA chiefs of station not to let Washington be surprised by a coup; quoted in Phillips, *The Night Watch* (1978).

"[Enemy] documents call for all-out, coordinated attacks throughout South Vietnam utilizing both military and political means to achieve 'ultimate victory' in the near future. . . . The one conclusion that can be drawn from all of this is that the war is probably nearing a turning point and that the outcome of the 1967–1968 winter-spring offensive will in all likelihood determine the future direction of the war."

> Cable from CIA's Saigon Station, 8 December 1967; cited in Ford, *CIA and the Vietnam Policymakers* (1998). The warning was discounted at CIA Headquarters, and the Tet Offensive the following month was almost a complete surprise.

"The Egyptian-Syrian attack [of 6 October 1973] was a classic of strategic and tactical surprise. . . . Every Israeli (and American) analysis before October 1973 agreed that Egypt and Syria lacked the military capability to regain their territory by force of arms; hence there would be no war. The Arab armies must lose; hence they would not attack. The premises were correct. The conclusions were not."

> **HENRY KISSINGER**, *Years of Upheaval* (1982).

"In April 1977 the CIA made public an unclassified version of a study which concluded that before 1985 the Soviet Union would face a shortfall in domestic petroleum production [that] would necessitate net imports of oil. While this prediction was not borne out by later events, the study may not have been in error, even if the projection was. By 1978 it was evident that the Soviets were undertaking vigorous remedial actions to prevent the predicted shortfall. It is possible that the CIA report jarred the Soviet leaders into action to keep the prediction from coming true."

> **RAYMOND GARTHOFF**, *Detente and Confrontation* (1985).

"After every crisis there surfaces in the press some obscure intelligence report or analyst purporting to have predicted it, only to have been foolishly ignored by the policymakers. What these claims omit to mention is that when warnings become too routine they lose all significance; when reports are not called specifically to the attention of the top leadership they are lost in bureaucratic background noise, particularly since for every admonitory report one can probably find also its opposite in the files."

> **HENRY KISSINGER**, *White House Years* (1979).

"The Soviet leaders may be on the threshold of a decision to commit their own forces to prevent the collapse of the [Afghan] regime and to protect their sizable stakes in Afghanistan."

> DCI **STANSFIELD TURNER**, memorandum to President Carter, 14 September 1979; cited in Gates, *From the Shadows* (1996).

"In reading the history and Agency-conducted postmortems of past international crises in a search for what might have gone wrong when intelligence failed to provide advance warning, I was struck by one common denominator running through the incidents in which the Agency performed inadequately. From the Soviet invasion of Czechoslovakia in 1968 to the Egyptian-Syrian attack on Israel in 1973, to the secret deployment of Cuban troops in Angola in 1975, there were in each case bits and pieces of information collected in advance that should have alerted the intelligence analysts and policymakers to what was coming. But to find these germs of wheat in the abundant chaff and to understand their significance in time to affect decision making was no easy job in the face of a preponderance of evidence pointing the other way. More important, these intelligence gems usually contradicted the prevailing assumptions of the policymakers.... There was a persistent tendency to assume that our opponents on the world stage would act in a logical and rational manner, like Western statesmen, and intelligence that went against this prevailing preconception tended in some cases to be discounted."

> Former senior CIA official **CORD MEYER**, *Facing Reality* (1980).

"On balance, this activity does not necessarily indicate that a Soviet invasion is imminent. We believe that these preparations suggest, however, that a Soviet intervention is increasingly likely."

> CIA warning memorandum, 2 December 1980, hedging its bets on a Soviet invasion of Poland; quoted in Gates, *From the Shadows* (1996). One internal CIA training course used this quotation as an example of how *not* to warn.

"The primary problem in major strategic surprises is not intelligence warnings but political disbelief."

> **RICHARD K. BETTS**, *Surprise Attack* (1982).

"Only a fool would make predictions—especially about the future."

> Attributed variously to movie mogul Samuel Goldwyn and to Danish physicist Niels Bohr.

"Prophets of doom are nearly always right."

> **PATRICK O'BRIAN**, *The Far Side of the World* (1984).

"We cannot foresee the time, but we can see the tendency between social aspirations and regime control eventually to confront the regime with challenges to its political control that it cannot contain."

> CIA briefing on the USSR to President Reagan, November 1985; quoted by former DCI Robert Gates, conference

on "US Intelligence and the End of the Cold War," Texas A&M University, 19 November 1999.

"Every international problem is affected by the attitudes and actions of the United States. Unless you know what the United States intends to do in a crisis you cannot begin to predict how it will turn out."

> Former DDI **R. JACK SMITH**, *The Unknown CIA* (1989).

"His apparent impatience and determination to push reform simultaneously on many fronts could alienate so many groups that even Gorbachev's political skills will not be able to prevent a coalition from forming against him.... A growing perception within the leadership that reforms are threatening the stability of the regime could lead to a conservative reaction.... Should a sharp polarization of the leadership prevent it from acting resolutely to deal with a growing crisis, the prospects would increase for a conservative coup involving a minority of Politburo members supported by elements of the military and the KGB."

> CIA analysis, "Rising Political Instability Under Gorbachev," January 1989; cited in *Studies in Intelligence* 39/3 (fall 1995).

"By early 1989, CIA was warning policymakers of the deepening crisis in the Soviet Union and the growing likelihood of a collapse of the old order.... Preventing surprises was CIA's mission and, with respect to the Soviet collapse, it fulfilled that mission more than two years ahead of time. That was two more years warning than Gorbachev got. Prophesy beyond that was not in CIA's charter and, in the real world, speculation of a Soviet internal apocalypse much before then would have been ignored, if not ridiculed, by decision-makers."

> Former DCI **ROBERT GATES**, "CIA and the Cold War," address at the University of Oklahoma, 12 September 1997.

"Mysteries occur when all [intelligence] information—known and secret—still cannot determine a most likely estimate, or cannot determine which of two or more estimates is more likely.... Suppose, for example, that an intelligence analyst were tasked to predict the flip of a fair coin. He could report that there is a 50 percent probability of the coin landing 'heads' and an equal probability of it landing 'tails,' but, assuming the coin is indeed fair, no amount of analysis or information—chemical analysis of the coin's composition, aerodynamic modeling, radar analysis of the coin's trajectory, etc.—would enable him to predict the outcome."

> BRUCE BERKOWITZ and ALLAN GOODMAN, *Strategic Intelligence* (1989).

"When we saw [Iraqi] troops move forward toward Kuwait, we advised our senior policymakers that we anticipated an invasion within 12 to 24 hours. It actually came in four. While we cannot always tell the precise moment when someone will act, we can, through analytical methods, determine what is likely to happen."

> DCI WILLIAM WEBSTER, 8 February 1991; in *1991 Speeches*.

"Did the CIA tell President Bush on Inauguration Day that on Dec. 25, 1991, the Soviet Union was going to disappear? No. And if it had? The policymakers would have treated it as nothing more than an informed guess, perhaps better than many, but nevertheless a guess."

> BRENT SCOWCROFT, former national security advisor to President George H. W. Bush, letter to the *Washington Post*, 12 January 2000. Scowcroft is too kind: that kind of prediction rightly would have been met with the ridicule that attempts at such confident precision deserve.

"The widespread use of electronic communications and the interception thereof have not made politico-military surprises less prevalent in the modern world than before. Quite the contrary. The U.S. has been surprised by every major world event since 1960."

> ANGELO CODEVILLA, *Informing Statecraft* (1992). Codevilla's statement is surprising.

"Warning must lobby for attention. This does not work through anonymous, routine warning reports."

> PAUL WOLFOWITZ, Undersecretary of Defense for Policy, 1989–93; quoted in *Studies in Intelligence* 39/1 (spring 1995).

"As a general rule, the best way to achieve complete strategic surprise is to commit an act that makes no sense or is even self-destructive."

> Maxim on DCI Robert Gates's desk; cited in Andrew, *For the President's Eyes Only* (1995).

"It has become fashionable for historians and commentators, armed with perfect hindsight . . . to look back on the '20s and deprecate the statesmen of that period for not seeing what was coming—German rearmament and Nazism, Japanese militarism, Soviet imperialism. How could we have been so blind? But even Winston Churchill, who was more prescient than virtually anyone in the world on this subject, didn't see then what was coming. In the '20s most of these developments were clouds no larger than a hand on the horizon. Until the despair in the aftermath of the 1929 Depression substantially boosted his following, for example, Hitler was just a crazy painter and failed putschist with a limited number of followers. It is not reasonable to judge the people and the statesmen of the '20s harshly because they were not clairvoyant. But it is reasonable to judge them because they were not careful. And it is on this point, Mr. Chairman, although the problems we face are very different, that our predecessors' lack of care and their foolish belief that nothing could seriously disrupt their lovely world bear some distinct resemblances to the mood of today's Washington."

> Former DCI **R. JAMES WOOLSEY** in Senate testimony on 2 October 1996; quoted in the *Wall Street Journal*, 6 November 1996.

"There are two periods of the year when you can be sure there will be a crisis: August and Christmas."

> Former DCI **ROBERT GATES**; quoted in *USA Today*, 31 July 1998.

"We live in a world still in transition from something that was very well understood—the bipolarity of the Cold War—to something that has yet to crystallize into a system that can be readily named. As a result, I believe the potential for surprise is greater than at any time since the end of World War II."

> DCI **GEORGE TENET**, address at Georgetown University, 18 October 1999.

"There are no facts about the future."

> DIA Director Vice Admiral **THOMAS WILSON**, quoted in the *Detroit News*, 8 December 1999.

"I got the data far in advance and had the chance to warn him but decided against it. . . . I thought that Bill Clinton would find a way to deal with it."

> Former Russian President **BORIS YELTSIN** in an interview on Russian television on information he received from Russia's intelligence services that Republicans in the U.S. Congress were planning to make the Monica Lewinsky affair public; cited by Associated Press, 7 October 2000.

"The fact remains . . . that we in the government of the United States could neither prevent nor precisely predict the devastating tragedy of September 11th. . . . I personally doubt [that] anything short of a hijacker turning himself in to us would have given us sufficient foreknowledge to have prevented the horrendous slaughter that took place."

> CIA operations chief **JAMES PAVITT**, address at Duke University, 11 April 2002.

"Never assume that the other guy will never do something you would never do."

> Secretary of Defense **DONALD RUMSFELD**; quoted in the *Washington Post*, 9 January 2001.

"We issued between January and September [2001] nine warnings, five of them global, because of the threat information we were receiving from the intelligence agencies. . . . [DCI] George Tenet was around town literally pounding on desks saying something is happening, this is an unprecedented level of threat information. He didn't know where it was going to happen, but he knew it was coming."

> Deputy Secretary of State **RICHARD ARMITAGE**; quoted in the *Washington Post*, 25 July 2003.

"You have to avoid falling into the trap of letting [warning] be a cover-your-ass exercise. If you scare hell out of people too often, and nothing happens, that can also create problems. Then when you do finally get a valid threat and warn people and they don't pay attention, that's equally damaging."

> Vice President **RICHARD CHENEY** on warning the public about terrorist threats; quoted in the *Washington Post*, 21 October 2001.

"Analysts must issue a strategic warning far enough in advance of the feared event for US officials to take protective action, yet with the credibility to motivate them to do so. No mean feat."

JACK DAVIS, CIA's senior thinker on analysis, January 2002.

"The good news from history is that attackers often fail to win the wars that they start with stunning surprises: Germany was defeated after invading the Soviet Union, Japan after Pearl Harbor, North Korea after 1950, Argentina after taking the Falkland Islands, Iraq after swallowing Kuwait. The bad news is that those initial attacks almost always succeed in blindsiding the victims and inflicting terrible losses. Once a war is underway, it becomes much harder to surprise the victim. . . . But even in the midst of war, surprise attacks often succeed in doing real damage: recall the Battle of the Bulge or the Tet offensive. For Americans, September 11 was the Pearl Harbor of terrorism. The challenge now is to make the next attacks more like Midway than like Tet."

RICHARD K. BETTS, "Fixing Intelligence," *Foreign Affairs* (January–February 2002).

"He who speaks about the future lies even when he tells the truth."

Arab proverb quoted by Singapore diplomat Kishore Mahbubani, *Can Asians Think?* (2002).

"Intelligence will never give you one hundred percent predictive capability. . . . There is no perfection in this business."

DCI **GEORGE TENET** in congressional testimony, 6 February 2002.

"What I didn't like [after September 11] was the blame game that followed: 'The CIA should have known,' 'the CIA should have predicted.' . . . You cannot predict accurately the intentions of evil people. . . . You can measure where the forces are, but it's impossible to always know when something is going to happen. Yeah, it would have been nice [to have predicted the attacks], but that's not the way the real world works."

Former President (and former DCI) **GEORGE H. W. BUSH**; on *Today*, NBC, 9 September 2002.

"We don't have one-year anniversaries for the things that didn't happen."

Secretary of Defense **DONALD RUMSFELD**; quoted in *USA Today*, 10 October 2002.

"The threat environment we find ourselves in today is as bad as it was last summer, the summer before September 11th. It is serious, they've reconstituted, they are coming after us, they want to execute attacks. You see it in Bali, you see it in Kuwait. . . . They intend to strike again."

DCI **GEORGE TENET**, testimony before the House and Senate intelligence committees, 17 October 2002.

"There's a structural discounting [among policymakers] about what warning staffs do, because they warn—that's their job."

RICHARD HAASS, chief of the State Department's policy planning staff, at a CIA symposium on DI analysis, 8 November 2002.

"It sounds like maybe they got too imaginative in this area."

Deputy Secretary of Defense **PAUL WOLFOWITZ** in Senate testimony on 29 July 2003, referring to a Pentagon plan to invite market trading on futures of terrorist events. The plan was scotched, eliminated, terminated with extreme prejudice.

"Terror Alerts May Always Be Based on Partial Data."

Washington Post headline, 16 February 2003. No kidding.

WEAPONS OF MASS DESTRUCTION

Modern technology has proved both boon and curse to intelligence, as it has to civilization in general. The danger posed by nuclear, biological, and chemical weapons of mass destruction (WMD), whether wielded by terrorists or totalitarians, has made accurate and timely intelligence more important than ever—and has magnified the consequences of being wrong. At the same time, intelligence benefits from the latest technological means to detect and monitor WMD programs. We are all better off if the technology of intelligence improves faster than the technology of WMD spreads.

See also: Intelligence, the Missions of; Warning, Prediction, & Surprise

"You will Do well to try to Innoculate the Indians by means of Blankets, as well as to try Every other method that can serve to Extirpate this Execrable Race."

> British General Sir **JEFFREY AMHERST** to Colonel Henri Bouquet, 16 July 1763. Amherst, in charge of British forces in New York, was responding to the suggestion of Bouquet, a Swiss mercenary in British service, to distribute blankets infected with smallpox among the indigenous peoples. *Papers of Jeffrey Amherst,* Library of Congress.

"Yes, here is the pestilence imprisoned. Only break such a tube as this into a supply of drinking water . . . and death—mysterious, untraceable death, death swift and terrible, death full of pain and indignity—would be released upon this city. . . . Here he would take the husband from the wife, here the child from its mother, here the statesman from his duty, and here the toiler from his trouble. . . . He would soak into the soil, to reappear in springs and wells at a thousand unexpected places. Once start him on the water supply, and before

we could ring him in, and catch him again, he would have decimated the metropolis."

> **H. G. WELLS**, "The Stolen Bacillus" (1894).

"Recent developments in the field of new weapons have advanced the question of an efficient intelligence service to a position of importance, vital to the security of the nation in a degree never attained and never contemplated. It is now entirely possible that failure to provide such a system might bring national disaster."

> Joint Chiefs of Staff, memorandum to Secretary of War Henry Stimson and Secretary of the Navy James Forrestal, 19 September 1945; in *FRUS 1945–1950: Emergence of the Intelligence Establishment* (1996), document 13.

"I hate to say it, but this must be the fattest atomic-bomb target on the whole face of the globe."

> James Bond on visiting New York for the first time; in **IAN FLEMING**, *Live and Let Die* (1954).

"The atomic age has created the most deadly saboteur in the history of the world—the little man with the heavy suitcase."

> M, James Bond's fictional boss and chief of British intelligence, in **IAN FLEMING**, *Moonraker* (1955). In *Thunderball* (1961), which is a story of nuclear blackmail, M continues in this vein: "You could get the whole thing into something only about twice the size of a big golf bag . . . you could put it into the back of a big car, for instance, and just run the car into a town and leave it parked with the time fuse switched on. Give yourself a couple of hours' start to get out of range . . . and that would be that."

"The principal difference between a chemical weapons factory and a pharmaceutical factory lies in the contents of the vats at any given time."

> **ANGELO CODEVILLA**, *Informing Statecraft* (1992).

"Without a combination of traditional human spies and advanced technical intelligence, the

United States will find it impossible either to monitor or to slow down the proliferation of weapons of mass destruction."

CHRISTOPHER ANDREW, *For the President's Eyes Only* (1995).

"For those nations seeking to limit or prevent proliferation, intelligence will be a crucial factor. It will not compensate for . . . lacking the will to confront nations attempting to develop nuclear weapons. It will not guarantee success, but it will increase the probability of success."

JEFFREY RICHELSON, *A Century of Spies* (1995).

"Quite frankly, we have not followed religious cults around the world and we don't have, right now, the resources to be able to do that. I really don't see any inclination, here or abroad, to have the CIA running around peering into religious groups around the world, to see who's naughty and nice."

GORDON OEHLER, director of CIA's Nonproliferation Center, in Senate testimony after the Tokyo nerve gas attack by the Japanese sect Aum Shinrikio; quoted in the *Washington Post*, 2 November 1995.

"It is my view, and I believe the view of most intelligence officers, that Pakistan could not have tested a nuclear device a few weeks ago without the nuclear materials and technologies supplied by China."

Former CIA nonproliferation chief **GORDON OEHLER**; quoted in the *Washington Times*, 15 June 1998.

"The destructive power of these weapons is no less than that of nuclear weapons."

AYMAN AL-ZAWAHRI, Osama bin Ladin's strategist and al-Qaeda official, in an April 1999 memorandum on the terrorist group's program to produce biological and chemical weapons; cited in the *Wall Street Journal*, 31 December 2001. The *Journal* obtained the memorandum from the hard drive of an al-Qaeda computer in Kabul, Afghanistan.

"Over the next 15 years . . . our cities will face ballistic missile threats from a wider variety of actors —North Korea, probably Iran, and possibly Iraq."

DCI **GEORGE TENET**, Senate testimony, quoted by Reuters, 1 February 2000.

"We still cannot account for all of North Korea's plutonium. . . . Indeed, the North probably has one or two nuclear bombs—and it may also have biological weapons alongside its chemical ones. . . . And it is busy at work on new models [of missiles] that could reach the United States itself with nuclear-sized payloads."

DDCI **JOHN McLAUGHLIN**, remarks at Texas A&M University, 17 April 2001.

"There is worse to come even than the destruction of the World Trade Centre and the attack on the Pentagon. . . . The question, alas, is not whether the terrorists of the 21st century will use weapons of mass destruction but when and where they will do so."

CHRISTOPHER ANDREW in the *Times* (London), 13 September 2001.

"The Ministry of Defence has placed a step-by-step guide on how to build an atomic bomb in the Public Record Office for anybody to see. . . . The files relate to the construction of . . . the first British atomic bomb, which was built in the late 1940s and early 1950s after the Americans cut off cooperation because of fears over British security. . . . The ministry refused to comment."

"MoD Shows Terrorists How to Make an A-Bomb," *London Daily Telegraph*, 15 April 2002.

"In the four years since the [U.N.] inspectors left [Iraq], intelligence reports show that Saddam Hussein has worked to rebuild his chemical and biological weapons stock, his missile delivery capability, and his nuclear program. . . . It is clear, however, that if left unchecked, Saddam Hussein will continue to increase his capacity to wage biological and chemical warfare and will keep trying to develop nuclear weapons."

> Senator **HILLARY CLINTON**, statement during Senate discussion supporting the resolution to authorize the use of force against Iraq, *Congressional Record*, 10 October 2002.

"If the CIA's predictions about Iraqi weapons of mass destruction prove to be wrong, how can Americans have confidence in CIA intelligence warnings in the future? . . . Before the war the agency was as sure as intelligence professionals can be that Saddam Hussein possessed weapons of mass destruction and was prepared to use them. That wasn't a political judgment or even an American one. It was shared by the intelligence services of Britain, France, and other nations. And it dated back to the 1990s, long before George W. Bush came to Washington."

> **DAVID IGNATIUS**, "The CIA and WMD," *Washington Post*, 21 October 2003.

"Our thinking now is that the weapons of mass destruction might actually be in that other one, whaddyacallit, Iran. Or Michigan. We're pretty sure the letter 'I' is involved."

> Humorist **DAVE BARRY**, "quoting" DCI George Tenet, in "Between Iraq and a Hard Place," *Washington Post Magazine*, 28 December 2003.

"[The Iraqis have] weapons programs. And they had prohibited activities they had not declared or reported to the U.N. But with regard to large stockpiles of weapons, the best evidence is, they simply didn't exist at the time of Operation Iraqi Freedom. . . . I actually believe that Saddam and Iraq were becoming more dangerous to us, not less dangerous. It was a society that was breaking up. . . . It was a stockpile of scientists and technology and actual equipment for producing WMD, while we're in a world where terrorists and others are seeking those weapons. They would have acquired it."

> Former chief U.S. weapons inspector **DAVID KAY**, on *Wolf Blitzer Reports*, CNN, 28 January 2004. On NBC's *Today* show, 27 January 2004, Kay was asked whether going to war with Iraq was prudent; he answered: "It was absolutely prudent. . . . It was a country that had the capability in weapons of mass destruction areas and in which terrorists, like ants to honey, were going after it."

"To conclude before the war that Saddam had no interest in rebuilding his WMD programs, we would have had to ignore his long and brutal history of using them. . . . To conclude before the war that Saddam had destroyed his existing weapons, we would have had to ignore what the United Nations and allied intelligence said they could not verify. . . . And to come to conclusions before the war other than those we reached, we would have had to ignore all the intelligence gathered from multiple sources after 1998."

> DCI **GEORGE TENET**, remarks at Georgetown University, 5 February 2004.

WOMEN

Why a category on women and intelligence—and particularly as the final subject of this book? The Literary Spy knows that "the last shall be first"—and that inevitably, probably sooner than most guess, a woman will become Director of Central Intelligence. That elevation will come about because of merit—the high stakes of this business mean there is no room for political correctness—and it will be a fitting response to a centuries-old prejudice against women in intelligence work.

See also: Espionage & Spies; People

"[A tyranny] entails a secret police, like the female spies employed at Syracuse."

ARISTOTLE, *Politics* (4th century B.C.).

"In December 1777, as George Washington's Continentals began to huddle for the winter at Valley Forge, Pennsylvania, the British forces occupying Philadelphia were planning to finish them off. But one of Washington's spies, an old lady named Lydia Darragh, overheard some British officers talking about their route of march, and told Washington. The ensuing American ambush at Whitemarsh ended the threat to Valley Forge."

ANGELO CODEVILLA, *Informing Statecraft* (1992).

"By means of their Emisaries they were informed of every thing that passed among us. . . . Women were the most proper persons for that purpose."

American Revolutionary War spy on British intelligence, 1777; quoted in Bakeless, *Turncoats, Traitors and Heroes* (1998).

"I had the Opportunity of going through their whole Army Remarking at the same time the strength & Situation of each Brigade, & the Number of Cannon with the Situation and Weight of Ball each Cannon was Charged with."

ANN BATES, American who spied on George Washington's army for the British during the Revolutionary War; cited in Polmar and Allen, *Encyclopedia of Espionage* (1997).

"Her information as to Matter and fact, was far superior to every other intelligence."

Testimony of Colonel **DUNCAN DRUMMOND**, former aide to Sir Henry Clinton, commander of British forces during the Revolutionary War, regarding the espionage of American Ann Bates; cited in Bakeless, *Turncoats, Traitors and Heroes* (1998).

"Our President and our General direct me to thank you. The Confederacy owes you a debt."

Confederate spymaster **THOMAS JORDAN** to Rose Greenhow, Washington socialite and Southern sympathizer who gave information on Federal army movements before the first battle of Bull Run, July 1861; cited in Miller, *Spying for America* (1989).

"I will in a day or so send drawings of the Northern defences of the city. . . . You know my soul is in the cause. . . . Tell [General Pierre] Beauregard that in my imagination he takes the place of God."

Confederate spy **ROSE GREENHOW**, dispatch to Richmond from Washington, August 1861; cited in Fishel, *Secret War for the Union* (1996).

"A clothsline [*sic*] with one piece denotes that the [Confederate] forces in the vicinity of Fredericksburg are on the move. An empty line denotes that they have all gone away. Two pieces shows that they are in force as they have been since the fight, three pieces that they are being reinforced. One piece has been displayed all day yesterday and today."

Union intelligence officer to General Daniel Butterfield, 11 March 1863, on the "clothesline code" employed by a Union spy—a black woman never identified by name—in Fredericksburg; cited in Fishel, *Secret War for the Union* (1996).

"The greater portion [of our intelligence] in its collection and in good measure in its transmission, we owed to the intelligence and devotion of Miss Van Lew."

> Union Colonel **GEORGE SHARPE**, chief of the Bureau of Military Information, on Elizabeth Van Lew, who in 1864–65 ran a spy ring for the North in Richmond; cited in Miller, *Spying for America* (1989).

"Women are never to be entirely trusted—not the best of them."

> Sherlock Holmes to Doctor Watson in Sir **ARTHUR CONAN DOYLE**, *The Sign of Four* (1890). Watson chose not to argue over this "atrocious statement."

"I have seen too much not to know that the impression of a woman may be more valuable than the conclusion of an analytical reasoner."

> Sherlock Holmes in Sir **ARTHUR CONAN DOYLE**, "The Man with the Twisted Lip" (1891). Holmes enigmatically distrusts women yet values their judgment.

"How can a man follow . . . the Great Game when he is so-always pestered by women?"

> **RUDYARD KIPLING**, *Kim* (1901).

"When women are employed as secret service agents, the probability of success and the difficulty of administration are alike increased. Women are frequently very skilful at eliciting information; they require no disguise; if attractive they are likely to be welcome everywhere, and may be able to seduce from their loyalty those whose assistance or indiscretion may be of use. On the other hand, they are variable, easily offended, seldom sufficiently reticent, and apt to be reckless."

> The first official British intelligence manual, April 1904, by Colonel **DAVID HENDERSON**; cited in Haswell, *Spies and Spymasters* (1977).

"The greatest obstacle to the employment of women as diplomatic agents is their well known inability to keep a secret."

> Unidentified Assistant U.S. Secretary of State, 1909; quoted in Martin Mayer, *The Diplomats* (1983).

"Telephone, telegraph, tell a woman."

> Sexist saying of unknown provenance.

"She had completed 25 years of continuous work and very useful service for Moscow Okhrana. . . . Her motivation for hard agent work came from her strong personal convictions. She hated sedition in all forms and performed her assignments against subversives as an idealist, having little interest in monetary remuneration. . . . She kept secrets even from her family. Accepting the job of clandestine employment among the revolutionaries, she had to reconcile herself to exposing her own children to revolutionary propaganda by holding meetings of subversives in her home. . . . Despite the emotional and spiritual conflicts she had to suppress unshared with anyone, her devotion to duty never failed."

> Tsarist Russian secret police memorandum of 31 January 1911 on agent Anna Serebryakova; in Ben Fischer, *Okhrana* (1997).

"I have always lived for love and pleasure. A courtesan, I admit it. A spy, never!"

> Famed exotic dancer and supposed spy **MATA HARI** at her trial by a French military court, 1917; quoted in *U.S. News and World Report* (3 February 2003). She had been employed as a spy by the French, who executed her for allegedly spying for Germany.

"Personally, I'm quite fond of women, and attracted sometimes by their very faults. But as the officer responsible for supplying my government with foreign intelligence, I had to regard them as unreliable and insecure elements in the organization, to be used only when all circumstances chanced to be favorable or when I had no choice. An agent should be calm, unostentatious, and reticent. Women are emotional, vain, loquacious. They fall in love easily and without discrimination. They are impatient with the strict requirements of security measures. They withstand hardships poorly. Moreover, they tend to become even less capable physically and less responsible mentally for several days out of every month. I'm talking about European women, of course. American women may be quite different, for all I know."

Anonymous "prewar European intelligence chief," "A Dim View of Women," *Studies in Intelligence* 6 (spring 1962). His reasons for anonymity are clear.

"I will not have any of your organization run by a woman. They simply are not trustworthy. . . . I can't have sex interfering with our work."

SIS official **CLAUDE DANSEY**, 1941, when he learned that a successful agent recruiter in France was "a she"; quoted in West, *Faber Book of Espionage* (1993). According to former DCI Richard Helms, Dansey was described by another senior SIS official as "the kind of a shit that gives other shits a bad name"; see Helms, *A Look over My Shoulder* (2003).

"Women are absolutely unfit for espionage work. They have no understanding of political and other affairs, and I have never received satisfactory information from them. Since they were useless to me, I did not employ them in my group."

Famed Soviet spy **RICHARD SORGE** after he had been caught by the Japanese in 1941; quoted in Dulles, *Great True Spy Stories* (1968).

"Initially it was considered improper to employ women in [SOE] operations. . . . Churchill was asked to adjudicate and deferred on the side of reality. Of the 52 female agents sent by SOE into France, 17 were arrested, of whom 12 died in concentration camps."

MARK LLOYD, *Guinness Book of Espionage* (1994).

"Keep mum—she's not so dumb!"

World War II poster in the British Imperial War Museum, depicting a blond beauty at a party being fawned on by garrulous senior officers. Memorable but politically incorrect today.

"In all, over 21,000 people worked for OSS during [World War II,] 4,000 of whom were women. One of its agents in France was Virginia Hall— even though she had an artificial leg. Working under cover as a foreign correspondent for the *New York Post*, Hall established contact with the French Underground. She organized sabotage and guerrilla units and arranged parachute drops of weapons and supplies. Her teams blew up bridges, sabotaged rail lines, and disrupted enemy communications. After the war, Virginia Hall went on to serve as one of the first women operations officers in the new Central Intelligence Agency."

DCI **ROBERT GATES**, 21 March 1992, in *Speeches* (1993).

"The great majority of women who worked for [OSS] spent their war years behind desks and filing cases in Washington, invisible apron strings of an organization which touched every theater of war. They were the ones at home who patiently filed secret reports, encoded and decoded messages, answered telephones, mailed checks and kept the records. . . . There were some, however, who had important administrative positions and others with regional and linguistic knowledge of great value in research, whose special skills were employed in exact and painstaking work such as map making and cryptography."

> OSS director **WILLIAM DONOVAN**, 1947; cited in McIntosh, *Sisterhood of Spies* (1998).

"If you don't send Registry that report we need, I shall fill the next Washington pouch with itching powder and virulent bacteriological diseases, and change all the numbers, as well as translating the material into Singhalese, and destroying the English version."

> OSS clerk **JULIA McWILLIAMS**—later famous as the French chef Julia Child—to OSS Headquarters from her unit in Ceylon, May 1944; quoted in McIntosh, *Sisterhood of Spies* (1998). Child says she joined OSS "because I was too tall to get into the WACs or WAVEs."

"I wasn't thinking in career terms. There weren't many careers to have. There wasn't anything [else] really open. Who knows? I might have ended up an alcoholic, since there wasn't anything [else] to do."

> **JULIA CHILD** on her OSS service; quoted in Tom Brokaw, *The Greatest Generation* (1998).

"Women in CIA undergo much the same training as men and can qualify for the same jobs except that overseas assignments for women are more limited. One reason for this is the ingrained prejudice in many countries of the world against women as 'managers' of men—in their jobs, that is."

> Former DCI **ALLEN DULLES**, *The Craft of Intelligence* (1963).

"There were [in the 1960s] plenty of women in CIA—clerks, typists, analysts, photo interpreters, even case officers—but none ever seems to have reached a level where she might play a leading role in the sort of things which excited the admiration or outrage of her countrypersons."

> **THOMAS POWERS**, *The Man Who Kept the Secrets* (1979). The word "countryperson" itself is an outrage, whether used by a man or a woman.

"It soon became clear to me that a strict sex discrimination policy was in place at MI5. . . . Men were recruited as what were called 'officers' and women had their own career structure, a second-class career, as 'assistant officers.' . . . I often wonder why I took the job."

> Dame **STELLA RIMINGTON** on reporting to work at MI5 in 1969, in *Open Secret* (2001). She rose to become director of MI5, 1992–96.

"In 1976 . . . of the Agency's 98 key officials, only one was a woman."

> CIA historian **ROBERTA KNAPP**; quotation in CIA's Historical Intelligence Collection.

"For brilliant and effective espionage, and for courage that is truly awe-inspiring."

> CIA citation for **JEANNIE ROUSSEAU**, who as a young woman survived three Nazi concentration camps after providing London with crucial intelligence on the Nazi V-1 and V-2 rockets, 1993; quoted in the *Washington Post*, 28 December 1998.

"He thought the mole hunt was being led by two dumb broads . . . and that he was smarter than we were."

> CIA counterintelligence officer **JEANNE VERTEFEUILLE**, who with colleague Sandra Grimes identified Aldrich Ames—who also worked in CIA counterintelligence—as a spy for Moscow; quoted in *Chicago Tribune*, 6 March 1997.

"We lied about our husband's jobs, stalled inquisitive policemen, befriended ministers' wives, kept our ears open at parties, deflected the children's questions, and worried in silence alone. We were the CIA wives. You never knew us."

BINA CADY KIYONAGA, *My Spy: Memoir of a CIA Wife* (2000).

"From Mata Hari to the 'great granny spy,' Melita Norwood, the media have found revelations about women in the traditionally male world of secret intelligence irresistibly attractive."

CHRISTOPHER ANDREW, in the *Times* (London), 17 September 2001.

"The CIA teaches its recruits how to lie, manipulate, and keep secrets. What woman isn't better at that than a man?"

Former CIA officer **LINDSAY MORAN**, "Why Women Make Better Spies," *Washingtonian* (September 2003).

"I've always wanted to be a spy, and frankly I'm a little surprised that British intelligence has never approached me."

Widely attributed to supermodel **ELIZABETH HURLEY**.

Selected Bibliography

Agee, Philip. *Inside the Company: CIA Diary.* New York: Bantam, 1975.

Allen, George W. *None So Blind: A Personal Account of the Intelligence Failure in Vietnam.* Chicago: Ivan R. Dee, 2001.

Andrew, Christopher. *For the President's Eyes Only: Secret Intelligence and the American Presidency from Washington to Bush.* New York: HarperCollins, 1995.

Andrew, Christopher, and Oleg Gordievsky. *KGB: The Inside Story.* New York: HarperCollins, 1990.

Andrew, Christopher, and Vasili Mitrokhin. *The Sword and the Shield: The Mitrokhin Archive and the Secret History of the KGB.* New York: Basic Books, 1999.

Austin, N. J. E., and N. B. Rankov. *Exploratio: Military and Political Intelligence in the Roman World.* London: Routledge, 1995.

Bakeless, John. *Turncoats, Traitors and Heroes: Espionage in the American Revolution.* New York: Da Capo, 1998.

Berkowitz, Bruce D., and Allan Goodman. *Strategic Intelligence for American National Security.* Princeton: Princeton University Press, 1989.

Bissell, Richard, Jr., with Jonathan Lewis and Frances Pudlo. *Reflections of a Cold Warrior: From Yalta to the Bay of Pigs.* New Haven: Yale University Press, 1996.

Brugioni, Dino A. *From Balloons to Blackbirds: Reconnaissance, Surveillance, and Imagery Intelligence—How It Evolved.* McLean, Va.: Association of Former Intelligence Officers, 1993.

Burrows, William E. *Deep Black: Space Espionage and National Security.* New York: Random House, 1986.

Central Intelligence Agency. *Symposium on Teaching Intelligence.* Washington, D.C.: Center for the Study of Intelligence, 1994.

Central Intelligence Agency. *The Origin and Development of the CIA in the Administration of Harry Truman: A Conference Report.* Washington, D.C.: Center for the Study of Intelligence, 1995.

Central Intelligence Agency. *Studies in Intelligence,* unclassified or declassified articles.

Clarridge, Duane R., with Digby Diehl. *A Spy for All Seasons: My Life in the CIA.* New York: Scribner, 1997.

Cline, Ray S. *Secrets, Spies and Scholars: Blueprint of the Essential CIA.* Washington, D.C.: Acropolis, 1976.

Clinton, Sir Henry. Letters and other papers, 1750–1838. The Henry Clinton collection, William L. Clements Library, University of Michigan.

Codevilla, Angelo. *Informing Statecraft: Intelligence for a New Century.* New York: Macmillan, 1992.

Colby, William, and Peter Forbath. *Honorable Men: My Life in the CIA.* New York: Simon and Schuster, 1978.

Council on Foreign Relations. *Making Intelligence Smarter.* Washington, D.C., 1996.

Darling, Arthur. *The Central Intelligence Agency: An Instrument of Government, to 1950.* University Park: Penn State University Press, 1990.

Dulles, Allen. *The Craft of Intelligence.* New York: Harper and Row, 1963.

Dulles, Allen, ed. *Great True Spy Stories.* New York: Harper and Row, 1968.

Dulles, Allen, ed. *Great Spy Stories from Fiction.* New York: Harper and Row, 1969.

Dvornik, Francis. *Origins of Intelligence Services: The Ancient Near East, Persia, Greece, Rome, Byzantium, the Arab Muslim Empires, the Mongol Empire, China, Muscovy.* New Brunswick: Rutgers University Press, 1974.

Earley, Pete. *Confessions of a Spy: The Real Story of Aldrich Ames.* New York: Putnam's, 1997.

Fialka, John J. *War by Other Means: Economic Espionage in America.* New York: W. W. Norton, 1997.

Fischer, Benjamin B., ed. *At Cold War's End: U.S. Intelligence on the Soviet Union and Eastern Europe, 1989–1991.* Washington, D.C.: CIA History Staff, 1999.

Fishel, Edwin C. *The Secret War for the Union: The Untold Story of Military Intelligence in the Civil War.* Boston: Houghton Mifflin, 1996.

Ford, Harold P. *CIA and the Vietnam Policymakers: Three Episodes 1962–1968.* Washington, D.C.: CIA History Staff, 1998.

Furse, George Armand. *Information in War: Its Acquisition and Transmission.* London: William Clowes and Sons, 1895.

Gates, Robert M. "The CIA and American Foreign Policy." *Foreign Affairs* 66 (winter 1987–88): 215–30.

Gates, Robert M. "An Opportunity Unfulfilled: The Use and Perceptions of Intelligence at the White House." *Washington Quarterly* 12 (winter 1989): 35–44.

Gates, Robert M. *Speeches, 1991–1992.* Washington, D.C.: CIA internal publication, 1993.

Gates, Robert M. *From the Shadows: The Ultimate Insider's Story of Five Presidents and How They Won the Cold War.* New York: Simon and Schuster, 1996.

Godson, Roy. *Dirty Tricks or Trump Cards: U.S. Covert Action and Counterintelligence.* Washington, D.C.: Brassey's, 1995.

Grose, Peter. *Gentleman Spy: The Life of Allen Dulles.* London: André Deutsch, 1994.

Haines, Gerald, and Robert Leggett, eds. *CIA's Analyses of the Soviet Union, 1947–1991: A Documentary Collection.* Washington, D.C.: CIA History Staff, 2001.

Haswell, Jock. *Spies and Spymasters: A Concise History of Intelligence.* London: Thames and Hudson, 1977.

Heinl, Robert Debs Jr. *Dictionary of Military and Naval Quotations.* Annapolis, Md.: U.S. Naval Institute, 1966.

Helgerson, John. *Getting to Know the President: CIA Briefings of Presidential Candidates, 1952–1993.* Washington, D.C.: CIA History Staff, 1996.

Helms, Richard, with William Hood. *A Look over My Shoulder: A Life in the Central Intelligence Agency.* New York: Random House, 2003.

Hilsman, Roger. *To Move a Nation: The Politics of Foreign Policy in the Administration of John F. Kennedy.* New York: Doubleday, 1967.

Holmes, W. J. *Double-Edged Secrets: U.S. Naval Intelligence Operations in the Pacific During World War II.* Annapolis, Md.: Naval Institute Press, 1979.

Hood, William. *Mole: The True Story of the First Russian Spy to Become an American Counterspy.* Washington, D.C.: Brassey's edition, 1993.

Horning, Jane. *The Mystery Lovers' Book of Quotations.* New York: Mysterious Press, 1989.

Jeffreys-Jones, Rhodri. *The CIA and American Democracy.* New Haven: Yale University Press, 1989.

Jeffreys-Jones, Rhodri, and Andrew Lownie, eds. *North American Spies: New Revisionist Essays.* Lawrence: University of Kansas Press, 1991.

Jeffreys-Jones, Rhodri, and Christopher Andrew, eds. *Eternal Vigilance? Fifty Years of the CIA.* London: Frank Cass, 1997.

Kahn, David. *The Codebreakers,* rev. ed. New York: Scribner, 1996.

Kalugin, Oleg, with Fen Montaigne. *The First Directorate: My Thirty-Two Years in Intelligence and Espionage Against the West.* New York: St. Martin's, 1994.

Katz, Barry M. *Foreign Intelligence: Research and Analysis in the Office of Strategic Services, 1942–1945.* Cambridge: Harvard University Press, 1989.

Keegan, John. *Intelligence in War: Knowledge of the Enemy from Napoleon to al-Qaeda.* New York: Knopf, 2003.

Kent, Sherman. *Strategic Intelligence for American World Policy.* Princeton: Princeton University Press, 1949.

Knightley, Phillip. *The Second Oldest Profession: Spies and Spying in the Twentieth Century.* London: Penguin, 1988.

Knott, Stephen F. *Secret and Sanctioned: Covert Operations and the American Presidency.* New York: Oxford University Press, 1996.

Koch, Scott A., ed. *Selected Estimates on the Soviet Union: 1950–1959.* Washington, D.C.: CIA History Staff, 1993.

Kuhns, Woodrow J., ed. *Assessing the Soviet Threat: The Early Cold War Years.* Washington, D.C.: CIA History Staff, 1997.

Laqueur, Walter. *A World of Secrets: The Uses and Limits of Intelligence.* New York: Basic Books, 1985.

Leary, William M., ed. *The Central Intelligence Agency: History and Documents.* University, Ala.: University of Alabama Press, 1984.

Levin, Walter. "The Efficacy of Propaganda in Global Conflict During the Twentieth Century." Ph.D. dissertation, Fletcher School of Law and Diplomacy, Tufts University, 1999.

Lloyd, Mark. *The Guinness Book of Espionage.* Middlesex, England: Guinness, 1994.

Mackenzie, Compton. *Water on the Brain.* New York: Penguin, 1959.

Mangold, Tom. *Cold Warrior: James Jesus Angleton, the CIA's Master Spy Hunter.* London: Simon and Schuster, 1991.

Marchetti, Victor, and John Marks. *The CIA and the Cult of Intelligence.* New York: Dell, 1975.

McAuliffe, Mary S., ed. *CIA Documents on the Cuban Missile Crisis, 1962.* Washington, D.C.: CIA History Staff, 1992.

McIntosh, Elizabeth. *Sisterhood of Spies: The Women of the OSS.* Annapolis, Md.: Naval Institute Press, 1998.

Meyer, Cord. *Facing Reality: From World Federalism to the CIA.* New York: Harper and Row, 1980.

Miller, Nathan. *Spying for America: The Hidden History of U.S. Intelligence.* New York: Dell, 1989.

Montagu, Ewen. *The Man Who Never Was.* Philadelphia: Lippincott, 1954.

Moravec, Frantisek. *Master of Spies: The Memoirs of General Frantisek Moravec.* New York: Doubleday, 1975.

Pedlow, Gregory, and Donald Welzenbach. *The CIA and the U-2 Program, 1954–1974.* Washington, D.C.: CIA History Staff, 1998.

Penkovskiy, Oleg. *The Penkovskiy Papers.* New York: Avon, 1966.

Petersen, Martin. "What We Should Demand from Intelligence." *National Security Studies Quarterly* 12 (spring 1999): 107–13.

Philby, Harold "Kim." *My Secret War.* London: Granada, 1968.

Phillips, David Atlee. *The Night Watch.* London: Robert Hale, 1978.

Pisani, Sallie. *The CIA and the Marshall Plan.* Lawrence: University Press of Kansas, 1991.

Polmar, Norman, and Thomas B. Allen. *The Encyclopedia of Espionage.* New York: Random House, 1997.

Powers, Richard Gid. *Not Without Honor: The History of American Anticommunism.* New York: Simon and Schuster, 1995.

Powers, Thomas. *The Man Who Kept the Secrets: Richard Helms and the CIA.* New York: Knopf, 1979.

Prange, Gordon W. *At Dawn We Slept: The Untold Story of Pearl Harbor.* New York: McGraw-Hill, 1981.

Ranelagh, John. *The Agency: The Rise and Decline of the CIA, from Wild Bill Donovan to William Casey.* New York: Simon and Schuster, 1986.

Richelson, Jeffrey T. *A Century of Spies: Intelligence in the Twentieth Century.* New York: Oxford University Press, 1995.

Ruffner, Kevin C., ed. *CORONA: America's First Satellite Program.* Washington, D.C.: CIA History Staff, 1995.

Russell, Francis. *The Secret War.* Alexandria, Va.: Time-Life Books, 1981.

Sayle, Edward F. "The Historical Underpinnings of the U.S. Intelligence Community." *International Journal of Intelligence and Counterintelligence* 1 (spring 1986): 1–27.

Schecter, Jerrold L., and Peter S. Deriabin. *The Spy Who Saved the World: How a Soviet Colonel Changed the Course of the Cold War.* Washington, D.C.: Brassey's, 1995.

Shulsky, Abram N. *Silent Warfare: Understanding the World of Intelligence,* 2nd rev. ed. Washington, D.C.: Brassey's, 1993.

Smith, Russell Jack. *The Unknown CIA: My Three Decades with the Agency.* Washington, D.C.: Pergamon-Brassey's, 1989.

Stafford, David. *Churchill and Secret Service.* New York: Overlook, 1998.

Steury, Donald P., ed. *Intentions and Capabilities: Estimates on Soviet Strategic Forces, 1959–1983.* Washington, D.C.: CIA History Staff, 1996.

Sullivan, William C. *The Bureau: My Thirty Years in Hoover's FBI.* New York: W. W. Norton, 1979.

Sun Tzu. *The Art of War.* I have used both the version edited by James Clavell (New York: Dell, 1983) and the translation by Ralph D. Sawyer (Boulder: Westview, 1994).

Taylor, Stan A., and Daniel Snow. "Cold War Spies." *Intelligence and National Security* 12 (April 1997): 101–25.

Treverton, Gregory F. *Covert Action: The Limits of Intervention in the Postwar World.* New York: Basic Books, 1987.

Troy, Thomas F. *Donovan and the CIA: A History of the Establishment of the Central Intelligence Agency.* Frederick, Md.: University Publications of America, 1981.

Turner, Stansfield. *Secrecy and Democracy: The CIA in Transition.* New York: Harper and Row, 1985.

U.S. Department of State. *Foreign Relations of the United States, 1945–1950: Emergence of the Intelligence Establishment.* Washington, D.C.: Government Printing Office, 1996.

U.S. Senate. *Alleged Assassination Plots Involving Foreign Leaders: Interim Report of the Senate Select Committee to Study Governmental Operations with respect to Intelligence Activities* [the Church Committee]. Washington, D.C.: Government Printing Office, November 1975.

U.S. Senate. *Final Report of the Senate Select Committee to Study Governmental Operations with respect to Intelligence Activities* [the Church Committee], *Books I–VI.* Washington, D.C.: Government Printing Office, April 1976.

Walters, Vernon. *Silent Missions.* New York: Doubleday, 1978.

Warner, Michael, ed. *The CIA Under Harry Truman: CIA Cold War Records.* Washington, D.C.: CIA History Staff, 1994.

Warner, Michael. *The Office of Strategic Services: America's First Intelligence Agency.* Washington, D.C.: Central Intelligence Agency, 2000.

Warner, Michael, ed. *Central Intelligence: Origin and Evolution.* Washington, D.C.: CIA History Staff, 2001.

Weber, Ralph, ed. *Spymasters: Ten CIA Officers in Their Own Words.* Wilmington, Del.: Scholarly Resources, 1999.

Webster, William H. *Speeches.* Washington, D.C.: CIA internal series, 1988–91.

West, Nigel, ed. *The Faber Book of Espionage.* London: Faber and Faber, 1993.

West, Rebecca. *The New Meaning of Treason.* New York: Time, 1966.

Winks, Robin. *Cloak and Gown: Scholars in the Secret War, 1939–1961.* New York: Morrow, 1987.

Zacharias, Ellis M. *Secret Missions: The Story of an Intelligence Officer.* New York: G. P. Putnam's Sons, 1946.

Index of Sources

Anonymous individuals and sources that, in my judgment, suffer from obscurity, are omitted. Each source may have more than one quotation on each page. Categories are listed for sources with more than three quotations. Quotations from coauthored works are indexed under the leading author's name.

Subject Index